Pastor Edward J. M...

26549 Pennie Rd.

Dearborn Hgts., MI 48125

SERMONS
IN
AMERICAN HISTORY

SERMONS
IN
AMERICAN HISTORY

Selected Issues in the American Pulpit 1630-1967

PREPARED UNDER THE AUSPICES OF THE SPEECH COMMUNICATION ASSOCIATION

DEWITTE HOLLAND, EDITOR

HUBERT VANCE TAYLOR AND JESS YODER, ASSISTANT EDITORS

SERMONS IN AMERICAN HISTORY

Copyright © 1971 by Abingdon Press

ISBN 0-687-37794-3

Library of Congress Catalog Card Number: 76-148072

SET UP, PRINTED, AND BOUND BY THE
PARTHENON PRESS, AT NASHVILLE,
TENNESSEE, UNITED STATES OF AMERICA

This volume is gratefully dedicated to Kenneth G. Hance, past president of the Speech Association of America, author, lecturer, master teacher and methodologist in rhetorical criticism, Christian gentleman, and supremely a friend. Through his years at Northwestern and Michigan State Universities he has successfully encouraged and directed massive amounts of research in preaching and religious communciation. Several of the contributors to this volume received their training in rhetorical theory and criticism from him.

Much of the current renewal of interest and research in contemporary preaching has been promoted by men and institutions stimulated by Dr. Hance. May this collection of materials on American preaching help to provide insight into the institution that he serves so well—the American church.

PREFACE

This work is a companion volume to *Preaching in American History*, Abingdon Press, 1969. Even so, each book is designed to stand alone. The former was intended to describe and analyze in some detail some of the major topics of the American pulpit, Catholic, Protestant, and Jewish, from 1630 to 1967. Only brief excerpts of sermons were presented. The purpose of this volume is to describe and analyze preaching itself and to present representative sermons on the major issues covered in the first book. The concern of both volumes is not with great pulpit personalities, sermonic technique, theory or theology of preaching, or inspiration to preach the Word; the focal point is issues.

But more than an anthology is involved here. The sermons are presented in a framework which, hopefully, allows for a balanced interpretation. We provide brief analyses of selected issues and then proffer sermons representing differing, even conflicting, views. In some cases the texts are the work of noted men; but often we have included the craft of little known people, because they, too, argued our issues and we have a record of their words.

Except in the case of the church-state issue between Roger Williams and John Cotton, the researchers have provided authentic sermon manuscripts. In the Williams-Cotton case, the substance of sermons was reconstructed from rhetorical writings on the issue involved. In not a few cases, the researchers have come upon rare and valuable manuscripts. They are drawn from published books, pamphlets, unpublished mimeographed texts, newspapers, broadcast transcripts, and denominational records. Many of the contemporary sermons were obtained directly from records of ministers who preached them. The collection is an imposing one not known to be approximated in other anthologies.

7

Most of the manuscripts have been shortened in the interest of space economy. However, the editor has been careful not to excise any point made in any of the sermons. All ideas in the complete manuscripts remain in the edited versions. Material cut was judged unnecessary or redundant and care was taken not to skew apportionment or style. In most cases archaic spelling has been retained as well as some word usage which now seems strange and even amiss. This will be noted especially in sermons prior to our Revolutionary period. Sources of complete texts are indicated for those who would pursue them.

The sermons should not be used as models of homiletical excellence, but as illustrative material of the varying positions that may be taken on a given topic. Significant topics have not been covered; for example, "Church Unity through Restoration," and "New Sects Challenge the Orthodox Concept of the Church," both especially relevant to the history of the church in America. Other omissions will surely occur to readers, but time and space have dictated limits. However, since a good sampling of issues of the American pulpit have been covered, the layman and the theological student may find the study useful in reconstructing the basic framework of what have been the major concerns of the church in America. The practicing minister, in examining the spectrum of views on a given topic, may well clarify and crystallize his own positions on the issues covered.

This work originated, as did the companion volume, in the casual interchanges of minds working in the Speech for Religious Workers Interest Group of the Speech Association of America. There a committee was appointed to draw together and publish a history of preaching in the United States. Plans were drawn and amended ad infinitum, work assigned, and after so long a time the volumes developed. Contributors were recruited primarily from the ranks of the interest group, but in a few cases specialists were invited to prepare specific chapters. The contributors have graduate degrees in rhetoric and public address and/or in theology. They are university, college, or seminary teachers or professional religious workers. Royalties have been assigned gratefully to the Speech Association of America.

DeWITTE HOLLAND
TEMPLE UNIVERSITY
PHILADELPHIA, PENNSYLVANIA

CONTENTS

1

SERMONS IN AMERICAN HISTORY: AN INTRODUCTION
DeWitte T. Holland

This book is about preaching in American history. It is peculiarly concerned
with preaching that surfaced in the ebb and flow of the tide of historical
factors in the American experience. The preaching that seems to have left
its mark is that which took on something of the character of the time of its
being. Here we describe and illustrate with sermons the polarity of views on
nineteen distinct issues that have been faced by the American pulpit. This
introduction seeks to explain why the pulpit took on paramount importance
from the earliest colonial period. It then presents a broad overview of the
issues treated in the remainder of the book.

In early colonial New England the minister, by virtue of his office, was
a great power. He headed the local congregation of the community church.
Protestant, Anglo-Saxon, and dissenting, the church was *the* social institution of the day. The power of the minister of that church was both open
and subtle. It extended directly into civil affairs because he often served as
magistrate. It reached into civic affairs more subtly because he controlled
church membership, a requirement for holding civil office and first-class
citizenship.

The primary vehicle for the subtle exercise of power was the sermon,
which from the time of the Reformation had become the major instrument
for exhortation and teaching the Bible. Preaching, then, was important in the
exercise of the ministerial office. Its greatest inherent strength, however, seems
to have derived from its replacement of the Mass as a means of grace.

A sacerdotal system of the eucharist, centuries old, was not easily forgotten.

Its undisputed bedrock authority was more easily deflected to another office or function. This basically was what happened in the Reformation. The Mass has stood in the center of faith and worship. To be caught up in the mystery of the Mass required little if any preaching. As the participant believed in the affirmations of the Mass, the experience of it enfolded him. Preaching, then, on the fundamentals of the faith was hardly necessary, though occasionally preaching missions were held to raise money for church renovation or to decry a specific local sin. The other sacraments, while important, pointed to or from the central sacrament of the Mass. The priesthood, then, was the messenger of saving grace through administration of the sacramental system.

The Reformation sought to rip away the sacramental system intervening between the individual believer and God, thus making each his own priest through the doctrine of the priesthood of all believers. However, only a few stalwart souls were able to shoulder the awesome responsibility of deciding for themselves the nature of their faith in God by examining all available evidences. Indeed, it would be a long time before brave souls in any significant numbers would be willing to put away not only the church, but Holy Writ as final authority in religious matters and willingly be their own priests. Desirous of changing from the sacerdotal system, but unwilling to trust fully in the new doctrine of individualism inherent in the priesthood of all believers, Christians sought some additional support. This they found in the scriptures. The Bible then came to be the undisputed highest authority.

With the exit of the sacramental system as assurance of a solid grace connection with God, the great Universal Church became superfluous among Protestants. Its chief meaning had been to guarantee the genuine character of the priesthood and saving sacraments. If each man was to be his own priest before God, then any mediating church was an insolence. As a result, church services dropped their mediating functions and instead provided preaching—a spiritual exercise attributing choice and dignity to its hearers. Very often the content of the preaching dealt with explication of the several ramifications of the priesthood of all believers doctrine. This is how it happened that in much of Protestantism and especially in Puritan New England, the Bible took the place of pope and historic church as primal authority in the Christian life; preaching of the Bible from the pulpit took the place of sacraments as the essential means of grace.

Examination of the debates surrounding religious motivation for founding of the colonies leads to the conclusion that freedom for one's own brand of gospel was not the only reason for crossing the ocean. Even so, the early leaders in New England and in the Middle Colonies, some sixty years later, were religious people. If these leaders were not themselves ministers, they

14

were closely counseled by ministers. It is beyond question that the experience of emigration and settlement was profoundly influenced by preaching—preaching by one who felt himself called by the Holy Spirit to lead but not to mediate; preaching designed to bring the word which would explain to the people what was God's will and design for them on this earth and thereafter.

Worshipers at Sunday services often sat for as long as two hours listening to doctrinal preaching and exhortation. Strong religious motivation and amazing physical endurance were no doubt prerequisite to such feats of attendance to the Word. Likely then, as now, the ministers simply overestimated the abilities of the people to absorb lengthy dry discourses.

Special counsel on the crises of famines, Indian attacks, epidemics, or civil strife came from the minister in the pulpit. Through biblical allusions and analogies, often quite farfetched, the preacher sought to bring some solace or guidance from the Book. New migrations into the wilderness had to be explained in biblical terms to this New Israel. Clearly, the early colonial communities, especially of New England and the Middle Colonies, had a dependence upon God and his Word in the scriptures. The minister was primarily the man of God, a guide in the quest to know and do God's will as revealed in the scriptures.

The local minister, in the remote parts of Massachusetts or Pennsylvania, was intertwined in his own shifting culture. This gave him a perspective necessarily different from that to be had in London or Leyden. He would then translate his perception of the Word into the unique historical millieu before him. Such speaking to Anglo Saxon, dissenting minds inevitably produced varying emphases and interpretations with resulting controversies on issues in vogue. It brought to the surface perceived conflicts in popular religious topics and produced a gradual movement toward objectives clustered around the priesthood of all believers. Indeed, the long backward view of major topics of the American pulpit illustrates how religious diversity of free men moved clearly away from traditionalism toward personal decision and freedom in all matters religious—a state akin to the social and political philosophy of modern America.

We turn now to a brief tracing of the major pulpit topics covered in subsequent chapters. We are concerned with what was said in the pulpit and how it interacted with and related to historical events.

John Cotton was a severe Puritan minister who presided over the church in Boston from 1635 until 1652. In England he stressed the volition of man in religious matters almost to the point of voluntarism or free will. The mental machinations occurring in his mind after he arrived in America are not fully known, but among all the first generation Puritan ministers he took the strongest stand on the absolutism of God.

People and ministers agreed with the general Protestant theme that God and man were eternally separated by sin. God was perfect, all powerful, incomprehensible, and absolute. The basic question for each person then was "What shall I do to be saved?" The orthodox Puritan answered, "Nothing. You, as Natural man, cannot do good. Salvation cannot be earned. It is a gift of God, if you are of the elect." Answers of this stripe made the rounds without satisfying everyone. Other ministers, including Peter Bulkeley, who is described in chapter 2, stressed God's conditional promises and mercy, lending hope to sinful man, especially if he were faithful to the church and moral in his behavior.

With preachers and laity, then, agreeing upon basics of God, man, and sin, the first major debate of Puritan America centered around the question of man's function in the scheme of salvation. This question, peaked in interest in the middle seventeenth century, was revived in the great awakening of the eighteenth century, and was renewed yet again by the conservatives of the mid-nineteenth century. The question still occupies some, but few now seem to hold to the absolute passivity of man in being "found of God."

The ship bringing him to Boston in 1631 had hardly returned over the eastern horizon before Puritan Roger Williams challenged the Boston church state oligarchy on religious grounds. Not only did he refuse the proffered post as teacher in the Boston church, but he refused even to join the congregation of these unseparated brethren. This conflict began a series of incidents leading to Williams' banishment from the Massachusetts Colony in 1635. On fleeing to the Providence area he engaged in an extended literary debate with John Cotton who ultimately took the vacant post at the Boston church.

This controversy grew out of the charges leading to Williams' banishment and centered around the relationship of church and state and collorary arguments. Motivation for the radical position of Williams originally seems to have been a desire to keep the church undefiled from secular power and control. His insistence on complete freedom (for purity) drove him to found Rhode Island, the ultimate political implication of the Reformation, the really historic foundation of modern United States. Chapter 3 traces this conflict.

The Great Awakening, described in chapter 4, is the label attached to widespread religious manifestations, both in the colonies and in England, taking place from 1730 to 1750. In the colonies the eastern seaboard revivals decried the growing intellectualism and rationalism in religion, while hitting hard on sin and the justice of God in the punishment of sinners. Advocates for and against the revivals entered sermonic controversy on whether the heart and emotions were to be involved in religious experience. As leading apologist for the revivalists, Jonathan Edwards developed an early unitary view of man. While Edwards stressed the majesty and sovereignty of God, his new doctrine of man was at least a crack in the wall of rigid orthodoxy.

Growing out of rationalism, humanism, and Arminianism which stressed man's ability to choose or resist God, the early nineteenth-century American Unitarian movement affirmed man's basic goodness and ability to work toward his own holiness. Orthodox Calvinists, of course, had not given up the bastions of original sin, predestination, and limited grace, so it was inevitable that conflict follow. Chapter 5 of our study describes and illustrates the rise of the Unitarianism controversy on the basic question of man's activity in the salvation experience. The seventeenth-century American Puritan had been concerned with much the same thing. The emphasis, however, shifted from the degree of absoluteness of God to the degree of activity of man in establishing the God-man relationship.

While the emerging Unitarians and the Orthodox were warring on the eastern seaboard over the nature of man and his potential relationship to God, the institutionless frontier was forcing another issue to the fore. That issue pertained to the nature of man and his responsibility for personal choice in all matters. On the frontier men had not the protection of law and social order against the threat of wilderness and savages, so self-reliance and individual initiative became prime character virtues. Orthodox religion, however, taught through the "Representation" thesis that man's eternal and social destiny was in charge of appointed officials. This did not fit the frontier experience where a man's success depended largely on his own initiative.

Frontier camp-meeting, revival religion flourished without inhibition and restraint and again emphasized the personal factor. The place of the individual will in religious experience was stressed. This undergirded anew the spirit of democracy and individualism so necessary to building a responsible citizenship for the yet formless institutions in a new land. Chapter 6 describes this debate more fully and illustrates it with sermons by Charles G. Finney and George Junkin.

The nature of the conversion experience emerged as a major issue in the Christian church during the fourth decade of the nineteenth century when Horace Bushnell challenged the dramatic concept of entering the kingdom by rigorous conversion or by being born again. He did not disparage that sort of experience for some, but argued it to be unnecessary for the youth nurtured in a Christian home. Chapter 7 depicts and illustrates the direct clash between Edward D. Griffin, prominent revivalist of the day, and Horace Bushnell of the North Church (Congregational) Hartford, Connecticut. Bushnell essentially stood alone in his challenge of the orthodox, but since his time an increasing number of clergymen conclude that God communicates through the organic nature of natural family relationships. To these clergymen such relationships are used of God as a means of grace to renew the heart.

Until 1831, the vast majority of the abolition societies were in the South. The coming of William Lloyd Garrison and his *Liberator* polarized the country on the issue of slavery. The pulpit followed suit. In both North and South denominations split and drove preachers to the Bibles to seek support for their sectional positions. The ministers found their proof texts and interpreted scripture to make it seem to approve slavery for the planter while condemning it for the abolitionist.

Prior to the Civil War, Theodore Parker of Boston, the most incisive of the many articulate abolitionist preachers, thundered against slavery as not only unchristian, but anti-Christian. Meanwhile, James H. Thornwell, a South Carolinian, built a carefully framed theological basis for slavery. Unfortunately, both of these men preached in areas increasingly sympathetic to, if not convinced, of the views that they advanced. Sympathetic audiences do not really need arguments. This issue is chronicled in chapter 8.

The polarization of the country following the onslaught of Garrisonians impelled the country toward the inevitable confrontation on slavery. The depth of the Yankee conscience on slavery and the roots of slavery in the South were equally underestimated, leaving the politicians unable to affect a compromise. Civil war erupted with the election of Lincoln, and the religious folk listened for what the pulpit would say. In those pre-Darwinian days, clerics and laity alike generally believed that God directly controlled all actions in the universe. The war, then, was brought on by God for his own purposes. Then, depending on one's theology, culture, and sectionalism, other basics were fed into sermonizing. In general, success or failure of a given side was interpreted by the pulpit in terms of that side's repentance, prayer, and purity of heart. Fortunes of the war changed radically, but the essential pulpit voice was the same: "We win or lose because we please or displease God." Chapter 9 treats the polarity of preaching on the Civil War.

Shortly after the Civil War, the impact of Charles Darwin's *Origin of Species* shook the religious minds of America. These minds were steeped in a God of creation and design, a God immanent in human affairs. The pulpit could not be silent in the face of such audacious claims, and a series of responses to Darwinism ensued. They ranged from ridicule of Williams Jennings Bryan to adoption by Henry Ward Beecher. Such responses did not come all at once, but most persevere to this day, although fewer voices outrightly reject the basic claims of emergent evolution. What happened was a reinterpretation of the concept of divine design and a recognition of latitude in the theory of nature described in the scriptures. This controversy, which had been semidormant in America, was renewed in the 1918–1925 period when William Jennings Bryan reintroduced it to the scene of the fundamentalist-modernist squabble. This heated controversy is described in chapter 10.

With the rise of industrial capitalism in the United States which followed the Civil War, the church studiously tried not to rock the boat by fulfilling its prophetic role. As social, economic, and industrial conditions went from bad to worse, just about every institution save the church protested the abuses of corporate interests which, they claimed, were oriented to social Darwinism. Finally, a few voices from the pulpits began to be heard. Many, of course, had long since proclaimed the "gospel of wealth," for those who paid the bills needed to hear that philosophy. In the main, however, the pulpit talked about salvation, glory, grace, and eschatology, matters plainly related to the accepted centrality of the gospel.

The country was rife with class conflict. A few pulpiteers began to ask, "Is not the church responsible for the whole man, including his environment?" The demands of this "love-thy-neighbor-as-thyself" philosophy gnawed at the vast, vested interests, and as the social gospellers grew strong enough to contest the orthodox, a vigorous debate followed. That debate is still going on in some quarters, but more often the question for the church-man has now become "How can I best love my neighbor as myself?" The developments in this struggle are described in chapter 11.

Endorsement of, or resistance to, war and all the positions in between have found voice in the American pulpit of the twentieth century. Predominant sentiment favored participation in World War I. It became a "holy crusade for liberty," a drive for democracy, concepts thought to be inherently Christian. Retrospection following the war, however, seemed to bring much regret for quasi-official endorsement of the war by the churches. Some had seen the war as a just one, as a position somewhat akin to the neo-orthodox position in World War II: It is unchristian to allow tyrants to kill. The historic Peace Churches were vocal in World War I and seem to have spread their doctrine to ministers of many other denominations by the time of World War II. During the Korean conflict of the 1950's and the Viet Nam involvement of the 1960's, the peace movement has gained momentum from persons and institutions outside the organized church. Chapter 12 offers a spectrum of views on the issue of war as a vehicle for solving human problems.

The Social Gospel Movement described in chapter 11 gave way to a broader liberalism that cut its moorings from many traditions. Then immediately following World War I, a conservative reaction set in. These conservatives set forth certain fundamentals of the Christian faith and forthwith were labeled fundamentalists. Opponents to them were called modernists; and together with fundamentalists they were found in most Protestant groups. The focus of the modernists was relevance, rationalism, and empiricism with some reservations.

The conflict between the modernists and the fundamentalists, covered in chapter 13, had been gathering ominously for at least a decade when Harry Emerson Fosdick preached a sermon in 1922 that was intended to conciliate the two philosophies. This sermon was pamphleted throughout the country with the title "Shall the Fundamentalists Win?" Clarence Macartney of Philadelphia answered Fosdick with "Shall the Unbelievers Win?" a sermon which was also circulated widely. The exact lines of the controversy were drawn, and the infamous debate between the modernists and the fundamentalists shook American Protestantism for the next few years. The intensity of the conflict subsided by 1930, with each side feeling vindicated, if not victorious. With the exception of regular outcries by a few professional fundamentalists, the controversy now only occasionally gains strength enough to be heard.

Neo-orthodoxy developed on the American religious scene around 1930. It was a clear reaction to the easy optimism of rising liberalism which suggested that the kingdom would come out of human effort or some blind forces within the universe. Neo-orthodoxy was a renewal of faith in the grace of God as a solution to human problems. This new thrust in religion sought to deflate human vanity in order to inflate once again the sovereignty and eminence of God. Thus the debate clearly centered on the doctrine of God issue.

Liberals were quick to respond to the challenge, lest a reaction to neo-orthodoxy demean and demoralize men and move them to withdraw from social responsibility. The two thrusts served as sounding boards for each other, and in the process both seemed to develop a more balanced view on man's responsibility in God's world. The interesting interchange is developed and illustrated in chapter 14.

By the dawn of the twentieth century a free church in a free American society fragmented itself almost beyond recognition. However, to counterbalance that trend organized efforts sought to remold the body of Christ into a visible and functioning unity. They were active at least by the time of the early nineteenth century restorationists who must certainly be identified as early ecumenists. The current ecumenical movement grew out of missionary and other potentially cooperative interdenominational programs. The local councils of churches, the National Council of Churches, and the World Council of Churches, together with several newly reunited church groups, stand as a monument to the tireless efforts of the cooperators. Further, dating from Pope John XXIII, promising dialogues between Catholic and Orthodox leaders have taken place as well as meaningful Protestant-Catholic conversations.

The ecumenical movement was not without its critics who attacked from several points of view. The heart of the criticism centered on the nature of the institutions of the movement. They are charged with being essentially human rather than divine. This charge was supported quite incisively by Carl F. H. Henry, former Dean of Fuller Theological Seminary and editor of *Christianity Today*, in his sermon in this volume. Eugene Carson Blake argued a radical ecumenical position in his sermon proposing a massive union of Protestants in America. This debate is described in chapter 15.

The several ecumenical bodies of the United States had hardly become oriented to their existence when they became the objects of wrath for an assortment of ardent conservatives of the radical right. These critics were the extreme right wing of the reaction to the liberalism of the 1920's and 1930's and in a sense a continuation of some of the more obsessive fundamentalists of the 1920's. Independent, individualistic, mistrustful of men, and irrepressibly vocal, these gentlemen of the radical right led the ecumenics a dogged and frustrating chase. Chapter 16 describes their encounter, giving broad space to ecumenical critics and some attention to the ecumenics.

"Popular" and "experimental" are names given to emphases in churchmanship immediately following World War II. Each type developed its own style of preaching. The former was an effort to return to the normalcy of using Bible-based "obvious" truth, while the latter was a fluid, subjective orientation perceiving truth experimentally in human events. These differences, described and illustrated in chapter 17, inspired some unique sermonizing because they concerned themselves with a common issue: What is the vehicle of religious knowledge?

At least as far back as 1631, when Roger Williams disallowed the magistrate (state) jurisdiction in the first four commandments, separation of church and state has been an issue in American life and in the American pulpit. Until recently, when the economic facts of life threatened the existence of parochial schools and encouraged states to aid religious schools, the complete separation of church and state had increasingly become reality in the United States.

In 1960, when Roman Catholic John F. Kennedy was nominated to be the Democratic candidate to the United States presidency, one of the hottest of campaign issues was the separation of church and state. The American pulpits joined the debate. On being elected, Kennedy laid fears to rest when he seemed to make political decisions independent of Vatican control. He left most people with the feeling that a United States President could at one and the same time be a free man and a good Roman Catholic.

The rulings of the Supreme Court on cases of prayer and Bible reading in the schools completed another chapter in the separation of church and state. Widespread pulpit reaction to both of these church-state topics is shown in chapter 18.

The one domestic issue which has increasingly concerned all of America since the Civil War is that of civil rights and race relations. That issue has broad and strong religious connotation. Chapter 19 must merely scratch the surface of this most relevant and intensive pulpit issue because it can treat only the single aspect of racial segregation. A radical change in attitude has swept the nation so that one hardly now hears an open apology for racial segregation. That a preponderance of Americans act so as to insure the continuation of segregation is plain enough, but it is no longer popular to advocate it openly and vocally. Even so, a few ministers still persist in doing so, and the sermon of one of them is reproduced in this volume. But the church, or at least segments of it, has aroused the conscience of America on racial discrimination. The vast majority of the leadership of the Negro revolt came from the pulpit.

Blacks have not as yet been granted full citizenship in the minds of white America, but apparently both blacks and whites are now moving in the right direction—toward each other as people. Whether they finally meet on common ground of basic human values remains to be seen.

The challenge of the secular is currently in vogue in the American pulpit. Responses range from further disengagement to total dissolution of the institutional church and the mingling of sacred and secular as one. Those who would disengage, however, accept a responsibility for changing society but insist that they will do the changing on an individual, noninstitutional basis. They seek to motivate men to improve society. On the other hand, the church secularists define religion in a broader way and move the province of the church to whatever ground it may define as within its boundary. Simply stated, the disengagers focus on doctrines and church-building-centered religious activities while the engagers focus on activities in society beyond the church edifice walls. The disengagers try to draw the world to the church and the engagers try to draw the church to the world. A very different form and style of preaching results from this polarity. Chapter 20 traces the challenge of the secular.

The rise and fall of events and ideas in our history are clearly reflected in the sermons emanating from the American pulpit. The preacher, though a spokesman for the eternal Kingdom of God, is inextricably bound to the times in which he lives. What he sees and is able to understand is largely affected by the social millieu out of which he came and in which he travels. His is ever a struggle to rise above history, to cast off cultural filters, to lay aside the blinders of vested interests so that he may see and share God's changeless truth and love for all men. Fallible men sit before the minister

23

to learn, but they see through filters and listen sporadically, thus perceiving only in part. As different men see different parts of God's truth, differing and even contradictory emphases in the church emerge. Even confusion may appear for a time. Happily, though, free men in a free church, sitting before a free pulpit have not only potential for confusion, but potential for self-correction through self-criticism. Ultimately, this is the only real human correction.

2

PURITAN PREACHING AND THE AUTHORITY OF GOD

Eugene E. White

Before Puritanism crossed the ocean, English system-atizers had thrust a protective theology of multiple covenants between man and the blinding glare of a completely transcendent God. Perhaps borrowed from the Rhineland reformers during the reign of Henry VIII, the covenantal theories were brought to mature fruition during the last years of the sixteenth century and the early decades of the seventeenth. In evolving the complicated dialectics of Puritan theology, the English divines were responding to the felt—if not expressed—need of making the Reformed God seem less remote and more believable and servable. Accepting as ultimate truths the individual responsibility of man, election, and the antithetical natures of God and man, the theologians developed a system of interlocking covenants, including the covenant of grace, the social covenant, and the church covenant.

No sharp break with the *Institutes* or with Reformed Orthodoxy, the "new" theology was based upon the conditional promises by God and the matching requirement of faith and obedience by man. According to this equation, God offered salvation to all men who fulfill his condition: to have faith, as manifested by union with

25

Christ. Only God, however, could supply the means of satisfying his condition. Saving faith could not be achieved by man. It was a divine free gift from a sovereign God who had arbitrarily predestined those who would receive it. Despite such absolutism, which ultimately exposed naked man to an all-powerful God, the analogy of the covenants provided the means of acquiring a better apprehension of God's nature, and the conditional promises of the covenants filtered the unbearable harshness of absolutism, mitigating his terrifying unpredictability, partially penetrating his awesome mystery, and rendering less than perfect his authority. This leavening of Calvinism and Reformed theology met the theological, logical, and psychological needs of the times and the circumstances. It provided an unobtrusively rationalized basis for the relationship between God and man; it identified sin as the enemy; it prescribed continuous, conscious striving for regeneration by the individual as a means of securing the fulfillment of the covenants; it endorsed the preaching of the Word as the chief ordinary means of communication from God to man, of eradication of sin, and of attainment of salvation.

Although the covenant theology was based upon thoroughly orthodox absolutist principles, its conditional promises encouraged a posture which tended to magnify man's efforts and to minimize the doctrine of election. In the writings of English Puritans, such as William Perkins, John Preston, William Ames, Paul Baynes, and Richard Sibbes, there runs a recurrent emphasis upon the conditional aspects of the covenants, frequently at the expense of the absolutist values. This focus upon the mercy of God, the willingness of God to bind himself in contracts with man, and the efficacy of the covenants, perhaps, can be epitomized by these representative extracts from the sermons of John Preston:

God made the world . . . for His glories sake, to make manifest that now . . . was to communicate His mercy and His goodness to the creature. . . . His mercy then must needs be His glory. . . . Doubt not then, but that when you come to ask at His hand any request that is meet for you, He will be ready to grant it, for it is His glory to shew mercy.

. . . So then if you will desire salvation, and happiness, and the strength of the *Inward man*, you shall have it. . . . Saith the *Lord* . . . I am willing to enter into covenant with thee, that is, I will bind myself, I will engage myself, I will enter into bond, as it were, I will not be at liberty any more. . . . If one plead the *covenant* hard with *God* . . . He cannot deny thee, He will put away thy sins.

When transported to New England, the covenant theology shaped the form and substance of Puritan preaching, as well as the Puritan concept of the authority of God. In responding to the unique conditions of the wilderness Zion, however, the generality of the first-generation colonial ministers perhaps stressed more consistently the terrors of the Law and the absolutist aspects of the covenants than did the English Puritans. Of the New England ministers, the most extreme exponent of absolutism was John Cotton, teacher of the Boston church. Before leaving England in 1633, upon occasion, at least, Cotton had emphasized the initiative powers of man, almost to the point of teaching voluntarism; he had stressed sanctification, accepting it as a valid indication of justification and very nearly expounding a doctrine of salvation by good works; he had endorsed liberal conditions for church membership and for admission to the Lord's Supper. Within the first year after his arrival in Boston, however, Cotton had reversed his earlier "liberal" positions. An excellent example of his "new" severe interpretations of covenant theology and church membership is found in his Salem sermon of 1636, which appears as a selection in our volume.

Although influenced by Cotton, the other New England ministers departed from his Reformed absolutism by accepting the necessity of preparation and the validity of sanctification as a probable indicator of saving grace. At the opposite end of the spectrum from Cotton was Peter Bulkeley, pastor of the Concord church. In contrast to Cotton, who asserted the total spiritual passivity of man and the necessary union with Christ *before* faith, Bulkeley preached in the most liberal accents of the English Puritans. To some extent Bulkeley helped prepare

27

the way for future changes of emphasis by stressing God's mercy, by bringing salvation within the reach of the sincere seeker, by advocating liberal requirements for church membership, and by connecting morality so closely with grace that pious behavior became a "safe" indicator of justification. A representative example of his thinking, excerpted from his *The Gospel Covenant*, is presented in this volume also.

Despite the acceptance of Cotton as being the most distinguished spokesman for the New England experiment, the way of the future lay in the increased emphasis upon God's conditional promises. Sustained by their belief in the covenant of grace, the church covenant, and the social covenant, John Winthrop's people subdued the wilderness and built a vigorous, aggressive order, devoted to the service of God and the extirpation of sin. In the process of causing New England to blossom, the people themselves changed—imperceptibly, yet ineluctably. From the beginning it had been possible for them to feel some protection from the awesomeness of an absolute God: If God had voluntarily entered into compact with the elect, then God had bound himself and, therefore, was not unlimited in the application of his power. During the passage of years the will-to-believe induced many minds to leap progressively from the wish to the hope and, ultimately, to the active acceptance of this crucial extension: If, as the covenantal theories taught, it were possible not only for the elected person to enter into covenant with God, but also for the imperfect individual church and the imperfect society to do so, perhaps man was not totally impotent, without hope or merit; perhaps he possessed within himself substantial means to further his own salvation.

The encouragement of hope contained in the covenants had helped the original colonists to endure the frequent preachments of carnal man's abject depravity and impotency. Then, as civilization moved up the rivers and spread over the land, and as liberating currents of enlightenment, of tolerance, and of recognition of the innate dignity and worth of man reached New England

and penetrated the thinking of the people, the hope for personal salvation very likely grew stronger and the fears of an incomprehensible, capricious God diminished. Although during the first century of the New England experience the Puritan doctrine remained essentially the same, the nature of society had altered to such an extent that the social covenant disintegrated and virtually disappeared; the church covenant was forced into configurations which would have seemed strange and alien to John Cotton; the stress of Cotton and his followers upon the absolutist values of the covenant of grace gave way to a greater emphasis upon conditional values, the efficacy of man's striving for faith, and the automatic, causal relationship between faith and salvation.

By the 1730's societal attitudes and practices had so magnified man and, thereby, diminished the majesty and authority of an unknowable God, that New Englanders were unprepared for the absolutist preaching of Jonathan Edwards. Brushing aside the protectiveness of the conditional aspects of covenant theology, Edwards taught that totally depraved man could achieve salvation only through the mercy of a totally sovereign God. Responding to his preaching with the flash fire of the Great Awakening, New England soon flinched from the awful consciousness of an absolute God, and in 1750 the people of Northampton drove Edwards from his pulpit.

Puritan theology had partially humanized the Reformation God, and societal practices had carried the transformation even further; by rejecting Edwards' attempt to return to the intense purity of John Cotton's Reformation ideal, New England had irrevocably committed itself to the uncharted reaches of the modern age.

JOHN COTTON

John Cotton was born at Derby England, in 1584. He received the B.A. in 1602, the M.A. in 1606, and the B.D. in 1613 from Cambridge University. Becoming a fellow of Emmanuel College, Cambridge, in 1603, he later served as head lecturer, dean, and catechist of that college. Ordained to the ministry in 1610, he became vicar of St. Botolph's Church, Lincolnshire. In 1630, he preached the farewell sermon to John Winthrop's company departing from Southampton. Three years later he and his family left for the Massachusetts Bay Colony, where he became teacher of the Boston church. A central figure in the Antinomian confrontation, the Roger Williams controversy, and the defense of the Congregational way, he remained one of the most influential—and most conservative—colonial leaders until his death in 1652.

A Sermon*

A SERMON PREACHED BY THE REVEREND, MR. JOHN COTTON, TEACHER OF THE FIRST CHURCH IN BOSTON IN NEW-ENGLAND. DELIVER'D AT SALEM, 1636. *To which is Prefixed, a Retraction of his former Opinion concerning* Baptism, *utter'd by him immediately Preceeding the Sermon here Emitted.*

Having been moved by your Reverend Elders, and some Others, to Speak a Word of *Instruction* and *Exhortation;* I thought it meet to begin with some word of *Confession.* . . . [Here follows a five-to-seven minute retraction of a position which Cotton had taken on local church control of baptism.]

Now having expressed this Word of *Confession,* together with my acknowledgment of my dependance upon the Lord for grief and sorrow; I this desire, That if my Letter Remain Written in any of your hands, you would not now look at it as my judgment; though sometime it was, yet now you have heard it retracted again by me, Professing also, that if any thing which I have since Written or Spoken, God give me to see it, appear different from the Truth, I will retract it also; in the mean time blame me not, if I do not retract it.

Jeremiah L.5.

Come, and let us cleave unto the Lord in a *Perpetual* and *Everlasting* Covenant which shall never be forgotten.

Some Translations reads it:

Come, and let us joyn our selves to the Lord in a Perpetual Covenant that shall never be forgotten.

* (Boston, printed in the year 1713).

30

These be the words which were foretold by Jeremiah, which the People of God Returning out of Captivity of Babel should use for the incouragement of one another to return to Sion, and there to bind themselves in Church Covenant with the Lord; for so you read it in the verse foregoing: *In those days (when the Lord shall destroy Babel) the Children of Israel shall come, and the Children of Judah together, going, and weeping as they go: and seek the Lord their God.* They shall ask the way to Zion with *their faces thitherward saying, Come, and let us joyn our selves to the Lord in a Perpetual Covenant, that shall not be forgotten.*

In these words of encouragement or exhortation you may observe.

1. The encouragement to the Work, *Come, and let us joyn our selves to the Lord.*

2. This joyning is set forth.

(1.) By the means of it: by a Covenant.

(2.) That Covenant is here amplifyed by a double adjunct of a double Eternity.

1. Here is the Covenant it self, that is Perpetual.

2. Set forth not only by the durance of it, but by the Report and Memory of it unto all Ages: *that shall never be forgotten.*

To speak to joyning to the Lord at large, is neither the Principal intendment of my Text, nor may it be so convenient to speak only to it. I shall have occasion to open it in shewing the way in which they do joyn to the Lord.

The Doctrine which I would Commend to your Christian consideration, is this;

DOCTRINE.

That the Church-Covenant, where-with the People of Israel & Judah did joyn themselves to the Lord, especially after their return from Babel; and yet more especially under the days of the New Testament, was a Perpetual Covenant.

Come, let us joyn our selves to the Lord. Israel and Judah spake this as they were a Church, and as they were about to renew Church Fellowship; *let us joyn our selves to the Lord in a Perpetual Covenant that shall never be forgotten.* You read the like Expression, Jer. 31. 31,32,33,34. *This shall be my Covenant with the House of Israel, saith the Lord, I will put my Law in their inward parts, and write it in their hearts, and I will be their God, and they shall be my People.* And verse 34. *I will forgive their Iniquities, and remember their Sins no more.* It is therefore an Everlasting Covenant; and He doth make the main difference between this and the

31

former Covenant to lie in this; whereas they break that Covenant, v.32. *This Covenant shall not be broken.* . . . In the Old Covenant you may observe a four-fold act of God, and a double act of the People.

First. The Lord doth prepare his People, and calleth them to Mount *Sinai,* and there revealeth Himself in Thundrings and Lightnings, and flames of Fire, so that the stoutest Spirits amongst them quaked; and *Moses* tho' a Man full of faith, yet he saith of himself, *I exceedingly tremble and fear;* and so did all the People; and when they heard the voice of the Thunders, and saw the Lightnings: *Exod.* 20. 18 *to* 21. They said to *Moses, Speak thou with us, and we will hear, but let not God Speak with us lest we die.* Thus did the Lord prepare them by breaking, for if the Lord do intend some real and serious work, He will then shake the foundation of the stubborness of their hearts, and bring them to see their own stubborness and baseness, for else they would despise it.

Secondly. The Second act of God is a Commandment which He doth put forth, wherein He doth require an exact Obedience unto all the Commandments of the Law, and to his Statutes & Judgments: Exod. 19.5. *If you will obey my voice indeed, saith the Lord, and keep my Covenant; then you shall be my peculiar treasure above all People.* Now this Covenant of God consisteth of Moral Laws, and Statutes and Judgments, unto all which He doth require Obedience, even to all that is written in the Law, *Deut.* 27.27.

Thirdly. The Lord doth profess unto them all that should keep Covenant, That they should Live by keeping Covenant. And this is the Grand and Principle Promise wraping up all other, *Lev.* 18.5. And the Apostle doth Interpret the meaning of that Promise: Gal. 3. 12. *The Law is not of faith, but the man that doth these things shall Live in them:* and this is the Promise of Life which God giveth to those that keep Covenant.

Fourthly. The fourth act of God in making this Covenant is, a heavy threatning of a curse to any that shall break these Commandments, *Deut.* 27. 22. Gal. 3. 10. *Cursed is every one that continueth not in all things that are written in the Law to do them.*

Now there are two acts of the People.

1. They do profess universal Obedience unto all the Commandments, *Deut.* 5.27. *Exod.* 19.8. Twice they repeat it, *All that the Lord shall say unto us, we will hear it, and do it.* Only consider this, They Promise it in some kind of opinion of their own Strength, without any sense or feeling of their own Insufficiency; like men under pangs of Conscience, they do believe that they shall be able to keep and do all that the Lord shall say unto them. *O that there were such an heart in them!* saith the

Lord, *Deut.* 5.29. Or as the word is in the Original; *Who shall give them such a heart?* But this they Promise.

2. They yield themselves to be accursed of God, if they shall not keep that Covenant; and therefore when it was pronounced, *Cursed is every one that continueth not in all things that are written in the Law to do them, all the People did say, Amen;* and so their faith lay upon a curse: This is the Old Covenant that God made with his People, and is called a Covenant of Works; the Lord requireth Righteousness and Works, He Promiseth Life to their Works, and they say, *Amen,* to enter into a curse. Now this was a temporal Covenant; this my Covenant they brake, saith the Lord; and they did quickly turn aside from the wayes of the Lord, and therefore *Moses* when he cometh and seeth the Calf which they had made, he brake the Tables of the Covenant.

Now for the Covenant that is Everlasting, we may observe therein also four acts of God towards his People.

First. Look as He prepareth the other by a Spirit of Bondage, so he doth prepare these for His Everlasting Covenant, by a Spirit of Poverty; and they are Poor and Afflicted in Spirit, in sense of their own Unworthiness & Insufficiency, that which the Lord doth wish to the other, *Deut.* 5.29. He worketh in these: Zeph. 3.12. *There shall be brought home to Zion a Poor and an Afflicted People:* He meaneth not in respect of their civil Estates, for there was not a feeble People amongst them; but as they stood in their Spirits, they were empty, and as they thought destitute of God, and therefore should seek the Lord and his Face, and his Strength, like those that had lost both Church and Covenant; unto those the Lord will have an Eye, and He will dwell with men of a contrite Spirit, *Isai.* 57.15, 16. . . .

Secondly. When the Lord hath brought His People to be Poor in Spirit, He doth then Promise them,

1. *Christ:* He giveth Him for a Covenant: Isai. 42.6. *I have called thee in Righteousness: I will give thee for a Covenant unto the Gentiles.* When the Lord maketh a Covenant of Grace, this is the gift of God; this is the Principal blessing of the Covenant, *Isai.* 49.8. And the Lord will not give Life in them to keep, and by them to uphold, but Jesus Christ for both.

2. In Jesus Christ He doth give Everlasting Communion with Him. Through Christ He will take away the Stony heart, and give a heart of flesh; and He will bring with Him Everlasting Righteousness, *Dan.* 9.24. That is to say, Such Pardon of Sin as He will never revoke more, that Justification which He will work in Christ, He will never repent of. . . .

Thirdly. These three things the Lord doth require.

1. *Faith:* That is to say a yielding of the Soul to the Lord, as unable

33

for this work, and yet to wait upon Him for Righteousness: *Ezek.* 36.37. *I will be enquired for this of the house of Israel to do it for them.* Not only to be sought unto for the Mercy, but I will be sought, that is, They shall seek me, they shall seek his face and his strength to do it all for them.

2. He doth require the *Obedience* of Faith: and this is expressly called for, *Rom.* 16.26. That is, for such Righteousness, as none can work by any Graces of their own; but which being wrought in them doth put life and strength into all their duties.

3. He doth require of his People that they should be of a Melting frame of Spirit, in regard of all their Whorishness, whereby they have prophaned His Name; they shall wail and bemone this: and therefore it is said of them in the verse before the Text, That Weeping they should go, for all the Evils that they have wrought in God's sight: And this is that which we read: *Ezek.* 6.9. *They that escape of you shall remember me among the Nations whither they shall be carried Captives, because I am broken with their whorish heart, which hath departed from me, and with their eyes which go a whoring after their Idols: and they shall loath themselves for the evils which they have committed in all their abominations.* This doth the Lord require of his People: but observe this withal, that He doth not require it in a way of a Legal command, but with an alsufficient Vertue, whereby He will work in them what He doth require; so that doth He require, that they should walk holily before Him, He Himself doth also work this. . . . The Lord prepareth the heart: certain duties indeed he doth lay upon them; as to believe in his Name, to yield the obedience of Faith, and to mourn for him; and he doth convey an effectual Power to work them.

Fourthly. The fourth act is an act of Cursing belonging to this Covenant.

1. To them that do not receive it.

2. To those that do Apostate from it: To them that do not receive it: *Heb.* 2.2, 3. If the word spoken by Angels was stedfast, and every transgression and disobedience, received a just recompence of reward, how shall we escape if [we] neglect so great Salvation? The neglecting of it brings desperate Misery.

To those that do Apostate from it: Heb. 10.29. *Of how much sorer Punishment shall they be thought worthy of who have trodden under foot the Son of God. . . .* Deut. 30.17,18. *If thy heart turn away that thou will not bear, but shalt be drawn away, and worship other gods, and serve them, I denounce unto you this day, that ye shall surely perish, and that ye shall not prolong your dayes upon the Land whither thou passeth over Jordan to possess it.* And that it is the Covenant of Grace, we may perceive by comparing, *Deut.* 30 v.11, to the 14, with, *Rom.* 16.6. So that we may see the Lord doth threaten a heavy curse to fall upon them that transgress this Covenant.

Now for the Peoples part: Their acts are two.

1. They fall down before the Lord confessing their Unworthiness of any Mercy.

2. Confessing their own Inability and want of Strength; and this is that which Joshua laboureth to possess the People with, *Josh.* 24. 19. There he telleth them, *Ye cannot serve the Lord your* GOD; that they might not trust in their own Strength: and therefore when the Lord doth make this Covenant with *Abraham,* he fell on his face, *Gen.* 17.3 in sense of his own Unworthiness.

Why this Covenant is such an Everlasting Covenant?

Reas. 1. Is from the Root & Fountain of it: Jer. 31.3. *I have loved thee with an Everlasting love, therefore with Mercy have I drawn thee.* What moveth the Lord to be thus earnest and zealous in drawing men to Christ? *No man can come to me,* saith Christ, *except the Father which hath sent me draw him,* Joh. 6.44. How cometh this to pass? *I have loved thee with an Everlasting love, therefore have I drawn thee.* Now He will carry his work an end in His with a mighty Power, thro' all the backwardness of their own Spirits; And this is the ground mentioned: Psal. 111. 4,5,9. *The Lord is Merciful and full of Compassion, He will be mindful of his Covenant for ever: He hath sent Redemption to his People, and commandeth his Covenant for ever. . . .*

2. Another principal Reason is taken from the Surety; though the Israelites had *Moses* for a Mediator, yet they had him not for a Surety. Now Jesus Christ is made the Surety of the Covenant, *Heb.* 4.6. A Surety is not for a Testament, but for a Covenant; no need is of a Surety on God's part, He never brake Covenant with any: but if a Surety be needful, doubtless it lyeth on our part; and therefore it is said, *I will give thee for a Covenant,* even Christ Himself: Isai. 55.2,3. *I will make an everlasting Covenant with thee, even the sure Mercies of David: Behold, I have given him for a witness to the People.* And hence it is that all the Promises of this Covenant are made directly to Jesus Christ; the Old Covenant was made to the People, but this is made to Christ. . . . So long as this Covenant is kept, and so long as the Members of the Church keep close to Christ, so long this Covenant is not broken. And hence it is that when the Jews had committed the greatest Sin that ever was committed upon the face of the Earth, yet the Apostles did not break Communion with them, notwithstanding that fearful injury of putting to death the Lord of Life; because they might have done it of Ignorance, and therefore, *Act.* 3.1. they went and joyned with him in Prayer; why did not they know that they had Crucified a just Man?

35

and is not this a horrible Prophanation of the Covenant? No, no, Brethren, this will not break an Everlasting Covenant. *Father, forgive them, they know not what they do;* our Saviour Prayeth for them, the Apostles keep Communion with them; here is the Spirit of a Saviour, and of his blessed Apostles: but when they do put away known Christ, *Act.* 13. 45, 46, when they contradicted and blasphemed, then what sayes the Apostles? *It was necessary the word of God should first have been spoken unto you, but seeing ye put it from you, and judge your selves unworthy of everlasting life, lo, we turn to the Gentiles.* And so also it was a dreadful proceeding which they use in this case: Act. 19. 7,8,9. *He went into the Synagogue & spake boldly for the space of three months, disputing & perswading the things concerning the kingdom of God. But when divers were hardened and believed not, but spake evil of that way before the multitude, he departed from them, and separated the Disciples,* . . . So mark you what it is that doth dissolve this Everlasting Covenant; not this that they Kill the Messias; it was a horrible Murder, but yet they may not separate for Murder: What! if it be the Eternal Son of God! You may not separate for that neither, so long as you do not Sin against Knowledge; but when they do Sin against Knowledge, and after they have been taught and convinced, do yet rebel, then is this Everlasting Covenant broken, else it is not broken till they come to this desperate extremity.

USE. I. The Use of this point in the first Place, may shew us from hence, a ground of that which some of us (yet but few) saw the truth of, in our Native Country, namely the Necessity of a *Church Covenant* to the Institution of a Church, *Come, and let us joyn our selves to the Lord:* That which doth make a People a joyned People with God, that doth make a Church: What is that? The Covenant of Grace doth make a People, a joyned People with God, and therefore a Church of God: and therefore you shall find that when the Lord Establishes Israel for a Church unto Himself, He maketh this Covenant; not only that in Mount Horeb, but He doth make another covenant with them in the Plains of Moab, Deut. 29. . . . And so by this means they came to be established to be a Church. . . .

. . . You are here this day that the Lord might establish you to be his People, *Deut.* 28. 12, 13. And how was the Church renewed, but by the renewing of this Covenant in the days of *Asa,* 2 *Chron.* 15. 12. And so in the days of *Ezra* and *Nehemiah, Chap.* 9. 38. *Chap.* 10. 29. And afterwards when the Lord would cast off his People: Zech. 11. 10, 14. *He brake the staff of Beauty, and the staff of Bands:* This now followeth, that so many of us, as have come to the Ordinances of God, and have partaken of the Seals of the Covenant, and have not entred into a Covenant, have violated the Seals of the Covenant which have not been given to the Elect of God in general, but to the Church of God; and therefore look at the Covenant by which you have entred here, as the ability of your State, which by no changes you are for ever to be removed from, but may for ever keep it by fellowship with Jesus Christ.

USE. II. In the Second Place, Let me provoke my Self, and all my Brethren, and all the Churches to Consider, What kind of Covenant you have entred, or will enter into: If you shall come hither into this Country, and shall here confess your Sins, that you have prophaned the Name of God withal, if you take Christ for your King, and Priest & Prophet, and if you shall profess to walk in all his ways, this may all be but a Covenant of works.

The Elders of the Church propound it, Will you renounce all your Sinful Pollutions? Will you keep Covenant? And enter into a Covenant with the Church, and take Christ, and promise to walk after all God's Ordinances? You Answer, All this we will do; all this is not more than the Old Covenant: For you are much deceived if you think there was no speech of Christ in the Covenant of works. What were the Ceremonies but shadows of Christ? What was the laying the hand on the head of the Sacrifice, but the laying hold upon Christ Jesus? What was the blood of the Sacrifice? Was it not the blood of Christ? And what was the Atonement by that blood? Was it not the Atonement which is by Christ? All the understanding Israelites did see that these things did point at Christ. Now, if we do enter into a Covenant to keep the Ordinances of the Law, of the Gospel, and of the Civil State, (for that was the tripartive Covenant) all this may be but a Covenant of Works. What then must we do? We must fall down before the Lord in our Spirits, and profess our selves insufficient to keep any Covenant, and profess our selves unworthy that the Lord should keep any Covenant with us; as to say, *Lord! who am I? Or what is my Fathers house, that the Lord should ever look upon such a poor Soul as I am?* What doth the Church lay hold upon duties, and there's an end? No, no, There are no true Servants of Jesus Christ, but they must be drawn out of themselves by a Spirit of Bondage, and unto Christ by a Spirit of Poverty; and then a Soul seeth there is much in Christ, but he cannot hope there is any thing for him: Now the Lord doth draw a man on to Christ Jesus, and calleth him to believe in Christ, but yet he is not able to reach Him. Now then, if the Lord draw the Soul to depend upon Christ, and shall go forth, and not undertake any thing in his own Strength; so you will keep it by the Strength of the Lord also; now the Lord will have Peace with you, and the gates of Hell shall never prevail against you. Build a Church upon any other foundation but Faith, and the profession of

Faith, and it will break into manifold distempers. But if the Church be built upon this Rock: Storms and Winds will not so much as shake it, it being built upon Faith, and Faith upon Christ Jesus: by this means the Covenant will keep us constantly, sweetly, and fruitfully, in an everlasting kind of Serviceable-usefulness one to another.

USE. III. The Use in the third Place, is of Direction, Upon what terms you may Separate. Suppose the Church Promise never to defile themselves more with any Pollutions of the Sons of men, but they do defile themselves, then Covenant is broken; they did Covenant they would not come into false Assemblies, & that they would have no fellowship with them, that did allow of false Assemblies; but this Covenant cometh to be broken: If this be your Covenant, it is but a Covenant of Works, and then no marvel tho' it do break & fail, seeing it stands upon duties, and keeping of duties; for being built upon the condition of duties, and standing upon performance of duties, and being broken upon neglect of duties, this is but a Covenant of Works; and yet you may be Married to Christ in this. You come and resolve to walk in all Ordinances, and undertake to reform both Church & Common Wealth; in such a Covenant the Lord is content to take you by the hand and become a Husband to you, *Jer.* 31.32. And what will a Husband do, he will rejoyce with you, and you will find comfort in duties; your heart hath been refreshed that you may see you have Jesus Christ in your bosome, He will also reveal Secrets unto you, he will cast in Seeds of sundry good things among you, so that you shall Prophecy in his Name, and have a Seed of Prayer, and many good things, and yet may want Everlasting love; you may find much comfort, and yet you will find some or other to give offence, or some or other to take offence, and you will break with breaking upon breaking, until you be like Sheep without a Shepherd. This is not the Covenant, therefore Brother, upon which thou & I must live in Church-fellowship everlastingly, tho' herein thou hast had comfort, & that unspeakable; such thou mayest have & yet run upon a Covenant of Works.

2. A second branch of this use may be to teach us where-upon a Man may build Separation Not upon breach of duty tho' they transgress, & prostrate their Sabbaths, defiling themselves with unclean devices of men. Is the Covenant of Grace broken? It is not broken until you have convinced this People of their Sin, *Act.* 3. 17. Because, if the Covenant be a Covenant of Grace, Jesus Christ doth step in, & all the breaches are fastened upon him. When then is the Church of Christ broken from him? Not when she doth Crucifie Him, nor when she doth pluck the Crown of Soveraignty from His Head; these things she may do of Ignorance: but when they are convinced that they have broken his Will, and transgressed the rule of

His Gospel: Now, if out of haughtiness of Spirit, they will not see an error, but will have their own ways still; now it is no Sin of Ignorance, no Sin of Infirmity. Now when men Sin not in Infirmity, not in Pang of a Passion, as *Peter* denied his Master, nor in Pang of a Lust, as *David* when he committed Adultery, but when in cool blood, Men do reject the word of Life: Now, since they have put the word of God from them, you may break off from them, and the blessing of Him that dwelt in the bush will be on your heads. . . .

USE. IV. The fourth Use may serve, to teach any Private Christian, whether thou be oft joyned to the Lord in an Everlasting Covenant. If thou buildest upon a Covenant of works, the end of all thy faith will be to say *Amen* to a curse, *Deut.* 27.21. If thou hast entred into a Covenant of Grace the end of thy faith will be the Salvation of thy Soul, and this is the faith of the Gospel, I *Pet.* 1. 8, 9.

Quest. But how shall I know whether I have built upon an Everlasting Covenant, or not?

Ans. 1. The Lord hath drawn thee to make this Everlasting Covenant, thou didst not take it upon thy own accord. Mind therefore what I say, The Lord draweth partly by a Spirit of Bondage, partly by a Spirit of Adoption: If you never found yourself a fire-brand of Hell, if your conscience were never afflicted with your dangerous Estate by Nature, you were never yet in Jesus Christ. You will say, *I trust in Christ, and look to be saved by his Righteousness.* Were you ever afflicted with sense of your own unrighteousness? If you say, No, I Pray you read, Joh. 8. 30. *As he spake these things, many believed on him.* They trusted on Him for Salvation. Did you then take the Covenant? see what followeth; *Jesus saith unto them, If you continue in my word, then are ye my Disciples indeed. And you shall know the truth, and the truth shall make you free.* They answered him, *We be Abrahams seed, & were never in bondage to any man:* They were never acquainted with bondage; they hoped bondage belonged to any rather than to them, and was more fit for Gentiles than for Jews. But what saith Christ? *Whosoever committeth Sin, the same is the Servant of Sin. If the Son shall make you free, then shall you be free indeed.* And afterwards he telleth them, *You are of your Father the Devil.* For if a Soul were never yet bruised with Sin, and with the sense of Sin, he never yet laid hold upon Christ, with a true Justifying Faith; such an one will not continue in Gods house for ever.

Object. You will say, Those that are brought up under Christian Parents, they are not affected with such Terrors as others are, that have lived in roaring distempers, of them, it is great reason that God should so bring them on by shewing them their fearful Misery; but these have been well trained up, and I for my part, saith one, cannot tell whether ever God did work this upon me?

Ans. If the State of such Persons be good, I profess, I do not know how to Intrepret the Speech of Christ. These men are the Children of *Abraham,* and yet if they do not see their bondage, they are not free by the Son; there is difference in the measure of the Spirit of bondage; as there is difference betwixt the Launcing and Pricking of a Boil, and yet both let out the Corruption, the one with a lesser, the other with a greater issue: therefore if the Lord doth not cut thee off from all thy good Education, believe it, thou art not yet in Christ, this faith of thine will fail thee, if thou so livest, and so dyest.

Object. But thou wilt say, I know the Pangs of Conscience, and the terrors of it, and I have seen the error of my way, and have cast off my leud Company; and since I know that the Lord requireth that I should seek him in Church Estate; I have come some thousands of Miles for that end, and I could not endure to see such things as are done by the devices of men: will not this hold?

Ans. I beseech you consider it, you have fallen upon this Reformation, you have undertaken a Covenant, yet now you have failed, and what then have you done? I go to Christ, and desire him to sprinkle me with the blood of his Covenant. Is not this a safe Estate? Truly this is no more than the very Covenant of Works, which the People of Israel entred into at *Horeb,* the Lord shook the foundations of their hearts; upon it they entred into a Covenant; *All that God commandeth us, we will hear it and do it;* and if they did offend, they then go to the appointed Sacrifice, and what, saith the Soul in such a case? *I thank God, I find some Peace to my Conscience.* All this you may do, you may reform your Selves and Families, and Churches; and when you fail at any time, you may return to Christ, and He may give you some remorse, as he did to the Israelites, *Psal.* 78. 34, 35, 36. All this may be by a Spirit of Bondage: *He in Mercy forgave their Iniquities, and destroyed them not.* So they may come to have their Sins Pardoned, but this kind of Pardon, is but a reprievment; it is not in everlasting Righteousness & Mercy: they Pray for Christ, and Mercy, and He doth sprinkle them, and then they see & find, that the Lord hath been Merciful unto them: but this will not do, the Lord will soon call back such Pardon. . . . When men have received ease from God, and then are streightlaced towards their Brethren, then doth the Lord revoke his Pardon. So that Reformation is no assurance that God hath made an everlasting Covenant with us. And mind you further, All the Graces that you have laid hold upon, have sprung from your own Righteousness. Thou hast taken a Promise, Did it belong to thee? if not it will fail you; you say you have been humbled, and come to Christ, and He hath refreshed you, mark where upon it is built; upon your humiliation? No, but I come to Christ, Do you so? Who brought you to Christ? He saith, *No man can come to me except the Father draw him.* Now, come to such an one, and say, Go to Prayer; saith the poor Soul, I cannot Pray; Be humbled, I cannot be humbled; apply Promises, they belong to any rather than to me: Such a frame of Spirit there is in every one whom the Father draweth: If you come to Christ by vertue of any thing which is in you, it is but a legal work. And I pray consider, what it will amount unto, you will find, that these men will breed distraction in your Churches, such Members will make no choice how they hear, or how they deal with their Brethren; look to it therefore carefully, when they come into the Church, for otherwise you will find everlasting confusion, rather than an everlasting Covenant.

2. Now then, doth the Lord draw you to Christ, when you are broken in the sense of your own Sins, and of your own Righteousness? When you look at duties you are not able to do them, not able to hear or pray aright. If the Lord do thus draw you by his Everlasting Arm, He will put a Spirit into you, that will cause you to wait for Christ, and to wait for Him until He doth shew Mercy upon you; and if you may but find Mercy at the last, you will be quiet and contented with it. And whilst you do with Patience & Constancy wait, you are drawn with Everlasting Love; now you have Christ in you, though you do not feel him: for as the Earth is hanged upon nothing, *Job* 26.7. So now there is a Place for Christ in the heart, when it is emtied of every thing besides; and such a man hath Christ, and is blessed, and the Covenant of Grace is his, you may safely receive him into your Church fellowship; and tho' he do neither know Christ nor his Covenant to be his, yet he will wait for him, knowing there is none in Heaven but Him, or in Earth in comparison of Him. . . . Now cometh the Son with his Personal work, (as he saith, Joh. 6.44. *No man knows the Father but the Son, & he to whom the Son reveals him:*) in which he doth show the Soul, that all this former work was the mighty Hand of God, whereby he hath drawn the Soul unto Jesus Christ, & afterwards doth assure and clear it unto the Soul in some measure, that this way is the way wherein God leadeth all his Elect Ones. Now where the Son leadeth, the Holy Ghost beginneth to work his proper work in the Soul, and Sealeth all this to the Soul; for the Soul will not rest in a weak hope that Jesus Christ is his, but doth seek for more & better security of Jesus Christ. If he have a Promise never so clear, yet it doth not quiet his Spirit fully, it doth stay him from sinking, but not from searching. . . . And thus he wrestles with God and prays for it [further mercy]; according to what the Apostle speaks: Eph. 1. 13. *In whom after ye believed, ye were sealed with*

41

the holy Spirit of Promise. And when the Soul hath received this, then doth he Sleep in quietness, and hath full contentment, and still he doth yet depend on Christ Jesus, fearing lest he should grieve & quench the Spirit; and such a Soul it is unto whom the Lord hath made an Everlasting Covenant.

If this man have broken any Law of God, you shall soon bring him about to see his Errors; and all this doth shew a man, he is a poor empty Creature; and this Soul is brought lower and lower, and nearer and nearer to Jesus Christ. So if we do wisely consider this, it may serve to give us a taste of discerning whether we be in an Everlasting Covenant, or no.

USE. V. The Use in the fifth Place, is of *Consolation* unto all the faithful Servants of God, whom God hath made this Everlasting Covenant withal: You will find that this will never be forgotten. You have entred into such a Covenant, wherein Christ is yours, and the Covenant yours, and all the Promises yours, and all the Blessings yours, and the whole World yours, and that which is the strength or the Consolation, they are yours Everlastingly, if the Lord bring you out of your selves, by a Spirit of Bondage, and unto Christ by a Spirit of Poverty; so that you wait upon him and cannot rest, until Christ hath revealed Himself to you by his Spirit: here is your Comfort, the Lord hath made with you an Everlasting Covenant which shall never be forgotten. . . . When *Moses* came and saw the Israelites worshipping the golden Calf, *Exod.* 32. 19. because he saw they had broken Covenant with God, therefore he brake the Tables of the Covenant; to shew the Lord would have no fellowship with them; and if the Covenant had not been renewed, they had perished. But come you to *Davids* Covenant: Psal. 89. 28. to the 34 *verse. My Covenant,* saith the Lord, *shall stand fast for ever: if his Children forsake my Law, I will visit their transgressions with a Rod; but my loving kindness will I not take from them.* This Covenant doth not stand on keeping Commandments, but this is all our delight, That the Lord will not break Covenant with us, nor alter the thing that is gone out of his Lips. Consider therefore, for here is a great deal of difference, your Covenant is not a point of order only, but the foundation of all your comfort; and therefore look not at it as a complement, for it is the well-ordered Covenant of God, even the Security of your Souls.

Object. *But some will say, This would indeed much comfort me, that hath been delivered, but if a man touch any Unclean thing, he is defiled, and if I touch him, that hath touched any Unclean thing, I am defiled also,* Numb. 19.13, 14. *Therefore sadness is upon me night and day for the Sins of the Church, and this doth eat up all my Comfort?*

Answ. I Pray you consider it: I will but interpret what it is to touch a dead man, and to touch dead Ordinances. I cannot give you a better Interpretation, than by that expression, which the Apostle useth: 2 Cor. 7.1. *It is good for a Man not to touch a Woman.* If so be a Man touch a strange Woman, so as to be familiar to plead for her, and to connive with her, this Man is defiled; and if I now touch this Man so as to be familiar with him, and to keep fellowship with him, I am also defiled. So in case the Church do tolerate these, that do defile themselves with any Sinful Pollution, do not I make my self Unclean now by touching this Church? God forbid, unless it be by touching them with familiar connivance. But If I do now touch them, with a sharp reproof, this doth indeed touch the Church, but it is so far from defiling, as that it doth hold forth the Purity of his heart that toucheth them: and if you do forbear Communion with the Church when you know the Church hath defiled her self, if you shall not come home to the Church, and bewail your Separation, your not touching the Church hath defiled you, *Lev.* 19. 17. You see the Church lye in Sin, you will not touch her, then you Sin against her, and have broken your Covenant. Will you suffer your Brother's Ox to lye in the Mire? and will not pluck it out? And are not Brethren more than Oxen. . . . I Pray you therefore consider it: I am marvellously afraid of Separation from Churches upon any breach of duty; they who do Separate for such causes, think they are sprinkled with the water of Separation: but believe it, they are Separated from Christ Jesus for ever, if they so live and so dye. Therefore if you belong to Christ, He will shew you it is not the water of Separation that will serve your turn, but getting Christ Jesus, and sitting closer to Him, and to your Brethren, by Admonishing and Reproving them, if you see them defiled. This will keep you clean, and your hearts clean, and your Souls comfortable: That the Lord hath made an Everlasting Covenant with you that shall never be *Forgotten.*

FINIS

PETER BULKELEY

Peter Bulkeley was born at Odell, England, in 1583. En-
rolling in St. John's College, Cambridge, he proceeded to the
B.A. in 1605 and the M.A. in 1608. He was appointed a
fellow in 1605 and University preacher in 1610. Upon suc-
ceeding his father as pastor at Odell, he served in that
charge until his suspension by Archbishop William Laud in
1635. Moving to Massachusetts Bay, in 1636 he became
the founder and the first minister of the Concord Church,
serving that congregation until his death in 1659. One of the
most liberal of the first-generation Puritans, he is chiefly
remembered for his widely read The Gospel Covenant, *which*
contains the ultimate development of covenant theology.

Three Differences More Betwixt the Two Covenants*

The third difference between the Covenant of workes, and of grace, is this; That in the covenant of works Gods acceptation begins with the worke, and so goes on to the worker or person working; but in the covenant of grace, his acceptation begins with the person, and so goes on to the work; In the one God accepts the person for the workes sake: In the other God rewards the worke for the persons sake. Hereof it is that the life promised in the Covenant of workes, is called ὀφείλημα, a debt, as due unto the worke unto which it is promised. But that which is promised in the Covenant of grace, is called χάρισμα, a gift, as being freely given to the person, without respect to any worke, or if to the worke, yet for the persons sake. This word (*gratis*) freely, puts the difference between the covenant of workes and of grace. In the covenant of workes, God justifies the doers of the law, but not (*gratis*) freely; but in the covenant of grace God justifies freely, without respect to the worke, out of love to the person. This is noted in the speech of *Moses* concerning *Abel*; *God had respect to Abel, and to his sacrifice*; Abel being a believer, and under grace, God had respect to his sacrifice, but it was because he first had

* Peter Bulkeley, *The Gospel Covenant . . . Preached in Concord in New England* (2nd ed., London, 1651), pp. 77-87.

respect to *Abel* himselfe. Hence also is that argument of theirs in *Judges* 13.23. *If* (say they) *the Lord would slay us; he would not have accepted an offering at our hands.*

They reason from the acceptance of their service, to the acceptance of their person; because the person is accepted first, and therefore if the offring be accepted, then the person much more. But on the contrary the Lord threatneth, that when he took no pleasure in their persons, then their offerings should not be regarded. And so when *Elijah* and the Priests of *Baal* offered the same kinde of sacrifice, God accepted the sacrifice of *Elijah*, but not of the other, because his person was accepted, but theirs were not. In I *Kings* 8. 52. God is said to have *his eyes open to heare the prayers of his people*; it is not the eye which heares, but the eare; yet God is said to have his eyes open to hear our prayers, because there is something first in Gods eye, which makes his eare to listen unto our cry: First, he lookes favourably upon our persons, and hath a gracious respect unto ourselves, and then he bowes his eare to the prayer which we make before him. According to that, *Psal.* 34.15. *The eyes of the Lord are upon the righteous, and his ear is open to their prayers*; Thus in Psal. 102. 19, 20. God is said to *look downe* from heaven, *that he may hear &c.* Thus it is in the Covenant of grace, Gods acceptance beginneth first with the person. And hence it is that when God hath cast favour upon the person, then he accepts weake services from him. A cup of cold water is better accepted from such an one, then a thousand rivers of oyle from another hand; yea though there be imperfections and weaknesses in the thing done, yet God passeth by the weaknesses for the favour he bears unto the person. As we may see in *Jacob*, he seeks the blessing, but mixeth so much imperfection and sin in it, that if God had not accepted his person, he might have brought a curse upon himselfe instead of a blessing; but God had said, *Jacob have I loved*, and therefore though he like not his dissembling, yet he passed by his infirmity, and *Jacob* got the blessings. And so *David*, though the thing which he had done displeased the Lord, yet God took not his mercy from him, as he took it from *Saul*; for *Saul* was under a covenant of works, and *David* under a covenant of grace. Herein the Lord would shew, that it was the person, not the work which had respect unto. But *Adam* being under a covenant of workes, he finds acceptance with God no longer then his worke is found perfect before him. All his personall indowments, excellent gifts, and the image of God which was stamped upon him, by which he was but little inferiour to the Angels, all these could procure him no favour or acceptance any longer then his worke was right; because hee was under the Covenant of Workes, his person is accepted according to his worke.

For all such as are under the Law, and have not yet made their refuge unto grace to finde acceptance in Christ, nothing that they do hath any acceptance with God. Themselves are abominable, and so are all their works abominable. And till they come to have their persons accepted in Christ, it's in vaine to tell God of their services, and what great things they have done; he regards none of their works, they are to him as the filthiness of a menstruous woman. Though they doe such things as are highly esteemed amongst men, yet they are but abomination in the sight of God. In *Luk.* 18. the Pharisee tells the Lord what a number of good works he had done; fasting, praying, paying tythes, dealing justly, &c. But what doth all this availe him? he goes away without any acceptance before God. So *Mat.* 7.22. and *Luke* 13.26. they shall come and say unto Christ, We *have eaten and drunke in thy presence, and prophesied in thy Name, and done many great workes*; But see what the Lord saith, *Depart away from me I know ye not.* Their persons were never accepted by grace in Christ, and therefore all that they had done; was but as if they had brought a carrion for sacrifice, or had offered Swines blood before the Lord. Here therefore begin, if we would have our works accepted, come before God in humility, and sense of our owne vileness, as the Publican did, and seek to be accepted through grace in Christ, and then come and offer thy gift and so coming, both thou and thy sacrifice shall finde acceptance with God....

For singular comfort unto all such, as having made their refuge unto grace, have found acceptance through faith in Christ. Be herein comforted, that the weakest and poorest services that you put up to God in Christ, are accepted of him. These are many times discouraged by reason of their weak performances; Oh! there is so much deadnesse, coldnesse, dulnesse, so many by-thoughts, such hypocrisie in their best actions, that they cannot think that ever such sorry services, such lame and sick sacrifices should be accepted of God. But tell me, you that thus complaine; To what do you look, that you may find acceptance of God? To your workes, or to the riches of grace revealed in the covenant of grace, accepting your person through Christ? Do you look that your work should be accepted of its owne sake, or through grace in Christ; your persons being first accepted in him? If you look to your workes, God regards neither you nor them; but if you fly to the abundance of grace, looking for your acceptance there, then feare not, thy weakest endeavours are accepted before God, and doe find favour in his sight. Our comfort lyes not in the excellencie of our duties, but in our free acceptance in Christ. . . . Gods acceptance begins in the person, not in the worke, accepting the worke for the persons sake.

46

And therefore if God have accepted thy person, he will accept thy worke also.

The fourth difference is this; In the Covenant of workes, a man is left to himselfe, to stand by his own strength; But in the Covenant of grace, God undertakes for us, to keep us through faith. The reason of this difference is, because when God comes to make a Covenant of workes with *Adam*, he finds him furnished with a sufficiency of power which was put into him in his creation. But when he comes to make with us a Covenant of grace in this estate of sin, he finds us of no strength *Rom.* 5.6. impotent, feeble, possessed with the spirit of infirmity, made up of weaknesses, having no power; and therefore *Isa.* 40. 29. the Lord promiseth unto such that *he wil give strength unto them, and increase power.* The Lord knowes the infirmitie of our flesh, how impossible it is for us to fulfill any part of the righteousness which the Law requires, *Rom.* 8.3. He knows also what powers we have against us, *Ephes.* 6. and therefore he tells us, that we are kept not by our own power, but by his power through faith unto salvation, I *Pet.* 1.5. And hence is that in *Joh.* 10.28. Christ tells us, that none shall pluck us out of his hand. And this is the reason, that though *Adam* fell from his first estate, and lost the life promised in that Covenant made with him, yet *we* fall not; he had more strength of grace then wee, and we have more corruption then he, (for he was then pure without sin) yet being left to his owne liberty, he willingly forsook the commandment of God, and fell into a state of perdition. But we being weaker then he, (yet being once taken into the covenant of grace) though we have the same powers of darknesse against us as he had, yet we fall not so as to sin unto perdition, as he did; because we are supported by the power of God. . . .

See hence the ground of that which sometimes seem marvellous in our eyes; we see men of different abilities, some simple, weak, and despised, others indued with eminent gifts, and excellent parts; yet those that so excell, many times fade, and fall away; their graces wither, their light is extinct, and they goe out like smoke of a Candle, with an ill favour; whereas the weake and simple ones are upholden, and go from strength to strength, and increase with the increasings of God. . . . the one sort viewing themselves in their owne excellencies in the glasse of their own conceit, they trust in themselves, and in their own strength, and do not commit their souls to God to be kept by him, and so are left unto themselves. And then at length, meeting with some temptation, which is stronger then they, their confidence and their strength fails them, and so they fall, and being left unto themselves, they are never able to rise anymore; whereas the other being sensible of their owne infirmity, and casting themselves on the power of God to be kept thereby, they are hereby preserved, and upholden against

47

all the powers of darknesse which are against them; so that either they fall not; or if they do fall, yet they rise againe. . . .

This may stay the minds of those that are weake, they think they shall never hold out. They cannot deny but the Lord hath shewed mercy on them, and wrought his grace in their hearts, but they feare they shall not hold out; they feel such a power of corruption in themselves, so many lusts, such strong temptations, who can endure? True, not of your selves, but God is able to make you stand. . . . If a friend relying upon thy trust and faithfulnesse should bring a Jewel to thee, and intreat thee to keep it carefully, thou wouldst be ashamed to be carelesse of it. Christ is the faithfull and true witnesse; therefore commit thy soule to him, and he will keep it, he can do it, *Jude* 24, and he is faithfull and will do it, I *Thes.* 5.24. it being his covenant and promise; and he cannot deny himselfe.

In the covenant of works, Gods highest end is the glorifying of his justice; In the Covenant of grace, it is to glorifie his Grace: In the Covenant of works, God reveals himselfe a just God, rewarding good, and punishing evil, condemning sin; but in the Covenant of grace, he shews himself a God gracious and mercifull; forgiving iniquity, &c. as *Jer.* 31. 31, 32. *I will be mercifull to your iniquity, &c.* The covenant of works forgiveth no sin, there is nothing but strict justice in that covenant. . . . in Gods Court of Justice, which he keeps according to the tenor of the Covenant of works, Justice acts and does all. Justice indictes, Justice examines; Justice pronounceth sentence, Justice executes the punishment; and so whosoever hath sinned, receives according to the evill that he hath done. And hence it is, that when *Adam* has sinned, the inquisition is not, whether he repented him of the evill that he had done; but, what hast thou done? Hast thou eaten of the Tree, whereof I said unto thee, thou shalt not eat? and the Lord finding that he had offended, pronounces curses and death. But in the Covenant of grace it is otherwise. There God looks at the repentance of his people, and accepts of humiliation, and faith in Christ. . . . The voyce of the Covenant of works, is like the first speech of *Nathan* to *David, thou art a child of death;* the voice of the Covenant of Grace, is like his after speech, when he saw *Davids* humiliation and repentance, *The Lord hath put away thy sin:* In the Covenant of Works, God speaks, as, *Ezek.* 18. *The soul that sinneth, it shall dye:* In the Covenant of Grace, he speaks as *Ezek.* 33. 11. *As I live, saith the Lord, I desire not the death of a sinner.* They are both expressed in one place, *Exod.* 34. 6. *The Lord gracious and mercifull, slow to anger,* yet not acquitting the wicked, but visiting iniquity, &c. In one covenant God condemns both sin and sinner; in the other, he condemns the sin, but spares, and gives life to the sinner, to glorifie his grace thereby. . . . God . . . will have his power and wisedome knowne in the creation of the world, his goodnesse knowne in the continuation and preservation and ordering of it, his faithfulnesse in keeping covenant with us, according to the Covenant made, his justice in a covenant of works, his grace in a covenant of grace which he makes with us in Christ Jesus.

This may smite feare and terror into the hearts of all such as are strangers unto the covenant of grace, such as never yet entred into a new covenant with God, by *that new and living* way which is opened to them in Christ. Let such consider what hath been said, that in the covenant of workes (under which yet they stand) there is no grace shewed, but strict justice without any mercy. Let such therefore bethink themselves, what a God they must meet withall, and with whom they must have to doe, even with a just God, a God of judgement, a God of vengeance, that will not spare their misdeeds. . . . This is an hard saying, but a true saying, as God is true; therefore *Isa.* 27.11. God speaking of the wicked people of the *Jewes,* saith he, *He that made them will not have mercy on them, neither shew them any favour.* And in *Ezek.* 5. 11. He threatens that his Eye *shall not spare, neither will he have any pitie.* And *Hos.* 1.6. *I will no more have mercy, &c.* And *James* 2.13. *They shall have judgement without mercy.* As God will be made marveilous in his mercy toward those that are vessels of mercy prepared unto glory, 2 *Thes.* 1. 10. so as men shall wonder at the abundance of grace shewed towards them; so on the contrary, God will be admired and wondred at in his judgements upon all sinfull and ungodly ones; he will *make their plagues wonderfull, Deut.* 28.59. He will deal with his owne servants onely in a way of grace, with these onely in a way of justice. And if so, what will their end be? Justice will spare neither high nor low, it is impartiall, and alike towards all. Justice will passe by no transgression, but will have an account for all, greater or lesse, wicked thoughts, idle words, foolish jests; Justice will not remit any part of the punishment which the Lord calls for, but it will have the full to the utmost farthing. Let this strike all their hearts, who are yet under a covenant of works, with a feare of this just God, who will judge them without mercy. And let this cause them to fly to the throne of grace, and there to enter into a new covenant with God. As the Angel counselled *Lot,* so do I counsell thee, hasten to get shelter under the wings of grace, that thou mayst be freed from the wrath of the just God.

Seing Gods end in the Covenant of grace is to glorifie his grace in us, we may by this in some measure discerne what part we have in the grace of this Covenant. And we may do it by this, if *our* ayms, and *Gods* ayms, our ends and Gods ends meet in one, when we come to seek grace in his sight. Many an one comes before God, begs mercy, and yet obtains it not; as *Pro.* 1.28. because they aske amisse, they seek it not in Gods way. Consider therefore, what seekest thou in begging mercy at his hand? Dost thou seek only to have thy sin pardoned? *only* to be saved from wrath? this wil not argue thy peace, that thou art under grace. But dost thou as well seek the glorifying of his grace towards thee, as the obtaining of thine own peace with him? If God hath put this disposition of heart into thee, that thou couldest be content to lye downe in the dust, and to take shame for thy sin before Angels and men, so that the aboundant riches of his grace may be glorified in the taking away of thy sin, if thy desire be not onely that thou maist see his salvation, but that the Lord himselfe may be made marveilous, and his grace magnified in thee, then thou art herein another *David*, a man after Gods own heart, thy thoughts are as Gods thoughts, thy intents and ends the same with Gods ends. Take this therefore as a pledge of his grace towards thee. Never couldest thou so desire the glorifying of that grace, if God had not a purpose of grace towards thee. . . .

For comfort unto such as see their own unworthiness, and are discouraged thereby from seeking after grace with God; They are so vile in their own eyes, that they thinke it is impossible, that ever such as they are, should find favour and acceptance with God. But let me aske, cannot the riches of grace, when it shall set it selfe on purpose to glorifie it selfe to the full, cannot such grace make thee accepted? Thou darest not deny it, Hold here then, grace can make thee accepted, if it will please to glorifie it selfe. . . . When God will glorifie himself in a way of justice, he will abase all the haughtinesse of man; no excellency of man can then stand in his presence; so on the contrary, when God will glorifie himself in a way of grace, there is no unworthinesse of man can hinder it; he will exalt the most vile, the abject, the most despised, and contemptible, that not we, but grace it selfe may be glorified, I *Cor.* 1. 27, 28. Therefore do not wrong the grace of God, but fly thereto in the sense of thine owne basenesse, and this is the readiest way to find acceptance.

It may serve for direction unto all such, as desire to enjoy the blessings of this grace which God offers in his Covenant; let them seek it with the same minde that God offers it, with a purpose and desire to have grace exalted and magnified; doe not onely seek it, that *you may be exalted* by grace, but that *grace may be exalted in you*. Goe to God for grace with the same minde as *Moses* did, and then we shall obtaine it, as he did. Now *Moses* sought it for this end, that his mercy might appeare, *Exod.* 32.32. *If thou wilt pardon their sin, thy mercy shall appeare*, (this reading I chuse and embrace as the best) as if he should say, they have indeed committed a great sin, but the greater the sin is, the more shall thy mercy and grace appeare, if thou wilt forgive. Thus *Moses* prayes, and see how it prevailes with God: In *ver.* 10 the Lord seemed to have been resolved to consume them, and bids *Moses* let him alone, that his wrath might wax hot against them; *I will destroy them,* (saith God) *I will not be intreated for them;* yet *Moses* notwithstanding goes before God, confessing their vile and hainous sin, but withall prayes, *Oh yet forgive, and then thy mercy shall be magnified.* And this prayer of his prevailed with God, he stayed his hand, he changed his minde; as *ver.* 14. and destroyed them not. These are prevailing requests with God, when we plead for the glorifying of his owne grace. In *John.* 12.28. our Saviour prayed to his Father, *Father glorifie thy name,* and there comes a voice out of the cloud, *I have glorified it, and will glorifie it againe:* so let us seek grace from God for this end, that it may be glorified in us. Father glorifie thy grace; and then the Lord in his time will answer us; I have both glorified it, and will now glorifie it again. In this way we cannot misse of obtaining the thing we seek for at Gods hand.

3

MAN AND HIS GOVERNMENT: ROGER WILLIAMS VS. THE MASSACHUSETTS OLIGARCHY

John W. Reed

When Roger and Mary Williams came to America in 1631, Roger was offered the choice opportunity of becoming the teacher in the church in Boston. To accept this position would have placed him in the most influential position in the new world. His Cambridge training and ability as a scholar well suited him for the responsibility. But Roger Williams interrogated the officials of the Boston church and declared them to be an "unseparated" people. They claimed to be faithful to the mother church in England while in the remoteness of the new world they did things in their own way. Such hypocrisy was too much for Williams. He went to Salem and then to the separatist people of Plymouth. Here he set up a trading post, learned the language of the Indians, and preached in the church. His influence with the Indians became quite strong. He wrote a *Treatise* concerning what he felt was the King's lack of authority over Indian lands and fell under great suspicion from the General Court of Massachusetts. He was submissive and they withdrew their threats. Williams returned to Salem, became teacher, and due to his continued radical preaching concerning the Indian controversy and the right of the

52

magistrates to demand that unregenerate men swear oaths of allegiance to the Bay Colony, he was summoned before the court on several occasions.

Roger Williams was finally offered a chance to debate before the General Court. He did debate but no opinions were changed. The decree of banishment was read to him, and he was told that he could stay until spring if he would not preach. He apparently could not be silent and when the General Court heard of his continued preaching, officers were sent to put him on a ship back to England. Friends had warned Williams of this plan and he fled into the wilderness to stay with the Indians until spring. When spring came, he went to the Narragansett Bay, bought land from the Indians, and founded Providence.

While Roger Williams was earning a reputation for being a dissident and radical preacher worthy only of banishment, John Cotton was establishing himself as the leading preacher in New England. Arriving in America in 1633, he was offered the position that Williams had refused in the Boston church. Cotton gladly accepted and became an artful exponent of the "middle way." He maintained the Puritan form of worship in New England and held tightly to the strings of the Anglican church back in England. He seemed soon to forget that he had been the object of persecution in England for his religious views—having come to America to escape appearing before the Court of the High Commission in 1632. John Cotton proceeded to become the leader of the Massachusetts Oligarchy and refused to tolerate any who could not bring themselves to hold the same views of the Bible that he held.

In the primitive surroundings of the Providence plantations, Roger Williams preached to the Indians and dreamed of the day when his silenced voice could speak once more. He exchanged some letters with the Bay Colony, but the controversy did not break open again until Williams went to London in 1643 to seek a charter for his colony. On the way to England he wrote a book on Indian customs and language entitled *A Key into the Language of America*. The book was published in London and created much interest and an audience for Williams.

Someone published a letter that John Cotton had written to Williams some time before defending the banishment proceedings. Williams immediately answered this publication with a letter that answered Cotton's contentions. He then entered into the pamphlet controversy over liberty of conscience, addressing John Cotton as a primary audience. His secondary audience was the Parliament and the clergy of England and America. His greatest work was entitled *The Bloudy Tenent of Persecution for cause of Conscience.* It set forth in dialogue form his arguments against John Cotton, refuting him on almost a word-for-word basis. Williams maintained his views on separation from the "apostate" Church of England. He firmly attacked the belief of the Bay Colony that they were the "New Israel" of God planted in the wilderness and therefore having every right to incorporate the church and the state into one commonwealth. The emergent and enduring issue of Williams' debate with John Cotton and the Massachusetts Oligarchy became that concerning liberty of conscience. He insisted that the civil state had no right to punish those who held divergent religious views. Spiritual matters were of concern only to the church and the civil state had no mandate to interfere with matters of a man's conscience. He demanded that freedom of conscience and freedom of worship be made available to all regardless of creed.

Roger Williams finally gained a charter from the Parliament for the Providence plantations and returned triumphantly in 1644.

John Cotton studied the *Bloudy Tenent* and in 1647 published his rebuttal entitled *The Bloudy Tenent, Washed, and made white in the bloud of the Lambe.* He maintained his views vigorously and added more scripture to his case.

Williams returned to London in 1652 and found that there was much interest in liberty of conscience. He had many interviews with Cromwell, Milton, and other important individuals and published his rebuttal to Cotton, *The Bloody Tenent yet More Bloody: By Mr. Cottons endevour to wash it white in the Blood of the Lambe.* Cotton died in 1652, probably before he saw Williams' rebuttal, or the debate might have been more extended. Williams finished his business in London and returned to America in 1654. Here he carried on an active life, dying in 1683.

Almost all of the major issues of the debate centered around the interpretation of biblical texts and concepts. Both men spoke to a limited audience of "initiated" people whose training would enable them to untangle the intricacies of Puritan dialectic. Cotton and Williams clashed over biblical typology, the interpretation of the parable of the wheat and the tares, and principles of separation of church and state. Williams always took the hard line of complete church purity and Cotton was the exponent of the "middle way." Williams summarized his case with a demand for complete liberty of conscience. Cotton died without shifting from his position of defending the "Puritan Oligarchy" and its right to suppress those who "sinned against their own consciences" after having been presented the truth by the Colonial Magistrates.

In the controversy between Roger Williams and the Massachusetts Bay Colony, blind conformity to tradition and authority was met in collision course by the startling new idea of complete freedom in matters of conscience concerning religion. The controversy itself helped to cast the American experience in a mold of agitation for change and constant modification of existing institutions that has helped to make America the leading nation in our present world. Although this tangled maze of seventeenth-century dialectic often leaves the modern reader exhausted, one reads with a spirit of expectancy—for here were minds in conflict over the primary issues of American freedom. After reading and reviewing the ebb and flow of this colonial controversy, an inescapable concept emerges— this is worth the time spent in study, for the America we know began here. Our America began with the birth of freedom and freedom was born in Rhode Island, the child of conformity and authority. Rhode Island was considered by the Massachusetts Bay Colony to be a disinherited son, unworthy of status or consideration. Yet freedom in America saw its first day there. Roger Williams was denied his pulpit, but the rhetoric of this great debate deserves a place in the history of those great preachers who helped shape the America that emerged with religious toleration and separation of church and state. The long shadow of this first great American dissenter hovers over our nation as a reminder that a free people must not be pressed into an authoritarian religious mold.

John Cotton[*]

John Cotton, noted for his extreme views as to the power of civil authority in religious matters, was a voluminous writer. He was author of nearly fifty books including The Keys of the Kingdom of Heaven, and the Power Thereof (1644), *where he presented his theocratic ideas of government; and* The Bloudy Tenent Washed and made White in the Bloud of the Lamb (1647), *in which he defended himself against the charges of Roger Williams.*

John Cotton here acknowledges the right of the civil magistrates to establish and reform religion. Cotton's degree of commitment to this principle is revealed in his justification of the use of capital punishment in such establishment or reformation of religion by the civil magistrates.

Civil Magistrates and Religion[**]

The matters which concern the civill peace, wherein Church-subjection is chiefly attended are of four sorts.

1. The first sort be civil matters, "the things of this life," as is the disposing of men's goods or lands, lives, or liberties, tributes, customes, worldly honours, and inheritances. In these the church submitteth, and referreth it self to the civill State. Christ as minister of the circumcision, refused to take upon him the dividing of Inheritances amongst Brethren, as impertinent to his calling. Luke 12:13, 14. "His kingdome" (he acknowledgeth) "is not of this world," Job 18:36. Himself payed tribute to Caesar, (Matthew 17:27.) for himself and his disciples.

2. The second sort of things which concern civil peace is the establishment of pure religion, in doctrines, worship, and government, according to the word of God: as also the reformation of all corruptions in any of these. On this ground the good Kings of Judah, commanded "Judah to seek the Lord God of their fathers," and to worship him according to his own statutes and commandments: and the contrary corruptions of strange gods, high places, Images, and Groves, they removed, and are commended of God, and obeyed by the Priests and people in so doing, 2 Chronicles 14:3, 4, 5. The establishment of pure Religion, and the reformation of corruptions in Religion, do

---

[*] See Chapter 2 for additional biographical data on John Cotton.
[**] *The Keys of the Kingdom of Heaven* (London, 1644) pp. 50-53.

much concerne the civill peace. If Religion be corrupted, there will be "warre in the gates." Judges 5:8 and "no peace to him, that cometh in, or goeth out." 2 Chronicles 15:3, 5, 6. But where Religion rejoyceth, the civill State flourisheth. Haggai 2:15 to 19. It is true, the establishment of pure Religion, and reformation of corruptions pertain also to the churches and Synodicall Assemblies. But they go about it onely with spiritual weapons, ministry of the Word, and Church censures upon such as are under Church-power. But Magistrates addresse themselves thereto, partly by commanding, and stirring up the Churches and Ministers thereof to go about it in their spiritual way: Partly also by civil punishments upon the wilfull opposers, and disturbers of the same. As Jehosophat sent Priests and Levites (and them accompanied and countenanced with Princes and Nobles) "to preach and teach in the Cities of Judah," 2 Chronicles 17: 7, 8, 9. So Josiah put to death the idolatrous Priests of the high places, 2 Kings 22:20. Nor was that a peculiar duty or priviledge of the Kings of Judah, but attended to also by heathen Princes, and that to prevent the wrath of God against the Realme of the King and his sons. Ezra 7:23. Yea, and of the times of the New Testament it is prophesied, that in some cases, capitall punishment shall proceed against false prophets, and that by the procurement of their neerest kindred. Zechariah 13:3. And the execution thereof is described, Revelation 16:4 to 7. where the "rivers and fountains of waters (that is, the Priests and Jesuites, that conveigh the Religion of the Sea of Rome throughout the countreys) are turned to blood," that is, have "blood given them to drink," by the civill Magistrate.

Neverthelesse, though we willingly acknowledge a power in the Civill Magistrate, to establish and reform Religion, according to the Word of God: yet we would not be so understood, as if we judged it to belong to the civill power, to compell all men to come and sit down at the Lords table, or to enter into the communion of the Church, before they be in some measure prepared of God for such fellowship. For this is not a Reformation, but a Deformation of the Church, and is not according to the Word of God, but against it, as we shall shew (God willing) in the sequell, when we come to speak of the disposition of Church-members.

3. There is a third sort of thing which concern the civill peace, wherein the Church is not to refuse subjection to the Civill Magistrate, in the exercise of some publick spiritual administrations, which may advance and help forward the publick good of Civill State according to God. In time of warre, or pestilence, or any publick calamitie or danger lying upon a Commonwealth, the Magistrate may lawfully "proclaim a fast as Jehosaphat did," 2 Chronicles 20:3. and the Churches ought not neglect an administration, upon such a just occasion. Neither doth it impeach the power of the Church to call a Fast, when themselves see God calling them to publick humiliation.

For as Jehosophat called a Fast: so the Prophet Joel stirreth up the Priests to call a Fast in time of a famine threatening the want of holy Sacrifices, Joel 1:13, 14.

It may fall out also, that in undertaking a warre, or in making a league with a forraine State, there may arise such cases of conscience as may require the consultation of a Synod. In which case, or the like, if the Magistrate call for a Synod, the Churches are to yeeld him ready subjection herein in the Lord. Jehosaphat thought he was out of his place, when he was in Samaria visiting an idolatrous King: yet he was not out of his way, when in case of undertaking the war against Syria, he called for counsell from the mouth of the Lord, by a Councell or Synod of Priests and Prophets. 1 Kings 22:5, 6, 7.

4. A fourth sort of things, wherein the church is not to refuse subjection to the Civil Magistrate, is in patient suffering their unjust persecutions without hostile or rebellious resistance. For though persecutions of the churches and servants of Christ will not advance the civill peace, but overthrow it; yet for the church to take up the sword in her own defence, is not a lawfull means of preserving the church peace, but a disturbance of it rather. In this case, when Peter drew his sword in defence of his Master, (the Lord Jesus) against an attachment served upon him, by the Officers of the high Priests and Elders of the people: our Saviour bad him "put up his sword into his sheath again; for (saith he) all they that take the sword, shall perish by the sword," Matthew 27:50, 51, 52. Where he speaketh of Peter, either as a private Disciple, or a church-officer, to whom, though the power of the keys was committed, yet the power of the sword was not committed. And for such to take up the sword, though in the cause of Christ, it is forbidden by Christ: and such is the case of any particular church or of a synod of churches. As they have received the power of the keys, not of the sword, to the power of the keys they may, and ought to administer, but not of the sword. Wherein neverthelesse, we speak of churches and Synods, as such, that is, as church-members, or church-assemblies, acting in a church way, by the power of the keys received from Christ. But if some of the same persons be also betrusted by the civill State, with the preservation and protection of the Lawes and Liberties, peace and safety of the same state, and shall meet together in a publike civill assembly (whether in councell or Camp) they may there provide by civil power (according to the wholesome lawes and liberties of the countrey) ... If King Saul swear to put Jonathan to death, the Leaders of the people may by strong hands rescue him from his fathers unjust and illegall fury. 1 Samuel 14:44, 45. But if Saul persecute David (though as unjustly as Jonathan) yet if the Princes and Leaders of the people will not rescue him from the wrath of the King, David (a private man) will not draw out

59

his sword in his own defence, so much as to "touch the Lords anoynted," 1 Samuel 24:4 to 7.

To conclude this *Corollary*, touching the subjection of churches to the civill State, in matters which concern the civill peace, this may not be omitted, that as the Church is subject to the sword of the Magistrate in things which concern the civill peace: so the Magistrate (if Christian) is subject to the keys of the Church, in matters which concern the peace of his conscience and the kingdome of heaven. Hence it is prophesied by Isaiah, that Kings and Queens, who are nursing fathers and mothers to the church, "shall bow down to the Church, with their faces to the earth," Isaiah 49:23. That is, they shall walk in professed subjection to the Ordinances of Christ in his Church. Hence also it is, that David prophecieth of "a two edged sword, (that is, the sword of the Spirit, the word of Christ) put into the hands of the Saints" (who are by calling the Members of the Church) as to subdue the nations by the ministery of the Word, to the obedience of the Gospel (Psalm 149:6, 7) so "to binde their Kings with chaines and their Nobles with fetters of iron, to execute upon them the judgment written" (that is written in the Word) Psalm 149: v. 8, 9.

[The debate between Roger Williams and John Cotton rambled on for some fifteen hundred pages of Puritan dialectic that tends to be quite confusing to the modern reader. The extract below is chapter six from Cotton's *The Bloudy Tenent Washed*, published in London in 1647. Cotton drew his issues directly from chapter six of Roger Williams' *Bloody Tenent of Persecution*. The clash over these issues gives an insight into the typical rhetoric of the debate. The "Discusser" is Roger Williams.]

A Reply to his sixth Chapter Discussing Civill peace, and the Disturbance of it.

In this Chapter, the Discusser undertaketh to declare what Civill peace is, and to shew, that the Toleration of different Religions, is no Disturbance of Civill Peace.

"First, for Civill peace, what is it," saith he, "but Pax Civitatis, whether English, or Irish, Spanish, or Turkish City."

Reply.

Be it so, and if the Civill State, or Common-wealth containe many Citties, or Townes, and so become a whole Countrey or Common-wealth, let Civill Peace be the peace of the Countrey, or of the Common-wealth. But what is then the peace of the Citty, or Countrey? Is it not *Tranquillitas Ordinis*

MAN AND HIS GOVERNMENT

the tranquility of order in every Society, wherein the Publicke Weale of the Citty, or Countrey is concerned? And is it not the proper worke of the Civill Magistrate to preserve the Civill Peace, and to prevent or reforme the disturbance of the Tranquility or Peace of any such Societyes, in whose Peace, the Peace or Weale of the Citty or Society is concerned? Suppose a Society of Merchants or Cloathyers, or Fishmongers, or Drapers, or the like: If the Weale of the Citty or Countrey be concerned in these, (as it is much concerned in them all): It is not for the safety of the Civill State to suffer any of these so to be disturbed, as wholely to breake up, and to be dissolved.

"No matter" (saith the Discusser) "though they due wholly breake up into pieces and dissolve into nothing. For neverthelesse the Peace of the Citty is not thereby in the least measure impaired or disturbed: because the Essence or being of the Citty is Essentially distinct from these particular Societyes etc. The Citty was before them, and standeth absolute and Entire, when they are taken downe etc."

Reply.

If by Peace be meant (as in Scripture Language it is) all welfare, It would argue a man that liveth in the world, to be too much Ignorant of the state of the world, "to say that in the breaking up and dissolving of such perticular Societyes, the Peace of the Citty or Countrey is not in the least measure impaired, or disturbed."

For 1. Though such Societyes of Merchants and other Trades, be not of the Essence of the Citty; yet they be of the integrety of the Citty. And if the defect of one Tribe In Israel was a great trouble to all the Common-wealth of Israel (Judges 21:2, 3.) then sure the breaking up and dissolving of so many particular useful Societyes cannot but much impaire and disturbe the Peace and wellfare of the Citty and Countrie.

2. Though these Societyes of Trades be not of the Essence of the Citty, yet they are amongst the conservant causes of the Citty: as without which the Citty cannot long flourish, no nor well subsist. Common sense will acknowledge so much.

Now then if all these particular Societyes and severale Companyes of Trades, they and their peace and wellfare doe much concerne the wellfare and peace of the Citty and Countrey, and therefore it behooveth the Civill Government to provide for their peace and wellfare: I demand, whether the Church also, (which is a particular Society of Christians) whether, I say, the Peace and wellfare of it, doe not concerne the Peace and wellfare of the Citty or Countrey where they live?

If it be denyed it is Easily proved:

First, David saith they shall prosper that love the Peace of Jerusalem, and

61

seeke the good of it; Psalm 122:6. etc. And Solomon saith, "where the Righteous rejoyce there is great Glory," Proverbs 28:12. And what is the Church, but a Congregation of Righteous men? If the Rejoycing of the Church be the glory of a Nation, surely the disturbing, and distracting, and dissolving of the Church, is the shame and Confusion of a Nation.

2. Consider the Excellency and Preheminence of the Church above all other Societyes. "She is the fairest amongst women," Song of Solomon 1:8 and 6:1. "She is the Citty and House of God," Revelation 21:2; Psalm 98:1; 1 Timothy 3:15. The world and all the Societyes of it, are for the Church, 1 Corinthians 3:21, 22. The world would not subsist, but for the Church: nor any Countrey in the world, but for the service of the Church. "And can the Church then breake up, into peices, and dissolve into nothing, and yet the Peace and wellfare of the Citty, not [be] in the least measure impaired or disturbed?"

3. It is a matter of just displeasure to God, and sad greife of heart to the Church, when Civill States looke at the estate of the Church, as of little, or no concernment to themselves. Zechariah 1:15. Lamentations 1:12.

Objection 1. [By Williams] "Many glorious and flourishing Cittyes of the world maintaine their Civill Peace: yea the very Americans, and wildest Pagans, keep the Peace of their Townes, and Cittyes, though neither in the one, nor in the other can any man prove a true Church of God in these places."

Answer. It is true, where the Church is not, Cittyes and Townes may enjoy some measure of Civill Peace, yea and flourish in outward prosperity for a time, through the Patience and Bounty and Long-sufferance of God. "The times of Ignorance God winketh at" Acts 17:30. But when the Church cometh to be Planted amongst them, If then Civill States doe neglect them, and suffer the Churches to corrupt, and annoy themselves by pollutions in Religion, the staffe of the Peace of the Common-wealth will soone be broken, as the Purity of Religion is broken in the Churches. The Common-wealth of Rome flourished five hundred yeares before the Kingdome of God in his Church came amongst them: and the decayes of the Common-wealth occasioned by the persecutions of the Church, were Repaired by the Publick establishment of the Churches peace in Christian Emperors. But when the Churches begun to pollute themselves by the Idolatrous worship of Images, and the Christian Emperors tooke no care to reforme this abuse in Churches, the Lord sent in (amongst other barberous nations) the Turkes to punish, not onely degenerate Churches, but also the Civill State for this wickednesse. And therefore the Holy Ghost upbraideth them for their continuance in Image worship, though the Turke were let loose from the River Euphrates, to scourge them for it, Revelation 9:14.20. Goe now, and say, the estate of the

Church whether true, or false, (pure or corrupt) doth not concerne the Civill Peace of the State.

Objection 2. "The Peace of the Church (whether true or false) is spirituall, and so of an higher and farre different nature from the peace of the Countrey, or People, which is meerely and Essentially Civill and humane."

Answer 1. Though the inward peace of the Church be spirituall and heavenly: Yet there is an outward peace of the Church due to them (even from Princes and Magistrates) in a way of godlinesse and honesty, 1 Timothy 2:1, 2. But in a way of ungodlinesse, and Idolatry, it is an wholesome faithfulnesse to the Church if Princes trouble the outward peace of the Church, that so the Church finding themselves wounded and pricked in the house of their friends, they may repent, and returne to their first Husband, Zechariah 13:6; Hosea 2:6,7.

Answer 2. Though the peace of the Countrey or Common-wealth be Civill and humane, yet it is distracted and cutt off, by disturbing the spirituall purity, and peace of the Church. Jehu cutting short his Reformation, God cutt short the coasts of the Civill State. 2 Kings 10:31, 32.

Answer 3. Civill Peace (to speake properly) is not onely a peace in civill things, for the Object; but a peace of all the persons of the Citty, for the Subject. The Church is one Society in the Citty, as well as is the Society, of Merchants, or Drapers, Fishmongers, and Haberdashers, and if it be a part of Civill Justice, out of regard to Civill Peace, to protect all other Societyes in peace according to the wholesome Ordinances of their Company, is it not so, much more to protect the Church-Society in peace, according to the wholesome Ordinances of the Word of Christ?

ROGER WILLIAMS

*Roger Williams, the son of a London shopkeeper, was
born about 1603. He earned his B.A. degree from Cambridge in 1627. Williams emerged from his early years as a
Separatist and came to America in 1631.*

*Upon arriving in New England, he was offered the post of
teacher in the church in Boston. After finding that the
church had not separated from the Church of England, he
declined the post. For a time he was teacher at Salem, and
later at Plymouth. He set up a trading post, learned the
language of the Indians, and preached in the church. He
gained great influence with the Indians. He preached with
fervor against the King's practice of taking lands from the
Indians and the Boston Magistrate's right to demand unregenerate men to swear oaths of allegiance to the Bay
Colony. He was subsequently charged before the General
Court of Massachusetts and finally banished.*

*Williams escaped to his Indian friends and from them
purchased the Providence Plantations where civil democracy
and religious liberty were first practiced in America. He
carried on a prolonged debate with John Cotton concerning
freedom of conscience and separation of church and state.
The most notable of his writings was* The Bloudy Tenent of
Persecution.

*The quotation below is Roger Williams' answer to Cotton's
arguments in chapter six of* The Bloudy Tenent Washed.
The excerpt is chapter six from The Bloudy Tenent Yet
More Bloudy *written by Williams and published in London
in 1652. Williams used a dialogue between "Peace" and
"Truth" as the stylistic form for his presentation.*

The Bloudy Tenent Yet More Bloudy

Peace.

But to proceed to the sixth Chapter, in which is handled that which more
especially concerns my self. It is too lamentably known, how the furious
troopes of persecutors in all States, Cities, Towns, etc. have ever marched
under my name, the white colours of peace, civil peace, publike peace.

Truth. Yet Master Cotton confesseth, that the Cities peace is an humane
and civil peace, as was further explained in many instances from Babylon,
Ephesus, Smyrna, etc. against which Master Cotton excepts not.

Peace. The difference or controversie in this Chapter lies in two things.

64

First, In the similitudes used from companies and societies, voluntarily entering into combinations, which are distinct from the City.

2. In the nature of the Church, which he maintaines to be a society, whose order the City is bound to preserve, as well as any of their civil orders or societies.

Truth. To begin with the first, Master Cotton replies, "That although such societies be not of the essence of the City, yet they are of the integral and conservant causes of the City, and so the disturbance of any of those orders or societies in the City, disturbes the City it self."

But I answer, the similitude was used more especially from a colledge of Physitians, or a society of Merchants, Turkish, East-Endies, etc. and consequently any other of that kinde, voluntarily combining together for the better inriching of themselves in the improvement of their faculties for publike good (at least so pretended.) It was never intended, that if such necessary Trades, Callings, etc. as he mentioneth, be dissolved and ruined, that there would be no disturbance of the peace of the City: But that if such or such a way and order of men of those faculties I mentioned voluntarily combine, and voluntarily also dissolve; yet all this may be, without any breach of civil and publike peace.

Peace. If so, much more the church of Christ, which is a spiritual society voluntarily uniting, may dissolve; I say, much more, without the breach of the peace of the city, which is of a civil and humane nature, as is confessed, and was urged in the instances of Ephesus, etc.

Truth. 2. We are wont when we speak of keeping or breaking the Peace, to speak of Words or Actions of Violence, Sedition, Uproare, etc. for, Actions of the Cases, Pleas, and Traverses may be, and yet no peace broken, when men submit to the Rule of State, for the composing of such differences, etc. Therefore it is that I affirme, that if any of Christs Church have difference with any other man in civill and humane things, he ought to be judged by the Law: But if the Church have spiritual controversies among themselves or with any other, or if God take away the Candlestick as he threatened the Church in Ephesus, all this may be, and yet no civil peace broken: Yea, amongst those that profess the same God and Christ, as the Papists [Catholics] and Protestants, or the same Mahomet, as the Turks and Persians, there would no civil Peace be broken, notwithstanding their differences in Religion, were it not for bloody Doctrine of Persecution, which alone breaks the bounds of civil peace, and makes Spiritual causes the causes of their bloodie dissentions.

I observe therefore, a twofold Fallacie in Master Cottons reply. First, he fallaciously mingles Peace and Prosperity together: for though it be true, that under the terme Peace all good things are sometimes concluded, yet

65

when we speak of Hereticks or Schismaticks breaking the civil peace, or strowing Doctrines tending to break the civill peace, we must understand some such words or acts of violence, wherein the bounds and orders of the City, Laws, and Courts are violated: taking it for granted (for this is the Supposition) that the Lawes of the City be meerely civil and humane. Hence then I affirme, that there is no Doctrine, no Tenent so directly tending to break the Cities peace, as this Doctrine of persecuting or punishing each other for the causes of conscience or Religion.

Againe, it is a second Fallacie to urge your order of the Church, and the Excellency thereof, and that therefore it is a Breach of the civil peace, when the Order of the church is not preserved: For although it is most true, that sooner or later the God of heaven punisheth the nations of the world, for their Idolatries, Superstitions, etc. yet Master Cotton himself acknowledgeth (as was affirmed) that many glorious flourishing cities there are all the world over, wherein no church of Christ is extant: Yea, that the Commonweale of Rome flourished five hundred years together, before ever the name of Christ was heard in it; which so great a Glory of so great a continuance, mightily evinceth the distinction of the civill peace of a State from that which is Christian Religion.

It is true (as Master Cotton tells us) that the Turks have plagued the Antichristian world, for their Idolatries: Yet History tels us, that one of their Emperours (Mahomet) was the man that first broke up and desolated two most glorious ancient cities, Constantinople (which had flourished 1120 yeares since its first building by Constantine) and Athens, which from Solons giving of it Laws, had flourished two thousand yeares, notwithstanding their Idolatries, etc.

Truth. It is apparent that then the Christian Religion gloriously flourished (contrary to Master Cottons observation) when the Roman Emperours took not power to themselves to reform the abuses in the Christian Church, but persecuted it; and then the church was ruined and overwhelmed with Apostacy and Antichristianism, when the Emperours took that power unto themselves: And then it was (as Master Cotton elsewhere confesseth) that Christianitie lost more, even in Constantines time, then under bloody Nero, Domitian, etc.

Peace. It cannot be denied (dear Truth) but that the Peace of a civil State (of all States, excepting that of typical Israel) was and is meerly and essentially civil. But Master Cotton saith further, Although the Inward Peace of a church is Spiritual, yet the outward Peace of it, Magistrates must keep in a way of Godliness and Honestie, 1 Timothy 2:1.

Truth. The Peace of a church of Christ (the onely true Christian State, Nation, Kingdom, or city) is Spiritual, whether internal in the Soul, or ex-

66

ternal in the administration of it; as the peace of a civil State is civil, internal in the mindes of men, and external in the administration and conversation of it; and for that place of Timothy, it hath been fully spoken to in this discourse, and the Discusser hath as yet seen no exception against what hath been spoken.

Peace. But further, saith Master Cotton, although the peace of a Country be civil, yet it is distracted by disturbing the peace of the Church for God cut short the Coasts of the civil State when Jehu shortned his Reformation, 2 Kings 10:31, 32.

Truth. Master Cotton denies not (but confessed in his discourse concerning Baptism) that Canaan was Typical, and to be cast out of that Land, was to be cast out of Gods sight: which proves thus much, That the church of Christ, the Israel now, neglecting to reform, God will cut this Israel short. But what is this to a meerly civil State, which may flourish many hundreds, yea some thousands of years together (as I before instanced) when the Name of the true Lord Jesus Christ is not so much as heard of within it?

Peace. Lastly, (saith he) the church is a Society, as well as the Societies of Merchants, Drapers, etc. and it is just to preserve the Society of the church, as well as any other Society.

Truth. When we speak of the balances of Justice, we must distinguish between the Balances of the Sanctuary, and the Balances of the World or civil States. It is Spiritual justice to preserve spiritual right; and for that end, the spiritual King [Christ] thereof hath taken care. It is civil Justice to preserve the civil rights; and the Rights of a civil society ought justly to be preserved by a civil State: (and yet if a company of men combine themselves into a civil society by voluntary agreement, and voluntarily dissolve it, it is not justice to force them to continue together.)

Peace. The church can least of all be forced: for as it is a spiritual society, and not subject to any civil Judicature: (though some say that a church in New England was cited to appear before a civil Court:) so is the combination of it voluntary, and the dissolution of it in part or whole is voluntary, and endures no Civil violence, but as a virgin (in point of marriage) *nec cogit, nec cogitur*, she forceth not, nor can be forced by any civil power.

Truth. But lastly, if it be justice to preserve the Society of the church, is it not partiality in a meer civil State to preserve one onely society, and not the persons of other Religious societies and consciences also? But the Truth is, this mingling of the church and the world together, and their orders and societies together, doth plainly discover, that such churches were never called out from the world, and that this is only a secret policy of flesh and blood, to get protection from the world, and so to keep (with some little stilling of conscience) from the Cross or Gallowes of Jesus Christ.

Truth. Yea, but hear (saith Master Cotton) those excellent penmen of the Spirit (both the Father and the Son) David and Solomon. First David (Psalme 122:6.) They shall prosper that love the peace of Jerusalem: and Solomon, Where the righteous rejoyce, there is great glory, Proverbs 28. Now (saith he) what is the church but a congregation of righteous men? If the rejoycing of the Church be the glory of a Nation, surely the disturbing, and destroying, and dissolving the church is the shame and confusion of a Nation.

Truth. The outward prosperity of a Nation, was a typical figurative blessing, of that national and figurative church of Israel in Canaan. It is now made good spiritually to them that love the spiritual Jerusalem: for though godliness hath a promise of things of this life convenient; yet persecution is the common and ordinary portion of the Saints under the Gospel, though that cup be infinitely sweetened also to them that drink of it with Christ Jesus, by the measure and increase of a hundred fold for one, even with persecution in this life.

2. It is true, the rejoycing of a Church of Christ, is the glory of any Nation, and the contrary a shame: yet this proveth not that God vouchsafeth to no state, civil peace, and temporal glory, except it establish and keep up a Church of Christ by force of armes; for the contrary we have mentioned, and Master Cotton confesseth the flourishing of States ignorant of Christ, from Age to Age, yea, and as I have mentioned, even to two thousand yeers in Athens: six generations before it heard of Christ, and fourteen generations since, with the sprinking (for some time) of the knowledge of Christ Jesus in it.

Peace. 2. But consider (saith Master Cotton) the excellency and preheminence of the church, that the world is for it, and would not subsist but for it, etc.

Truth. Tis true, glorious things are spoken of the City of God, etc. yet for many Ages together Master Cotton confesseth the Nations of the world may subsist and flourish without it: and though it be the duty of the Nations of the world to countenance and cherish the church of Christ; yet where is there any commission, either in the New or Old Testament, that the Nations of the world should be the judges, governors, and defenders of Christ Jesus his spiritual kingdome, and so bound to take up Armes and smite with the civil sword (among so many pretenders) for that which they believe to be the church of Christ?

Peace 3. (saith he) It is matter of just displeasure to God, and sad grief of heart to the church, when civil states looke at the state of the church, as of little or no concernment to themselves, Zechariah 1:19; Lamentations 1:13.

Truth. Grant this, and that the most jealous God will awake in his season, for these sins, and for the persecutions, idolatries, and blasphemies which the Nations live in: yet what is this for warrant to the Nations (as before) to judge and rule the church of Christ, yea, and under the colour of defending Christs faith, and preserving Christs church pure, to tear Christ out of heaven, by persecuting of his Saints on earth; and to fire the world with devouring flames of bloody wars, and this onely for the sweet sake of the prince of peace?

Peace. Dear Truth, we are now upon an high point, and that which neerly concerns my self, the peace of the world, and the Nations of it. Master Cotton saith further, God winketh at the Nations in the time of their ignorance, and suffers the Nation to flourish many hundred yeers together, as did the Empire of Rome; yet when the church of Christ comes to be planted amongst them, then, as he brought the Turkes upon the Romans, for their persecuting the church, and not preserving it in purity; so consequently will he do unto the Nations of the world.

Truth. I answer, the most righteous Judge of the whole world hath plagued the Nations of the World, both before Christs coming, and since, for their pride and cruelty against his people, for their idolatries, blasphemies, etc. Yet Master Cotton acknowledgeth that many states have flourished many hundred yeers together, when no true church of Christ hath been found in them: and Master Cotton will never prove, that God ever commanded the Nations and governments of the world, to gather or constitute his churches, and to preserve them in purity: For God gave his ordinances, both before and since Christ, to his people onely, whom he chuseth and calleth out of the World, and the Nations of it: and he hath punished and dissolved them for their obstinate neglect thereof. And for the Roman Empire, and the Emperors thereof, the Christian Religion, and the purity thereof, never lost so much, as when the Emperor were perswaded of Master Cottons bloody Tenent, as Master Cotton and all men seen in History and Christianity must confess.

Peace. But further, although (saith Master Cotton) the peace of the church be a spiritual inward peace, yet there is an outward peace of the church due to them from Princes and Magistrates, in a way of godliness and honesty, 1 Timothy 2:2. But in a way of ungodliness, and idolatry, it is an wholesome faithfulness to the church, if Princes trouble the outward peace of the church, that so the church finding themselves wounded, and pricked in the house of their friends, they may repent, and return to their first husband, Zechariah 13:6; Hosea 2:7.

Truth. The peace of the Church is not only inward, between God and themselves; but as the Argument importeth, to which Master Cotton answereth, the peace of the Church external and outward, is spiritual, essentially differing from the peace of the civil state, which is meerly civil and humane. When the peace of the churches, Antioch, Corinth, Galatia, was disturbed by spiritual oppositions, the Lord never sent his Saints for civil help to maintaine their spirituall peace, though the Lord did send Paul to the higher civill powers, to preserve his civill peace, when he was molested and oppressed by the Jews and Romans.

2. For that place of Timothy, [1 Timothy 2:1-2] though I have fully spoken to it in this discourse elswhere, yet this now: It proves not, because the church must pray for civil Rulers, that so they may live a quiet and peaceable life in all godliness and honesty, that therefore civil rulers are supream rulers and judges Ecclesiastical, next unto Christ Jesus, of what is godliness, holiness, etc. since God hath chosen few wise or noble, to know godliness: And although it is true that Gods end of vouchsafing peace and quietness, is, that his Churches might walk in his fear, and in the wayes of godliness; yet it doth not hence follow, that Magistrates were the causes of the Churches walking in the fear of God, and being edified, but only of enjoying Rest from Persecution, Acts 9:31.

3. Although Gods chastisement call to repentance, and although the false prophet in the church of Israel was to be wounded and slaine (as they are now to be cut off spiritually from the church of spiritual Israel) yet was it so in all the other Nations of the world? Or did Christ Jesus appoint it to be so in all the Nations of the world, since his coming, which is the great question in difference?

4. And indeed, what is this, but to add coals to coals, and wood to fire, to teach the Nations of the world, to be briars and thorns, butchers and tormentors to the Lilies and Lambes of the most holy and innocent Lamb of God Christ Jesus?

Peace. But God (saith Master Cotton) cut Israel short in their civil state or Nation, when they cut short their reformation, 1 Kings 10:32.

Truth. Master Cotton elsewhere denying a National church, which is bounded with natural and earthly limits, it is a wonder how he can apply that instance of National Israel, to the now spiritual Nation and Israel of God? May he not as well promise earthly peace and prosperity then most to abound to Gods people, when they most prosper and flourish in holiness, zeal, etc. The contrary whereof, to wit, persecution, is most evident in all the New Testament, and all mens new and fresh experience.

Peace. To end this chapter, Master Cotton affirmes, that civil peace (to speak properly) is not only a peace in civil things for the object, but the peace of all the persons in the City for the subject. The church is one society in the City, as well as the society of Merchants, Drapers, etc. And if it be civil justice to protect one, then the other also.

Truth. Civil peace will never be proved to be the peace of all the subjects or Citizens of a City in spiritual Things: The civil state may bring into order, make orders, preserve in civil order all her members: But who ordained, that either the spiritual estate should bring in and force the civil state to keep civil order, or that the civil state should sit, judge, and force any of her subjects to keep spiritual order?

The true and living God, is the God of order, spiritual, civil and natural: Natural is the same ever and perpetual: civil alters according to the constitutions of peoples and nations: spiritual he hath changed from the national in one figurative land of Canaan, to particular and congregational churches all the world over; which order spiritual, natural or civil, to confound and abrogate, is to exalt mans folly against the most holy and incomprehensible wisdome of God, etc.

4

The Rhetoric of Sensation Challenges The Rhetoric of the Intellect
Edward M. Collins, Jr.

The religious posture of the eighteenth century reached the point where orthodoxy needed to be challenged. The prevailing doctrines of Arminianism, Stoddardism, and Calvinism challenged the intellect, created a salvation by works, and succeeded rather nicely in keeping God and man at arms' length.

Orthodoxy was challenged at its most vulnerable point, the doctrine of regeneration, or how a man might be born anew into the Kingdom of God. The challenge took the form of revivals, spread in space over the entire eastern seaboard and in time from 1734–1735 to the decade of 1740–1750. A study of the forces and counterforces in these revivals is beyond the scope of our present purpose. It is enough to say that Charles Chauncy of Boston and Jonathan Edwards of Northampton emerged as the chief combatants, with James Davenport as an extremist in itinerant emotional evangelism.

Jonathan Edwards made four defenses of revivalism. The first two dealt with the 1734–1735 revival and the renewed activity in 1740. The first came in a letter to Benjamin Colman in which he described the happenings in his own parish in Northampton in 1734–1735.[1] His second defense of the revival, presented here as an example, was a sermon, *The Distinguishing Marks of a Work of the Spirit of God, Applied to that Uncommon Operation that has lately appeared on the Minds of Many of the People in New England,* preached at Yale University in September, 1741.[2] The 1734-1735 revivals had created curiosity; people wanted to hear about the effects of the work of the Spirit of God; but by 1741 interest had shifted from description of the events to an explanation of their significance. For a long while Edwards had studied the effects of revivalism and had had firsthand experience with it, while to most of the persons to whom he spoke in New Haven revivalism was unknown and trifling. In this sermon Edwards stated that if the revival were truly of God it would (1) raise esteem for Jesus, (2) operate against the interests of Satan's kingdom, (3) cause a greater regard for holy Scripture, (4) lead people to truth, and (5) operate as a spirit of love to God and man. Since Edwards had seen evidences of these criteria throughout the course of the revival, he reasoned that it must be of God. Extending his reasoning, since the revival was the work of God not only was no man to oppose it; on the contrary, he was to do everything in his power to promote it. Thus, Edwards in very bold terms had defended the revival and had attempted to pry his New Haven audience away from apathy toward the movement. He was not invited to speak at Yale again.

The third defense of the revival by Edwards came in 1743, when he published *Some Thoughts Concerning the Present Revival of Religion in New England.*[3] This work amplified the Yale sermon by defending the revival as the true work of God.

In the fourth defense, A *Treatise Concerning Religious*

---

[1] A *Faithful Narrative of the Surprising Work of God in the Conversion of Many Hundred Souls in Northampton, Massachusetts, A.D. 1735* (London, printed for John Oswald 1735). Edwards described the various ways that conversion could be brought about and gave in detail a description of the conversion experience of Abigail Hutchinson and Phebe Bartlet.

[2] (New York, 1832).

[3] (New York: Dunning and Spalding, 1832).

Affections,[4] published in 1746, Edwards attempted to define the soul's relation to God. Historian Frank Foster points out that the primary thesis of this work is "that religion consists in the holy choice of the will accompanied by the lively play of the appropriate emotions."[5] In other words, true religion will reside basically in the heart.

The writings and preaching of Edwards and other apologists of revivalism called forth intense opposition from some of the more moderate among the New England clergy, of whom the most prominent was Charles Chauncy, minister of the First Church in Boston.

Chauncy attacked revivalism through two writings. His first direct attack came in a sermon preached the Sunday after the Harvard Commencement of 1742. A copy of it is presented here showing his analysis. The sermon was entitled *Enthusiasm Described and Caution'd Against,*[6] and contained a rather lengthy preface in the form of a letter to the Rev. Mr. James Davenport. A complimentary copy of the sermon was sent to Davenport accompanied by Chauncy's wish that "it may be of service to you, as I hope it will to others, guarding themselves against the wilds of a heated imagination."[7] In the letter Chauncy chided Davenport for what he considered to be all of the evils of revivalism:

What good you may have been the means of elsewhere, I know not: But I am well assured, instead of good, you will be the occasion of much hurt, to the interest of religion in these churches. Your manner in speaking, as well as what you say, seems rather calculated, at least at some times, to disturb the imagination, than inform the judgment: And I am fully perswaded, you too often mistake the mechanical operations of violent voice and action, for impressions of another kind. . . .[8]

[4] Ed. John E. Smith (New Haven; Yale University Press, 1959).
[5] *A Genetic History of the New England Theology* (New York: Russell & Russell, 1963), p. 57.
[6] . . . *A Sermon Preach'd at the Old Brick Meeting House in Boston, The Lord's Day After the Commencement,* 1742 (Boston, 1742).
[7] *Ibid.,* p. i.
[8] *Ibid.,* p. ii.

74

The sermon itself equated revivalism to antinomianism and all of the evils that should fall under the classification. F. M. Davenport pointed out that "Chauncy was a great protagonist of order and righteous conduct as over against 'the things of a bad and dangerous tendency,' of which he wrote in his famous sermon published in 1742." [9]

Chauncy's second defense of the established order came as direct refutation to the expansion of Edwards' sermon at New Haven, published as *Some Thoughts Concerning the Present Revival of Religion in New England.* Feeling that Edwards' work needed answering, Chauncy wrote to his cousin, the Rev. Nathanael Chauncy of Durham, Connecticut:

Mr. Edwards' book of 378 pages upon the good work is at last come forth; and I believe will do much hurt; and I am the rather inclined to think so, because there are some good things in it. Error is much more likely to be propagated, when it is mixed with truth. . . . I am preparing an antidote, and if the world should see cause to encourage it, it may be time to come to light. [10]

The antidote that Chauncy brought forth was the work, *Seasonable Thoughts on the State of Religion in New England, A Treatise in Five Parts.* [11] This work was patterned point by point after Edwards' five-part work and condemned the revival as a whole and Edwards in particular. The revival was disavowed for errors of doctrine, emotion, censoriousness, claims of immediate inspiration, and itinerant preaching. Over three fourths of the book was devoted to refuting these dangerous activities. His indictment lay basically in his belief that "there is a Religion of the Understanding and Judgment, and Will, while Stress is laid upon the latter, it can't be but People should run into Disorders." [12]

The will and the affection occupied the central point of controversy in revivalism's challenge to orthodoxy.

[9] *Primitive Traits in Religious Revivals: A Study in Mental and Social Evolution* (New York, 1917), p. 117.
[10] *New England Historical and Genealogical Register* X, 332. Letter dated March 16, 1742/43.
[11] (Boston, 1743).
[12] *Ibid.,* p. 422.

Chauncy argued that revivalism must be of the devil because it directed itself to men's emotions which were independent and separate from the will. Davenport was cited as the prime example of what could happen when the emotions were allowed to go unchecked.

Chauncy was thoroughly correct in charging extravagance and excess to the itinerants. To the extreme revivalists the degree of emotion became the test of conversion, which meant that the more violent the shriekings, fainting, tremblings, and impulses the stronger was the conversion experience.

While disagreeing with Chauncy over the dichotomy of emotion and reason, Edwards, nevertheless, would not go so far as to support the position of the extreme revivalists. His position transcended both and in so doing served as a bridge to make the contrast of Chauncy and the itinerants less sharp. He agreed with the revivalists that true religion is centered in the heart. This concept in turn shifted the whole thrust of preaching from homiletical beauty to pragmatic effect. Yet, in spite of his emphasis on a religion of the heart, he still sided with Chauncy by affirming that uncontrolled emotionalism is just as heretical as complete dependence on the intellect for salvation. Edwards' synthesizing position thus was the realization that both the heart and the intellect are necessary in the religious experience.

The following sermons by Jonathan Edwards and Charles Chauncy demonstrate the intellectual polarity of a religion of the heart as opposed to a religion of the intellect that was created in the eighteenth century when revivalism challenged the established religious order.

Jonathan Edwards (October 5, 1703–March 22, 1758) was the fifth child and only son of the Reverend Timothy Edwards of East Windsor, Conn. His schooling consisted of private tutoring by his mother and father and later Yale College where he enrolled in 1716. He remained at Yale after graduation to spend two additional years in theological study.

He began his career as minister to a Presbyterian church in New York. The church was unable to support him, and he resigned on May 21, 1724, to accept a position as tutor at Yale. In September, 1725, because of illness he resigned the Yale position and in 1726 became the colleague of his grandfather, Solomon Stoddard, in Northampton, Mass. Almost a quarter of a century later by a vote of 200 of the 230 voting members of the church, Edwards was asked, because of varying conflicts with his parishioners, to resign his position. Slightly over a year afterward he accepted a position as missionary to the Indians in Stockbridge and pastor of a church composed mostly of Indians. His final position came in September, 1757, when he was chosen to succeed his son-in-law, Aaron Burr, as president of the College of New Jersey, which in 1756 had moved from Newark to Princeton. On March 22, 1758 following an inoculation against smallpox, he died and was buried in Princeton.

Edwards was a pastor, theologian, philosopher, and clearly the most influential thinker of his time. In appearance he was tall, slender, with piercing eyes, thin lips, and a prominent nose. He used the plain style and read his sermons. Yet, through his preaching and writing he became the chief spokesman for Calvinism and the recorder and defender of the first great religious revival on this continent.

The Marks of a Work of the True Spirit*

Beloved, believe not every Spirit, but try the Spirits whether they are of God, because many false prophets are gone out into the world.—I JOHN IV. 1.

In the apostolic age, there was the greatest out-pouring of the spirit of God that ever was; both as to his extraordinary influences and gifts, and his ordinary operations, in convincing, converting, enlightening and sanctifying the

* The Distinguishing Marks of a Work of the Spirit of God (Boston, 1751)

souls of men. But as the influences of the true spirit abounded, so counterfeits did also abound: The Devil was abundant in mimicking, both the ordinary and extraordinary influences of the spirit of God, as is manifest by innumerable passages of the apostles' writings. This made it very necessary that the church of Christ should be furnished with some certain rules, distinguishing and clear marks, by which she might proceed safely in judging of the true from the false without danger of being imposed upon. The giving of such rules is the plain design of this chapter, where we have this matter more expressly and fully treated of than any where else in the Bible. . . .

The words of the text are an introduction to this discourse of the distinguishing signs of the true and false spirit. . . . Hence we are to look upon these words as a direction to examine and try their pretences to the spirit of God, in both these respects.

My design therefore at this time is to show what are the true, certain and distinguishing evidences of a work of the spirit of God, by which we may safely proceed in judging of any operation we find in ourselves, or see in others. And here I would observe, that we are to take the *scriptures* as our guide in such cases. This is the great and standing rule which God has given to his church, in order to guide them in things relating to the great concerns of their souls; and it is an infallible and sufficient rule. . . . so that in my present discourse I shall go no where else for rules or marks for the trial of spirits, but shall confine myself to those that I find in this chapter.—But before I proceed particularly to speak to these, I would prepare my way by, FIRST, observing *negatively*, in some instances, what are *not signs* or evidences of a work of the spirit of God.

SECT. I.

NEGATIVE SIGNS; *or, What are no signs by which we are to judge of work—and especially, What are no evidences that a work is not from the spirit of God.*

I. Nothing can be certainly concluded from this, That a work is carried on in in a way very unusual and extraordinary; provided the variety or difference be such, as may still be comprehended within the limits of scripture rules. What the church has been used to, is not a rule by which we are to judge; because there may be new and extraordinary works of God, and he has heretofore evidently wrought in an extraordinary manner. He has brought to pass new things, strange works; and has wrought in such a manner as to surprise both men and angels. And as God has done thus in times past, so we have no reason to think but that he will do so still. . . . We ought not to limit God where he has not limited himself.

Therefore it is not reasonable to determine that a work is not from God's holy spirit because of the extraordinary degree in which the minds of persons are influenced. If they seem to have an extraordinary conviction of the dreadful nature of sin, and a very uncommon sense of the misery of a Christless condition—or extraordinary views of the certainty and glory of divine things, —and are proportionably moved with very extraordinary affections of fear and sorrow, desire, love or joy . . . these things are no argument that the work is not of the spirit of God. . . . When things are in small degrees, though they be really agreeable to the rule, it is not so easily seen whether their nature agrees with the rules.

There is a great aptness in persons to doubt of things that are strange; especially elderly persons, to think that to be right which they have never been used to in their day and have not heard of in the days of their fathers. But if it be a good argument that a work is not from the spirit of God, that it is very unusual, then it was so in the apostles' days. The work of the spirit then, was carried on in a manner that, in very many respects, was altogether new; such as never had been seen nor heard since the world stood. . . .

It may be reasonably expected that the extraordinary manner of the work then, will bear some proportion to the very extraordinary events, and that glorious change in the state of the world which God will bring to pass by it.

II. A work is not to be judged of by any effects on the bodies of men; such as tears, trembling, groans, loud outcries, agonies of body, or the failing of bodily strength. The influence persons are under, is not to be judged of one way or other, by such effects on the body; and the reason is, because the scripture nowhere gives us any such rule. We cannot conclude that persons are under the influence of the true spirit because we see such effects upon their bodies, because this is not given as a mark of the true spirit; nor on the other hand, have we any reason to conclude, from any such outward appearances, that persons are not under the influence of the spirit of God, because there is no rule of scripture given us to judge of spirits by, that does either expressly or indirectly exclude such effects on the body, nor does reason exclude them. . . . If we should suppose that a person saw himself hanging over a great pit, full of fierce and glowing flames, by a thread that he knew to be very weak, and not sufficient to bear his weight, and knew that multitudes had been in such circumstances before, and that most of them had fallen and perished, and saw nothing within reach, that he could take hold of to save him, what distress would he be in? How ready to think that *now* the thread was breaking, that now *this minute*, he should be swallowed up in those dreadful flames? And would not he be ready to cry out in such circumstances? How much more those that see themselves in this manner hanging over an infinitely more dreadful pit, or held over it in the hand of God, who at the same time they see to be exceedingly provoked? No wonder that the wrath of God, when manifested but a little to the soul, overbears human strength.

So it may easily be accounted for, that a true sense of the glorious excellency of the Lord Jesus Christ, and of his wonderful dying love, and the exercise of a truly spiritual love and joy, should be such as very much to overcome the bodily strength. We are all ready to own, that no man can see God and live, and that it is but a very small part of that apprehension of the glory and love of Christ, which the saints enjoy in heaven, that our present frame can bear; therefore it is not at all strange that God should sometimes give his saints such foretastes of heaven, as to diminish their bodily strength.
. . .

Some object against such extraordinary appearances, that we have no instances of them recorded in the New Testament, under the extraordinary effusions of the Spirit. Were this allowed, I can see no force in the objection, if neither reason, nor any rule of Scripture exclude such things; especially considering what was observed under the foregoing particular. I do not know that we have any express mention in the New Testament of any person's weeping, or groaning, or sighing through fear of hell, or a sense of God's anger; but is there any body so foolish as from hence to argue, that in whomsoever these things appear, their convictions are not from the spirit of God? . . . And there is also reason to think, that such great outpouring of the spirit, was not wholly without those more extraordinary effects on persons' bodies. The jailor in particular, seems to have been an instance of that nature, when he, in the utmost distress and amazement, came trembling, and fell down before Paul and Silas. His falling down at that time does not seem to be a designed putting himself into a posture of supplication, or humble address to Paul and Silas; for he seems not to have said any thing to them then; but he first brought them out, and then he says to them, Sirs, what must I do to be saved? Acts xvi. 29 and 30. But his falling down seems to be from the same cause as his trembling. . . .

It is a weak objection, that the impressions of enthusiasts have a great effect on their bodies. That the Quakers used to tremble, is no argument that Saul, afterwards Paul, and the jailor, did not tremble from real convictions of conscience. Indeed all such objections from effects on the body, let them be greater or less, seem to be exceeding frivolous; they who argue thence, proceed in the dark, they know not what ground they go upon, nor by what rule they judge. The root and course of things is to be looked at, and the nature of the operations and affections are to be inquired into, and examined by the rule of God's word, and not the motions of the blood and animal spirits.

III. It is no argument that an operation on the minds of people, is not the work of the spirit of God, that it occasions a great deal of noise about religion. For though true religion be of a contrary nature to that of the Pharisees—which was ostentatious, and delighted to set itself forth to the view of men for their applause—yet such is human nature, that it is morally impossible there should be a great concern, strong affection, and a general engagedness of mind amongst a people, without causing a notable, visible, and open commotion and alteration amongst that people. . . .

Indeed, Christ says, Luke xvii.20. "The kingdom of God cometh not with observation." That is, it will not consist in what is outward and visible; it shall not be like earthy kingdoms, set up with outward pomp, in some particular place, which shall be especially the royal city, and seat of the kingdom; as Christ explains himself on the words next following, "Neither shall they say, Lo here, or lo there; for Behold the kingdom of God is within you. . . ."

IV. It is no argument that an operation on the minds of a people, is not the work of the Spirit of God, that many who are the subjects of it, have great impressions made on their imaginations. That persons have many impressions on their imaginations, does not prove that they have nothing else. It is easy to be accounted for, that there should be much of this nature amongst a people, where a great multitude of all kinds of constitutions, have their minds engaged with intense thought and strong affections about invisible things; yea, it would be strange if there should not. Such is our nature, that we cannot think of things invisible, without a degree of imagination. I dare appeal to any man, of the greatest powers of mind, whether he is able to fix his thoughts on God; or Christ, or the things of another world, without imaginary ideas attending his meditations? . . .

It is no argument that a work is not of the Spirit of God, that some who are the subjects of it have been in a kind of extacy, wherein they have been carried beyond themselves, and have had their minds transported into a train of strong and pleasing imaginations, and a kind of visions, as though they were wrapt up even to heaven, and there saw glorious sights. I have been acquainted with some such instances, and I see no need of bringing in the help of the devil into the account that we give of these things, nor yet of supposing them to be of the same nature with the visions of the prophets, or St. Paul's rapture into paradise. Human nature, under these intense exercises and affections, is all that need be brought into the account.

81

If it may be well accounted for, that persons under a true sense of the glorious and wonderful greatness and excellency of divine things, and soul-ravishing views of the beauty and love of Christ, should have the strength of nature overpowered, as I have already shewn that it may; then I think it is not at all strange, that amongst great numbers that are thus affected and overborn, there should be some persons of particular constitutions that should have their imaginations thus affected. . . . Some are ready to interpret such things wrong, and to lay too much weight on them, as prophetical visions, divine revelations, and sometimes significations from heaven of what shall come to pass; which the issue, in some instances I have known has shewn to be otherwise. But yet, it appears to me that such things are evidently sometimes from the Spirit of God, though indirectly; that is, their extraordinary frame of mind, and that strong and lively sense of divine things which is the occasion of them, is from his Spirit; and also as the mind continues in its holy frame, and retains a divine sense of the excellency of spiritual things even in its rapture; which holy frame and sense is from the Spirit of God, though the imaginations that attend it are but accidental, and therefore there is commonly something or other in them that is confused, improper and false.

V. It is no sign that a work is not from the Spirit of God, that example is a great means of it. It is surely no argument that an effect is not from God, that means are used in producing it; for we know that it is God's manner to make use of means in carrying on his work in the world. . . .

And as it is a *scriptural* way of carrying on God's work, by example, so it is a *reasonable* way. It is no argument that men are not influenced by reason, that they are influenced by example. . . . Words are of no use any otherwise than as they convey our own ideas to others; but actions, in some cases, may do it much more fully. There is a language in actions; and in some cases, much more clear and convincing than in words. It is therefore no argument against the goodness of the effect, that persons are greatly affected by seeing others so; yea, though the impression be made only by seeing the tokens of great and extraordinary affection in others in their behaviour, taking for granted what they are affected with, without hearing them say one word. There may be language sufficient in such a case in their behaviour only, to convey their minds to others, and to signify to them their sense of things more than can possibly be done by words only. If a person should see another under extreme bodily torment, he might receive much clearer ideas, and more convincing evidence of what he suffered by his actions in his misery, than he could do only by the words of an unaffected indifferent relator. In like manner he might receive a greater idea of any thing that is excellent and very delightful, from the behaviour of one that is in actual enjoyment, than by the dull narration of one which is inexperienced and insensible himself. I desire that this matter may be examined by the strictest reason.—Is it not manifest, that effects produced in persons' minds are rational, since not only weak and ignorant people are much influenced by example, but also those that make the greatest boast of strength of reason, are more influenced by reason held forth in this way, than almost any other way. Indeed the religious affections of many when raised by this means, as by hearing the word preached, or any other means, may prove flashy, and soon vanish, as Christ represents the stony ground hearers; but the affections of some thus moved by example, are abiding, and prove to be of saving issue. . . .

It is no valid objection against examples being so much used, that the Scripture speaks of the word as the principle means of carrying on God's work; for the word of God is the principle means, nevertheless, by which other means operate and are made effectual. Even the Sacraments have no effect but by the word; and so it is that example becomes effectual; for all that is visible to the eye is unintelligible and vain, without the word of God to instruct and guide the mind. It is the word of God that is indeed held forth and applied by example, as the word of the Lord sounded forth to other towns in Macedonia, and Achaia, by the example of those that believe in Thessalonica. . . .

VI. It is no sign that a work is not from the Spirit of God, that many, who seem to be the subjects of it, are guilty of great imprudences and irregularities in their conduct. We are to consider that the end for which God pours out his Spirit, is to make men holy, and not to make them politicians. It is no wonder that, in a mixt multitude of all sorts—wise and unwise, young and old, of weak and strong natural abilities, under strong impressions of mind—there are many who behave themselves imprudently. . . .

We have a remarkable instance, in the New Testament, of a people that partook largely of that great effusion of the Spirit in the Apostles' days, among whom there nevertheless abounded imprudences and great irregularities; viz. the church at Corinth. There is scarce any church more celebrated in the New Testament for being blessed with large measures of the Spirit of God, both in his ordinary influences, in convincing and converting sinners, and also in his extraordinary and miraculous gifts; yet what manifold imprudences, great and sinful irregularities, and strange confusion did they run into, at the Lord's Supper, and in the exercise of Church Discipline? . . .

The Apostle Peter himself, who was a great, eminently holy, and inspired apostle—and one of the chief instruments of setting up the Christian Church in the world—when he was actually engaged in this work, was guilty of a great and sinful error in his conduct; of which the Apostle Paul speaks, Gal. ii.11, 12, 13. "But when Peter was come to Antioch, I withstood him to the face, because he was to be blamed; for before that certain came from James, he did eat with the Gentiles, but when they were come, he withdrew, and separated himself, fearing them that were of the circumcision; and the other Jews dissembled likewise with him; insomuch, that Barnabas also was carried away with their dissimulation." If a great pillar of the Christian church—one of the chief of those who are the very foundations on which, next to Christ, the whole church is said to be built— was guilty of such an irregularity; is it any wonder if other lesser instruments, who have not that extraordinary conduct of the divine Spirit he had, should be guilty of many irregularities?

And in particular, it is no evidence that a work is not of God, if many who are either the subjects or the instruments of it, are guilty of too great forwardness to censure others as unconverted. For this may be through mistakes they have embraced concerning the marks by which they are to judge of the hypocrisy and carnality of others; or from not duly apprehending the latitude the Spirit of God uses in the methods of his operations; or, from want of making due allowance for that infirmity and corruption that may be left in the hearts of the saints; as well as through want of a due sense of their own blindness and weakness, and remaining corruption, whereby spiritual pride may have a secret vent this way, under some disguise, and not be discovered.—If we allow that truly pious men may have a great deal of remaining blindness and corruption, and may be liable to mistakes about the marks of hypocrisy, as undoubtedly all will allow, then it is not unaccountable that they should sometimes run into such errors as these. It is as easy, and upon some accounts more easy to be accounted for, why the remaining corruption of good men should sometimes have an unobserved vent this way, than most other ways; and without doubt (however lamentable) many holy men have erred in this way.

Lukewarmness in religion is abominable, and zeal an excellent grace; yet above all other Christian virtues, this needs to be strictly watched and searched; for it is that with which corruption, and particularly pride and human passion, is exceedingly apt to mix unobserved. And it is observable, that there never was a time of great reformation, to cause a revival of zeal in the church of God, but that it has been attended, in some notable instances, with irregularity, and a running out some way or other into an undue severity. . . .

VII. Nor are many errors in judgment, and some delusions of Satan intermixed with the work, any argument that the work in general is not of the spirit of God. However great a spiritual influence may be, it is not to be expected that the spirit of God should be given now in the same manner as to the apostles, infallibly to guide them in points of Christian doctrine, so that what they taught might be relied on as a rule to the Christian church. And if many delusions of Satan appear, at the same time that a great religious concern prevails, it is not an argument that the work in general is not the work of God, any more than it was an argument in Egypt, that there were no true miracles wrought there, by the hand of God, because Jannes and Jambres wrought false miracles at the same time by the hand of the devil. . . . Many godly persons have undoubtedly in this and other ages, exposed themselves to woful delusions, by an aptness to lay too much weight on impulses and impressions, as if they were immediate revelations from God, to signify something future, or to direct them where to go, and what to do.

VIII. If some, who were thought to be wrought upon, fall away into gross errors, or scandalous practices, it is no argument that the work in general is not the work of the spirit of God. That there are some counterfeits, is no argument that nothing is true: such things are always expected in a time of reformation. If we look into church history, we shall find no instance of any great revival of religion, but what has been attended with many such things. Instances of this nature in the apostles' days were innumerable; some fell away into gross heresies, others into vile practices, though they seemed to be the subjects of a work of the spirit—and were accepted for a while amongst those that were truly so, as their brethren and companions—and were not suspected till they went out from them. And some of these were teachers and officers—and eminent persons in the Christian church—whom God had endowed with miraculous gifts of the Holy Ghost; as appears by the beginning of the 6th chapter of the Hebrews. An instance of these was Judas, who was one of the twelve apostles, and had long been constantly united to, and intimately conversant with a company of truly experienced disciples, without being discovered or suspected, till he discovered himself by his scandalous practice. . . .

So in the time of the reformation from Popery, how great was the number of those who for a while seemed to join with the reformers, yet fell away into the grossest and most absurd errors, and abominable practices. And it is particularly observable, that in times of great pouring out of the spirit to revive religion in the world, a number of those who for a while seemed to partake in it, have fallen off into whimsical and extravagant errors, and gross enthusiasm, boasting of high degrees of spirituality and perfection, censuring and condemning others as carnal. Thus it was with the Gnosticks in the Apostles' time. . . . Thus also in England, at the time

85

when vital religion much prevailed in the days of king Charles I. the inter-regnum, and Oliver Cromwell, such things as these abounded. And so in New England, in her purest days, when vital piety flourished, such kind of things as these broke out. Therefore the devil's sowing such tares is no proof that a true work of the Spirit of God is not gloriously carried on.

IX. It is no argument that a work is not from the Spirit of God, that it seems to be promoted by ministers insisting very much on the terrors of God's holy law, and that with a great deal of pathos and earnestness. If there be really a hell of such dreadful, and never-ending torments, as is generally supposed, of which multitudes are in great danger—and into which the greater part of men in Christian countries do actually from generation to generation fall, for want of a sense of its terribleness, and so for want of taking due care to avoid it—then why is it not proper for those who have the care of souls to take great pains to make men sensible of it? Why should they not be told as much of the truth as can be? If I am in danger of going to hell, I should be glad to know as much as possibly I can of the dreadfulness of it. If I am very prone to neglect due care to void it, he does me the best kindness, who does most to represent to me the truth of the case, that sets forth my misery and danger in the liveliest manner.

I appeal to every one, whether this is not the very course they would take in case of exposedness to any great temporal calamity? If any of you who are heads of families saw one of your children in a house all on fire, and in imminent danger of being soon consumed in the flames, yet seemed to be very insensible of its danger, and neglected to escape after you had often called to it—would you go on to speak to it only in a cold and indifferent manner? Would not you cry aloud, and call earnestly to it, and represent the danger it was in, and its own folly in delaying, in the most lively manner of which you was capable? . . .

When ministers preach of hell, and warn sinners to avoid it in a cold manner—though they may say in words that it is infinitely terrible—they contradict themselves. For actions, as I observed before, have a language as well as words. If a preacher's words represent the sinner's state as infinitely dreadful, while his behaviour and manner of speaking contradict it—shew-ing that the preacher does not think so—he defeats his own purpose; for the language of his actions, in such a case, is much more effectual than the bare signification of his words. Not that I think that the law only should be preached: ministers may preach others things too little. The gospel is to be preached as well as the law, and the law is to be preached only to make way for the gospel, and in order that it may be preached more effectually. The main work of ministers is to preach the gospel: "Christ is the end of the law for righteousness." So that a minister would miss it very much if he should insist so much on the terrors of the law, as to forget his Lord, and neglect to preach the gospel; but yet the law is very much to be insisted on, and the preaching of the gospel is like to be in vain without it.

And certainly such earnestness and affection in speaking is beautiful, as becomes the nature and importance of the subject. Not but that there may be such a thing as an indecent boisterousness in a preacher, something besides what naturally arises from the nature of his subject, and in which the matter and manner do not well agree together. Some talk of it as an unreasonable thing to fright persons to heaven; but I think it is a reasonable thing to endeavour to fright persons away from hell. They stand upon its brink and are just ready to fall into it, and are senseless of their danger. Is it not a reasonable thing to fright a person out of a house on fire? The word *fright* is commonly used for sudden, causeless fear, or groundless surprise; but surely a just fear, for which there is good reason, is not be spoken against under any such name.

SECT. II

What are distinguishing, scripture evidences of a work of the Spirit of God.

Having shewn, in some instances, what are not evidences that a work wrought among a people, is not a work of the Spirit of God, I now proceed, in the second place, as was proposed, to shew positively what are the sure, distinguishing, scripture evidences and marks of a work of the Spirit of God, by which we may proceed in judging of any operation we find in ourselves, or see among a people, without danger of being misled.—And in this, as I said before, I shall confine myself wholly to those marks which are given us by the apostle in the chapter wherein is my text, where this matter is particularly handled, and more plainly and fully than any where-else in the Bible. And in speaking to these marks, I shall take them in the order in which I find them in the chapter.

I. When the operation is such as to raise their esteem of that Jesus who was born of the Virgin, and was crucified without the gates of Jerusalem; and seems more to confirm and establish their minds in the truth of what the gospel declares to us of his being the Son of God, and the Saviour of men; is a sure sign that it is from the Spirit of God. This sign the apostle gives us in the 2 and 3 verses, "Hereby know ye the Spirit of God; and every spirit that confesseth that Jesus Christ is come in the flesh is of God; and every spirit that confesseth not that Jesus Christ is come in the flesh is not of God." This implies a confessing not only that there was such a person who appeared in Palestine, and did and suffered those things that are recorded of him, but that he was Christ, i.e. the Son of God, anointed to be Lord and Saviour, as the name Jesus Christ implies. That thus much is implied in the apostle's meaning, is confirmed by the 15th verse, where the apostle is still on the same subject of signs of the true spirit; "Whosoever shall confess that Jesus is the Son of God, God dwelleth in him, and he in God." And it is to be observed that the word *confess,* as it is often used in the New Testament, signifies more than merely *allowing:* It implies an establishing and confirming of a thing by testimony, and declaring it with manifestation of esteem and affection; so Matt. x.32. "Whosoever therefore shall *confess* me before me, him will I *confess* also before my Father which is in heaven." . . .

So that if the spirit that is at work among a people is plainly observed to work so as to convince them of Christ, and lead them to him—to confirm their minds in the belief of the history of Christ as he appeared in the flesh—and that he is the Son of God, and was sent of God to save sinners; that he is the only Saviour, and that they stand in great need of him; and if he seems to beget in them higher and more honourable thoughts of him than they used to have, and to incline their affections more to him; it is a sure sign that it is the true and right Spirit; however incapable we may be to determine, whether that conviction and affection be in that manner, or to that degree, as to be saving or not. . . .

The devil has the most bitter and implacable enmity against that person, especially in his character of the Saviour of men; he mortally hates the story and doctrine of his redemption; he never would go about to beget in men more honourable thoughts of him, and lay greater weight on his instructions and commands. The spirit that inclines men's hearts to the seed of the woman, is not the spirit of the serpent that has such an irreconcileable enmity against him. He that heightens men's esteem of the glorious Michael, that prince of the angels, is not the spirit of the dragon that is at war with him.

II. When the spirit that is at work operates against the interests of Satan's kingdom, which lies in encouraging and establishing sin, and cherishing men's worldly lusts; this is a sure sign that it is a true, and not a false spirit. This sign we have given us in the 4th and 5th verses. "Ye are of God, little children, and have overcome them; because greater is he that is in you, than he that is in the world. They are of the world, therefore speak they of the world, and the world heareth them." . . .

What the apostle means by *the world,* or "the things that are of the world," we learn by his own words, in the 2d chapter of this epistle, 15th and 16th verses. "Love not the world, neither the things that are in the world: If any man love the world, the love of the Father is not in him: for all that is in the world, the lust of the flesh, and the lust of the eyes, and the pride of life, is not of the Father, but is of the world." So that by the world the apostle evidently means everything that appertains to the interest of sin, and comprehends all the corruptions and lusts of men, and all those acts and objects by which they are gratified. . . .

It is not to be supposed that Satan would convince men of sin, and awaken the conscience; it can no way serve his end, to make that candle of the Lord shine the brighter, and to open the mouth of that vicegerent of God in the soul. It is for his interest, whatever he does, to lull conscience asleep, and keep it quiet. . . .

Possibly some may say, that the devil may even awaken men's consciences to deceive them, and make them think they have been the subjects of a saving work of the Spirit of God, while they are indeed still in the gall of bitterness. But to this it may be replied, that the man who has an awakened conscience, is the least likely to be deceived of any man in the world; it is the drowsy, insensible, stupid conscience that is most easily blinded. The more sensible conscience is in a diseased soul, the less easily is it quieted without a real healing. The more sensible conscience is made of the dreadfulness of sin, and of the greatness of a man's own guilt, the less likely is he to rest in his own righteousness, or to be pacified with nothing but shadows. . . . We may certainly conclude that it is from the Spirit of God, whatever effects this concern has on their bodies; though it cause them to cry out aloud, or to shriek, or to faint; or, though it throw them into convulsions, or whatever other way the blood and spirits are moved. . . .

III. The spirit that operates in such a manner, as to cause in men a greater regard to the holy Scriptures, and establishes them more in their truth and divinity, is certainly the Spirit of God. This rule the apostle gives us in the 6th verse: "We are of God; he that knoweth God heareth us: he that is not of God heareth not us: hereby know we the spirit of truth, and the spirit of error." *We are of God*; that is, "We the apostles, are sent forth of God, and appointed by him to teach the world, and to deliver those doctrines and instructions, which are to be their rule; *he that knoweth God, heareth us, &c.*"—The apostle's argument here equally reaches all that in the same sense are *of God*; that is, all those that God has appointed and inspired to deliver to his church its rule of faith and practice; all the prophets and apostles, whose doctrine God has made the foundation on which he has built his church, as in Eph. ii. 20. in a word, all the penmen of the holy Scriptures. The devil never would attempt to beget in persons a regard to that divine word which God has given to be the great and standing rule for the direction of his church in all religious matters, and all concerns of their souls, in all ages. . . . Every text is a dart to torment the old serpent. He has felt the stinging smart thousands of times; therefore he is engaged against the Bible, and hates every word in it: and we may be sure that he never will attempt to raise persons' esteem of it, or affection to it. And accordingly we see it common in enthusiasts, that they depreciate this written rule, and set up the light within or some other rule above it.

IV. Another rule to judge of spirits may be drawn from those compellations given to the opposite spirits, in the last words of the 6th verse, "The spirit of truth and the spirit of error." These words exhibit the two opposite characters of the Spirit of God, and other spirits that counterfeit his operations. And therefore, if by observing the manner of the operation of a spirit that is at work among a people, we see, that it operates, as a spirit of truth, leading persons to truth, convincing them of those things that are true, we may safely determine that it is a right and true spirit. For instance, if we observe that the spirit at work, makes men more sensible than they used to be, that there is a God, and that he is a great and a sin-hating God; that life is short, and very uncertain; and that there is another world; that they have immortal souls, and must give account of themselves to God; that they are exceeding sinful by nature and practice; that they are helpless in themselves; and confirms them in other things that are agreeable to some sound doctrine; the spirit works thus, operates as a spirit of truth; he represents things as they truly are. . . . If I am brought to a sight of truth, and am made sensible of things as they really are, my duty is immediately to thank God for it, without standing first to enquire by what means I have such a benefit.

V. If the spirit that is at work among a people operates as a spirit of love to God and man, it is a sure sign that it is the spirit of God. This sign the apostle insists upon from the 6 verse, to the end of the chapter. "Beloved, let us love one another; for love is of God, and every one that loveth is born of God, and knoweth God: He that loveth not, knoweth not God, for God is love, &c." Here it is evident, that the apostle is still comparing those two sorts of persons that are influenced by the opposite kinds of spirits; and mentions love as a mark by which we may know who has the true spirit: but this is especially evident by the 12th and 13th verses, "If we love one another, God dwelleth in us and his love is perfected in us: hereby know we that we dwell in him, and he in us, because he hath given us of his spirit." In these verses love is spoken of as if it were that wherein the very nature of the holy spirit consisted; or, as if *divine love* dwelling in us, and the *spirit of God* dwelling in us, were the same thing; as it is also in the last two verses of the foregoing chapter; and in the 16th verse of this chapter. Therefore this last mark which the apostle gives of the true spirit he seems to speak of as the most eminent; and so insists much more largely upon it, than upon all the rest; and speaks expressly of both love to God and men; of *love to men* in the 7th, 11th, and 12th verses; and of *love to God*, in the 17th, 18th, and 19th verses; and of both together, in the last two verses; and of love to men, as arising from love to God, in these last two verses.

. . . The spirit that excites to love on these motives, and makes the attributes of God as revealed in the gospel, and manifested in Christ, delightful objects of contemplation; and makes the soul to long after God and Christ—after their presence and communion, acquaintance with them, and conformity to them—and to live so as to please and honour them: the spirit that quells contentions among men, and gives a spirit of peace and good will, excites to acts of outward kindness, and earnest desires of the salvation of souls—and causes a delight in those that appear as the children of God, and followers of Christ; I say, when a spirit operates after this manner among a people, there is the highest kind of evidence of the influence of a true and divine spirit.

Indeed there is a counterfeit love, that often appears among those who are led by a spirit of delusion. There is commonly in the wildest enthusiasts, a kind of union and affection, arising from self-love, occasioned by their agreeing in those things wherein they greatly differ from all others, and from which they are objects of the ridicule of all the rest of mankind. This naturally will cause them so much the more to prize those peculiarities that make them the objects of others' contempt. Thus the ancient Gnosticks, and the wild fanaticks that appeared in the beginning of the reformation, boasted of their great love one to another; one sect of them in particular, calling themselves the *family of love*. But this is quite another thing than that christian love I have just described: it is only the working of a natural self-love, and no true benevolence, any more than the union and friendship which may be among a company of pirates, that are at war with all the rest of the world. . . . What kind of love that is, we may see best in what appeared in Christ's example. The love that appeared in that Lamb of God, was not only a love to friends, but to enemies, and a love attended with a meek and humble spirit. "Learn of me," says he, "for I am meek and lowly in heart."—Love and humility are two things the most contrary to the spirit of the devil, of anything in the world; for the character of that evil spirit, above all things, consists in pride and malice.

Thus I have spoken particularly to the several marks the apostle gives us of a work of the true spirit. There are some of these things which the devil *would not* do if he could: thus he would not awaken the conscience, and make men sensible of their miserable state by reason of sin, and sensible of their great need of a saviour; and he would not confirm men in the belief that Jesus is the Son of God, and the Saviour of sinners, or raise men's value and esteem of him: he would not beget in men's minds an opinion of the necessity, usefulness, and truth of the holy scriptures, or incline them to make much use of them; nor would he shew men the truth, in things that concern their soul's interest; to undeceive them, and lead them out of darkness into light, and give them a view of things as they really are. And there are other things that the devil *neither can nor will* do: he will not give men a spirit of divine love, or christian humility and poverty of spirit; nor *could* he if he would. He cannot give those things he has not himself: these things are as contrary as possible to his nature. And therefore when there is an extraordinary influence or operation appearing on the minds of a people, if these things are found in it, we are safe in determining that it is the work of God, whatever other circumstances it may be attended with, whatever instruments are used, whatever methods are taken to promote it; whatever means a sovereign God, whose judgments are a great deep, employs to carry it on; and whatever motion there may be of the animal spirits, whatever effects may be wrought on men's bodies. . . .

But here some may *object* to the sufficiency of the marks given, what the apostle Paul says, in 2 Cor. xi. 13, 14. "For such are false apostles, deceitful workers, transforming themselves into the apostles of Christ; and no marvel, for Satan himself is transformed into an angel of light."

To which I *answer*, that this can be no objection against the sufficiency of these marks to distinguish the true from the false spirit, in those false apostles and prophets, in whom the devil was transformed into an angel of light, because it is principally with a view to them that the apostle gives these marks; as appears by the words of the text, "Believe not every spirit, but try the spirits, whether they are of God; and this is the reason he gives, because many false prophets are gone out into the world: *viz.* 'There are many gone out into the world who are the ministers of the devil, who transform themselves into the prophets of God, in whom the spirit of the devil is transformed into an angel of light; therefore try the spirits by these rules that I shall give you, that you may be able to distinguish the true spirit from the false, under such a crafty disguise.' Those *false prophets* the apostle *John* speaks of, are doubtless the same sort of men with those *false apostles*, and deceitful workers, that the apostle *Paul* speaks of, in whom the devil was transformed into an angel of light: and therefore we may be sure that these marks are especially adapted to distinguish between the true spirit, and the devil transformed into an angel of light, because they are given especially for that end; that is the apostle's declared purpose and design, to give marks by which the true spirit may be distinguished from that sort of counterfeits. . . .

Having thus fulfilled what I at first proposed, in considering what are the certain, distinguishing marks, by which we may safely proceed in judging of any work that falls under our observation, whether it be the work of the spirit of God or no. I now proceed to the APPLICATION.

SECT. III.

Practical inferences.

I. From what has been said, I will venture to draw this inference, viz. *That the extraordinary influence that has lately appeared, causing an uncommon concern and engagedness of mind about the things of religion, is undoubtedly, in the general from the spirit of God.* There are but two things that need to be known in order to such a work's being judged of, viz. *Facts* and *rules.* The *rules* of the word of God we have had laid before us; and as to *facts,* there are but two ways that we can come at them, so as to be in a capacity to compare them with the rules, either by our own observation or by information from others who have had opportunity to observe them.

As to this work, there are many things concerning it that are notorious, and which, unless the apostle John was out in his rules, are sufficient to determine it to be in general the work of God. The spirit that is at work, takes off persons' minds from the vanities of the world, and engages them in a deep concern about eternal happiness, and puts them upon earnestly seeking their salvation, and convinces them of the dreadfulness of sin, and of their own guilty and miserable state as they are by nature. It awakens men's consciences, and makes them sensible of the dreadfulness of God's anger, and causes in them a great desire and earnest care and endeavour to obtain his favour. It puts them upon a more diligent improvement of the means of grace which God has appointed; accompanied with a great regard to the word of God, a desire of hearing and reading it, and of being more conversant with it than they used to be. And it is notoriously manifest, that the spirit that is at work, in general, operates as a spirit of truth, making persons more sensible of what is really true in those things that concern their eternal salvation: As that they must die, and that life is very short and uncertain; that there is a great sin-hating God, to whom they are accountable, and who will fix them in an eternal state in another world; and that they stand in great need of a Saviour. It makes persons more sensible of the value of Jesus who was crucified, and their need of him; and that it puts them upon earnestly seeking an interest in him. It cannot be but that these things should be apparent to people in general through the land; for these things are not done in a corner; the work has not been confined to a few towns, in some remoter parts, but has been carried on in many places all over the land, and in most of the principal, the populous, and public places in it. Christ in this respect has wrought amongst us, in the same manner that he wrought his miracles in Judea. It has now been continued for a considerable time; so that there has been a great opportunity to observe the manner of the work. And all such as have been very conversant with the subjects of it, see a great deal more, that by the rules of the apostle, does clearly and certainly shew it to be the work of God.

And here I would observe, that the nature and tendency of a spirit that is at work, may be determined with much greater certainty, and less danger of being imposed upon, when it is observed in a great multitude of people of all sorts, and in various places, than when it is only seen in a few, in some particular place, that have been much conversant one with another. . . .

And here it is to be observed, that for persons to profess that they are so convinced of certain divine truths, as to esteem and love them in a *saving manner*; and for them to profess, that they are *more convinced* or confirmed in the truth of them, than they used to be, and find that they have a greater regard to them than they had before, are two very different things. Persons of honesty and common sense, have much greater right to demand credit to be given to the latter profession, than to the former. Indeed in the former, it is less likely that a people in general should be deceived, than some particular persons. But whether person's convictions, and the alteration in their dispositions and affections, be in a degree and manner that is saving, is beside the present question. If there be such effects on people's judgments, dispositions and affections, as have been spoken of, whether they be in a degree and manner that is saving or no, it is nevertheless a sign of the influence of the Spirit of God. Scripture rules serve to distinguish the common influences of the Spirit of God, as well as those that are saving, from the influence of other causes.

And as, by the providence of God, I have for some months past, been much amongst those who have been the subjects of the work in question; and particularly, have been in the way of seeing and observing those extraordinary things with which many persons have been offended;—such as persons crying out aloud, shrieking, being put into great agonies of body, &c.—and have seen the manner and issue of such operations, and the fruits of them, for several months together; many of them being persons with whom I have been intimately acquainted in soul concerns, before and since; so I look upon myself called on this occasion to give my testimony, that—

94

so far as the nature and tendency of such a work is capable of falling under the observation of a by-stander, to whom those that have been the subjects of it have endeavoured to open their hearts, or can be come at by diligent and particular enquiry—this work has all those marks that have been pointed out. And this has been the case in very many instances, in *every article*; and in many others, all those marks have appeared in a very *great degree*.

The subjects of these uncommon appearances, have been of two sorts; either those who have been in great distress from an apprehension of their sin and misery; or those who have been overcome with a sweet sense of the greatness, wonderfulness and excellency of divine things. Of the multitude of those of the former sort, that I have had opportunity to observe, these have been very few, but their distress has arisen apparently from real proper conviction, and being in a degree sensible of that which was the truth. And though I do not suppose, when such things were observed to be common, that persons have laid themselves under those violent restraints to avoid outward manifestations of their distress, that perhaps they otherwise would have done; yet there have been very few in whom there has been any appearance of feigning or affecting such manifestations, and very many for whom it would have been undoubtedly utterly impossible for them to avoid them. Generally, in these agonies they have appeared to be in the perfect exercise of their reason; and those of them who could speak, have been well able to give an account of the circumstances of their mind, and the cause of their distress, at the time, and were able to remember, and give an account of it afterwards. I have known a very few instances of those, who, in their great extremity, have for a short space been deprived, in some measure, of the use of reason; but among the many hundreds, and it may be thousands, that have lately been brought to such agonies, I never yet knew one, lastingly deprived of their reason. In some that I have known, melancholy has evidently been mixt; and when it is so, the difference is very apparent; their distresses are of another kind, and operate quite after another manner, than when their distress is from mere conviction. It is not truth only that distresses them, but many vain shadows and nations that will not give place either to scripture or reason. Some in their great distress have not been well able to give an account of themselves, or to declare the sense they have of things, or to explain the manner and cause of their trouble to others, that yet I have had no reason to think were not under proper convictions, and in whom there has been manifested a good issue. . . . Some, who on first enquiry, said they knew not what was the matter with them, have on being particularly examined and interrogated, been able to represent their case, though of themselves they could not find expressions, and forms of speech to do it.

Some suppose, that terrors producing such effects, are only a fright. But certainly there ought to be a distinction made between a very great fear, or extreme distress arising from an apprehension of some dreadful truth—a cause fully proportionable to such an effect—and a needless, causeless fright. The latter is of two kinds; either, first when persons are terrified with that which is not the truth; (of which I have seen very few instances unless in case of melancholy;) or, secondly, when they are in a fright from some terrible outward appearance and noise, and a general notion thence arising. These apprehend, that there is something or other terrible, they know not what; without having in their minds any particular truth whatever. Of such a kind of fright I have seen very little appearance, among either old or young.

Those who are in such extremity, commonly express a great sense of their exceeding wickedness, the multitude and aggravations of their actual sins: their dreadful pollution, enmity, and perverseness. . . . Very many, in the midst of their extremity, have been brought to an extraordinary sense of their fully deserving that wrath, and the destruction which was then before their eyes. They feared every moment, that it would be executed upon them; they have been greatly convinced that this would be altogether just, and that God is indeed absolutely sovereign. Very often, some text of scripture expressing God's sovereignty, has been set home upon their minds, whereby they have been calmed. They have been brought, as it were, to lie at God's feet; and after great agonies, a little before light has arisen, they have been composed and quiet, in submission to a just and sovereign God; but their bodily strength much spent. Sometimes their lives, to appearance, were almost gone; and then light has appeared, and a glorious Redeemer, with his wonderful, all-sufficient grace, has been represented to them often, in some sweet invitation of scripture. Sometimes the light comes in suddenly, sometimes more gradually, filling their souls with love, admiration, joy, and self-abasement. . . .

Some object against it as great confusion, when there is a number together in such circumstances making a noise; and say, God cannot be the author of it; because he is the God of order, not of confusion. But let it be considered, what is the proper notion of confusion, but the breaking that order of things, whereby they are properly disposed, and duly directed to their end, so that the order and due connection of means being broken, they fail of their end. Now the conviction of sinners for their conversion is the obtaining of the end of religious means. Not but that I think the persons thus extraordinarily moved, should endeavour to refrain from such outward manifestations, what they well can, and should refrain to their utmost, at the time of their solemn worship. But if God is pleased to convince the consciences of persons, so that they cannot avoid great outward manifestations, even to interrupting, and breaking off those public means they were attending, I do not think this is confusion, or an unhappy interruption, any more than if a company should meet on the field to pray for rain, and should be broken off from their exercise by a plentiful shower. . . .

Besides those who are overcome with conviction and distress, I have seen many of late, who have had their bodily strength taken away with a sense of the glorious excellency of the Redeemer, and the wonders of his dying love; with a very uncommon sense of their own littleness and exceeding vileness attending it, with all expressions and appearances of the greatest abasement and abhorrence of themselves. Not only new converts, but many who were, as we hope, formerly converted, have had their love and joy attended with a flood of tears, and a great appearance of contrition and humiliation, especially for their having lived no more to God's glory since their conversion. . . .

Providence has cast my lot in a place where the work of God has *formerly* been carried on. I had the happiness to be settled in that place two years with the venerable STODARD: and was then acquainted with a number who, during that season, were wrought upon under his ministry. I have been intimately acquainted with the experiences of many others who were wrought upon under his ministry, before that period, in a manner agreeable to the doctrine of all orthodox Divines. And of late, a work has been carried on there, with very much of uncommon operations; but it is evidently the same work, that was carried on there, in different periods, though attended with some new circumstances. And certainly we must throw by all talk of conversion and christian experience; and not only so, but we must throw by our Bibles, and give up revealed religion, if this be not in general the work of God. Not that I suppose the degree of the spirit's influence, is to be determined by the degree of effect on men's bodies; or, that those are always the best experiences, which have the greatest influence on the body.

And as to the imprudencies, irregularities, and mixture of delusion that has been observed; it is not at all to be wondered at, that a reformation, after a long continued and almost universal deadness, should at first, when the revival is new, be attended with such things. . . .

The imprudencies and errors that have attended this work, are the less to be wondered at, if it be considered, that chiefly young persons have been the subjects of it, who have less steadiness and experience, and being in the heat of youth, are much more ready to run to extremes. Satan will keep men secure as long as he can; but when he can do that no longer, he often endeavours to drive them to extremes, and so to dishonour God, and wound religion in that way. And doubtless it has been one occasion of much misconduct, that in many places, people see plainly that their ministers have an ill opinion of the work; and therefore, with just reason, durst not apply themselves to themselves to them as their guides in it; and so are without guides.—No wonder then that when a people are as sheep without a shepherd, they wander out of the way. A people in such circumstances, stand in great and continual need of guides, and their guides stand in continual need of much more wisdom than they have of their own. . . . The happy influence of experience is very manifest at this day, in the people among whom God has settled my abode. The work which has been carried on there this year, has been much purer than that which was wrought there six years before: it has seemed to be more purely spiritual; free from natural and corrupt mixtures, and any thing savouring of enthusiastic wildness and extravagance. . . . Many among us who were wrought upon in that former season, have now had much greater communications from heaven than they had then. Their rejoicing operates in another manner; it abases them, breaks their hearts, and brings them into the dust. When they speak of their joys, it is not with laughter, but a flood of tears. Thus those that laughed before, weep now, and yet by their united testimony, their joy is vastly purer and sweeter than that which before did more raise their animal spirits. They are now more like Jacob, when God appeared to him at Bethel, when he saw the ladder that reached to heaven, and said, "How dreadful is this place?" And like Moses, when God shewed him his glory on the mount, when he made haste and "bowed himself unto the earth."

II. Let us all be hence warned, *by no means to oppose, or do any thing in the least to clog or hinder the work; but, on the contrary, do our utmost to promote it.* Now Christ is come down from heaven in a remarkable and wonderful work of his spirit, it becomes all his professed disciples to acknowledge him, and give him honour.

The example of the Jews in Christ's and the apostle's times, is enough to beget in those who do not acknowledge this work, a great jealousy of themselves, and to make them exceeding cautious of what they say or do. Christ then was in the world, and the world knew him not: he came to his own professing people, and his own received him not. That coming of Christ had been much spoken of in the prophecies of Scripture which they had in their hands, and it had been long expected; and yet because Christ came in a manner they did not expect, and which was not agreeable to their carnal reason, they would not own him. Nay they opposed him, counted him a madman, and pronounced the spirit that he wrought by to be the spirit of the devil. They stood and wondered at the great things done, and knew not what to make of them; but yet they met with so many stumbling blocks, that they finally could not acknowledge him. . .

There is another, a spiritual coming of Christ, to set up his kingdom in the world, that is as much spoken of in scripture prophecy as that first coming and which has long been expected by the church of God. We have reason to think, from what is said of this, that it will be, in many respects parallel with the other. And certainly, that low state into which the visible church of God has lately been sunk is very parallel with the state of the Jewish church, when Christ came; and therefore no wonder at all, that when Christ comes, his work should appear a strange work to most; yea, it would be a wonder if it should be otherwise. Whether the present work be the beginning of that great and frequently predicted coming of Christ to set up his kingdom, or not, it is evident, from what has been said, that it is a work of the same spirit, and of the same nature. And there is no reason to doubt, but that the conduct of persons who continue long to refuse acknowledging Christ in the work—especially those who are set to be teachers in his church—will be in like manner provoking to God, as it was in the Jews of old, while refusing to acknowledge Christ; notwithstanding what they may plead of the great stumbling blocks that are in the way, and the cause they have to doubt of the work. . . .

It is not to be supposed that the great Jehovah has bowed the heavens, and appeared here now for so long a time, in such a glorious work of his power and grace—in so extensive a manner, in the most public places of the land, and in almost all parts of it—without giving such evidences of his presence, that great numbers, and even many teachers in his church, can remain guiltless in his sight, without ever receiving and acknowledging him, and giving him honour, and appearing to rejoice in his gracious presence; or without so much as once giving him thanks for so glorious and blessed a work of his grace, wherein his goodness does more appear, than if he had bestowed on us all the temporal blessings that the world affords. A long continued silence in such a case is undoubtedly provoking to God; especially in ministers. It is a secret kind of opposition, that really tends to hinder the work. . . . Let all to whom this work is a cloud and darkness—as the pillar of cloud and fire was to the Egyptians—take heed that it be not their destruction, while it gives light to God's Israel.

I would intreat those who quiet themselves, that they proceed on a principle of prudence, and are waiting to see the issue of things—and what fruits those that are the subjects of this work will bring forth in their lives and conversations—to consider, whether this will justify a long refraining from acknowledging Christ when he appears so wonderfully and graciously present in the land. It is probable that many of those who are thus waiting, know not for what they are waiting. If they wait to see a work of God without difficulties and stumbling blocks, it will be like the fool's waiting at the river side to have the water all run by. . . .

It is probably that the stumbling blocks that now attend this work, will in some respects be increased, and not diminished. We probably shall see more instances of apostacy and gross iniquity among professors. And if one kind of stumbling blocks are removed, it is to be expected that others will come. It is with Christ's works as it was with his parables; things that are difficult to men's dark minds are ordered of purpose, for the trial of their dispositions and spiritual sense; and that those of corrupt minds and of an unbelieving, perverse, cavilling spirit, "seeing might see and not understand." Those who are now waiting to see the issue of this work, think they shall be better able to determine by and by; but probably many of them are mistaken. . . .

This pretended prudence, in persons waiting so long before they acknowedged this work, will probably in the end prove the greatest imprudence. Hereby they will fail of any share of so great a blessing, and will miss the most precious opportunity of obtaining divine light, grace and comfort, heavenly and eternal benefits, that God ever gave in New England. . . . That caution of an unbelieving Jew might teach them more prudence, Acts v. 38, 39. "Refrain from these men, and let them alone; for if this counsel, or this work be of men, it will come to nought; but if it be of God, ye cannot overthrow it; lest haply ye be found to fight against God." Whether what has been said in this discourse be enough to produce conviction, that this is the work of God, or not; yet I hope that for the future, they will at least hearken to the caution of Gamaliel, now mentioned; so as not to oppose it or say any thing which has even an indirect tendency to bring it into discredit, lest they should be found opposers of the Holy Ghost. There is no kind of sin so hurtful and dangerous to the souls of men, as those committed against the Holy Ghost. We had better speak against God the Father, or the Son, than to speak against the Holy Spirit in his gracious operations on the hearts of men. Nothing will so much tend for ever to prevent our having any benefit of his operations on our own souls. . . .

Since the great God has come down from heaven, and manifested himself in so wonderful a manner in this land, it is vain for any of us to expect any other than to be greatly affected by it in our spiritual state and circumstances, respecting the favour of God, one way or other. Those who do not become more happy by it, will become far more guilty and miserable. It is always so; such a season as proves an acceptable year, and a time of great favour to them who accept and improve it, proves a day of vengeance to others. Isai. lix. 2. When God sends forth his *word*, it shall not return to him void; much less his *Spirit*. . . .

III. To apply myself to those who are the friends of this work, who have been partakers of it, and are zealous to promote it. Let me earnestly exhort such to give diligent heed to themselves to avoid all errors and misconduct, and whatever may darken and obscure the work; and to give no occasion to those who stand ready to reproach it. The apostle was careful to cut off occasion from those that desired occasion. The same apostle exhorts Titus, to maintain a strict care and watch over himself, that both his preaching and behaviour might be such as "could not be condemned; that he who was of the contrary part might be ashamed, having no evil thing to say of them," Tit. ii. 7, 8. We had need to be wise as serpents and harmless as doves. . . .

Humility and self-diffidence, and an entire dependence on our Lord Jesus Christ, will be our best defence. Let us therefore maintain the strictest watch against spiritual pride, or being lifted up with extraordinary experiences and comforts, and the high favours of heaven, that any of us may have received. We had need after such favours, in a special manner to keep a strict and jealous eye upon our own hearts, lest there should arise self-exalting reflections upon what we have received, and high thoughts of ourselves as being now some of the most eminent of saints and peculiar favourites of heaven, and that the secret of the Lord is especially with us. . . .

Some of the true friends of the work of God's spirit have erred in giving too much heed to impulses and strong impressions on their minds, as though they were immediate significations from heaven to them, of something that should come to pass, or something that it was the mind and will of God that they should do, which was not signified or revealed any where in the bible without those impulses. These impressions, if they are truly from the spirit of God, are of a quite different nature from his gracious influences on the hearts of the saints: they are of the nature of the extraordinary *gifts* of the spirit, and are properly inspiration, such as the prophets and apostles and others had of old; which the apostle distinguishes from the *grace* of the Spirit. I Cor. xiii.

One reason why some have been ready to lay weight on such impulses, is an opinion they have had, That the glory of the approaching happy days of the church would partly consist in restoring those *extraordinary gifts* of the spirit. This opinion, I believe, arises partly through want of duly considering and comparing the nature and value of those two kinds of influences of the spirit, viz. those that are ordinary and gracious, and those that are extraordinary and miraculous. The former are by far the most excellent and

101

glorious; as the apostle largely shews. (I Cor. xii. 31, &c.) Speaking of the extraordinary gifts of the spirit, he says, "But covet earnestly the best gifts; and yet I shew you a more excellent way." i.e. a more excellent way of the influence of the spirit. And then he goes on, in the next chapter to shew what that more excellent way is, even the grace of that spirit, which summarily consists in charity, or divine love. And throughout that chapter he shews the great preference of that above inspiration. God communicates his own nature to the soul in saving *grace* in the heart, more than in all miraculous *gifts*. The blessed image of God consists in *that* and not in *these*. The excellency, happiness and glory of the soul, immediately consists in the former. That is a root which bears infinitely more excellent fruit. Salvation and the eternal enjoyment of God is promised to divine grace, but not to inspiration. A man may have those extraordinary gifts, and yet be abominable to God, and go to hell. . . . The influence of the Holy spirit, or divine charity in the heart, is the greatest privilege and glory of the highest archangel in heaven; yea, this is the very thing by which the creature has fellowship with God himself, with the Father and the Son, in their beauty and happiness. Hereby the saints are made partakers of the divine nature, and have Christ's joy fulfilled in themselves.

The ordinary sanctifying influences of the spirit of God, are the *end* of all extraordinary gifts, as the apostle shews, Ephes. iv. 11, 12, 13. They are good for nothing, any further than as they are subordinate to this end; they will be so far from profiting any without it, that they will only aggravate their misery. This is, as the apostle observes, the most excellent way of God's communicating his spirit to his church, it is the greatest glory of the church in all ages. This glory is what makes the church on earth most like the church in heaven, when prophecy, and tongues, and other miraculous gifts cease. And God communicates his spirit only in that more excellent way of which the apostle speaks, viz. *charity* or divine love, "which never faileth." Therefore the glory of the approaching happy state of the church does not at all require these extraordinary gifts. As that state of the church will be the nearest of any to its perfect state in heaven, so I believe it will be like it in this, that all extraordinary gifts, shall have ceased and vanished away; and all those stars, and the moon, with the reflected light they gave in the night, or in a dark season, shall be swallowed up in the sun of divine love. . . . When the expected glorious state of the church comes, the increase of light shall be so great, that it will in some respect answer what is said, ver. 12, of *seeing face to face*. (see Isa. xxiv. 23. and xxv. 7.)

Therefore I do not expect a restoration of these miraculous gifts in the approaching glorious times of the church, nor do I desire it. It appears to me, that it would add nothing to the glory of those times, but rather diminish from it. For my part, I had rather enjoy the sweet influences of the spirit, shewing Christ's spiritual divine beauty, infinite grace, and dying love, drawing forth the holy exercises of faith, divine love, sweet complacence, and humble joy in God, one quarter of an hour, than to have prophetical visions and revelations the whole year. It appears to me much more probable that God should give immediate revelations to his saints in the dark times of prophecy, than, now in the approach of the most glorious and perfect state of his church on earth. It does not appear to me that there is any need of those extraordinary gifts to introduce this happy state, and set up the kingdom of God through the world; I have seen so much of the power of God in a more excellent way, as to convince me that God can easily do it without.

I would therefore entreat the people of God to be very cautious how they give heed to such things. I have seen them fail in very many instances, and know by experience that impressions being made with great power, and upon the minds of true, yea, eminent saints—even in the midst of extraordinary exercises of grace, and sweet communion with God, and attended with texts of scripture strongly impressed on the mind—are no sure signs of their being revelations from heaven. I have known such impressions fail, in some instances attended with all these circumstances. They who leave the sure word of prophecy—which God has given us as a light shining in a dark place—to follow such impressions and impulses, leave the guidance of the polar star, to follow *a Jack with a lanthorn*. No wonder therefore that sometimes they are led into woful extravagancies.

Moreover, seeing inspiration is not to be expected, *let us not despise human learning.* They who assert that human learning is of little or no use in the work of the ministry, do not well consider, what they say; if they did, they would not say it. By human learning I mean, and suppose others mean, the improvement of common knowledge by human and outward means. And therefore to say, that human learning is of no use, is as much as to say that the education of a child, or that the common knowledge which a grown man has, more than a little child, is of no use. At this rate, a child of four years old, is as fit for a teacher in the church of God, with the same degree of grace—and capable of doing as much to advance the kingdom of Christ, by his instruction—as a very knowing man of thirty years of age. If adult persons have greater ability and advantage to do service, because they have more knowledge than a little child, then doubtless if they have more human knowledge still, with the same degree of grace, they would have still greater ability and advantage to do service. An increase of knowledge, without doubt, increases a man's advantage either to do good or hurt, according as he is disposed. It is too manifest to be

103

denied, that God made great use of human learning in the apostle Paul, as he also did in Moses and Solomon.

And if knowledge, obtained by human means, is not to be despised, then it will follow that the means of obtaining it are not to be neglected, *viz.* *study*; and that this is of great use in order to a preparation for publicly instructing others. And though having the heart full of the powerful influences of the spirit of God, may at some time enable persons to speak profitably, yea, very excellently without study; yet this will not warrant us needlessly to cast ourselves down from the pinnacle of the temple, depending upon it that the angle of the Lord will bear us up, and keep us from dashing our foot against a stone, when there is another way to go down, though it be not so quick. And I would pray, that *method*, in public discourses, which tends greatly to help both the understanding and memory, may not be wholly neglected.

Another thing I would beg the dear children of God more fully to consider of, is: how far, and upon what grounds the rules of the holy scriptures will truly justify their passing censures upon other professing Christians, as hypocrites, and ignorant of real religion. We all know that there is a judging and censuring of some sort or other, that the scripture very often and very strictly forbids. I desire that those rules of scripture may be looked into, and thoroughly weighted; and that it may be considered whether our taking it upon us to discern the state of others—and to pass sentence upon them as wicked men, though professing Christians, and of a good visible conversation—be not really forbidden by Christ in the new Testament. If it be, then doubtless the disciples of Christ ought to avoid this practice, however sufficient they may think themselves for it; or however needful, or of good tendency they may think it. . . .

Again, whatsoever kind of judging is the proper work and business of the day of judgment, is what we are forbidden, as in I Cor. iv. 5. "Therefore judge nothing before the time, until the Lord come; who both will bring to light the hidden things of darkness, and will make manifest the counsels of the heart; and then shall every man have praise of God." But to distinguish hypocrites, that have the form of godliness and the visible conversation of godly men, from true saints; or, to separate the sheep from the goats, is the proper business of the day of judgment; yea, it is represented as the main business and end of that day. They therefore do greatly err who take it upon them positively to determine who are sincere, and who are not—to draw the dividing line between true saints and hypocrites, and to separate between sheep and goats, setting the one on the right hand and the other on the left—and to distinguish and gather out the tares from amongst the wheat. . . . I know there is a great aptness in men who suppose they have had some experience of the power of religion, to think themselves sufficient to discern and determine the state of others by a little conversation with them; and experience has taught me that this is an error. I once did not imagine that the heart of man had been so unsearchable as it is. I am less charitable, and less uncharitable than once I was. . . .

The instance of *Judas* is remarkable; whom—though he had been so much amongst the rest of the disciples, all persons of true experience, yet —his associates never seemed to have entertained a thought of his being any other than a true disciple, till he discovered himself by his scandalous practice—And the instance of *Ahitophel* is also very remarkable, David did not suspect him, though so wise and holy a man, so great a divine, and had such great acquaintance with scripture. He knew more than all his teachers, more than the ancients, was grown old in experience, and was in the greatest ripeness of his judgment. He was a great prophet, and was intimately acquainted with Ahitophel, he being his familiar friend, and most intimate companion in religious and spiritual concerns. Yet David not only never discovered him to be a hypocrite, but relied upon him as a true saint. He relished his religious discourse, it was sweet to him, and he counted him an eminent saint; so that he made him above any other man his guide and counsellor in soul matters; but yet he was not only, no saint, but a notoriously wicked man, a murderous, vile wretch. . . .

To suppose that men have ability and right to determine the state of the souls of visible Christians, and so to make an open separation between saints and hypocrites, that true saints may be of one visible company, and hypocrites of another, separated by a partition that men make, carries in it an inconsistency: for it supposes that God has given men power to make another visible church, within his visible church; for by visible Christians or visible saints; i.e. persons who have a right to be received as such in the eye of a public charity. None can have right to exclude any one of this visible church but in the way of that regular ecclesiastical proceeding, which God has established in his visible church.—I beg of those who have a true zeal for promoting this work of God, well to consider these things. I am persuaded, that as many of them as have much to do with souls, if they do not hearken to me now, will be of the same mind when they have had more experience.

And another thing that I would entreat the zealous friends of this glorious work of God to avoid, is managing the controversy with opposers with too much heat, and appearance of an angry zeal; and particularly insisting very much in public prayer and preaching, on the persecution of opposers. If their persecution were ten times so great as it is, methinks it would not be best to say so much about it. . . . God's zealous ministers would do well to think of the direction the apostle Paul gave to a zealous minister, 2 Tim. ii. 24-26. "And the servant of the Lord must not strive, but be gentle unto all men, apt to teach, patient, in meekness instructing those that oppose themselves, if God peradventure will give them repentance, to the acknowleding of the truth, and that they may recover themselves out of the snare of the devil, who are taken captive by him at his will."

I would humbly recommend to those that love the Lord Jesus Christ, and would advance his kingdom, a good attendance to that excellent rule of prudence which Christ has left us, Matt. ix. 16, 17. "No man putteth a piece of new cloth into an old garment; for that which is put in to fill it up, taketh from the garment, and the rent is made worse. Neither do men put new wine into old bottles; else the bottles break and the wine runneth out, and the bottles perish. But they put new wine into new bottles, and both are preserved." I am afraid that the wine is now running out in some part of this land, for want of attending to this rule. . . . Therefore that which is very much beside the common practice, unless it be a thing in its own nature of considerable importance, had better be avoided. Herein we shall follow the example of one who had the greatest success in propagating the power of religion. I Cor. ix. 20-23. "Unto the Jews, I become as a Jew, that I might gain the Jews; to them that are under the law, as under the law, that I might gain them that are under the law; to them that are without law, as without law, (being not without law to God, but under to Christ) that I might gain them that are without law. To the weak became I as weak that I might gain the weak. I am made all things to all men, that I might by all means save some. And this I do for the gospel's sake that I might be partaker thereof with you."

CHARLES CHAUNCY

Charles Chauncy (January 1, 1705–February 10, 1787) was the son of Charles Chauncy, a Boston merchant, and the great-grandson of Charles Chauncy, second president of Harvard College. In preparation for the ministry, his education consisted of the Boston Latin School followed by two degrees at Harvard College in 1721 and 1724. On October 25, 1727, he was ordained minister of the First Church in Boston and continued as a clergyman for sixty years. In physical appearance he was small and slender.

Chauncy became the acknowledged leader of the liberals of his day, and was the most influential clergyman in the Boston area. His views caused him to engage in three major controversies: Revivalism, Episcopacy, and the Benevolence of God. In his first controversy he fought every thing that in the least hinted of revivalism even to the point of praying that God would keep him from being an orator (one of his friends remarked that unquestionably the prayer had been answered). The second controvery concerned the Episcopacy and its relation to church polity. The royal governors argued that the Episcopal form was the only form of church government while Chauncy devoted nine years of his life to arguing against this position. The third controversy was theological in character, primarily in the form of rebuttal to Edwards' Calvinistic doctrine of grace. This controversy led to the publication in 1784 by Chauncy of The Benevolence of the Deity and in 1785 of Dissertation on the Fall and Its Consequences.

A Caveat Against Enthusiasm*

If any Man among you think himself to be a PROPHET, or SPIRITUAL, let him acknowledge that the Things that I write unto you are the Commandments of the LORD.—I COR. XIV. xxxvii.

Many Things were amiss in the *Church of Corinth*, when *Paul* wrote this Epistle to them. There were envyings, strife and divisions among them, on account of their ministers. Some cried up one, others another: one said, I am of PAUL, another I am of APPOLLOS. They had form'd themselves into parties, and each party so admired the teacher they followed, as to reflect unjust contempt on the other.

* *Enthusiasm Described and Cautioned Against* (Boston: J. Draper, 1742).

Nor was this their only fault. A spirit of pride prevailed exceedingly among them. They were conceited of their gifts, and too generally dispos'd to make an ostentatious shew of them. From this vain glorious temper proceeded the forwardness of those that had the *gift* of *tongues*, to speak in languages which others did not understand, to the disturbance, rather than edification of the church: And from the same principle it arose, that they spake not by turns, but several at once, in the same place of worship, to the introducing such confusion, that they were in danger of being tho't mad.

Nor were they without some pretence to justify these disorders. Their great plea was, that in these things they were guided by the Spirit, acted under his immediate influence and direction. This seems plainly insinuated in the words I have read to you. *If any man think himself to be a prophet, or spiritual, let him acknowledge that the things that I write unto you are the commandments of the Lord.* As if the apostle had said, you may imagine your selves to be *spiritual* men, to be under a divine afflatus in what you do; but 'tis all imagination, meer pretence, unless you pay a due regard to the *Commandments* I have here *wrote to you*; receiving them not as the *word of man, but of* GOD. Make trial of your spiritual pretences by this rule: If you can submit to it, and will order your conduct by it, well; otherwise you only cheat yourselves, while you think yourselves to be *spiritual* men, or *prophets*: You are nothing better than *Enthusiasts*; your being acted by the SPIRIT, immediately guided and influenced by him, is meer pretence; you have no good reason to believe any such thing.

From the words thus explained, I shall take occasion to discourse to you upon the following Particulars.

 I. I shall give you some account of *Enthusiasm*, in its *nature* and *influence*.

 II. Point you to a rule by which you may judge of persons, whether they are under the influence of *Enthusiasm*.

 III. Say what may be proper to guard you against this unhappy turn of mind.

The whole will then be follow'd with some suitable Application.

I. I am in the first place, to give you some account of *Enthusiasm*. And as this is a thing much talk'd of at present, more perhaps than at any other time that has pass'd over us, it will not be tho't unseasonable, if I take some pains to let you into a true understanding of it.

The word, from its Etymology, carries in it a good meaning, as signifying *inspiration from* GOD: in which sense, the prophets under the old testament, and the apostles under the new, might properly be called *Enthusiasts*. For they were under a divine influence, spake as moved by the HOLY

GHOST, and did such things as can be accounted for in no way, but by recurring to an immediate extraordinary power, present with them.

But the word is more commonly used in a bad sense, as intending an *imaginary*, not a *real* inspiration: according to which sense, the *Enthusiast* is one, who has a conceit of himself as a person favoured with the extraordinary presence of the *Deity*. He mistakes the workings of his own passions for divine communications, and fancies himself immediately inspired by the SPIRIT of GOD, when all the while, he is under no other influence than that of an over-heated imagination.

The cause of this *enthusiasm* is a bad temperament of the blood and spirits; 'tis properly a disease, a sort of madness: And there are few; perhaps, none at all, but are subject to it; tho' none are so much in danger of it as those, in whom *melancholy* is the prevailing ingredient in their constitution. In these it often reigns; and sometimes to so great a degree, that they are really beside themselves, acting as truly by the blind impetus of a wild fancy, as tho' they had neither reason nor understanding.

And various are the ways in which their *enthusiasm* discovers itself.

Sometimes, it may be seen in their countenance. A certain wildness is discernable in their general look and air; especially when their imaginations are mov'd and fired.

Sometimes, it strangely loosens their tongues, and gives them such an energy, as well as fluency and volubility in speaking, as they themselves, by their utmost efforts, can't so much as imitate, when they are not under the enthusiastick influence.

Sometimes, it affects their bodies, throws them into convulsions and distortions, into quakings and tremblings. This was formerly common among the people called *Quakers*. I was myself, when a Lad, an eye-witness to such violent agitations and foamings, in a boisterous female speaker, as I could not behold but with surprize and wonder.

Sometimes, it will unaccountably mix itself with their conduct, and give it such a tincture of that which is freakish or furious, as none can have an idea of, but those who have seen the behaviour of a person in a phrenzy.

Sometimes, it appears in their imaginary peculiar intimacy with heaven. They are, in their own opinion, the special favourites of GOD, have more familiar converse with him than other good men, and receive immediate, extraordinary communications from him. The tho'ts, which suddenly rise up in their minds, they take for suggestions of the SPIRIT; their very fancies are divine illuminations; nor are they strongly inclin'd to any thing, but 'tis an impulse from GOD, a plain revelation of his will.

And what extravagances, in this temper of mind, are they not capable of, and under the specious pretext too of paying obedience to the authority of GOD? Many have fancied themselves acting by immediate warrant from heaven, while they have been committing the most undoubted wickedness. There is indeed scarce any thing so wild, either in *Speculation* or *practice*, but they have given into it: They have, in many instances, been blasphemers of GOD, and open disturbers of the peace of the world.

But in nothing does the *enthusiasm* of these persons discover it self more, than in the disregard they express to the Dictates of *reason*. They are above the force of argument, beyond conviction from a calm and sober address to their understandings. As for them, they are distinguish'd persons; GOD himself speaks inwardly and immediately to their souls. "They see the light infused into their understandings, and cannot be mistaken; 'tis clear and visible there, like the light of bright sunshine; shews it self and needs no other proof but its own evidence. They feel the hand of GOD moving them within, and the impulses of his SPIRIT; and cannot be mistaken in what they feel. Thus they support themselves, and are sure reason hath nothing to do with what they see and feel. What they have sensible experience of, admits no doubt, needs no probation." And in vain will you endeavour to convince such persons of any mistakes they are fallen into. They are certainly in the right; and know themselves to be so. They have the SPIRIT opening their understandings and revealing the truth to them. They believe only as he has taught them: and to suspect they are in the wrong is to do dishonour to the SPIRIT; 'tis to oppose his dictates, to set up their own wisdom in opposition to his, and shut their eyes against that light with which he has shined into their souls. They are not therefore capable of being argued with; you had as good reason with the wind.

And as the natural consequence of their being thus sure of every thing, they are not only infinitely stiff and tenacious, but impatient of contradiction, censorious and uncharitable: they encourage a good opinion of none but such as are in their way of thinking and speaking. Those, to be sure, who venture to debate with them about their errors and mistakes, their weaknesses and indiscretions, run the hazard of being stigmatiz'd by them as poor unconverted wretches, without the SPIRIT, under the government of carnal reason, enemies to GOD and religion, and in the broad way to hell.

They are likewise positive and dogmatical, vainly fond of their own imaginations, and invincibly set upon propagating them: And in the doing of this, their Powers being awakened, and put as it were, upon the stretch, from the strong impressions they are under, that they are authorized by the immediate command of GOD himself, they sometimes exert themselves, with a sort of *extatic* violence: And 'tis this that gives them the advantage, among the less knowing and judicious, of those who are modest, suspicious of themselves, and not too assuming in matters of conscience and salvation.

The extraordinary fervour of their minds, accompanied with uncommon bodily motions, and an excessive confidence and assurance, gains them great reputation among the populace; who speak of them as *men of* GOD in distinction from all others, and too commonly hearken to, and revere their dictates, as tho' they really were, as they pretend, immediately communicated to them from the DIVINE SPIRIT.

This is the nature of *Enthusiasm,* and this its operation, in a less or greater degree, in all who are under the influence of it. 'Tis a kind of religious Phrenzy, and evidently discovers it self to be so, whenever it rises to any great height. . . .

But I come

II. In the second place, to point you to a *rule* by which you may judge of persons, whether they are *enthusiasts,* meer pretenders to the immediate guidance and influence of the SPIRIT. And this is, in general, *a regard to the bible, an acknowledgment that the things therein contained are the commandments of* GOD. This is the rule in the text. And 'tis an infallible rule of tryal in this matter: We need not fear judging amiss, while We keep closely to it.

'Tis true, it wont certainly follow, that a man, pretending to be a *prophet,* or *spiritual,* really is so, if he owns the *bible,* and receives the truths therein revealed as the mind of GOD: But the conclusion, on the other hand, is clear and certain; if he pretends to be conducted by the SPIRIT, and disregards the scripture, pays no due reverence to *the things there delivered as the commandments of* GOD, he is a meer pretender, be his pretences ever so bold and confident, or made with ever so much seeming seriousness, gravity, or solemnity.

And the reason of this is obvious; viz. that the things contained in the scripture were wrote by holy men as they were moved by the HOLY GHOST: they were received from GOD, and committed to writing under his immediate, extraordinary influence and guidance. And the divine, ever-blessed SPIRIT is consistent with himself. He cannot be suppos'd to be the author of any *private* revelations that are contradictory to the *public standing* ones, which he has preserved in the world to this day. This would be to set the SPIRIT of truth at variance with himself; than which a greater reproach can't be cast upon him. 'Tis therefore as true, that those are *enthusiastical,* who pretend to the SPIRIT, and at the same time express a disregard to the scripture, as that the SPIRIT is the great revealer of the things therein declared to us. And we may depend upon the certainty of this conclusion. . . .

But the *rule* in the text is yet more particular. It refers especially to *the things wrote by the apostle* PAUL, *and which he wrote to the church*

111

of *Corinth*, to rectify the *disorders* that had crept in among them. And whoever the person be, that pretends to be *Spiritual*, to be under the extraordinary guidance of the SPIRIT, and yet acts in contradiction to what the apostle has here wrote, he vainly imagines himself to be under the special guidance of the SPIRIT; he is a downright *enthusiast*.

And here suffer me to make particular mention of some of the things, the apostle has wrote in *this Epistle*, which, whoever will not acknowledge, in *deed* as well as *word*, to be the *commandments of* GOD, they are not guided by the SPIRIT, but vainly pretend to be so.

The first thing, in this kind, I would mention, is that which relates to *Ministers*; condemning an undue preference of one to another, the holding one in such admiration as to reflect disgrace on another. This was one of the disorders the Apostle takes notice of, as prevailing in the *church* of *Corinth*; and he is particular in his care to give check to this unchristian spirit, which had crumbled them into parties, and introduced among them faction and contention.

Now, whoever, under the pretence of being guided by the spirit, set up one minister in opposition to another, glory in this minister to the throwing undue contempt on that, thereby obstructing his usefulness, and making way for strife and divisions, they are not really acted by the SPIRIT, whatever they may pretend. For they evidently contradict what the apostle has wrote upon this very head: And if *he was inspired, the spirit they* are influenced by, cannot be the SPIRIT of GOD.

Not that one minister may not be preferr'd to another; this is reasonable: But no minister ought to be regarded, as tho' he was the author of our faith; nor let his gifts and graces be what they will, is he to be so esteemed, as that others must be neglected, or treated in an unbecoming manner. . . .

Another thing the apostle is particular in writing upon, is the *commandment* of *charity*. And this he declares to be a matter of such essential importance in true christianity, that if a man is really destitute of it, he is nothing in the sight of GOD: Nay, tho' his pretences, his attainments, his gifts, be ever so extraordinary or miraculous; still, if he is without charity he will certainly be rejected of GOD and the LORD JESUS CHRIST. This is beautifully represented in the three first verses of the 13th chapter of this Epistle, in some of the boldest figures. "Tho' I speak, says the apostle, with the tongues of men and of angels, and have not charity, I am become as sounding brass, or a tinkling cymbal. And tho' I have the gift of prophecy, and understand all mysteries and all knowledge; and tho' I have all faith, so that I could remove mountains, and have not charity, I am nothing. And tho' I bestow all my goods to feed the poor, and tho' I give my body to be burned, and have not charity, it profiteth me nothing."

112

. . . I say, if he was without this charity, this love of his neighbour, these things would be all nothing; he would notwithstanding be out of favour with GOD, without any interest in CHRIST, and in such circumstances, as that unless there was a change in them, he would certainly perish.

This, in sum, is what the apostle has, in a distinct and peremptory manner, delivered concerning charity. . . .

Charity, my brethren, is the commandment of the gospel by way of eminence. 'Tis the grand mark by which christians are to distinguish them-selves from all others. . . . To pretend therefore that we are led by the SPIRIT, and are under his extraordinary influence, when, in contradiction to the plain laws of JESUS CHRIST, revealed by the SPIRIT, we *judge our brother*, and *set at naught our brother*, and plead a right to do so, and are in a disposition TO THANK GOD, THAT WE ARE ENABLED TO DO SO; there is not a more sure mark, in all the revelations of GOD, of a BAD HEART, or a DISTEMPERED MIND. If any thing will evidence a man to be a *prophet* and *spiritual*, only in his own conceit, this must do it: And if this is not allow'd to be sufficient proof, there is no knowing, when a man is under the influence of *enthusiastick* heat and zeal.

Another thing the apostle bespeaks this church upon, is that *self-conceit* which appear'd among them in the exercise of *spiritual gifts*: And 'tis more than probable, there were those among them, who being vainly puffed up in their minds, behaved as tho' they were *apostles*, or *prophets*, or *teachers*; leaving their own station, and doing the work that was proper to others. It was to rectify such disorders, that the apostle, in the 12th chapter, addresses to them in that language, v. 29. *Are all apostles? Are all prophets? Are all teachers?* The question carries with it it's own answer, and means the same thing, as when he affirms in the foregoing verse *God hath set some in the church, first apostles, secondarily prophets, thirdly teachers,* and so on. 'Tis evident from what the apostle here writes, and indeed from the current strain of this whole chapter, that there is in the body of CHRIST, the Church, a distinction of members; some intended for one use, others for another; and that it would bring confusion into the *body mystical,* for one member to be employed in that service which is adapted to another, and is its proper business.

'Tis not therefore the pretence of being moved by the SPIRIT, that will justify *private christians* in quiting their own proper station, to act in that which belongs to another. Such a practice as this naturally tends to destroy that order, GOD has constituted in the church, and may be followed with mischiefs greater than we may be aware of.

'Tis indeed a powerful argument with many, in favour of these persons, their pretending to *impulses,* and a call from GOD; together with their

113

insatiable thirst to do good to souls. And 'tis owing to such pretences as these, that encouragement has been given to the rise of such numbers of *lay-exhorters and teachers,* in one place and another, all over the land. But if 'tis one of the things wrote by the apostle as the commandment *of* GOD, that there should be *officers* in the church, an *order of men* to whom it should belong, as their *proper, stated work,* to exhort and teach, this cannot be the business of others: And if any who think themselves to be *spiritual,* are under *impressions* to take upon them *this ministry,* they may have reason to suspect, whether their *impulses* are any other than the workings of their own imaginations: And instead of being under any divine extraordinary influence, there are just grounds of fear, whether they are not acted from the vanity of their minds: Especially, if they are but beginners in religion; men of weak minds, babes in understanding; as is most commonly the case. The apostle speaks of *novices,* as in danger of being *lifted up with pride, and falling into the condemnation of the devil:* And it is a seasonable caution to this kind of persons. . . .

And it deserves particular consideration, whether the suffering, much more the encouraging WOMEN, yea, GIRLS to speak in the assemblies for religious worship, is not a plain breach of that *commandment of the* LORD, wherein it is said, *Let your* WOMEN *keep silence in the churches; for it is not permitted to them to speak—It is a shame for* WOMEN *to speak in the church.* After such an express constitution, designedly made to restrain WOMEN from speaking in the church, with what face can such a practice be pleaded for? . . .

The last thing I shall mention as written by the apostle, is that which obliges to a *just decorum in speaking* in the *house of* GOD. It was an extravagance these *Corinthians* had fallen into, their speaking many of them together, and upon different things, while in the same place of worship. *How is it, brethren,* says the apostle? *When ye come together, every one hath a psalm; hath a doctrine; hath a tongue; hath a revelation; hath an interpretatien.* It was this that introduced the confusion and noise, upon which the apostle declares, if an unbeliever should come in among them, he would take them to be mad. And the *commandment* he gives them to put a stop to this disorder, is, that they should *speak in course, one by one,* and so as that *things might be done to edifying.*

And whoever the persons are, who will not acknowledge what the apostle has here said is the *commandment of* GOD, and act accordingly, are influenced by another spirit than that which moved in him, be their impressions or pretences what they will. The disorder of EXHORTING, and PRAYING, and SINGING, and LAUGHING, *in the same house of worship, at one and the same time,* is as great as was that, the apostle blames in the *church* of *Corinth:* And whatever the persons, guilty of such gross irregularity may imagine, and however they may plead their being under the influence of the SPIRIT, and mov'd by him, 'tis evidently a breach upon common order and decency; yea, a direct violation of the *commandment of* GOD, written on purpose to prevent such disorders: And to pretend the direction of the SPIRIT in such a flagrant instance of extravagant conduct, is to reproach the blessed SPIRIT, who is not, as the apostle's phrase is, *the author of confusion, but of peace, as in all the churches of the saints.*

In these, and all other instances, let us compare men's pretences to the SPIRIT by the SCRIPTURE: And if their conduct is such as can't be reconcil'd with an *acknowledgment of the things therein revealed, as the commandments of* GOD, their pretences are vain, they are *prophets* and *spiritual,* only in their own proud imaginations. I proceed now to

III. The third thing, which is to caution you against giving way to *enthusiastic impressions.* And here much might be said,

I might warn you from the *dishonour* it reflects upon the SPIRIT of GOD. And perhaps none have more reproach'd the blessed SPIRIT, than men pretending to be under his extraordinary guidance and direction. . . . And what a stone of stumbling has the wildness of *Enthusiasm* been to multitudes in the world? What prejudices have been hereby excited in their minds against the very being of the SPIRIT? What temptations have been thrown in their way to dispute his OFFICE as the SANCTIFYER and COMFORTER of God's people? And how have they been over-come to disown HIS WORK, when it has been really wro't in the hearts of men?

I might also warn you from the damage it has done in the world. No greater mischiefs have arisen from any quarter. It is indeed the genuine fource of infinite evil. POPERY it self han't been the mother of more and greater blasphemies and abominations. It has made strong attempts to destroy all property, to make all things common, *wives* as well as *goods.*— It has promoted faction and contention; filled the church oftentimes with confusion, and the state sometimes with general disorder.—It has, by its pretended spiritual interpretations, made void the most undoubted laws of GOD. It has laid aside the *gospel sacraments* as weak and carnal things; yea, this *superior light within* has, in the opinion of thousands, render'd the *bible* a *useless dead letter.*—It has made men fancy themselves to be *prophets* and *apostles;* yea, some have taken themselves to be CHRIST JESUS; yea, the blessed GOD himself. It has, in one word, been a pest to the church in all ages, as great an enemy to real and solid religion, as perhaps the grossest *infidelity.*

I might go on and warn you from the danger of it to yourselves. If you should once come under the influence of it, none can tell whither it would carry you. There is nothing so wild and frantick, but you may be reconcil'd to it. And if this shou'd be your case, your recovery to a right mind would be one of the most difficult things in nature. There is no coming at a thorow-pac'd *enthusiast.* He is proof against every method of dealing with him. Would you apply to him from reason? That he esteems a carnal thing, and flees from it as from the most dangerous temptation. Would you rise higher, and speak to him from *Scripture?* It will be to as little purpose. For if he pays any regard to it, 'tis only as it falls in with his own pre-conceiv'd notion. . . .

But as the most suitable guard against the first tendencies towards *enthusiasm,* let me recommend to you the following words of counsel.

1. Get a true understanding of the *proper work of the* SPIRIT; and don't place it in those things wherein the gospel does not make it to consist. The work of the SPIRIT is different now from what it was in the first days of christianity. Men were then favoured with the extraordinary presence of the SPIRIT. He came upon them in miraculous gifts and powers; as a spirit of prophecy, of knowledge, of revelation, of tongues, of miracles; But the SPIRIT is not now to be expected in these ways. His grand business lies in preparing men's minds for the grace of GOD, by true *humiliation,* from an apprehension of sin, and the necessity of a *Saviour;* then in working in them *faith* and *repentance,* and such a *change* as shall *turn them from the power of sin and Satan unto* GOD; and in fine, by carrying on the good work he has begun in them; assisting them in duty, strengthening them against temptation, and in a word, preserving them blameless thro' faith unto salvation: And all this he does by the *word* and *prayer,* as the great means in the accomplishment of these purposes of mercy.

Herein, in general consists the work of the SPIRIT. It does not lie in giving men *private revelations,* but in opening their minds to understand the *publick ones* contained in the scripture. It does not lie in *sudden impulses* and *impressions,* in *immediate calls* and *extraordinary missions.* Men mistake the business of the SPIRIT, if they understand by it such things as these. And 'tis, probably, from such unhappy mistakes, that they are at first betrayed into *enthusiasm.* Having a wrong notion of the *work of* the SPIRIT, 'tis no wonder if they take the uncommon sallies of their own minds for his influences.

You cannot, my brethren, be too well acquainted with what the *bible* makes the *work* of the HOLY GHOST, in the affair of salvation: And if you have upon your minds a clear and distinct understanding of this, it will be a powerful guard to you against all *enthusiastical impressions.*

2. Keep close to the *Scripture,* and admit of nothing for an impression of the SPIRIT, but what agrees with that unerring rule. . . . And let it

be your care to compare the motions of your minds, and the workings of your imaginations and passions, with the *rule* of GOD's *word*. And see to it, that you be impartial in this matter: Don't make the rule bend to your pre-conceiv'd notions and inclinations; but repair to the *bible*, with a mind dispos'd, as much as may be, to know the truth as it lies nakedly and plainly in the *scripture* it self. . . .

This adherence to the bible, my brethren, is one of the best preservatives against *enthusiasm*. If you will but express a due reverence to this *book* of GOD, making it the great rule of judgment, even in respect of the SPIRIT's *influences* and *operations*, you will not be in much danger of being led into delusion. Let that be your inquiry under all suppos'd *impulses* from the SPIRIT, *What saith the scripture? To the law, and to the testimony:* If your impressions and imagined spiritual motions agree not therewith, 'tis because there is no hand of the SPIRIT of GOD in them: They are only the workings of your own imaginations, or something worse; and must at once, without any more ado, be rejected as such.

3. Make use of the *Reason* and *Understanding* GOD has given you. This may be tho't an ill-advis'd direction, but 'tis as necessary as either of the former. Next to the *Scripture*, there is no greater enemy to *enthusiasm*, than *reason*. 'Tis indeed impossible a man shou'd be an *enthusiast*, who is in the just exercise of his understanding; and 'tis because men don't pay a due regard to the sober dictates of a well inform'd mind, that they are led aside by the delusions of a vain imagination. Be advised then to shew yourselves men, to make use of your reasonable powers; and not act as the *horse* or *mule*, as tho' you had no understanding.

'Tis true, you must not go about to set up your own *reason* in *opposition* to *revelation*: Nor may you entertain a tho't of making *reason* your *rule* instead of *scripture*. The *bible*, as I said before, is the *great rule* of religion, the grand test in matters of salvation: But then, you must use your reason in order to understand the *bible*: Nor is there any other possible way, in which, as a reasonable creature, you shou'd come to an understanding of it.

You are, it must be acknowledged, in a corrupt state. The fall has introduc'd great weakness into your reasonable nature. You can't be too sensible of this; nor of the danger you are in of making a wrong judgment, thro' prejudice, carelessness, and the undue influence of sin and lust. And to prevent this, you can't be too solicitous to get your *nature sanctified:* Nor can you depend too strongly upon the divine grace to assist you in your search after truth: And 'tis in the way of due dependance on GOD, and the influences of his SPIRIT, that I advise you to the use of your reason: And in this way, you must make use of it. How else will you know what is a revelation from GOD? . . .

117

You may, it is true, misuse your reason: And this is a consideration that shou'd put you upon a due care, that you may use it well; but no argument why you shou'd not use it at all: And indeed, if you shou'd throw by your reason as a useless thing, you would at once put your selves in the way of all manner of delusion.

But, it may be, you will say, you have committed yourselves to the *guidance* of the SPIRIT; which is the best preservative. Herein you have done well; nothing can be objected against this method of conduct: Only take heed of mistakes, touching the SPIRIT's *guidance*. Let me enquire of you, how is it the SPIRIT preserves from delusion? Is it not by opening the understanding, and enabling the man, in the due use of his reason, to perceive the truth of the things of GOD and religion? Most certainly: And, if you think of being led by the SPIRIT without understanding, or in opposition to it, you deceive yourselves. The SPIRIT of God deals with men as *reasonable* creatures: And they ought to deal with themselves in like manner. And while they do thus, making a wise and good use of the understanding, GOD has given them, they will take a proper means to prevent their falling into delusions; nor will there be much danger of their being led aside by *enthusiastic* heat and imagination.

4. You must not lay too great stress upon the *workings* of your *passions* and *affections*. These will be excited, in a less or greater degree, in the business of religion: And 'tis proper they shou'd. The passions, when suitabley mov'd, tend mightily to awaken the *reasonable powers*, and put them upon a lively and vigorous exercise. And this is their proper use. . . . The *soul* is the *man: And unless the reasonable nature* is suitably wro't upon, the *understanding* enlightened, the *judgment* convinc'd, *the will* perswaded, and the *mind* intirely chang'd, it will avail but to little purpose; tho' the passions shou'd be set all in a blaze. This therefore you shou'd be most concern'd about. . . .

5. In the last place here, you must not forget to go to GOD by *prayer*. This is a duty in all cases, but in none more than the present. If left to yourselves, your own wisdom and strength, you will be insufficient for your own security; perpetually in danger from your *imaginations*, as well as the other enemies of your *souls*. . . . You must daily commit the keeping of your soul to him; and this you must particularly be careful to do in times of more special hazard; humbly hoping in GOD to be your help: And if he shall please to undertake for you, no delusion shall ever have power over you, to seduce you; but, possessing a sound mind, you shall go on in the uniform, steady service of your maker and generation, till of the mercy of GOD, thro' the merits of the REDEEMER, you are crowned with eternal life.

But I shall now draw towards a close, by making some suitable *application* of what has been said, And,

1. Let us beware of charging GOD *foolishly*, from what we have heard of the *nature*, and *influence* of *enthusiasm*. This may appear a dark article in GOD's government of the world; but it stands upon the same foot with his permission of other evils, whether *natural* or *moral*. And, if we shou'd not be able to see perfectly into the reason of this dispensation, we shou'd rather attribute it to our own ignorance, than reply against GOD. We may assure ourselves, a wise, and good, and holy GOD, would not have suffered it thus to be, if there were not some great and valuable ends to be hereby answered.

Greater advantages may, in the end, accrue to true religion, by the sufferance of an *enthusiastic* spirit, and the prevalence of it, at certain times, than we may be capable of discerning at present.

It may furnish both opportunity and occasion for the trial of those, who call themselves christians; whether they have just notions of religion, and courage and faithfulness to stand up for *real* truths, against meer *imaginary* ones. . . . In a word, It may put men upon a more thorough examination into the grounds of the christian religion, and be the means of their being, more generally, established in its truth, upon the best and most reasonable evidence.

. . . The persons, heated with *enthusiastic* imaginations, are either, in a faulty sense, accessory to this unhappy turn of mind, or they are not: If the *latter*, they may depend upon the pity and mercy of GOD, notwithstanding the extravagancies they may run into; yea, if they are good men, as is, doubtless, sometimes the case, it may be hoped, that this evil which has happened to them, will, after the manner of other sufferings, work together for good to them: But if thro' the pride of their hearts; a vainglorious temper, accompanied with rashness and arrogance, or the like, they are really accessary to their own delusion, and mad conduct following therefrom, let them not think to cast the blame on GOD: They do but reap the fruit of what they themselves have sown. . . .

2. Let none, from what has been offered, entertain prejudices in their minds against the *operations* of the SPIRIT. There is such a thing as his influence upon the hearts of men. No consistent sense can be put upon a great part of the *bible*, unless this be acknowledged for a truth: Nor is it any objection against its being so, that there has been a great deal of *enthusiasm* in the world, many who have mistaken the motions of their own passions for divine operations. . . . But at the same time, 'tis no reason, why we shou'd think the worse of the blessed SPIRIT, of or those influences that are really *his*.

119

Let us be upon our guard as to this matter. Many from what they have seen or heard of the strange conduct of men, pretending to be under *divine impressions,* have had their minds insensibly leaven'd with prejudices against the things of the SPIRIT. O let it be our care, that we be not thus wro't upon! And the rather, least it shou'd prove the ruin of our souls. This, perhaps, we may not be afraid of: But the danger is great, if we take up wrong notions of the SPIRIT, or encourage an unbecoming tho't of his influences in the business of salvation, least we shou'd grieve the *good* SPIRIT, and he shou'd leave us to perish in a state of alianation from GOD, and true holiness.

'Tis worthy our particular remark, it is by the powerful operation of the holy SPIRIT on the hearts of men, that they are chang'd from the love and practice of sin, to the love and practice of holiness; and have those tempers form'd in them, whereby they are made meet for the glory to be hereafter revealed: Nor can this be done, in any way, without the *special influence* of the blessed SPIRIT. . . .

Only let us look to it, that we take no *impressions* for his but such as really are so: And let us not be satisfied, 'till we experience within ourselves the *real effects* of the SPIRIT's operations; such as are common to all that are in CHRIST JESUS; and always have been, and always will be, accompanied with a *holy frame of soul,* and a *conversation becoming the Gospel.*

3. Let not any think *ill* of religion, because of the *ill* representation that is made of it by *enthusiasts.* There may be danger of this; especially, in regard of those who have not upon their minds a serious sense of GOD and the things of another world. They may be ready to judge of religion from the *copy* given them of it, by those who are too much led by their fancies; and to condemn it, in the gross, as a wild, imaginary, inconsistent thing. But this is to judge too hastily and rashly. . . .

But however religion may appear as viewed in the lives, even of the best men, 'tis a lovely thing, as required by GOD, and pourtrayed in the bible. We shou'd take our sentiments of it from this *book of* GOD; and this, in the calm and sober exercise of our understandings: And if we view it, as 'tis here delineated, we can't but approve of it, the *doctrines* it teaches, and the *duties* it requires, whether they relate to GOD, ourselves, or our neighbour; they are all so reasonable in themselves, and worthy of the GOD, the stamp of whose authority they bear.

Let us fetch our notions of religion from the scripture: And if men, in their practice, set it in a disadvantageous light, let us be upon our guard, that we don't take up prejudices against it. This will blind our eyes, and may, by degrees, prepare the way to our throwing off all concern about religion; yea, we may bro't to treat it even with contempt; than which, nothing can be more dangerous, or put our salvation to a greater risque.

4. Let us esteem those as *friends* to religion, and not *enemies*, who warn us of the danger of *enthusiasm*, and would put us upon our guard, that we be not led aside by it. As the times are, they run the hazard of being call'd *enemies* to the *holy* SPIRIT, and may expect to be ill spoken of by many, and loaded with names of reproach. . . .

'Tis really best, people shou'd know there is such a thing as *enthusiasm*, and that it has been, in all ages, one of the most dangerous enemies to the church of GOD, and has done a world of mischief: And 'tis a kindness to them to be warn'd against it, and directed to the proper methods to be preserved from it. 'Tis indeed, one of the best ways of doing service to *real* religion, to distinguish it from that which is *imaginary*: Nor shou'd ministers be discouraged from endeavouring this, tho' they shou'd be ill-tho't, or evil-spoken of. They shou'd beware of being too much under the influence of that *fear of man, which bringeth a snare*; which is evidently the case, where they are either silent, or dare not speak out faithfully and plainly, lest they shou'd be called PHARISEES or HYPOCRITES, and charged with LEADING SOULS TO THE DEVIL. . . .

There is, I doubt not, a great deal of *real, substantial* religion in the land. The SPIRIT of GOD has wro't effectually on the hearts of many, from one time to another: And I make no question he has done so of late, in more numerous instances, it may be, than usual. But this, notwithstanding, there is, without dispute, a *spirit of enthusiasm*, appearing in one place and another. There are those, who make great pretences to the SPIRIT, who are carried away with their imaginations: And some, it may be, take themselves to be *immediately and wonderfully conducted by him*; while they are led only by their own fancies. . . .

The good Lord give us all wisdom; and courage, and conduct, in such a Day as this! And may both *ministers* and *people* behave after such a manner, as that religion may not suffer; but in the end, gain advantage and be still more universally established.

And, may that grace of GOD, which has appeared to all men, bringing salvation, teach us effectually, to deny ungodliness and worldly lusts, and to live soberly and righteously, and godlily in the world: so may we look with comfort for the appearing of our SAVIOUR JESUS CHRIST: And when he shall appear in the glory of his FATHER, and with his holy angels, we also shall appear with him, and go away into everlasting life: Which GOD of his infinite mercy grant may be the portion of us all; for the sake of CHRIST JESUS.

AMEN.

121

5

THE RISE OF UNITARIANISM IN AMERICA
Thomas Olbricht

For the first fifty years of the nineteenth century, theology in New England was in continual upheaval because of new modes of thinking which crystalized into the American Unitarian Association. The new ways of thought began to appear at the middle of the eighteenth century in the form of Arminianism. Arminianism emphasized the ability of man to choose God or evil on his own, while traditional Calvinism insisted on God as sovereign over the created order and human history. But it was after the turn of the century before cracks began to show in the fellowship of churches and ministers. A famous Arminian in the eighteenth century was Charles Chauncy. In the early part of the nineteenth century one finds reoccuring in the controversy the names of Aaron Bancroft (1755–1839), William Emerson (1769–1811), Joseph S. Buckminster (1784-1812), Thaddeus Harris (1768–1842), and James Freeman (1759–1835). Then somewhat later the names of Andrews Norton (1786–1852)), William Ellery Channing (1780–1842), and Henry Ware, Jr. (1794–1843) became well known. Among the orthodox who exercised leadership for the opposition were Nathanael Emmons (1745–1840) and Lyman Beecher (1775–1863).

THE RISE OF UNITARIANISM IN AMERICA

Much more was at stake in the Unitarian controversy than the doctrine of the Trinity, though the name itself might imply otherwise. Orthodox Calvinism emphasized original sin, predestination both to heaven and hell, the idea that salvation is the result of God's unmerited grace, and that the one who is saved first becomes aware of this grace through the action of the Holy Spirit in his conversion. The Unitarians objected to these doctrines, affirming the ability of man to work toward his own holiness. In addition, they criticized the orthodox for the doctrine of the Trinity, which they charged was irrational.

The two speeches, one by Bancroft and one by Emmons, printed here indicate the polarity in the controversy, even though not all the areas of difference are introduced. A leading polemicist among the Unitarians was Aaron Bancroft of the Second Church in Worcester. His sermon was not as developed in detail as William Ellery Channing's "Unitarian Christianity," nevertheless it clearly set forth the heart of the controversy as most Unitarians saw it. It was the first sermon of a series which attacked the orthodox position. Thus, it presented in an overall manner the main issues at stake. The sermon by Nathanael Emmons focused specifically on the doctrine of the Trinity, but even so, the grounds on which the dispute revolved are obvious. Emmons' view of the Trinity was similar to that of the orthodox, even though he favored the "New Divinity" theology. Since Emmons sided with those who supported the awakening it is surprising that he was willing to argue the doctrine of the Trinity in terms of reasonableness, but then emotion was emphasized as the avenue for conversion, not as the tool for theological construction. In this conflict both sides were willing to settle the argument in terms of reasonableness. As the result, the opposing views drew nearer one another and by 1830, for example, even the orthodox had ceased emphasizing the doctrine of election.

In his sermon "Religion in Man a Rational and Voluntary Service," Aaron Bancroft argued that man is not under compulsion but is free to make his own decisions in Jesus Christ. Such decisions, in this sermon at least, are doctrinal decisions, not moral ones. Bancroft's main concern was with doctrine, a focus not true of all Unitarians, especially William Ellery Channing who emphasized the moral life. In the last part of the sermon, Bancroft was willing to admit that the freedom for each to decide the doctrines of Christianity would result in differences. But these differences he saw as healthy as long as charitableness prevailed. The sermon makes it obvious that Bancroft saw the Unitarians as being irenic in spirit while the orthodox were uncharitable. If Conrad Wright is correct in *The Beginnings of Unitarianism in America*, Bancroft's conclusion has considerable evidence to support it. It is interesting, however, that not more than twenty years later a new generation arose within Unitarian ranks to accuse the orthodox Unitarian of uncharitableness. In the remainder of the sermon Bancroft set forth the doctrinal differences as he saw them. This delineation is valuable as a means for discerning what was at the heart of the controversy. As one reads the sermon he is impressed with its clear structure, its precise language, and the cogency of the argument.

In his address on the "Doctrine of the Trinity," Nathanael Emmons presented arguments for the orthodox point of view. He opposed both those who emphasized the mystery in revelation and those who found no place for it. He concerned himself, however, with those who denied mystery: those who later accepted the name Unitarian. He made the point that while a mystery cannot be comprehended, it can be distinguished from an absurdity, a point which the Unitarians were unwilling to admit. He set forth the orthodox view that God is one in three persons, which he considered a mystery. Though he claimed biblical support for this formula, he made no effort to find it so stated in the Scriptures, but assumed that various statements therein established it. If he was aware of the historical background of the formula he did not indicate that awareness in this sermon. He presented a number of analogies for understanding the doctrine which have a long historical background, but he did not refer to that background. He claimed that though these analogies have some value, they all fail and the mystery remains.

It was the "three persons" aspect of the formula to which Emmons directed his attention, for that was the phrase particularly ridiculed by the Unitarians. But even though the three is a mystery he contended it was not an absurdity, as, for example, a claim that two equals three. The claim was not, he pointed out, that three Gods are one, but that one God exists in three persons. Just what is meant by persons is hence the mystery. But the Unitarians should not be so concerned about mysteries since there are those which they themselves are willing to accept, for example, that God is self-existent, or is his own cause. In the last part of the sermon Emmons attempted to show that the doctrine of the Trinity was compatible with the biblical views concerning God's work in the universe and his relationship with men.

A cogency of argument marks this sermon, but one which is not immediately obvious. As one reads he must give close attention so as to grasp the development of thought. The argument is concise; only in doxology does it tend to get wordy. The sermon shows the manner in which some orthodox ministers, at least, were willing to meet the Unitarians in direct clash. It may be that Emmons was more fair in representing the views of the Unitarians than they in representing orthodox views. But there was a reason for this, and not that the Unitarians were vicious in intent. What they precisely denied was the validity of the older theology, and for this reason they did not have much stomach for learning its subtleties.

AARON BANCROFT

Aaron Bancroft was born in Reading, Massachusetts, November 10, 1755. His schooling was interrupted by the early battles of the Revolutionary War. He served as a Minuteman and was present at the battles of Lexington Green and Bunker Hill. Shortly afterward he entered Harvard where he took his A.B. Degree in 1778. He then turned to teaching and at the same time studied theology. After being licensed to preach he spent three years in missionary type efforts in Yarmouth, Nova Scotia. In 1785 he was settled with the Congregational Church in Worcester, Massachusetts. He was associated with this church for fifty-four years until his death, August 19, 1839. Bancroft was active in church councils and conventions and as a result Harvard conferred the D.D. Degree upon him. His church was the second parish in Worcester and was made up of a large proportion of the distinguished people of the town. In theology, Bancroft was Arminian. In his early years in Worcester he had considerable difficulty associating with other ministers in the area. Bancroft printed a number of sermons including one volume from which the sermon printed here is taken. His sermon style is cogent and forceful, and often polemical. He also served a term as president of the American Unitarian Association.

Religion in Man a Rational and Voluntary Service*

Ye can discern the face of the sky, and of the earth; but how is it, that ye do not discern this time?—LUKE XII. 56.

Jesus Christ, in the establishment of his religion, did not adopt measures of compulsion. He taught men every essential religious truth, propounded laws for the government of their conduct, and addressed them with the most persuasive motives. He then left men to act freely, that the happiness of his disciples might be the reward of obedience, which flows from an enlightened mind and a teachable temper.

Our Saviour exhibited the clearest proof of a divine mission. By his life, he displayed the moral worth of his character. To the Jews he stated, that

* Sermons on those Doctrines of the Gospel and on those Constituent Principles . . . of Controversy (Worcester: Wm. Manning & Son, 1822).

in him their prophecies were fulfilled: in the presence of those who followed him, he wrought miracles; and he called on his countrymen to examine his doctrines, to reflect on his works, and to weigh the actions of his life; and for themselves determine, whether they might not confidently receive his communications, obey his precepts, and rely on his promises.

This is the substance of the appeal in our text. In the previous verses, Jesus had observed to those who accompanied him, When ye see a cloud rise out of the west, straightway ye say, there cometh a shower, and so it is; and when ye perceive the south wind to blow, ye say, there will be heat, and it cometh to pass. Ye hypocrites! ye can discern the face of the sky, and of the earth; but how is it, that ye do not discern this time? From usual appearances, you form a correct judgment of the effects of natural principles; why do ye not seriously attend to the moral dispensations of God, and, by the evidence produced, become satisfied of the divine origin of the doctrines I inculcate? In our subsequent context, our Saviour prefaces a case of moral duty with the question, Why, even of yourselves, judge ye not what is right? It is then evident, that Christ recognized powers in man to judge of the evidence on which his religion is founded, and to perceive that his instructions are conformable to the unchangeable laws of truth and rectitude.

A number of important inferences may be drawn from this appeal of our Saviour to the human mind.

1. Religion in man is a rational and voluntary service.

God has imparted to man the attributes of reason and liberty. These constitute him the subject of a moral government, and make him capable of virtuous action. Take away these faculties, and he ceases to be the proper object of rewards or punishment. Without moral liberty, man may be the instrument of actions which in their effects are salutary or pernicious; but in the agent there can be neither virtue nor vice. . . . The manner in which the faculties of the human mind are used, determines the moral character. The intention fixes the moral complexion of human conduct. The same action in this man is a virtue, and in that a vice. An example will fully illustrate this remark. Two men unite to feed and clothe a hungry and naked fellow-being; one discharges this humane office from a conviction that it is a social duty, of indispensable obligation—and in him the duty is virtuous and worthy of praise; the other adopts this form of benevolence towards a suffering object, as the means to gain his confidence, and thereby to ensnare and ruin him—and this malignant intention renders the action vile and wicked. Reason to distinguish good from evil, and liberty to choose the one and refuse the other, render men capable of moral conduct and moral government. This distinction between free and necessary agents being taken away, men are let down to the level of beasts, or they become mere machines, and there is no more moral worth in their actions than there is in the effects produced by the established laws of the natural kingdom. To suspect the motive, would be uncharitable, when the conduct is habitually good—because the life furnishes to us the best evidence of the state of the heart; but God judgeth not as men judge: he looketh at the heart, and decideth on the moral worth of our conduct from our secret intention and purpose. From every view we can take of our subject, it will appear, that as rational and free beings we are subjected to moral laws, and that it is in the right exercise of our reason and liberty that we become religious men.

2. I infer, it is the duty of men to improve all the means they enjoy, to enlighten their minds on the subject of religion.

To act rationally and freely in the important concerns of religion, we must know its foundation, and be made acquainted with its essential truths and duties. We cannot consistently perform the offices of religion, while ignorant of its first principles, any more than we can converse intelligibly in a language with which we are unacquainted. Suppose an individual educated in a country where the true religion is professed—yet a traditional reception of it, without a knowledge of the grounds of his faith or the reasons of his hope, would not entitle him to praise. Had he been born in a different country, he would have embraced its religion, however false and absurd. Is there no advantage, then, it will be asked, in the traditional reception of the true religion? Much every way; chiefly because this is a providential means of acquiring the knowledge of many religious truths and moral duties, of which an individual would otherwise have been ignorant: these he admits on divine authority; and, to maintain a good conscience, he lives in their habitual exercise, and is thereby formed to a virtuous disposition. But his faith, being founded on an accidental circumstance of his nativity, and not being the result of inquiry and conviction, has in itself no worth. The Parent of Life favourably appointed the place of his birth, and by this circumstance his religious superstructure is erected on the basis of truth; but from it he himself can claim no merit. But in the man, who cultivates his intellectual powers, who examines the foundation of his religion, weighs its evidence, and adopts it on conviction of its truth, faith is a moral exercise, acceptable to God. This man has preserved his mind free from the influence of prejudice, and his heart from the bias of sin; and obedience in him is the act of an enlightened judgment, as well as of a sound conscience.

The observations made respecting religion as a system will apply to its several parts. If our understanding must be convinced before we can consistently profess the belief that a particular religion is true, then its peculiar doctrines must be examined and understood before we can consistently embrace them. To believe as this master in theology, or as that church believes, is not to give a sufficient reason for our faith. We stand on our own foundation, not theirs; their answers will not be accepted as ours in the day of judgment. The right of private judgment will not be questioned. If we voluntarily resign it, we part withour religious capacity, we undermine the foundation of personal religion, and can no longer live in the rational exercise of faith or hope. Implicit confidence can never be safely reposed on human authority. Religious instructers are forbidden to exercise dominion over the faith of their fellow-men, but they are directed to be the helpers of their joy.

We are commanded to call no man father, knowing that one is our Father, who is in heaven. We are solemnly warned not to judge one another, knowing that every one shall account for himself to God. When we resign our understandings and consciences to fallible men, and receive human formularies as the standard of sound doctrine, we remove ourselves from the foundation of the gospel, and have no sure basis on which to rest; and we shall be exposed to all the impositions which the weakness or ignorance, the worldly interests or the personal ambition of men can introduce into the Christian church. Reason and revelation, I think, warrant the position, that every man who seriously endeavours to acquire the knowledge of divine truth, and habitually practises according to the dictates of an enlightened conscience, will be accepted at the final judgment; but the individual who complies with this condition of acceptance can be positively *ascertained* only by him who knows the heart. To the serious consideration of those who feel disposed to condemn a brother merely for his Christian opinions, I present the reproof of our Saviour to his disciples, Ye know not what spirit ye are of.

As the understanding of a man must be enlightened, and his judgment convinced, before he can consistently embrace any system of doctrine, I infer,

3. That uniformity of religious opinion is not to be expected even among Christians.

The natural understandings of men differ, their education is dissimilar, and their course of life is various. These circumstances lead to different views of religion and of all other subjects. A truth that is plain and evident to the man of ten talents, may be unintelligible to him who possesses but one. What you deem to be a mere rite of religion, your neighbour may hold as a fundamental principle of the gospel. No one ought to adopt the opinion of another against the dictates of his own mind. Speculative differences, when accompanied with Christian virtues in the life, should not be made the occasion of uncharitableness among disciples who acknowledge a common Master. Is this opening too widely the door of charity? Look into the New Testament, and there learn the term of admission into the Christian church. This is simply a confession of faith in Jesus as the Messiah. Such was the confession of Peter—*We believe and are sure that thou art the Christ, the Son of the living God.* And of Mary—*I believe that thou art the Christ, the Son of God.* On this confession, Philip baptized the Samaritan converts and the eunuch of Ethiopia. On a similar profession of faith, St. Paul baptized the jailer and other Gentile disciples. If the acknowledgment of Jesus Christ as the Son of God was all the apostles required for admission into the Christian community, shall we demand more, and deny the Christianity of the man who, professing the name of Christ, manifests by his life that he faithfully observes the directions of his divine Lord? Shall we exclude from our fellowship all who do not receive the whole system of doctrines which we believe to be revealed in the gospel? We shall then probably exclude from our charity the greater number of Christian professors. Should our principle of fellowship be generally adopted, the Christian church could never be relieved from bitter disputes and destructive divisions.

The signs of the times led my reflections to our present subject. Many of this audience know that the history of American Unitarianism, originally issued from a British press, has lately been re-published in our Commonwealth, and a strong appeal made to the publick on the system of doctrine therein unfolded. The purpose of the Editors probably was to depress Unitarianism in our country, by the weight of publick odium. They insinuated that Unitarian Ministers, in the apprehension that their cause would not bear the light, were endeavouring to promote it in a secret and insidious manner. On this representation of timidity and concealment, the Editors exclaim, "Are these the true representatives of the Apostles and martyrs, glorifying God by an *open profession* of his gospel, and not ashamed to own their Lord before men? Is this the *simplicity* and *godly sincerity* of the gospel?" Thus assailed, Unitarian Ministers were compelled publickly to vindicate themselves. They corrected the gross errours in the statement of their opponents, explained their opinions, and adduced scriptural authority for their support....

The time for inquiry and investigation is come; and our citizens, liberated from the shackles of a national establishment, will not receive the dogmas of schoolmen as the truths of revelation. On the minds of the clergy of our Commonwealth there is no bias from a view to the emolument of high ecclesiastical offices, nor from a fear of ecclesiastical censures, which the civil power will enforce by the forfeiture of salaries, by fines and imprisonment. These circumstances are highly favourable to free and candid inquiry, and they tend to elevate the character of a Christian community. But all human advantages are attended with inconvenience, and are liable to abuse. When men think for themselves, they form different opinions even on subjects the most important; and if they hold their peculiar sentiments with an uncandid spirit, and refuse Christian fellowship with those who differ from them, the society of Christians must be divided into numberless sects, and few of them will possess the means to support the publick institutions of the gospel in a respectable manner. Most of those who acknowledge the divine origin of Christianity embrace all the principles that are essential to its effectual establishment. Let Christians, then, in forbearance and charity, permit each other to judge for themselves respecting doctrines, in the explanation of which the wisest and best men have disagreed, and then they may mutually co-operate in promoting the reign of their common Lord.

Professors with us, at the present day, may be classed in two great divisions, Calvinists and Liberal or Unitarian Christians. Perhaps the most distinguishing point of difference between them respects the office of reason in the sacred concerns of religion. The Calvinists style themselves the orthodox, evangelical professors; and they require that the mysteries of revelation, as they denominate them, should be received, though these cannot be explained, in humble submission to Divine Wisdom. Numbers of this class seem disposed to attribute opposition to their peculiar system of faith to the obstinacy of a mind not rectified by divine grace. Some more ardent, altogether deny the Christianity of those who reject their peculiar views. In answer to these allegations, we say, that, among all denominations, worthy and unworthy professors may be found—that, in each, the most perfect disciples have occasion to lament their weakness and their failings—and that, with every denomination, the fruits manifested by the life and conversation should furnish the rule of charitable judgment, and not doctrinal opinions.

In respect to the office of reason in religious concerns, we hold, that without the exercise of reason, no man can be a consistent disciple of Jesus Christ. Indeed, we perceive that Calvinists never reject the authority of reason, when it can be brought to support their positions. We hold, that by the exercise of reason a judgment is formed of the evidence by which our religion is proved to be true—by reason we make up our opinions of the doctrines contained in the sacred scriptures—and by reason we pronounce on the purity and excellence of the precepts and institutions of the gospel. Though we do not pretend to comprehend God in his attributes, in his works or ways, yet we say that our duty extends no further than our capacity for knowledge extends; and that we cannot consistently admit any position as a doctrine of divine revelation, which consists of a set of terms conveying no distinct ideas to the mind, much less if it involve a direct contradiction, or is manifestly opposed to admitted principles of rectitude and goodness. Deny this, and we are denied the power to distinguish between a true and false religion, between good and evil, between virtue and vice.

You, my candid hearers, are witnesses that, in my general course of preach-

131

ing, I have dwelt on the undisputed doctrines of revelation, and on the important duties of the Christian character; though I have not studied concealment of my opinion on any religious subject, but as occasion dictated have, as far as I understood it, declared unto you the whole counsel of God. Unusual attention is at this day given to doctrinal questions on which Christians have divided. Disquisitions on these subjects are now circulated among every class in society, by the distribution of sermons, religious tracts, and theological journals; and the peculiar tenets of the two great divisions of believers are frequently made the subject of conversation in our families. . . .

In conclusion,

Let us, my respected hearers, improve the means we enjoy for the acquisition of Christian knowledge. May we not hold the truth in unrighteousness, but live in the maintenance of a conscience void of offence towards God and man. Then we shall be able to give an answer to every man who asketh us the reason of the hope which is in us. The moral excellence of the gospel will not only entertain our minds, but also purify our hearts, and form us to the disposition requisite to enjoy the future rewards it promises to its obedient disciples. In this world we shall realize the support, the consolation, and joy, which Christianity is fitted to yield to those who are imbued with its spirit; and at the close of our probation, we shall be found of our Judge in peace; and the approving sentence will be pronounced on us individually, Well done, good and faithful servant, enter thou into the joy of thy Lord.

Nathanael Emmons was born in East Haddam, Connecticut, April 20, 1745. He attended Yale University from which he received the A.B. Degree in 1767. At Yale he read the writings of Jonathan Edwards and thus was influenced in the direction of the New Divinity or Hopkinsian theology. He was related, through marriage, to a number of well-known Hopkinsian ministers. Emmons studied theology under John Smalley and was licensed to preach on October 3, 1769. From this time he preached among churches in central and western New York and northern New Hampshire before finally settling with the Second Church of Franklin, Massachusetts, in April 1773. This church he served for sixty-seven years until his death in 1840 at Franklin. Emmons was actively engaged in the various church activities of his time, including missions to the Indians and education. A number of young men studied theology with him, perhaps as many as a hundred. He engaged in the theological controversies, disputing not only with orthodox Calvinists, but with the Arminians and then Unitarians. He served as president of the Massachusetts Missionary Society and editor of the Massachusetts Missionary Magazine. He participated in various efforts such as the anti-Masonic, and antislavery movements even into his ninetieth year. He published numerous sermons. He was clear in style and forceful in argument, but not always economical in the use of language.

On the Doctrine of the Trinity*

For there are three that bear record in heaven, the Father, the Word, and the Holy Ghost: and these three are one.—I JOHN v, 7.

In treating on revealed religion, men have often run into two extremes. Some have been fond of finding mysteries every where in the Bible; while others have been equally fond of exploding all mysteries from divine revelation. Here the truth seems to lie in the medium. Many parts of scripture are plain and easy to be understood; but some parts are truly mysterious, and surpass the utmost limits of human comprehension. Of all religious mysteries, the distinction of persons in the Divine Nature, must be allowed to be the greatest. Accordingly upon this subject, there has been the greatest absurdity as

* *Sermons on Some . . . Doctrines of True Religion* (Wrentham, Mass.: Nathaniel and Benjamin Heaton, 1800).

well as ingenuity displayed, in attempting to explain a realy mystery. But though a mystery cannot be comprehended, nor consequently explained; yet it may be stated, and distinguished from a real absurdity. And this is the only object of the present discourse.

The words, which I have read, plainly represent the Divine Being as existing in a mysterious manner; though their primary intention is, to point out the united testimony of each person in the Godhead to the divinity of Christ. "There are three that bear record in heaven, the Father, the Word, and the Holy Ghost." The Father testified to the divinity of Christ at his baptism, when he declared with an audible voice from heaven, "This is my beloved Son, in whom I am well pleased." The Holy Ghost testified to his divinity at the same time, by "descending upon him in the form of a dove." And Christ testified to his own divinity, by his public declarations and miraculous works. "And these three are one;" that is, one God, one Divine Being. This, indeed, is a profound mystery, which calls for peculiar precaution in both speaker and hearer, lest the one should say or the other receive any thing, which should be derogatory to the supreme and incomprehensible Jehovah.

I shall, first, attempt to state the doctrine of the Trinity according to scripture; and then endeavor to make it appear, that there is nothing in this doctrine, which is repugnant to the dictates of sound reason.

I. I shall attempt to show what conceptions the Scripture leads us to form of the peculiar mode of the divine existence. And here I may observe,

1. The Scripture leads us to conceive of God, the first and supreme Being, as existing in three distinct persons. I use this word, because there appears to be no better, in our language, by which to express that Trinity in Unity, which is peculiar to the one living and true God. Indeed, there is no word, in any language, which can convey a precise idea of this incomprehensible distinction in the divine nature; for it is not similar to any other distinction in the minds of moral beings. So that it is very immaterial, whether we use the name person, or any other name, or a circumlocution instead of a name, in discoursing upon this subject. Let me say, then, the one living and true God exists in such a manner, that there is a proper foundation in his nature, to speak of himself, in the first, second, and third person, and say I, Thou, and He, meaning only Himself. This is a mode of existence, which is peculiar to the first and Supreme Being. No created being can properly speak of himself in any other than the first person, I. Thou and He, among creatures, denote another being as well as another person. But God can, with propriety, say I, Thou, and He, and mean only Himself. There is a certain SOMETHING in the divine Nature, which lays a proper foundation for such a personal distinction. But what the SOMETHING is, can neither be *de-*

scribed, nor *conceived.* Here lies the whole mystery of the Trinity. And since this mystery cannot be comprehended, it is absurd to borrow any similitudes from either matter, or spirit, or from both united, in order to explain it. All the illustrations, which have ever been employed upon the mysterious mode of the divine existence, have always served to obscure, rather than elucidate the subject; because there is nothing in the whole circle of nature, which bears the least resemblance of three persons in one God.

Some have supposed, there is a resemblance between this doctrine and the union of soul, spirit, and body in one man. But allowing, that man is made up of these three constituent parts; yet it is easy to perceive, that these three parts make but one person, as well as one man. For a man, speaking of himself, cannot say, *thy* soul, nor *his* soul; *thy* spirit, nor *his* spirit: *thy* body, nor *his* body; but only *my* soul, *my* spirit, *my* body. The single man, who is composed of soul, spirit, and body, is also a single person; but God is one Being in three persons. And here the similitude totally fails of illustrating the principal thing intended.

Some have endeavored to illustrate the distinction of persons in the divine Nature, by what they call the cardinal properties of the soul; namely, understanding, will, and affections. But supposing this to be a proper analysis of the human mind; yet the similitude drawn from it, fails in the same respect, that the former did. For these three properties of the soul are not *personal* properties; and *my* understanding, *my* will, *my* affections, are not *thine,* nor *his,* nor any second, nor third person's. Hence the similitude exhibits no illustration of three distinct persons, in the one undivided essence of the Deity.

Some would consider the Father, Son, and Holy Ghost as one person as well as one being, acting in three distinct offices; as those of Creator, Redeemer, and Sanctifier. And this idea of the Trinity in Unity, they would illustrate, by one man's sustaining three distinct offices; such as Justice, Senator, and Judge. But this, like every other similitude, only serves to sink or destroy the scripture doctrine of three persons in the one supreme, self-existent Being. The profound mystery of the Trinity, as represented in Scripture, necessarily carried in it a distinction of persons in the divine Essence. For nothing short of three distinct persons in the one undivided Deity, can render it proper for him to speak of Himself in the first, second, and third person, *I, Thou,* and *He.* Hence the Scripture represents the Father, Son, and Holy Ghost, as distinctly possessed of personal properties. . . .

2. The Scripture represents the three Persons in the sacred Trinity, as absolutely equal in every divine perfection. We find the same names, the same attributes, and the same works ascribed to each person. Is the Father called GOD? the same name is given to the Son and Spirit. Are eternity, omni-

presence, omniscience, and omnipotence ascribed to the Father? the same divine attributes are ascribed to the Son and Spirit. . . .

3. The Scripture represents the three equally divine Persons in the Trinity, as acting in a certain Order, in the work of redemption. Though they are absolutely equal, in Nature; yet in Office, the first person is superior to the second, and the second is superior to the third. The Father holds the office of Creator, the Son the office of Redeemer, and the Holy Ghost the office of Sanctifier. . . .

4. The Scripture teaches us, that each of the divine Persons takes his peculiar Name from the peculiar office, which he sustains in the Economy of redemption. Each person has a peculiar name given to him in the text. "There are three that bear record in heaven, the Father, the Word, and the Holy Ghost." . . .

5. The Scripture represents these three divine Persons as *One God*. This is the plain language of the text. "There are three that bear record in heaven, the Father, the Word, and the Holy Ghost: and *these three are one*." Our Lord clearly taught the union between Himself and the Father. He asserted, that he dwelt in the Father, and the Father in him. And he said in plain terms, "I and my Father are one." It appears from the light of nature, that there is *one* God; and it appears from the light of divine revelation, that there is *but One*. . . .

II. That this Scriptural account of the mysterious doctrine of the sacred Trinity, is not repugnant to the dictates of sound Reason. Those, who disbelieve, that God exists a Trinity in Unity, suppose, that such a mode of existence is not only above reason, but contrary to its plainest dictates. They consider the doctrine of three Persons in one God, not as a profound mystery, but as a gross absurdity. And it must be granted, that any doctrine is absurd, and ought to be exploded, which is really contrary to the dictates of sound reason. The only wise God can no more require us to believe that, which is absurd, than he can command us to do that, which is sinful. If we can clearly perceive, therefore, that there is a real absurdity in the doctrine of the Trinity, we ought not to believe it. But, perhaps, if we candidly attend to what may be said, under this head of discourse, we shall be convinced, that the Scriptural doctrine of the Trinity is no absurdity, but a great and glorious mystery; which lays a broad and solid foundation, upon which we may safely build our hopes of a blessed immortality. Here it may be proper to observe,

1. The doctrine of the Trinity, as represented in Scripture, implies no contradiction. Any doctrine, which necessarily involves a contradiction, is repugnant to reason, and demonstrably false. For it is out of the power of the human mind to conceive, that a real contradiction should be true. We can-

not conceive, that two and three are equal to ten, nor that ten and five are equal to twenty. We cannot conceive, that a part should be equal to the whole; or that a body should move east and west at the same time. As soon as these propositions are understood, they instantly appear to be plain contradictions. And did the doctrine of the Trinity, according to Scripture, imply that *three* Persons are *one* Person, or *three* Gods are *one* God, it would necessarily involve a plain contradiction. But the Scripture speaks more consistently upon this subject. It asserts, that there is but *one* God, and yet three divine Persons. This only implies, that *three* divine *Persons* are *one God*; and who can perceive a contradiction in this representation of a Trinity in Unity? We find no difficulty in conceiving of three divine Persons. It is just as easy to conceive of three *divine* persons, as of three *human* persons. No man, perhaps, ever found the least difficulty, in conceiving of the Father as a distinct Person from the Son, nor in conceiving of the Son as a distinct Person from the Holy Ghost, nor in conceiving of the Holy Ghost as a distinct Person from both the Father and Son. But the only difficulty, in this case, lies in conceiving these *three* persons to be but *one*. And it is evident, that no man can conceive three *divine* Persons to be *one* divine Person, any more than he can conceive *three* Angels to be but *one* Angel. But it does not hence follow, that no man can conceive, that *three* divine Persons should be but *one* divine Being. For, if we only suppose, that Being may signify something different from Person, in respect to Deity; then we can easily conceive, that God should be but *one* Being, and yet exist in *three* Persons. It is impossible, therefore, for the most discerning and penetrating mind, to perceive a real contradiction, in the Scriptures representing the *one* living and true God, as existing in *three* distinct Persons. There may be, for aught we know, an incomprehensible SOMETHING in the One selfexistent Being which lays a proper foundation for *his existing a Trinity in Unity*.

2. If it implies no contradiction, that the one living and true God should exist in three Persons, then this mysterious mode of the divine existence is *agreeable* to the dictates of sound reason. We cannot suppose, that the *uncreated* Being should exist in the same manner, in which we and other *created* beings exist. And if he exists in a different manner from created beings, then his mode of existence must necessarily be mysterious. As creatures, we must expect to remain forever unacquainted with that mode of existence, which is peculiar to the great Creator. To suppose, that God does not exist in a manner absolutely *mysterious* to creatures, is virtually to deny his existence. And if his existing a Trinity in Unity does not involve a plain contradiction, then it amounts to no more than a *profound mystery*, which we might reasonably expect to find in his mode of existence, had the Scripture been silent upon the subject. Though, perhaps, the bare unassisted

137

power of reason would have never discovered, that God exists in three Persons; yet since the Scripture has revealed this great mystery in the divine existence, reason has nothing to object against it. Reason can see and acknowledge a mystery, though it cannot comprehend it. Hence the Scripture doctrine, that the one living and true God exists in three Persons, is as agreeable to the dictates of sound reason as any mystery can be, or as any other account of the mode of the divine existence could have been. If the Scripture had given any true account of the mode of God's existence, that mode must have appeared to such finite, imperfect creatures as we are, truly mysterious, or incomprehensible. And whoever now objects against the Scripture account of the sacred Trinity, would have equally objected against any other account, which God could have given of his peculiar mode of existence. I may add,

3. The doctrine of the Trinity, as represented in Scripture, is no more repugnant to the dictates of sound reason, than many other doctrines, which all Christians believe concerning God. God is truly incomprehensible by creatures. "Canst thou by searching find out God? canst thou find out the Almighty unto perfection?" All, who believe the existence of the Deity, must believe mysteries, which no human understanding can fathom. Here permit me to mention several things respecting God, which are commonly believed, and which are as mysterious as his existing in three Persons.

It is generally believed, that God is a *selfexistent* Being, or that there is no cause or ground of his existence out of Himself. But who can explain this mode of existence, or even form any clear conception of it? . . . Is it not as repugnant to the dictates of sound reason to say, that the ground of God's existence is mysterious, as to say that the ground of his existing in three Persons is mysterious? These two cases are exactly parallel. There is a certain SOMETHING in the divine Being, which renders his existence absolutely necessary. This all must believe, who believe, that God exists. And so there is a certain SOMETHING in the divine being, which renders it equally necessary, that he should exist in three Persons. It is, therefore, easy to see, that there is nothing more repugnant to right reason, in the doctrine of the Trinity, than in the doctrine of God's selfexistence. Again,

It is generally believed, that God is constantly present in all places, or that his presence perpetually fills the whole created universe. But can we frame any clear ideas of this universal presence of the Deity? It seems to be repugnant to reason, to suppose that his presence is *extended*, because extension appears to be incompatible with the nature of a pure Spirit. And if his presence be not extended, it is impossible for us to conceive, how it should reach and fill all places, at all times. The moment we attentively consider the universal presence of the supreme Being, we are involved in a mystery, as profound as that of three Persons in one God. Once more,

It is generally believed, that God is the Creator, who has made all things out of nothing. But it was a maxim with the antient atheistical philosophers, that it is a contradiction to say, that God made all things out of nothing; that is, without any pre-existent materials. And it is supposed by many, who have had more light upon this subject, that creation is no more than an *emination* of the Deity, or that God only *diffuses* his own existence in giving existence to other beings. Indeed, a strict and proper creation of all things out of nothing, has appeared to many great and learned men, as *contrary* to every dictate of reason. They have considered it, not merely as a difficulty, or mystery, but as a real absurdity. And whoever will critically attend to the subject, will probably find it as difficult to reconcile the doctrine of a strict and proper creation to the dictates of his own reason, as the doctrine of three Persons in one God. That a fountain should be diffused into streams, or the whole be divided into parts, is easy to conceive; but these similitudes do not touch the case of a strict and proper creation. For in creation, God does not diffuse himself; since created objects are no part of the Deity: nor does he divide himself; since the Creator is not capable of a division into a multiplicity of parts. God neither made the world of pre-existent materials, nor of Himself; but he made it out of nothing, that is, gave it a proper and real existence, distinct from his own. Creation is the effect of nothing but mere Power. But of that Power, which is able to create, or produce something out of nothing, we can form no manner of conception. This attribute of the Deity, therefore, is as really mysterious and incomprehensible, in its operation, as the doctrine of the Trinity. Or it is a mystery, that looks as much like an absurdity, as that of God's existing in three Persons. There is nothing in the doctrine of the Trinity, as represented in this discourse, which is more repugnant to the dictates of sound reason, than the doctrine of a strict and proper creation, the doctrine of the divine omnipresence, or even the doctrine of the divine existence. And we must be extremely inconsistent, if we believe the Being, and works of the great Creator; and, at the same time, disbelieve that he exists one God in three Persons, according to the general representation of the sacred Scriptures.

I shall now close the subject, with a few brief remarks.

REMARK 1.

If the doctrine of the sacred Trinity has been properly stated in this discourse, then there seems to be no just foundation for the doctrine of the Eternal Generation of the Son, and of the Eternal Procession of the Holy Ghost. . . .

139

REMARK 2.

The doctrine of the sacred Trinity, as represented in Scripture, gives us a clear and striking view of the All-sufficiency of God. Since he exists in three equally divine Persons, there is a permanent foundation in his own Nature, for the most pure and perfect blessedness. Society is the source of the highest felicity. And that society affords the greatest enjoyment, which is composed of persons of the same character, of the same disposition, of the same designs, and of the same pursuits. The Father, Son, and Holy Ghost, who are three equally divine Persons in the one living and true God, are perfectly united in all these respects; and therefore God's existing a Trinity in Unity, necessarily renders him the all sufficient source of his own most perfect felicity. . . .

REMARK 3.

What has been said, in this discourse, may show us the importance of understanding and believing the Scripture doctrine of the ever blessed Trinity. Unless we understand and believe this great and mysterious doctrine, it will be extremely difficult to answer the objections of the Deists against the Bible, which plainly represents the Father, Son, and Holy Ghost, as three equally divine Persons, and yet asserts there is but one God. And this doctrine is so interwoven with the whole scheme of the gospel, that we cannot possibly explain the great work of Redemption, in a clear and consistent manner, without adopting and believing the personal characters and offices of the three divine Persons in the sacred Trinity. This is evident from the peculiar phraseology of Scripture; and no less evident from observation. All who have exploded the mystery of the Trinity from the Bible, have shaken, if not destroyed, the fundamental doctrines of Christianity. The gospel is so absolutely and obviously founded on the doctrine of three Persons in one God, that whoever denies this great and fundamental truth, must, in order to be consistent, deny all the peculiarities, which distinguish *revealed* religion from *natural*. And if this be true, every friend of divine Revelation must feel the importance of understanding, believing, and maintaining the first principle of his religion.

REMARK 4.

The joint operations of the ever blessed Trinity, lay a foundation for the most perfect and blessed Union, among all *holy* Beings. Each divine Person bears a distinct part in the work of redemption; and each will be infinitely well pleased with the conduct of each. . . .

6

Building Men for Citizenship
Raymond Bailey

The successful revolt of the American colonies gave them new status among the nations of the world. The intellectual development of the new world came to be strongly influenced by the ideas of the enlightenment with their intense focus on the worth and dignity of the individual. The military conflict with the Empire was a prelude to the internal ideological conflict which followed. In politics the conflict was polarized in the Federalists, devoted to a strong central government to be composed of an intellectual and propertied aristocracy, and the democrats with their emphasis on the individual.

The social and economic life of America was shaped by the unlimited opportunities of the frontier. On the frontier a man was limited only by his own vision and resourcefulness. The unique mentality of the American frontiersman altered significantly the European institutions which he had brought from the Old World, and created new ones to meet his needs in the New.

Religion did not escape the ferment of postrevolution America. A representative at the General Assembly of the Presbyterian Church in 1798 reported on the status of religion:

141

We perceive with pain and fearful apprehension a general disreliction [sic] of religious principles and practice among our fellow citizens, a visible and prevailing impiety and contempt for the laws and the institutions of religion, and an abounding infidelity which, in many instances, tends to atheism itself.[1]

Albert Barnes, a dynamic new-school Presbyterian who was tried for heresy as a result of his liberal theology, expressed the need for a new approach to religion.

. . . This is an age of freedom, and man will be free. The religion of forms is the stereotyped wisdom or folly of the past, and does not adapt itself to free movement, the enlarged views, the varying plans of this age. The spirit of this age demands that there shall be freedom in Religion; that it shall not be fettered or suppressed, that it shall go forth to the conquest of the world. . . .[2]

A new mode and a new content for religion in America was not long in coming.

The Americanization process occurred in three stages. The first was the explosive camp meetings which began in Kentucky and soon spread like a prairie fire across the frontier. These revivals were completely uninhibited; they were crude and loud, characterized by unchecked emotionalism. In the camp meetings, the unrestrained spirit of boundless space and the feeling of personal liberation found religious expression.

The second stage in the religious revolution took place in the East under the leadership of the astute Lyman Beecher. Beecher and his followers attempted to adapt orthodox theology, which was strongly Calvinistic, to evangelical Christianity. The revivalist movement had evolved a doctrine of conversion which placed stress on the role of man in the salvation process. "The theology of the revival reflected the new spirit of democracy. It stood for the sovereignty of God, but departed from

---

[1] B. B. Tyler, "A Chapter in American Church History," *The Magazine of Christian Literature* IV (July, 1891), 193.

[2] Richard Niebuhr and Daniel D. Williams, *The Ministry in Historical Perspective* (New York: Harper and Brothers, 1956), p. 247.

Calvinism in its emphasis on the work of man." [3] Beecher, although loudly proclaiming his Calvinist orthodoxy, articulated a theological position to support revivalist activity and preaching. He declared that "men are free agents" and thus capable of doing whatever is required of them to be redeemed.[4] Beecher led the second wave in the assult on Calvinistic conservatism in America and thus prepared the way for the final grand assault of Charles G. Finney.

The attack on traditional Calvinism reached its climax in Charles Grandison Finney, the nineteenth century's clearest and boldest exponent of the doctrine of individual responsibility. Nearing his thirtieth birthday, Finney was turned from the study of law by a dramatic conversion experience. He enjoyed great popularity as an evangelist, for he spoke the language of the common people spicing his sermons with vivid and rustic illustrations. Finney declined to attend seminary, choosing rather to shape his own theology through personal Bible study.

Charles Finney many times expressed his disdain for manuscript sermons or even the use of notes; therefore, all we have extant of his early sermons are reports which were printed in newspapers and journals. In 1834 he began to prepare sermons on selected subjects for publication. The subsequent publication of *Sermons on Important Subjects* provided his critics with concrete evidence to charge him with Arminianism. The first sermon, "Sinners Bound to Change Their Own Hearts," was a broadside against traditional Calvinism and a declaration of the individual's role and responsibility in achieving salvation. Its ideas were not inconsistent with those expressed in Finney's sermons from the beginning of his ministry. However, this sermon presented here as a model has special significance because of the uncompromising enunciation of individual responsibility and its ridicule of the Calvinist position.

[3] Clifton E. Olmstead, *History of Religion in the United States* (Englewood Cliffs, N. J.: Prentice Hall, 1960), p. 257.

[4] Barbara Cross, ed., *The Autobiography of Lyman Beecher,* I (Cambridge: The Belknap Press, 1961), 412.

Even before the formulation of a supporting philosophy, the death knell of hyper-Calvinism had been sounded. Pragmatic Americans responded not to that which sounded good but to that which worked. Revivalism worked and personal discipline and responsibility were the democratic way. It was characteristic of the Early National period that theory developed from practice. Man was free, socially, politically, and religiously.

The Rev. George Junkin was among the most vigorous adversaries of the revivalist theology which made man responsible for his soul. Junkin was the grand inquisitor for the Calvinists and he was passionate in his attack upon the proponents of revivalism. It was he who brought heresy charges against Albert Barnes.

Junkin's tenets were most clearly expressed in an address delivered before the General Assembly of the Presbyterian Church on May 15, 1845. He entitled the treatise "Truth and Freedom." The sermon is a strong affirmation of man's helplessness before the throne of God. Implicit in the declaration is the idea that man must accept, without question, the unalterable decrees of the Almighty.

The political conflict of the time is readily visible in Junkin's "Representation" thesis. There are in the world he contended, duly elected representatives whose decisions must be accepted. Man's eternal destiny, as his social destiny, must be left to duly appointed officials.

The concept of man as a responsible creature under God was coterminus with the democratic ideal. The Americanization of religion had a tremendous impact upon the entire spectrum of American life. The philosophy of the revivalists had the effect of providing a divine seal to the hope for a free society of promise. The direct and indirect contributions of the development of religious thought in the nineteenth century were extremely significant. They provided the people with a faith which, while making demands in terms of personal conduct, did not degrade them as worthy individuals. The new theology further provided them with a sustaining confidence and continuing hope. The humanitarian movements of the

144

latter part of the nineteenth century grew out of the rich soil of evangelical religion.[5] Of no less importance was the influence of revival theology on the later missionary and educational ministries of American Protestantism.

[5] This theme is developed in the excellent work of Timothy L. Smith, *Revivalism and Social Reform* (Nashville: Abingdon Press, 1957).

CHARLES GRANDISON FINNEY

Charles Grandison Finney was born August 29, 1792, in Warren, Connecticut. In 1794, the Finney family moved to Oneida County, New York. After two years at the Oneida Academy, young Charles began the private study of law. His legal studies brought him into contact with Mosaic law and the Bible.

A traumatic religious conversion in 1823 turned Finney from law to theology. He declined seminary attendance and chose instead a personal study of the Scriptures. In spite of his unorthodox view of the atonement, he was ordained in July, 1824.

Finney spent the major part of his life as a dynamic evangelist who roamed the West in search of souls. The "free will" tone of his sermons shook the theological foundations of Calvinist orthodoxy and he met with great popular acceptance. Moving his vast audiences with simple folksy illustrations and everyday language, he made American religion personal and available to all.

In 1837, Finney assumed the presidency of Oberlin College. For the remainder of his life he presided over that institution and taught young ministers theology and evangelistic methodology. For most of his life he continued to make occasional preaching forays across America and, in 1847–1850, to Great Britain.

The principle focus of Finney's theology was individual responsibility. He declared that salvation was available to all who would accept it.

Finney's publications include Lectures on Systematic Theology *(2 vols., 1846, 1847);* Sermons on Important Subjects *(1836);* Sermons on Gospel Themes *(published posthumously 1876).*

Sinners Bound to Change Their Own Hearts*

"Make you a new heart and a new spirit, for why will ye die?"—EZEK. XVIII, 31.

These words were addressed to the house of Israel, who, from their history and from the verses in connexion with the text, were evidently in a state of impenitency; and the requirement to make them a new heart and a new

* Sermons on Important Subjects (New York: John S. Taylor, 1836), pp. 3-42.

spirit, was enforced by the weighty penalty of death. The death mentioned in the text cannot mean natural death; for natural death is common both to those who have, and to those who have not, a new heart. Nor can it mean spiritual death, which is a state of entire sinfulness; for then it should have read, Why are ye already dead? The death here spoken of, must mean, eternal death, or that state of banishment from God and the glory of his power, into which the soul shall be cast, that dies in its iniquities.

The command here addressed to the Israelites, is binding upon every impenitent sinner, to whom the Gospel shall be addressed. He is required to perform the same duty, upon the same penalty. It becomes, therefore, a matter of infinite importance that we should well understand, and fully and immediately obey, the requirement. The questions that would naturally arise to a reflecting mind on reading this text, are the following:

1. What are we to understand by the requirement to make a new heart and a new spirit?

2. Is it reasonable to require the performance of this duty on pain of eternal death?

3. How is this requirement, that we should make to us a new heart and a new spirit, consistent with the often repeated declarations of the Bible, that a new heart is the gift and work of God?

Does God require of us the performance of this duty, without expecting its fulfilment, merely to show us our impotency and dependence upon him? Does he require us to make to ourselves a new heart, on pain of eternal death, when at the same time he knows we have no power to obey; and that if ever the work is done, he must himself do the very thing which he requires of us?

[1.] In order to answer these questions satisfactorily, I will attempt to show,

I. What is *not* the meaning of this requirement; and

II. What *is*.

. . . Our present business is, to ascertain its meaning as used in the text; for it is in this sense, that we are required to make us a new heart and a new spirit. I begin, therefore, by saying,

1. That it does not mean the fleshly heart, or that bodily organ which is the seat of animal life.

2. That it does not mean a new soul. We have one soul, and do not need another. Nor,

3. Are we required to create any new faculties, of body or mind. We now have all the powers of moral agency; we are just as God made us, and do not need any alteration in the substance of soul or body. Nor,

4. Does it mean that we are to bring to pass any *constitutional* change

in ourselves. We are not required to add to the constitution of our minds or bodies any new principle or taste. Some persons speak of a change of heart as something miraculous—something in which the sinner is to be entirely passive, and for which he is to wait in the use of means, as he would wait for a surgical operation, or an electric shock. . . .

Again—A constitutional alteration, and the implantation of a new principle, in the substance of his soul, or diffusing a new taste which is incorporated with, and becomes an essential part of his being, would destroy all the virtue of his obedience. . . .

Again—The constitutional implantation of a principle of holiness in the mind, or the creation of a constitutional taste for holiness, if such a thing were possible, would render the perseverance of the saints physically necessary, make falling from grace a natural impossibility, and would thus destroy all the virtue of perseverance.

Again—A constitutional change would dispense with the necessity of the Spirit's agency, after conversion. . . .

But this implantation of a new principle, which dispenses with the necessity of the special influences of the Spirit in after life, is contrary to experience; for those who have a new heart, find that his constant agency is as indispensable to their perseverance in holiness, as it was to their conversion.

Again—The idea of a constitutional change is inconsistent with backsliding. For if the constitution of the mind were changed, and a taste for holiness and obedience were implanted in the substance of the soul, it is manifest that to backslide, or to fall from grace, would be naturally as impossible as to alter the constitutional appetites of the body.

. . . All holiness, in God, angels, or men, must be *voluntary*, or it is not holiness. To call any thing that is a part of the mind or body, holy— to speak of a holy substance, unless it be in a figurative sense, is to talk nonsense. Holiness is virtue; it is something that is praiseworthy; it cannot therefore be a part of the created substance of body or mind, but must consist in voluntary obedience to the principles of eternal righteousness. . . .

But I come now to show what we are to understand by the command of the text. The Bible often speaks of the heart, as a fountain, from which flow the moral affections and actions of the soul, as in Matt. xv. 19, "Out of the heart proceed evil thoughts, murders, adulteries, fornications, thefts, false witness, blasphemies." The term *heart*, as applied to mind, is figurative, and recognizes an analogy between the heart of the body, and the heart of the soul. The fleshly organ of the body called the *heart*, is the seat and fountain of animal life, and by its constant action, diffuses life through the animal system. *The spiritual heart, is the fountain of spiritual life, is that deep seated but voluntary preference of the mind, which lies back of all its other voluntary affections and emotions, and from which they take their character.* In this sense I understand the term heart to be used in the text. It is evidently something over which we have control; something voluntary; something for which we are to blame, and which we are bound to alter. . . .

A change of heart, then, consists in changing the controling preference of the mind in regard to the *end* of pursuit. The selfish heart is a preference of self-interest to the glory of God and the interests of his kingdom. A new heart consists in a preference of the glory of God and the interests of his kingdom to one's own happiness. In other words, it is a change from selfishness to benevolence, from having a supreme regard to one's own interest to an absorbing and controling choice of the happiness and glory of God and his kingdom.

It is a change in the choice of a *Supreme Ruler.* The conduct of impenitent sinners demonstrates that they prefer Satan as the ruler of the world, they obey his laws, electioneer for him, and are zealous for his interest, even to martyrdom. They carry their attachment to him and his government so far as to sacrifice both body and soul to promote his interest and establish his dominion. A new heart is the choice of JEHOVAH as the supreme ruler; a deep-seated and abiding preference of his laws, and government, and character, and person, as the supreme Legislator and Governor of the universe.

. . . Adam was perfectly holy, but not infinitely so. As his preference for God was not infinitely strong, it was possible that it might be changed, and we have the melancholy fact written in characters that cannot be misunderstood, on every side of us, that an occasion occurred on which he actually changed it. . . . Now suppose God to have come out upon Adam with the command of the text, "Make to you a new heart, for why will you die." Could Adam have justly answered, Dost thou think that I can change my own heart? Can I, who have a heart totally depraved, can I change that heart? Might not the Almighty have answered him in words of fire, Rebel, you have just changed your heart from holiness to sin, now change it back from sin to holiness. . . .

In proof that the change which I have described constitutes a change of heart, if any proof is necessary—I observe, first, that he who actually does prefer the glory of God, and the interest of his kingdom, to his own selfish interest, is a Christian; and that he who actually prefers his own selfish interest to the glory of God, is an impenitent sinner.

The fundamental difference lies in this ruling preference, this fountain, this heart, out of which flows their emotions, their affections, and actions. As the difference between them consists not in the substance of their minds or bodies, but in the voluntary state of mind in which they are, it is just as unphilosophical, absurd, and unnecessary, to suppose that a physical or constitutional change has taken place in him who has the new heart, as to infer, that because a man has changed his politics, therefore his nature is changed. . . .

Once more—If a change of heart was physical, or a change in the constitution of the mind, it would have no moral character. The *change*, to have moral character, must be *voluntary*. To constitute a change of *heart*, it must not only be voluntary, but must be a change in the *governing preference of the mind*. It must be a change in regard to the supreme object of pursuit. . . .

2. The second inquiry is, whether the requirement of the text is reasonable and equitable. The answer to this question must depend upon the nature of the duty to be performed. If the change be a physical one, a change in the constitution or substance of the soul, it is clearly not within the scope of our ability, and the answer to the question must be, No, it is not reasonable nor equitable. To maintain that we are under obligation to do what we have no power to do, is absurd. If we are under an obligation to do a thing, and do it not, we sin. For the blame-worthiness of sin consists in its being the violation of an obligation. But if we are under an obligation to do what we have no power to do, then sin is unavoidable; we are forced to sin by a natural necessity. But this is contrary to right reason, to make sin to consist in any thing that is forced upon us by the necessity of nature. . . . It will be seen, that the answer to the question, whether the requirement in the text is just, must turn upon the question of man's ability; and the question of ability must turn upon the nature of the change itself. If the change is physical, it is clearly beyond the power of man; it is something over which he has no more control than he had over the creation of his soul and body. But if the change is moral—in other words, if it be voluntary, a change of choice or preference, such as I have described, then the answer to the question, Is the requirement of the text just and reasonable? clearly is, Yes, it is entirely reasonable and just. . . .

3. I come now to the third and last inquiry, viz: How is this requirement, to "make to yourself a new heart," consistent with the often repeated declarations of the Bible, that a new heart is the gift and work of God. The Bible ascribes conversion, or a new heart, to four different agencies. Oftentimes it is ascribed to the Spirit of God. And if you consult the Scriptures, you will find it still more frequently ascribed to the truth; as, "Of his own will begat he us by the word of truth"—"The truth shall make you free" —"Sanctify them through thy truth"—"The law of God is perfect, converting the soul." It is sometimes ascribed to the preacher, or to him who

presents the truth; "He that winneth souls is wise:" Paul says, "I have begotten you through the Gospel"—"He that converteth a sinner from the error of his ways, shall save a soul from death, and hide a multitude of sins." Sometimes it is spoken of as the work of the sinner himself; thus the apostle says, "Ye have purified yourselves by obeying the truth;" "I thought on my ways," says the Psalmist, "and turned unto the Lord." Again he says, "When thou saidst, Seek ye my face; my heart replied, Thy face, Lord, will I seek." Now the question is, Are all these declarations of Scripture consistent with each other? They are all true; they all mean just as they say; nor is there any real disagreement between them. There is a sense in which conversion is the work of God. There is a sense in which it is the effect of truth. There is a sense in which the preacher does it. And it is also the appropriate work of the sinner himself.

The fact is, that the actual turning, or change, is the sinner's own act. The agent who induces him, is the Spirit of God. A secondary agent, is the preacher, or individual who presents the truth. The truth is the instrument, or motive, which the Spirit uses to induce the sinner to turn. Suppose yourself to be standing on the bank of the Falls of Niagara. As you stand upon the verge of the precipice, you behold a man lost in deep reverie, approaching its verge unconscious of his danger. He approaches nearer and nearer, until he actually lifts his foot to take the final step that shall plunge him in destruction. At this moment you lift your warning voice above the roar of the foaming waters, and cry out, *Stop.* The voice pierces his ear and breaks the charm that binds him: he turns instantly upon his heel, all pale and aghast he retires, quivering, from the verge of death. He reels, and almost swoons with horror; turns and walks slowly to the public house; you follow him; the manifest agitation in his countenance calls numbers around him: and on *your* approach, he points to you, and says, That man saved my life. Here he ascribes the work to you; and certainly there is a sense in which you had saved him. But, on being further questioned, he says, *Stop!* how that word rings in my ears. Oh, that was to me the word of life. Here he ascribes it to the word that aroused him, and caused him to turn. But, on conversing still further, he said, had I not turned at that instant, I should have been a dead man. Here he speaks of it, and truly, as his own act; but directly you hear him say, O the mercy of God; if God had not interposed, I should have been lost. Now the only defect in this illustration is this: In the case supposed, the only interference on the part of God, was a *providential* one: and the only sense in which the saving of the man's life is ascribed to him, is in a providential sense. But in the conversion of a sinner there is something more than the providence of God employed; for here not only does the providence of God so order it, that the preacher cries, *Stop,* but the

Spirit of God forces the truth home upon him with such tremendous power as to induce him to turn.

. . . Some months since a tract was written, the title of which was, "Regeneration is the effect of Divine Power." The writer goes on to prove that the work is wrought by the Spirit of God, and there he stops. Now it had been just as true, just as philosophical, and just as Scriptural, if he had said, that conversion was the work of man. It was easy to prove that it was the work of God, in the sense in which I have explained it. The writer, therefore tells the truth, so far as he goes; but he has told only half the truth. For while there is a sense in which it is the work of God, as he has shown, there is also a sense in which it is the work of man, as we have just seen. The very title to this tract is a stumbling block. It tells the truth, but it does not tell the whole truth. And a tract might be written upon this proposition that *"conversion or regeneration is the work of man;"* which would be just as true, just as Scriptural, and just as philosophical, as the one to which I have alluded. Thus the writer, in his zeal to recognize and honor God as concerned in this work, by leaving out the fact that a change of heart is the sinner's *own act,* has left the sinner strongly intrenched, with his weapons in his rebellious hands, stoutly resisting the claims of his Maker, and waiting passively for God to make him a new heart. Thus you see the consistency between the requirement of the text, and the declared fact that God is the author of the new heart. God commands you to do it, expects you to do it, and if it ever is done, you must do it.

I shall conclude this discourse with several inferences and remarks.

1st. *Sinners make their own wicked hearts.*

Their preference of sin is their own voluntary act. They make self-gratification the rule to which they conform all their conduct. . . .

2dly. *From what has been said, the necessity of a change of heart is most manifest.*

The state of mind in which impenitent sinners are, is called by the apostle the "carnal mind;" or as it should have been rendered, "the minding of the flesh is enmity against God." . . . This state of mind, is the direct opposite of the character and requirements of God. With this heart, the salvation of the sinner is a manifest impossibility.

3d. *In the light of this subject, you can see the nature and degree of the sinner's dependence on the Spirit of God.*

The Spirit's agency is not needed to give him power, but to overcome his voluntary obstinacy. Some persons seem to suppose that the Spirit is employed to give the sinner *power*—that he is *unable* to obey God, without the Spirit's agency. . . .

. . . To illustrate both the nature and degree of man's dependence on the Spirit, suppose a man to be bent upon self-murder; in the absence of his wife he loads his pistols, and prepares to commit the horrid deed. His little child observes the disorder of his mind, and says, Father, what are you going to do? *Be still*, he replies, I am going to blow my brains out. The little one weeps, spreads out its little beggar hands, beseeches him to desist, and pours out his little prayers, and tears, and agonizing entreaties, to spare his life. Now if the eloquence of this child's grief, his prayers, and tears, could prevail to change the obstinacy of his purpose he would need no other influence to subdue and change his mind. But the parent persisting, the child screams to his mother, who flies at the voice of its entreaty, and on being told the cause of its anguish, hastens, upon the wings of terror, to her husband's apartment, and conjures him to change his purpose. By his love for his family—by their love for him—by their dependence upon him—in view of the torn heart, and distraction of the wife of his bosom—by the anguish, the tears, the helplessness of his babes—by the regard he has for his own soul—by the hope of heaven—by the terrors of hell—by every thing tender and persuasive in life—by all that is solemn in the final judgment, and terrible in the pains of the second death, she conjures him, over and over again, not to rush upon his own destruction. Now if all this can move him, he needs no other and higher influence to change his mind. But when she fails in her efforts, suppose she could summon all the angels of God, and they also should fail to move and melt him by their unearthly eloquence; here, then, some higher power must interfere, or the man is lost. But just as he puts his pistol to his ear, the Spirit of God, who knows perfectly the state of his mind, and understands all the reasons that have led him to this desperate determination, gathers such a world of motive, and pours them in such a focal blaze upon his soul, that he instantly quails, drops the weapon from his nerveless hand, relinquishes his purpose of death for ever, falls upon his knees, and gives glory to God. Now it was the strength of the man's voluntary purpose of self-destruction alone, that made the Spirit's agency at all necessary in the case. Would he have yielded to all the motives that had been before presented, and should have subdued him, no interposition of the Holy Spirit had been necessary. . . . The degree of his dependence upon the Spirit, is just the degree of his obstinacy; were he but slightly inclined to pursue the road to death, *men* could change him without calling upon God for help; but just in proportion to the strength of his preference for sin, is it necessary that the Spirit should interpose or he is lost. Thus you see, the sinner's dependence upon the Spirit of God, instead of being his excuse, is that which constitutes his guilt.

4th. Again—*You see from this subject the* NATURE *of the Spirit's agency.*

153

That he does not act by direct physical contact upon the mind, but that he uses the truth as his sword to pierce the sinner; and that the motives presented in the Gospel are the instruments he uses to change the sinner's heart. . . . The strivings of the Spirit of God with men, is not a physical scuffling, but a debate; a strife not of body with body, but of mind with mind; and that in the action and reaction of vehement argumentation. From these remarks, it is easy to answer the question sometimes put by individuals who seem to be entirely in the dark upon this subject, whether in converting the soul the Spirit acts directly on the mind, or on the truth. This is the same nonsense as if you should ask, whether an earthly advocate who had gained his cause, did it by acting directly and physically on the jury, or on his argument.

5th. Again—*It is evident from this subject that God never does, in changing the sinner's heart, what he requires the sinner to do.*

Some persons, as I have already observed, seem disposed to be passive, to wait for some mysterious influence, like an electric shock, to change their hearts. But in this attitude, and with these views, they may wait till the day of judgment, and God will never do their duty for them. The fact is, sinners, that God requires you to turn, and what he requires of you, he cannot do for you. It must be your own voluntary act. It is not the appropriate work of God to do what he requires of you. Do not wait then for him to do your duty, but do it immediately yourself, on pain of eternal death.

6th. *This subject shows also, that if the sinner ever has a new heart, he must obey the command of the text, and make it himself.*

But here some one may interpose and say, Is not this taking the work out of God's hands, and robbing him of the glory? No. It is the only view of the subject that gives the glory to God. Some in their zeal to magnify the grace of the Gospel, entirely overthrow it. They maintain the sinner's *inability*, and thereby do away his guilt. . . .

7th. But again—*The idea that the Spirit converts sinners by the truth, is the only view of the subject that honours either the Spirit, or the truth of God.*

The work of conversion is spoken of in the Bible as a work of exceeding great power. . . . Now when we consider the deep-rooted selfishness of the sinner; his long cherished habits of sin; his multifarious excuses and refuges of lies; it is a most sublime exhibition of wisdom and of moral power to pursue him step by step with truth, to hunt him from his refuges of lies, to constrain him by the force of argument alone, to yield up his selfishness and dedicate himself to the service of God. This reflects a glory and a lustre over the truth of God and the agency of the Holy Spirit, that at once delights and amazes the beholder.

8th. But again—*The idea that the Spirit uses motives to change the heart, is the only view that gives consistency, and meaning to the often repeated injunction, not to resist the Holy Ghost—not to strive with his Maker.*

For if the Spirit operated upon the mind by direct physical contact, the idea of effectually resisting physical omnipotence is ridiculous. The same thought applies to those passages that caution us against grieving and quenching the Spirit.

9th. Again—*You see from this subject that a sinner, under the influence of the Spirit of God, is just as free as a jury under the arguments of an advocate.*

Here also you may see the importance of right views on this point. Suppose a lawyer, in addressing a jury, should not expect to change their minds by any thing he could say, but should wait for an invisible and physical agency, to be exerted by the Holy Ghost upon them. And suppose, on the other hand, that the jury thought that in making up their verdict, they must be passive, and wait for a direct physical agency to be exerted upon them. In vain might the lawyer plead, and in vain might the jury hear, for until he pressed his arguments as if he was determined to bow their hearts, and until they make up their minds, and decide the question, and thus act like rational beings, both his pleading and their hearing is in vain. . . . Ministers should labour with sinners, as a lawyer does with a jury, and upon the same principles of mental philosophy; and the sinner should weigh his arguments, and make up his mind as upon oath and for his life, and give a verdict upon the spot, according to law and evidence. . . .

10th. But, says the objector, *if right apprehensions of truth presented by the Spirit of God convert a sinner, does it not follow that his ignorance is the cause of his sin?*

. . . Every sinner . . . at first sins against what knowledge he has by overlooking the motives to obedience, and yielding himself up to the motives to disobedience, and when once he has adopted the selfish principle, his ignorance becomes wilful and sinful, and unless the Spirit of God induce him, he *will* not see. He knows the truth to a sufficient extent to leave him without excuse, but he will not *consider* it and let it have its effect upon him. . . .

It is indeed the pressing of truth upon the sinner's consideration that induces him to turn. But it is not true that he is ignorant of these truths before he thus considers them. He knows he must die—that he is a sinner—that God is right and he is wrong—that there is a heaven and a hell—but, as the prophet says, "They will not see"—and again, "My people will not *consider.*" It is not mainly then to *instruct,* but to lead the sinner to *think upon his ways,* that the Spirit employs his agency.

I have already shown why he will not be converted when truth is forced upon him in hell.

11th. But here some one may say, *Is not this exhibition of the subject inconsistent with that mystery of which Christ speaks, when he says, "The wind bloweth where it listeth, thou hearest the sound thereof, but canst not tell whence it cometh nor whither it goeth; so is every one that is born of the Spirit?"*

Says the objector, I have been in the habit of considering the subject of a new heart, as a very mysterious one; but you make it very plain. How is this? Does not Christ, in the text I have quoted, represent it as mysterious? In answer to this I would ask, Wherein does Christ, in that text, represent the mystery of the new birth as consisting? Not in the effects which the Spirit produces, for the effects are matters of experience and observation. Not in the instrumentality used, for this is often revealed in the Bible. But the mystery lies in the manner of the Spirit's communicating with mind. How disembodied spirits communicate with each other, we are unable to say—or how a disembodied spirit can communicate with one that wears a body, we do not know. We know that we communicate with each other through the medium of our bodily senses. The particular manner in which the Spirit of God carries on his debates and strivings with the mind, is what, in this life, we shall probably never know. Nor is it important that we should. Every Christian knows that in some way the truth was kept before his mind, and made to bear, and press upon him, and hedge him in, until he was constrained to yield. These are matters of experience; but in what particular manner the Holy Spirit did this, is just as mysterious as millions of other facts, which we daily witness, but cannot explain.

12th. But here perhaps another objection may arise—*If the sinner is able to convert himself, why does he need the Spirit of God?*

Suppose a man owed you one hundred dollars, was abundantly able, but wholly unwilling to pay you; you obtain a writ, and prepare, by instituting a suit against him, to ply him with a motive that will constrain him to be honest and pay his debts. Now suppose that he should say, I am perfectly able to pay this hundred dollars, of what use then is this writ, and a sheriff, and a lawsuit? The answer is, It is to make him willing—to be sure, he is able but he is unwilling. Just so with the sinner—he is able to do his duty, but is unwilling, therefore the Spirit of God plies him with motives to make him willing.

13th. Again—*You see that sinners should not content themselves with praying for a new heart.*

It has been common for those who believe that sinners are *unable* to change their own heart, when sinners have inquired what they should do to be saved, to substitute another requirement for that contained in the text, and instead of commanding them to make to them a new heart, have told them to pray that God would change their heart. . . .

Sinner! instead of waiting and praying for God to change your heart, you should at once summon up your powers, put forth the effort, and change the governing preference of your mind. But here some one may ask, Can the carnal mind, which is enmity against God, change itself? I have already said that this text in the original reads, "The minding of the flesh is enmity against God." This minding of the flesh, then, is a choice or preference to gratify the flesh. Now it is indeed absurd to say, that a choice can change itself; but it is not absurd to say, that the agent who exercises this choice, can change it. The sinner that minds the flesh, can change his mind, and mind God.

14th. *From this subject it is manifest that the sinner's obligation to make to himself a new heart, is infinite.*

Sinner! your obligations to love God is equal to the excellence of his character, and your guilt in not obeying him is of course equal to your obligation. You cannot therefore for an hour or a moment defer obedience to the commandment in the text, without deserving eternal damnation.

15th. *You see it is most reasonable to expect sinners, if they are converted at all, to be converted under the voice of the living preacher, or while the truth is held up in all its blaze before the mind.*

An idea has prevailed in the church, that sinners must have a season of protracted conviction, and that those conversions that were sudden were of a suspicious character. But certainly "this persuasion cometh not from God." We nowhere in the Bible read of cases of lengthened conviction. Peter was not afraid on the day of Pentecost that his hearers had not conviction enough. He did not tell them to pray and labour for a more impressive sense of their guilt, and wait for the Spirit of God to change their hearts, but urged home their immediate duty upon them. . . . And now, sinner, if you go away without making up your mind, and changing your heart, it is most probable that your mind will be diverted—you will forget many things that you have heard—many of the motives and considerations that now press upon you may be abstracted from your mind—you will lose the clear view of the subject that you now have—may grieve the Spirit, defer repentance, and push your unbroken footsteps to the gates of hell.

16th. *You see the importance of presenting those truths, and in such connexions and relations, as are calculated to induce the sinner to change his heart.*

. . . The spirit selects such considerations, at such times and under such circumstances, as are naturally calculated to disarm and confound the sinner; to strip him of his excuses, answer his cavils, humble his pride, and break his heart. The preacher should therefore acquaint himself with his refuges of lies, and as far as possible take into consideration his whole history, including his present views and state of mind; should wisely select a subject; so skilfully arrange, so simply and yet so powerfully present it, as to engage the sinner's whole attention, and then lay himself out to the utmost to bring him to yield upon the spot. He who deals with souls should study well the laws of mind, and carefully and prayerfully adapt his matter and his manner to the state and circumstances, views and feelings, in which he may find the sinner at the time. He should present that particular subject, in that connexion and in that manner, that shall have the greatest *natural tendency* to subdue the rebel at once. If men would act as wisely and as philosophically in attempting to make men Christians, as they do in attempting to sway mind upon other subjects; if they would suit their subject to the state of mind, conform "the action to the word and the word to the action," and press their subject with as much address, and warmth, and perseverance, as lawyers and statesmen do their addresses; the result would be the conversion of hundreds of thousands, and converts would be added to the Lord "like drops of the morning dew." . . .

17th. *From this subject you may see the importance of pressing every argument, and every consideration, that can have any weight.*

And now, sinner, while the subject is before you, will you yield? To keep yourself away from under the motives of the Gospel, by neglecting church, and neglecting your Bible, will prove fatal to your soul. And to be careless when you do attend, or to hear with attention and refuse to make up your mind and yield, will be equally fatal. And now, "I beseech you, by the mercies of God, that you at *this time* render your body and soul, a living sacrifice to God, which is your reasonable service." Let the truth take hold upon your conscience—throw down your rebellious weapons—give up your refuges of lies—fix your mind steadfastly upon the world of considerations that should instantly decide you to close in with the offer of reconciliation while it now lies before you. Another moment's delay, and it may be too late for ever. The Spirit of God may depart from you—the offer of life may be made no more, and this one more slighted offer of mercy may close up your account, and seal you over to all the horrors of eternal death. Hear, then, O sinner, I beseech you, and obey the word of the Lord—"Make you a new heart and a new spirit, for why will ye die?"

George Junkin

George Junkin, born November 1, 1790, in Cumberland County, Pennsylvania, was one of fourteen children and was reared in the austere atmosphere of the rugged western frontier. He graduated from Jefferson College in 1813. Having studied theology in New York, he was licensed to preach in 1816. Two years later Junkin was ordained by the Associate Reformed Presbytery of Philadelphia.

Junkin was engaged in missionary work until he was installed as pastor of the Presbyterian church at Milton, Pennsylvania. He served this congregation for eleven years and then resigned to become head of the Manual Labor Academy at Germantown, Pennsylvania. The rest of his career was devoted to educational administration and to defending the faith.

From the time of his appointment as a commissioner to the General Assemby of the Presbyterian Church in 1826, until his death in 1868, George Junkin remained in the maelstrom of theological controversy. He was an unrelenting antagonist of the New School party, especially in the great schism of the Presbyterian Church in 1837–38. It was he who brought charges of heresy against Albert Barnes. Junkin fought vigorously and bitterly against any and all who would soften the traditional Calvinist double-predestination formula for salvation and damnation.

Junkin's publications include The Vindication, Containing a History of the Trial of the Rev. Albert Barnes (1836); The Integrity of American National Union vs. Abolitionism (1843); A Treatise on Justification (1849); A Treatise on Sanctification (1864); A Commentary Upon the Epistle to the Hebrews (1873); and many other tracts and pamphlets.

Truth and Freedom*

"The truth shall make you free."—JOHN VIII, 32.

In the absence of practical holiness there can be no sufficient evidence of true piety. Speculative orthodoxy, deep and pungent conviction, emotions of joy

* (Cincinnati: R. P. Donogh & Co., 1845) p. 3 ff. There is a copy of this sermon in the library of Columbia Theological Seminary, Decatur, Georgia.

even to ecstacy, high-toned and fiery zeal may all have existed, and most of them may co-exist, and yet the heart not be right with God. It is easy to say Lord, Lord; to avow our belief in the doctrines of the Word made flesh; to love in tongue; to attach ourselves to some division of the great Christian army and swear allegiance to its standard: but to fight the good fight of faith; to evince the truth and reality of our love by our actions; to embody the doctrines of religion in a life of holiness, and make it appear unto all men that we are freed from the bonds of corruption;—this is no easy task. Yet this is indispensable among the evidences of discipleship. . . . "The truth shall make you free."

To sons of Abraham, primarily were these words addressed—a race who had not been in a state of servile bondage from the days of Egypt, and consequently, such bondage cannot be correlate to the freedom in question—this enfranchisement cannot be deliverance from bondage in a merely domestic or a civil sense. The same we learn from the context. "We were never in bondage to any man." Which misrepresentation or quibble, the Saviour immediately corrects, by pointing out a slavery more debasing and ruinous than that of Egypt—a voluntary bondage which the wicked endure when they serve the malignant enemy of souls. . . . Such is the wretched condition in which our text contemplates the race, and from which it proclaims deliverance to Jew and Gentile, through the Truth.

We are called upon to consider,

I. MAN'S ESTATE OF SLAVERY TO SIN,

II. HIS RESTORATION TO FREEDOM,

III. THE MEANS OF THIS RESTORATION.

I. *The bondage condition.*—And here a few items, very briefly stated by way of analysis must suffice.

1st. It was through the door of the understanding that sin entered. . . . Nothing can become a prevalent motive to action, but that which appears a good. Our first mother "being deceived, was in the transgression." Until a delusion was practiced upon her understanding, she maintained her integrity. When the evil, in her conception of it, *appeared* a good, it became the object of definite desire: and this false apprehension was brought about by the belief of a lying testimony. Hence:

2dly. Blindness of mind, darkness, ignorance of God and of ourselves and of the relations we sustain to Him and to one another, belong to the degradation of our natural condition. Professing themselves to be wise men became fools, they know not God, nor regard the doing of his hand.

3dly. The pride of free-will is the strongest link in the chain of human bondage. . . . Scorning subordination to the will of his Maker, man threw himself upon his own sovereignty, and plunged into the abyss of woe.

I found them free, and free they must remain,
Till they enthrall themselves; I else must change
Their nature, and revoke the high degree,
Unchangeable, eternal, which ordained,
Their freedom; they themselves ordained their fall.

4thly. Let us note; The total debasement of his affections, hence resulting, rivets his manacles in a hopeless bondage. . . . The inmost feelings of his soul are tainted with evil and can, by no possibility originate a movement tending toward holiness and heaven. Like a whited sepulchre, indeed, he may appear fair and beautiful to the eye of external observation; but like it, he is inwardly furnished with all uncleanness, loathesome as dead men's bones.

5thly. The last item, which for our purposes, it may be necessary to mention, is the utter incapacity of this slave of sin, to break off his chains and restore himself to true moral freedom. The fact, good men every where confess and lament. The philosophy of the fact, sound reasoners duly appreciate; whilst the scripturalness of the doctrine every simple hearted reader of the Bible, discovers at a glance. "Ye are dead and your life is hid with Christ in God.—Without me ye can do nothing.—No man can come unto me, except the Father which hath sent me draw him.—Can the Ethiopian change his skin, or the leopard his spots? no more can ye who have been accustomed to do evil, learn to do well." According to the obvious necessity created by this doctrine; or rather, by the facts it rests on, the word of God everywhere represents regeneration, faith, repentance as graces of God's Holy Spirit, wrought in his people, by his Almighty energies and leading them in the way, by the truth to the enjoyment of life everlasting. . . .

II. *Man's restoration to freedom*, now demands our attention. The question, What is freedom? thus broadly stated, is rendered difficult by the variety of aspects it assumes, and answers, which it admits. . . . We, however, must limit our field of inquiry to man's moral or spiritual freedom: and toward the ascertainment of what it is, and how it may be secured, the following remarks are offered.

1st. A rule of action is indispensable to a moral and accountable agent. Where there is no law, there can be no transgression; no obedience; no virtue; no vice; no development of moral character; no test of principle; no rule of judgment. . . .

2dly. But again, if the idea of morality necessarily involves the notion of law or rule, what shall we say of the obligation to comply with it? Can a man be *obliged* to obey, and yet be free? Does obligation destroy liberty? A man is peremptorily bound by the command of another, is he therefore not free? Or is moral liberty consistent with the most peremptory authority? Should this last question be answered in the negative: should the obligations of law be deemed and held inconsistent with freedom; then, in the nature of things, moral government is an impossibility. But if the contrary answer be returned, we have the conception, that the kind of obligation and necessity imposed by law is not inconsistent with liberty, but is involved in it. No possible force of moral obligation; no conceivable power of motive to right action; not all the authority of God himself; not all the lures presented in the glory and felicity of the heavenly state, can in the least degree trench upon the freedom of a moral agent. . . .

With a little explanation, I can adopt the definition of the great and good Edwards on this subject. "The plan and obvious meaning of the word *Freedom* and *Liberty*, in common speech, is, *The power, opportunity, or advantage that any one has, to do as he pleases*. Or, in other words, his being free from hindrance or impediment in the way of doing, or conducting in any respect as he wills. And the contrary to liberty, whatever name we call that by, is a person's being hindered or unable to conduct as he will, or being necessitated to do otherwise. I say not only *doing*, but *conducting*. Because a voluntary forbearing to do, sitting still, keeping silence, etc., are instances of persons' *conduct*, about which liberty is exercised; though they are not so properly called *doing*."

Here it is evident that by *doing* and *conduct*, Edwards means the *physical*, or bodily action, or inaction, whereby the volitions of the mind are or might be carried out and expressed: and the *hindrance* or *impediment*, is any thing which prevents the bodily act from following the volition. Wherever there is no "*constraint*—otherwise called *force, compulsion and co-action; or restraint*, which is being hindered and not having power to do *according* to his will," there man is free, or at liberty. But farther, according to this definition he is called *free*, whom the Bible calls a slave of sin, a child of the devil, and an enemy of all righteousness. For nothing is more obvious than that such are not hindered or impeded in the embodiment of their volitions, in acts of rebellion against the will of their Creator. "Whilst they promise them liberty, they themselves are the servants of corruption." Here is intellectual liberty, if I may so speak; and moral bondage co-existing—rather co-alescing and identical. On the other hand, we have the same intellectual liberty, co-alescing and identical with moral subjection and true spiritual freedom. "As free, and not using your liberty for a cloak of maliciousness, but as the servants of God." True liberty—the spiritual liberty of a moral agent consists not in acting as a man pleases; unless, indeed, he pleases to act *rightly*. It is doing the will of God. He whose volitions are put forth in accordance with the Divine law, and find no impediment to their embodiment in action, is Christ's freeman: and his freedom will be perfect, whensoever his will and his Creator's become perfectly coincident. Happy—infinitely and forever happy, the man who shall truly say, "my meat is to do the will of Him that sent me." How shall man attain to this felicity?

1st. We must know what God will have him to do:—he must understand the things freely given to him of God:—must have his mind enlightened in Divine Truth. By this door sin entered, darkness triumphed, Satan domineered; by the same door must sin be expelled, darkness dissipated, and Satan be despoiled of his tyrannic rule. Without a knowledge of God's law, there can be no thorough conviction of sin,—no feeling and realizing sense of man's lost condition—no brokenness of heart, no contrition of spirit, no prostration of soul before the sovereignty of Divine grace. . . .

2dly. But farther:—This illumination must involve the presentation of other objects of desire. A good, external to itself, the immortal mind must have; this, whatever it be, is the soul's God, and to him the pathway must be pointed out. It must be made to appear that there is another and a better portion. The former master he will not quit and abandon, until he sees one more desirable, whose yoke is easier, his burden lighter, the rewards of his service better adapted to secure the blessedness of his being.

3dly. This enfranchisement requires the removal of the corrupt lusts. . . . Until this do occur, until he obtain a new heart, man is a slave to sin; when he hath it, he is a servant of God, and a freedman of Christ. On this point there is a very general harmony amongst christians. All who occupy any thing like evangelical ground, agree that this internal change of affections and will is indispensable to spiritual life and liberty. We therefore pass on to the

III. General head of discussion—*The Means of this Restoration*. THE TRUTH shall make you free. *What truth?* How shall it make you free? *Efficiently?* or *Instrumentally?*

These questions cover all our remaining ground; but they divide the christian world. We may even drop the epithet and say they divide the world of mankind into two great schools. Let us address ourselves to these two questions of *matter* and *manner*.

1st. *What is Truth?*

The previous context directs us to the true answer in general. The twelfth verse [John 8] teaches the doctrine of spiritual illumination as emanating from Christ. "I am the light of the world, he that followeth me shall not walk in darkness, but shall have the light of life." Here we have a corroboration of what has been already advanced, relative to the understanding as the leading faculty both into slavery and into freedom.

In verse 14, he refers to his mission from the Father, which implies the relationship of son, and embraces substantially the doctrine of the Trinity in unity. In this, and in verses, 21, 24, and 28, he alludes to his vicarious death and the consequent rescue of his own people from sin and death. In short, the whole train of his remark is designed to lead their minds to the great and glorious gospel Scheme of Redemption; and, therefore, the fair and true answer to the question propounded will be found in a brief, compendious, summary statement of the gospel scheme.

But, as the Gospel is a remedial law; and, as every remedial law goes to establish the principle of the original institute, and thereby to achieve its end, and cannot be properly understood unless the original be first understood; it seems necessary, or at least highly expedient, that we bring the original covenant relation of man distinctly before our minds. . . .

Man, having been created with physical, intellectual, and moral susceptibilities, rendering it possible for him to become both a rational and a moral agent, was immediately furnished with that measure of knowledge which was necessary to make him such. From this moment he became a subject of law, responsible to his Maker, whose will for that purpose revealed, became the rule of his action. Resistance to this will must lay him under the displeasure of the law-giver: compliance with it must secure God's approbation, and consequently man's happiness. Such is the moral law of his creation. But, additional to this, it pleased the Creator to throw this law into the form of a covenant, thereby limiting the field and the duration of a man's state of trial. He proposed to Adam, as the test of his obedience, a specific and positive command, requiring thereto prompt and perfect submission:—"Of the tree of the knowledge of good and evil thou shalt not eat of it." Under this negative form as the easiest conceivable, God was pleased to test the spirit of man's subjection.

As the reward of obedience, and as a motive conducing towards it, life was promised—present and everlasting happiness to the whole man. Death, on the contrary, was threatened as the consequence of disobedience—"In the day thou eatest thereof, thou shalt surely die;" which involves the promise of the opposite result to the opposite conduct. Obedience and life; disobedience and death; this is the divine ordinance.

Moreover, as there must, . . . be a limit to probation, or a state of trial—a period beyond which trial shall cease and reward be administered according to conduct and character, we conclude, without its having been mentioned in this very brief record, that had Adam maintained his integrity during this period, he would have been entitled, on the ground of his obedience or good works, to the promised life; just as, on the ground of his disobedience or wicked works, he was brought into a state of suffering and death.

To all these propositions, flowing from divine condescension, man assented. From them he could not either rationally or morally dissent. And an evidence most conclusive to this amount we have in the fact, that, when the sin of eating was charged upon him and the death sentence pronounced, he put in no plea of ignorance; he attempted no excuse in bar of punishment, on the ground of his not having, at first, agreed to the terms of the covenant; which plea would have been valid, if true; and which, undoubtedly, he would have laid in, if possible: because he did manifest an earnest desire to excuse himself.

Thus we have all the essentials of a covenant transaction: here are stipulation and re-stipulation; condition and corresponding condition; reward and penalty; and consent of parties. Nothing is wanting that is properly essential to a federal transaction. But, besides all that belongs to moral government and the federal compact, we have the great social principle of representation. Adam stands revealed to us as a public person—a representative head; he acts in all this, not in his personal character and responsibility only, but also for the race—for all human persons. The existence of this moral, federal, or representative headship—this legal relationship—is abundantly set forth in Scripture. There is a sense in which "all die in Adam—by one man's disobedience many were made sinners—by one man sin entered into the world." Here we have the germ—the prime element of all social order. Without this moral transfusion of intelligent agency and legal responsibility—this doctrine of federal headship and representation, there could be no imputation of one man's action, as to its legal effect, to another. Adam's sin could not be imputed to his natural descendents, nor Christ's righteousness to his spiritual seed. How preposterously absurd the idea of visiting the legal consequences of Adam's act, in all the fearfulness of deserved wrath, upon persons who stand in no sense legally connected with him! Take away this doctrine—deny the federal representative character of the first man and you must do the same concerning the second; and in so doing you demolish the theology of the Bible; you obliterate the sun from the theological hemisphere, and hurl all things back to chaos and old night; system and order and law are annihilated, and not an element is left by which to reorganise the universe of moral truth.

Nor would the confusion and wild uproar of elemental strife be less confounded in the merely moral—the civil and political world. Everywhere the representative principle is the master element—the *primum mobile*. Without it, free government, among men, is impracticable. It is the life-blood, which courses all the arteries and veins of the body politic: sluice it off and all is gone; the pulse stands still; the flaccid muscle no longer wields the bony frame; the nerves no longer string the system to vigorous action: but paralyzed, drop, and all is death.

Let us now glance at these doctrines, as they are embodied in the remedial law, covenant of grace, or gospel System of Salvation; bearing in mind that

165

it is a remedial law. The Scriptures everywhere represent it as such; and, of course, it must establish the principle of the original institute, which is the covenant of works; and thereby remedy the evils resulting from the perversion of its principles and secure the good originally proposed.

Now, the grand and glorious end toward which the covenant of works was directed and which it was adapted to secure, was the life and everlasting happiness of all Adam's natural posterity for whom he acted. This it failed to accomplish by reason of sin:—"The law which was ordained unto life, I found to be unto death." The new covenant must therefore remove death from and secure life to all the spiritual seed of the second Adam. He must take away sin by the sacrifice of himself—by bearing it in the punishment of it in his own body on the tree, and secure the removal of its pollution by the graces of his Holy Spirit. But in order to do both these he must first become a representative head, precisely as the first Adam did. . . . But for this doctrine of vicarious substitution, the agonies of Gethsemane and of Calvary, the death of Jesus by appointment of the Father protrudes itself to our view, an awful deformity upon the otherwise fair face of the Divine Administration— a terrible, an appalling, unexplained, and unexplainable fact. . . . This same covenant transaction between the Father and the Son, is referred to in numerous passages of Scripture; for example,—"Who verily was foreordained, before the foundation of the world, but was manifest in these last times for you, who by him do believe in God. In hope of eternal life, which God that cannot lie promised before the world began. According as he hath chosen us in him before the foundation of the world, that we should be holy and without blame before him in love: having predestined us unto the adoption of children by Jesus Christ, to himself, according to the good pleasure of his will. . . .

From these, to which many other texts might be added, it is fairly deduced:—

That a covenant existed in eternity, before the world was, analagous to, and indeed the prototype of, that which in time was entered into by God and Adam.

That the Son was constituted the moral or representative head of his elect body, which consists of that immense multitude which no man can number; even all the sons that he will bring unto glory—the whole body of God's redeemed.

That the Father requires the Son to bring these unto glory, and of course to do and to suffer all that might be necessary as means; to which the latter cheerfully assented.

That, as a reward for this service, the Father promised to his Son the whole body of the saved and all the glory resulting from the work: viz: the glory of revealing the new and illustrious attribute of divine mercy to the admiring gaze of the moral and intelligent universe.

That, in execution of this blessed covenant, the Son created this world, placed man over it and in it, giving him a rule of obedience, and leaving to his own choice to obey and disobey; man sinned, and in consequence of his failure, the obligations of law fell upon his surety; consequently, it became necessary for the Son to obey and to die in the very nature that had disobeyed—the Word was made flesh, obeyed, died, rose again, ascended, lives, reigns over the universe, and is still carrying out the gospel scheme in its practical application to those whom the Father gave to him.

That having, in his representative character,—as the surety of his people in that better covenant—fulfilled the law in its precept and endured its penalty in a painful death, he reckons or imputes his righteousness, or the merits of his active obedience to them for their justification; and the efficacy of his atoning blood, or the satisfaction his death rendered to Divine Justice for their sins, to them, and secures their pardon.

That on the grounds of his own merits, Jesus sends the Holy Spirit to regenerate, convert, and sanctify them wholly. In this he changes the temper and disposition of the hearts, works in the soul true faith and sincere repentance, and all those heavenly affections by which they are fitted for that pure and holy state to which his own death and obedience hath entitled them.

And, that when this work of preparation is duly forwarded he takes them, first the soul, and in due time, the entire persons, to dwell with himself in glory, when he as the final act of his mediatorial office shall pronounce the sentence of an unchangeable judgment; and as Mediator, covenant Head, and Surety, shall deliver up the kingdom to God even the Father.

Such is the free grace scheme, such the system which stains the pride of all human glory, prostrates man in the dust, rejects all his works as the basis and ground of salvation, yet requires good works as the fruits and evidences of a gracious union with Christ: which denies free-will, self-conversion, and the efficiency of mere moral suasion; and maintains God's sovereignty in grace, and conversion by the almighty and resistless energies of the Holy Ghost; which finds a man bond-slave to sin and restores him to freedom, yet teaches in the words of our Confession, that "the will of man is made perfectly and immutably free to good alone, in the state of glory only."

Such is *the Truth* of our text, as we understand the Bible.—But as intimated before, the questions,—*what* truth? and *how* does it make free, divide the world. There is a view, considerably different from the preceding, taken and held by a large number who hold to the Scriptures as inspired, and by a still greater number who do not so view them. We mean, of course, the free-will scheme, whose distinguishing feature is a denial of the doctrine of the two covenants as above set forth, and as held by the unanimous consent of all the reformation churches. This scheme rejects the doctrine of particular election; the federal headship or representative character of Adam and of Christ, the imputation of Adam's sin and of Christ's righteousness, the vicarious nature and, of course, the definite character of the atonement, original sin, including total depravity, and inability of will, irresistible grace in conversion, and the perseverance of the saints. It affirms conversion by moral suasion, through some intrinsic efficacy in the truth; that the soul is active (as an agent we suppose) in its own regeneration, which is merely a change of its governing purpose—a change effected by itself, or its own free will; that sufficient grace is given to and possessed by all, in consequence of Christ's death, and the soul's salvation or loss is conditioned upon its own improvement or neglect in the exercises of free-will; that faith, admitted to be necessary to salvation, is a human work; that under the gospel, there is thus a new law of grace requiring only sincere obedience in order to live.

Such is the brief and necessarily imperfect summary of the free-will scheme. Not that we suppose every item is maintained by any one sect. But they are affiliated sentiments, and are therefore found commonly together. They characterise a system which has existed more or less in the church for about fourteen centuries and, according to the degree of their predominance, has eaten in upon the spirit of its piety, and disturbed its peace and quietness.

Thus much for the question of doctrine: let us proceed to that of method. *How* does the truth make you free: Is it by an intrinsic *efficiency?* or by its *instrumentality?*

The former is affirmed, of course, by the advocates of the human ability or free-will scheme; the latter, by the friends of the free-grace system. We suppose there is no intrinsic power in the truth to effect a change; taking the word power in its plain ordinary meaning, as that energy or activity which produces its effect without anything beyond itself giving it force.—Thus, we should say that a sword has no power to cut and to kill. It has an adaptation as an instrument, but the power to kill lies in the arm that wields it. So, we say, the truth hath an adaptation, as an instrument, to break off the chains, and restore man to freedom; but the power is in the divine Spirit. . . . Nothing short of a creating energy, such as that exerted in the raising of Christ from the dead, can give spiritual life to the dead soul, and fill the agonized heart with joy unspeakable and full of glory.

THE APPLICATION

From this discussion, we perceive the high importance of doctrinal instruction as a means. Unless you sever the chains of ignorance, you can never sunder the bonds of corruption. . . .

2. We see a philosophical reason for the fact, that the most successful and influential of the apostles, was a man of pre-eminent intellectual culture. . . . Hence, the preparation and vocation of Saul in Tarsus, in whose writing, more than in any other portion of the Scriptures, are developed and systematized, the great doctrines of the covenants.

3. We learn further, why it is, that wherever these doctrines have been prevailed, high and noble efforts have been put forth to secure a well-educated ministry, and to advance the cause of popular education. Be-hold the reformed churches. No sooner were they awakened to spiritual life by the Holy Ghost, through *the truth*, than they were engrossed with this business. Contemplate for a moment what these doctrines did for the English universities in the days of the commonwealth. The puritans breathed a soul of intelligence and life into the hitherto dead and inanimate bodies of these great national establishments. Look to North Britain. What transformed her barren crags into beacon lights for the moral and intellectual world, and made Scotland a vast Normal Seminary? What, but the energy naturally accompanying her religious doctrines? What does not America owe to the might of her principles? . . . .

4. Not without some hazard of being reputed invidious, we venture the correlate observation, that the higher branches of literature and science, in conjunction with efforts toward universal popular education, have not flourished permanently any where in christendom, under the free-will scheme of religion. . . .

No doubt, as contrary to this we will be referred to the Jesuits. Have they not been the very patrons of learning? We object to this exception. The followers of Loyola do indeed hold the free-will doctrine and they have labored with great success in education. But education of what kind? That of the mass of the people? or even of their own church? Not at all. Their efforts have been directed mainly to the children of the nobility, with the view of securing their consciences under their own control, and thus of promoting the aggrandizement of Rome. Indeed, this was the original design of their order, as formally declared in their application to the Pope for a charter, and if they received other children, the object was the same. And, even now, in our own country, it is the children of Protestants chiefly, whom they endeavor to bring under their own power and influence; whilst the vast masses of their own people are left in ignorance. . . .

5thly. *The Truth* naturally and necessarily meliorates the condition of man, in reference to bondage of every kind, personal, social, civil, religious, or political. By the mild effulgence of its light, beaming upon moral relations; by the love which is shed abroad in the heart by the accompanying Spirit, the soul of the master and slave; the sovereign and his subject; the

169

despotic lord and his cringing serf; the victorious conqueror and his vanquished foe: are all placed under the power of one common law and made the voluntary servants of one blessed Master, whose yoke is easy and his burden light. . . .

6thly. We learn the philosophy of the fact, that the system of free-will and conditional salvation has been generally found in alliance with strong government, ecclesiastical and civil; whilst, on the contrary, the free-grace system, which makes divine sovereignty the foundation whence flow the waters of human salvation, is always allied to the popular element in government, civil and ecclesiastical. Here let us first attend to the fact and then to its philosophy. . . .

That the Roman Catholic apostacy embodies the system of free-will and conditional salvation will be questioned by none. It builds salvation upon human merit, and rejects the sovereign grace of God. And that this apostate and secularized church towers pre-eminent upon the page of history, above all despots and tyrants, is surely not less evident, than that the dragon himself took up his abode in the seven hilled city.

On the other hand, during the same extended period, there were many within her polluted pale, who held in fact to the doctrines of truth. And there is a sense, too, in which the Papacy, in its worst estate held to them, viz: by approving, in general terms the fathers and the creeds of the early centuries, which embraced these doctrines: whilst, at the same time, they were entirely inoperative and neglected, and the contrary was the real, practical system of Rome. Luther's testimony is direct to the point. In his reply to Erasmus, he says, "you are the only one, who, among all my adversaries in this religious cause, has attempted to handle the real matter in dispute; nor have you fatigued me with extraneous matter about the papacy, purgatory, indulgences and such like trifles, about which I have hitherto been hunted on all sides, to no purpose. You, and only you, have seen the true hinge on which all turned and have aimed your blow at the throat." How clearly did the penetrating eye of the great Reformer see the true position of the free-will doctrine, as being the very foundation of the entire papal structure! Moreover, during the whole of this dark period, there was always a body of non-conformists, and, to a considerable extent, of separatists from the Romish communion, who held the self-denying system of free-grace. We may mention the Novatians of the third and fourth centuries; the Donatists of the fourth, fifth, and sixth; the Paulicians of the seventh, eight, and ninth; the Waldenses of the ninth, tenth, eleventh, twelfth, and thirteenth; the Wickliffites and Hussites of later periods: all these maintained all the essential features of this system, and protested against the corruptions of Rome. Their tendency toward free government is manifest from their claim of religious liberty, as expressed in their choosing their own spiritual rulers and teachers; and waiting upon their ministrations. Millions of them sealed their testimony with their blood, rather than forego this high privilege. Perfectly submissive to the civil authorities in things temporal, they claimed the right of worshipping God according to conscience.

The great moral revolution of the sixteenth century, is our next reference, in proof of the fact, that free-grace leads to liberty and free-will to despotism. All the churches of the Reformation, without exception, as their published creeds do fully shew, held to divine sovereignty and free-grace; and rejected conditional salvation and free-will. Luther and Melanchthon, in Germany; Zwingli and Calvin, in Switzerland; Ridley and Cranmer in England, Hamilton, Wishart, and Knox, in Scotland; are so many impersonations of the reformed doctrines; and are their opinions unknown! Has history entered up no record about the controversy between Eccius, as the advocate of free-will, and Luther and Carlstadt defending free-grace and unconditional salvation? Nothing about the Diatribe of Erasmus?—a labored argument which that able scholar wrote at the earnest and oft-repeated solicitations of the Pope, and his friends, and after his Holiness had sent him a present of two hundred florins. It is a defence of free-will, and an assault upon Luther. Has history been silent on the subject of the Reformer's treatise in reply, *concerning the bondage of the will?* These are undoubted facts: and equally true it is, that all these champions of the reformation were most decided friends of free government and opposed to despotic rule in church and state. How could they possibly be otherwise, when the very matters which brought them into collision and conflict was the abridgement of liberty of speech, of the press, and of choosing their own spiritual guides? Let their history answer.

We may refer for farther proof of the fact in question, to the controversy within the pale of the Roman sect, between the Molinists and the Dominicans; and also, between the Jesuits and Jansenists. The Molinists and Jesuits maintained the free-will scheme; the Dominicans and Jansenists, the free-grace system. Pope Urban the VIII, condemned the book of Jansenius, and thus, with perfect consistency, upheld the free-will scheme. Which of these parties leaned toward freedom of opinion, and free government, we need not here stop to enquire.

Again, from the 10th of December, 1520, when Luther publicly burnt the Pope's bull, and the decretals and canons concerning his supremacy, until the rise of Arminianism in Holland, the Protestant Churches were not troubled with the free-will doctrine; and then it was introduced by recent converts from popery, and was sustained by the same identical arguments

171

and sophism practiced by the Jesuits. They refused to submit to an ecclesiastical council; but sought the aid of the civil power, and took decidedly
Erastian ground. All this, the candid reader of Dr. Thomas Scott's transla-
tion of the history of the Synod of Dort, will see abundantly stated.

Prior, in some degree, to this fermentation of the free-will leaven in
Belgium, the republican tendency of the opposite scheme, had proved somewhat annoying to the monarchy, and aristocracy in Britain. The Puritans
of England and Scotland, who were all at this time Presbyterian, had given
trouble to Elizabeth and James. Hume, speaking of the year 1604, the
second of James' English reign, says,—"The more he knew of the Puri-
tanical clergy, the less favor he bore to them. He had remarked in their
Scottish brethren, a violent turn toward republicanism, and a zealous attachment to civil liberty; principles nearly allied to that with which they were
actuated.—The Church of England, he adds, has not yet abandoned the
rigid doctrines of grace and predestination." The Presbyterians had applied
to the King for liberty to hold religious meetings. But James shortly replied,
*"If you aim at a Scottish presbytery, it agrees as well with monarchy, as
God and the Devil."* Such was the feeling of the high aristocracy, toward
the free-grace system and its advocates, just preceding the introduction of
Arminianism. Arminius died in 1609, before a full development and detec-
tion and condemnation of his doctrine. James [died] in 1625, seven years
after the meeting of the Synod of Dort. . . . The king, though at this time his
Calvanistic education had rivetted him in the doctrine of absolute decrees,
yet, being a zealous partisan of episcopacy, was insensibly engaged, towards
the end of his reign, to favor the milder theology of Arminius. Even in so
great a doctor, the genius of the religion prevailed over its speculative tenets,
and with him the whole clergy, gradually dropped the more rigid principles
of absolute reprobation, and unconditional decrees: some noise was made
about these innovations."

Thus, the open apologist of the house of Stuart, and zealous advocate of
strong monarchy, distinctly points out the history and the adaptation of the
free-will scheme, to high toned episcopacy, and so to civil monarchy. Hence,
the desperate and bloody efforts to force both upon Scotland. These same
views pervaded the court of Charles I. Laud was their guardian angel; their
history is written in blood, and known and read of all men.

But even Presbyterian Scotland, whose "democratic religion," as Edmund
Burke called that of their American descendants, the house of Stuart with
the arms of all England at their command, could not subdue to prelacy and
Arminianism,—even Scotland failed of preserving her integrity intact, against
the seductive influence of the latter, when it came without epaulette sword
or gun. The free-will system, produced the moderate party in the Scotch

Church, with all its leanings upon and towards aristocratic power, and all its spiritual paralysis and reduced standard of piety and morals. This philosophy, we mean to intimate, is generally accompanied by a lowered standard of piety and morals. The Scottish Moderates and the English high Church parties, are splendid but mournful illustration and proof of this truth. The Belgic Remonstrants, the Molinists, the Jesuits and the Papists in general, fill up the back ground and complete the shading of this dark and melancholy picture.

America, on the eve of the Revolution, shall furnish us with the last item in support of our general fact. The churches in the New World knew little of the free-will leaven, prior to '76. That branch of the great puritan family, which in, and immediately after the Westminster age, forsook the platform of representative democracy as embodied in the Presbyterian form of government, and adopted the Independent or Congregational form, still adhered steadfastly to the doctrinal standards of the Reformation. The other large branch, which still held to the original form of the Presbyterian government, continued also to maintain, with equal zeal and strenuousness, the free-grace system. The opposite theory had scarcely the semblance of an organized advocacy on this continent. High Church Episcopacy, at least and especially in Virginia, was decidedly Arminian, and of course, leaned toward toryism and the crown; and, accordingly, when the crisis arrived, fled to England and basked in the sunshine of royal favor, until the storm passed away. Whilst both the Congregational and Presbyterian branches of the great Puritan family, stood firm, unmoved and undismayed by the standard of freedom, and contended unto death for that representative principle in politics, which they had so long enjoyed and practiced in religion.

Thus much for the *fact*; we now proceed to the *philosophy*.

"Shew me," says Luther in his argument against Erasmus and free-will, "Shew me any one instance of a man, who, through the pure efficacy of free-will, even in the smallest degree, either mortified his appetites or forgave an injury. On the contrary, I can easily shew you, that the very holy men whom you boast of as free-willers, always in their prayers to God, totally laid aside every idea of free-will, and had recourse to nothing but grace, pure grace." And again, he remarks, "Then where are the desires, the endeavors, the merits of free-will, and what are their uses? Suppose we admit that the advocates of free-will allow only exceedingly little to that faculty; they nevertheless make that little the foundation of justification; because they represent the grace of God as obtained by that little. Indeed, they have no other mode of answering the question, Why does God justify one man and not another? But by having recourse to the different use which they suppose men to make of their free-will; namely, that in one case there are exertions, in the

173

other no exertions; and that God approves of one man on account of his exertions, and punishes the other for the neglect of them: not to say that they imagine he would be unjust if he did otherwise. Thus our gracious God is described as a respecter of works; and thus, whatever may be pretended to the contrary, the dignity of merits is maintained and inculcated."

In the former of these quotations, the Reformer points out the irreligious an immoral tendency of the system he opposes; and hence, we can see its incongruity with free government in church or state: for such government is impracticable, except where there is a considerable amount of truth and virtue in the mass of the people. The latter quoted passage, shews that free-will leads away from the foundation rock of salvation, and builds upon human merit. . . .

On the other hand the free-grace scheme stains the pride of all human glory, and prostrates the haughtiness of man in the dust before the sovereignty of the Divine will, the best of all temperaments to bring the heart into humble and quiet subjection to the will of the supreme Lawgiver. He who has learned to bow to the simple sovereign pleasure of God, in the great matter of his personal salvation . . . will find less difficulty in subordinating his desires and his entire conduct to the same holy, sovereign will, as it may be embodied in the movements of Providence and the wholesome restraints of law in a free church and a free commonwealth. Accustomed to look to the will of God as his rule in spirituals, it is exceedingly natural that he should do the same in things temporal.

But the principal point of special adaptation in the free-grace scheme, to be the precursor to a free system of government, is found in its federative or representative principle. We have only to transfer this prominent feature of our theology, into government, ecclesiastical and civil, and religious and political liberty are both secured. . . . The churches in the very first age organized their government on this principle. . . . Thus sprang up, under the forming hand of the Christian ministry, a representative government, limited, in its action, to matters purely religious, and interfering not at all with the civil affairs of the empire; but always seeking the peace of the world and the glory of God. The light of this spiritual rule continued to shine upon the path of the Roman monarch, pagan and Christian, until finding itself in peril of sinking under accumulating difficulties, the monarchy threw out its arms for help and grasped the church. From this coalition resulted the hybrid monster of the Papal despotism. Upon its development, the true church—Christ's own holy spouse—the republic ecclesiastical, retired into the fastness of the Alps, the Appenines, the Grisons, the Pyrennees, the Mountains of Bohemia, the hills of Caledonia, the wilds of America. In this last wilderness retreat, after centuries of iron oppression and compression, the distinguishing feature soon found room to expand itself in the ecclesiastical and to pass over into the civil: the result is, a vast, free, republican empire, founded upon the broad basis of federal representation. How interesting the *fact!* how beautiful the *philosophy! The truth shall make you free.*

One remark more, Fathers and Brethren Beloved! and I have done. To you more than to any other body of men on the globe, is entrusted the maintainance, defense and dissemination of these blessed and soul-emancipating doctrines. You,—and thereby I mean the General Assembly of this Presbyterian Church; and in this I mean no offence at all to other denominations, who (I rejoice to know) hold the same great doctrines. You have a fearful responsibility in reference *to the truth.* To your hands hath the Captain of Salvation committed the Protestant Banner. Yours is the honor and yours let it be, of rallying around the flag of the covenants during the conflicts of the present times and during that fearful war of opinion to which all the nations of Christendom look forward with such trembling solicitude. Yours, I confidently believe, is the glorious destiny of bearing it onward o'er hill and dale, valley, moor, and mountain, until, beneath its ample folds and heavenly sway, all the nations of the world shall rejoice in the freedom of THE TRUTH.

7

ON ENTERING THE KINGDOM: NEW BIRTH OR NURTURE?

D. Ray Heisey

One of the theological issues which engaged the pulpit during the first half of the nineteenth century was: What should be the method by which a person enters the kingdom of God? Should it be an instantaneous conversion or a process of growth?

According to New England Calvinism, man was considered innately sinful, but capable of responding to "special divine interposition" with a dramatic change of mind and life. This conversion experience, even for children of religious homes, was not only the surest means of entering the kingdom, but was traditionally obtained under the influence of religious revival. It was therefore by periodic revivals that churches increased their membership lists and enlarged their influence in the communities.

Among the outstanding revivalists of the time, though not so well known as Lyman Beecher or Charles Finney, was Edward D. Griffin. The impact that Griffin had may be seen in the numerous conversions for which he reportedly was responsible. One biographer, for example, compares him in this respect to Whitefield.[1] As a revivalist, Griffin deplored the erratic and extravagant measures used in later revivals. His preaching has been described by various contemporaries as "brilliant" and "surpassingly eloquent." [2] It is said that "his polished rhetoric and magnificent voice made [his sermons] sound like works of genius." [3] Standing six feet three inches tall and weighing 250 pounds, he presented an impressive figure in the pulpit, where he is said to have been more "in his element" than anywhere else.

When orthodoxy was thrown on the defensive by the popularity of Unitarianism in the early 1800's, Griffin was an important figure in two different attempts made by the Calvinists to regain the "faith once delivered to the saints." Andover Theological Seminary, begun near Boston in 1808 as an orthodox answer to Harvard, invited him to come there as a professor of sacred rhetoric.[4] Also, the Park Street Church, Boston, established in 1811 as a conservative stronghold in the heart of the "liberal" city, called him to be their first minister. Though Griffin failed to restore Calvinism, he was an articulate spokesman for the orthodox view of regeneration and revivalism. He believed that regeneration was a supernatural phenomenon—an intervention of God's sovereign will—which resulted in instantaneous conversion.

Griffin's sermon, "Regeneration Not Progressive," is important for two reasons. First, it incorporates the substance of the revivalistic–new-birth rhetoric. (1) Man,

[1] William B. Sprague, *Sermons by the Late Rev. Edward D. Griffin* I (New York: John S. Taylor, 1839), 258-59.
[2] L. W. Spring, A *History of Williams College* (Boston: Houghton Mifflin, 1917), p. 149.
[3] Allen Johnson, ed., *Dictionary of American Biography* IV (New York: Charles Scribner's Sons, 1960), 620.
[4] In his inaugural oration, in which he says that "the perfection of pulpit eloquence consists in displaying the most affecting gospel truths, in the most impressive manner," Griffin's orthodoxy is central. He adds, "But the success of the gospel is ensured, not by human eloquence, but by the *interpositions of omnipotent grace.*" [Italics mine] See Edward D. Griffin, *An Oration Delivered June 21, 1809, on the Day of the Author's Induction into the Office of Pulpit Eloquence, in the Divinity College, at Andover* (Boston: Farrand, Mallory and Co., [n.d.]) A copy is located in the Oberlin College Library.

being in a state of "supreme selfishness," is entirely hostile to God and thus totally morally depraved. (2) The moral change from "unabated enmity to supreme love" for God must be instantaneous. (3) The sinner must turn from sin in an individual act of repentance and by faith believe in Christ. (4) Regeneration depends upon the supernatural power of God's sovereign will. The sinner cooperates, says Griffin, "in no other sense than the rebel who is subdued by force of arms assists his prince in vanquishing himself."

The second reason is that the sermon provides an excellent example of Griffin's rhetorical method, not unrepresentative of revivalistic preaching generally. The introduction offers the essence of Griffin's argument: Since the native character of man is destitute of true love for God, and, since holiness is universal love, it therefore follows that the change which occurs in regeneration must be instantaneous. The body of the sermon consists of an explication of these two points. The argument of the sermon is argument by definition. The definitions of the nature of man and of the nature of regeneration force Griffin to the categorical conclusion that the change "is as sudden as the entrance of the first drop that falls into a vessel." Rhetorical questions are used very frequently to phrase supposed objections to his position. He then answers these objections by his so-called "reasonings," based on his interpretation of scripture and "truths already established." The conclusion, a disproportionate one third of the entire discourse, consists of two "inferences" drawn from his main argument.[5]

Revivalism, with its overemphasis on conversion, was brought under the fire of numerous critics, chief of whom was Horace Bushnell of Hartford's North Church. The critics maintained that an overemphasis on conversion and revivals fostered an unnatural attitude toward promoting religion and encouraged a neglect of "the ordinary

---

[5] Compare the approach here to that of Finney in his "Sinners Bound to Change Their Own Hearts." The introduction announces the proposition, the discourse proper is highly argumentative, supplying reasons based on scripture and on analogy, and the conclusion offers certain "inferences."

means of grace." Careful Christian nurture of children, once an important part of New England theology, was neglected in the contemporary scheme of salvation. As a young Congregational minister, Bushnell grew steadily uneasy with the kind of emphasis being given to revivals and conversions.[6] He had tried using this method but failed. From a theological as well as a practical standpoint, he felt that the approach was highly questionable. In 1838, only one year after the death of Griffin, Bushnell published in the *Christian Spectator* an essay on "Spiritual Economy of Revivals of Religion" in which he attempted "to secure to the cause of evangelical religion a more natural, satisfactory, and happy, as well as a more constant movement," than that associated with revivals. Six years later another essay was issued, "Growth, not Conquest, the True Method of Christian Progress." These two essays reveal the roots of his Christian nurture philosophy.

In 1846 he was invited by his ministerial association to discuss the subject of Christian nurture. The two discourses which he delivered were then published by the Massachusetts Sabbath School Society, but had to be withdrawn from sale due to the fierce opposition which they created. The following year he republished the discourses along with a forceful defense of them, and the two earlier essays. In 1861 he published in final book form his thinking on Christian nurture which remains the classic statement on this subject.[7] The first two chapters of this volume are entitled "What Christian Nurture Is" and are believed to be the original two sermons on Christian nurture.

The first of the two discourses is the more comprehensive. It not only advances the proposition, explaining its meaning, and develops in detail the evidence for his

[6] For biographies, see Mary Bushnell Cheney, *Life and Letters of Horace Bushnell* (New York: Harper and Brothers, 1880); T. T. Munger, *Horace Bushnell: Preacher and Theologian* (Boston: Houghton Mifflin, 1899); and Barbara Cross, *Horace Bushnell* (Chicago: University of Chicago Press, 1958).

[7] The most recent edition is *Christian Nurture* (New Haven: Yale University Press, 1967) with an introduction by Luther A. Weigle.

argument from what he calls "the human side," but it also incorporates the essence of his argument from the theological side, which is then given elaboration and more structure in the second discourse.[8]

Whereas Griffin's proposition is that regeneration is not progressive, but instantaneous, Bushnell's proposition is "that the child is to grow up a Christian, and never know himself as being otherwise." He develops this thesis by extended and well-organized argument. His reasoning throughout is built upon two supporting propositions. One is psychological, that the organic nature of the family relationship is such that the life and spirit of the Christian parents are the matrix for the child's life, flowing into him all the time, forming his character. The other is theological, that the relation between the natural and the supernatural is such that God uses the family unit as a means of grace to accomplish the renewal of the heart. Bushnell does not deny regeneration,[9] but he rejects the "one-sided, distorted" view of conversion for the more natural means of growth in the organic relationship of the Christian family. Christ himself, he says, should be infused in this way into the mind of the child.

Both Griffin and Bushnell came from religious homes, graduated from Yale, were interrupted in their plans to enter law,[10] became Congregational clergymen, were pastors of important churches, and were offered the presi-

[8] The second discourse, not included in the present volume, gives attention, as well, to the rite of baptism as it relates to nurture, to the answering of possible objections to the doctrine of Christian nurture, and to practical conclusions.

[9] Bushnell does not clarify as well as he might in "What Christian Nurture Is" the relationship between regeneration for non-Christian and Christian families. For those persons who do not grow up in the nurture of the Christian home, Bushnell would require "a great spiritual change" in their "ruling love" as necessary to salvation. See his sermon, "Regeneration," in *Sermons for the New Life*, 5th ed. (New York: Charles Scribner, 1859), pp. 106-26.

[10] Griffin intended to study law, but "a serious illness and a fall from a horse precipitated him into the ministry." *Dictionary of American Biography*, p. 619. Bushnell was already embarked on his study of law when an invitation came to be a tutor at Yale College which he accepted. His experience there turned him to theology. Munger, *Horace Bushnell*, p. 27.

dency of New England colleges. Despite these similarities in their backgrounds, their divergent views on the nature of entering the kingdom are aptly symbolized in two ways. First, their relationships to Harvard were wholly dissimilar. Griffin was so disliked by the Harvard authorities for his unyielding orthodoxy that they resorted to amending their charter twice in order to prevent him from exercising his functions as an *ex officio* member of the board. Bushnell, on the other hand, not only was invited to Harvard to address anniversary occasions, but was awarded an honarary D.D. degree. Second, their preaching styles were dissimilar. Of Griffin it is said: "Lacking range and depth of thought and the distinction of style necessary to great literature, dwelling too constantly upon the terrors of the law, these sermons had only an immediate and passing mission, and that in spite of their admirable clearness, their driving force, their resounding rhetoric, and not infrequent beauty of phrase." [11] Of Bushnell it is said: "The flights of his imagination were not rhetorical strivings, but the simple rehearsals of what he saw. . . . He follows the wide sweep of the thought which yet never wanders from the theme." [12]

His sermons are said to belong to that class of literature called "the literature of power," and may be expected to live on because they are "timeless in their truth, majestic in their diction, commanding in their moral tone, penetrating in their spirituality, and are pervaded by that quality without which a sermon is not one,—the divine uttering itself to the human." [13]

In these two men, and in their representative sermons, we see the religious mind of America in ferment. On the one hand, there was an effort to retain the old ways of thinking—in this case, about how to enter the kingdom of God. Griffin was holding to New England Calvinism, arguing that sinners, destitute of true love, needed to be changed instantaneously. Bushnell was departing from the revivalistic movement, proposing that a radical conversion

[11] Spring, *History of Williams College*, p. 150.
[12] Munger, *Horace Bushnell*, pp. 279, 284.
[13] *Ibid.*, pp. 287-88.

experience be replaced with the more natural and constant process of Christian growth. Whereas revivalism and the new birth appealed to the rugged individualism of the young nation and the frontier, Christian nurture appealed to the emerging sense of social responsibility that was to appear dominant later in American life.

EDWARD D. GRIFFIN

Edward D. Griffin (1770-1837), son of a prosperous farmer, was born in East Haddam, Connecticut. Upon his graduation from Yale College in 1790, he studied theology, was ordained pastor at New Hartford in 1795, and later served at the First Presbyterian Church in Newark, New Jersey. In 1809 he was appointed professor of pulpit eloquence in Andover Theological Seminary and two years later was installed as the first minister of the Park Street Congregational Church, Boston. After spending four years in an effort to restore Calvinism in the Unitarian stronghold, and six more years at Newark, he accepted in 1821, an invitation to become president of Williams College, where he served for fifteen years. He is credited with having saved the college from dissolution. Remembered for his commanding presence, his magnificent voice, his polished sermons, his Calvinist orthodoxy, and his emphasis on revivals, Griffin was one of the leading pulpit orators during the early national period.

Regeneration Not Progressive*

I will put a new spirit within you; and I will take the stony heart out of their flesh, and will give them a heart of flesh.—EZEKIEL XI. 19.

There is a phenomenon in the moral world for which no adequate natural cause has ever yet been assigned. I mean a great and sudden change of temper and character, brought about under a strong impression of scriptural truths; a change in many cases from habitual vice and malignity, to the sweetness and purity of the Christian spirit, and continuing to manifest itself in a new character through life, accompanied, if you will believe the subjects, with new views of God, and Christ, and divine things in general, and with new feelings towards them. This change is discovered in people of all temperaments; in the phlegmatick as well as the ardent, in the slow and cautious as well as the impetuous and sanguine, in minds wholly subject to the understanding, as well as those that submit more to the dominion of the imagination. It takes place in people of all ranks and conditions, in the wise and

---

* *A Series of Lectures Delivered in Park Street Church, Boston on Sabbath Evenings* (Boston: Nathaniel Willis, 1813), pp. 111-35. A copy of this volume is in the Oberlin College Library.

learned as well as the simple and ignorant, in persons insulated by society of a different cast, and strongly prejudiced against the belief of such a change. Thousands who are not mad, but cool, dispassionate, and wise, the ornaments of society and of learning, whose word would be taken in any other case, and who certainly ought to be regarded as competent judges, tell you that they have had opportunity to *see both sides*, as the revilers of this doctrine have not; that they once looked upon the subject with the eyes of their opponents, but have since seen for themselves, and do assuredly know that there is such a thing as a spiritual change of heart. And what witnesses can you oppose to these? Men who offer mere *negative* testimony,—who can only say, they know of no such thing.

To this spiritual change . . . I am now to draw your attention. But as the reasonings will be founded on truths already established, it is necessary to lay these truths before you again, and at one view. It has been proved that holiness radically consists in universal love, which fixes the heart supremely on God; that sin has its root in affections limited to an individual or a private circle, but chiefly in selfishness, including, as a main part, the love of the world; that every man makes either God or himself the object of his chief regard; that supreme self-love necessarily produces enmity to God, to the utter exclusion of every better affection towards Him; that they who do not love God supremely are destitute of true charity to *man*, and altogether without holiness; that this is the native character of all who are born into the world, whether in pagan or Christian countries.

Out of these truths arises the necessity of that moral change which is denominated Regeneration. The reason of this necessity is here laid open to the core. It is the same that our Saviour assigned to the wondering Nicodemus. He had astonished that Jewish ruler with the solemn asseveration, "Verily, verily I say unto thee, Except a man be born again he cannot see the kingdom of God;" and while the Jew stood doubting and amazed, He added as the sole ground of this necessity, "That which is born of the flesh is flesh:" in other words, that which is born by natural generation is "carnal," is "enmity against God," and must be born again.

These truths disclose also the precise *nature* of the change which is necessary. It is a transition from supreme selfishness to universal love,—from enmity against God to supreme attachment to Him. It is readily seen of course that it must be the greatest change that ever takes place in the human affections.

The first question that will come before us is, *Whether Regneration is progressive or instantaneous*. From the truths already established and other considerations I shall attempt to prove it *instantaneous*. It is not necessary however to suppose that the precise time is always *known*. Conceive of a man sitting in a dungeon, so occupied in thought as not to notice the change gradually produced by a light approaching at a distance. Turning his eye at length he discerns objects, and perceives that there is light in the room; but when it began to enter he cannot tell. Yet there was a moment when the first ray passed the window. Can we not find the idea of such an instantaneous change more than implied in the text? What is the blessing promised? Not the *gradual* improvement of an *old* temper, but "a new spirit;"—"the stony heart," not softened *by degrees* into flesh, but by one decisive effort removed, and a heart of flesh substituted in its room.

You are told by some that no other change is necessary than what is accomplished by reason, *gradually* resuming its empire over the passions and appetites. But this theory overlooks the *enmity of heart* that refuses to yield to reason. It arrays its ethicks against the grosser ebullitions of sin, but leaves the seat of the disorder untouched. You are told by others that through the influence of instruction, example, one's own exertions, and the common operations of the Spirit, the enmity is gradually weakened till it is destroyed, and the taste of the mind, as in many other instances, is brought over by degrees from aversion to love. But does not this, and every other theory which recognises the principle of progressive Regeneration, wholly overlook the nature of the disease, and the real ground of the native enmity? The disease is supreme self-love; the ground of enmity, that God requires upon penalty of eternal death that universal love which will fix the heart supremely on Him. This enmity will remain and exclude every particle of love, as long as self-love is supreme. Now self-love will remain supreme till the chief regard is transferred to another object. But in the universe there is not another object to receive it but God Himself. Self-love then will remain supreme and support the enmity in all its vigour, till God is supremely loved. As long as the sinner loves himself chiefly he is the enemy of God, to the utter exclusion of every better affection towards Him: the moment he ceases to love himself supremely his highest affection centres in God. There is no intermediate space. No time can elapse between the last moment in which he loves himself supremely, and the first moment in which he does not.

You talk of the taste being brought over by a gradual process from enmity to love: but can you find any step in that process at which the man does not either love the *world* better than God, or God better than the world? If he loves the world better than God he has made no progress at all; for "if any man love the world *the love of the Father is not in him*": and if no love, then enmity: "He that is not *with* me is *against* me." "The *friendship* of the world is *enmity* with God; whosoever therefore will be a *friend* of the world is the *enemy* of God." "Either he will *hate* the one and love the other, or else he will hold to the one and *despise* the other." On the other hand, if he

185

loves God better than the world Regeneration is consummated, and there is no room for progress. Either then he has made no advance, or the work is complete. In every step of the supposed progress he is either an enemy to God or loves him supremely.

Yielding then the point that the man is an enemy to God till the change is complete, it may yet be asked, is not that enmity *gradually weakened?* It cannot be *radically* weakened till its *cause* is weakened, which is supreme self-love, (or more generally the love of *the creature,* for the *social* affections too may set up their objects in opposition,) struggling against the law and administration of God. . . .

But you ask, May not new *light* thrown upon the conscience convince the mind of the *unreasonableness* of its opposition, and thus sooth and allay the enmity? I answer: by reasoning you may compose the passions of an angry man without at all changing his disposition. After you have calmed the risings of enmity against God, I ask, *is the dominion of the limited affections in the least abated?* This is the decisive question: for supreme attachment to the creature comprehends the root and essence of the whole disease. Now can you weaken the love of the creature *by light?* Or to confine the question to a part of the evil, can you by light and conscience weaken the power of *self-love?* Can you reason a man out of his attachment to himself? Will all the light of the Last Day abate in the least the selfishness of the wicked? Will not light and conscience in their highest degrees act together in the regions of despair, without producing any other effect than rage and gnashing of teeth? No, but the *living,* you say, possess *hope.* Hope! and can you then *bribe* a man to be *less selfish?* What, bribe a man to *hate a bribe!* If enmity against God were only a *prejudice,* arising from a misconception of His true character, it might indeed be removed by light. In that case it would not be a sin but a virtue; for to hate a *false* image of God, in other words, a false *God,* is our duty. But if the *heart* of sinners is depraved, if they hate the *true* character of God in whatever form it appears, they will hate it the more the more it is seen, and light, so far from abating, will only rouse the enmity to stronger action. . . .

But you say again, May not the divine *Spirit,* before the love of God is implanted, bring the mind to a better frame by weakening its prejudices against religion, and exciting reflections, desires, and resolutions which come nearer to a holy character? All that the Spirit does before Regeneration, I suppose is to pour *light* upon the mind; thus awakening remorse of conscience, and by alarming self-love occasioning various and strong actings of that principle. If this is all that the Spirit does before Regeneration, the question has been already answered in what was said of the influence of *light.* But whatever the Spirit does, He certainly does not perform impossibilities.

. . . But I have another thing to say. The feelings of the convicted are holy, or sinful, or neither. If neither, they have no moral nature, that is, are deserving neither of praise or blame, and of course have nothing to do with our subject. If they are sinful, what approaches, I pray, can *sin* make to *holiness?* even to the *lowest* degree of holiness? What approaches can total *darkness* make to the lowest degree of *light?* or total *deadness* to the lowest degree of *life?* Will you say then that they are *holy?* What, holy without love to God! without a particle of that "love" which "is the *fulfilling* of the law!" . . .

In every view then it appears that there can be no approaches toward Regeneration in the antecedent temper of the heart. The moment before the change the sinner is as far from sanctification as darkness is from light, as death is from life, as sin is from holiness. Admitting that his passions are somewhat allayed, and the *actings* of self-love not so *violent*, (a concession by no means to be made, certainly not in every case, considering the strong light in which he views the objects of his aversion and dread,) still the least action of enmity to God is as far removed from the lowest degree of holiness, as an object which God *infinitely hates*, from an object which He infinitely *loves*,—as far as a thing which deserves everlasting shame and contempt, from a grace that will receive endless and inconceivable rewards. And the two can never approach nearer together.

I have now finished one train of reasoning, and will enter on another. I prove that Regeneration is instantaneous from the established truth that mankind by nature are destitute of holiness. Regeneration is nothing more nor less than the *commencement* of holiness in the soul,—the *increase* of that principle being not Regeneration but sanctification. If the soul is wholly destitute of holiness there must be a moment when it first receives that principle, provided the principle itself is specifically different from any thing preexisting in the mind, and is not a *compound* gradually formed out of the natural affections. Even in that case there would be a moment when by *increase*, or by a *perfect process of combination*, it would first become entitled to the name of holiness. . . .

This idea may be further illustrated by a recurrence to some of the images under which this change is represented. It is set forth by the figure of light created in the midst of total darkness: "God who commanded the light to shine out of darkness, hath shined in our *hearts*, to give the light of the knowledge of the glory of God in the face of Jesus Christ." It is called the opening of blind eyes, and the unstopping of deaf ears. It is called a resurrection from the dead: "You hath He quickened who were dead in trespasses and sins." It is called a new creation: "If any man be in Christ he is a new creature." "We are His workmanship created in Christ Jesus unto good works." "Put on the new man which after God is created in righteousness and true holiness." It is called the removal of a heart of stone and introduction of a heart of flesh. It is called a new birth. Now all these figures import an instantaneous change. There is a moment when the first ray of light enters a region of total darkness. There is a moment when the blind man begins to see. There is a moment when the deaf man hears the first sound. There is a moment when life begins to animate a dead body. The creation of a *simple substance* is instantaneous. The formation of the various objects that were to compose *a world*, admitted of successive acts; and to this is analogous the new creation of the whole body of the elect in successive generations: but when a simple substance was to be produced, "God said, Let there be light, and there was light." The removal of a heart of stone, likewise, and substitution of a heart of flesh, must be instantaneous, or according to the figure there is a time when either there are two hearts or no heart at all. And in regard to a birth, there is a moment in every case in which it may be first said, a child is born into the world.

Regeneration has sometimes been compared to the struggle of *light* with darkness and its *gradual* prevalence at the *dawn of day*. But what do they mean by *light*? If it is *holiness* that they mean, they assume what has been proved to be false, that there is holiness in the heart before the completion of Regeneration. Show me a man in whom holiness and sin are struggling for dominion, and I will show you one who is already born again. But if they mean any thing *besides holiness*, any thing besides *the identical principle whose prevalence is to constitute the change*, the change itself bears no resemblance to the progress of the dawn,—the progress of the same light that makes the day. It might more fitly be compred to the first ray that strikes the eastern horizon, or rather to the first ray that enters a region of *total* darkness. And between the last moment of total darkness and the first moment of commencing light no time can elapse. . . .

It affords much support to these reasonings that the Scriptures divide the whole human race into two classes,—saints and sinners, the good and the bad, believers and unbelievers, natural men and spiritual men, those who are *in* Christ and those who are *out*, they who are still under condemnation and they who are justified, the heirs of heaven and the heirs of hell. There is not a third class. "He that is not *with* me is *against* me." It follows that every man, at every moment of his life, belongs to one or the other of these two classes. Then he belongs to one *till the moment* he enters the other. Were it otherwise, there would be a time in which he is neither good nor bad, neither *in* Christ nor *out*, neither condemned nor justified, neither an heir of heaven nor an heir of hell. What is he then? To whom does he belong? Whither would he go if he should die? Is there a purgatory?

I might add to these reasonings that Regeneration is represented to be a great exhibition of *power*,—as great as the resurrection of Christ: "The eyes of your understanding being enlightened, that ye may know—what is *the exceeding greatness of His power* to us-ward who *believe*, according to the working of His *mighty power* which He wrought in Christ when He raised Him from the dead, and set Him at His own right hand in the heavenly places." This certainly favours the idea at least of a *sudden* change. Divine power is doubtless as much *exerted* in the gradual motion of the heavenly bodies, and in the slow process of vegetation, as it was in stopping the sun over Gibeon; but when men are summoned to witness a great *exhibition* of power, they naturally look for a *sudden* effect, as the burst of a volcano, or the sweep of a whirlwind. But if instead of one grand effort Regeneration is brought about by a lingering influence, it is no more an exhibition of power than the growth of a plant, or the alteration of any of our tastes. And if it is produced by the slow operation of *reason* and *knowledge*, it manifests no special power at all.

But after all the question chiefly turns on these two points,—the supreme selfishness or total depravity of the human heart, and the nature of holiness. No one who admits this view of the native character, and believes that holiness is a simple principle, not a compound formed out of preexisting properties, can doubt that there is a moment when it is first introduced. *What is the character of the natural heart?* and *What is holiness?* are the two questions which on this subject must divide the world. For if holiness is a simple principle, and first introduced in Regeneration, especially if it is a principle of supreme love to God following supreme selfishness, nothing can be plainer than that the change is as sudden as the entrance of the first drop that falls into a vessel, or the first ray that penetrates a dungeon.

This doctrine however does not militate against the idea of an *antecedent preparation* in the conscience, wrought by the means of grace and the enlightening influences of the Spirit. . . . At present I shall content myself with two inferences from the doctrine already established.

(1) It inevitably follows from the foregoing exposition that none of the feelings, or actions, or duties, (as they are called,) of the unregenerate, (so far as they partake of a *moral* nature, that is, so far as they are entitled to praise or blame from the moral Governour of the world,) *are otherwise than sinful.* They are sinful, or holy, or neither. If neither, they receive no praise or blame from the moral Governour. For whatever may be said of God in the character of *temporal* head of the Jewish nation, or as accommodating, in these days, His *visible* dispensations to *visible* characters, yet as *moral Governor* He praises nothing but holiness, or *real* conformity to His *law*, and blames nothing but sin, which "is the transgression of the law." For to govern

ACCORDING TO LAW enters into all our ideas of a righteous Governour. That some of the feelings and actions of the unregenerate are of a neutral character is not denied, but these are to be set aside as of no account. The rest are either sinful or holy. But they are not holy, for the *beginning* of holiness is Regeneration: of course they must be sinful.

It is not denied that the *form* of their actions is often right; and if the form *by itself* is respected in the divine law, it is, as far as it goes, real obedience. But *is* the form so divided by the divine law from the disposition, that, standing alone, it constitutes any part of obedience? If so, the form without the disposition must constitute some part of *transgression;* and then, in the eye of the divine law, a man in part commits murder who kills his neighbour by accident, or in a paroxysm of madness. The truth is that no action is rewarded or punished by God or man, (unless by God accommodating His *visible* dispensations to the *apprehensions* of mankind,) otherwise than as it is known, or supposed to be, the index of the heart. Separate from murder all ideas of malicious intent, and it is no longer murder in the eyes of God or man. Separate from prayer all ideas of pious design, and in the eyes of God and man it is no longer prayer. No law human or divine ever thought of forbidding a *mad* man to kill his neighbour: (no matter for what reason.) No law human or divine ever thought of requiring a *mad* man to perform deeds of charity. It is then a *fact* that no law ever forbade or required an external action *but as an expression of mind, of choice, of disposition.* The external action in its naked form, exclusive of the choice and disposition, *is not required,* and the action thus alone is no part of obedience, no part of holiness. But if *any thing* in the mind is necessary to impart a holy character to an action, it must be HOLINESS *in the mind.* For certainly nothing but the thing itself can instamp its own character. Where therefore there is no holiness in the heart, there can be, in the view of Him who tries the reins, no holy action.

But while I neglect to ascribe *holiness,* I do not mean to impute *sin,* to the bare form of actions. In strictness of speech the form distinct from the mind no more partakes of a moral nature than the motions of a clock. All that I affirm of the sinfulness of the actions of the unregenerate is, that *so far* as those actions, considered in both the outward and inward part, partake of a moral nature, they are sinful, and *that* whether the external form is right or wrong. In strictness of speech the sin lies not in the outward form even when that form is wrong, certainly not when it is right. Yet in the popular language of Scripture, as in the common language of mankind, the form and disposition are both comprehended in the action. Now what I assert is, that the action, thus complexly considered, takes its moral character, not from the form, but from the disposition; and where the disposition is wrong the general action is pronounced sinful. "The Lord seeth not as man seeth; for man looketh on the outward appearance, but the Lord looketh on the heart." The widow's mite He affectionately approves, while He rejects the man who without evangelical love bestows all his goods to feed the poor, and then with a martyr's zeal gives his body to be burned. He accepts "the willing mind" even where no action follows, while He pronounces the very "sacrifice of the wicked—an abomination." While "a cup of cold water," administered in love, is rewarded with eternal life, "he that turneth away his ear from hearing the law, even his prayer [is] abomination." And *that* not merely when he *intends* to mock: "The sacrifice of the wicked is abomination, *how much more when he bringeth it with a wicked mind.*" Nor let it be supposed that his *sacrifices* are singled out to bear this reproach: "The *plowing* of the wicked is sin." His commonest actions are an offence to God, because they proceed from a heart "deceitful above all things and desperately wicked." . . .

The case is not altered by any convictions which the Spirit may excite, by any anxieties of the sinner, by any attention to the means of grace. If Regeneration is the *commencement* of holiness, all the feelings and actions to that moment, so far as they partake of a moral nature, must be sinful. So far as the moral Governour is at all affected, He is disgusted and offended till the very moment of the change.

(2) It follows that the unregenerate, even under their highest convictions, and however near they may have approached the time of conversion, still lie at the *uncovenanted* mercy of God. By this I do not mean that no promises are held out to them *on condition* of their returning; I only mean that nothing which they *now* do has the promise of any reward or notice from God. The moral Governour of the world cannot pledge Himself to reward sinful actions, nor actions barely neutral. . . . The following passage reveals the *sole* condition, (unless you profanely suppose *two* conditions, like the *two prices* of the petty merchant) on which all temporal blessings were promised that people: "And it shall come to pass, if you shall hearken diligently unto my commandments which I command you this day, TO LOVE THE LORD YOUR GOD, and to serve Him WITH ALL YOUR HEART, AND WITH ALL YOUR SOUL, that I will give you the rain of your land in his due season, the first rain and the latter rain, that thou mayest gather in thy corn, and thy wine, and thine oil." . . .

There is another insuperable difficulty in the way of extending promises to the unregenerate; they are not *united to Christ.* The great bond of union is *faith;* but "whosoever believeth—is *born of God.*" "If any man be *in Christ* he is a *new creature.*" . . . "The Scripture hath concluded *all* under sin, that *the promise by faith of Jesus Christ* might be given to them that *believe.*" How then can any promise reach those who are out of Christ? The promise chiefly contended for is one that shall ensure to the unregenerate an answer to their *prayers:* But if such prayers are answered it must be *without the influence of Christ;* of course they might have been answered if Christ had never died. Why then did He die? If *one prayer* of a sinner could ascend to God without going through, *a whole soul* might, and if *one* soul might, a *whole world* might. If in *one act* a sinner can be accepted without a Saviour, he may be so accepted in his general conduct; and if *one* may, a *whole world* may: why then was a Saviour provided? But far from us be such a thought. Infinite Purity cannot commune with pollution, (no not in a single instance,) nor look upon a sinner except through a Mediator. What mean you to contend for the privilege of going to God without a Mediator? to contend for the privilege of being *pagans?* Hope a prayer may reach the mercy seat without going through Christ!—if this is not *self-righteousness* expunge the word from the language. Further, a promise implies a *reward.* Now if the unregenerate are rewarded they are *rewarded* before they are *pardoned.* They receive tokens of favour while they remain objects of wrath. And for what are they rewarded? Not for the merits of Christ, for they have no part in Him; but for their own works,—works too which are indifferent or sinful. This is "confusion worse confounded." But charge not this upon the *Bible.* From Genesis to Revelation no such promise is found. "Ask and ye shall receive," is indeed said to all; but when you inquire the meaning of that condition, the answer is, "ASK IN FAITH, NOTHING WAVERING." . . . In short all the promises addressed to the unregenerate are summed up in either of the following texts: "Ye shall seek me and find me, *when ye shall search for me* WITH ALL YOUR HEART." "If—thou shalt seek the Lord thy God, thou shalt find him *if thou seek Him* with ALL THY HEART, AND WITH ALL THY SOUL."

HORACE BUSHNELL

Horace Bushnell (1802–1876), a descendant of early colonial settlers, was born in Litchfield, Connecticut. He grew up in a home where religion was "a constant atmosphere, a commanding but genial presence." He was graduated from Yale College in 1827 and later from Yale Divinity School. Ordained pastor of the North Church (Congregational), Hartford, in 1833, he continued in that position until 1859, when ill health forced his resignation. He used his pulpit and the lecture platform to speak on social and political questions as well as theological issues. His speaking did not draw the crowds; his depth and independence of thought were more suitable to select audiences. He did influence contemporary preaching, however, in both content and style, bringing freshness and life to the pulpit where there had been structure and dogma. He provided new direction and added considerable substance to nineteenth-century theology by his books, God in Christ *(1849),* Nature and the Supernatural *(1858),* Christian Nurture *(1861),* and *The Vicarious Sacrifice *(1866).*

What Christian Nurture Is*

"Bring them up in the nurture and admonition of the Lord."—EPHESIANS VI. 4.

There is then some kind of nurture which is of the Lord, deriving a quality and a power from Him, and communicating the same. Being instituted by Him, it will of necessity have a method and a character peculiar to itself, or rather to Him. It will be the Lord's way of education, having aims appropriate to Him, and, if realized in its full intent, terminating in results impossible to be reached by any merely human method.

What then is the true idea of Christian or divine nurture, as distinguished from that which is not Christian? What is its aim? What its method of working? What its powers and instruments? What its contemplated results? Few questions have greater moment; and it is one of the pleasant signs of the times, that the subject involved is beginning to attract new interest and

* Christian Nurture (New Haven: Yale University Press, 1967), pp. 3-23.

excite a spirit of inquiry which heretofore has not prevailed in our churches.

. . . What is the true idea of Christian education?—I answer in the following proposition, which it will be the aim of my argument to establish, viz.:

That the child is to grow up a Christian, and never know himself as being otherwise.

In other words, the aim, effort, and expectation should be, not, as is commonly assumed, that the child is to grow up in sin, to be converted after he comes to a mature age; but that he is to open on the world as one that is spiritually renewed, not remembering the time when he went through a technical experience, but seeming rather to have loved what is good from his earliest years. I do not affirm that every child may, in fact and without exception, be so trained that he certainly will grow up a Christian. The qualifications it may be necessary to add will be given in another place, where they can be stated more intelligibly.

This doctrine is not a novelty, now rashly and for the first time propounded, as some of you may be tempted to suppose. I shall show you, before I have done with the argument, that it is as old as the Christian church, and prevails extensively at the present day in other parts of the world. Neither let your own experience raise a prejudice against it. If you have endeavored to realize the very truth I here affirm, but find that your children do not exhibit the character you have looked for; if they seem to be intractable to religious influences, and sometimes to display an apparent aversion to the very subject of religion itself, you are not of course to conclude that the doctrine I here maintain is untrue or impracticable. You may be unreasonable in your expectations of your children. . . .

Perhaps they will go through a rough mental struggle, at some future day, and seem, to others and to themselves, there to have entered on a Christian life. And yet it may be true that there was still some root of right principle established in their childhood, which is here only quickened and developed, as when Christians of a mature age are revived in their piety, after a period of spiritual lethargy; for it is conceivable that regenerate character may exist, long before it is fully and formally developed.

But suppose there is really no trace or seed of holy principle in your children, has there been no fault of piety and constancy in your church? no want of Christian sensibility and love to God? no carnal spirit visible to them and to all, and imparting its noxious and poisonous quality to the Christian atmosphere in which they have had their nurture? For it is not for you alone to realize all that is included in the idea of Christian education. It belongs to the church of God, according to the degree of its social power over you and in you and around your children, to bear a part of the responsibility with you.

. . . You must not assume that we, in this age, are the best Christians that have ever lived, or most likely to produce all the fruits of piety. An assumption so pleasing to our vanity is more easily made than verified, but vanity is the weakest as it is the cheapest of all arguments. We have some good points, in which we compare favorably with other Christians, and Christians of other times, but our style of piety is sadly deficient, in many respects, and that to such a degree that we have little cause for self-congratulation. . . .

For some reason, we do not make a Christian atmosphere about us—do not produce the conviction that we are living unto God. There is a marvelous want of savor in our piety. It is a flower of autumn, colored as highly as it need be to the eye, but destitute of fragrance. It is too much to hope that, with such an instrument, we can fulfill the true idea of Christian education. Any such hope were even presumptuous. At the same time, there is no so ready way of removing the deficiencies just described, as to recall our churches to their duties in domestic life; those humble, daily, hourly duties, where the spirit we breathe shall be a perpetual element of power and love, bathing the life of childhood.

Thus much it was necessary to say, for the removal of prejudices that are likely to rise up in your minds, and make you inaccessible to the arguments I may offer. Let all such prejudices be removed, or, if this be too much, let them, at least, be suspended till you have heard what I have to advance; for it can not be desired of you to believe any thing more than what is shown you by adequate proofs. Which also it is right to ask that you will receive, in a spirit of conviction, such as becomes our wretched and low attainments, and with a willingness to let God be exalted, though at the expense of some abasement in ourselves. In pursuing the argument, I shall—

I. Collect some considerations which occur to us, viewing the subject on the human side, and then—

II. Show how far and by what methods God has justified, on his part, the doctrine we maintain.

There is then, as the subject appears to us—

1. No absurdity in supposing that children are to grow up in Christ. On the other hand, if there is no absurdity, there is a very clear moral incongruity in setting up a contrary supposition, to be the aim of a system of Christian education. There could not be a worse or more baleful implication given to a child, than that he is to reject God and all holy principle, till he has come to a mature age. What authority have you from the Scriptures to tell your child, or, by any sign, to show him, that you do not expect him truly

to love and obey God, till after he has spent whole years in hatred and wrong? . . . Meantime, wherein would it be less incongruous for you to teach your child that he is to lie and steal, and go the whole round of the vices, and then, after he comes to mature age, reform his conduct by the rules of virtue? Perhaps you do not give your child to expect that he is to grow up in sin; you only expect that he will yourself. That is scarcely better: for that which is your expectation, will assuredly be his; and what is more, any attempt to maintain a discipline at war with your own secret expectations, will only make a hollow and worthless figment of that which should be an open, earnest reality. You will never practically aim at what you practically despair of, and if you do not practically aim to unite your child to God, you will aim at something less; that is, something unchristian, wrong, sinful.

But my child is a sinner, you will say; and how can I expect him to begin a right life, until God gives him a new heart? This is the common way of speaking, and I state the objection in its own phraseology, that it may recognize itself. Who then has told you that a child can not have the new heart of which you speak? Whence do you learn that if you live the life of Christ, before him and with him, the law of the Spirit of Life may not be such as to include and quicken him also? And why should it be thought incredible that there should be some really good principle awakened in the mind of a child? For this is all that is implied in a Christian state. The Christian is one who has simply *begun* to love what is good for its own sake, and why should it be thought impossible for a child to have this love begotten in him? Take any scheme of depravity you please, there is yet nothing in it to forbid the possibility that a child should be led, in his first moral act, to cleave unto what is good and right, any more than in the first of his twentieth year. He is, in that case, only a child converted to good, leading a mixed life as all Christians do. The good in him goes into combat with the evil, and holds a qualified sovereignty. And why may not this internal conflict of goodness cover the whole life from its dawn, as well as any part of it? And what more appropriate to the doctrine of spiritual influence itself, than to believe that as the Spirit of Jehovah fills all the worlds of matter, and holds a presence of power and government in all objects, so all human souls, the infantile as well as the adult, have a nurture of the Spirit appropriate to their age and their wants? What opinion is more essentially monstrous, in fact, than that which regards the Holy Spirit as having no agency in the immature souls of children who are growing up, helpless and unconscious, into the perils of time?

2. It is to be expected that Christian education will radically differ from that which is not Christian. Now, it is the very character and mark of all

unchristian education, that it brings up the child for future conversion. No effort is made, save to form a habit of outward virtue, and, if God please to convert the family to something higher and better, after they come to the age of maturity, it is well. Is then Christian education, or the nurture of the Lord, no way different from this? Or is it rather to be supposed that it will have a higher aim and a more sacred character?

And, since it is the distinction of Christian parents, that they are themselves in the nurture of the Lord, since Christ and the Divine Love, communicated through him, are become the food of their life, what will they so naturally seek as to have their children partakers with them, heirs together with them, in the grace of life? I am well aware of the common impression that Christian education is sufficiently distinguished by the endeavor of Christian parents to teach their children the lessons of Scripture history, and the doctrines or dogmas of Scripture theology. But if they are given to understand, at the same time, that these lessons can be expected to produce no fruit till they are come to a mature age—that they are to grow up still in the same character as other children do, who have no such instruction —what is this but to enforce the practical rejection of all the lessons taught them? And which, in truth, is better for them, to grow up in sin under Scripture light, with a heart hardened by so many religious lessons; or to grow up in sin, unvexed and unannoyed by the wearisome drill of lectures that only discourage all practical benefit? Which is better, to be piously brought up in sin, or to be allowed quietly to vegetate in it?

These are questions that I know not how to decide; but the doubt in which they leave us will at least suffice to show that Christian education has, in this view, no such eminent advantages over that which is unchristian, as to raise any broad and dignified distinction between them. We certainly know that much of what is called Christian nurture, only serves to make the subject of religion odious, and that, as nearly as we can discover, in exact proportion to the amount of religious teaching received. And no small share of the difficulty to be overcome afterwards in the struggle of conversion, is created in just this way.

On the other hand, you will hear, for example, of cases like the following: A young man, correctly but not religiously brought up, light and gay in his manners, and thoughtless hitherto in regard to any thing of a serious nature, happens accidentally one Sunday, while his friends are gone to ride, to take down a book on the evidences of Christianity. His eye, floating over one of the pages, becomes fixed, and he is surprised to find his feelings flowing out strangely into its holy truths. He is conscious of no struggle of hostility, but a new joy dawns in his being. Henceforth, to the end of a long and useful life, he is a Christian man. The love into which he was surprised

197

continues to flow, and he is remarkable, in the churches, all his life long, as one of the most beautiful, healthful, and dignified examples of Christian piety. Now, a very little miseducation, called Christian, discouraging the piety it teaches, and making enmity itself a necessary ingredient in the struggle of conversion, conversion no reality without a struggle, might have sufficed to close the mind of this man against every thought of religion to the end of life.

Such facts . . . compel us to suspect the value of much that is called Christian education. They suggest the possibility also that Christian piety should begin in other and milder forms of exercise than those which commonly distinguish the conversion of adults; that Christ himself, by that renewing Spirit who can sanctify from the womb, should be practically infused into the childish mind; in other words, that the house, having a domestic Spirit of grace dwelling in it, should become the church of childhood, the table and hearth a holy rite, and life an element of saving power. . . .

3. It is a fact that all Christian parents would like to see their children grow up in piety; and the better Christians they are, the more earnestly they desire it, and, the more lovely and constant the Christian spirit they manifest, the more likely it is, in general, that their children will early display the Christian character. This is current opinion. But why should a Christian parent, the deeper his piety and the more closely he is drawn to God, be led to desire, the more earnestly, what, in God's view, is even absurd or impossible? And, if it be generally seen that the children of such are more likely to become Christians early, what forbids the hope that, if they were riper still in their piety, living a more single and Christ-like life, and more cultivated in their views of family nurture, they might see their children grow up always in piety towards God? Or, if they may not always see it as clearly as they desire, might they not still be able to implant some holy principle, which shall be the seed of a Christian character in their children, though not developed fully and visibly till a later period in life?

4. Assuming the corruption of human nature, when should we think it wisest to undertake or expect a remedy? When evil is young and pliant to good, or when it is confirmed by years of sinful habit? And when, in fact, is the human heart found to be so ductile to the motives of religion, as in the simple, ingenuous age of childhood? How easy is it then, as compared with the stubbornness of adult years, to make all wrong seem odious, all good lovely and desirable. . . .

He can not understand, of course, in the earliest stage of childhood, the philosophy of religion as a renovated experience, and that is not the form of the first lessons he is to receive. He is not to be told that he must have a new heart and exercise faith in Christ's atonement. We are to understand that a right spirit may be virtually exercised in children, when, as yet, it is not intellectually received, or as, a form of doctrine. . . . The operative truth necessary to a new life may possibly be communicated through and from the parent, being revealed in his looks, manners, and ways of life, before they are of an age to understand the teaching of words, for the Christian scheme, the gospel, is really wrapped up in the life of every Christian parent, and beams out from him as a living epistle, before it escapes from the lips or is taught in words. And the Spirit of truth may as well make this living truth effectual as the preaching of the gospel itself.

Never is it too early for good to be communicated. Infancy and childhood are the ages most pliant to good. And who can think it necessary that the plastic nature of childhood must first be hardened into stone, and stiffened into enmity towards God and all duty, before it can become a candidate for Christian character! There could not be a more unnecessary mistake, and it is as unnatural and pernicious, I fear, as it is unnecessary.

There are many who assume the radical goodness of human nature, and the work of Christian education is, in their view, only to educate or educe the good that is in us. Let no one be disturbed by the suspicion of a coincidence between what I have here said and such a theory. The natural pravity of man is plainly asserted in the Scriptures, and, if it were not, the familiar laws of physiology would require us to believe what amounts to the same thing. And if neither Scripture nor physiology taught us the doctrine, if the child was born as clear of natural prejudice or damage as Adam before his sin, spiritual education, or, what is the same, probation, that which trains a being for a stable, intelligent virtue hereafter, would still involve an experiment of evil, therefore a fall and a bondage under the laws of evil; so that, view the matter as we will, there is no so unreasonable assumption, none so wide of all just philosophy, as that which proposes to form a child to virtue, by simply educing or drawing out what is in him.

The growth of Christian virtue is no vegetable process, no mere onward development. It involves a struggle with evil, a fall and a rescue. The soul becomes established in holy virtue, as a free exercise, only as it is passed round the corner of fall and redemption, ascending thus unto God through a double experience, in which it learns the bitterness of evil and the worth of good, fighting its way out of one, and achieving the other as a victory. The child, therefore, may as well begin life under a law of hereditary damage, as to plunge himself into evil by his own experiment, which he will as naturally do from the simple impulse of curiosity, or the instinct of knowledge, as from any noxious quality in his mold derived by descent. For it is not sin which he derives from his parents; at least, not sin in any sense which imports blame, but only some prejudice to the perfect harmony of this mold, some kind of pravity or obliquity which inclines him to evil. These suggestions are offered, not as necessary to be received in every particular, but simply to show that the scheme of education proposed is not to be identified with another, which assumes the radical goodness of human nature, and according to which, if it be true, Christian education is insignificant.

5. It is implied in all our religious philosophy, that if a child ever does any thing in a right spirit, ever loves any thing because it is good and right, it involves the dawn of a new life. This we can not deny or doubt without bringing in question our whole scheme of doctrine. Is it then incredible that some really good feeling should be called into exercise in a child? In all the discipline of the house, quickened as it should be by the Spirit of God, is it true that he can never once be brought to submit to parental authority lovingly and because it is right? Must we even hold the absurdity of the Scripture counsel—"Children obey your parents in the Lord, for this is right?" When we speak thus of a love for what is right and good, we must of course discriminate between the mere excitement of a natural sensibility to pleasure in the contemplation of what is good (of which the worst minds are more or less capable) and a practicable subordination of the soul to its power, a practicable embrace of its law. The child must not only be touched with some gentle emotions towards what is right, but he must love it with a fixed love, love it for the sake of its principle, receive it as a vital and formative power....

6. Children have been so trained as never to remember the time when they began to be religious. Baxter was, at one time, greatly troubled concerning himself, because he could recollect no time when there was a gracious change in his character. But he discovered, at length, that "education is as properly a means of grace as preaching," and thus found the sweeter comfort in his love to God, that he learned to love him so early. The European churches, generally, regard Christian piety more as a habit of life, formed under the training of childhood, and less as a marked spiritual change in experience. In Germany, for example, the church includes all the people, and it is remarkable that, under a scheme so loose, and with so much of pernicious error taught in the pulpit, there is yet so much of deep religious feeling, so much of lovely and simple character, and a savor of Christian piety so generally prevalent in the community. So true is this, that the German people are every day spoken of as a people religious by nature; no other way being observed of accounting for the strong religious bent they manifest. Whereas it is due, beyond any reasonable question, to the fact that children are placed under a form of treatment which expects

them to be religious, and are not discouraged by the demand of an experience above their years. . . .

Once more, if we narrowly examine the relation of parent and child, we shall not fail to discover something like a law of organic connection, as regards character, subsisting between them. Such a connection as makes it easy to believe, and natural to expect, that the faith of the one will be propagated in the other. Perhaps I should rather say, such a connection as induces the conviction that the character of one is actually included in that of the other, as a seed is formed in the capsule; and being there matured, by a nutriment derived from the stem, is gradually separated from it. It is a singular fact that many believe substantially the same thing in regard to evil character, but have no thought of any such possibility in regard to good. There has been much speculation, of late, as to whether a child is born in depravity, or whether the depraved character is superinduced afterwards. But, like many other great questions, it determines much less than is commonly supposed; for, according to the most proper view of the subject, a child is really not born till he emerges from the infantile state, and never before that time can he be said to receive a separate and properly individual nature.

The declarations of Scripture, and the laws of physiology, I have already intimated, compel the belief that a child's nature is somewhat depravated by descent from parents, who are under the corrupting effects of sin. But this, taken as a question relating to the mere *punctum temporis*, or precise point of birth, is not a question of any so grave import as is generally supposed; for the child, after birth, is still within the matrix of the parental life, and will be, more or less, for many years. And the parental life will be flowing into him all that time, just as naturally, and by a law as truly organic, as when the sap of the trunk flows into a limb. We must not govern our thoughts, in such a matter, by our eyes; and because the physical separation has taken place conclude that no organic relation remains. Even the physical being of the child is dependent still for many months, in the matter of nutrition, on organic processes not in itself. Meantime, the mental being and character have scarcely begun to have a proper individual life. Will, in connection with conscience, is the basis of personality or individuality, and these exist as yet only in their rudimental type, as when the form of a seed is beginning to be unfolded at the root of a flower.

At first the child is held as a mere passive lump in the arms, and he opens into conscious life under the soul of the parent streaming into his eyes and ears, through the manners and tones of the nursery. The kind and degree of passivity are gradually changed as life advances. A little farther on it is observed that a smile wakens a smile; any kind of sentiment or passion, playing in the face of the parent, wakens a responsive sentiment or passion.

201

Irritation irritates, a frown withers, love expands a look congenial to itself, and why not holy love? Next the ear is opened to the understanding of words, but what words the child shall hear, he can not choose, and has as little capacity to select the sentiments that are poured into his soul. Farther on, the parents begin to govern him by appeals to will, expressed in commands, and whatever their requirement may be, he can as little withstand it as the violet can cool the scorching sun, or the tattered leaf can tame the hurricane. Next they appoint his school, choose his books, regulate his company, decide what form of religion, and what religious opinions he shall be taught, by taking him to a church of their own selection. In all this they infringe upon no right of the child, they only fulfill an office which belongs to them. Their will and character are designed to be the matrix of the child's will and character. Meantime, he approaches more and more closely, and by a gradual process, to the proper rank and responsibility of an individual creature, during all which process of separation, he is having their exercises and ways translated into him. Then, at last, he comes forth to act his part in such color of evil, and why not of good, as he has derived from them.

The tendency of all our modern speculations is to an extreme individualism, and we carry our doctrines of free will so far as to make little or nothing of organic laws; not observing that character may be, to a great extent, only the free development of exercises previously wrought in us, or extended to us, when other wills had us within their sphere. We have much to say about the beginning of moral agency, and we seem to fancy that there is some definite moment when a child becomes a moral agent, passing out of a condition where he is a moral nullity, and where no moral agency touches his being. Whereas he is rather to be regarded, at the first, as lying within the moral agency of the parent, and passing out, by degrees, through a course of mixed agency, to a proper independency and self-possession. The supposition that he becomes, at some certain moment, a complete moral agent, which a moment before he was not, is clumsy and has no agreement with observation. The separation is gradual. He is never, at any moment after birth, to be regarded as perfectly beyond the sphere of good and bad exercises; for the parent exercises himself in the child, playing his emotions and sentiments, and working a character in him, by virtue of an organic power.

And this is the very idea of Christian education, that it begins with nurture or cultivation. And the intention is that the Christian life and spirit of the parents, which are in and by the Spirit of God, shall flow into the mind of the child, to blend with his incipient and half-formed exercises; that they shall thus beget their own good within him—their thoughts, opinions, faith, and love, which are to become a little more, and yet a little more, his own separate exercise, but still the same in character. . . .

All society is organic—the church, the state, the school, the family; and there is a spirit in each of these organisms, peculiar to itself and more or less hostile, more or less favorable to religious character, and to some extent, at least, sovereign over the individual man. A very great share of the power in what is called a revival of religion is organic power; nor is it any the less divine on that account. The child is only more within the power of organic laws than we all are. We possess only a mixed individuality all our life long. A pure, separate, individual man, living *wholly* within and from himself, is a mere fiction. No such person ever existed or ever can. I need not say that this view of an organic connection of character subsisting between parent and child lays a basis for notions of Christian education far different from those which now prevail, under the cover of a merely fictitious and mischievous individualism.

Perhaps it may be necessary to add, that, in the strong language I have used concerning the organic connection of character between the parent and the child, it is not designed to assert a power in the parent to renew the child, or that the child can be renewed by any agency of the Spirit less immediate than that which renews the parent himself. When a germ is formed on the stem of any plant, the formative instinct of the plant may be said in one view to produce it; but the same solar heat which quickens the plant must quicken also the germ and sustain the internal action of growth by a common presence in both. So, if there be an organic power of character in the parent, such as that of which I have spoken, it is not a complete power in itself, but only such a power as demands the realizing presence of the Spirit of God, both in the parent and the child, to give it effect. As Paul said, "I have begotten you through the gospel," so may we say of the parent, who, having a living gospel enveloped in his life, brings it into organic connection with the soul of childhood. But the declaration excludes the necessity of a divine influence, not more in one case than in the other.

Such are some of the considerations that offer themselves, viewing our subject on the human side, or as it appears in the light of human evidence— all concurring to produce the conviction that it is the only true idea of Christian education that the child is to grow up in the life of the parent and be a Christian in principle from his earliest years.

8

Preaching on Slavery
Hubert Vance Taylor

The issue was slavery. Strategists plotted pulpit silence to insure both ecclesiastical and political peace, but competing spokesmen sought biblical arguments and stubbornly voiced them in sermons, church courts, and journals. For Protestants, both North and South, Christian duty was prescribed by the Bible. If scripture sanctioned slavery the planter should extend and perpetuate his peculiar institution; if scripture condemned slavery, advocates of immediate emancipation were duty bound to halt the extension of slavery and persuade planters to set their captives free. Pro-slavery advocates erected elaborate and systematic scriptural defenses—perhaps the most elaborate and systematic of all its arguments; abolitionism had religious roots and employed religious methods and appeals. Thus entangled in the issue, the American churches contributed spokesmen.

Prior to 1820, American Protestants officially sought emancipation. The Methodist General Conference of 1784 proscribed slaveholding and the Presbyterian General Assembly of 1818 ruled slavery inconsistent with God's law. But the invention of the cotton gin had begun rapid expansion of the cotton kingdom, firm establishment of the plantation system, and stimulation of the domestic slave trade. Sectional tensions were voiced in the debates leading to the 1820 Missouri Compromise. That decision limited the extension of slavery and the South developed an aggressive minority stance within the next decade. Although as late as 1826, of 143 emancipation societies in the nation 103 were in the South, preachers opposed slavery there with mounting difficulty and many deserted the South. Before 1830, slavery was defended as a positive good in the South and traditional Protestant opposition to it was challenged.

When, in 1831, Garrison's call for immediate emancipation was followed by the Southampton slave insurrection and the Virginia decision to maintain slavery, the South strengthened slave codes and closed her borders to abolitionists. In 1833, the immediatists formed the American Anti-Slavery Society that declared slaveholding sin, flooded the South with pamphlets calling slaveholders to repentence, organized revivals in the North to recruit crusading emancipationists, attempted to win denominational adoption of their doctrine and church court enforcement of it. Southern preachers rejected their doctrine, searched for scriptural refutation of it, and sought silence on the slavery issue in national denominational meetings. They argued that slavery was a civil, not a church, matter.

Church schisms followed these struggles: Presbyterians formed two separate bodies in 1838; Methodists and Baptists divided into sectional groups in 1844 and 1845, respectively. Methodist abolitionists unsuccessfully sought restoration of the Rule of Discipline proscribing slaveholding in 1840, and then pro-slavery forces demanded the election of a slaveholding bishop in 1844. When their demand was rejected, the southern members formed a sectional church. Baptists split over refusal of their missionary agency to appoint slaveholders for foreign service. Moderates had sought compromises that would restore peace and maintain national churches, but once sectional churches were established, antithetical sectional positions were propagated without the benefit of clash in national church deliberative assemblies.

New England was the center of abolitionist activity. Garrison circulated his *Liberator* from Boston, where reform sentiment flourished. At Harvard Divinity School, in 1834, were two young preachers who would soon be heard on this slavey issue: Theodore Parker and James H. Thornwell. Alienated by the social and intellectual climate, after only one summer of study, Thornwell returned to South Carolina. Parker completed his study, participated in the Boston ferment, and accepted the abolitionists' philosophical and theological stance. When he first preached on slavery in 1841, he exposed their fully developed doctrine—a doctrine developed in the speeches and sermons of the preceding decade. His address, "A Sermon of Slavery," presented here, vehemently proclaims intolerance for slavery.

Thornwell's South Carolina was the center of proslavery activity. In Washington her senator, John C. Calhoun, was the planters' militant spokesman. He first sought silence on slavery by arguing that Congress lacked power to interfere with state institutions. Later he argued that Congress lacked power to exclude slavery from new territories. Shortly before his death, in the debate on the 1850 compromise, he deplored congressional efforts to limit the expansion of slavery. Shortly after Calhoun's death Thornwell, influential professor at South Carolina College exposed the fully developed theological justification of slavery in his sermon at Charleston. Here were the convictions that enabled planters to view the expanding cotton kingdom as a good land. That sermon, "Rights and Duties of Masters" is presented in this volume.

The nation now moved rapidly toward the war of 1861. The Kansas-Nebraska Act of 1854 removed the 1820 geographical barrier erected against slavery's expansion. Persuaded that slavery was a local rather than a national issue, legislators turned Kansas into a bloody battleground. The Dred Scott decision of 1857 seemed to remove the issue from even local debate, for it denied territorial or state governments power to outlaw slavery. Lincoln now charged slavery forces with conspiracy to make slavery national and perpetual. No longer could he be silent. The nation must not be indifferent to such a moral question. In 1858, his speeches rang with the prophetic indignation articulated by abolitionists in the thirties, echoed and developed by men like Parker and Henry Ward Beecher during the succeeding two decades. The expansion of evil slavery must be halted, he cried. In 1860, the nation elected him President.

Southern congregations in 1860 were challenged to perpetuate and extend slavery as a Christian duty. Thornwell now justified the political concepts of the Confederacy while William Swan Plumer, in his New Orleans sermon on Thanksgiving Day, restated the biblical justification for slavery: A divine providence entrusted the South with her unique institution. Christian duty seemed to demand antithetical postures in different parts of the nation. Presbyterians in the South, forming their sectional denomination in 1861, addressed to the churches of the Christian world a statement justifying slavery.

Time had made ancient good uncouth. In four decades, new understanding of God's will had so dominated American minds that men sought solutions in pitched battle rather than in parliamentary debate. Demands for peace in church courts had silenced debate of the nation's dominant issue there. Denied opportunity to meet argument with argument, appeal with appeal, unable to test biblical interpretation against biblical interpretation, actually denied freedom of speech and discussion, American Christians played a major role in the greatest tragedy of our history. Sectional preachers sanctioned opposite positions in sermons. Scripture sanctioned slavery for the planter but condemned it for the abolitionist. Regardless of the circumstances that apparently justified their decisions, failure to maintain open communication between Christian brothers and to insist upon continuing debate within Christian fellowship must be seen as an early failure with serious consequences in the developing tragedy. When deliberative speech was silenced in national forums, sermons became demonstrative and served to harden antithetical positions rather than to search for alternative solutions.

THEODORE PARKER

Theodore Parker was born in Lexington, Massachusetts, in 1810 and died in Florence, Italy, in 1860. He was a Unitarian clergyman, theologian, and author. He was graduated from Harvard Divinity School in 1836, ordained at the West Roxbury, Massachusetts, Church in 1837, and served the 28th Congregational Society of Boston from 1845 until his death.

Parker articulated a new radical theology that rated Christianity as man's highest experience of God. For knowledge of God he depended upon the immanence of God in nature and human experience, rather than upon supernatural revelation. From his pulpit in Boston's Music Hall, through wide-ranging lecture tours, and through the press, he promoted human welfare, for he defined the church as a union to cultivate love of God and man. Ignoring the demand of conservative and moderate churchmen for separation of political and church affairs, he boldly attacked social wrongs and political policies. Slavery felt the full force of his prophetic condemnation. For him God was infinitely perfect and his justice would be done. Therefore, not even the perpetuation of the Union was worth compromise with slavery. Webster's support of the 1850 Compromise was an offense, the 1854 Kansas-Nebraska Act was merely prelude to civil war, and John Brown's 1858 project received his aid as a means of inciting the inevitable conflict. Parker's influence upon political figures such as Sumner, Chase, and Lincoln has been acknowledged.

A Sermon of Slavery*

Know ye not that to whom ye yield yourselves servants to obey, his servants ye are whom ye obey; whether of sin unto death, or of obedience unto righteousness?—ROM. VI. 16.

In our version of the New Testament the word *servant* often stands for a word in the original, which means *slave*. Such is the case in this passage just read, and the sense of the whole verse is this:—"If a man yields unconditional service to sin, he is the *slave* of sin, and gets death for his reward." Here,

* *The Works of Theodore Parker*, ed. Francis Power Cobbe (London: Trubner and Company, 1843).

however, by a curious figure of speech, not uncommon in this apostle, he uses the word *slave* in a good sense—*slave* of obedience unto righteousness. I now ask your attention to a short sermon of slavery.

A popular definition has sometimes been given of common bodily slavery, that it is the holding of property in man. In a kindred language it is called body-property. In this case, a man's body becomes the possession, property, chattel, tool, or thing of another person, and not of the man who lives in it. This foreign person, of course, makes use of it to serve his own ends, without regard to the true welfare, or even the wishes, of the man who lives in that body, and to whom it rightfully belongs. Here the relation is necessarily that of force on one side and suffering on the other, though the force is often modified and the suffering sometimes disguised or kept out of sight.

Now man was made to be free, to govern himself, to be his own master, to have no cause stand between him and God, which shall curtail his birthright of freedom. He is never in his proper element until he attains this condition of freedom; of self-government. Of course, while we are children, not having reached the age of discretion, we must be under the authority of our parents and guardians, teachers, and friends. This is a natural relation. There is no slavery in it; no degradation. The parents, exercising rightful authority over their children, do not represent human caprice, but divine wisdom and love. They assume the direction of the child's actions, not to do themselves a service, but to benefit him. The father restrains his child, that the child may have more freedom, not less. Here the relation is not of force and suffering, but of love on both sides; of ability, which loves to help, and necessity, which loves to be directed. The child that is nurtured by its parent gains more than the parent does. So is it the duty of the wise, the good, the holy, to teach, direct, restrain the foolish, the wicked, the ungodly. If a man is wiser, better, and holier than I am, it is my duty, my privilege, my exaltation to obey him. For him to direct me in wisdom and love, not for his sake but for my own, is for me to be free. He may gain nothing by this, but I gain much.

As slavery was defined to be holding property in man, so freedom may be defined as a state in which the man does of his own consent, the best things he is capable of doing at that stage of his growth. Now there are two sorts of obstacles which prevent, or may prevent, man from attaining to this enviable condition of freedom. These are:—

I. Obstacles external to ourselves, which restrict our freedom; and

II. Obstacles internal to ourselves, which restrict our freedom.

A few words may be said on the condition to which men are brought by each of these classes of objects.

I. Of the slavery which arises from a cause external to ourselves. By the blessing of Providence, seconding the efforts, prayers, tears of some good men, there is no bodily, personal slavery sanctioned by the law amongst us in New England. But at the South we all know that some millions of our fellow-citizens are held in bondage; that men, women, and children are bought and sold in the shambles of the national capital; are owned as cattle; reared as cattle; beaten as cattle. We all know that our fathers fought through the War of Independence with these maxims in their mouths and blazoned on their banners: that all men are born free and equal, and that the God of eternal justice will at last avenge the cause of the oppressed, however strong the oppressor may be; yet it is just as well known that the sons of those very fathers now trade in human flesh, separating parent and child, and husband and wife, for the sake of a little gain; that the sons of those fathers eat bread not in the sweat of their own brow, but in that of the slave's face; that they are sustained, educated, rendered rich, and haughty, and luxurious by the labour they extort from men whom they have stolen, or purchased from the stealer, or inherited from the purchaser. It is known to you all, that there are some millions of these forlorn children of Adam, men whom the Declaration of Independence declares "born free and equal" with their master before God and the Law; men whom the Bible names "of the same blood" with the prophets and apostles; men "for whom Christ died," and who are "statues of God in ebony"—that they are held in this condition and made to feel the full burden of a corrupt society, and doomed from their birth to degradation and infamy, their very name a mock-word; their life a retreat, not a progress, —for the general and natural effect of slavery is to lessen the qualities of a man in the slave as he increases in stature or in years,—their children, their wives, their own bones and sinews at the mercy of a master! That these things are so, is known to all of us; well known from our childhood.

Every man who has ever thought at all on any subject, and has at the same time a particle of manhood in him, knows that this state of slavery would be to him worse than a thousand deaths; that set death in one scale, and hopeless slavery for himself and children in the other, he would not hesitate in his choice, but would say, "Give me death, though the life be ground out of me with the most exquisite tortures of lingering agony that malice can invent or tyranny inflict." To the African thus made the victim of American cupidity and crime, the state of slavery, it will be said, may not appear so degrading as to you and me, for he has never before been civilized, and though the un-taught instinct of man bid him love freedom, yet Christianity has not re-vealed to him the truth, that all men are brothers before God, born with equal rights. But this fact is no excuse or extenuation of our crime. Who would justify a knave in plundering a little girl out of a fortune that she in-herited, on the ground that she was a little girl "of tender years," and had never enjoyed or even beheld her birthright? The fact, that the injured party was ignorant and weak, would only enhance and aggravate the offence, adding new baseness and the suspicion of cowardice to guilt. If the African be so low, that the condition of slavery is tolerable in his eyes, and he can dance in his chains—happy in the absence of the whip—it is all the more a sin, in the cultivated and the strong, in the Christian(!) to tyrannize over the feeble and defenceless. Men at the South with the Bible in one hand—with the Declaration of Independence in the other hand—with the words of Jesus, "Love your neighbour as yourself," pealing upon them from all quarters, attempt to justify slavery; not to excuse, to cloak, or conceal the thing, but to vindicate and defend it. This attempt, when made by reflecting men in their cool moments, discovers a greater degree of blackness of heart than the kidnapping of men itself. It is premeditated wickedness grown conscious of itself. The plain truth of the matter is this:—Men who wish for wealth and luxury, but hate the toil and sweat, which are their natural price, brought the African to America; they make his chains; they live by his tears; they dance to the piping of his groans; they fatten on his sweat and are pampered by his blood. If these men spoke as plainly as they must needs think, they would say openly; "our sin captured these men on the African sands; our sin fettered them in slavery; and, please God, our sin shall keep them in slavery till the world ends." This has been thought long enough, it is high time it was said also, that we may know what we are about and where we stand.

Men at the North sometimes attempt to gloss the matter over, and hush it up by saying the least possible on the subject. They tell us that some masters are "excellent Christians." No doubt it is so, estimating these masters by the common run of Christians,—you find such on the deck of pirate ships; in the dens of robbers. But suppose some slaveholders are as good Christians as Fenelon or St Peter; still a sin is a sin, though a Christian commit it. Our fathers did not think "taxation without representation" any the less an evil because imposed by "his most Christian Majesty," a King of Christians.

Then, too, it is said, "the slaves are very happy, and it is a great pity to disturb them," that "the whole mass are better fed and clothed, and are troubled with fewer cares, than working men at the North." Suppose this true also, what then? Do you estimate your welfare in pounds of beef; in yards of cloth; in exemption from the cares of a man! If so all appeal to you is vain, your own soul has become servile. The Saviour of the world was worse fed and clothed, no doubt, than many a Georgian slave, and had not where to lay his head, wearied with many cares; but has your Christianity taught you that was an evil, and the slave's hutch at night, and pottage by day, and exemption from a man's cares by night and day, are a good, a good to be weighed against freedom! Then are you unworthy the soil you stand on; you

211

contaminate the air of New England, which free men died to transmit to their children free!

Still further it is said, "the sufferings of slaves are often exaggerated." This may be true. No doubt there have been exaggerations of particular cases. Every slave-owner is not a demon, not a base man. No doubt there are what are called good Christians, men that would be ornaments to a Christian church, among slaveholders. But though there have been exaggerations in details, yet the awful sum of misery, unspeakable wretchedness, which hangs over two millions of slaves is such that eye hath not seen it; nor ear heard it; nor heart conceived of it. It were so if all their masters were Christians in character, in action, still retaining slaves. How much deeper and wilder must swell that wide weltering sea of human agony, when the masters are what we know so many are, hard-hearted and rapacious, insolent and brutal!

This attempt to gloss the matter over and veil the fact, comes from two classes of men.

1. Some make the attempt from a real design to promote peace. They see no way to abate this mischief; they see "the folly and extravagance" of such as propose "dangerous measures," and therefore they would have us say nothing about it. The writhing patient is very sick; the leech more venturesome than skilful; and the friends, fearful to try the remedy, unwilling to summon wiser advice, declare the sick man is well as ever if you will only let him alone! These men mourn that any one should hold another in bondage; they think our fathers were illustrious heroes, for fighting dreadful wars with the parent country rather than pay a little tax against their will, but that this evil of slavery can never be healed; therefore, in the benevolence of their heart, they refuse to believe all the stories of suffering that reach their ears. The imagination of a kind man recoils at the thought of so much wretchedness; still more, if convinced that it cannot be abated. Now these men are governed by the best of motives, but it does not follow that their opinions are so just as their motives are good.

2. But there are others, who are willing to countenance the sin and continue it, well knowing that it is a sin. They would not have it abated. They tell you of the stupidity of the African; that he is made for nothing but a slave; is allied to the baboon and the ape, and is as much in his place when fettered, ignorant and savage, in a rice field, to toil under a taskmaster's whip, as a New Englander, free and educated, is in his place, when felling forests, planning railroads, or "conducting" a steam-engine. Hard treatment and poor fare, say they, are the black man's due. Besides, they add, there is a natural antipathy between the black race and the white, which only the love of money, or the love of power, on the part of the white is capable of overcoming; that the blacks are an inferior race, and therefore the white Saxons

are justified in making them slaves. They think the strong have a right to the services of the weak, forgetting that the rule of reason, the rule of Christianity, is just the other way; "We that are strong ought to bear the infirmities of the weak." They would have us follow the old rule, "that they should get who have the power, and they should keep who can." Of this class nothing further need be said save this: that they are very numerous, and quote the New Testament in support of slavery, thus contriving to pass for Christians, and have made such a stir in the land that it is scarce safe to open one's mouth and strip the veil from off this sin. . . .

The opinion of good and religious men here amongst us seems to be, that slavery is a great sin and ought to be abolished as soon as possible; that the talent and piety of the nation cannot be better employed than in devising the speediest and most effectual way of exterminating the evil. Such of them as see a way to abolish the wrong cry aloud and publish the tidings; others who see no way state that fact also, not failing to express their dread of all violent measures. Such is the conviction of good and religious men at the North. But there is another opinion a little different, which is held by a different class of men at the North;—they think that slavery is a great sin, and ought to be kept up so long as men can make money by it. But if the suppression of slavery could be effected—not as our fathers won their freedom, by blood and war—so gently as not to ruffle a sleeping baby's eyelid, yet if it diminished the crop of rice, or cotton, or tobacco, or corn, a single quintal a year, it would be a great mistake to free, cultivate, Christianize, and bless these millions of men! No one, I take it, will doubt this is a quite common opinion here in New England. The cause of this opinion will presently be touched upon. To show what baseness was implied in holding such opinions, would be simply a waste of time.

We all know there is at the North a small body of men, called by various names, and treated with various marks of disrespect, who are zealously striving to procure the liberation of slaves, in a peaceable and quiet way. They are willing to make any sacrifice for this end. They start from the maxim, that slavery is sin, and that sin is to be abandoned at once, and for ever, come what will come of it. These men, it is said, are sometimes extravagant in their speech; they do not treat the "patriarchal institution" with becoming reverence; they call slave-holders hard names, and appeal to all who have a heart in their bosoms, and to some who find none there, to join them and end the patriarchal institution by wise and Christian measures. What wonder is it that these men sometimes grow warm in their arguments! What wonder that their heart burns when they think of so many women exposed to contamination and nameless abuse; of so many children reared like beasts, and sold as oxen; of so many men owning no property in their hands, or their feet, their hearts, or their lives! The wonder is all the other side, that they do not go to further extremities, sinful as it might be, and like St. John in his youth, pray for fire to come down from heaven and burn up the sinners, or like Paul, when he had not the excuse of youthful blood, ask God to curse them. Yet they do none of these things; never think of an appeal to the strong arm, but the Christian heart. . . . There is no doubt that these men are sometimes extravagant! There need be no wonder at that fact. The best of men have their infirmities, but if this extravagance be one of them, what shall we call the deadness of so many more amongst us? An infirmity? What shall we say of the sin itself? An infirmity also? Honest souls engaged in a good work, fired with a great idea, sometimes forget the settled decorum of speech, commonly observed in forum and pulpit, and call sin SIN. If the New Testament tell truth, Paul did so, and it was thought he would "turn the world upside down," while he was only striving to set it right. John the Baptist and Jesus of Nazareth did the same thing, and though one left his head in a charger, and the other his body on a cross, yet the world thinks at this day they did God's great work with their sincerity of speech.

The men who move in this matter encounter opposition from two classes of men; from the moderate, who do not see the wisdom of their measures, and who fear that the slave if set free will be worse off than before, or who think that the welfare of the masters is not sufficiently cared for. These moderate men think "we had better not meddle with the matter at present," but by and by, at a convenient season, they will venture to look into it. . . .

Then too they encounter opposition from the selfish, who see, or think they see, that the white masters will lose some thousands of millions of dollars, if slavery be abolished! Who has forgotten the men that opposed the introduction of Christianity at Ephesus,—the craftsmen that made silver shrines for Diana!

I know some men say, "we have nothing to do with it. Slavery is the affair of the slave-owners and the slaves, not yours and mine. Let them abate it when they will." A most unchristian saying is this. Slavery! we have something to do with it. The sugar and rice we eat, the cotton we wear, are the work of the slave. His wrongs are imported to us in these things. We eat his flesh and drink his blood. I need not speak of our political connection with slavery. You all know what that is, and its effect on us here. But socially, individually, we are brought into contact with it every day. If there is a crime in the land known to us, and we do not protest against it to the extent of our ability, we are partners of that crime. It is not many years since it was said, temperate men had nothing to do with the sin of drunkenness; though they paid for it out of their purse! When they looked they found they had much to do with it, and sought to end it. . . .

Such then is slavery at the South; such the action of men at the North to attack or to defend it. But look a moment at the cause of this sin, and of its defence. It comes from the desire to get gain, comfort, or luxury; to have power over matter, without working or paying the honest price of that gain, comfort, luxury, and power; it is the spirit which would knowingly and of set purpose injure another for the sake of gaining some benefit to yourself. Such a spirit would hold slaves everywhere, if it were possible. Now when the question is put to any fair man,—Is not this spirit active at the North as well as the South? there is but one answer. The man who would use his fellow-man as a tool merely, and injure him by that use; who would force another in any way to bend to his caprice; who would take advantage of his ignorance, his credulity, his superstition, or his poverty, to enrich and comfort himself; in a word, who would use his neighbour to his neighbour's hurt,—that man has the spirit of slave-holding, and were circumstances but different, he would chain his brethren with iron bonds. If you, for your own sake, would unjustly put any man in a position which degrades him in your eyes, in his own eyes, in the eyes of his fellow-men, you have the spirit of the slave-holder. There is much of this spirit with us still. . . . Doubtless we have still social institutions which eyes more Christian than ours shall one day look upon as evils, only less than that of slavery itself. But it is gradually that we gain light; he that converts it to life as fast as it comes, does well.

II. Let a word be said on the other kind of slavery; that which comes from a cause internal to ourselves. This is common at the North, and South, and East, and West. In this case the man is prevented from doing what is best for him, not by some other man who has bound him, but by some passion or prejudice, superstition or sin. Here the mischief is in his own heart. If you look around you, you find many that bear the mark of the beast; branded on the forehead and the right hand; branded as slaves. "He that committeth sin is the slave of sin." The avaricious man is a slave. He cannot think a thought but as his master bids. He cannot see a truth if a dollar intervene. He cannot relieve the poor, nor sympathize with the distressed, nor yield to the humane impulse of his natural heart. If he sees in the newspaper a sentence on the wastefulness or the idleness of the poor, he remembers it for ever; but a word in the Bible to encourage charity,—he never finds that.

The passionate man is a slave; he lies at the mercy of the accidents of a day. If his affairs go well he is calm and peaceful; but if some little mistake arise he is filled with confusion, and the demon that rules him draws the chain. This master has many a slave under his yoke. He is more cruel than any planter in Cuba or Trinidad. He not only separates friend from friend, parent from child, and husband from wife, but what is worse yet, prevents their loving one another while they are together. This makes man a tyrant, not a husband; woman a fiend, not an angel, as God made her to be. This renders marriage a necessary evil, and housekeeping a perpetual curse, for it takes the little trifles which happen everywhere, except between angels, and makes them very great matters; it converts mistakes into faults, accidents into vices, errors into crimes; and so rends asunder the peace of families, and in a single twelvemonth disturbs more marriages than all the slave-holders of Carolina in a century.

So the peevish man is a slave. His ill humour watches him like a demon. Ofttimes it casteth him into the fire, and often into the water. In the morning he complains that his caprice is not complied with; in the evening that it is. He is never peaceful except when angry; never quiet but in a storm. He is free to do nothing good; so he acts badly, thinks badly, feels badly,—three attributes of a devil. A yoke of iron and fetters of brass were grievous to bear, no doubt; the whip of a task-master makes wounds in the flesh; but God save us from the tyranny of the peevish, both what they inflict and what they suffer.

The intemperate man also is a slave; one most totally subjugated. His vice exposes him to the contempt and insult of base men, as well as to the pity of the good. Not only this, but his master strips him of his understanding; takes away his common sense, conscience, his reason, religion,—qualities that make a man differ from a beast; on his garments, his face, his wife and child, is written in great staring letters, so that he may read that runs—This man also has sold his birthright and become a slave. . . .

Bodily slavery is one of the greatest wrongs that man can inflict on man; an evil not to be measured by the external and visible woe which it entails on the victim, but by the deep internal ruin which it is its direct tendency to produce. If I had the tongue of the Archangel I could not give utterance to the awfulness of this evil. There is no danger that this be exaggerated,—no more than that the sun in a picture be painted too bright. . . .

I know men say that you and I ought not to move in this matter; that we have nothing to do with it. They urge in argument that the Constitution of the United States is the supreme law of the land, and that sanctions slavery. But it is the supreme law made by the voters, like the statutes denouncing capital punishment. What voters have made can voters unmake. There is no supreme law but that made by God; if our laws contradict that, the sooner they end or the sooner they are broken, why, the better. It seems to be thought a very great thing to run counter to a law of man, written on parchment; a very little thing to run counter to the law of Almighty God, Judge of the quick and the dead. Has He sanctioned slavery? "Oh yes," say some, and cite Old Testament and New Testament in proof thereof. It has been said, "The devil can quote Scripture for his purpose." We need not settle that question now, but it is certain that men can quote it to support despotism when that is the order of the day,—or freedom when that is the "law of the land;" certain that men defend drunkenness and war, or sobriety and peace, out of its pages. A man finds what he looks for. . . .

Bodily slavery, though established by the powers that be, is completely in the hands of the voters, for they are the powers that be, is no more sanctioned by the supreme law of the land than stealing or murder. No enactment of man can make that right which was wrong before. It can never be abstractly right in any circumstances to do what is abstractly wrong.

But that other slavery, which comes from yourself, that is wholly within your power. And which, think you, is the worse, to be unwillingly the slave of a man and chained and whipped, or to be the voluntary slave of avarice, passion, peevishness, intemperance! It is better that your body be forcibly constrained, bought and sold, than that your soul, yourself, be held in thraldom. The spirit of a slave may be pure as an angel's; sometimes as lofty and as blessed too. The comforts of religion, when the heart once welcomes them, are as beautiful in a slave's cabin as in a king's court. When death shakes off the slave's body, the chain falls with it, and the man, disenthralled at last, goes where the wicked cease from troubling, where the weary are at rest, where the slave is free from his master; yes, where faithful use of the smallest talent and humblest opportunity has its reward, and unmerited suffering finds its ample recompense. But the voluntary slavery under sin— it has no bright side. None in life; in death no more. You may flee from a taskmaster, not from yourself.

Body-slavery is so bad that the sun might be pardoned if it turned back, refusing to shine on such a sin; on a land contaminated with its stain. But soul-slavery, what shall we say of that? Our fathers bought political freedom at a great price; they sailed the sea in storms; they dwelt here aliens on a hostile soil, the world's outcasts; in cold and hunger, in toil and want they dwelt here; they fought desperate wars in freedom's name! Yet they bought it cheap. You and I were base men, if we would not give much more than they paid, sooner than lose the inheritance.

But freedom for the soul to act right, think right, feel right, you cannot inherit; that you must win for yourself. Yet it is offered you at no great price. You may take it who will. It is the birthright of you and me and each of us; if we keep its conditions it is ours. Yet it is only to be had by the religious man—the man true to the nature God gave him. Without His Spirit in your heart you have no freedom. Resist His law, revealed in nature, in the later scripture of the Bible, in your own soul; resist it by sin, you are a slave, you must be a slave. Obey that law, you are Christ's freeman; nature and God are on your side. How strange it would be that one man should be found on all the hills of New England, of soul so base, of spirit so dastardly, that of his own consent took on him the yoke of slavery; went into the service of sin; toiled with that leprous host, in hopeless unrecompensed misery, without God, without heaven, without hope. Strange, indeed, that in this little village there should be men who care not for the soul's freedom, but consent to live, no, to die daily, in the service of sin.

James Henley Thornwell was born in Marlboro District, South Carolina, in 1812 and died in 1862. He was a Presbyterian clergyman, theologian, professor at South Carolina College from 1837 until 1851, and then president from 1851 until 1855. From 1855 until the year of his death he was professor at Columbia Theological Seminary.

During Thornwell's undergraduate days his South Carolina College experienced turbulent opposition to the liberalism of President Thomas Cooper. Theological study at both Andover Seminary and Harvard Divinity School in 1834 led Thornwell to reject the liberal Massachsuetts intellectual climate, and he returned to Carolina without completing his formal theological study. Soon his orthodox theology and effective preaching secured election to a professorship in his alma mater. Combining rigorous logic and emotional fervor he gained greater fame as preacher and controversialist than as educator. Such fame and influence was extended through the Southern Presbyterian Review *that he founded in 1847.*

As a churchman Thornwell attended ten Presbyterian general assemblies between 1837 and 1860, and was elected moderator of that court in 1847. When the Presbyterian Church in the Confederate States of America was organized in 1861, he wrote its address that justified the pro-slavery doctrine before the churches of the world.

A major Southern ploy secured pulpit silence on slavery through insistence that civil matters were no concern of the church. After 1833, Southern preachers seldom discussed slavery, for it was regulated by civil law. When this silence was broken the sermons were usually of special significance. Thornwell preached his Charleston sermon entitled "The Rights and Duties of Masters" soon after the death of John C. Calhoun, in the middle of the Congressional debates that led to the 1850 Compromise. Again he broke the silence in 1860, when South Carolina proclaimed a Fast Day amidst legislative preparations for secession from the Union. The timing of these pulpit statements by a spokesman revered in Southern civil and church circles is significant.

The Rights and the Duties of Masters*

(The following Sermon was preached on Sunday evening, May 26, 1850, before a large assembly of intelligent and respectable citizens of Charleston, at

*(Charleston: Steam Power Press of Walker and James, 1850).

the dedication of a Church erected for the religious instruction of the Negroes. This building has been put up under the supervision of the Second Presbyterian Church. The congregation worshipping in it are under the ecclesiastical watch and control of the Session of that Church, into which will be received all those who may become Church members. There is, therefore, no separate ecclesiastical organization of this congregation. . . .

At the Sunday School connected with this Church, there are generally present about one hundred and eighty scholars, who are taught by the Minister and some twenty or thirty ladies and gentlemen. Their improvement in religious knowledge and orderly behaviour, during two years of instruction, is very manifest.

The Session of the Second Presbyterian Church, anxious that the profound and comprehensive views of Dr. THORNWELL, upon *the* question of our country and our day, should not be confined to those who heard his Discourse, have requested and obtained from him a copy for publication. It is, accordingly, now sent forth as another Scriptural exhibition of the Rights and the Duties of Masters.)

Masters, give unto your Servants that which is just and equal; knowing that ye also have a master in Heaven.—COLOSSIANS IV: 1.

God has not permitted such a remarkable phenomenon as the unanimity of the civilized world, in its execration of slavery, to take place without design. This great battle with the Abolitionists, has not been fought in vain. The muster of such immense forces—the fury and bitterness of the conflict—the disparity in resources of the parties in the war—the conspicuousness—the unexampled conspicuousness of the event, have all been ordered for wise and beneficent results; and when the smoke shall have rolled away, it will be seen that a real progress has been made in the practical solution of the problems which produced the collision. . . .

. . . Truth must triumph. God will vindicate the appointments of His Providence—and if our institutions are indeed consistent with righteousness and truth, we can calmly afford to bide our time—we can watch the storm which is beating furiously against us, without terror or dismay—we can receive the assault of the civilized world—trusting in Him who has all the elements at His command, and can save as easily by one as a thousand. . . . It is not the narrow question of abolitionism or of slavery—not simply whether we shall emancipate our negroes or not; the real question is the relations of man to society—of States to the individual, and of the individual to States; a question as broad as the interests of the human race.

These are the mighty questions which are shaking thrones to their centres —upheaving the masses like an earthquake, and rocking the solid pillars of this Union. The parties in this conflict are not merely abolitionists and slave-holders—they are atheists, socialists, communists, red republicans, jacobins, on the one side, and the friends of order and regulated freedom on the other. In one word, the world is the battle ground—Christianity and Atheism the combatants; and the progress of humanity the stake. One party seems to regard Society, with all its complicated interests, its divisions and sub-divisions, as the machinery of man—which, as it has been invented and ar-ranged by his ingenuity and skill, may be taken to pieces, re-constructed, altered or repaired, as experience shall indicate defects or confusion in the original plan. The other party beholds in it the ordinance of God; and con-templates "this little scene of human life," as placed in the middle of a scheme, whose beginnings must be traced to the unfathomable depths of the past, and whose development and completion must be sought in the still more unfathomable depths of the future—a scheme, as Butler expresses it, "not fixed, but progressive—every way incomprehensible"—in which, conse-quently, irregularity is the confession of our ignorance—disorder the proof of our blindness, and with which it is as awful temerity to tamper as to sport with the name of God....

The part accordingly, which is assigned to us in the tumult of the age, is the maintenance of the principles upon which the security of social order and the development of humanity depends, in their application to the dis-tinctive institutions which have provoked upon us the malediction of the world. The Apostle briefly sums up all that is incumbent, at the present crisis, upon the slaveholders of the South, in the words of the text—Masters, give unto your servants that which is just and equal, knowing that ye also have a Master in Heaven. It would be an useless waste of time to spend many words in proving, that the servants contemplated by the Apostle were slaves. Finding it impossible to deny that slavery, as an existing element of society, is actually sanctioned by Christ and His Apostles, those who would preserve some show of consistency in their veneration of the Scriptures, and their con-demnation of us, resolve the conduct of the founders of Christianity into motives of prudence and considerations of policy. While they admit that the letter of the Scriptures is distinctly and unambiguously in our favour, they maintain that their spirit is against us, and that our Saviour was content to leave the destruction of whatsoever was morally wrong in the social fabric, to the slow progress of changes in individual opinions, wrought by the silent influence of religion, rather than endanger the stability of governments by sudden and disastrous revolutions....

But it may be worth while to expose the confusion of ideas, from which this distinction, betwixt the letter and the spirit of the Gospel, has arisen, and which has been a source of serious perplexity, both to the defenders

221

and the enemies of slavery. . . . If it can be shown that slavery contravenes the spirit of the Gospel—that as a social relation it is essentially unfavourable to the cultivation and growth of the graces of the Spirit—that it is unfriendly to the development of piety and to communion with God—or that it retards the onward progress of man—that it hinders the march of society to its destined goal, and contradicts that supremacy of justice, which is the soul of the State, and the life-blood of freedom—if these propositions can be satisfactorily sustained, then it is self-condemned—religion and philanthropy alike require us to labour for its destruction, and every good man amongst us would feel bound to contribute to its removal; and even the voice of patriotism would demand that we should wipe from our country the foul reproach of standing in the way of the destined improvement of mankind.

The confusion upon this subject has arisen from a two-fold misapprehension—in relation to the nature of the slavery tolerated in the letter of the Scriptures, and the other in relation to the spirit of Christianity itself.

It is common to describe slavery as the property of man in man—as the destruction of all human and personal rights, the absorption of the humanity of one individual into the will and power of another. "The very idea of a slave," says Dr. Channing, "is that he belongs to another, that he is bound to live and labour for another, to be another's instrument, and to make another's will his habitual law, however adverse to his own." "We have thus," says he in another place, "established the reality and sacredness of human rights, and that slavery is an infraction of these, is too plain to need any laboured proof. Slavery violates not one but all, and violates them not incidentally, but necessarily, systematically, from its very nature." In other words, in every system of slavery, from the operation of its inherent and essential principles, the slave ceases to be a person—a man—and becomes a mere instrument or thing. Dr. Channing does not charge this result upon the relation as it obtains under particular codes, or at particular times, or in particular places. He says, distinctly and emphatically, that it violates all human rights, *not incidentally*, but *necessarily, systematically* from *its very nature*. It belongs to the very essence of slavery to divest its victims of humanity.

"Slavery," says Professor Whewell, "is contrary to the fundamental principles of morality. It neglects the great primary distinction of Persons and Things—converting a person into a thing, an object merely passive, without any recognized attributes of human nature. A slave is, in the eye of the State which stamps him with that character, not acknowledged as a man. His pleasures and pains, his wishes and desires, his needs and springs of action, his thoughts and feelings, are of no value whatever in the eye of the community. He is reduced to the level of the brutes. . . ."

222

If this be a just description of slavery, the wonder is, not that the civilized world is now indignant at its outrages and wrongs, but that it has been so slow in detecting its enormities, that mankind, for so many centuries, acquiesced in a system which contradicted every impulse of nature, every whisper of conscience, every dictate of religion—a system as monstrously unnatural as a general effort to walk upon the head or think with the feet. I have, however, no hesitation in saying, that whatever may be the technical language of the law, in relation to certain aspects in which slavery is contemplated, the ideas of personal rights and personal responsibility pervade the whole system. It is a relation of man to man—a form of civil society, for which persons are the only elements, and not a relation of man to things. Under the Roman code, in which more offensive language than that employed by ourselves was used in reference to the subject, the Apostles did not regard the personality of the slave, as lost or swallowed up in the propriety of the master. They treat him as a man—possessed of certain rights, which it was injustice to disregard, and make it the office of Christianity to protect these rights by the solemn sanctions of religion—to enforce upon masters the necessity, the moral obligation, of rendering to their bondmen that which is just and equal. Paul treats the services of slaves as *duties*—not like the toil of the ox or the ass—a labor extracted by the stringency of discipline—but a moral debt, in the payment of which they were rendering a homage to God. "Servants," says he, "be obedient to them that are your masters, according to the flesh, with fear and trembling, in singleness of your heart, as unto Christ; not with eye-service, as men-pleasers, but as the servants of Christ, doing the will of God from the heart; with good will doing service, as to the Lord, and not to men; knowing that whatever good thing any man doeth, the same shall he receive of the Lord, whether he be bond or free." I need not say to those who are acquainted with the very elements of moral philosophy, that obedience, except as a figured term, can never be applied to any but rational, intelligent, responsible agents. It is a voluntary homage to law—implies moral obligation, and a sense of duty, and can only, in the way of analogy, be affirmed of the instinctive submission of brutes, or the mechanical employment of instruments and things.

The apostle not merely recognizes the moral agency of slaves, in the phraseology which he uses, but treats them as possessed of conscience, reason and will—by the motives which he presses. He says to them in effect that their services to their masters are duties which they owe to God—that a moral character attaches to their works, and that they are the subjects of praise or blame according to the principles upon which their obedience is rendered. . . .

The state of things so graphically described and eloquently deplored by the great father of Unitarian Christianity in America, is a palpable impossibility. The constitution of the human mind is in flagrant contradiction to the absorption of the conscience, will, and understanding of one man into the personality of another—it is a thing which cannot be conceived—and if it ever could take place, the termination of all responsibility on the part of the slave would render it ridiculous to labour for his spiritual improvement, or attribute to him any other immortality, than that which Indian fables ascribe to the dog as the faithful companion of his master. And yet upon this absurdity, that slavery divests its victims of humanity—that it degrades them from the rank of responsible and voluntary agents to the condition of tools or brutes—the whole philosophical argument against the morality of the system, as an existing institution—is founded. . . . We grant most cheerfully, and we make an admission in no way inconsistent with Southern slavery, or the slavery sanctioned in the Bible, that though "the human soul may be lost, it cannot either be sold or be made a gift of to another—that conscience may be bound or may be slaughtered, but cannot be transferred to another's keeping—that moral responsibility, instead of being shifted entirely from one to another, or instead of being shared between two, each taking a half or a portion, is doubled, whenever it is attempted to be transferred, or to be deposited, or to be pawned."

The property of man in man—a fiction to which even the imagination cannot give consistency—is the miserable cant of those who would storm by prejudice what they cannot demolish by argument. We do not even pretend that the organs of the body can be said strictly to belong to another. The limbs and members of my servant are not mine, but his—they are not tools and instruments which I can sport with a pleasure, but the sacred possession of a human being, which cannot be invaded without the authority of law, and for the use of which he can never be divested of his responsibility to God.

If, then, slavery is not inconsistent with the existence of personal rights and of moral obligation, it may be asked in what does its peculiarity consist? What is it that makes a man a slave? We answer, the obligation to labour for another, determined by the Providence of God, independently of the provisions of a contract. The right which the master has is a right, not to the *man*, but to his *labour*; the duty which the slave owes is the service which, in conformity with this right, the master exacts. The essential difference betwixt free and slave-labour is, that one is rendered in consequence of a contract; the other is rendered in the consequence of a command. The labourers in each case are equally moral, equally responsible, equally men. But they work upon different principles. . . .

224

. . . The Providence of God marks out for the slave the precise services, in the lawful commands of the master, which it is the Divine will that he should render; the painful necessities of his case are often as stringent upon the free labourer, and determine, with as stern a mandate, what contracts he shall make. Neither can he be said to select his employments. God allots to each his portion—places one immediately under command—and leaves the other not unfrequently a petitioner for a master.

Whatever control the master has over the person of the slave, is subsidiary to this right to his labour; what he sells is not the man, but the property in his services—true he chastises the man, but the punishments inflicted for disobedience are no more inconsistent with personal responsibilities than the punishments inflicted by the law for breaches of contract. On the contrary, punishment in contradistinction from suffering, always implies responsibility, and a right which cannot be enforced, is a right, which society, as an organized community, has not yet acknowledged. The chastisements of slaves are accordingly no more entitled to awaken the indignation of loyal and faithful citizens—however pretended philanthropists may describe the horrors of the scourge and the lash—than the penalties of disgrace, imprisonment, or death, which all nations have inflicted upon crimes against the State. All that is necessary in any case, is that the punishment should be *just*. . . . It is not part of the essence of slavery, however, that the rights of the slave should be left to the caprice or to the interest of the master; and in the Southern States, provisions are actually made—whether adequate or inadequate it is useless here to discuss—to protect him from want, cruelty, and unlawful domination. Provisions are made which recognize the doctrine of the Apostle, that he is a subject of rights, and that justice must be rendered to his claims. . . .

This view of the subject exposes the confusion, which obtains in most popular treatises of morals, of slavery with involuntary servitude. The service, in so far as it consists in the motions of the limbs or organs of the body, must be voluntary, or it could not exist at all. If by voluntary be meant, however, that which results from hearty consent, and is accordingly rendered with cheerfulness, it is precisely the service which the law of God enjoins. Servants are exhorted to obey from considerations of duty; to make conscience of their tasks, with good will doing service, as to the Lord, and not to men. Whether, in point of fact, their service, in this sense, shall be voluntary, will depend upon their moral character. But the same may be said of free labour. There are other motives beside the lash that may drive men to toil, when they are far from toiling with cheerfulness or good will. . . .

There is a moral bondage, the most galling and degrading species of

225

servitude, in which he may be held, as with chains of brass, who scorns to call any man master on earth. Those who have most patiently studied the ends of government and the theory of political society, who are best prepared to solve the problems connected with the nature and extent of the individual restraints, which the security of public order demands—those who have most profoundly investigated the whole question of civil and political liberty, may yet be slaves. They may submit to the sway of a fiercer and more cruel tyrant than any despot who ever wielded a sceptre on earth. "Jesus answered them, Verily, verily I say unto you, whosoever committeth sin is the servant or slave of sin." There is a freedom which is the end and glory of man; the only freedom which the pen of inspiration has commended, and which, from its very nature, is independent of the decrees of kings, or the mandates of States. It is *the* freedom which God approves; which Jesus bought by his blood, and the Holy Spirit effectually seals by His grace; the liberty wherewith Christ has made us free. It consists essentially in the dominion of rectitude, in the emancipation of the will from the power of sin, the release of the affections from the attractions of earth, the exemption of the understanding from the deceits of prejudice and error. It is a freedom which the *truth* of God brings with it—a freedom enjoyed by the martyr at the stake, a slave in his chains, a prisoner in his dungeon, as well as the king upon his throne. Independent of time or place, or the accidents of fortune, it is the *breath* of the soul as regenerated and redeemed; and can no more be torn from us than the atmosphere of Heaven can be restrained. If the Son shall make you free, you shall be free indeed. . . . This freedom makes man truly a man; and it is precisely the assertion of this freedom—this dominion of rectitude—this supremacy of right, which the Apostle enjoins upon slaves—when he exhorts them to obey their masters in singleness of heart as unto Christ—to despise eye-service, but to do their work as in the eye of God. To obey under the influence of these motives, is to be slaves no longer. This is a *free* service—a service which God accepts as the loyal homage of the soul—and which proclaims them to be the Lord's freed-men, while they honour their masters on earth. Such slavery might be their glory—might fit them for thrones in the kingdom of God. So far was the Apostle, therefore, from regarding involuntary servitude as the characteristic of slavery, that he condemns such servitude as a sin. He treats it as something that is abject, mean, despicable; but insists on the other hand, that slavery dignifies and ennobles the servant, who obeys from the heart.

But while it may be admitted that slavery is not absolutely inconsistent with moral responsibility, nor the freedom of a moral agent, it may be asked whether the slave is not stripped of some of the rights which belong to him essentially as a man; and in this view, whether the relation is not incompatible with the spirit of the Gospel, which asserts and promotes the dignity and perfection of our race. In other words, whether there is not a limitation upon the moral freedom of the slave—whether his situation does not preclude him from discharging his *whole* duty as a man; and, therefore, whether the relation is not ultimately destructive of the full complement of human rights.

This question, it seems to me, comprises the whole moral difficulty of slavery; and it is at this point of the discussion, that the friends and enemies of the system are equally tempted to run into extravagance and excess; the one party denying the inestimable value of freedom; the other exaggerating the nature and extent of human rights, and both overlooking the real scope and purpose of the Gospel, in its relation to the present interests of man.

That the design of Christianity is to secure the perfection of the race, is obvious from all its arrangements; and that when this end shall have been consummated, slavery must cease to exist, is equally clear. This is only asserting that there will be no bondage in heaven. Among beings of the same nature, each relatively perfect, there can be no other inequalities than those which spring from superior endowments—the outward advantages of all must be of the same kind, though they may vary in degrees proportioned to the capacities of the individuals to enjoy them. If Adam had never sinned and brought death into the world, with all our woe, the bondage of man to man would never have been instituted; and when the effects of transgression shall have been purged from the earth, and the new heavens and the new earth, wherein dwelleth righteousness, given to the saints, all bondage shall be abolished. In this sense, slavery is inconsistent with the spirit of the Gospel, that it contemplates a state of things—an existing economy, which it is the design of the Gospel to remove. Slavery is a part of the curse which sin has introduced into the world, and stands in the same general relations to Christianity as poverty, sickness, disease or death. In other words, it is a relation which can only be conceived as taking place among fallen beings—tainted with a curse. It springs not from the nature of man as man, nor from the nature of society as such, but from the nature of man as sinful, and the nature of society as disordered.

Upon an earth radiant with the smile of heaven, or in the Paradise of God, we can no more picture the figure of a slave than we can picture the figures of the halt, the maimed, the lame and the blind; we can no more fancy the existence of masters and tasks than we can dream of hospitals and beggars. These are the badges of a fallen world. That it is inconsistent with a perfect state—that it is not absolutely a good—a blessing—the most

227

strenuous defender of slavery ought not to permit himself to deny; and the devout believer in Revelation would be made to close his eyes to the fact, that the form in which it is first threatened, in the Bible, is as a punishment for crime. . . . When we consider the diversities in moral position, which sin has been the means of entailing upon the race, we may be justified in affirming, that, relatively to some persons and to some times, slavery may be a good, or to speak more accurately, a condition, though founded in a curse, from which the Providence of God extracts a blessing. We are not to judge of the institutions of the present, by the standard of the future life—we are not to confound the absolute and relative. For aught that we know slavery may stand in somewhat the same relation to political society, in a world like ours, in which mortality stands to the human body; and it may be as vain to think of extirpating it, as to think of giving man immortality upon earth. It may be, and perhaps is, in some of its forms, essential to an imperfect society; and it may be, and perhaps is, the purpose of God that it should be found among men, as long as the slime of the serpent is over the earth. Admit, then, that slavery is inconsistent with the spirit of the Gospel, as that spirit is to find its full development in a state of glory—yet the conclusion by no means follows, that it is inconsistent with the spirit of the Gospel, as that spirit operates among rebels and sinners, in a degraded world, and under a dispensation of grace. The real question is, whether it is incompatible with the spiritual prosperity of individuals, or the general progress and education of society. It is clearly the office of the Gospel to train men, by virtue of the discipline of temptation, hardship and evil, for a state of perfection and glory. Nothing is inconsistent with it which does not present obstacles to the practice of duty, which its own grace is inadequate to surmount. Whoever, therefore, would maintain that slavery is incompatible with the present relations of the Gospel to man, must maintain that it precludes him, by its very nature, from the discharge of some of the duties which the Gospel enjoins. It is nothing to the purpose to speak of it generally and vaguely as an evil—it must be shown to be an evil of that specifick kind which necessitates the commission of sin, and the neglect of duty. Neither is it sufficient to say that it presents strong temptations to sin, in the violent motives which a master may press upon a slave, to execute unlawful commands. This can be affirmed of numberless other situations, in which none will contend that it is unlawful to be found. The question is—not whether it is the state most favourable to the offices of piety and virtue—but whether it is essentially incompatible with their exercise. This is the true issue.

The fundamental mistake of those who affirm slavery to be essentially sinful, is that the duties of all men are specifically the same. . . . The argument, fully and legitimately carried out, would condemn every arrangement of society, which did not secure to all its members an absolute equality of position; it is the very spirit of socialism and communism.

The doctrine of the Bible, on the other hand, is that the specifick duties —the things actually required to be done, are as various as the circumstances in which men are placed. . . . The circumstances in which men are placed in this sublunary state are exceedingly diversified, but there is probably no external condition in which the actual discipline to which men are subjected may not terminate in the temper of universal holiness. Some are tried in one way, some in another—some are required to do one set of things, some another—but the spirit of true obedience is universally the same—and the result of an effectual probation is, in every case, a moral sympathy with the moral perfections of God. The lesson is the same, however different the textbooks from which it has been taught.

Now, unless slavery is incompatible with the habitudes of holiness— unless it is inconsistent with the spirit of philanthrophy or the spirit of piety—unless it furnishes no opportunities for obedience to the law, it is not inconsistent with the pursuit or attainment of the highest excellence. It is no abridgement of moral freedom; the slave may come from the probation of *his* circumstances as fully stamped with the image of God, as those who have enjoyed an easier lot—he may be as completely in unison with the spirit of universal rectitude, as if he had been trained on flowery beds of ease. Let him discharge his *whole* duty in the actual circumstances of his case, and he is entitled to the praise of a perfect and an upright man. The question with God is—not *what* he has done—but *how;* —man looketh at the outward circumstances, but God looketh at the heart. . . . The slave is to show his reverence for God—the freedom of his inward man—by a cheerful obedience to the lawful commands of his master;—the master, his regard for one who is his master in heaven, by rendering to the slave that which is just and equal. The character of both is determined, in the sight of God, by the spirit which pervades their single acts, however the acts may differ in themselves.

If slavery is not essentially incompatible with the discharge of the essential duties, as a spiritual service, it is not destructive of the essential rights of humanity. All political organizations, our enemies themselves being judges, are subservient to the interests of the individual. . . .

All this the grace of God, through the instrumentality of the gospel, may accomplish in the person of one who is bound to labor under the direction and authority of another. The servant of men may be the freeman of the Lord. If his situation is compatible, as it confessedly is, with the achievement of the great end of his existence—if in the school of bondage he may be trained for the glorification and enjoyment of God, he is not divested of any of the rights which belong to him essentially as *man*. He may develop his moral and religious nature—the source and measure of all his rights—and must, consequently, retain every characteristick of essential humanity. . . .

. . . There are rights which belong to men in other situations, to which he is by no means entitled; the rights of the citizen, for example, and the free member of the commonwealth. They are not his, for the simple reason that they are not essential, but contingent; they do not spring from humanity simply considered, for then they would belong to women and children—but from humanity in such and such relations.

As to the influence of slavery upon the advancement of society, there can be no doubt, if the government of God be moral, that the true progress of communities and States, as well as the highest interests of individuals, depend upon the fidelity with which the duties are discharged, in every condition of life. It is the great law of providential education, that to every one that hath shall be given and he shall have abundance; but from him that hath not shall be taken away even that which he hath. In this way the reign of universal justice is promoted, and wherever that obtains, the development of the individual, which is the great end of all social and political institutions, must infallibly take place. The prosperity of the State at the same time is secured, and secured, too, without the necessity of sudden changes or violent revolutions. . . .

Beside the arguments drawn from considerations of justice and the essential rights of humanity, the incompatibility of slavery with the spirit and temper of the Gospel, is not unfrequently attempted to be made out, from the injunction of the Saviour to love our neighbor as ourselves, and to do unto others as we would have them to do unto us. The principle, however, upon which the precept of universal benevolence is interpreted in this case, makes it the sanction of the grossest wickedness. If we are to regulate our conduct to others by the arbitrary expectations which, in their circumstances, our passions and selfishness might prompt us to indulge, there ceases to be any other standard of morality than caprice. The humour of every man becomes law. The judge could not condemn the criminal, nor the executioner behead him—the rich man could not claim his possessions nor the poor learn patience from their sufferings. If I am bound to emancipate my slave because if the tables were turned and our situations reversed, I should covet this boon from him, I should be bound, upon the same principle, to promote my indigent neighbors around me, to an absolute equality with myself. That neither the Jews, in whose law the precept was first formally announced, nor the Apostles, to whom it was more fully expounded by the Saviour, ever applied it in the sense of the Abolitionists, is a strong presumption against their mode of interpretation. The truth is, it is nothing but the inculcation of *justice* from motives of love. Our Saviour directs us to do unto others what, in their situations, it would be right and reasonable in us to expect from them. We are to put ourselves in their situations, that we may duly weigh the circumstances of their case, and so be prepared to apply to it the princi- ples of universal justice. . . .

The instances which are usually urged to prove that slavery is inconsistent with the rights of man, unfortunately for the argument, are not peculiar to slavery. They are incidents to poverty, wherever it prevails in a distressing form; and a wise system of legislation could much more easily detach them from the system of slavery than from the deep indigence which is sure to crush the laborer where a crowded population obtains. They are, at best, only abuses in the one case which might be corrected, while in the other, they seem to be inseparable elements.

Enough has been said to show that slavery is not repugnant to the spirit of the Gospel, in its present relations to our race. It is one of the conditions in which God is conducting the moral probation of man—a condition not incompatible with the highest moral freedom, the true glory of the race, and, therefore, not unfit for the moral and spiritual discipline which Christianity has instituted. It is one of the schools in which immortal spirits are trained for their final destiny. If it is attended with severer hardships, these hardships are compensated by fewer duties, and the very violence of its temptations gives dignity and luster to its virtues. The slave may be fitted, in his humble, and if you please, degraded lot, for shining as a star in the firmament of heaven. In his narrow sphere, he may be cherishing and cultivating a spirit which shall render him meet for the society of angels and the everlasting en- joyment of God. The Christian beholds in him, not a tool, not a chattel, not a brute or thing—but an immortal spirit, assigned to a particular position in this world of wretchedness and sin, in which he is required to work out the destiny which attaches to him, in common with his fellows, as a man. . . .

The important question among us is, that which relates to the discharge of our own duties as masters—what are the things which are just and equal that we are required to render to our slaves.

But before attending to this inquiry, it may be well to notice the popular argument against slavery, drawn from the fact, that as it must have begun in the perpetration of grievous wrong, no lapse of time can make it subsequently right. Prescription can never sanctify injustice. The answer turns upon the distinction between the wrong itself and the effects of the wrong. The criminal act, whatever it may have been, by which a man was reduced to the condition of bondage, can never cease to be otherwise than criminal, but the relations to which that act gave rise, may, themselves, be consistent with the

231

will of God and the foundation of new and important duties. The relations of a man to his natural offspring, though wickedly formed, give rise to duties which would be ill-discharged by the destruction of the child. No doubt the principle upon which slavery has been most largely engrafted into society as an integral element of its complex constitution—the principle, that captivity in war gives a right to the life of a prisoner, for which his bondage is accepted in exchange, is not consistent with the truth of the case. But it was recognized as true for ages and generations—it was a step in the moral development of nations, and has laid the foundation of institutions and usages, which cannot now be disturbed with impunity, and in regard to which, our conduct must be regulated by the fact of their existence, and not by speculation upon the morality of their origin. Our world exhibits, every where, the traces of sin—and if we tolerate nothing but what we may expect to find in a state of perfection and holiness, we must leave this scene of sublunary distraction. The education of States is a slow process. Their standards of rectitude slowly approximate the standard of God, and in their ages of infancy, ignorance and blindness, they establish many institutions upon false maxims, which cannot subsequently be extirpated without abandoning the whole of the real progress they have made, and reconstituting society afresh. . . .

In treating slavery as an existing institution, a fact involving most important moral relations, one of the prime duties of the State is to protect, by temporal legislation, the real rights of the slave. The moral sense of the country acknowledges them—the religion of the country to a large extent, ensures their observance, but until they are defined by law and enforced by penalties there is no adequate protection of them. They are in the category of imperfect and not of perfect rights. The effect of legal protection would be to counteract whatever tendencies slavery may be supposed to possess to produce servility and abjectness of mind. It would inspire a sense of personal responsibility—a certain degree of manliness and dignity of character, which would be, at once, a security to the master and an immense blessing to the slave. The meanness, cunning, hypocrisy lying and theft, which accompany a sense of degradation, would give place to the opposite virtues, and there would be no foundation in our social relations for that slavery which Cicero defines—*obedientia fracti animi et abjecti, et arbitrio carentis suo.*

In the different systems of slavery, taken collectively, all the essential rights of humanity have been recognized by law—showing that there is nothing in the relation itself, inconsistent with this legal protection. The right to acquire knowledge—which is practically admitted by us, though legally denied, was fully recognized by the Romans, whose slaves were often the teachers of their children, and the scholars of the commonwealth. The right of the family was formally protected among the Spaniards; and the right to personal safety is largely protected by ourselves. But, without stopping to inquire in what way temporal legislation may, most effectually, protect the rights of the slave, we hesitate not to affirm that one of the highest and most solemn obligations which rests upon the masters of the South, is to give to their servants, to the utmost extent of their ability, free access to the instructions and institution of the Gospel. The injustice of denying to them food and raiment, and shelter, against which the law effectually guards, is nothing to the injustice of defrauding them of that bread which cometh down from Heaven. Their labor is ours. From infancy to age, they attend on us—they greet our introduction into the world with smiles of joy, and lament our departure with a heartfelt sorrow; and every motive of humanity and religion exacts from us, that we should remunerate their services by putting within their reach, the means of securing a blessed immortality. The meanest slave has, in him, a soul of priceless value. "No earthly or celestial language can exaggerate its worth. . . ." That soul has sinned—it is under the curse of the Almighty, and nothing can save it from an intolerable hell but the redemption that is in Christ Jesus. They must hear this joyful sound or perish. For how shall they believe in Him of whom they have not heard, and how shall they hear without a preacher, and how shall they preach except they be sent? Our design in giving them the Gospel, is not to civilize them—not to change their social condition—not to exalt them into citizens or freemen—it is to save them. The Church contemplates them only as sinners, and she is straitened to declare unto them the unsearchable riches of Christ. . . . Christian knowledge inculcates contentment with our lot; and in bringing before us the tremendous realities of eternity, renders us comparatively indifferent to the inconveniences and hardships of time. It subdues those passions and prejudices, from which all real danger to the social economy springs. "Some have objected," says a splendid writer*, "to the instruction of the lower classes, from an apprehension that it would lift them above their sphere, make them dissatisfied with their station in life, and by impairing the habits of subordination, endanger the tranquillity of the State; an objection devoid surely of all force and validity. It is not easy to conceive in what manner instructing men in their duties can prompt them to neglect those duties, or how that enlargement of reason which enables them to comprehend the true grounds of authority, and the obligation to obedience, should indispose them to obey. . . .

Our highest security in these States, lies in the confidence and affection of our servants, and nothing will more effectually propitiate their regards than consistent efforts, upon our part, to promote their everlasting good. They will feel that those are not tyrants who are striving to bring them unto

* Robert Hall. Advantages of Knowledge to the lower classes. Works. Vol. I, p. 202.

God; and they will be slow to cast off a system which has become associated in their minds with their dearest hopes and most precious consolations. Brutal ignorance is indeed to be dreaded—the only security against it, is physical force—it is the parent of ferocity, of rashness, and of desperate enterprizes. But Christian knowledge softens and subdues. Christ Jesus in binding his subjects to God, binds them more closely to each other in the ties of confidence, fidelity and love. We would say, then, to you and to all our brethren of the South, go on in your present undertaking; and though our common enemies may continue to revile, you will be consolidating the elements of your social fabrick, so firmly and compactly, that it shall defy the storms of fanaticism, while the spectacle you will exhibit of union, sympathy and confidence, among the different orders of the community, will be a standing refutation of all their accusations against us. Go on in this noble enterprise, until every slave in our borders shall know of Jesus and the resurrection; and the blessing of God will attend you—and turn back the tide of indignation which the public opinion of the world is endeavouring to roll upon you. Go on in this career, and afford another illustration of what all experience has demonstrated, that Christianity is the cheap defence of every institution which contributes to the progress of man.

9

Civil War Preaching
Charles Stewart

Few groups were more deeply involved in the sectional disputes prior to the American Civil War than the clergy. Slavery became increasingly a moral and religious issue during the early decades of the nineteenth century, and the pulpit found itself in a growing entanglement from which it could not escape. Clergymen tended to migrate to sections of the country most compatible with their personal views. This migration made the United States more divided than ever, and left ardent abolitionists and slavery proponents without effective oppositions.

Charles Darwin's theories did not invade the United States until after the Civil War, so the fundamental religious premise, that God controlled the universe and everything and actions in it, remained an important factor in the thinking of pre-Civil War Americans. At mid-century then, the pulpit was still a significant molder of public opinion. Abolitionists and defenders of slavery naturally turned to the Bible for proof that God did or did not approve of slavery, and the clergy, as authorities on biblical teachings, became spokesmen for both sides of the controversy.

Regardless of geographic separation, clerics found it increasingly difficult to avoid sectional issues, for their annual denominational assemblies brought representatives together from all geographical sections. The inevitable conflicts occurred. By 1845, long before the nation experienced actual political division, the Baptist and Methodist Churches split into separate Northern and Southern Churches. Presbyterians, Episcopalians, and Lutherans maintained shaky unities until the nation itself divided, then, they too separated into Northern and Southern factions.

When Southern states began to secede in the months after Lincoln's election, clerical reaction was as mixed as public reaction. Some preachers felt that secession would not last, while others seemed to believe that a division would have its advantages. Some argued that peace could be maintained if the anti- and pro-slavery radicals would moderate their views, while others warned that a division of states so closely related for decades could only result in a horrible military conflict. Some clergy pleaded for compromise, and others demanded a stern maintenance of "principle" at any cost.

In the early morning of April 12, 1861, public and clerical speculations became purely academic, for the bombardment of Fort Sumter in Charleston harbor had begun. The nation was at war with itself. All serious attempts at compromise ended, and the majority of clergymen became ardent supporters of either the Union or the Confederacy. Preachers soon discovered that they could avoid partisan politics in their sermons, but silence on supporting their respective governments would lead to severe criticism from their congregations. On Sundays, days of fast and days of thanksgiving, clergy preached sectional unity and loyalty before church congregations, before mass meetings of citizens, and before state legislatures and assemblies.

During the four long and bloody years of the Civil War, Union and Confederate preachers never ceased to sermonize on the conflict, nor did they fail to base their sermons on the fundamental religious premise generally accepted in pre-Darwinian America: God controls the universe and everything and action in it. This belief led clerics to conclude that God caused the war for his own purposes: for example, to punish the nation for its sins, to end or to protect slavery, to end rebellion or to assure Southern independence. Neither section could be victorious, they argued, without first turning humbly to God. When their side was winning, clergymen saw the victories as a direct result of prayer; when they were losing, they charged congregations and the populace of their sections with skepticism, sin, and turning from God.

During the early period of the war, April, 1861, to January, 1862, the war began to look like the bloody stalemate it was later to become. However, Confederate armies did score several victories—notably the first battle at Manassas or Bull Run. The majority of clergymen in both sections wisely avoided citing slavery as the cause for which their side was fighting. Abolitionism was still unpopular in the North, and slaveholders represented a small minority of the Southern population. Southern preachers declared that Confederate armies were fighting for Southern independence, while Northern clerics declared that Union forces were fighting to preserve divinely established government. Clergy in the North tended to stress the holy nature of war, the sacred duty of protecting one's government. The war became a grand religious crusade. Confederate clergymen seemed content with their victories, and inferred that these victories were signs of God's approval of the Confederacy.

Preaching during the middle period of the war, January, 1862, to July, 1863, was greatly influenced by the status of the military conflict, and clerical pessimism and optimism went with the side succeeding or failing on the battlefield. God had caused the war, clergy agreed, but Northerners now saw God demanding an end to slavery. Southerners, on the other hand, were certain that God was punishing a sinful, corrupt North, and they pointed to impressive Confederate victories as proof of God's approval of the Southern fight for independence. Confederate preaching of this period generally ignored slavery, while Union preachers, hesitant to mention slavery in the early period, seemed obsessed with the issue during the middle period. Slavery was a cause of the war, a cause of Union defeats, a cause for which to fight, and, if it were abolished, a means of gaining God's favor. Lincoln's Emancipation Proclamation was doubtless a factor in the pulpit's increased interest in the abolition of slavery.

The final period of the war, July, 1863, to April, 1865, was the longest, the bloodiest, and saw the gradual strangulation of the Confederacy by powerful Union armies. Preachers of both sides tried to convince their audiences that victory alone was acceptable, and not surrender or compromise. The cost in lives and wealth was irrelevant, they argued. Sermons were still based on the premises that God was all powerful and that he had caused the war, but less attention was given to these premises. Victories were the result of prayer, preachers contended, while defeats were the result of unrepented sin and a turning from God. The Northern cause, for which God was giving it many victories, was the restoration of divine government to all of the nation. Unlike the middle period, slavery was rarely mentioned as the Northern cause. Southern sermons reflected the worsening plight of the Confederacy. Such sins as profiteering, extortion, speculation, desertion, treason, discontent, factionalism, and religious skepticism were cited by a large number of ministers. Northern clergymen said that God condemned all revolutions and, thus, would give final victory to the Union forces. Southern clerics presented a variety of rationalizations why the Confederacy could not lose: God wanted to protect slavery and therefore had to protect the South; God approved the purposes of the Confederate states (slavery, self-defense, independence); God knew the North was intent on destroying his heritage on earth; God would not abandon the South after giving it victories in 1861, 1862, 1863; God always makes evil forces lose after initial successes (the fact was ignored that the South itself was losing after initial successes); God chooses new nations after a time of affliction; and God was using the South as defender of true republicanism.

In conclusion, Civil War sermons were based on the fundamental religious tradition of America, that God controls all earthly things and actions. Clergymen argued that God, and not science, armies, human leaders, or industry could grant final victory. This meant also that

238

no matter how severely a side was defeated there was still hope. Sermons reflected clearly the varying fortunes of war, and exhibited what could be regarded as blind loyalty to the geographic sections of the speakers. The two sermons contained here, "Thanksgiving Discourse" by H.A. T. Tupper, Confederate, and "Our National Reverses" by Unionist James D. Liggett, appropriately represent the ideas described above.

HENRY ALLEN TUPPER

Henry Allen Tupper was born in Charleston, South Carolina, on February 29, 1828. He was converted and baptized during a great revival in 1846, and became a voluntary missionary in the Charleston area. Licensed to preach in 1847, he went on to receive a Bachelor of Arts Degree in 1848 and a Master of Arts Degree in 1852 from Madison University in New York. Meanwhile, in 1850 Tupper graduated from the Theological Seminary at Madison and was ordained at Charleston. After poor health prevented his becoming a foreign missionary, he became pastor of the Baptist Church in Washington, Georgia, where he remained for nearly twenty years. During the Civil War the Confederate government commissioned Tupper as chaplain of the 9th Georgia regiment. In 1872, Tupper accepted the office of corresponding secretary of the Board of Foreign Missions of the Southern Baptist Convention. He delivered his "Thanksgiving Discourse" in Washington, Georgia, on September 18, 1862.

A Thanksgiving Discourse*

*"If it had not been the Lord who was on our side,—now may Israel say;
If it had not been the Lord who was on our side,—when men rose up against us:
Then they had swallowed us up quick,—when their wrath was kindled against us:
Then the waters had overwhelmed us,—the stream had gone over our soul:
Then the proud waters had gone over our soul.*
BLESSED BE THE LORD—WHO HATH NOT GIVEN US AS A PREY TO THEIR TEETH.
*Our soul is escaped as a bird out of the snare of the fowlers:
The snare is broken and we are escaped.
Our help is in the name of the Lord,—who made heaven and earth."*—PSALM CXXIV.

* (Macon, Ga.: Burke, Boykin & Co., 1862). This sermon was delivered in response to the proclamation of Jefferson Davis: "Now, therefore, I, JEFFERSON DAVIS, President of the Confederate States, do issue this, my proclamation, setting apart Thursday, the 18th day of September, instant, as a day of prayer and thanksgiving to Almighty God, for the great mercies vouchsafed to our people, and more especially for the triumph of our arms at Richmond, Ky., and at Manassas; and I do hereby invite the people of the Confederate States to meet on that day at their respective places of public worship, and to unite in rendering thanks and praise to God for these great mercies, and to implore Him to conduct our country safely through the perils which surround us to the final attainment of the blessings of peace and security."

The Psalmist praises God as the author of his people's deliverance—deliverance from an enemy, whose power he compares with the overwhelming waters; whose ferocity, with the beast of prey; and whose wiliness with the snare of the fowler. He rejoices that the net in which they were held a prey is broken—that they had escaped that danger; and trusts that the Lord, who had not suffered them to be swallowed up when the enemy's wrath was kindled against them, would still be on their side and their God.

And similar praise and rejoicing, and prayer, are we called upon to-day to make before the Lord.

I. Blessed be God, our powerful, and fierce and subtile enemy has not swallowed us up. His huge power was gradually coiled around us; and he gloated over the prospect of crushing our existence as a people. And judging from the threats of his lips, the injury actually inflicted, all his feelings and conduct towards us, and the natural course of revenge for our breaking the bands which held us in his power—depriving him of such profitable possession, and humbling his pride at home and abroad—there is no room to doubt that his most cruel intents would have been fully executed, had his success been equal to his wrath. But, blessed be the name of the Lord, He has thus far been on our side. He broke the snare for us, and permitted us to escape. He has struck heavy blows for us—heavy blows at Sumter, and Manassas, and Carthage, and Lexington, and Shiloh, and Richmond, and in every part of the monstrous coil of living venom, rage, and power; and has begun again at the head and neck in the late decisive strokes at Manassas, and Richmond, Ky. And the monster has recoiled from his position, and stretched himself out in slow and sullen retreat, leaving unguarded even the way of entrance to his own domain.

If heavy wounds have been inflicted upon us—and terrible indeed have they been—they have only served, (while we confess that they are not greater than our sins,) to make us realize the cruelty and power of our adversary, that we might raise our eyes to Him who made heaven and earth, and controls all, and bless His name, that in mercy, He has not "given us as a prey to his teeth."

II. And the developments of this struggle only make us rejoice the more that the ties which bound us together—the meshes which secured us an easy prey to our enemy—have been broken, and that we have escaped from an unnatural, and destructive union.

1. I say unnatural union: for this war has demonstrated what has long been felt, that difference in pursuits, and interests, and institutions, and education, and manners, and political and social views, has made us virtually two people—as much two as any people could be of the same language and color. And the latent prejudices and adverse sentiments, and hostilities, which have

241

originated in this obvious and conscious difference in circumstance and character, and which have been strengthened by political and religious contentions, by mutual criminations, and re-criminations, have now been brought forth, by the clash of arms, to their full extent, and exposed our spirits to each other, and to the world, as almost antipodal, utterly devoid of the sympathy and good will for each other necessary to keep a republic together, and which made our union a sham and a mockery—a thing unnatural and impossible.

2. And as destructive to us, as unnatural:

(1). A radical change had taken place in our Government. By a series of encroachments upon the reserved rights of the States, the Federal Government had assumed powers never delegated to it, and was fast tending to consolidation, where the will of the numerical majority was tantamount to the law of the land. The temptation to this change was too great for selfish human nature to withstand, where there was the consciousness of superior numbers, and where the change was of such advantage to local interests. And adverse parties of the one section, influenced by these interests, united upon measures for their common benefit; and thus the other section, in a hopeless minority, was the constant victim of unconstitutional legislation, leading directly to Northern aggrandizement, and the impoverishment of the South.

No wonder "the Union" was so much beloved. It was not the principles on which the Union was founded. These were not so profitable. They furnished a shield to the weaker, and a check to the stronger. They had long since been disregarded, and are now shamelessly trampled under feet, while "the Union —the glorious Union," which bound us as a prey to Northern rapacity, is extolled above the skies, and made the idol—a perfect Moloch—to which the dearest rights and interests of humanity are to be immolated.—Surely *coveteousness is idolatry; and the love of money is the root of all evil.*

This was our danger and death in the Union. By legalized processes, our life's blood was being extracted: while to talk of escape was arrant treason, which must be crushed by the strong arm of usurped authority.

(2). And more destructive, "the peculiar sentiment" of the North. It may be laid down as a settled principle, that any sentiment, as well as interest, which is predominant in the mind of a people who have the power, will enter into the government, and be carried out to the fullest extent practicable and profitable. This sentiment had grown and spread with fearful power and rapidity. And forcing itself into the legislation of the country, through the breaches of the Constitution, it was destined to rule and to ruin. No obstacle could impede its progress. No argument, no law, no expostulation, could influence the fanaticism, which has neither reason, conscience, nor mercy.

It was as deaf as an adder, as hard as a stone, as cruel as death. It pro-created the doctrine of a "higher law," by which the Constitution was to be adjudged. It declared an "irrepressible conflict," by which the interests of one section were to be ruined by the opinions of the other. It resisted the laws for our safety, in their execution; ruptured the ties of sister churches; elected a purely sectional President, in clear violation of the Federal Compact, and against an aggregate majority of nearly one million of votes; and now it is rioting in monstrous barbarities against us, only surpassed by the designs they avow, should opportunity open the way to their madness. Surely union with such sentiment was hugging death to the bosom. The ruin might have been gradual, but it was none the less ruin. And between these two engines of destruction, an unrestrained majority, and unconscionable fanaticism, we were truly between the upper and the nether stones, which sooner or later would have ground us to powder.

3. We cannot but rejoice, therefore, that we have been delivered from the unnatural and destructive alliance, though it be at the necessary expense of this terrible war. I say necessary expense of this war. With such gains from the Union, no less than *two hundred millions* a year, would the North have ever listened to peaceable separation? If Pharaoh will not let us go after all his afflictions, would he have been persuaded by the voice of reason, and the appeals to mercy? The present struggle shows how desperate was their love of the Union. No expense, no principles, no reputation, no blood, was too much to be offered upon its altar. The God Dagon fell down, and was smashed, before the ark of the Covenant, but this idol is not to bow to the power of reason, nor the providence of God. Against hope, they hope; against defeat, they contend; against the protests of nations, they persevere; against the voice of God, they cling to the golden calf. No! never would they have been guilty of the sacrilege of severing the "sacred Union." Sooner would the craftsmen of Ephesus have demolished, at the instance of Paul, the temple of the great Diana, from which they got their gains. Deliberation would only have given time for further circumvention, and to bar the possibility of rupture. The only way was to burst the fetters at once; and to resort to our powers of defence, and to the God of Righteousness and of Hosts. SEPARATION WAS NECESSARY TO SALVATION, AND WAR TO FINAL SEPARATION.

Hence, the Lord, who would deliver us from the snare, led providentially and imperceptibly into the war.

(1). Had it not been for the blindness of our enemy, in attempting, contrary to all reason and right, to preserve the Union by force, would the mass of our people ever have been so united in the determination to be freed forever from the Central Tyranny? New compromises and reconstruction might have been resorted to; and thus the injustice and injury saddled on coming generations. But God used our foes to accomplish the very object against which they desperately strove.

(2). Had it not been for our ignorance of the immense resources of the enemy—the money he could command, the men he could bring into the field, the damage he could do us, and the vast proportions the war would assume—had it not been for our delusive hopes of dissensions among their parties, the uprising of their populace, their succumbing to national bankruptcy, of the necessity of European interference for "King Cotton," and the efficiency of our "Militia of the seas," "which were to penetrate into every sea, and find splendid prizes in the silk ships of China, and the gold-freighted steamers of California," would we have been so ready to plunge ourselves into these billows of blood?

These are only hints of the many providences by which God over-ruled to our acceptance of the only alternative to our political and social degradation and ruin. And terrible though it be, the progress of the conflict develops evils tenfold more terrible to which we would inevitably have been subjected, as the hampered prey to our enemy's teeth; and we are summoned to-day, amid the troubles of the land, to rejoice that the net is broken, and we have escaped, as among the great mercies which God has shown us as a people.

III. And since our escape, how merciful has God been to us, as a Government, a people, and an army!

1. As a Government how great has been the Divine favor to us. It was indeed, as a nation, born in a day; and it came into the world with no patrimony for its support. But He who feeds the ravens, and clothes the lily with its glory, did not forget the new-born Republic. A substantial basis of credit was growing in the fields; the vaults of the banks were thrown open, as by some magic *sesame*, to the public exigency; one hundred and fifty thousand of the most approved arms were found in our arsenals; without discord, a Constitution was adopted, duly acknowledging the Lord, guarding against the corruptions of the old Government, and more strongly setting forth the great principles of Republicanism; five hundred thousand men were soon in the field; and the people, as one family—conspicuous among them the women of the country—(God bless them!) to whom the Provisional Government voted "a public acknowledgment of their faithfulness in the glorious work of effecting our independence"—massed to their support, and furnished, in one quarter of a year, provisions valued at $3,000,000. And now the child of yesterday stands a full match for its rival of near a century's growth; and extorts the reluctant admiration of nations, who lack the candor or manliness to openly acknowledge what they secretly feel. Never was a great government so rapidly organized in all its departments—never was one more signally crowned with the blessings of God.

2. And as a people, how blessed! The pillars of a nation have been torn down, but no ruins of anarchy and confusion are scattered abroad. The excellence of the principles of State-independence, for which we contend, has appeared in the perfect order with which the affairs of each State have gone on while the Confederacy has been going through the bloodiest revolution the world has ever known. Except where the foot of the enemy treads all continues as if peace prevailed. And with social peace, there has been plenty. Deducting the loss, in whole or part of several crops, and not underrating the commercial pressure, which, however, may only make us feel our dependency on God, and develop the invention and industry, and resources of the country, there is abundance given to keep the people at home content, and to support our brethren in the field. And choicest of all have been the blessings of Divine Grace bestowed upon many parts of the land, which come as special comfort at this time of distress, as evidence of the Divine presence and favor, and we trust, as the earnest of more abundant blessings, both temporal and spiritual.

3. And to our arms, how signal has been His favor! Upon the mere doctrine of chances, what hope was there that our forces, so inferior in numbers and equipments, could succeed? But men strike bolder, and mightier, who strike for right and home, and all; and men strike mightiest who strike under a sense of the Divine approval of their cause. And upon every fair field of battle, they have struck victoriously, and so manifestly by the aid of God, that spontaneously, Commanders and commands have been ready to give the praise to Him. The late victories have been signal and decisive. The blows at Manassas demolished the enemy's toils of a year. The Confederate Capital was the great longing—the coveted prize at which the hydra-tongues were licking-out on every side. But God banded the heads together for the well-aimed and stunning blow, which has driven the monster to his den, and calls us out to bless the Lord, who has not given us a prey to his teeth. And in Kentucky a new phase has been put upon the face of things. The way has been opened, by our successes, to the rich fields of the West, into which, God grant, that we may fully enter, and make just and ample restitution for the unjust and wholesale spoliations to which we have been subjected. As we glance to-day over the position of things, what a prospect of success looms up before the vision! In the midst of our anxieties and afflictions, the heart thrills with gratitude to God.—Truly He has done great things for us, whereof we are glad. Let us come before Him with the voice of praise and thanksgiving; let us rejoice—though with chastened joy—and be exceeding glad; and let the unfeigned sentiment of our heart be: "Not unto us, O Lord, not unto us, but unto thy name give glory for thy mercy, and for thy truth's sake."

IV. And the mercies of the past should only encourage us to implore further and greater favors. We are not to boast as those who put off the harness. We are still in the midst of the bloody contention. Success is far from being decided. All that has been done and felt—all our progress and hopes, would only make defeat more terrible to us. Every victory has but sharpened the teeth, and strengthened the jaws of the enemy's resentment. The crisis is really upon us. Our forces are in the enemy's country; the energy of despair is massing materials of war against us; the proud waters driven back, only rise up higher to overwhelm us; foreign powers have clearly deserted us; and there is nothing to look to—and God be thanked for it—but our own manhood, and our God. But manhood is nothing without God. Let us come, then, before His Throne, while we praise Him with the spirit of united and ardent prayer. If anything can inspire our hearts, and fire our tongues, surely it is the blessings of success, the horrors of defeat—the dear objects, temporal and spiritual, wrapped up in the destiny of our beloved country. Yes, our beloved country—the country which gave us birth, and affords protection, and bestows such benefits, and to which God has bound our hearts as to a mother. Our country, whose sacred soil has been polluted by the monster's trail; whose noble daughters have been threatened with dishonor; whose gallant sons lie slain upon her gory bosom; and whose outrage cries to heaven to avenge her cruel wrongs. Oh God, look down upon our bleeding country —hear the cries of our distracted mother—and arm her sons with hearts of fire, and sinews of steel, and let future ages know, in our rescue from the jaws of ruin, the glory of thy mercy, and the terribleness of thy wrath.

And no song of praise would we write to celebrate the wonders of our arms; no traditions of heroic deeds would we hand down to our children, to fill their minds with the greatness of their sires; no monuments of marble and brass would we erect to perpetuate our day to future generations. But in the hearts of a grateful and Godly-people, would we commemorate this deliverance from worse than Babylonish captivity, and from generation to generation, hymn the praise of our Great Deliverer, the sentiments of divine inspiration:

"If it had not been the Lord who was on our side,—
If it had not been the Lord who was on our side—when men rose up against us:
Then they had swallowed us up quick—when their wrath was kindled against us:
Then the waters had overwhelmed us,—the stream had gone over our soul:
Then the proud waters had gone over our soul.
Blessed be the Lord—who hath not given us as a prey to their teeth.
Our soul is escaped as a bird out of the snare of the fowler:
The snare is broken, and we are escaped.
Our help is in the name of the Lord,—who made heaven and earth."

And let all respond: Amen, and Amen, to the glory of God.

JAMES D. LIGGETT

The Rev. James D. Liggett was born in Warren County, Ohio, on December 10, 1821. He graduated from Miami University, Oxford, Ohio, in 1843 and went on to study and practice law in Ohio until 1849. In that year Liggett established the Peninsular Freeman in Detroit. He later returned to Ohio and published the Xenia News until 1858. In 1858 he began to study theology and was ordained in the Congregational Church a year later. His first pastorate was the First Congregational Church in Leavenworth, Kansas. Liggett moved to the First Congregational Church in Hiawatha, Kansas in 1873 and, in 1877, left the ministry to found the Detroit Home and Day School in Detroit, Michigan. He delivered the sermon "Our National Reverses" in the First Congregational Church of Leavenworth on September 7, 1862.

Our National Reverses*

*And the Children of Israel inquired of the Lord, saying, Shall I again go out to battle against the children of Benjamin my brother, or shall I cease? And the Lord said, go up; for to-morrow I will deliver them into thine hand.—*JUDGES, 20TH CHAPTER, 27TH AND 28TH VERSES.

The facts connected with this passage of Scripture are such as to present a question in relation to God's dealings with his people of great interest and practical importance.

A few wicked and worthless men of Gibeah, of the tribe of Benjamin, committed a most horrible outrage upon a Levite and his wife, who had taken lodgings for a night in their town. No reason for the act is given in the narrative, and none can be supposed by us except their own devilish desire to commit wickedness. It was unprovoked and devilish. As the news of it spread through all the tribes of Israel, the greatest indignation was excited in all hearts; and the people came together en masse to decide what to do. With one voice they said, the perpetrators of so great a crime must be speedily and terribly punished; and they demanded of the Benjamites that the criminals be delivered up for punishment. But, instead of complying with this reasonable and righteous demand, the whole tribe of Benjamin

* Unpublished manuscript, Civil War Collection, Yale University.

took offense at the action of the other tribes and prepared to resist them by force of arms.

Under these circumstances no choice of action was left to the other tribes but to enforce justice and assert the authority of the nation by the sword. Hence they went out against Benjamin with four hundred thousand trained men of war, many of whom had seen actual service in the battle-field, thus arraying at once the whole military power of the nation against one little tribe. Their purpose seems to have been to make sure and thorough work. There were no delays or want of earnestness in the prosecution of the war. The cause was doubtless just; the nation was united in its support; the symbols of national authority were with them; and the result shows that God himself was on their side, and against Benjamin. Yet the Israelites were unexpectedly and disgracefully beaten in the first battle; and also in the second.

There were four hundred thousand men of valor, representing the national authority, with justice and the divine approval, on the one side; and only twenty-six thousand rebels and wrongdoers on the other; yet the wrong-doers triumphed in two successive pitched battles, slaying in the two engagements fourteen thousand more than their own entire army.

Now, on the theory that God has something to do in these conflicts of men, and that all his attributes are always pledged to the side of justice and right; how shall we explain this remarkable piece of history? Certainly not by the more than semi-infidel saying attributed to Napoleon, that "God favors the strongest battalions."

Surely some superhuman influence was in the conflict, otherwise the result in the first battles would have been different. Taking merely human power and valor into the account, it is incredible that 26,000 men could defeat and rout an army of 400,000 men of equal valor in a fair and open conflict. Shall we say then that God was, even temporarily, on the side of wicked men and wrongdoers, and gave them the victory? Certainly not. But we must say that his power was exerted on their side; and yet his favor was not with them. His power was so exerted as to result ultimately in the greatest good to Israel, whom he did really favor; and the greatest evil to Benjamin, whom it was his will and purpose to punish with a most signal punishment. The facts will make this interpretation clear.

(a) Israel did not consult God, their king and leader, as was his duty to do before making that war; but a mass meeting of the people was called, and a Congress of the chief men of the tribes deliberated and determined for themselves the question of duty.

(b) They were evidently actuated by a wrong spirit; that of revenge rather than an humble and conscientious desire to vindicate the cause of justice in the fear of God.

(c) In the heat and haste of passion, they evidently sought to glorify themselves rather than God.

(d) They evidently trusted in their own superiority of strength for an easy victory, and forgot their dependence on the God of battles. God required of them when they went to war at all, not only and solely that it should be in a just cause, but that they should first submit the decision of that matter to him; and then prosecute it with motives and feelings consistent with a holy cause, and in a confident dependence upon himself for success. In this way he undertook to train them to follow him as their leader, and to educate them for his own peculiar people, ready to acknowledge and glorify him at all times and in all things.

But you will observe that the only question which they at the outset submitted to him for decision was one of minor importance, which doubtless arose from ambitious rivalry. It was "who shall lead us?" Who shall have the most responsible position and reap the most glory from the war? Who shall be the Commander-in-Chief of the united armies? The Lord nevertheless decided this question for them. He said "Judah shall go up first," and of course the chief man of Judah became the chief man of all. Nor can we doubt that he was the right man in the right place, because God chose him. But with all that, they were not prepared for victory. The conditions upon which God could grant them success were not complied with.

After their first defeat they were greatly mortified and grieved, even wept out their tears of bitterness before God; but evidently had not really discovered the true cause of their failure and disaster.

They encouraged themselves, instead of seeking direction from God; and set themselves in battle array the second time, and then after having done so, sought God's advice whether to fight or not. Having first decided the question of duty for themselves, the act of submitting it to God was doubtless a formal, rather than a sincere submission to his will. Their purpose was already fixed, and no answer contrary thereto would have been heeded. But God's answer was again given. He said "go up." He approved the war. His will was that they should prosecute it still further and to the bitter end; yet he determined in his wisdom, to make it the means of correcting Israel, as well as of punishing Benjamin, and the former object had to be first accomplished.

Israel had one Bull Run disaster, and had passionately resolved to avenge it, and wipe out the disgrace at all hazards; and their feelings of pride and unholy ambition, alike dishonoring to God and degrading to themselves made another such disaster necessary. Again they are defeated and massacred in heaps on the same bloody and fatal field. This second defeat brought them to a proper sense of their own weakness and error. While in their vain glory and zeal, they undertook the correction of other transgressors, they found themselves corrected. This time they go to God with fastings, tears and confessions. This time their tears are not those produced solely by regrets for their losses and disgrace; but there are also tears of penitence for their own sins in forgetting and departing from the Living God; and they for the first time humbly and honestly submit the question to him: "Shall we go out and fight against Benjamin, our brother, again, or shall we cease?" This time, there was a sincere willingness either to fight or not, as God's will should indicate; a willingness to obey him, even though it involved their own disgrace by a base submission to the victorious arms of an inferior foe. The answer of God, as before, is "go up," and with it the promise also "tomorrow I will deliver them into your hands."

The state of mind to which they had been brought, and the lesson of dependence which they had learned, were such as to make victory a blessing, and not a curse to them, as it would have been under their former state of feelings.

This then, makes this seemingly dark chapter of the Divine Providence luminous and instructive. God is always consistent with himself, and works for righteous ends. If his hand is for a time against even his own people, it is not in anger, not without a just reason, and for a glorious purpose. If he uses his enemies to scourge his own people, and to correct them, it is in mercy, and it does not follow that his favor is even temporarily with his enemies, and against his own people, but the contrary.

This history and its lessons of instruction are old, but today they seem to us new and profitable.

Almost the very same history is being acted over again in our country. Thus far the parallel is almost, if not entirely perfect; and if as a nation we shall only heed the lessons which the past and the present teach us, it will be perfect to the end. If by our past reverses we shall be made willing to be corrected as Israel was, then shall we yet be victorious over all our enemies. Let us trace the parallel briefly.

Certain wicked men, of the Southern tribes of our Confederacy, inaugurated rebellion by the commission of the greatest crimes known to the laws of God or man, and have continued to prosecute it in the same spirit of wickedness. The effect of their acts of rebellion was to arouse the loyal people of the whole land to a pitch of excitement and indignation very much like that excited in the tribes of Israel, when they heard the news of the crime of the men of Gibeah. The hearts of the people, as in that case, were also knit together as the heart of one man. The unanimous decision was that the rebellion must be subdued.

The laws of God and man, the welfare of the whole nation, and the interests of the human race at large, and of future generations seemed plainly to every right-hearted and right-minded man, to require that these criminals must be punished. In this the whole nation, the slaveholders and those who sincerely sympathized with them excepted, was heartily agreed. And for this object it was determined that the whole power of the nation should be at once employed. The first campaign was inaugurated, and after some successes, ended with a great defeat. The people wept sorely and were greatly disheartened, but they encouraged themselves, and again set themselves in battle array against the enemy. The second campaign was inaugurated on a scale much larger than the first. We felt that no power could withstand our new armies as disciplined, equipped and commanded; and with impatient confidence, we sent them forth to wipe away the disgrace of former defeats. Again after various successes and doubtful victories, this campaign also has ended in failure; and our national existence, involving the cause of liberty and justice, is in greater peril than ever. The men of Belial, and the tribes that sustain them in their great wickedness are again triumphant and defiant.

A loyal people are again in mourning for the thousands of good and valiant men who have fallen in disastrous conflicts. Why is it? O God of Justice! why is it?

There is an adequate reason for these terrible calamities and disappointments. But God does not in fact look with favor upon such schemes of conspiracy against liberty and humanity as the authors of the rebellion are endeavoring to carry out. That cannot be. God forbid that any man should think so for a single moment! All the attributes of his nature are clearly against that system of human bondage which they are avowedly fighting to establish; which they have boastingly laid down as the corner stone of the frail superstructure of the aristocratic and military government which they hope to erect upon it.

We cannot come to the conclusion that our enemies are in the right and that God is with them; and if they are in the wrong God cannot be the friend of their cause.

Where then is the trouble? If the question is put, "Shall we go out again and fight against the rebels?" the principles of justice and right, and the law of self-preservation, as plainly answer in the affirmative and as authoritatively as if an audible voice from Heaven uttered the words of permission, "Go up." Look at this question in whatever light we may,— religiously, politically, socially, and with reference to the welfare of other nations as well as our own, and the answer is the same. No choice of action is or ever has been left to us but to fight, or treasonably betray the high trusts which the past has committed to us; and which the generations of all the future plead with us to sacredly guard for them. But notwithstanding all this, the promise does not seem to come as yet—"tomorrow I will deliver them into your hands." As to what seems to be duty, all agree, and there can be no mistake; but as to what is to be the result, and when it shall be attained, all are equally in darkness and doubt. Such perils and uncertainties surround us, that we can only walk by faith. And if, indeed, our reverses have brought us, or shall soon bring us, to this point, there is good hope for us yet. If as a people we shall thus walk, God will then speedily lead us to victory, but by the path of righteousness.

Such questions, as who shall lead our armies, may well be laid aside if God shall be pleased to lead them. Well may we lay aside our confidence in merely human leadership, since all our most competent military commanders, separately and unitedly, have been unequal to the task of achieving victory either by genius, science, numbers or personal prowess. Our armies have always fought bravely and well; and the tens of thousands of our noblest ones have fallen as heroes only fall. We could not, in reason, ask them to do more. Yet, in the main, we are defeated. The stubborn hosts, after the fortunes of hundreds of important and bloody battles, face each other on substantially the first battle-fields of the war. It is time then to lay aside the question of leadership, since thus far there has been neither success, nor glory for any. If other conditions of success were complied with, we have men enough competent in skill and courage for any responsibilities that may be imposed upon them.

But rather let us define our objects and settle our policy, and see to it that they are such as we can confidently ask God to maintain for us. What, then, are we fighting for? Is it for what we often meaninglessly call "our glorious Union"? Is it for a Union representing the principles of justice and liberty to all, or merely a Union in name and form, without regard to what it represents? If it is for the Union as it recently was, corrupted and perverted by the very men who have destroyed it, to sub-serve in all possible ways the base ends of the slavery power and interest, then that is one of the things that can never be again. The antagonisms of the old Union— Liberty and Slavery—destroyed it; and the same antagonisms, if attempted to be preserved, will forever keep its fragments asunder. Is it for the old Union, under which free men of the North were made, like blind Samson, to grind in the mills of the political Philistines of the South? Then, God in his mercy has saved us by our defeats from such a fate. Is it that we may again be made like poor, eyeless Samson, an object of sport and derision for these same Philistines of the South? Then, God give us strength to shake down the old fabric ourselves, and let us, like men, perish in the ruins. But that question is already settled by the past. Let the dead bury their dead. The question is now, whatever it may have been twelve months ago, no such thing as "the restoration of the Union as it was." Let that most stupid and transparent of all fallacies, which has already cost so much blood and treasure, be abandoned. Let us break away from the fallacies and prejudices of the past which, like withes, have bound us in helplessness; and in manly strength grapple with the living issue of the agonizing Present. That issue is Liberty or Slavery. The rebels have resolved to destroy the nation that they may establish Slavery. Shall we hesitate to destroy Slavery that we may preserve the nation? Because it has come to this, that the nation must perish or that which strikes at the nation's life must perish. Our President has said, and all his policy has been, to preserve the national life and slavery too, if he can. He has tried it, and the experiment has certainly been tried long enough. The nation faints under the terrible and protracted torture. God thunders in his ears from the rivers and valleys of the West and mountain fastnesses and plains of the East, which the blood of our slain has made red in vain—"You cannot." The honest judgment of all loyal men decrees to him in terms that are imperial—"You cannot," and, what is more, "You shall not." All the sacrifices which a noble people have made and are pledged still to make, protest against a longer continuance of the ruinous experiment. Why, then, is what seems to be the will of the whole nation thus balked by the stubborn will of one man? In the midst of all the popular outcry for Liberty and the destruction of Slavery, I think I hear God saying to us—"Are you as a people, after all, ready to do justice? The rebels are fighting for Slavery; are you fighting for Liberty in the true sense, and from principle? Is it from a sense of justice to the slave, or a feeling of revenge and hatred towards the master that you ask Slavery to be destroyed? Is this nation fit in heart to do this great work of God?" If not, then must He, by still greater reverses and afflictions, prepare our hearts and make us fit to receive upon our brows the wreath of victory which His own holy hands shall place there. Our God is a jealous God and looks on the heart. Let us endeavor, through outward signs, to look a little further into this nation's heart. What means the heathenish and God-defying sentiment uttered by a distinguished orator and applauded by a great crowd, "I hate the Negro, but am willing, for my own safety, to let him shoot a rebel, reserving the privilege of scorning and persecuting him afterwards?" What means the recently enacted black code of the great, patriotic and Liberty professing State of Illinois? Do the sons of that would-be-glorious State die by the thousands for the liberty of the black man, as of the white man, and then by a vote almost unanimous, deny him a resting place for the sole of his weary foot on their own boasted free soil? What means all the howl of objection against allowing black men, who were good enough to fight the battles of our country under Washington and Jackson, to bear arms and help to fight the same battles under Lincoln? What means the most extraordinary spectacle of the President of our great nation, inviting to his own council chamber a large number of as intelligent and respectable colored men as he could find, to insult and degrade them by telling them, "Your presence in this country is offensive, injurious and intolerable to the white race, and I am authorized, by the representatives of the nation in Congress assembled, to say to you that your expenses shall be paid, if you will be gone from our sight and the land of your unfortunate birth forever"? What mean these and very many other things, to which I cannot now allude, but that there is yet in the heart of the nation a deep-seated and unjustifiable hatred of the enslaved race of this country?—a spirit which is at once the root and the fruit of Slavery. "Whosoever hateth his brother, is a murderer." And shall we not, from this divine rule of judgment, also say that whoever hateth an oppressed race of men in our midst is an oppressor? This hatred is the very essence and soul of the system of Slavery. It has kept, and it today keeps it in existence. Judged by this just rule, we are a nation of slaveholders still. Is this nation then prepared in heart to take off the shackles from four millions of black men and do justice by them? If God will punish the slaveholder for his sin, as we believe He will, is it not just in him first to correct the spirit of the slaveholder in the hearts of those whom he intends to make the instruments of that punishment? Will he honor this generation with the championship of freedom, while it is imbued with the principles and feelings of despotism? I believe he will indeed thus honor this generation, but not until he has made it fit to bear the honor; not until he has purged the nation's heart of the poison of Slavery.

These facts and principles, thus merely hinted, are sufficient, as it seems to me, to explain to us God's dealings with us; how he is against us, and yet not against us, as he was against Israel and yet all the time for him. If our pro-slaveryism is not the particular and only cause of his chastisements—if I am wholly mistaken in this, then there is some other cause; and still the general principle upon which I have explained His dark providence is undoubtedly true. Let him that has a better solution or a more faithful admonition to give, not for a moment hold his peace, but cry aloud, spare not, and show this people their transgression.

In the vast changes wrought already in the hearts of the people by the defeats we have suffered and not by the victories we have won, we can plainly see that God and not man is working a mighty and rapid revolution for us. It may seem to us to move slowly, too slowly while the life of the nation is wasting away in torrents of blood, but the engine of God's power propels it; and it must and will move on, through all the friction and weight of man's opposition—"through on time." This is our faith; and let it be the ground of our hope. In the meantime let us be patient and not despair, but work on, seeking to work in the line of God's direction. The Lord says "Go up." Other defeats and greater may yet be necessary; how many and how great He only knows, yet He says, "Go up again," and again. When the nation is fit for final victory He will grant it; and it will be signal and complete. What the near future has in store for us no man can tell; yet having faith in God and the certainty of human progress under God, though your eyes and mine may not behold it, I believe that the future of this nation shall be more glorious than the past; and that no drop of precious blood will have baptised the yet virgin soil of our beloved land in vain. Unborn generations will yet praise God for the defeats of our armies, as well as the victories which He shall hereafter grant unto them. These are not the bitter words of treason, but the joyful words of loyal faith and hope. But for this interpretation of what is otherwise dark and inscrutable, I should despair of the present and the future of my country. If God be indeed against us, then are we undone. Let our constant and submissive prayer be—"Thy will be done, O God, and fit us to do it."

10

THE VOICE OF GOD:
NATURAL OR SUPERNATURAL?
Harold Miller

To the American Christian of the eighteenth and early nineteenth centuries the natural world could be explained by references to biblical texts, such as "The Heavens declare the glory of God and the Firmament showeth His Handiwork." In Judeo-Christian concepts, the intricacies of the natural world were often used to prove that the universe had design and, therefore, a designer. Throughout the early nineteenth century in England and America, apologists for Christian thought referred to evidences of God's handiwork, such as the eye, to show that chance alone could not have produced such marvels. During that century the watch was often used to show design. Of course, the watch needed the watchmaker to construct it and to make it keep accurate time. Thus, the universe needed a designer to construct it and keep it going.

The American theologian in the nineteenth century reflected the Hebrew-Christian tradition that the natural world confirmed, rather than denied the existence of a God of design. Historian Stowe Persons writing on "Evolution and Theology in America" declares: "In early years of the nineteenth century, Orthodox Protestant

256

Christian thinkers, both in England and in America, absorbed the Deist argument in its rationalistic aspects by harmonizing natural religion with revelation. The one was found to strenghten and confirm the other." [1] Thus, for the nineteenth century American Christian, science served rather than hindered the cause of religion.

But the spirit of congeniality between science and religion was shattered by the publication and rapid scientific acceptance of *Origin of Species* by Charles Darwin, so that by 1902, William James was prompted to say:

As for the argument from design, see how Darwin's ideas have revolutionized it. Conceived as we now conceive them, as so many fortunate escapes from almost limitless processes of destruction, the benevolent adaptations which we find in nature suggest a deity very different from the one who figured in the earlier versions of the argument. [2]

But the advocates of the doctrine of design did not give up as easily as might be assumed from all this. The years from 1859 to 1902 provided the setting for a vigorous fight between the advocates of the traditional view of design and those willing to accept the view of gradual improvement of the species by natural selection.

A close look at the Christian preaching in America during the late nineteenth century reflects this struggle between evolution and traditional religion. While it is fairly evident that there were several concurrent efforts to relieve tension between science and religion, there were four distinct stages which eventually culminated in the accommodation and, in some circles, endorsement of some variation of the evolutionary theory by the major body of Christendom.

The first reaction of the church in an effort to relieve the tension between science and religion was to ridicule the statements of Darwin. Within weeks after the publication of *Origin* the first famous confrontation took place.

[1] *Evolutionary Thought in America*, ed. Stowe Persons (New Haven: Yale University Press, 1950), p. 423.
[2] *Varieties of Religious Experience* (New York: Modern Library, 1929), pp. 427-28.

257

Though it was staged in England, what was said in that confrontation was to be repeated throughout the late nineteenth century and well into the twentieth both in England and America.

In the June, 1860, meeting of the British Association at Oxford, Bishop Samuel Wilberforce delivered the first public attack on Darwin's theories. It was lengthy, and, while it appeared to start out with great regard for Mr. Darwin's findings, it gradually moved into the strategy of ridicule as the technique for attack. By the conclusion Wilberforce was saying:

The whole world of nature is laid for such a man under a fantastic law of glamour, and he becomes capable of believing anything: to him it is just as probable that Dr. Livingston will find the next tribe of negroes with their heads growing under their arms as fixed on the summit of the cervical vertebrae; and he is able, with a continually growing neglect of all the facts around him, with equal confidence and equal delusion, to look back to any past and to look on to any future.[3]

While Bishop Wilberforce's speech at the British Association meeting was the initial attack which received public attention upon the works of Darwin, it was not the last. Writing in the *New England Quarterly*, historian Bert J. Loewenberg suggests that wholesale denunciation of the kind used by Wilberforce was "the distinguishing note" of the American period from 1859 to the death of Louis Agassiz in 1873. Loewenberg attaches this strategy to "the newness of the evolutionary idea and the doubtful attitude of the scientists." [4]

The strategy of scorn did not entirely end with the death of Agassiz, as anyone who is familiar with the fundamentalist controversy in the early twentieth century knows. While William Jennings Bryan's speech "God and Evolution" is not analyzed in detail in this volume, it incorporates many of the arguments of Wilberforce and other preachers who chose to fight the scientists by attacks

[3] "The Origin of Species," *Quarterly Review* CVIII (July, 1860), 230.
[4] "The Controversy over Evolution in New England," *New England Quarterly* VIII (June, 1935), 234.

upon their character, as well as their logic. It is presented here to characterize opposition to evolution. Mr. Bryan, in that speech assails the intellectual honesty of the Darwinists of his day:

Evolutionists, not being willing to accept the theory of creation, have to explain everything, and their courage in this respect is as great as their efforts are laughable. The eye, for instance, according to evolutionists, was brought out by "the light beating upon the skin"; the ears came out in response to "air waves"; the leg is the development of a wart that chanced to appear on the belly of an animal; and so the tommyrot runs on *ad infinitum* and sensible people are asked to swallow it.

Recently a college professor told an audience in Philadephia that a baby wiggles its big toe without wiggling its other toes because its ancestors climbed trees; also that we dream of falling because our forefathers fell out of trees fifty thousand years ago, adding that we are not hurt in our dreams of falling because we descended from those that were *not killed.*[5]

So for some preachers in the early struggle the ridicule of unwelcome ideas seemed the best course to take. That strategy stayed with many of the more orthodox segments of the church in America well into the twentieth century.

It should, however, not be inferred that the only weapon of orthodoxy was insult and character assassination. Professor Charles Hodge, in 1874, published an orderly and somewhat scholarly work, *What Is Evolution?* In that volume, Hodge stated his objections to the theory. These objections served orthodox churchmen for some years as a handbook for debating the theory of evolution.

Dr. James I. McCosh, to the left of Hodge and leaning to the acceptance of some form of evolution as an explanation for life, was concerned about the effect a flat rejection of evolution would have on bright students. In 1888, he published a series of lectures on the topic. McCosh said in the initial lecture:

The great body of naturalists, all younger than forty, certainly all younger than thirty, are sure that they see evolution in nature; but they are assured by their teachers or the religious

[5] *Evolution and Religion,* ed. Gail Kennedy (Boston: D. C. Heath & Co., 1957), p. 25.

press that, if evolution does everything there is nothing left for God to do, and they see no proof of his existence.[6]

Thus, McCosh allowed for some development of the species within the framework of traditional beliefs of design.

At the pole opposite from Wilberforce, Bryan, and Hodge stood a number of the liberal American preachers. By 1885, one of America's most eloquent pulpiteers made his stand for theistic evolution. His name was Henry Ward Beecher, pastor of Brooklyn's Plymouth Church. In 1885, Beecher preached a series of sermons which explained his views on the topic to his congregation. These sermons were later published in a volume, *Evolution and Religion*. His sermon "Divine Providence and Design" reproduced here readily incorporates Evolution into Design.

Beecher admitted his indebtedness to the writings of Herbert Spencer and endorsed the view that survival of the fittest implied a God of grand design. In the introduction to his volume of sermons on evolution he says:

For myself, while finding no need of changing my idea of the Divine personality because of new light upon His mode of working, I have hailed the Evolutionary philosophy with joy. . . . the underlying truth, as a Law of Nature (that is, a regular method of the divine action), I accept and use, and thank God for it![7]

While more orthodox churchmen had condemned the ideas of Darwin as analogous to asking a watch to form itself and to keep perfect time by the order of chance, Beecher argues that accepting the idea of evolution does not rule out the concept of a God of design. Indeed, Beecher feels that evolution allowed for a more grand interpretation of design:

If it be an argument of design that a man could make one watch, is it not a sublimer argument of design that there is a man existing who could create a manufactory turning out

[6] *The Religious Aspect of Evolution* (New York: Charles Scribner's Sons, 1890), p. 6.

[7] (New York: Fords, Howard, and Shilbert, 1885), p. 3.

millions of watches, and by machinery too, so that the human hand has little to do but to adjust the parts already created by machines? . . . Is not the Creator of the system a more sublime designer than the creator of any single act? [8]

And so the argument from design had been revolutionized. Beecher saw the "benevolent adaptations found in nature" to suggest an industrial-age God who built and managed the factory of the universe.

When theologians were faced with a theory of nature which ran directly counter to what they had believed, they had to react. Historically, the reactions were not neat and orderly and did not proceed in a step-by-step adjustment of beliefs. Through that period some men insisted on the literal biblical view of creation. It was their strategy to deny the fact of evolution and to say that acceptance of any form of that belief was a denial of the inspiration of the Bible and would lead ultimately to atheism. To these men, the ridicule of Wilberforce and Bryan and the logic of Hodge were pertinent and useful.

But for the large segment of the church which bowed to the growing acceptance of evolutionary theory, a re-explanation of design was necessary. An interpretation of science allowing for: "In the beginning God created"; and an interpretation of scripture which would grant some form of modification and selection of characteristics was the goal of much of Christian belief about natural law since Darwin. The tension which was precipitated in the American church by the publication of *Origin of Species* was relieved by the acceptance of the possibility of changing species as long as that change was not accompanied by an insistence on a denial of design.

[8] *Ibid.*, p. 116.

WILLIAM JENNINGS BRYAN

William Jennings Bryan, the politician-orator of the early twentieth century, is well known for his arguments for the prosecution in the Scopes evolution trial in Tennessee. Bryan had, for some years, been involved in the fundamentalist movement and in its struggle against evolution. He was elected the first president of the World Fundamentalist Association, an organization devoted to forcing the teaching of evolution out of public schools by legislative action. It is not surprising, therefore, that The New York Times invited Mr. Bryan to submit one of his speeches against evolution to the Times for publication. The text of this speech was printed February 26, 1922.

God and Evolution*

I appreciate your invitation to present the objections to Darwinism, or evolution applied to man, and beg to submit to your readers the following:

The only part of evolution in which any considerable interest is felt is evolution applied to man. A hypothesis in regard to the rocks and plant life does not affect the philosophy upon which one's life is built. Evolution applied to fish, birds and beasts would not materially affect man's view of his own responsibilities except as the acceptance of an unsupported hypothesis as to these would be used to support a similar hypothesis as to man. The evolution that is harmful—distinctly so—is the evolution that destroys man's family tree as taught by the Bible and makes him a descendant of the lower forms of life. This, as I shall try to show, is a very vital matter.

I deal with Darwinism because it is a definite hypothesis. In his "Descent of Man" and "Origin of Species" Darwin has presumed to outline a family tree that begins, according to his estimate, about two hundred million years ago with marine animals. He attempts to trace man's line of descent from this obscure beginning up through fish, reptile, bird and animal to man. He has us descend from European, rather than American, apes and locates our first ancestors in Africa. Then he says, "But why speculate?"—a very significant phrase because it applies to everything that he says. His entire discussion is speculation.

DARWIN'S "LAWS"

Darwin set forth two (so-called) laws by which he attempts to explain the changes which he thought had taken place in the development of life from the earlier forms to man. One of these is called "natural selection" or "survival of the fittest," his argument being that a form of life which had any characteristic that was beneficial had a better chance of survival than a form of life that lacked that characteristic. The second law that he assumed to declare was called "sexual selection," by which he attempted to account for every change that was not accounted for by natural selection. Sexual selection has been laughed out of the class room. Even in his day Darwin said (see note to "Descent of Man" 1874 edition, page 625) that it aroused more criticism than anything else he had said, when he used sexual selection to explain how man became a hairless animal. Natural selection is being increasingly discarded by scientists. John Burroughs just before his death, registered a protest against it. But many evolutionists adhere to Darwin's *conclusions* while discarding his *explanations*. In other words, they accept the line of descent which he suggested *without any explanation whatever* to support it.

Other scientists accept the family tree which he outlined, but would have man branch off to a point below, or above, the development of apes and monkeys instead of coming through them. So far as I have been able to find, Darwin's line of descent has more supporters than any other outlined by evolutionists. If there is any other clearly defined family tree supported by a larger number of evolutionists, I shall be glad to have information about it that I may investigate it.

The first objection to Darwinism is that it is only a guess and was never anything more. It is called a "hypothesis," but the word "hypothesis," though euphonious, dignified and high-sounding, is merely a scientific synonym for the old-fashioned word "guess." If Darwin had advanced his views as a *guess* they would not have survived for a year, but they have floated for a half a century, buoyed up by the inflated word "hypothesis." When it is understood that "hypothesis" means "guess," people will inspect it more carefully before accepting it.

NO SUPPORT IN THE BIBLE

The second objection to Darwin's guess is that it has not one syllable in the Bible to support it. This ought to make Christians cautious about accepting it without thorough investigation. The Bible not only describes man's creation, but gives a reason for it; man is a part of God's plan and is placed on earth for a purpose. Both the Old and New Testament deal with man and with man only. They tell of God's creation of him, of God's dealings with him and of God's plans for him. Is it not strange that a Christian will accept Darwinism as a substitute for the Bible when the Bible not only does not support Darwin's hypothesis but directly and expressly contradicts it?

Third—Neither Darwin nor his supporters have been able to find a fact in the universe to support their hypothesis. With millions of species, the investigators have not been able to find *one single instance* in which one species has changed into another, although, according to the hypothesis, *all* species have developed from one or a few germs of life, the development being through the action of "resident forces" and without outside aid. Wherever a form of life, found in the rocks, is found among living organisms, there is no material change from the earliest form in which it is found. With millions of examples, nothing imperfect is found—nothing in the process of change. This statement may surprise those who have accepted evolution without investigation, as most of those who call themselves evolutionists have done. One preacher who wrote to me expressing great regret that I should dissent from Darwin said that he had not investigated the matter for himself, but that nearly all scientists seemed to accept Darwinism.

The latest word that we have on this subject comes from Professor Bateson, a high English authority, who journeyed all the way from London to Toronto, Canada, to address the American Association for the Advancement of Science the 28th day of last December. His speech has been published in full in the January issue of *Science*.

Professor Bateson is an evolutionist, but he tells with real pathos how every effort to discover the origin of species has failed. He takes up different lines of investigation, commenced hopefully but ending in disappointment. He concludes by saying, "Let us then proclaim in precise and unmistakable language that our faith in evolution is unshaken," and then he adds, "our doubts are not as to the reality or truth of evolution, but as to the origin of species, a technical, almost domestic problem. Any day that mystery may be solved." Here is optimism at its maximum. They fall back on faith. They have not yet found the origin of species, and yet how can evolution explain life unless it can account for change in species? Is it not more rational to believe in creation of man by separate act of God than to believe in evolution without a particle of evidence?

Fourth—Darwinism is not only without foundation, but it compels its believers to resort to explanations that are more absurd than anything found in the "Arabian Nights." Darwin explains that man's mind became superior to woman's because, among our brute ancestors, the males fought for their females and thus strengthened their minds. If he had lived until now, he

would not have felt it necessary to make so ridiculous an explanation, because woman's mind is not now believed to be inferior to man's.

AS TO HAIRLESS MEN

Darwin also explained that the hair disappeared from the body, permitting
man to become a hairless animal because, among our brute ancestors, the
females preferred the males with the least hair and thus in the course of
ages, bred the hair off. It is hardly necessary to point out that these explanations conflict; the males and the females could not both select at the same
time.

Evolutionists, not being willing to accept the theory of creation, have to
explain everything, and their courage in this respect is as great as their efforts
are laughable. The eye, for instance, according to evolutionists, was brought
out by "the light beating upon the skin"; the ears came out in response to
"air waves"; the leg is the development of a wart that chanced to appear on
the belly of an animal; and so the tommyrot runs on *ad infinitum* and
sensible people are asked to swallow it.

Recently a college professor told an audience in Philadephia that a baby
wiggles its big toe without wiggling its other toes because its ancestors climbed
trees; also that we dream of falling because our forefathers fell out of trees
fifty thousand years ago, adding that we are not hurt in our dreams of
falling because we descended from those that were *not killed*. (If we descended from animals at all, we certainly did not descend from those that were
killed in falling.) A professor in Illinois has fixed as the great day in history
the day when a water puppy crawled upon the land and decided to stay
there, thus becoming man's first progenitor. A dispatch from Paris recently
announced that an eminent scientist had reported having communicated
with the soul of a dog and learned that the dog was happy.

I simply mention these explanations to show what some people can believe who cannot believe the Bible. Evolution seems to close the heart of
some to the plainest spiritual truths while it opens the mind to the wildest
of guesses advanced in the name of science.

GUESSING IS NOT SCIENCE

Guesses are not science. Science is classified knowledge, and a scientist
ought to be the last person to insist upon a guess being accepted until
proof removes it from the field of hypothesis into the field of demonstrated
truth. Christianity has nothing to fear from any *truth*; no *fact* disturbs the
Christian religion or the Christian. It is the unsupported *guess* that is sub-

stituted for science to which opposition is made, and I think the objection is a valid one.

But, it may be asked, why should one object to Darwinism *even though it is not true?* This is a proper question and deserves a candid answer. There are many guesses which are perfectly groundless and at the same time entirely harmless; and it is not worth while to worry about a guess or to disturb the guesser so long as his guess does not harm others.

The objection to Darwinism is that it is *harmful,* as well as groundless. It entirely changes one's view of life and undermines faith in the Bible. Evolution has no place for the miracle or the supernatural. It flatters the egotist to be told that there is nothing that his mind cannot understand. Evolution proposes to bring all the processes of nature within the comprehension of man by making it the explanation of everything that is known. Creation implies a Creator, and the finite mind cannot comprehend the infinite. We can understand some things, but we run across mystery at every point. Evolution attempts to solve the mystery of life by suggesting a process of development commencing "in the dawn of time" and continuing uninterrupted up until now. Evolution does not explain creation: it simply diverts attention from it by hiding it behind eons of time. If a man accepts Darwinism, or evolution applied to man, and is consistent, he rejects the miracle and the supernatural as impossible. He commences with the first chapter of Genesis and blots out the Bible story of man's creation, not because the evidence is insufficient, but because the miracle is inconsistent with evolution. If he is consistent, he will go through the Old Testament step by step and cut out all the miracles and all the supernatural. He will then take up the New Testament and cut out all the supernatural—the virgin birth of Christ, His miracles and His resurrection, leaving the Bible a story book without binding authority upon the conscience of man. Of course, not all evolutionists are consistent; some fail to apply their hypothesis to the end just as some Christians fail to apply their Christianity to life.

EVOLUTION AND GOD

Most of the evolutionists are materialists; some admitting that they are atheists, others calling themselves agnostics. Some call themselves "theistic evolutionists," but the theistic evolutionist puts God so far away that He ceases to be a present influence in the life. Canon Barnes of Westminster, some two years ago, interpreted evolution as to put God back of the time when the electrons came out of "stuff" and combined (about 1740 of them) to form an atom. Since then, according to Canon Barnes, things have been developing to God's plan but without God's aid.

It requires measureless credulity to enable one to believe that all that we see about us came by chance, by a series of happy-go-lucky accidents. If only an infinite God could have formed hydrogen and oxygen and united them in just the right proportions to produce water—the daily need of every living thing—scattered among the flowers all the colors of the rainbow and every variety of perfume, adjusted the mocking bird's throat to its musical scale, and fashioned a soul for man, why should we want to imprison God in an impenetrable past? This is a living world. Why not a living God upon the throne? Why not allow Him to work now?

Theistic evolutionists insist that they magnify God when they credit Him with devising evolution as a plan of development. They sometimes characterize the Bible God as a "carpenter god," who is described as repairing His work from time to time at man's request. The question is not whether God could have made the world according to the plan of evolution—of course, an all-powerful God could make the world as He pleased. The real question is, Did God use evolution as His plan? If it could be shown that man, instead of being made in the image of God, is a development of beasts we would have to accept it, regardless of its effect, for truth is truth and must prevail. But when there is no proof we have a right to consider the effect of the acceptance of an unsupported hypothesis.

DARWIN'S AGNOSTICISM

Darwinism made an agnostic out of Darwin. When he was a young man he believed in God; before he died he declared that the beginning of all things is a mystery insoluble by us. When he was a young man he believed in the Bible; just before his death he declared that he did not believe that there had ever been any revelation; that banished the Bible as the inspired Word of God, and, with it, the Christ of whom the Bible tells. When Darwin was young he believed in a future life; before he died he declared that each must decide the question for himself from vague, uncertain probabilities. He could not throw any light upon the great questions of life and immortality. He said that he "must be content to remain an agnostic."

And then he brought the most terrific indictment that I have read against his own hypothesis. He asks (just before his death): "Can the mind of man, which has, as I fully believe, been developed from a mind as low as that possessed by the lowest animal, be trusted when it draws such grand conclusions?" He brought man down to the brute level and then judged man's mind by brute standards.

This is Darwinism. This is Darwin's own testimony against himself. If Darwinism could make an agnostic of Darwin, what is its effect likely to be upon students to whom Darwinism is taught at the very age when they are throwing off parental authority and becoming independent? Darwin's guess gives the student an excuse for rejecting the authority of God, an excuse that appeals to him more strongly at this age than at any other age in life. Many of them come back after a while as Romanes came back. After feeding upon husks for twenty-five years, he began to feel his way back, like a prodigal son, to his father's house, but many never return.

Professor Leuba, who teaches psychology at Bryn Mawr, Pennsylvania, wrote a book about six years ago entitled "Belief in God and Immortality," . . . in which he declared that belief in God and immortality is dying out among the educated classes. As proof of this he gave the results which he obtained by submitting questions to prominent scientists in the United States. He says that he found that more than half of them, according to their own answers, do not believe in a personal God or a personal immortality. To reinforce his position, he sent questions to students of nine representative colleges and found that unbelief increases from 15 per cent in the freshman year to 30 per cent in the junior class, and to 40 to 45 per cent (among the men) at graduation. This he attributes to the influence of the scholarly men under whose instruction they pass in college.

RELIGION WANING AMONG CHILDREN

Anyone desiring to verify these statistics can do so by inquiry at our leading state institutions and even among some of our religious denominational colleges. Fathers and mothers complain of their children losing their interest in religion and speaking lightly of the Bible. This begins when they come under the influence of a teacher who accepts Darwin's guess, ridicules the Bible story of creation and instructs the child upon the basis of the brute theory. In Columbia a teacher began his course in geology by telling the children to lay aside all that they had learned in Sunday School. A teacher of philosophy in the University of Michigan tells students that Christianity is a state of mind and that there are only two books of literary value in the Bible. Another professor in that university tells students that no thinking man can believe in God or in the Bible. A teacher in the University of Wisconsin tells his students that the Bible is a collection of myths. Another state university professor diverts a dozen young men from the ministry and the president of a prominent state university tells his students in a lecture on religion to throw away religion if it does not harmonize with the teaching of biology, psychology, etc.

The effect of Darwinism is seen in the pulpits; men of prominent denominations deny the virgin birth of Christ and some even His resurrection. Two

Presbyterians, preaching in New York state, recently told me that agnosticism was the natural attitude of old people. Evolution naturally leads to agnosticism. Those who teach Darwinism are undermining the faith of Christians; they are raising questions about the Bible as an authoritative source of truth; they are teaching materialistic views that rob the life of the young of spiritual values.

Christians do not object to freedom of speech; they believe that Biblical truth can hold its own in a fair field. They concede the right of ministers to pass from belief to agnosticism or atheism, but they contend that they should be honest enough to separate themselves from the ministry and not attempt to debase the religion which they profess.

And so in the matter of education. Christians do not dispute the right of any teacher to be agnostic or atheistic, but Christians do deny the right of agnostics and atheists to use the public school as a forum for the teaching of their doctrines.

The Bible has in many places been excluded from the schools on the ground that religion should not be taught by those paid by public taxation. If this doctrine is sound, what right have the enemies of religion to teach irreligion in the public schools? If the Bible cannot be taught, why should Christian taxpayers permit the teaching of guesses that make the Bible a lie? A teacher might just as well write over the door of his room, "Leave Christianity behind you, all ye who enter here," as to ask his students to accept a hypothesis directly and irreconcilably antagonistic to the Bible.

Our opponents are not fair. When we find fault with the teaching of Darwin's unsupported hypothesis, they talk about Copernicus and Galileo and ask whether we shall exclude science and return to the dark ages. Their evasion is a confession of weakness. We do not ask for the exclusion of any scientific truth, but we do protest an atheist teacher being allowed to blow his guesses in the face of the student. The Christians who want to teach religion in their schools furnish the money for denominational institutions. If atheists want to teach atheism, why do they not build their own schools and employ their own teachers? If a man really believes that he has brute blood in him, he can teach that to his children at home or he can send them to atheistic schools, where his children will not be in danger of losing their brute philosophy, but why should he be allowed to deal with other people's children as if they were little monkeys?

We stamp upon our coins "In God We Trust"; we administer to witnesses an oath in which God's name appears, our President takes his oath of office upon the Bible. Is it fanatical to suggest that public taxes should not be employed for the purpose of undermining the nation's God? When we defend the Mosaic account of man's creation and contend that man has no

269

brute blood in him, but was made in God's image by separate act and placed on earth to carry out a divine decree, we are defending the God of the Jews as well as the God of the Gentiles, the God of the Catholics as well as the God of the Protestants. We believe that faith in a Supreme Being is essential to civilization as well as to religion and that abandonment of God means ruin to the world and chaos to society.

Let these believers in "the tree man" come down out of the trees and meet the issue. Let them defend the teachings of agnosticism or theism if they dare. If they deny that the natural tendency of Darwinism is to lead many to a denial of God, let them frankly point out the portions of the Bible which they regard as consistent with Darwinism, or evolution applied to man. They weaken faith in God, discourage prayer, raise doubt as to a future life, reduce Christ to the stature of a man, and make the Bible a "scrap of paper." As religion is the only basis of morals, it is time for Christians to protect religion from its most insidious enemy.

HENRY WARD BEECHER

Henry Ward Beecher served one of the largest and most influential congregations in America in the late nineteenth century. In addition, he edited one of the largest religious papers of the day: The Christian Union (circulation 100,-000). Thus, his ideas on evolution had a large and significant audience. After reading several of Hebert Spencer's works on the subject, Mr. Beecher became what he termed a "congenial evolutionist." In early 1885 he devoted seven Sunday sermons to the discussion of the effects of evolutionary philosophy on some of the fundamental doctrines of Christianity: revelation, the question of human sinfulness, the inspiration of the Bible, divine providence, evolution of man's consciousness of God, the new birth, and the church. "Divine Providence and Design" was the sixth of these sermons. It was delivered on Sunday, June 28, 1885, to the congregation assembled in Plymouth Church in Brooklyn, New York.

Divine Providence and Design[*]

"To whom will ye liken me, and make me equal, and compare me, that we may be like?"—Isa. xlvi: 5.

There is no attempt in the Hebrew Scriptures to give definite form to God, nor strict analysis, nor any comprehensive theory; as we formulate in modern times "the philosophy of things," there is no philosophy of God made known in the Bible,—any more than there is science in nature. Science is the recognition by men of things pre-existing in the world of matter; and theologies are the consciousness and the intellectual views of men respecting the facts that are set forth in the Bible. It was expressly forbidden, indeed, that there should be any form given to God in carved statues. They were not to be allowed to make images, and the spirit of the command is equally strong against pictures and against fashioning in the imagination any definite conception of form. It degrades God in the mind and imagination of men to limit him by forms of matter. There is, to be sure, addressed not to the senses but to the imagination, some form given to God by descriptions— Isaiah, Daniel, John, the Apocalyptic writer; yet even then there was but sublime indefiniteness. There was the declaration of will, the quality of

---

[*] *Evolution and Religion* (New York: Fords, Howard, and Shilbert, 1885).

271

disposition, the attributes of power and of glory; but they were all diffused through time and space, and with no definite outlines. The "word-pictures" in Isaiah and Daniel and the Revelation of John, though descriptions, are symbols and figures playing on the imagination; . . . Any formulation of the divine nature, which becomes definite, crystalline, philosophic, is a perpetual affront to the method of God's revelation, whether in Scripture or in science.

Science, at length, is tending to relieve the world of the idealizations of the Greek philosophy and of the hard and organic materialism of the Roman mind; also of the ignorant analyses and quibbling refinements of the school-men of Mediaeval ages. It is not without reason, then, that Christian men have looked upon the tendency of science to destroy the beliefs of men in certain fundamental notions of God, with apprehension and alarm.

The theory of Design has been supposed to be overthrown by the in-evitable tendencies of science. The existence of a general and special Provi-dence of God has been supposed to be incompatible with the deductions of science. The scope and use of Prayer have been ridiculed by some votaries of science. The apparent scientific denial of the possibility of Miracles— ending in the impossibility of that greatest of all, the incarnation of Jesus Christ—all these have troubled men of faith without any just reason.

It will be my design this morning, therefore, to discuss at least two of these matters—the question of Design in creation and the question of a general and a special Providence, as they stand related, not to the Scriptural testimony alone, but to what we now know of the course of natural law in this world. . . .

Atheism taxes credulity a great deal more than even the most superstitious notions do. There is nothing in human experience which can furnish a basis for believing the origin and the progress of the world of its own self without any external influence. Time and matter being given and certain forces established, then the world, to be sure, could be unfolded as it is taught by Evolution; but where was the matter and where were the laws that directed it through uncountable periods, and gave to it system, progress, direction not only, but organic symmetry? No man can believe that things happen of themselves. There is always a force prior to an effect, and that fact is wrought into the very (I had almost said) common-sense of man-kind. But the origin of matter, and what matter is, we do not know any better than we do what the spirit is, the mind, the soul. We are absolutely ignorant of what matter is. You can tell what forms matter takes, what functions it performs, but what it is, in and of itself, no man can tell.

The men that ridicule the doctrine of the soul or spirit as something separate from matter, and defy an intelligent definition of it, are no better

272

off in their mud than we are in our mire. The origin of matter, the existence of tendencies or laws in matter, of itself, is simply inconceivable.

The law of cause and effect is fundamental to the very existence of science, and, I had almost said, to the very operation of the human mind. So, then, we gain nothing by excluding divine intelligence, and to include it smooths the way to investigation, and is agreeable to the nature of the human mind. It is easier to conceive of the personal divine being with intelligence, will and power, than it is to conceive of a world of such vast and varied substance as this, performing all the functions of intelligence and will and power. That would be giving to miscellaneous matter the attributes which we denied to a personal God.

The doctrine of Evolution, at first sight, seems to destroy the theory of intelligent design in creation, and in its earlier stages left those who investigated it very doubtful whether there was anything in creation but matter. or whether there was a knowable God.

So sprang up the Agnostic school, which includes in it some of the noblest spirits of our day. "God may exist, but we do not know it." That is what the Bible says from beginning to end; that is what philosophy is now beginning to explain. We cannot understand the divine nature, so exalted above everything that has yet been developed in human consciousness, except it dawns upon us when we are ourselves unfolding, and rising to such a higher operation of our own minds as does not belong to the great mass of the human race. God is to be seen only by those faculties that verge upon the divine nature, and to them only when they are in a state of exaltation. Moral intuitions are not absolute revelations, but they are as sure of higher truths as the physical senses are of material truths.

But the question of design in creation, which has been a stable argument for the proof of the existence of God and his attributes, seems to have been shaken from its former basis. It is being restored in a larger and grander way, which only places the fact upon a wider space, and makes the outcome more wonderful. Special creation, and the adaptation in consequence of it, of structure to uses in animals, and in the vegetable kingdom to their surroundings, has always been an element of God's work regarded as most remarkable. How things fit to their places! how regular all the subordinations and developments that are going on! how fit they are to succeed one another! Now the old theory conceived God as creating things for special uses. When the idea of the lily dawned on him, he smiled and said: "I will make it;" and he made it to be just as beautiful as it is. And when the rose was to be added, like an artist God thought just how it should be all the way through. That is the old view—that some plants were made to do without

273

water and could live in parched sands; and that some could live only in the tropics; and thus God adapted all his creation to the climate and the soil and the circumstances, and it was a beautiful thing to see how things did fit, by the divine wisdom, the places where they were found.

Then comes Evolution and teaches that God created through the mediation of natural laws; that creation, in whole or detail, was a process of slow growth, and not an instantaneous process; that plants and animals alike were affected by their surrounding circumstances favorably or unfavorably; and that, in the long-run, those which were best adapted to their environment survived, and those perished which could not adapt themselves to the conditions of soil, climate, moisture, cold or heat which in the immeasurable periods of creation befell them. The adaptation then of plants to their condition did not arise from the direct command of the Great Gardener; but from the fact that, among these infinite gradations of plants, only those survived and propagated themselves which were able to bear the climate and soil in which they found themselves; all others dwindled and perished. Of course there would be a fine adjustment of the plant to its condition; it came to this by a long preparation of ancestral influences.

How beautiful it is to see a plant growing right under the cheek of a precipice or a snow-bed, or by the edges of winter through the year! Men say how beautiful the thought was that God should create life in vegetables and flowers right alongside the snow, as it were, to cheer the bosom of winter: whereas it turned out that everything that could not live there died; and, by and by, there were some plants so tough that they could live there, and they did; and the adaptation was the remainder after a long series of perishings. Men say, What a remarkable instance of divine design that the cactus can live on arid deserts, where water scarcely falls more than once or twice a year; and what a special creation and adaptation it was on the part of God that he should make such plants as that! But the Evolutionist says that all the plants were killed in succession until it came about, in the endless variations of the vegetable kingdom, that a plant developed whose structure was covered, as it were, with an india-rubber skin, and whose leaves were substantially little cisterns, which drank up all the water they wanted to use through the summer, and so continued to live in spite of their dry surroundings, when others could not live because they could not adapt themselves. So the argument for special design, as we used to hold it, fails there.

Through long periods all things tended to vary more or less from their original forms, and adapted themselves to their necessary conditions; and what could not do this perished; for the theory of Evolution is as much a theory of destruction and degradation as of development and building up.

As the carpenter has numberless shavings, and a vast amount of wastage of every log which he would shape to some use, so creation has been an enormous waste, such as seems like squandering, on the scale of human life, but not to Him that dwells in Eternity. In bringing the world to its present conditions, vast amounts of things have lived for a time and were unable to hold on, and let go and perished. We behold the onflowing, through immeasurable ages of creation, of this peculiar tendency to vary, and in some cases to improve. The improvement is transmitted; and in the battle of life, one thing conflicting with another, the strong or the best adapted crowd out the weak, and these continue to transmit their qualities until something better yet shall supplant them.

Vast waste and the perishing of unfit things is one of the most striking facts in the existence of this world; for while life is the consummation, death seems to be the instrument by which life itself is supplied with improvement and advancement. Death prepares the way for life. Things are adapted thus to their condition, to their climate, to their food; or by their power of escape from their adversaries, or their power of establishing themselves and of defending their position, they make it secure. The vast universe, looked at largely, is moving onward and upward in determinate lines and directions, while on the way the weak are perishing. Yet, there is an unfolding process that is carrying creation up to higher planes and upon higher lines, reaching more complicated conditions in structure, in function, in adaptation, with systematic and harmonious results, so that the whole physical creation is organizing itself for a sublime march toward perfectness.

If single acts would evince design, how much more a vast universe, that by inherent laws gradually builded itself, and then created its own plants and animals, a universe so adjusted that it left by the way the poorest things, and steadily wrought toward more complex, ingenious, and beautiful results! Who designed this mighty machine, created matter, gave to it its laws, and impressed upon it that tendency which has brought forth the almost infinite results on the glove, and wrought them into a perfect system? Design by wholesale is grander than design by retail.

You are all familiar with the famous illustration of Dr. Paley, where a man finds a watch, and infers irresistibly that that watch was made by some skillful, thoughtful watchmaker. Suppose that a man, having found a watch, should say to himself, "Somebody thought this out, somebody created this; it is evidently constructed and adapted exactly to the end in view—the keeping of time." Suppose, then, that some one should take him to Waltham, and introduce him into that vast watch-factory, where watches are created in hundreds of thousands by machinery; and suppose the question should be put to him, "What do you think, then, about the man who created this machinery, which of itself goes on cutting out wheels, and springs, and pinions, and everything that belongs to making a watch? If it be an argument of design that a man could make one watch, is it not a sublimer argument of design that there is a man existing who could create a manufactory turning out millions of watches, and by machinery too, so that the human hand has little to do but to adjust the parts already created by machines?" If it be evidence of design in creation that God adapted one single flower to its place and functions, is it not greater evidence if there is a system of such adaptations going on from eternity to eternity? Is not the Creator of the system a more sublime designer than the creator of any single act? . . .

It may be safely said, then, that Evolution, instead of obliterating the evidence of divine Design, has lifted it to a higher plane, and made it more sublime than it ever was contemplated to be under the old reasonings.

Next, it has been thought that science, by introducing the doctrine of the universality and invariableness of law, and giving it a larger and a more definite field of operation, destroys all possibility of a special Providence of God over men and events. It has been said that everything that we know anything about in this world has happened by the force of law, and that it is not likely that God will turn law aside or change law and interject his immediate creative will for the sake of any favorites that he had in this world. I need hardly say to you, after the reading of the passage (Matt. vi: 19-34) this morning in our opening services, that no doctrine is taught more explicitly by the Lord Jesus Christ than this doctrine of the personal watch and care of God over men and things,—that nothing happens without his inspection. The theist admits that there may be a general Providence supervising the machinery of the universe. But the Christian doctrine of special Providence,—the adaptation of all the forms of nature to the welfare of particular individuals, races and nations,—if this doctrine of Providence were to be overthrown by science, I need not say that it would make a very great breach in our faith, in the New Testament and as to the divinity of Christ himself. One of the things that makes life endurable is that we are not like so many stones, rolled, broken and rattling down by violent torrents, without any particular force of design; but that we are grouped together in communities and in families; and, as individuals, under the beneficent inspection of God, who has a continual thought of our welfare. The world would seem to me a very dreary place if I did not believe in the immanence of the divine Mind and the interference of the divine Will. The belief in a special divine Providence brings with it great peace and confidence, and is exactly suited to the ignorance and helpless condition of the human race. A chariot with no driver, an engine with no engineer, a voyage and no captain or officers, a raging battle and no commander—what would all these events be in comparison with undirected human life upon this whirling globe, in its endless passage through time? The world is full of ignorance, disease, revolution, wars, pestilence, and immeasurable disasters. They spring from definite laws; but laws are cruel to those who are too ignorant to obey them. All this does not establish the doctrine of a divine special Providence, but it makes it devoutly to be wished that such a government may be proved to exist. It should make one very unwilling to destroy the teaching of Jesus and thus reduce the world to orphanage.

But is there any *reason* in the doctrine of a Natural Law which controls all things, and no God who controls law itself? It is said that a special divine Providence implies an interference with the regular action of natural laws; a direct exercise of the divine will aside from or even opposed to their uniform operation; that it is not philosophical to suppose that God shows partiality—that he sets aside for some men the laws which regulate the conduct of others; that he favors particular persons, families, and nations. It is said also that God works only through laws and never sets them aside. But this is begging the question. What are natural laws? In the lower elements of creation they may be described as the behavior of matter. Under the same conditions, matter, so far as we know, behaves in the same manner. What the compelling influence is that produces uniform sequences to certain antecedents, we do not know. We can conceive of a Being from whom goes forth an energy, generic and unconscious, quite aside from conscious will and purpose. To a limited extent this condition exists in man. Men call it magnetic force, or personal atmosphere. We can imagine that as the sun fills the world with light and heat, not by any volition, but by the nature given to it by God, so there may be in God himself a radiancy of power separable from thought or purpose, and which fills the universe with the energy that men call Force or Natural Law. But to say that God's will never interferes with this ordinary effluence of force, to control or direct, is an assumption of knowledge which no man can possess. Using the term Law, for convenience in its popular sense, as a ruling and uniform action of force inherent in matter and pervading creation, it may be pointed out, that, while the inorganic materials of creation are held in the grasp of law with the greatest constancy, yet, as matter rises upon the scale through mechanical, chemical forces to organic life, and again from the lower forms of life to higher organization, the forces and their laws become more complex and diversified. What are called laws of nature seem to occupy, among the lower conditions of matter, the place of mind in higher animals and in the human family. But as the human mind rises in the scale it gives evidence of more and more control over the laws of matter; and this fact seems to suggest the possibility that the mind, in its highest development, is of all natural forces itself the greatest and most universally active and efficient.

But, leaving this suggestion, there can be no doubt of the control which the human mind exercises over those forces which men call natural laws. The popular idea is, and it is partaken of very largely by philosophical men, that laws are unchangeable, irresistible in their sphere, that they are not to be controlled, and that they compel all. It is felt as though they were great energies that moved as bars of steel would move through crowds, overturning, bruising and destroying all that came in their way. The irresistibleness of natural law is an illusion. Of all the things within the conception of the imagination, there is nothing gentler, nothing more pliable, nothing more applicable, nothing more controllable, than natural physical laws. They are a great deal more like the silk thread than they are like the needle that carries it, or than they are like a bar of iron or steel. Only obey a natural law, and it becomes your servant; you must break yourself in as you would a steed, whose broad back then carries you whithersoever you will.

Natural laws are constantly checked, constantly contradicted and made inoperative. They are set in conflict one against the other. The laws of chemical affinity are perpetually thwarted in the laboratory. The acid cannot have its way when it meets with an alkali, or the alkali when it meets an acid; they make a compromise. In mechanics the law of gravity cannot pull down the stone which you put an iron pillar under to support. . . .

Laws depend upon human intelligence for their achievements. In their wildest state natural laws are only half fruitful. Winds have roamed like wild giants over the globe, roaring hither and thither, before there was a human population; but now they grind the food of man by turning windmills, or swell the sails that carry men for all their purposes round and round the world. The wild wind that knew no master is apprenticed to ten thousand masters to-day. Human reason has taken possession of it and made it work for its living. Water floated in the clouds or stormed on the sea, or rushed forth in useless rivers. It, too, has been reduced to service, everywhere turning wheels, everywhere replenishing the supplies of society through the medium of manufactories; and even in the desert, by irrigation, making the wilderness to bud and blossom as the rose. Water had never done that of itself; water inspired by human will does it. . . .

Not by violating, either, but by *using* the laws of nature, men can and do create a providence; and thus we come back to the gist of the matter. I can use the laws of nature so that they shall be a providence to me, and I can use them so that they shall be a providence to my family. It is by the use of natural laws, not by violating them, by harnessing them and making them work, that I can make my family respectable and send out my children to the vocations of life. . . .

Not only can a man take care of himself and of his household, but of all his neighbors as well. He can impart the benefit of his knowledge to his whole neighborhood. Surely, God ought to be able to do almost as much as that in the wider use of natural law!

One single combination of laws in a machine revolutionizes the industry of the globe. It gives to the poor man what before only the princely loom gave to the rich sovereigns of the earth; and a man's invention of a machine made cotton the fabric of the world, on whose existence statesmanship turned and nations lived and throve, or perished. A man can, by discoveries of the functions of natural law, bless the age in which he lives. What are the steamboats that ply the world around, what are the factories that are turning out wondrous things for the whole population of the globe, and what is the world itself but a wise subjugation of natural laws by human intelligence directed by the human will?

If, then, God cannot create a providence by using, not violating, natural laws, he cannot do what the meanest creatures on earth can do in some degree and measure. All the talk about the inevitableness of natural laws and their being utterly irresistible is inconsiderate and unfounded. He can use these laws without violating them, just as men use them. He can exert, directly or indirectly, upon the consciousness of men, an influence which shall make them enactors of his decree. Theists recognize a general Providence, by which the world and all its laws and apparatus are preserved and kept in working order. But Jesus taught more than this; he taught that God uses the machinery of the world for his own special ends. It does not follow that God overrides stated forces; he can, with superior skill, direct the great powers of Nature to special results. God's will, or mind, may be supposed to act upon the human mind, either through ordinary laws, or directly, without any intermediate instruments.

In the case of direct influence the effect may be supposed to be an exaltation of the whole mind or of special parts of it. The result would be not merely a quickening of faculties, but an exaltation of the mind to a higher plane, on or around which play new energies or forces; and to this superior condition of mind there would be easily opened new vision, new powers—especially the power to more wisely adapt, direct, and use natural laws, even those which pertain to the higher planes.

In this direction, it may be, we shall find a philosophy of miracle, of the powers of faith, of prophecy, of a human control of matter which allies exalted manhood to the creative power of God. Such an augmented power of the human soul was unquestionably taught by Jesus. As science is teaching us that hitherto men have known but little of the infinite truths of the material world, so we are beginning to find out that there are infinite possibilities in the human soul which have never been included in our philosophies.

He who enters upon the theme of the interaction of the human mind and the Divine mind, launches upon a wide and solemn sea, fathomless, shoreless, and dark, as yet. Better than Columbus sailing westward, will come Jesus to quell the wave, illumine the darkness, and reveal the shore. The human mind is the kernel; the material world is but the shell or rind. As yet science has chiefly concerned itself with the shell. The unexplored soul is yet to be found out.

When men have gone out of the simple faith of childhood by the misinterpretation of the theory and philosophy of natural law, it ought to be to them a source of great joy and rejoicing that science itself, which misled them, has been appealed from—science not well informed, to science better informed; and that this royal doctrine, in which is so much hope, so much courage, so much rest, is returning to its place for women and children, for heroic men in straits, for all men who find themselves outside of those normal and ordinary influences upon which prosperity depends. When men are hampered and find themselves in such emergencies, if they are right-minded, if they can lift themselves higher than flesh and blood, higher than the lower forms of material law, into the communion of God, they have a right to believe that there is a divine influence, an atmospheric one, shall I call it?—something like sunlight to the leaves and flowers; that which will lift them up and compel such laws to serve them; and, what is better, will direct them in such a way that they shall come under the influence of those laws which should give them relief.

There is one other view, however, that may supplement this, namely, that we are to take into consideration the location of this life and its relation to the life to come. As in autumn the leaves fall gently from the trees without harming the tree, externally stripped and apparently dead, whose life is yet in it, and which waits the snowy season through for resurrection which is to come, so is it with human life. Our seeking is often folly, and our regrets often more foolish. We lose to gain, and gain to lose. In short, God's Providence is wiser than man's judgment of his own needs. We are to bear in mind that this life is a mere planting-time. We are started here; we await transplantation through resurrection, and what may seem the neglect of God and a want of providence will reveal itself a step beyond, as being an illustrious Providence, watchful, tender, careful.

So, brethren, be not in haste to cast away, on the instruction or the misinterpretation of science, yet crude in many of its parts, that faith of childhood, that faith of your fathers, that faith which is the joy and should be the courage of every right-minded man, the faith that God's eye is on you, and that he cares, he guides, he defends, and will bring you safely from earth to life eternal.

11

THE SOCIAL GOSPEL: PREACHING REFORM
1875-1915

William Bos
Clyde Faries

As Americans struggled to adjust to industrialization, the church battled to maintain its influence upon their lives. Social, economic, and political upheavals, however, so dominated the years from 1875 to 1915 and class consciousness so permeated attitudes and actions, that Christian leaders encountered increasing difficulty in persuading people to look to the church for leadership. Workers formed unions; industrialists formed cooperatives. The producing class became silverites; the controllers of production became monometalists. The poor grew wretched; the wealthy grew greedy. The deprived looked for aid and comfort from the pulpit; the rich demanded loyalty to the gospel of wealth from their preachers.

Corporate profits climbed higher and higher while farmers, laborers, and small businessmen sank lower and lower in the economy. Farmers saw their produce drop in price by more than a third from 1873 to 1896, while the amount they paid for manufactured goods rose by a similar amount. They saw their families hungry and ill-clothed, while the wealthy spoke of the healthy economy. Workers, already inadequately paid, found themselves replaced by imported labor, and they were dissatisfied. Small businessmen pressured from their shops by powerful combinations, tried unsuccessfully to compete in the overcrowded labor market, and they were depressed. As the gulf widened between the poor and the wealthy, ministers of the gospel searched for the way to give spiritual guidance that would avert social disruption.

The pulpit extended little support to labor, prison reform voting, temperance, and monetary reform movements at the outset. When labor disputes burst into street violence, pulpits rang with bitter denunciation of those unwilling to accept "their station in life." Some ministers called for the Gatling gun to be used indiscriminately against those who would disturb the public tranquility by their wage demands. In fact, something of a national crusade was aroused by the Grangers' revolt, the railway strike of 1877, and the Haymarket riot. Such church organs as the *Watchman,* the *Independent,* the *Congregationalist,* the *Christian Advocate* and the *Christian Union* spoke as one great chorus calling for bullets and bayonets to be used without mercy against those making public protest against low wages.

Many ministers urged the producing class to accept poverty without trying to reform the social and economic order. The poor merely needed to tighten their belts and learn to want less, counseled these preachers, for if God had not meant them to have less he would have given them more. Besides, others argued, poverty needed to exist in abundance so that the wealthy could express their Christianity through charity to the needy.

But a few used the pulpit to launch a crusade against social and economic inequities. They wanted to change sweatshops into well-ordered places of work, to take children from the factories and put them in school. They preached that laborers and farmers must organize and demand a greater share of the wealth they produced. Peter Dietz, John Ryan, Walter Rauschenbusch, George Herron, William Kerby, Washington Gladden, Samuel Fielden, and William Carwardine, among others, worked for the kind of reform that they believed would infuse a "love-thy-neighbor-as-thyself" attitude into the business world.

Most preachers ignored the gathering storm of class conflict. They urged people to be saved, explained doctrine, pictured the glories of heaven, and warned of the torments of hell, but did not mention the crises that tore at the soul of the country. The church is a house of worship, not a union hall, they maintained, and the minister is a preacher of the Gospel, not a political advocate. A popular theme explained that if everyone were to accept Christ, there would be no need for reform movements. Published sermons of the era are mostly untimely and often innocuous.

Time, reason, declining church membership, decreasing influence of ministers, worsening economic conditions, and persistence of reformers, however, gradually forced the church to change. Changes were slight at first but soon swept over most American pulpits. Fewer preachers denounced the strike of 1886 than did the strike of 1877, and those who did condemn the 1886 labor action did so with less vehemence. Those who had preached the gospel of wealth now were saying that a man's value lay not in his control of material goods but in his usefulness to others. Church papers that twenty years earlier had called for use of the Gatling gun against strikers now blamed manufacturers for heartless, arbitrary, and ruthless acts against striking employees. Many who had carefully skirted worldly controversy now found some good in the new social gospel. By the turn of the century many ministers had developed a new, compassionate attitude toward the plight of the poor. They believed that the church should give Christian leadership to reform movements, and they viewed the Bible as a guide to social reform.

Social gospelers reasserted the spiritual leadership of the pulpit. By condemning those who wronged the poor and by urging all to work for improvement of living conditions for everyone, ministers slowed the trend of the church toward following rather than guiding public opinion. In so doing they found approval among the wealthy as well as among the poor. The church had erred by fighting farm and labor movements, argued these social gospelers, and it should now make amends by actively seeking equality for everyone, especially in law, education, and physical care.

They pumped new enthusiasm into the pulpit by associating Jesus Christ with the preacher of reform. Jesus fought disease, ignorance, and poverty, they told congregations, and it was high time that Christians should follow in his steps. A man cannot amass wealth or wisdom without the aid of his fellows, and should only use his talents and his goods to make the world a more livable place for everyone. Some advocated making the church more homelike so that it would be more inviting to people and would serve as the very spring of reform activity. The most visionary of the social gospelers even looked forward to the day when poverty, disease, and jails would no longer exist.

The age of reform was an era of great preachers. Henry Van Dyke, Dwight Moody, Peter Dietz, John Ryan, Walter Rauschenbusch, George Herron, William Kerby, Washington Gladden, Russell Conwell, William Lawrence, Alexander Maclaren, Nathaniel Butler, Charles Finney, and Shailer Mathews, to name but a few, electrified congregations with their Christian advocacy. As leadership in the church moved from those fighting reform to the social gospelers, two groups maintained the greatest congregational support. Whereas the reformers and the antireformers intensified the atmosphere within the church, it was those who remained silent on social issues and the moderates who were heard most frequently in the pulpit. The preaching of Henry Van Dyke, Dwight L. Moody, and Washington Gladden represent the efforts of the majority of ministers. Moody offered people frustrated by industrialization an escape into Christ; Van Dyke offered them the challenge of Christ; Gladden agitated for a stronger commitment to carry out Christ's work. Moody advised people to accept Christ and thereby attain the strength to face life's problems; Van Dyke identified accepting Christ with accepting the duty to try to solve economic and social problems; Gladden admonished all to seek Christ by rejecting greed and strife and administering the law of brotherly love.

DWIGHT L. MOODY

Dwight L. Moody was probably the leading evangelist of the nineteenth century. Born in Northfield, Massachusetts, February 5, 1837, he lived in relative poverty in a rural area the first sixteen years of his life. He went to Boston as a young man and became interested in the teachings of Christ because of the preaching of a certain Dr. Kirk.

After leaving Boston he traveled to Chicago, where he became a highly successful shoe salesman. He was also successful as a religious worker in his spare time. Through his work with the underprivileged and through the Young Men's Christian Association, he became known as a devout professor of Christ and an effective public speaker.

Although he was never ordained as a minister, he ministered to the sick and wounded of both armies during the Civil War. After the war he founded a church in Chicago and continued his preaching there. Perhaps his most important decision was to accompany the Rev. Ira Sankey to Britain for a series of evangelistic services. His speaking on that tour lasted two years and was so popular that it inspired a new evangelistic movement. Moody probably spoke to more people during his career than any other preacher of his time.

Evening Sermon*

"What must I do to be saved?"—ACTS 16:30.

I take my text this evening from the sixteenth chapter of Acts, thirtieth verse: "What must I do to be saved?" At our afternoon meeting there were quite a number got up and told how they had been saved in the past two weeks. One young man rose and said that he had been saved within the last hour. I asked him how it was, and he said it was in the noon prayer-meeting, when we were talking about believing on the Lord Jesus Christ. He said the Lord saved him right there in the meeting. And in thinking of that I thought I would try and get hold of someone else tonight, and in the same way. The only way to be saved is to believe in the Lord Jesus Christ. This question, asked of Paul and Silas, is the most important that can be asked by a human being in this world. I have no doubt that every man and woman in this house tonight has at some time or other asked this question,

* *Fifty Evenings with Dwight L. Moody* (Philadelphia: C. H. Yost, 1876), pp. 176 ff.

"What must I do?" many and many a time. I wish they would add the words "to be saved" to that last word. A man of business gets up in the morning and asks, "What must I do today? What shall I do to make the most money? It is hard times, and it is hard to make both ends meet. It is hard to meet the notes that are coming due." But there is a good deal more important question than that, when a man is sick and asks what he must do to save his life; and even that is not so important a question as we have before us tonight, A man had better lose the life of the body than the life of the soul; and it is better to go into bankruptcy, and lose all through failure in business than to fail to save your soul.

From the highest to the lowest, it is an everyday question, "What must I do?" Now I want you to put on the rest of that question, and ask, "What must I do to be saved?" It is not "What must my brother do?" or "What must my friends do?" but, "What must I do to be saved?" We want to bring out that cardinal idea tonight—to bring it home to ourselves. "What shall I do to be saved?" Now the answer was, "Believe on the Lord Jesus Christ and thou shalt be saved." Simply to believe! That Philippian jailor was like all the rest of mankind by nature. He was a sinner; he was already condemned, and what he wanted was salvation. What he wanted was to know what he should do to be saved—that is what every sinner wants to know when he becomes aroused and awakened. He thinks he has something to do. What was this Philippian jailor told to do? To pray earnestly, and weep, and mourn, and fast, and do penance, and cry aloud upon God? No; they did not tell him anything of the kind. They said, "Believe on the Lord Jesus Christ and thou shalt be saved, and not only thou, but thy whole house." Just simply "believe." A man's mind is always affected by the character of what he believes. If you believe that the Gospel is good news, it will make you glad. If you believe it is bad news, it will send you away sorrowful. We want to take God at His word, and believe that the Gospel is good news, and go on our way rejoicing. The Philippian jailor and his whole house rejoiced because they believed—so Paul and Silas say. In the next verse it says that he told how Christ died for sinners and a poor Philippian jailor, and he rejoiced. If we can make men believe that the Gospel is good news, it will fill them with gladness. I often hear people say, "Why do I not have the joy I have heard that others have when they are converted?" It is because you do not believe the Gospel is good news; if you did, it could not help making you glad. I had a friend who, last fall, came from Chicago with his wife and four children, who were going to France. After they sailed, as time went on, he kept looking at the papers to see if the steamer had arrived. As it did not arrive when due, he began to grow uneasy on the first day. On the second, they had not arrived, and he became alarmed. On the third, he was almost frantic with anxiety. One day when he had become almost mad with anxiety, and had been unable to sleep, a despatch came from his wife, saying, "Saved alone." All his children had gone to a watery grave. That was bad news, which made him very sad. I suppose if the despatch had said, "By the grace of God we are saved, not only myself, but all the family;" that would have been good news, and he would have rejoiced. When one hears good news, it makes him glad, and when he hears bad news, it makes him sad.

There were those four lepers, the messengers who brought the news that the Syrian army had gone, at which so many rejoiced. There are a great many who are willing to believe the Gospel if they can have some polite messenger. They say: "You do not believe we would go and hear such a minister, do you? We do not believe in that kind of preaching." Now, if a boy brings you a despatch containing good news, you do not look to see who the boy is, do you? It is so in preaching; never mind who brings you the news of the Gospel; what you want is to be saved. When the news was brought to Samaria, people rushed out of the gate, and came where they could get the good news. We see in the eighth chapter of Acts, that Philip went down and preached the gospel, and there was great joy in that city because they believed the Gospel of Jesus Christ. So there was good news brought to Samaria twice. Once was when the lepers brought the news that the army had left, and once when Philip went down and preached the gospel. Tonight I want to make it so plain that every soul can understand what it is to be saved. A man said in one of our meetings, some time ago, that he had been forty-two years in learning three things; the first thing was that he could not do anything toward his own salvation. I said to myself, "I have learned that, too." The second thing was that God did not require him to do anything; and the third thing was, that Christ had done it all Himself. These things are worth knowing, if it did take him forty years to learn them. You cannot do anything toward saving yourself, you cannot work for salvation. It is a work of the mind, and not of the body. Though it is an act of faith, it certainly is not working; you would not say that trusting is working; or that believing a man's testimony is working. The first thing was, that he could not do anything; the second was, that God did not require him to do anything; and the third was, that Jesus Christ had done it all. All that you have to do is to believe in the finished work of Jesus Christ. When He said, "It is finished," He meant what He said. It is finished, it is completed, and all that poor mortals have to do is to accept it.

What shall I do to be saved? Accept of Jesus Christ personally; take Him in your heart now; let go of your own self; cease all your efforts, and just lay hold on Him. There were once two millers who used to keep their mill running day and night. Every night at midnight the man would go down the stream in his boat, and get out a few hundred yards above the dam, and from there a brother miller would take the boat and row back. One night the miller fell asleep, and when he awoke he found he was only a few yards from the dam. He seized the oar, and pulled against the stream, but he found the current was so savage that he could make no headway. He managed in the darkness to get near enough the shore to get hold of a little twig; that twig began to give way near the roots, and he knew that if it did give way he would be lost. He had to stop trying to save himself: he gave a cry, "Help! help! help!" and at last someone heard his voice, and came and threw a rope from the shore. All that he had to do was to let go the twig and take hold of the rope, and they pulled him up from the jaws of death. Now, the rope let down into this unpleasant world is just the word "believe." Lay hold of this rope tonight; it is offered to every soul tonight, and all that you have to do is to lay hold of it. Another illustration I would give is about a dream—not that I believe in dreams, but sometimes they illustrate good truth. A woman was troubled about the condition of her soul, and tried to find peace by working her way up to heaven; but she felt as everyone else does who tries to do that. One night she dreamed that she was in a terrible pit; it was so steep that she could not climb out. She kept climbing up a little way and then slipping back until at last she got discouraged and gave up the whole thing. How many there are who have been saved just when they have got discouraged in trying to save themselves! So she threw herself down on the bottom of the pit to die. She looked up and saw a little star through the mouth of the pit and the star began to lift her up, and she was lifted higher and higher; then she took her eyes off and began to look at herself, and the moment she saw herself she went down again to the bottom of the pit. A second time she fixed her eyes upon the star and again it raised her higher, higher, higher; then again she looked at herself! What a picture it is of hundreds of sinners whom we meet every day! They take their eyes off of Christ and begin to look at themselves, and find they have the same old feelings again, and get discouraged. So when the woman looked at herself a second time, back she went again. The third time she fixed her eye on that star, and in her dream it lifted her, until at last she came out of the pit and her feet were landed safely. She has been looking at that star ever since and the darkness and clouds are now gone.

In order to be saved, you must look steadfastly unto the Lord. Jesus says to look into the ends of the earth and be saved, for God is able to give you help, and there is none else. Don't look into your own sinful hearts away from Christ, for He alone can quicken you. He can draw you out of the pit that Adam dug for you and into which you have fallen. When he fell into it, he drew us all into it, too. There are plenty of coal holes in America, and some pretty deep ones too; there are some hundreds and thousands of feet in depth, but I tell you that none of them are as deep as the one we are now in through Adam, and there is not one so hard to get out of as that same pit that Adam dug for us. Stop trying, therefore, for your efforts are fruitless; give up your own exertions and cry unto the Lord for succor. David says in the fortieth Psalm: "He brought me up also out of a horrible pit, out of the miry clay, and set my feet upon a rock and established my goings. And He hath put a new song into my mouth, even praise unto our God." Yes, He did it, He did it himself. The Lord wants to bring you up out of the horrible pit this very night, if you only let Him. "He heard my cry." There is not a poor penitent anywhere on this earth, no matter in how low a place he may be, but God will hear his cry. If you come from the very depths of sin and cry unto the Lord, He will hear and save you.

I remember when I was in the north of England—at Newcastle—one time I came home very late from the meeting, and sat down at table to take a little something to eat before going to bed; and the lady of the house set something before me and then said, "Mr. Moody, is there anything that you would like that is not on the table?" Well, I said there was nothing except, perhaps, a glass of water, as I felt thirsty. She went out and brought in a jug of water—they use jugs, earthen jugs in that part of the country, that keep the water nice and cool. Well, she brought in and set it before me, and then stepped aside. I took up the jug to pour out some of the water, when I saw a little fly in the water. I didn't want to trouble her again so late at night, and so didn't say anything to her about it—set down the jug of water without drinking it. Soon she perceived that I didn't pour any out, and said, "Why, Mr. Moody, what is the matter? I thought you were thirsty; why don't you drink? Is there anything the matter with the water?" Well, I didn't want to put her to any further trouble, and I said, "Oh, never mind; it's all right; thank you." "No; I am sure there is something wrong with the water," said she; and she came over and looked into the jug and found the fly. "Oh, it is a fly," she said; "now, if Edith were here"—Edith was a little girl about ten years of age—"she would have mercy upon the little fly and take it out." I immediately said, "Madam, Edith shan't be more merciful than I am," and I took the pickle-fork and put it down near the fly. The little thing had given up struggling, and had resigned itself to its fate. But as soon as it saw the fork it commenced struggling again, and when it had seized it, held on firmly with all its might, and I brought it out of its danger safely. I then placed in on my warm hand—it was so cold that it could hardly stir—and by and by it began to move its wings, and when it had them all free of the water, and felt they were strong enough to carry it, it left my hand and flew to the wall. It was rescued, and, no doubt, if it could have spoken, it would have said, "Thank you, thank you; you have saved me." That is just what Christ is doing now. He will save you if you trust in Him. You must have faith in heaven, and believe that help must come from above; it can come from nowhere else. Just stop trying; that is a lesson that God wants you to learn. "I will save you if you give up trying to save yourself," God says; give up all hope, and he will be near and bring you safely home. But men are all the time saying, "I must do something; I can't remain still; I must be up and doing." I tell you that God don't save until you give up all hope. When you come to the end of your struggles, then comes God and offers you salvation. A couple of men, two or three years ago, went out to bathe in Lake Michigan, in the month of July. They were both fine swimmers. But they had not been long in the water before one of them got attacked by the cramp. When he felt it in his limbs, he cried out to his friend to save him. Of course the man swam out to him, and came within his reach. But his drowning companion immediately seized him around the neck, notwithstanding his repeated warnings, and both went down together. By the greatest exertions his friend got away from him while under the water. When he rose to the surface, he said to his friend, who was but a few feet away from him, "Now, I can save you if you only let me. Don't seize me again, but let me take you by the collar, and I will bring you ashore. You give up all effort and I will save you. If you promise me you won't touch me it will be all right. If you seize me you will drown me as well as yourself." The drowning man promised all he was asked. Upon that his friend swam over to him again, but his terrified friend took hold of him again harder than ever. After a life-and-death struggle, however, he was shaken off, and his friend had, for safety, to swim away from him several yards. He dare not go near him again, and there he had to stay, and he heard the dying groans of his drowning friend, and saw him go down for the last time, never to breathe again. He might have been saved if he had stopped trying. And so it is with you now; and if you give up all hope of saving yourself, and fall quietly into the arms of Christ—into the loving arms of the Saviour—He will save you.

"What must I do to be saved?" the jailor cried. The answer was, "Believe in the Lord Jesus Christ, and thou shalt be saved." You can do nothing yourself. You, my friend, may have tried to stop swearing, but after a short period of endeavor you have failed, haven't you? You have tried to stop drinking, haven't you, and have failed too? You have a miserable, wretched temper, my friend, and have tried to overcome it and have failed, haven't you? You have tried, some of you have, to break off some sin or other, and you have failed. You have tried again, and failed again; tried and tried, and failed and failed, every time, haven't you? Now, if you give up all hope and stop trying, you will be strengthened by grace from above, and you will conquer. Stop trying, then, tonight, and fall into the arms of the loving Saviour. You should trust Him, and then how quick will your salvation come. Let Him come into your heart and dwell there, and create it into a new tabernacle of holiness. If the heart is right, the life is right. If the fountain is pure, the stream is pure. I remember some years ago I used to hold open-air meetings out in Illinois. In the summer evenings great crowds used to come out, and I noticed at one of the meetings a gentleman sitting in his carriage which was on the outskirts of the assembly, and he had a cigar in his mouth. And again the next morning he was there; and again the next evening. After the preaching was over, he always used to drive right away. One time I saw him take a great interest in what was said, and after a while I saw tears trickling down his cheeks. I made inquiries about him, and they told me who he was. I said to them that I must go and see him some day. They laughed. "Why, you don't know the man as well as we do. You have no idea of the ridicule he has made use of with respect to these meetings, and the lies he has told about you all around town." And they gave me his history. They said he was a man of large wealth, had a fine house, and had everything to make life pleasant to him, but he was a very profane, godless man. He would curse everything and everybody. Even the wife of his bosom has curses showered down upon her, and his children used to be witnesses of his frightful oaths. One day I set out to go to see him. I was near his house when he stepped out of the front door. I stepped up— "This is Mr. P., I believe?" "Yes, sir," in a gruff, unwelcome voice, "that is my name; what do you want?" He knew very well who I was; he mistrusted what I wanted. "I would like to ask you a question," I replied. "Well, what is it?" "I am told," I said, "that you are very wealthy, that God has blessed you with great wealth, that you have a beautiful wife and lovely children, and I just want to know why you treat God in this way you do?" The tears came out of his eyes, and he said, "Come in, come in." So I entered, and he told me that he had tried a thousand times to stop swearing, but he couldn't. I told him to trust Jesus and He would stop it for him—that's what He came into the world to do, and the result was that he let Christ take the burden. He confessed his sin, had the prayers of all the Christians round about, and in a year he became one of the elders of the church.

Then be saved, my friends, yourselves. Don't put it off. A Scotch lassie in Perth wanted somebody to pray for her in meeting once. The minister gave her afterward the fifty-third chapter of Isaiah to read. She said, in her Scotch language, "I canna read, I canna pray. Oh, Jesus, tak me just as I am." It is a mistake to send one away like that. Jesus can save you this very hour, this very minute. Oh sinner! let Him save you now. Throw yourself into His arms, and He'll save you. What must you do to be saved? Believe on the Lord Jesus Christ, and he will save you this very minute. When I was preaching once in Illinois, the next morning I had an inquiry meeting. I went around, speaking to this one and that one. And among them I saw a girl about seven years old—about as big as this girl here on the front seat. I I thought she was too young to know what an inquiry meeting was. But just as I got through, I thought I would say something to her. So I said, "How long have you been a Christian?" "Ever since last night," she said. "I was at the meeting, and I felt I was a sinner, and I went home and kneeled by the side of my bed, and I asked God to take away my sin, and He did it." And I said, "How do you know He did it?" And she said, "Why, He promised to." I couldn't say more. "He promised to." If you believe, He will save you. Oh, believe Him, trust Him; receive Christ and you are saved.

HENRY VAN DYKE

Henry Van Dyke was virtually born into the ministry. At the time of his birth, November 10, 1852, his father was a prominent Presbyterian preacher in Germantown, Pennsylvania, and his family had a long history of church leadership. At Princeton University young Henry Van Dyke won acclaim as a scholar in English and as a public speaker. After receiving his M.A. Degree at Princeton, he studied theology at the University of Berlin.

Although he served only two churches in his career, he became one of the best known preachers in the country. After serving only two years at the United Presbyterian Church in Newport, R.I., be moved to the Brick Presbyterian Church in New York City, where he remained from 1882 until 1900. In New York, he tripled the membership within a few years and often had congregations so large that they spilled over into the street to hear his sermons. He was the university preacher at Princeton, Cornell, Harvard, and Amherst and a lecturer at Yale. He was probably the most popular commencement speaker in the United States.

A noted writer of both prose and poetry, a successful teacher, and an author and editor of best-selling English textbooks, he was capable of challenging the intellect of the most sophisticated listeners. As a cautious liberal, he helped lead his church into the era of the social gospel. Although an artist, he never cared more for his art than for his people.

Salt *

BACCALAUREATE SERMON, HARVARD UNIVERSITY, JUNE, 1898

Text: *"Ye are the salt of the earth."*—MATTHEW 5:13.

This figure of speech is plain and pungent. Salt is savory, purifying, preservative. It is one of those superfluities which the great French wit defined as "things that are very necessary." From the very beginning of human history men have set a high value upon it and sought for it in caves and by the seashore. The nation that had a good supply of it was counted rich. A bag of salt, among the barbarous tribes, was worth more than a man. The Jews prized it especially because they lived in a warm climate where food was difficult to keep, and because their religion laid particular emphasis on cleanliness, and because salt was largely used in their sacrifices.

* *Masterpieces of Modern Oratory*, ed. Edwin DuBois Shurter (Boston: Ginn and Company, 1906), pp. 325-36.

Christ chose an image which was familiar when He said to His disciples, "Ye are the salt of the earth." This was His conception of their mission, their influence. They were to cleanse and sweeten the world in which they lived, to keep it from decay, to give a new and more wholesome flavor to human existence. Their character was not to be passive, but active. The sphere of its action was to be this present life. There is no use in saving salt for heaven. It will not be needed there. Its mission is to permeate, season, and purify things on earth. . . .

Men of privilege without power are waste material. Men of enlightenment without influence are the poorest kind of rubbish. Men of intellectual and moral and religious culture, who are not active forces for good in society, are not worth what it costs to produce and keep them. If they pass for Christians they are guilty of obtaining respect under false pretenses. They were meant to be the salt of the earth. And the first duty of salt is to be salty.

This is the subject on which I want to speak to you today. The saltiness of salt is the symbol of a noble, powerful, truly religious life. . . .

Think, first, of the influence for good which men of intelligence may exercise in the world if they will only put their culture to the right use. Half the troubles of mankind come from ignorance—ignorance which is systematically organized with societies for its support and newspapers for its dissemination—ignorance which consists less in not knowing things than in willfully ignoring the things that are already known. There are certain physical diseases which would go out of existence in ten years if people would only remember what has been learned. There are certain political and social plagues which are propagated only in the atmosphere of shallow self-confidence and vulgar thoughtlessness. There is a yellow fever of literature specially adapted and prepared for the spread of shameless curiosity, incorrect information, and complacent idiocy among all classes of the population. Persons who fall under the influence of this pest become so triumphantly ignorant that they cannot distinguish between news and knowledge. They develop a morbid thirst for printed matter, and the more they read the less they learn. They are fit soil for the bacteria of folly and fanaticism.

Now the men of thought, of cultivation, of reason in the community ought to be an antidote to these dangerous influences. Having been instructed in the lessons of history and science and philosophy they are bound to contribute their knowledge to the service of society. As a rule they are willing enough to do this for pay, in the professions of law and medicine and teaching and divinity. What I plead for is the wider, nobler, unpaid service which an educated man renders to society simply by being thoughtful and by helping other men to think.

The college men of a country ought to be its most conservative men; that is to say, the men who do most to conserve it. They ought to be the men whom demagogues cannot inflame nor political bosses pervert. They ought to bring wild theories to the test of reason, and withstand rash experiments with obstinate prudence. When it is proposed, for example, to enrich the whole nation by debasing its currency, they should be the men who demand time to think whether real wealth can be created by artificial legislation. And if they succeed in winning time to think, the danger will pass—or rather it will be transformed into some other danger requiring a new application of the salt of intelligence. For the fermenting activity of ignorance is so incessant, and perpetual thoughtfulness is the price of social safety. . . .

Think, in the second place, of the duty which men of moral principle owe to society in regard to the evils which corrupt and degrade it. Of the existence of these evils we need to be reminded again and again, just because we are comparatively clean and decent and upright people. Men who live an orderly life are in great danger of doing nothing else. We wrap our virtue up in little bags of respectability and keep it in the storehouse of a safe reputation. But if it is genuine virtue it is worthy of a better use than that. It is fit, nay it is designed and demanded, to be used as salt, for the purifying of human life.

There are multitudes of our fellowmen whose existence is dark, confused, and bitter. Some of them are groaning under the burden of want; partly because of their own idleness or incapacity, no doubt, but partly also because of the rapacity, greed, and injustice of other men. Some of them are tortured in bondage to vice; partly by their own false choice, no doubt, but partly also for want of guidance and good counsel and human sympathy. Every great city contains centers of moral decay which an honest man cannot think of without horror, pity, and dread. The trouble is that many honest folk dislike these emotions so much that they shut their eyes and walk through the world with their heads in the air, breathing a little atmosphere of their own, and congratulating themselves that the world goes very well now. But is it well that the things which eat the heart out of manhood and womanhood should go on in all our great towns?

> Is it well that while we range with science, glorying in
> the time,
> City children soak and blacken soul and sense in city
> slime?
> There, among the glooming alleys, progress halts on palsied
> feet;
> Crime and hunger cast our maidens by the thousand on
> the street.

There the smoldering fire of fever creeps across the
rotted floor,
    And the crowded couch of incest, in the warrens of the
poor.

Even in what we call respectable society, forces of corruption are at work. Are there no unrighteous practices in business, no false standards in social life, no licensed frauds and falsehoods in politics, no vile and vulgar tendencies in art and literature and journalism, in this sunny and self-complacent modern world of which we are a part? All these things are signs of decay. The question for us as men of salt is: What are we going to do to arrest and counteract these tendencies? It is not enough for us to take a negative position in regard to them. If our influence is to be real, it must be positive. It is not enough to say "Touch not the unclean thing." On the contrary, we must touch it, as salt touches decay to check and overcome it. Good men are not meant to be simply like trees planted by rivers of water, flourishing in their own pride and for their own sake. They ought to be like the eucalyptus trees which have been set out in the marshes of the Campagna, from which a healthful, tonic influence is said to be diffused to countervail the malaria. They ought to be like the tree of paradise, "whose leaves are for the healing of nations."

Where good men are in business, lying and cheating and gambling should be more difficult, truth and candor and fair dealing should be easier and more popular, just because of their presence. Where good men are in society, grossness of thought and speech ought to stand rebuked, high ideals and courtliness and chivalrous actions and "the desire of fame and all that makes a man" ought to seem at once more desirable and more attainable to everyone who comes into contact with them. . . .

There is a loftier ambition than merely to stand high in the world. It is to stoop down and lift mankind a little higher. There is a nobler character than that which is merely incorruptible. It is the character which acts as an antidote and preventive of corruption. Fearlessly to speak the words which bear witness to righteousness and truth and purity; patiently to do the deeds which strengthen virtue and kindle hope in your fellowmen; generously to lend a hand to those who are trying to climb upward; faithfully to give your support and your personal help to the efforts which men are making to elevate and purify the social life of the world,—that is what it means to have salt in your character. And that is the way to make your life interesting and savory and powerful. The men that have been happiest, and the men that are best remembered, are the men that have done good.

What the world needs today is not a new system of ethics. It is simply a larger number of people who will make a steady effort to live up to the system that they have already. There is plenty of room for heroism in the plainest kind of duty. The greatest of all wars has been going on for centuries. It is the ceaseless, glorious conflict against the evil that is in the world. Every warrior who will enter that age-long battle may find a place in the army, and win his spurs, and achieve honor, and obtain favor with the great Captain of the Host, if he will but do his best to make his life purer and finer for every one that lives. . . .

It remains only to speak briefly, in the third place, of the part which religion ought to play in the purifying, preserving, and sweetening of society. . . .

Religion is something which a man cannot invent for himself, nor keep to himself. If it does not show in his conduct it does not exist in his heart. If he has just barely enough of it to save himself alone, it is doubtful whether he has even enough for that. Religion ought to bring out and intensify the flavor of all that is best in manhood, and make it fit, to use Wordsworth's noble phrase, "For human nature's daily food." Good citizens, honest workmen, cheerful comrades, true friends, gentle men,—that is what the product of religion should be. And the power that produces such men is the great antiseptic of society, to preserve it from decay.

Decay begins in discord. It is the loss of balance in an organism. One part of the system gets too much nourishment, another part too little. Morbid processes are established. Tissues break down. In their debris all sorts of malignant growths take root. Ruin follows. . . .

Some people say that another revolution is coming in our own age and our own country. It is possible. There are signs of it. There has been a tremendous increase of luxury among the rich in the present generation. There has been a great increase of suffering among the poor in certain sections of our country. It was a startling fact that nearly six millions of people in 1896 cast a vote of practical discontent with the present social and commercial order. It may be that we are on the eve of a great overturning. I do not know. I am not a prophet nor the son of a prophet. But I know that there is one thing that can make a revolution needless, one thing that is infinitely better than any revolution, and that is a real revival of religion—the religion that has already founded the hospital and the asylum and the free school, the religion that has broken the fetters of the slave and lifted womanhood out of bondage and degradation, and put the arm of its protection around the helplessness and innocence of childhood, the religion that proves its faith by its works, and links the preaching of the fatherhood of God to the practice of the brotherhood of man. That religion is true Christianity, with plenty of salt in it which has not lost its savor.

WASHINGTON GLADDEN

Washington Gladden was born in 1836 and lived to the age of 82. Apparently, from an early age he prepared himself for the Christian ministry, for after graduation from Williams College he taught in the public schools for only a short time, meanwhile reading in theology, and was ordained to the Congregational ministry in 1860.

While he may not have been a profound scholar, he was one who tried to keep abreast of his time, and he saw the function of Christianity and the Church to be the molding of perfect man in a perfect society; and he found it impossible to separate individual man from his society. He believed the Kingdom of Heaven to include all of life; hence, it could not come into being except through a regenerate society.

He saw the institutional Church as an agency to improve the quality of society and its institutions; he had a keen awareness of the needs of mankind, collectively. He saw this application of Christian truth, not as antagonistic, but as complementary to preaching to individuals.

Gladden has long been recognized as one of the first and strongest of the "social gospelers." The following sermon has been selected to illustrate his philosophy of Christianity and the thrust of his preaching.

Spiritual Law in the Natural World *

And when even was come, the disciples came to him, saying, The place is desert, and the time is already past; send the multitudes away, that they may go into the villages, and buy themselves food. But Jesus said unto them, They have no need to go away; give ye them to eat. And they say unto him, We have here but five loaves and two fishes. And he said, Bring them hither to me. And he commanded the multitudes to sit down on the grass; and he took the five loaves and two fishes, and looking up to heaven, he blessed and brake and gave the loaves to the disciples, and the disciples to the multitudes. And they did all eat and were filled; and they took up that which remained over of the broken pieces, twelve baskets full. And they that did eat were about five thousand men, besides women and children.—MATT. 14:15-21

I do not wish to discuss with you this morning the miraculous features of this narrative. Suppose I should convince you that this thing here described

---

* *Where Does the Sky Begin* (Boston: Houghton Mifflin, 1904), pp. 267 ff.

could not have happened: what value would there be in that demonstration? Suppose that I should convince you that it did happen; how much would that help you? You, at least, have no expectation that anything of the sort will ever happen to you. Loaves are never going to be multiplied in your larder by miracle. It is only by labor that the supply can be maintained. Let us rather take the story as an illustration of a spiritual law. . . .

Christ's parables bring before us the similitude between certain physical facts and certain spiritual facts. . . . Between those spiritual laws which we know and those physical laws which we know, there are similitudes, and there are also contrasts. . . . Let us look at what lies on the surface of this narrative.

Here, to begin with, is a great result achieved with small resources. Five thousand and more are abundantly fed with five loaves and two fishes.

Do we ever see anything like this happening in the natural world? We do see under the power of life wonderful multiplications of natural organism. A single kernel of corn may multiply, in one summer, to hundreds of kernels; and there are many orders of plants and animals, which, if their geometrical increase were not checked, would soon cover the surface of the earth. Life is, in many of its tribes, marvelously prolific.

Yet this natural increase all goes on under the law of conservation of energy. There are marvelous transformations of the materials existing upon the surface of the earth, but there is no real addition to them. The kernel of corn becomes a great stalk, almost a tree, with its green bannerets, and its tufted plumes, and its branching ears; but for all that it has thus become, it is indebted to the earth and the air; every particle of the matter which is thus organized has been drawn out of the soil or the atmosphere; by as much as its life has been enriched, by so much are the earth and the air the poorer. Even in the kingdoms of life, what one existence has another has not—what one gains some other must lose.

Now it does not appear, in this narrative, that the multiplication of these loaves and fishes involved any diminution or loss of force or substance to anybody. There was a marvelous increase, at no cost to those by whom it was ministered. Nay, they seem to have been richer at the end of their ministry than they were at the beginning. Each of the twelve went out with a few fragments in his hand, kept giving them away, took nothing from any one, and came back with a basket full. This is a process for which the natural order, so far as we now understand it, furnishes no analogy.

Yet we constantly see, in the spiritual world, something very like this taking place. We see the smallest and feeblest resources multiplied indefinitely, with no apparent diminution anywhere to balance this increase; rather with evident gains to all by whom the increase comes.

Less than a hundred years ago a few young men were wont to meet behind a haystack, in the edge of a grove near Williams College, to pray that God would provide a way by which they might go forth as missionaries to the heathen. The new impulse which had taken possession of their souls sprang from the discovery of the truth that God loves all men, and is ready to save all men. Up to this time the general belief had been that Christ died for the elect only; that the heathen nations were not included in the plan of salvation. Now there were those who ventured to assert that the atonement was not limited; that Christ had tasted death for every man; that whosoever would might come and take of the water of life freely. This was considered before that day a great and dangerous heresy; those who taught it were believed to be the enemies of true religion; harder words were said about them than are said about any of the new theologians of this day. Nevertheless, they found in this heresy a great motive to work for the building of the kingdom; since the gospel was for all men they desired that all men should hear the gospel, those who were far off as well as those who were near. . . . It was only a year or two later, as the result of this little prayer meeting, that the American Board of Commissioners for Foreign Missions was formed; and out of that germ has sprung the whole great foreign missionary work in America, with its thousands of missionaries, and its hundreds of thousands of converts, and its millions of dollars annually contributed for the prosecution of the work, with colleges and high schools and schools for girls in every part of the world; with influences at work that are leavening many nations. The beginnings were small and feeble, but the issues are large and fair. Out of resources that seemed insignificant something very grand has been evolved.

Go a little further back in history. In an old manor house, in Scrooby, Nottinghamshire, England, a small company of religious outcasts were wont to meet in the early hours of the morning, to worship God according to the simple rites which they preferred. Not many of the wise or the mighty were among them; ecclesiastically they were pariahs; the great English Church had made the exercise of their religion a crime, and was hunting them, like venomous reptiles, out of her borders. Nobody who saw that little company hiding before day in the Scrooby manor house, could have supposed that anything important was likely to arise from such a meeting; yet that was the Pilgrim Church, which landed a few years later in Leyden, Holland, and a little later still, from the Mayflower, on the sands of Plymouth harbor, in Massachusetts Bay, and planted a germ which has developed into a nation of seventy millions. Whatever other beginnings may have been made upon the soil, the ideas and the forces which organized that Plymouth

301

Colony have been the constructive elements of this nation. They were all represented there in that little company at Scrooby manor.

Travel a little further back across the centuries, and look upon that small congregation of very common people assembled in an upper chamber in Jerusalem and waiting for the promise of the Father. There were about six score of them; and they, too, were despised and rejected of men; none of the magnates of their nation had anything but contempt and curses for them; but this was the germ of Christendom; it was by the testimony of these men, by the manifestation of the life that was in them, that the Christian church was formed, that the influences were set in motion by which one third of the population of the earth has been Christianized.

Such wonderful results as these we are often able to trace in the action of the spiritual forces. Nor am I able to find in these phenomena anything which indicates that they come under the law of the conservation of energy. I do not discover that spiritual effects of this nature, though they are stupendous in their range and reach, are produced by reducing life at other points, I do not see that the world is impoverished anywhere, in order that it may be enriched by this multiplication of spiritual energies.

In truth, the law of the spiritual life is unlike the law of the physical life in this, that it increases by what it imparts and lives by what it loses. We may say what we will about this story of the feeding of the five thousand; but we know that in all the *superior* realms of our life something exactly like what is said to have taken place here on the shores of Gennesaret is all the while going on. We go out very often, with a few fragments, and by dint of giving these away diligently, we come back with baskets full. We have but little ourselves, and are very conscious of the smallness of our resources; but the more we give to others the more we have left.

Take a man like Mark Hopkins, like Theodore Woolsey, like Noah Porter, like James Fairchild; the mind of any of them, in its youthful periods, is crude and comparatively barren. Good scholars they are; they master their books; certain amounts of knowledge they have accumulated, but how deficient are they in the larger quality of wisdom. The early essays of Dr. Hopkins are correct in form, and show a certain mental alertness, but how little there is in them compared with what we find in the later writings. But this man begins, in his youth, freely to impart what he has freely received. He has not much to bestow, at the beginning, but such as he has he gives. Year after year he pours out the treasures of his accumulated wisdom into the minds of his pupils. To one class after another, to one generation after another, he seeks to communicate the best he has—all he has; to keep back nothing; to share with these young minds his choicest gains. Scores and hundreds of them glean from his lips the fruit of ripe thought,

of large experience; their ideas are cleared, their mental processes are rectified, their judgment is steadied, their imagination is chastened, their whole
intellectual and moral life is invigorated and enriched by what he has given
to them. And how is it with him? Is he impoverished by this lavish bestowal?
No; every year his knowledge widens, his wisdom deepens, his insight
clarifies, his temper becomes more genial, his sympathies more comprehensive. He has given his best life to thousands, but not one of the thousands
of receivers has gained one-hundredth part of what he, the giver, has won.
Does any man believe that a closeted recluse, absorbing and hoarding
knowledge, could ever have become so large-minded, so large-hearted, so
full of benignant wisdom? No, it is the very act of giving by which this
mind has been enriched. It is not merely the exercise of the mental faculties,
it is their benevolent exercise, it is the use of these powers under the spiritual
law, that has wrought this enlargement of the nature.

Take a woman like Dorothy Pattison,—Sister Dora,—in her youth rather
wilful, passionate, inconsiderate of others, and watch the effect upon her
nature of a life of service. How steadily it broadens and ripens under this
regimen. She is giving herself more and more unreservedly to the care of the
needy and the suffering; she is never thinking about self-culture; she covets
only those gifts that can make her life more useful to those about her;
delicate lady that she is, her days are spent amid the most loathsome and
repulsive scenes; all that she studies to do is to give comfort and relief and
happiness to others. And how is her character affected by this discipline?
Those who estimate life by the common worldly standards should expect to
find her growing hard and sour and shrewish; they should look to see her
small stock of amiability and tenderness utterly exhausted by this daily ex-
penditure; surely one who has so little and spends so much must be impoverished. But this is not the law of the spiritual realm. The more she
gives of sympathy and tenderness the more she has to give; the sources of
her affection are deepened; new fountains of gracious compassion are un-
sealed; the rather hard-natured girl becomes the good angel of the suffering
poor of a whole city. There, today, in the market place of Walsall her
statute stands, the tribute of the people who loved her. Look into that
calm, strong, radiant face. You do not need to be assured that it is a good
likeness; the soul is shining through it. It is the glory of womanhood. And it
was won, as that glory is always won, not by grasping at personal good or
gain; not by seeking recognition and social distinction, but by giving—freely,
constantly, lavishly—service, ministry, love, life, to all who were in need.

There is no question about this law. The facts that I am reciting to you
can be multiplied in the observation of every thoughtful person. You know
by abundant evidence, that the goods of the spiritual realm are increased by

dispensing them; that those and those only are enriched who give abundantly, constantly, with no thought of return. Every spiritual power or possession is enhanced by sharing it with others. My faith is strengthened when I can inspire some other soul with confidence; if my hopefulness is caught by other hearts, my own hope is confirmed; if I can kindle joy in a sorrowing heart, my own beats with livelier pulsations.

No one can doubt that the whole superior realm of man's life is under this higher law. It is not the law of competition; it is not the law of mutual exclusion; it is not the law of the conservation of energy. We rise, in our moral and spiritual progress, into a region where these principles which are of the earth . . . no longer bear rule. The law of this higher realm is that which we see illustrated, symbolized, at any rate, in the narrative before us. It is the law which guarantees that those who go forth with fragments, if they but diligently give them away, shall come back with baskets full.

We can clearly see that this law rules in the realm of the spirit; but we are perplexed by the suggestion that it can also be made to rule in the material realm. When it comes to the matter of loaves and fishes, we think that we must fall back on the law of the material realm. We do not expect to see the principle of the spiritual realm prevailing over the principle of the material realm; to find our food and raiment, our goods and chattels, our dimes and dollars multiplying as we dispense them. No; I do not think that it would be wise for us to look for anything just like this. I do not, indeed, know how far this process of spiritualizing the material realm may yet be carried. I do not know what will happen when the day comes that the whole creation is waiting and longing for—the day when it shall be manifest that men are the sons of God. I imagine that what we call the powers and laws of nature will be supple and docile under their hands in ways that we do not now comprehend. I surmise that some things which we now call miracles will then become mere commonplaces. And when I see this man Jesus Christ, who stands at the summit of human perfection, wielding forces whose nature I do not understand, my reason is not confounded; it is what I expect. Certain it is that he seemed to possess powers, which some of us do not possess, of spiritualizing nature; of making the forces of the material realm conform to the laws of the spiritual realm. Every man in some measure does this who learns to rule impulse by reason, and to bring appetite under the dominion of love. But Jesus Christ did it in many ways, and with such demonstrations of spiritual power as are yet to our dull vision marvelous. I do not think that it is well for us to covet the powers that seem to us miraculous. The very fact that they seem so to us is proof that we do not know how to use them; that we would suredly do mischief with them.

But it is possible for us to bring large spaces of the lower realm under the influence of the spiritual laws; and when we come near enough to this Christ to catch his spirit and learn his methods we shall be doing this all the while. It may not be possible for us, always, to subjugate matter and its laws by the spiritual principle; but it is possible for us to make this principle regnant in our relations with men. If physical substances cannot be made to conform to spiritual laws, human relations can.

There is a book the title of which is "Natural Law in the Business World." The natural law which is expounded is Rob Roy's rule:

That he should get who has the power,

And he should keep who can.

It is the law which authorizes and encourages every man to get as much as he legally and safely can from every one of his fellows. That is what is generally meant by natural law in the business world. And the argument seeks to show that the operation of this law must bring the greatest good to the greatest number. This is precisely the point on which I must dissent from a great deal of current teaching. I do not believe that the business world or any other world can ever be peaceful and prosperous under the operation of this law. It seems to me that what we want is the substitution of spiritual law for natural law in the business world. What would that signify? Simply this: that each, instead of getting as much as he could away from everybody else for himself, should give as much as he could to everybody else. Do you think that that would be a quixotic rule in the business world? I do not think so. I believe that the most successful traders today are those who honestly try to give their customers as much as they can for their money—not as little as they can. I believe that this liberal policy proves to be good policy. As much as they can, I say. The business must be maintained; common prudence must be used; the methods must not be such as shall destroy the business or make its manager a pauper; but within the bounds of ordinary sagacity, the man who gives his customers as much as he can afford to give them for their money is more likely in the long run to succeed, than the man who gives them just as little for their money as he can prevail upon them to take. . . .

But let us try the principle in another realm where human relations are a larger factor in the problem. Let us think of the society which is composed of the employer and the employed. Would not a substitution of spiritual law for natural law increase the welfare, the material welfare, of the whole of this society? Take a great industry in which the employer, on his side, was trying to get just as much as he could out of his employees, and the employees, on their side, were trying to get as much as they could out of their employer; each side acting from the principle of sheer selfishness. Let the fundamental law of that society be changed. Let the spiritual principle be brought in to modify what men call the natural principle. Let the employer earnestly seek to give his men as much as he can for their service, and the employees honestly endeavor to give their master as much as they can for the wages he pays them; is not the prosperity of that industrial group likely to increase? Would not the product of such an industry be considerably enlarged, and would there not be more to divide between employer and employed? I am not saying anything about methods, now; I am only speaking of the spirit, the motive, that might control the relations of this industrial group. I am supposing, also, that this spirit is manifested on both sides of this relation. If the employer were utterly selfish, and the employees only were inspired with goodwill, the relation could not be prosperous; neither would it work when the employer was the only Good Samaritan and the employees were mostly shirks and sponges; but when each party heartily wishes to do all he can for the welfare of the other, there is, I say, a better promise of prosperity for both, than where each is determined to advance its own interests at the expense of the other. Can any sane man doubt this? . . . Does not the principle which we find in the story we are studying—the principle that our possessions are increased by sharing them —come pretty near fulfillment even here within the material realm? . . .

But whatever the effect of the observance of this law might be upon our material prosperity, whether or not it would enlarge our gains and our revenues, one effect it would certainly have; it would greatly enhance the value of what we do possess. The real question is not, after all, how much we have, but how much good it does us; how much real satisfaction we get out of it. There are millionaires, not a few, who get less enjoyment and less real benefit out of their vast incomes, than many a day laborer gets out of his wages, than many a hard-working clerk gets out of his small salary. The man whose character, whose manhood, whose essential happiness is most increased by his possessions, is the man whose portion is most to be coveted.

Now here is a fact that I know by experience, and so do many of you— a fact that is just as distinctly a part of our consciousness as is our personal identity. We know that when we divide our portion, for love's sake, with our brother, what we have left is worth more to us than the whole would have been if we had kept it all for ourselves. We know that the real value of our possessions is enhanced by sharing them with those that are in need. We know that it is only when the love that prompts us to do good and to communicate is in our hearts that we derive the highest enjoyment from our earthly possessions. We have gone out, more than once, with our fragments in our hands; we have distributed more freely, perhaps, than we thought prudent, and we have come back, if not with baskets full, at least with hearts full, which is the main thing, after all.

Here, then, are our everyday miracles. Whatever may have happened to those loaves and fishes, we know, that with the real bread of life, which is love, this very thing happens every day. We divide our portion with those less fortunate than ourselves, and what is left is more because of what was given; the part is larger than the whole. We give daily, all that is most truly ourselves,—give freely of thought and hope and love—and find our treasure daily growing; the more we bestow the larger is our store. How fast this world might grow rich if all men would stop hoarding their best, and would begin to give it away, with unstinted bounty to all who were able to receive it.

12

PREACHING ON ISSUES OF WAR AND PEACE DURING THE TWENTIETH CENTURY

Jess Yoder

The response of churchmen to war during the twentieth century has ranged from strong endorsement to categorical refusal to participate in it. Three responses to war which have a long standing tradition in the life of the church are: the crusade or holy war, the just war, and pacifism. These three positions have been represented with varying degrees of emphasis during the wars of this century. Crusaders participate in war with enthusiasm because it is a means of establishing the righteousness of God and removing evil from the world. Proponents of the just war doctrine are not willing to regard warfare as holy, rather they deem it as a necessary action in which men must participate out of a sense of duty to God and government. Even though warfare is sinful, they hold that men must fight and kill so that judgment will be meted out upon injustice and evil and that justice can be established. The pacifists refuse to take up arms because they regard war as sinful; they believe that men ought not to commit evil in order to cast out greater evils and restore righteousness. The distinction between the just war and the crusade is not always easy to draw because the positions are not mutually exclusive. However, the attitude of the American churches during World War I stands in sharp contrast to World War II; the former approaches the expression of the crusade, while the latter conforms more to the just war view.

At the turn of this century churchmen supported this nation's optimism, which was marked by new social reforms. Social legislation was passed to curb monopolies, prevent child labor, improve conditions for the working man, and establish human rights. Many envisioned a new era of world peace and brotherhood. Establishing the Hague Peace Palace and Pan-American cooperation gave encouragement to those hoping for a new era of international peace in the world. The activities of the Federal Council of Churches and the Church Peace Union, a unified effort of Catholics, Protestants, and Jews, illustrate the call for peaceful cooperation which came from religious leaders.

On the very day that churchmen were to hold the first World Peace Congress at Constance, Germany, in 1914, their meeting was canceled because Germany declared war and confiscated transportation for troop mobilization. The following year Germany sank the *Lusitania,* a "neutral" United States ship carrying munition supplies for the Allies. The summons for national preparedness and American involvement increased as the war progressed in Europe. The predominant emphasis of the clergy shifted from advocating neutrality and exploring peaceful negotiations to favoring participation in the war. By the time America entered the war in 1917, it had become a holy cause endorsed by most churchmen.

The well-known statement that "World War I was fought to make the world safe for democracy" was a common theme in World War I sermons. In an address before the Federal Council of Churches in 1917, the Rev. Henry Churchill King said, "the standards and ideals of Christ must prevail in our entire civilization" and that the church cannot be indifferent as to whether its fruits abide, "for Christianity is democratic to the core." The Rev. James Vance declared that "we have tried to keep out of this war, but we are in it because we believe that the cause is right, and because we feel that in it we can

309

serve Christ." Christ was proclaimed as "the greatest fighter the world has ever seen" by the Rev. Wesley Johnston and the Rev. Harold Bell identified "the sword of America" to be "the sword of Jesus." The Rev. Billy Sunday likened the German-American conflict to hell against heaven. A number of ministers, notably Dwight Hillis, filled their sermons with fantastic atrocity stories that were later found to be fabricated rumors.

While many preachers supporting the crusade or holy war position are properly regarded to be emotional and even chauvinistic in their appeals to listeners, this was not characteristic of all preachers who maintained this position during World War I. Many sermons that viewed fighting in the war as an act of righteousness employed effective reasoning and argument. Fosdick's sermons of this period are strong in their rational appeals. The sermon by Henry Van Dyke, "Peace on Earth Through Righteousness," which has been selected for this volume, not only is rich in emotional appeals but also reflects a well-articulated Christian doctrine of the just war. While the Rev. Van Dyke contended that "the Allies and America were forced to enter this war as a work of righteousness in order to make the world safe for peace," he also called upon the victors to administer justice rather than vengeance at the conclusion of the war. When the war was over, many clergymen gave full support to the League of Nations and other measures that would insure world peace.

Reflections on World War I had a sobering effect on many churchmen. Studies on war propaganda were disillusioning to ministers who afterward learned that they were misled and manipulated. Samuel McCrea Cavert, general secretary for the Federal Council of Churches, said that he slowly but clearly came to "the conclusion that the church in its official capacity should never again give its sanction to war or attempt to make war appear as holy." Rabbi Stephen S. Wise looked upon his support of World War I with regret and pledged never to support any war again. Other nationally known ministers who took the pacifist position included Bernard Iddings Bell, Harold Bosley, George Buttrick, Henry H. Crane, Edwin

T. Dahlberg, Albert E. Day, Sherwood Eddy, Charles E. Jefferson, E. Stanley Jones, Charles Morrison, Reinhold Niebuhr, Ralph Sockman, and Ernest F. Tittle. Some of these men were already pacifists during World War I but many of them had not come to this position until after the war. Ministers of the historic peace churches— Brethren, Mennonites, and Quakers—were traditionally pacifists.

The sermons of the pacifists emphasized that war conflicts with the scriptural teachings regarding the fatherhood of God and the brotherhood of man. They often appealed to the teachings and example of Jesus and the prophets, calling upon men to break the course of evil by loving their enemies. Their sermons reminded men of the futility of war, the grim statistics of war which show that not only the enemy is killed but also many innocent. Sermons often warned against the lure of war profits, the surrender of truth and moral judgment to hatred and hysteria; and they called upon men to redeem their enemies rather than destroy them. Many of these pacifist appeals and arguments are set forth in the accompanying sermon, "The Terrible Meek," by Albert Edward Day. In it he attempted to refute the arguments that pacifists are irresponsible, irrelevant, and indifferent people who withdraw from society rather than assume their Christian responsibilities. Day contended that the means must conform to the end. "The cross and not the sword is the nation's surest weapon of defense," he proclaimed; "The cross does not conquer enemies; it ends enmities."

As World War II approaches, the pacifist position came under sharp criticism by the ministers and theologians who embraced neo-orthodoxy. Reinhold Niebuhr, who was earlier a pacifist, became their severest critic. He charged that pacifists absolutize sacrificial love at the expense of social responsibility. He held that a war to defend men from wanton aggression is justifiable even though it is evil. Thus man must live in the tension between what he ought to do and what he does. According to Niebuhr, God's forgiveness does not make man's behavior righteous but it enables him to live in the face of his predicament.

311

Many of the World War II sermons regarded war as unholy and sinful. The sermon in this volume by Rolland Schloerb clearly articulates the neo-orthodox response to the problem of war. Schloerb said, "It is not Christian to kill. . . . But neither is it Christian to allow tyrants to use their power to kill." All the courses of action available to man have something bad in them, he pointed out, but killing men in war or threatening to kill them "may be the least unchristian of the courses open to us in this kind of world." The majority of the sermons treating the issues of war during the Second World War took this "lesser evil" position. They stressed the evils of the enemy but also admitted the evil of their own actions. The sermons emphasized the Christian's duty to establish justice, remove evil and tyranny, and restore peace. This war was not viewed as a crusade by the righteous to destroy a depraved enemy, as was the case in World War I. With the advent of the A-bomb at the close of the war and later the H-bomb, new dimensions were brought to the war issue. Some churchmen became "nuclear pacifists" because they believed the "lesser evil" position could not be maintained in a nuclear conflict.

This analysis has presented three positions on war advocated from the American pulpit during this century. No sermon can adequately represent the diversity within each of these positions. The three sermons presented here do illustrate striking contrasts as we examine their treatment of the war question.

ROLLAND W. SCHLOERB

Rolland Schloerb was born on March 1, 1893, at Oshkosh, Wisconsin. In 1915 he received the B.A. degree from North Central College, Naperville, Illinois. He received the B.D. from Evangelical Theological Seminary in 1917, the S.T.B. from Union Theological Seminary in 1920, the M.A. from Northwestern University in 1921, and in 1936 was awarded an honorary doctorate from North Central College. He married Edith Gransden June 12, 1920. Ordained to the ministry of the Evangelical United Brethren Church in Naperville he served as pastor of the First Evangelical Church in Naperville and the Hyde Park Baptist Church in Chicago. He was affiliated with the YMCA at the outbreak of World War I and served as an army chaplain during 1918 and 1919. He is author of God in Our Lives *(1938) and* The Preaching Ministry Today *(1946).*

An Uneasy Conscience About Killing*

It is not the will of your Father who is in heaven that one of these little ones should perish.—MATTHEW 18:14.

Many thoughtful young men in the armed forces today have an uneasy conscience about killing other men. And their uneasiness is shared by countless parents who are deeply pained because their sons must learn the art of destroying their fellow human beings.

The uneasy conscience grows out of the conflict that results from the fact that the nation says to him, "Thou shalt kill!" while a voice from his religious heritage says, "Thou shalt not kill!" Although he knows that the Hebrews did not apply the command to killing in war, he has been trained to nourish certain humanitarian impulses which summon him to heal and to build human lives rather than to destroy them.

This conflict within the hearts of men is revealed in two conversations which came to my attention within the past few weeks. A member of our church told about a chat which he overheard between two soldiers in a

---

smoking compartment of a Pullman car. These men had been in combat in the Far East, and they confessed to a sense of revulsion against killing people. One of the young men had been sufficiently troubled by this question to ask his chaplain if it is right to kill a man. The answer given was, "Yes, it is right to kill." But then the chaplain took the young man to task for some other lapses in his moral conduct. The soldier could not but muse upon the perspective of a religion that frowned upon the sins of the flesh and then condoned the taking of human life.

The other conversation took place between a soldier and Professor Conant of Harvard. The soldier, who was a sincere Christian and a member of the Episcopal Church, told the professor that he had decided not to take communion for the duration of the war. When asked for the reason, he responded that it did not seem right to share in the sacrament of the Lord's Supper when he was learning how to kill his fellow human beings in one of the most effective ways of killing in the service.

Each of these men had an uneasy conscience about the killing business that war demands of him. What can be said to those who have an uneasy conscience about killing? One hesitates to make any comment whatever, especially when he recalls a devastating sentence with which Professor Westermarck concludes a chapter in his *Christianity and Morals*. "War," says this not too friendly critic of Christianity, "is a rock on which Christian principles have suffered the most miserable shipwreck." And yet one ought to try to give the best response he knows to the person who is troubled by the terrible necessity of taking human life.

I

The first remark that I would like to make in this connection is not very illuminating or reassuring. But it ought to be said: *We are all in the killing business.* The young man who is being taught how to bayonet an enemy, or how to strangle a sentry on duty, is acutely conscious that he is learning how to kill. And the bombardier too is becoming aware that he may be the one to release the tons of metal that will bring death to civilians and soldiers alike.

But these men are not the only ones in the killing business. We are all in it. We who forge the iron into the bomb, we who put the weapon into the boy's hands, we who pay the bills to produce these materials of war—we are all in the killing business. Whenever a person purchases a war bond he may be thinking chiefly of the good investment that he is making, or of the fact that he is doing his part to prevent a ruinous inflation from descending upon the country. But he ought also to remember that he is having a part in the killing business.

Even the person who refuses to buy war bonds, but who pays his taxes, has a part in the killing. Most of his tax money is being used to support a war machine. He may not will it so, but neither does the young man want to devote himself to the killing business. And the man who refuses to cooperate with his government in any way, who is taken to jail, is drawing off man-power to care for him and to feed him and is thereby helping the killers on the other side.

It is impossible to escape from having a part in the killing business, we must at least say to the soldier with the uneasy conscience: You are not the only one with a troubled conscience—we are all in it with you.

II

Something further can be said: *The vast majority of the human race despise killing.* There may be a few sadistic individuals who enjoy inflicting suffering on their fellows, and who feel a sense of power in crushing the life out of people whom they fear. It is possible to quote individuals who think that this killing business is something desirable. One will suffice. Mussolini, who should have reason to ponder the wisdom of his words, said some years ago: "Fascism believes neither in the possibility nor in the usefulness of perpetual peace. War alone brings to its highest tension all human energy and puts the stamp of nobility upon the people who have the courage to engage in it."

This kind of talk is no doubt indulged in to whip up a nation to serve the purposes of power-seeking leaders. Most people would echo the feelings of Captain John Woodward Philip. During the Battle of Santiago, as his battleship Texas was sweeping past the burning ship Vizcaya, his men started to cheer. But he stopped them with the words: "Don't cheer, boys! The poor devils are dying."

The news that heavy losses are being inflicted upon the enemy brings some reassurance to us, but hearts are heavy at the thought of the wholesale destruction of human life and property. We are all in the killing business and we do not like it. But our comments on this matter cannot end there.

III

We have learned that *killing is not stopped just because we do not like it or refuse to participate in it.* In fact, there is some reason to believe that the fact that people refused to have anything to do with the forcible restraint of violators of international law, made it possible for them to build mighty war machines.

If powerful and responsible nations in the international community had been willing to threaten to resist by force those who violated the territories of others, they might have prevented the widespread slaughter that is going on now. It is not enough to hate killing and to refuse to kill. One does not prevent the growth of tyranny simply by refusing to kill.

IV

What shall we say then? Shall we agree with the chaplain who said, "Yes, yes, it is right to kill"? I would rather agree with those who say, "Killing is wrong. We cannot bless war. We cannot call war the coming of the Kingdom on earth. It is not the will of God that one of these little ones should perish."

It is not Christian to kill. But neither is it Christian to allow tyrants to use their power to kill. It is not right to sit back and assume that the refusal to participate in the struggle is Christian. *None of the possibilities with which a person is confronted during these days is absolutely Christian.* They all have something bad about them. Since our sinful acts have caused this kind of world to come to pass, we have no perfectly Christian alternative.

To kill men in war or to threaten to kill them is not Christian, but it may be the least unchristian of the courses open to us in this kind of world. Resort to war is no good, but it may be less evil than any other possibility confronting us.

A young man may still insist that this leaves him with an uneasy conscience. If he goes to war he is not certain that he is choosing the lesser of two evils. Likewise, if he goes to a conscientious objector camp he may not be certain that he is lending aid to the side that he believes in. Uneasy consciences everywhere! And thank God for them! Let us continue to keep our consciences uneasy, for this tension ought to be kept alive.

One of the Tawneys once said that "war is either a crime or a crusade." This is too simple a distinction. If war is a crime then it is completely bad. If it is a crusade then it may be interpreted as completely good. War is always bad, but it may be less evil than any other possibilities offered. There is a sense therefore in which we can reassure the young man by saying, "Peace, peace, when there is no peace." Your uneasy conscience should reassure you, for you are sensitive enough to know that killing is not Christian, even though it may be less evil than refusing forcibly to resist the tyrannical regimes that frankly disavow all Christian standards.

316

V

This leads us to a final assertion: *Since killing is so unchristian we ought to dedicate ourselves to do all we can to prevent this killing business from recurring.* The destruction that war brings is getting serious enough that mankind as a whole really ought to do something about it. War is a luxury that humanity cannot afford much longer. As long as little professional armies slaughtered each other from spring to autumn, nations could absorb the shock, but with the destruction of huge populations and property, war is becoming a very expensive luxury.

For many people the stopping of killing seems utterly hopeless. Their observation is: There will always be conflicts, and so there will always be war. One can agree with the first part of the statement without being compelled to accept the second part. There will always be conflicts of interest. But these do not necessarily always have to be settled by people killing each other. The reason that nations resort to war is that they have no other way of getting their rights. If some rough justice is approximated by other machinery, national leaders will not be able easily to whip their people into war frenzy.

For many generations England and Scotland were periodically at war with one another. It seemed to be a foregone conclusion that these two people would fight each other. But the time came, as Stephan Zweig points out, that this recurring warfare seemed to the dwellers on one island a "senseless iniquity." These two nations had too many common interests to destroy each other. And so in 1707 they united and for over two centuries they have settled their differences by other ways than killing each other.

The time will surely come when dwellers in One World will regard war as a senseless iniquity. They will seek other means than periodic bloodletting to settle their differences.

When I made a short trip through Europe nineteen years ago, two buildings impressed themselves indelibly upon my memory. One was the War Museum in Berlin. There in the dark corridors were displayed all the instruments of killing and destruction that man had devised. A heavy pall seemed to hang over the place as if the dead hand of the past were strangling the present.

The other building was the Hague Peace Palace in Holland, where the Permanent Court of Arbitration convened. The Palace itself was built of materials brought from many lands, and its rooms were dedicated to settling disputes by other means than by having the disputants try to kill each other.

The first museum seems most contemporary, and yet I believe that the

317

future lies with the kind represented by the Hague Peace Palace. *Killing is simply not Christian—War is not the fulfillment of the Christian ideal.* At any one time it may be the least evil of possibilities, but one must preserve an uneasy conscience about it, that he may do all in his power to prevent its recurrence and that he may always remember that "it is not the will of the Father in heaven that one of these little ones should perish."

Henry Van Dyke[*]

Peace on Earth Through Righteousness [**]

After we have found peace in our own souls through faith in God and in His Son, Jesus Christ our Saviour, if our faith is honest, we must feel the desire and the duty of helping to make peace prevail on earth.

But here we are, in a world of confusion and conflict. Darkness and ignorance strive against light. Evil hates and assaults good. Wrong take up arms against right. Greed and pride and passion call on violence to defeat justice and enthrone blind force. So has it been since Cain killed Abel, since Christ was crucified on Calvary, and so it is to-day wherever men uphold the false doctrine that "might makes right."

The Bible teaches us that there is no foundation for enduring peace on earth except in righteousness: that it is our duty to suffer for that cause if need be: that we are bound to fight for it if we have the power: and that if God gives us the victory we must use it for the perpetuation of righteous peace.

In these words I sum up what seems to me the Christian doctrine of war and peace,—the truth that in time of war we must stand for the right, and that when peace comes in sight, we must do our best to found it upon justice. These two truths cannot be separated. If we forget the meaning of the Christian duty to which God called us in the late war, all our sacrifice of blood and treasure will have been in vain. If we forget the watchword which called our boys to the colours, our victory will be fruitless. We have fought in this twentieth century against the pagan German doctrine of war as the supreme arbiter between the tribes of mankind. They that took the sword must perish by the sword. But in the hour of victory we must uphold the end for which we have fought and suffered,—the advance of the world towards a peaceful life founded on reason and justice and fair-play for every man.

So there are two heads to this sermon. First, the indelible remembrance of a righteous acceptance of war. Second, the reasonable hope of a righteous foundation of peace.

I. First of all, then, it must never be forgotten that the Allies and America were forced to enter this war as a work of righteousness in order to make the world safe for peace.

* See chapter 11 for biographical sketch.
** *What Peace Means* (New York: Fleming H. Revell, 1919).

Peace means something more than the mere absence of hostilities. It means justice, honour, fair-play, order, security, and the well-protected right of every man and nation to life, liberty, and the pursuit of happiness. It was the German contempt for these Christian ideals, it was the German idolatry of the pagan Odin, naked, cruel, bloody, god of war, it was the German will to power and dream of world-dominion, that made the world unsafe for real peace in 1914.

Never could that safety be secured until that enemy of mankind was overcome. Not only for democracy, but also for human peace, it was necessary, as President Wilson said, that "the German power, a thing without honour, conscience, or capacity for covenanted faith, must be crushed."

I saw, from my post of observation in Holland, the hosts of heathen Germany massing for their attack on the world's peace in the spring of 1914. Long before the pretext of war was provided by the murder of the Austrian Crown-Prince in Serajevo, I saw the troops, the artillery, the mountains of ammunition, assembled at Aix-la-Chapelle and Trier, ready for the invasion of neutral Belgium and Luxembourg, and the foul stroke at France.

Every civilized nation in Europe desired peace and pleaded for it. Little Servia offered to go before the Court of Arbitration at The Hague and be tried for the offense of which she was accused. Russia, Italy, France and England entreated Germany not to make war, but to submit the dispute to judicial settlement, to a righteous decision by a conference of powers. But Germany said no. She had prepared for war, she wanted war, she got war. And now she must abide by the result of her choice.

I have seen also with my own eyes the horrors wrought by Germany in her conduct of the war in Belgium and Northern France. Words fail me to describe them. Childhood has been crucified, womanhood outraged, civilization trampled in the dust. The nations and the men who took arms against these deviltries were the servants of the righteous God and the followers of the merciful Christ.

He told us, "If any man smite thee on the right cheek, turn unto him the left also." But never did He tell us to abandon the bodies and the lives of our women and children to the outrage of beasts in human form. On the contrary, He said to His disciples, in His parting discourse, "He that hath no sword let him sell his garment and buy one."

Does any silly pacifist say that means a spiritual sword? No. You could get that without selling your garment. It means a real sword,—as real as the purse and the scrip which Christ told His followers to carry with them. It means the power of arms dedicated to the service of righteousness without which the world can never be safe for peace.

Here, then, we may stand on the Word of God, on the work of righteousness in making the world safe for peace. Let me tell you of my faith that every one who has given his life for that cause, has entered into eternal rest.

II. Come we now to consider the second part of the text: "the effect of righteousness, quietness and confidence forever."

What shall be the nature of the peace to be concluded after our victory in this righteous war?

Here we have to oppose the demands of the bloodthirsty civilians. They ask that German towns should endure the same sufferings which have been inflicted on the towns of Belgium and Northern France. Let me say frankly that I do not believe you could persuade our officers to order such atrocities, or our soldiers to obey such orders. Read the order which one of the noble warriors of France, General Pétain, issued to his men:

"To-morrow, in order to better dictate peace, you are going to carry your arms as far as the Rhine. Into that land of Alsace-Lorraine that is so dear to us, you will march as liberators. You will go further; all the way into Germany to occupy lands which are the necessary guarantees for just reparation.

"France has suffered in her ravaged fields and in her ruined villages. The freed provinces have had to submit to intolerable vexations and odious outrages, but you are not to answer these crimes by the commission of violences, which, under the spur of your resentment, may seem to you legitimate.

"You are to remain under discipline and to show respect to persons and property. You will know, after having vanquished your adversary by force of arms, how to impress him further by the dignity of your attitude, and the world will not know which to admire most, your conduct in success or your heroism in fighting."

The destruction of the commonplace Cathedral of Cologne could never recompense the damage done to the glorious Cathedral of Rheims. Nor could the slaughter of a million German women and children restore the innocent victims of Belgium, France, Servia, and Armenia to life. We do not thirst for blood. We desire justice.

No doubt the ends of justice demand that the principal brigands who are responsible for the atrocities of this war should be tried before an international court. If convicted they should be duly punished. But not by mob-law or violence. Nothing could be less desirable than the assassination of William Hohenzollern. It would be absurd and horrible to give a martyr's crown to a criminal. Vengeance belongeth unto God. He alone is wise and great enough to deal adequately with the case. It is for us to keep our righteous indignation free from the poison of personal hatred, and to do no more than is needed to uphold and vindicate the eternal law.

William Hohenzollern, and his fellow-conspirators who are responsible for the beginning and the conduct of the dreadful war from which all the toiling

321

peoples of earth have suffered, must be brought to the bar of justice and sentenced; otherwise the world will have no defense against the anarchists who say that government is a vain thing; and the bloody Bolshevists who proclaim the Empire of the Ignorant,—the Boob-Rah,—as the future rule of the world, will have free scope.

It is evident that a league of free, democratic states, pledged by mutual covenant to uphold the settlement of international differences by reason and justice before the use of violence, offers the only hope of a durable peace among the nations. It is also the only defense against that deadly and destructive war of classes with which Bolshevism threatens the whole world. The spirit of Bolshevism is atheism and enmity; its method is violence and tyranny; its result would be a reign of terror under that empty-headed monster, "the dictatorship of the proletariat." God save us from that! It would be the worst possible outcome of the war in which we have offered and sacrificed so much, and in which God has given us the opportunity to make "a covenant of peace."

How vast, how immeasurable, are the responsibilities which this great victory in righteous war has laid upon the Allies and America. God help us to live up to them. God help us to sow the future not with dragon's teeth, but with seeds of blessed harvest. God paint upon the broken storm-cloud the rainbow of eternal hope. God help us and our friends to make a peace that shall mean good to all mankind. God send upon our victory the light of the cross of Christ our Saviour, where mercy and truth meet together, righteousness and peace kiss each other.

ALBERT EDWARD DAY

Albert Edward Day was born at Euphemia, Ohio, Nov. 18, 1884. He received the B.A. from Taylor University, 1904; the M.A. from the University of Cincinnati 1916; the D.D. from Ohio Wesleyan University in 1926 and Allegheny College in 1936; the Litt.D. from the University of Southern California in 1939. In 1904 he married Emma Reader, and the same year he was ordained in the Methodist Episcopal Church. He was pastor of a number of churches in Ohio; these included the Hyde Park Methodist Church in Cincinnati, William Street Methodist Church in Delaware, and the First Methodist Church in Canton. He was also pastor at the Christ Methodist Church in Pittsburgh, Pennsylvania; Mount Vernon Place Methodist Church in Baltimore, Maryland; and the First Methodist Church in Pasadena, California. He was a lecturer in preaching at Andover Newton Theological School (1949) and at Union Theological Seminary in Richmond (1951). He was a chaplain in World War I, he served on the Methodist Board of Foreign Missions, and was vice-president of the Federal Council of Churches in America from 1942 to 1944. He founded the Disciplined Order of Christ, edited New Life magazine, and chaired the National Conference on Church and War. He gave the Lyman Beecher Lectures at Yale in 1934 and also a number of other lectureships at seminaries and universities. His published works include Faith We Live By (1940), Discipline and Discovery (1946), and Autobiography of Prayer (1952). In a Christian Century poll of 1940 he was nominated as one of the six leading ministers in the nation.

The Terrible Meek*

Charles Rann Kennedy wrote a powerful one-act play entitled "The Terrible Meek." It is a drama of Calvary. There are only three characters: a soldier, his captain, and the mother of Jesus. The captain and the soldier have nailed Jesus to the cross, have watched his dying agony, and have finished him with a thrust of the spear into his heart. The crowd has departed. Darkness deeper than night has enveloped the hill. The captain and soldier are uneasy over what they have done. Neither of them knows any reason for it, except that they were ordered to do it and they did. That is a soldier's duty—"theirs not to reason why, theirs but to do and die." Behind their ghastly deed was a series of such duty-performances. Pilate did his duty by Rome; the Sanhedrin did its duty by the High Priest; the High Priest did his duty by the law. Each one of them did his blind, unexamined, conventional duty.

But something about Jesus broke the spell of routine duty with the captain. "It doesn't seem to be love or neighborliness or pity or understanding or anything that comes out hot . . . from the heart of man. Duty! Duty! We talk of duty. What sort of devil's duties are there in the world . . . when they lead blindly, wantonly, wickedly to the murder of such a man as this?"

So he turns from heartless duty to the heart broken on Calvary, surrenders his own heart to it, refuses to continue his blind obedience to Caesar's behest. And he says to the mother of Jesus: "We stretch out our hands to possess the earth—domination, power, glory, money, merchandise, luxury—these are the things we aim at; but what we really gain is pest and famine, grudge labor, the enslaved hate of men and women, ghosts, dead and death-breeding ghosts that haunt our lives forever. We have lost both the earth and ourselves in trying to possess it." And he adds with conviction "Something has happened up here on this hill today to shake all our kingdoms of blood and fear to dust. . . . The meek, the terrible meek, the fierce agonizing meek are about to enter into their inheritance."

WHAT PACIFISTS ARE NOT

There are increasing numbers who believe that Christ and his cross represent the only way to achieve justice and freedom and peace. They are called *pacifists*. Do not let the word confuse you. They are not neutrals; they distinguish clearly between right and wrong, between tyrant and democrat, between aggressor and victim. They can even draw a fine line between the older British and French imperialism and Germany's revolution of nihilism. They are not indifferentists, merely saying, "What goes on in Europe is no concern of ours. As long as our shores are not menaced, what do we care?" They do care. Their hearts have bled over Ethiopia and Spain, China and Czechoslovakia and Poland. They believe Hitler's triumph would be a disaster to civilization. They are not passivists "supinely acquiescent in highhanded wrong," surrendering precious values to anyone who challenges, bowing the knee to tyrants, taking aggression without protest. They do not propose that lovers of justice and liberty and decency and humanity should turn the world over to any lying, sadist gang of hoodlums anywhere. They do not believe that history should be a succession of Munichs—"if at first you don't succeed, fly, fly again." Not Mr. Chamberlain's umbrella, but the cross of Christ is their symbol of hope and power.

The proposal of this type of pacifists is a philosophy first and then an active procedure. They believe that war is wrong. War has often been glorified as a crusade, but most of the wars in history have been not crusades but crimes perpetrated for greed, nationalistic pride, imperialistic ambition, plunder of territory, raw materials and markets. No less a man than Aldous Huxley declared: "The ethics of international politics are persistently those of the gangster, the pirate, the swindler, the bold, bad baron." War has been the chief reliance of such politics. Even when war has been waged for justifiable ends, the means have corrupted the ends. The treaty of Versailles was the natural outcome of four years of terror, lust and murder.

THE POLICE FORCE ILLUSION

There is no comparison between armies in wartime and a police force. Police are nonpartisan instruments of law; armies are ex-parte contestants in a struggle which knows no law. The police arrest, or at worst kill the criminal; armies slay innocent women, children, and civilians. Police hale the offender into court where in an atmosphere of judicial calm his case is tried according to law; armies cannot arrest war instigators and cannot bring whole nations to trial. If armies compel an armistice, there is no court into which the disputants can be haled, or in which the accused can be fairly tried. The accuser, if victor, is both prosecuting attorney, judge and jury.

Equally false is the frequent comparison between a man defending his wife against an assailant and armies on the rampage. The husband, even if he kills the assailant, does not kill the assailant's wife or children or innocent neighbors. He does not upset the economic or industrial life of a whole city or state. He does not destroy liberty, his own and his neighbor's. Nor does he, in wrath, impose dangers against the assailant's children and grandchildren to the third and fourth generation. He does not compel all the rest of the community to arm itself with guns lest he turn on them next. Armies do all that and more.

WAR AND PREPARATION FOR WAR FUTILE

These pacifists believe that war is futile. The argument was presented last week, and I shall not repeat it now. I can take time only to quote what Premier Daladier wrote in an appeal to Hitler: "If French and German blood should flow again as it did twenty-five years ago in a still longer and more murderous war, then both nations would fight in confidence of victory. The victory, however, would be only destruction and barbarity." This is the terrible judgment upon war—"only destruction and barbarity" for victor and victim alike—the very quintessence of futility!

Do you remember the very last moment of the picture "All Quiet on the Western Front"? A German soldier in the trenches, still carrying in his heart a love of beauty, spies a butterfly just outside the horrid shelter. He reaches for it, and that moment a bullet from the trench opposite finds its mark. You see the hand that was reaching for beauty relax, turn over, grow limp— and you know the boy is dead. That is war! Millions of men like you and me, knowing no better, following their leaders, reaching for some butterfly of happiness and justice and peace, but finding only a bullet; seeking beauty, discovering only death!

These pacifists believe that preparation against war only creates the psychology which makes war inevitable. Over and over again we have heard in recent days, "America must build an army and a navy so strong that no one will dare attack her." Of all the fatuous hopes that have ever been indulged, this is the most fatuous. Strong armies and navies do not intimidate, they only irritate. For the armament that you think guarantees your security denies security to the other fellow. You may protest your peaceful intentions. You may declare that your armament is only for defense, but your protest is never convincing. The other fellow hears what you say, but he sees what you do. Actions speak louder than words with him. He therefore arms too. If he cannot alone stack arms against yours, he will seek allies to balance your power, and then you have the old balance-of-power game and the consequent power politics which perpetually keep Europe on the brink of war. Armaments do not guarantee security. They only create the fears and suspicions which destroy security and sooner or later lead to war. If history proves one thing, that is it!

These pacifists believe that the one adequate defense against enemies is to abolish enemies, not by destroying them but by making them your friends. That can be done only by creating confidence in your own friendliness, your own passion for peace, your own inflexible purpose to be just and generous, your own understanding of others' needs, your own desire to cooperate with them in building a world where they and you alike may have a chance for a decent human life.

They believe that can be accomplished only by reduction of armies and navies to the level of police power; by willingness to confer about raw materials and territories and markets and boundaries and tariffs; by relinquishment of that extreme national sovereignty which insists on being absolute judge of its own rights and claims; by consent to submit disputes to some international court. Mere treaties of peace are inadequate. Peace action is demanded based on a recognition "that the existing status has no inherent sanctity, since the world is a living, changing organism, but that change can and should be consistent with basic human rights."

NONVIOLENT RESISTANCE—HOW IT WORKS

But the real pacifist does not stop there. If he did he would not be a realist. He does not live in a world that has disarmed or has shown its willingness to revise the status quo and to meet the legitimate demands of underprivileged peoples with territorial and economic adjustments. He lives in an armed, selfish, rigid world where there is glaring injustice and where there are bound to be conflicts, as those who are impoverished struggle for a share in the world's goods. What does he propose should be done in such a world? What would he have a wronged, attacked, invaded, but peace-loving nation do?

Suppose Mr. Hitler and Mr. Stalin should conquer and divide Europe and then drunk with success swarm the Western hemisphere? What would the pacifist have America do? He would recommend not surrender, but resistance—nonviolent resistance! Instead of poison gas, vigorous protest against invasion and tyranny. Instead of cannon, courageous refusal to harbor the invaders, to obey their commands, to turn over to them commerce and industry and the machinery of government. Instead of war, words backed by conviction and action. Instead of an effort to kill, an attempt to conciliate and to convert. Instead of annihilation of the aggressor nation, an appeal to their better nature, and if invasion continued and tyranny waxed hot, a willingness to go to jail or to the concentration camp in persistent noncooperation with the enemy and in unsuppressed loyalty to American ideals and to Christian practices.

Americans would suffer in such a program, to be sure. Americans would fill jails and concentration camps. Americans would be stood up against the wall and shot. But do not forget that Americans would suffer if we went to war. They would be taken prisoners. They would be slain by thousands on the battlefield. American women and children would die in multitudes in bombed cities. Once armies are set in motion by a nation believing itself defrauded, a nation deceived by censorship and lashed into fighting fury by propaganda, there can be no stopping those armies, except by suffering and death. The pacifist knows that a price must be paid for peace and freedom.

KILLING TO MAKE MEN FREE

But he wants the price paid to purchase peace and freedom. He wants suffering and death to be effective. He wants them to be clean. If anybody must die, he believes it is better to be the killed than the killer. He is determined that he will not be one to bomb babies in the cradle and women in the kitchen.

What he proposes is a very definite loyalty to all the values of civilization and Christianity, an immovable determination that those values shall be preserved, a willingness to suffer and die for their preservation, a faith that suffering and death, endured rather than inflicted, are the way of the cross but also the way of redemption!

During the last war American audiences assembled to support war aims and foster the sale of liberty bonds, often sang those lines from the "Battle Hymn of the Republic": "As he died to make men holy, let us die to make men free." They seldom realized the utter contradiction between what they were proposing to do and what Jesus did. If they had sung the truth instead of a rhapsody, this would have been their refrain: "As he died to make men holy, let us *kill* to make men free." That is what war is—killing. And the pacifist's contention is that killing does not make men free; it enslaves both the killed and the killer. We killed to make men free in 1914–1918, but we only bred new tyrannies and fastened new dictatorships on the world and necessitated another war which is already turning England and France into wartime dictatorships and threatening us with the same fate.

The pacifist cannot imagine Jesus behind a machine gun or pushing a bayonet into another man's breast, or at the wheel of a bomber dropping death upon the innocent. The pacifist knows that we are not Christ. He had a vocation which is not ours. In him there was an absoluteness of character which no mortal among us shares. But the pacifist is sure that when Christ went to the cross, when "being reviled he reviled not again," when "being persecuted he threatened not but committed himself to him that judgeth righteously," he pointed the only way to the triumph of truth and righteousness. Only a kingdom built on love and sacrifice can endure. The cross and not the sword is the nation's surest weapon of defense. The cross does not conquer enemies; it ends enmities. Nothing but the death of enmity can bring the birth of peace.

AN EXAMPLE FROM HISTORY

Has anything like this ever been done? It sounds fantastic, doesn't it—like one of those ideals which are so remote from reality that they are not worth considering, like the dream of a dreamer who will never be under the necessity of testing his dreams by his deeds? Have you ever heard of Deak? Franz Josef, emperor of Austria, attempted the subordination of Hungary. War would have been lost before it began, Hungary was so weak. But Francis Deak aroused the nation: "Woe to the nation which raises no protest when its rights are outraged. The nation which submits to injustice and oppression without protest is doomed." He exhorted the people not to resort to violence. He organized a scheme for independent education, agriculture and industry. He urged Hungarians to refuse to recognize the Austrian government in any way and to carry on a boycott against Austrian goods. When the Austrian tax collector came the people did not beat him; they simply refused to pay. When the Austrian police seized their goods, no Hungarian auctioneer would sell them. When an Austrian auctioneer was brought on, the Hungarian people refused to buy. The government found it would have to import both auctioneer and buyers—a process more costly than profitable. Austria sent in soldiers, but the soldiers after trying to live in houses where everyone despised them protested strongly. Austria declared the boycott illegal, but the Hungarians continued to boycott. Austrian soldiers filled jails with Hungarians, but to no avail. Prisoners were released and partial self-government given, but Hungarians insisted on their full rights. In retaliation the emperor decreed compulsory military service, but Hungarians refused to obey. At last the emperor gave up and Hungary's constitution was won.

The complete story of this and other nonviolent campaigns waged by Mr. Gandhi in South Africa and in India are told in Gregg's *Power of Non-Violence*, which I urge you to read. They have demonstrated that moral power is more than a match for military power; that a people who have faith in their cause and in the human nature of their opponents in God can wield a force greater than that of arms; that the spirit that can suffer is a more powerful champion than the sword.

ADVANTAGES OF NONVIOLENT RESISTANCE

This is not a policy of weakness, but of strength. It requires all the military virtues—courage, endurance, discipline, sacrifice, and it accomplishes results which are beyond the power of military strategy.

It takes a far less fearful toll of human life. If there is any killing, it is done by the aggressor alone. And because he is a human being, he cannot go on killing people who are not harming him. The success of this strategy is epitomized in the assertion of one of the Indian police when their fierce onslaught failed to frighten Gandhi's followers and to provoke retaliation.

"You can't go hitting a blighter when he stands up to you like that." Even Lenin with all the fierce, intransigent philosophy of communism behind him admitted, "It was a hellishly hard task to execute people, ruthlessley to split skulls open." Ten million people lost their lives in the last world war. If France and England had adopted a policy of nonviolent resistance, not a fraction of that number would have perished.

Such a policy rallies world opinion. It is an unanswerable demonstration that the people who adopt it are not aggressors, that they have only a desire for peace and justice, that they believe in the righteousness of their cause. When a nation arms for war and goes to war, there is always a doubt about it from the very beginning. When it kills and destroys in the prosecution of the war, the very passions aroused carry it to ends which cannot be justified. Doubt concerning it is deepened. World conscience cannot be unanimous when armies are in motion because of that from which armies spring and that to which they tend. Sympathetic as we are to Britain, there is pertinence in the question of one columnist who asks, "Are we to underwrite the blunders and stupidities of British diplomacy every twenty-five years?" That question would not be asked if that diplomacy had not been based on a military victory in 1918, and on the possibility of summoning another war to atone for its failures. An armed Britain has the sympathy of a part of the world; a Britain committed to the policy of nonviolence and to such politics and economics as nonviolence could defend, would have the sympathy of all the world. In the long run world opinion is more decisive than war. Witness the frantic eagerness of the fighting nations to persuade the world that they and not their opponents are right!

THINKING WOULD KILL WAR

Such a policy wins the antagonist. It does not conquer; it converts. Frederick the Great, vigorous soldier, said: "If my soldiers began to think, not one would remain in the ranks." When soldiers encounter nonviolent people, they have to think. When they are met with guns, all they have to do is to keep on shooting. But when they are met with the grit that nevertheless offers no harm, they have to ask: "Why have we marshaled against such a people? Why are they so resolute and yet so harmless?" Thinking begins and morale crumbles. The Duke of Wellington, another great soldier, confessed, "No man with any scruples of conscience is fit to be a soldier." Conscience can be submerged when the other fellow is trying to kill you—the instinct of self-preservation smothers the voice of the soul. But when the other fellow is offering you no peril, when he meets your blows with kindness . . . your conscience inevitably becomes active. That is history. And it is religion. "If thine enemy hunger, feed him, if he thirst, give him drink; for in so doing thou shalt heap coals of fire upon his head."

IT IS TIME WE TRIED SOMETHING ELSE

Non-violence summons both the intelligence and the conscience of the opponent into action, and each of these two great soldiers, Frederick the Great and Wellington, has admitted that no army can hang together when its intelligence and conscience begin to function. Not defeat, but disintegration overtakes it. The passions of war subside. Men become once again human beings instead of fighting animals. And in their awakened humanity is the hope of conciliation and conference and peace!

I realize fully that what I have said this morning will seem to you like an oversimplification of the subject. It is an immense theme with many ramifications. What I have tried to do is not to answer every question involved, but to raise questions in your mind; not to cover the field, but to open the gates so that you might be tempted to enter. The world has tried war a long time. It is time we tried something else. I believe nonviolent resistance is that something. Unless we break the deadly circle of war breeding war, civilization is doomed.

I should like to send you home with a quotation worth remembering and pondering: "Dying for one's ideals with nonviolent resistance is one way to make those ideals live; killing or wounding for the sake of those ideals kills or wounds the ideals as well."

13

THE FUNDAMENTALIST–MODERNIST CONTROVERSY, 1918-1930

Allen H. Sager

Religious disputation in America was never more spectacular than during the decade of the twenties. Fundamentalists, militantly concerned with the consolidation and defense of staunch orthodoxy and active within almost every major Protestant denomination in the United States, were confronting liberals intent upon refashioning Christianity in the interests of vitality and relevancy. Also contested were those scientific or secular emphases, especially the theory of evolution, which challenged orthodox dogmas.

Within their respective denominations, fundamentalists attempted by creedal definition and imposition to exclude from the churches, and particularly from the control of their educational and missionary enterprises, those who did not ascribe to the conservative faith. Employing as channels for persuasion Bible and prophetic conferences, fundamentalist schools, special organizations, tractarian propaganda, ecclesiastical and legislative pressures, and polemical preaching and platform speaking, fundamentalist leadership rallied adherents whose mixed desires for religious security, theological uniformity, ecclesiastical power, and personal aggrandizement hardened into a movement of militant protestation and defensive maneuverings.

Modernism, both as a method for interpreting Christian scripture and tradition and a body of liberal teachings, launched itself as a movement determining to vindicate the relevancy and vitality of Christianity in the new age. From left-wing exponents of humanism in theological dress to right-wing evangelicals, all agreed that a relevant theology must allow for the change, modification, and growth characteristic of vital, systematized disciplines.

It was inevitable that the two different theological worlds should clash. Fundamentalists challenged modernists in the arena of higher criticism of the Bible, where skirmishing centered around three doctrines: biblical inspiration, the virgin birth, and the second coming.

Of all Protestant denominations, Baptists and Presbyterians were most immediately and most actively plunged into the controversy. Harry Emerson Fosdick, ordained as a Baptist in 1903 but called as the associate preaching minister of the First Presbyterian Church of New York City in 1918, bore impact on both denominations. Though controversy was well under way among the Northern Presbyterians when he accepted the call to First Presbyterian, Fosdick was not disposed to enter into the then-current doctrinal squabbles. A product of the liberal-oriented Union Theological Seminary, Fosdick had made it his apparent practice so to temper his sermons that his liberal theology disturbed neither Baptist nor Presbyterian conservatives. Indeed, his great rhetorical gift, his literary attainments, and his popularity in student meetings were such as to distract from much concern over his theology.

But conditions were to change. In the summer of 1921, under the auspices of the YMCA, Fosdick traveled to China and Japan to address some missionary conferences. While there he became alarmed, especially at the divisive impact of the Bible Union of China, founded in 1920 as a fundamentalist premillennial organization devoted to the maintenance of the Five Points (the Infallibility of the Bible, Christ's Virgin Birth, his Substitutionary Atonement, his Bodily Resurrection, and his Second Coming).

333

It was this condition, coupled with his observance upon return to America that reactionary Protestantism was increasing at home, that led him to preach on May 21, 1922, that sermon which Robert D. Clark has called "the most sensational and widely-publicized sermon of his generation,"[1] "Shall the Fundamentalists Win?" It is reproduced here to illustrate the controversy. Fosdick's own commentary on the nature and intent of the sermon follows:

My sermon, "Shall the Fundamentalists Win?," was a plea for tolerance, for a church inclusive enough to take in both liberals and conservatives without either trying to drive the other out. I stated the honest differences of conviction dividing these two groups on such matters as the virgin birth of Jesus, the inerrancy of the Scriptures and the second coming of Christ, and then made my plea that the desirable solution was not a split that would tear the evangelical churches asunder, but a spirit of conciliation that would work out the problem within an inclusive fellowship.[2]

Anything but "a spirit of conciliation" followed as Fosdick himself lamented in retrospect: "If ever a sermon failed to achieve its object, mine did. It was a plea for good will, but what came of it was an explosion of ill will, for over two years making headline news of a controversy that went the limit of truculence."[3] Interestingly, the congregation of the First Presbyterian Church detected nothing inflamatory about the sermon at the time of its delivery. However, the sermon in pamphlet form came to the attention of Ivy Lee, a liberal Presbyterian layman, who was determined, as head of one of the nation's foremost publicity organizations, to supply copies of the sermon to a nationwide audience. Lee divided the sermon into sections, supplied a series of captions, cut out parts of the conciliatory introduction and conclusion, and retitled it, "The New Knowledge and the Christian

[1] "Harry Emerson Fosdick," A History and Criticism of American Public Address III (New York: Speech Association of America, 1955), 425.
[2] "The Fundamentalist Controversy," The Living of These Days (New York: Harper & Row, 1956), p. 145.
[3] Ibid.

Faith." The effectiveness for arousal of Lee's version of the sermon cannot be disputed, for after its circulation the brewing controversy erupted into open conflict.

The first reply, a copy of which accompanies this analysis, came from Clarence E. Macartney, a stalwart Presbyterian clergyman of Philadelphia. In a sermon subsequently published under the title, "Shall Unbelief Win?" [4] Macartney praises Fosdick for his "lucidity of thought and outline," for his "charm of word grouping," and for the absence of intolerance, bigotry, and arrogance. While expressing a "sincere desire for the return of Dr. Fosdick to evangelical faith," Macartney believes himself called to "contend earnestly and intelligently and in a Christian spirit" for that Christian faith of which he argues Fosdick's views are subversive. Upon reviewing Fosdick's position on the virgin birth, the inspiration of the Bible, the second advent, and the atonement, Macartney concludes that it is neither possible nor desirable to effect a reconciliation. "Both positions cannot be right; one *must* be wrong." Fosdick's remarks likening disputes over doctrinal matters to petty quarrels over mint, anise, and cummin, he called "an almost unpardonable flippancy on the part of one who speaks as a teacher of Christianity." Denying charges that there existed a fundamentalist conspiracy to put liberals out of the church, Macartney assured Fosdick and his companions that they "need not worry about processes of excision and ecclesiastical trial, and so being put out of the church." Caustically he added: "The sad thing is that in the minds of thousands upon thousands of Christians, they are already *out* of the church, and no act of an ecclesiastical court could make the fact more real."

Prayers that "they may be brought back into the

[4] In speaking of Fosdick's sermon, "Shall the Fundamentalists Win?," Macartney says: "This extraordinary sermon I answered with one entitled, 'Shall Unbelief Win?' This sermon, too, was printed in pamphlet form and widely circulated." (Cf. Macartney's autobiography, *The Making of a Minister*, ed. J. Clyde Henry [Great Neck, N.Y.: Channel Press, 1961], p. 184). The sermon, published in pamphlet form by Wilber Hanf of Philadelphia, bears but few editorial changes from the one published in two parts in *The Presbyterian*, July 13, 1922, pp. 8-10, 26; and July 20, 1922, pp. 8-10.

church" were soon overshadowed by denunciations insisting that the Philadelphia Presbytery overture the General Assembly of the Presbyterian Church (USA) that doctrine contrary to the Presbyterian Confession of Faith was being preached from the pulpit of the First Presbyterian Church of New York City. The ensuing action of the Philadelphia Presbytery set off a chain reaction, so that by the time the General Assembly met in May of 1923, twelve separate overtures had been filed, ten of which were unfavorable toward Fosdick. The governing powers of the church were thus set to work on the case. The intricate involvements of this action have been traced in careful detail,[5] and need hardly be reproduced here. To make the broad outline of the narrative complete, however, it should be noted that after two years of General Assembly debate (in which William Jennings Bryan figured prominently), Judicial Commission rulings, minority reports, political maneuverings, drafting and redrafting of statements, and Presbytery and Session inquiries, Fosdick was asked to "regularize" his position by becoming a Presbyterian minister "subject to the jurisdiction and authority of the Church," or "not to continue to occupy a Presbyterian pulpit." Fosdick declined the invitational ultimatum to become a Presbyterian minister, feeling such action would represent a "retrograde sectarian movement," a "return to the principle of a denominationally 'closed shop' "—a principle completely unpalatable to him as a "convinced interdenominationalist." [6] His resignation followed. He preached his farewell sermon to the First Presbyterian Church of New York City on Sunday, March 1, 1925.

Largely because of the charismatic leadership of such men as William Jennings Bryan and William Bell Riley,

[5] Cf. *The First Presbyterian Church of New York and Dr. Fosdick* (pamphlet giving no publication details); *Fosdick Case, Complaint of Walter D. Buchanan and Others to the 136th General Assembly of the Presbyterian Church in the U.S.A. Against the Presbytery of New York in its Answer to the Mandate of the 135th General Assembly of the Presbyterian Church in the U.S.A.* (Grand Rapids, 1924); and Fosdick, "The Fundamentalist Controversy," *The Living of These Days*, pp. 144-76.

[6] "The Fundamentalist Controversy," *The Living of These Days*, p. 174.

fundamentalists had extended their battle front beyond the "Five Points" to take up also the issue of evolution. The battle against evolutionists similarly reached its climax in 1925 in the Scopes trial. Although fundamentalists were successful on both fronts, they found their power waning progressively after 1925, their year of "victory."

Depicted analogously, the situation was much the same as that described by a scientist, who, when asked who killed off the dinosaurs, replied: "Nobody, the climate changed and they died." Fundamentalists were not defeated in the late twenties and early thirties; the climate changed and they found themselves no longer a viable force on the American theological scene. By 1930, a whole new slate of issues had been drawn to the fore. In short, it was time to begin viewing the fundamentalist-modernist controversy as history.

Harry Emerson Fosdick

Harry Emerson Fosdick was born in Buffalo, New York, on May 24, 1878, and died Oct. 5, 1969. He was educated at Colgate University (A.B., 1900), Union Theological Seminary (B.D., 1904) and Columbia University (A.M., 1908). He became a member of Phi Beta Kappa. Ordained to the Baptist ministry in 1903, he served as pastor of the First Baptist Church in Montclair, New Jersey, from 1904 until 1915, and of the First Presbyterian Church, New York City, from 1919 to 1925. From 1926 until 1946 when he became pastor emeritus, he was minister of the Park Avenue Baptist Church (which became the Riverside Church), New York City. He also worked with the YMCA in France from 1917 until 1919. He taught at Union Theological Seminary from 1908 to 1915 as an instructor in homiletics, and from 1915 to 1946 as Professor of Practical Theology.

Fosdick's Lyman Beecher Lectures were published under the title The Modern Use of the Bible *in 1924. He was well known for his nationwide radio preaching on National Vespers. Some of his books are:* The Assurance of Immortality *(1913)*, Christianity and Progress *(1922)*, Adventurous Religion *(1926)*, As I See Religion *(1932)*, The Hope of the World *(1933)*, The Secret of Victorious Living *(1934)*, The Power to See It Through *(1935)*, Successful Christian Living *(1937)*, A Guide to Understanding the Bible *(1938)*, Living Under Tension *(1941)*, On Being a Real Person *(1943)*, A Great Time to Be Alive *(1944)*, On Being Fit to Live With *(1946)*, The Man from Nazareth *(1949)*, What Is Vital in Religion *(1955)*, The Living of These Days *(1956)*, Riverside Sermons *(1957)*.

Shall the Fundamentalists Win? *

This morning we are to think of the Fundamentalist controversy which threatens to divide the American churches, as though already they were not sufficiently split and riven. A scene, suggestive for our thought, is depicted in the fifth chapter of the Book of the Acts, where the Jewish leaders hale before them Peter and others of the apostles because they had been preaching Jesus as the Messiah. Moreover, the Jewish leaders propose to slay them,

* Ernest Wrage and Barnet Baskerville, *Contemporary Forum* (New York: Harper & Row, 1963), pp. 97 ff. Stenographically reported.

when in opposition Gamaliel speaks: "Refrain from these men, and let them alone: for if this counsel or this work be of men, it will be overthrown: but if it is of God ye will not be able to overthrow them; lest haply ye be found even to be fighting against God."

One could easily let his imagination play over this scene and could wonder how history would have come out if Gamaliel's wise tolerance could have controlled the situation. For though the Jewish leaders seemed superficially to concur in Gamaliel's judgment, they nevertheless kept up their bitter antagonism and shut the Christians from the synagogue. We know now that they were mistaken. Christianity, starting within Judaism, was not an innovation to be dreaded; it was the finest flowering out that Judaism ever had. When the Master looked back across his racial heritage and said, "I came not to destroy, but to fulfill," he perfectly described the situation. The Christian ideas of God, the Christian principles of life, the Christian hopes for the future, were all rooted in the Old Testament and grew up out of it, and the Master himself, who called the Jewish temple his Father's house, rejoiced in the glorious heritage of his people's prophets. Only, he did believe in a living God. He did not think that God was dead, having finished his words and works with Malachi. He had not simply a historic, but a contemporary God, speaking now, working now, leading his people now, from partial into fuller truth. Jesus believed in the progressiveness of revelation and these Jewish leaders did not understand that. Was this new gospel a real development which they might welcome or was it an enemy to be cast out? And they called it an enemy and excluded it. One does wonder what might have happened had Gamaliel's wise tolerance been in control.

We, however, face today a situation too similar and too urgent and too much in need of Gamaliel's attitude to spend any time making guesses at suppositious history. Already all of us must have heard about the people who call themselves the Fundamentalists. Their apparent intention is to drive out of the evangelical churches men and women of liberal opinions. I speak of them the more freely because there are no two denominations more affected by them than the Baptists and the Presbyterians. We should not identify the Fundamentalists with conservatives. All Fundamentalists are conservatives, but not all conservatives are Fundamentalists. The best conservatives can often give lessons to the liberals in true liberality of spirit, but the Fundamentalist program is essentially illiberal and intolerant. The Fundamentalists see, and they see truly, that in this last generation there have been strange new movements in Christian thought. A great mass of new knowledge has come into man's possession: new knowledge about the physical universe, its origin, its forces, its laws; new knowledge about human history and in particular about the ways in which the ancient peoples used to think in matters of religion and the methods by which they phrased and explained their spiritual experiences; and new knowledge, also, about other religions and the strangely similar ways in which men's faiths and religious practices have developed everywhere.

Now, there are multitudes of reverent Christians who have been unable to keep this new knowledge in one compartment of their minds and the Christian faith in another. They have been sure that all truth comes from the one God and is his revelation. Not, therefore, from irreverence or caprice or destructive zeal, but for the sake of intellectual and spiritual integrity, that they might really love the Lord their God not only with all their heart and soul and strength, but with all their mind, they have been trying to see this new knowledge in terms of the Christian faith and to see the Christian faith in terms of this new knowledge. Doubtless they have made many mistakes. Doubtless there have been among them reckless radicals gifted with intellectual ingenuity but lacking spiritual depth. Yet the enterprise itself seems to them indispensable to the Christian Church. The new knowledge and the old faith cannot be left antagonistic or even disparate, as though a man on Saturday could use one set of regulative ideas for his life and on Sunday could change gear to another altogether. We must be able to think our modern life clear through in Christian terms and to do that we also must be able to think our Christian life clear through in modern terms.

There is nothing new about the situation. It has happened again and again in history, as, for example, when the stationary earth suddenly began to move and the universe that had been centered in this planet was centered in the sun around which the planets whirled. Whenever such a situation has arisen, there has been only one way out: the new knowledge and the old faith had to be blended in a new combination. Now, the people in this generation who are trying to do this are the liberals, and the Fundamentalists are out on a campaign to shut against them the doors of the Christian fellowship. Shall they be allowed to succeed?

It is interesting to note where the Fundamentalists are driving in their stakes to mark out the deadline of doctrine around the church, across which no one is to pass except on terms of agreement. They insist that we must all believe in the historicity of certain special miracles, preeminently the virgin birth of our Lord; that we must believe in a special theory of inspiration—that the original documents of the scripture, which of course we no longer possess, were inerrantly dictated to men a good deal as a man might dictate to a stenographer; that we must believe in a special theory of the atonement—that the blood of our Lord, shed in a substitutionary death, placates an alienated deity and makes possible welcome for the returning sinner; and that we must believe in the second coming of our Lord upon the clouds of heaven to set up a millennium here, as the only way in which God may bring history to a worthy denouement. Such are some of the stakes which are being driven, to mark a deadline of doctrine around the church.

If a man is a genuine liberal, his primary protest is not against holding these opinions, although he may well protest against their being considered the fundamentals of Christianity. This is a free country and anybody has a right to hold these opinions or any others, if he is sincerely convinced of them. The question is: Has anybody a right to deny the Christian name to those who differ with him on such points and to shut against them the doors of the Christian fellowship? The Fundamentalists say that this must be done. In this country and on the foreign field they are trying to do it. They have actually endeavored to put on the statute books of a whole state binding laws against teaching modern biology. If they had their way, within the church they would set up in Protestantism a doctrinal tribunal more rigid than the pope's. In such an hour, delicate and dangerous, where feelings are bound to run high, I plead this morning the cause of magnanimity and liberality and tolerance of spirit. I would, if I could reach their ears, say to the Fundamentalists about the liberals what Gamaliel said to the Jews, "Refrain from these men, and let them alone: for if this counsel or this work be of men, it will be overthrown: but if it is of God ye will not be able to overthrow them; lest haply ye be found even to be fighting against God."

That we may be entirely candid and concrete and may not lose ourselves in any fog of generalities, let us this morning take two or three of these Fundamentalist items and see with reference to them what the situation is in the Christian churches. Too often we preachers have failed to talk frankly enough about the differences of opinion which exist among evangelical Christians, although everybody knows that they are there. Let us face this morning some of the differences of opinion with which somehow we must deal.

We may as well begin with the vexed and mooted question of the virgin birth of our Lord. I know people in the Christian churches, ministers, missionaries, laymen, devoted lovers of the Lord and servants of the gospel, who, alike as they are in their personal devotion to the Master, hold quite different points of view about a matter like the virgin birth. Here, for example, is one point of view: that the virgin birth is to be accepted as historical fact; it actually happened; there was no other way for a personality like the Master to come into this world except by a special biological miracle. That is one point of view, and many are the gracious and beautiful souls who hold it. But, side by side with them in the evangelical churches is a group of equally loyal and reverent people who would say that the virgin birth is not to be accepted as an historic fact.

To believe in virgin birth as an explanation of great personality is one of the familiar ways in which the ancient world was accustomed to account for unusual superiority. Many people suppose that only once in history do we run across a record of supernatural birth. Upon the contrary, stories of miraculous generation are among the commonest traditions of antiquity. Especially is this true about the founders of great religions. According to the records of their faiths, Buddha and Zoroaster and Lao-Tse and Mahavira were all supernaturally born. Moses, Confucius and Mohammed are the only great founders of religion in history to whom miraculous birth is not attributed. That is to say, when a personality arose so high that men adored him, the ancient world attributed his superiority to some special divine influence in his generation, and they commonly phrased their faith in terms of miraculous birth. So Pythagoras was called virgin born, and Plato, and Augustus Caesar, and many more. Knowing this, there are within the evangelical churches large groups of people whose opinion about our Lord's coming would run as follows: those first disciples adored Jesus—as we do; when they thought about his coming they were sure that he came specially from God—as we are; this adoration and conviction they associated with God's special influence and intention in his birth—as we do; but they phrased it in terms of a biological miracle that our modern minds cannot use. So far from thinking that they have given up anything vital in the New Testament's attitude towards Jesus, these Christians remember that the two men who contributed most to the church's thought of the divine meaning of the Christ were Paul and John, who never even distantly allude to the virgin birth.

Here in the Christian churches are these two groups of people and the question which the Fundamentalists raise is this: Shall one of them throw the other out? Has intolerance any contribution to make to this situation? Will it persuade anybody of anything? Is not the Christian church large enough to hold within her hospitable fellowship people who differ on points like this and agree to differ until the fuller truth be manifested? The Fundamentalists say not. They say that the liberals must go. Well, if the Fundamentalists should succeed, then out of the Christian church would go some of the best Christian life and consecration of this generation—multitudes of men and women, devout and reverent Christians, who need the church and whom the church needs.

Consider another matter on which there is a sincere difference of opinion between evangelical Christians: the inspiration of the Bible. One point of view is that the original documents of the scripture were inerrantly dictated by God to men. Whether we deal with the story of creation or the list of dukes of Edom or the narratives of Solomon's reign or the Sermon on the Mount or the thirteenth chapter of first Corinthians, they all came in the same way and they all came as no other book ever came. They were inerrantly dictated; everything there—scientific opinions, medical theories, historical judgments, as well as spiritual insights—is infallible. That is one idea of the Bible's inspiration. But side by side with those who hold it, lovers of the book as much as they, are multitudes of people who never think about the Bible so. Indeed, that static and mechanical theory of inspiration seems to them a positive peril to the spiritual life. The Koran similarly has been regarded by Mohammedans as having been infallibly written in heaven before it came to earth. But the Koran enshrines the theological and ethical ideas of Arabia at the time when it was written. God an oriental monarch, fatalistic submission to his will as man's chief duty, the use of force on unbelievers, polygamy, slavery—they are all in the Koran. The Koran was ahead of the day when it was written, but, petrified by an artificial idea of inspiration, it has become a millstone about the neck of Mohammedanism.

When one turns from the Koran to the Bible, he finds this interesting situation. All of these ideas, which we dislike in the Koran, are somewhere in the Bible. Conceptions from which we now send missionaries to convert Mohammedans are to be found in the Book. There one can find God thought of as an oriental monarch; there, too, are patriarchal polygamy, and slave systems, and the use of force on unbelievers. Only in the Bible these elements are not final; they are always being superseded; revelation is progressive. The thought of God moves out from oriental kingship to compassionate fatherhood; treatment of unbelievers moves out from the use of force to the appeals of love; polygamy gives way to monogamy; slavery, never explicitly condemned before the New Testament closes, is nevertheless being undermined by ideas that in the end, like dynamite, will blast its foundations to pieces. Repeatedly one runs on verses like this: "It was said to them of old time. . . . but I say unto you"; "God, having of old time spoken unto the fathers in the prophets by divers portions and in divers manners, hath at the end of these days spoken unto us in his Son"; "The times of ignorance therefore God overlooked; but now he commandeth men that they should all everywhere repent"; and over the doorway of the New Testament into the Christian world stand the words of Jesus: "When he, the spirit of truth is come, he shall guide you into all the truth." That is to say, finality in the Koran is behind; finality in the Bible is ahead. We have not reached it. We cannot yet compass all of it. God is leading us out toward it. There are multitudes of Christians, then, who think, and rejoice as they think, of the Bible as the record of the progressive unfolding of the character of God to his people from early primitive days until the great unveiling in Christ; to them the Book is more inspired and more inspiring than ever it was before; and to go back to a mechanical and static theory of inspiration would mean to them the loss of some of the most vital elements in their spiritual experience and in their appreciation of the Book.

Here in the Christian church today are these two groups, and the question which the Fundamentalists have raised is this: Shall one of them drive the other out? Do we think the cause of Jesus Christ will be furthered by that? If he should walk through the ranks of this congregation this morning, can we imagine him claiming as his own those who hold one idea of inspiration and sending from him into outer darkness those who hold another? You cannot fit the Lord Christ into that Fundamentalist mold. The church would better judge his judgment. For in the middle west the Fundamentalists have had their way in some communities and a Christian minister tells us the consequence. He says that all the educated people are looking for their religion outside the churches.

Consider another matter upon which there is a serious and sincere difference of opinion between evangelical Christians: the second coming of our Lord. The second coming was the early Christian phrasing of hope. No one in the ancient world had ever thought, as we do, of development, progress, gradual change, as God's way of working out his will in human life and institutions. They thought of human history as a series of ages succeeding one another with abrupt suddenness. The Graeco-Roman world gave the names of metals to the ages—gold, silver, bronze, iron. The Hebrews had their ages too—the original paradise in which man began, the cursed world in which man now lives, the blessed messianic kingdom some day suddenly to appear on the clouds of heaven. It was the Hebrew way of expressing hope for the victory of God and righteousness. When the Christians came they took over that phrasing of expectancy and the New Testament is aglow with it. The preaching of the apostles thrills with the glad announcement, "Christ is coming!"

In the evangelical churches today there are differing views of this matter. One view is that Christ is literally coming, externally on the clouds of heaven, to set up his kingdom here. I never heard that teaching in my youth at all. It has always had a new resurrection when desperate circumstances came and man's only hope seemed to lie in divine intervention. It is not strange, then, that during these chaotic, catastrophic years there has been a fresh rebirth of this old phrasing of expectancy. "Christ is coming!" seems to many Christians the central message of the gospel. In the strength of it some of them are doing great service for the world. But unhappily, many so over-emphasize it that they outdo anything the ancient Hebrews or the ancient Christians ever did. They sit still and do nothing and expect the world to grow worse and worse until he comes.

Side by side with these to whom the second coming is a literal expectation, another group exists in the evangelical churches. They, too, say, "Christ is coming!" They say it with all their hearts; but they are not thinking of an external arrival on the clouds. They have assimilated as part of the divine revelation the exhilarating insight which these recent generations have given to us, that development is God's way of working out his will. They see that the most desirable elements in human life have come through the method of development. Man's music has developed from the rhythmic noise of beaten sticks until we have in melody and harmony possibilities once un-dreamed. Man's painting has developed from the crude outlines of the cave-men until in line and color we have achieved unforeseen results and possess latent beauties yet unfolded. Man's architecture has developed from the crude huts of primitive men until our cathedrals and business buildings re-veal alike an incalculable advance and an unimaginable future. Development does seem to be the way in which God works. And these Christians, when they say that Christ is coming, mean that, slowly it may be, but surely, his will and principles will be worked out by God's grace in human life and institutions, until "he shall see of the travail of his soul and shall be satisfied."

These two groups exist in the Christian churches and the question raised by the Fundamentalists is: Shall one of us drive the other out? Will that get us anywhere? Multitudes of young men and women at this season of the year are graduating from our schools of learning, thousands of them Christians who may make us older ones ashamed by the sincerity of their devotion to God's will on earth. They are not thinking in ancient terms that leave ideas of progress out. They cannot think in those terms. There could be no greater tragedy than that the Fundamentalists should shut the door of the Christian fellowship against such.

I do not believe for one moment that the Fundamentalists are going to succeed. Nobody's intolerance can contribute anything to the solution of the situation which we have described. If, then, the Fundamentalists have no solution of the problem, where may we expect to find it? In two con-cluding comments let us consider our reply to that enquiry.

The first element that is necessary is a spirit of tolerance and Christian liberty. When will the world learn that intolerance solves no problems? This is not a lesson which the Fundamentalists alone need to learn; the liberals also need to learn it. Speaking, as I do, from the viewpoint of liberal opinions, let me say that if some young, fresh mind here this morning is holding new ideas, has fought his way through, it may be by intellectual and spiritual struggle to novel positions, and is tempted to be intolerant about old opinions, offensively to condescend to those who hold them and to be harsh in judgment on them, he may well remember that people who held those old opinions have given the world some of the noblest character and the most memorable service that it ever has been blessed with, and that we of the younger generation will prove our case best, not by controversial intolerance, but by producing, with our new opinions, something of the depth and strength, nobility and beauty of character that in other times were associated with other thoughts. It was a wise liberal, the most adventurous man of his day—Paul the apostle—who said, "Knowledge puffeth up, but love buildeth up."

Nevertheless, it is true that just now the Fundamentalists are giving us one of the worst exhibitions of bitter intolerance that the churches of this country have ever seen. As one watches them and listens to them, he remembers the mark of General Armstrong of Hampton Institute: "Cantankerousness is worse than heterodoxy." There are many opinions in the field of modern controversy concerning which I am not sure whether they are right or wrong, but there is one thing I am sure of: courtesy and kindliness and tolerance and humility and fairness are right. Opinions may be mistaken; love never is.

As I plead thus for an intellectually hospitable, tolerant, liberty-loving church, I am of course thinking primarily about this new generation. We have boys and girls growing up in our homes and schools, and because we love them we may well wonder about the church which will be waiting to receive them. Now, the worst kind of church that can possibly be offered to the allegiance of the new generation is an intolerant church. Ministers often bewail the fact that young people turn from religion to science for the regulative ideas of their lives. But this is easily explicable. Science treats a young man's mind as though it were really important. A scientist says to a young man: "Here is the universe challenging our investigation. Here are the truths which we have seen, so far. Come, study with us! See what we already have seen and then look further to see more, for science is an intellectual adventure for the truth." Can you imagine any man who is worth while turning from that call to the church, if the church seems to him to say: "Come and we will feed you opinions from a spoon. No thinking is allowed here except such as brings you to certain specified, predetermined conclusions. These prescribed opinions we will give you in advance of your thinking; now think, but only so as to reach these results." My friends, nothing in all the world is so much worth thinking of as God, Christ, the

Bible, sin and salvation, the divine purposes for humankind, life everlasting. But you cannot challenge the dedicated thinking of this generation to these sublime themes upon any such terms as are laid down by an intolerant church.

The second element which is needed if we are to reach a happy solution of this problem is a clear insight into the main issues of modern Christianity and a sense of penitent shame that the Christian church should be quarreling over little matters when the world is dying of great needs. If, during the war, when the nations were wrestling upon the very brink of hell and at times all seemed lost, you chanced to hear two men in an altercation about some minor matter of sectarian denominationalism, could you restrain your indignation? You said, "What can you do with folks like this who, in the face of colossal issues, play with the tiddledywinks and peccadillos of religion?" So, now, when from the terrific questions of this generation one is called away by the noise of this Fundamentalist controversy, he thinks it almost unforgivable that men should tithe mint and anise and cummin, and quarrel over them, when the world is perishing for the lack of the weightier matters of the law, justice, and mercy, and faith.

These last weeks, in the minister's confessional, I have heard stories from the depths of human lives where men and women were wrestling with the elemental problems of misery and sin—stories that put upon a man's heart a burden of vicarious sorrow, even though he does but listen to them. Here was real human need crying out after the living God revealed in Christ. Consider all the multitudes of men who so need God, and then think of Christian churches making of themselves a cockpit of controversy when there is not a single thing at stake in the controversy on which depends the salvation of human souls. That is the trouble with this whole business. So much of it does not matter! And there is one thing that does matter—more than anything else in all the world—that men in their personal lives and in their social relationships should know Jesus Christ.

Just a week ago I received a letter from a friend in Asia Minor. He says that they are killing the Armenians yet; that the Turkish deportations still are going on; that lately they crowded Christian men, women and children into a conventicle of worship and burned them together in the house where they had prayed to their Father and to ours. During the war, when it was good propaganda to stir up our bitter hatred against the enemy we heard of such atrocities, but not now! Two weeks ago, Great Britain, shocked and stirred by what is going on in Armenia, did ask the Government of the United States to join her in investigating the atrocities and trying to help! Our government said that it was not any of our business at all. The present world situation smells to heaven! And now, in the presence of colossal problems, which must be solved in Christ's name and for Christ's sake, the Fundamentalits propose to drive out from the Christian churches all the consecrated souls who do not agree with their theory of inspiration. What immeasurable folly!

Well, they are not going to do it; certainly not in this vicinity. I do not even know in this congregation whether anybody has been tempted to be a Fundamentalist. Never in this church have I caught one accent of intolerance. God keep us always so and ever increasing areas of the Christian fellowship: intellectually hospitable, open-minded, liberty-loving, fair, tolerant, not with the tolerance of indifference as though we did not care about the faith, but because always our major emphasis is upon the weightier matters of the law.

CLARENCE E. MACARTNEY

Clarence Macartney was born in Northwood, Ohio, September 18, 1879. He was graduated from the University of Wisconsin (B.A., 1901), Princeton University (M.A., 1904), and Princeton Theological Seminary (1905). He was ordained a Presbyterian minister in 1905, and served as pastor of the First Presbyterian Church, Paterson, New Jersey, from that time until 1914. From 1914 until 1927 he was minister at Arch Street Presbyterian Church, Philadelphia, Pennsylvania, and from 1927 until 1953 served at the First Presbyterian Church, Pittsburgh, Pennsylvania. He was Moderator of the Presbyterian Church in the U.S.A. from 1924 to 1925.

He wrote fifty-seven books in fields of history, biography, and religion, including: Lincoln and His Cabinet (1931), Sermons on Old Testament Heroes (1935), Peter and His Lord (1937), Facing Life and Getting the Best of It (1940), Preaching Without Notes (1946), Lincoln and the Bible (1949), Men of the Bible (1950), Chariots of Fire (1951), Grant and His Generals (1953), Faith Once Delivered (1953), and The Parables of the Old Testament (1955). He died February 19, 1957.

Shall Unbelief Win? *

There appeared recently in a number of the religious papers, and has since been distributed in pamphlet form, the copy of a sermon, entitled, "Shall the Fundamentalists Win?" preached by Dr. Harry Emerson Fosdick in the pulpit of the First Presbyterian Church, New York. The sermon has all the lucidity of thought and outline, and all the charm of word grouping which have won for Dr. Fosdick a well-deserved popularity. It is also free from the intolerance and arrogance which sometimes mar the writings of the so-called "liberal" school of theologians, and whose own illiberality and churlishness of spirit speak much more loudly than anything else they say.

This sermon by Dr. Fosdick will be read with varying emotions. Those who agree with the position held by Dr. Fosdick will hail it with delight as a sort of declaration of principles and an eloquent setting forth of the Fourteen Points of modernistic theology, a manual by which all on that side can

* Pamphlet (Philadelphia: Wilber Hanf, 1922).

march and drill and fight. Persons who are a-theological in their thinking, but who always applaud the revolt against what has been held, taught and believed in the Church will also rejoice in it. But there are not a few others, who do not think of themselves as either "Fundamentalists" or "Modernists," but as Christians, striving amid the dust and the confused clamor of this life to hold to the Christian faith and follow the Lord Jesus Christ, who will read this sermon with sorrow and pain. The Presbyterians who read it will deeply regret that such an utterance, so hopelessly irreconcilable with the standards of belief required by the Reformed Churches, could be made by the stated occupant of a Presbyterian pulpit, and apparently without any protest or wonder on the part of the Session of the Church, or the Presbytery to which the Church belongs. I have just read a letter from a minister in the West in which the writer expresses the earnest hope that Dr. Fosdick will awaken to the inconsistency of his position and the non-Christianity of his views, and return, like many another wanderer to the Cross of Christ. In this pious wish I am sure that all right-minded ministers who differ with Dr. Fosdick will join. One of his own school of thought in conversation with me, declared that Dr. Fosdick must be retained to the Church because of his splendid emphasis on the social side of Christianity. None would deny that emphasis. But why not keep him for a greater service, for an emphasis upon the redemptive side of Christianity, the truth that takes in all else? We may feel that there are few instances of men who have gone as far from historic Christianity as he has gone ever returning to the faith. But what about Romanes? What about Reginald Campbell and his "New" Theology, now long since recanted? The citation of these names gives one hope that Dr. Fosdick too may yet speak in accents which will rejoice the hearts of believers instead of causing them anxiety and sorrow.

But a sincere desire for the return of Dr. Fosdick to evangelical faith, and the sense of pain and anxiety which his sermon occasions, must not be permitted to stand in the way of an emphatic and earnest rejoinder on the part of those who hold the opposite views, and who believe that the views held by Dr. Fosdick are subversive of the Christian faith. The greatest need of the Church to-day is a few men of ability and faith who are not afraid of being called "bigots," "narrow," "mediaeval" in their religious thought. I do not mean to infer that Dr. Fosdick ever so thinks of those who repudiate his views, for he goes out of his way to rebuke those of his side who indulge in this childish pastime. But more and more there is a tendency to brand as illiberal, medieval and narrow any man who differs from the current of popular religious thought, and declares it to be non-Christian in its tendencies. There is a great discussion in the pulpit and out of it as to what the Church is to do or not to do. The state of opinion on this subject is singularly chaotic at present. But with all the diversity of opinion as to the work of the Church, there seems to be a pretty general agreement as to the one thing which the Church is not to do. Whatever the Church is to do or not to do, it is not to defend the faith; it is not to point out the errors and inconsistencies of those who stand as the interpreters of Christianity. This amazing agreement would have struck the Christian believers of almost any age in Church history, save our own, as a very extraordinary one. The writer of this article dissents entirely from this popular view, that when a Christian man hears or reads an utterance of Christian teachers and leaders which he believes to be irreconciliable with the Gospel the thing to do is to do nothing. Certainly this is not the course followed by those who are blasting at the Rock of Ages, and, consciously or unconsciously, adulterating distinctive and New Testament Christianity with the conclusions and vagaries of this world's life and thought. I do not believe in letting them hold the field all to themselves. I believe that in this day one of the greatest contributions that a man can make to the success of the Gospel is to contend earnestly and intelligently and in a Christian spirit, but nevertheless, CONTEND, for the faith.

Whatever one's theological position may be, one cannot but feel glad that Dr. Fosdick has spoken so frankly as he has. He, at least, cannot be charged with the offense of subtly corrupting Christian doctrines by pretending to honor them, while all the time evacuating them of their meaning. The recent book by Dr. Sterrett on "What Is Modernism?" is a good example of the fog and bog of much of the rationalistic movement in the Church. One is puzzled to know just what the man does believe. As an elder in one of our Presbyterian churches said of his own minister: "I really do not know what our minister believes!" He knew it was something strange, something perhaps out of harmony with historic Christianity, but just why or how, he could not tell. But none can charge Dr. Fosdick with such obfuscation. Both rationalistics and evangelicals, therefore, will rejoice that Dr. Fosdick in this sermon leaves no reader or hearer in the least doubt as to what he believes, or disbelieves, about the cardinal doctrines of the Christian religion.

It is unfortunate that Dr. Fosdick uses the name "Fundamentalist." It is a grand name, and the man who claims it certainly puts the burden of proof on those who differ from him. But in recent years the name has come to be applied to a group, who indeed hold to conservative views, but whose chief emphasis is upon the premillennial reign of Christ on this earth. In this sense we are not interested in the controversy, for we do not believe that an opinion, conviction or expectation as to the time of the second

351

Epiphany of Christ is a fundamental of the Christian faith. Historic Christianity has been wisely guided here, for no great body of the Christian Church has ever made an opinion about the TIME of Christ's advent an article of its creed. In any recent controversy between rationalists and evangelicals there has been a tendency on the part of the former to use chiliasm as a sort of smoke-screen and raise the cry of "premillenarian," whereas they know that the strongest and most influential currents of thought in conservative Protestantism run in an altogether different direction. The Princeton "school" of theology, for example, as summed up in Charles Hodge's famous eight reasons against premillennialism, has never had any chiliastic leanings whatever. But, as we shall see, Dr. Fosdick not only, and with some cause, protests against the premillenarian propaganda, but goes far beyond that and reduces the great New Testament teaching of the Second Advent of Jesus Christ to a "glittering generality."

Let us now take up, one by one, the different Christian doctrines mentioned in the sermon, and see how Dr. Fosdick views them. His claim is that a group of "Fundamentalists" are drawing a "dead line" in theology across which no man may step and live. In stating the views of the so-called "Fundamentalists," which is of little consequence, Dr. Fosdick states his own views and those of his school of thought, and this is of the greatest consequence, for it clears the atmosphere and lets us see the religious chaos which reigns in rationalistic circles. They who, above all others, ought to read this sermon, are not the conservatives and not the rationalists, but the middle-of-the-road people who are fondly hoping that these schools are divided only by a difference in words and names, and that the two positions can and will be reconciled. Dr. Fosdick's sermon shows the impossibility and the non-desirability of such reconciliation. If Dr. Fosdick is right, his views ought to prevail, and the creed of the Presbyterian Church and of every other Church in Christendom, save the smaller humanitarian bodies like the Unitarians, and which are really creedless, as to either a written or unwritten creed, ought to be revised. If this is truth, then let it prevail, no matter how many churches sink into oblivion. But whether he is right, or whether the evangelical position is right, one thing all must now admit: both positions cannot be right; one MUST be wrong.

I. *The Virgin Birth.* Dr. Fosdick does not accept the Virgin Birth as an historic fact. He rejects what he calls "a special biological miracle" as the explanation for the way in which Christ came into the world. The Virgin Birth to him is merely an effort on the part of religious devotion and faith to account for the manifest superiority of the character and person of Jesus. But lest I should do him any injustice in my summary of this paragraph of his sermon, let me quote his own words:

To believe in virgin birth as an explanation of great personality is one of the familiar ways in which the ancient world was accustomed to account for unusual superiority. Many people suppose that only once in history do we run across a record of supernatural birth. Upon the contrary, stories of miraculous generation are among the commonest traditions of antiquity. Especially is this true about the founders of great religions. According to the records of their faiths Buddha and Zoroaster and Lao-Tsze and Mahavira were all supernaturally born. Moses, Confucius and Mohammad are the only great founders of religions in history to whom miraculous birth is not attributed. That is to say, when a personality arose so high that men adored him, the ancient world attributed his superiority to some special divine influence in his generation, and they commonly phrased their faith in terms of miraculous birth. So Pythagoras was called virgin born, and Plato, and Augustus Caesar, and many more. Knowing this, there are within the evangelical churches large groups of people whose opinion about our Lord's coming would run as follows: those first disciples adored Jesus—as we do; when they thought about his coming, they were sure that he came specially from God—as we are; this adoration and conviction they associated with God's special influence and intention in his birth—as we do; but they phrased it in terms of a biological miracle that our modern minds cannot use. So far from thinking that they have given up anything vital in the New Testament's attitude toward Jesus, these Christians remember that the two men who contributed most to the Church's thought of the divine meaning of the Christ were Paul and John, who never even distantly allude to the virgin birth.

This speaks for itself. There was no Virgin Birth. The opening chapters of St. Matthew and St. Luke are pure myth, and the alleged facts and acts of those pages are merely a pious, devout and natural effort of believing men to account for the personality of Jesus, in much the same way that the followers of Buddha, Zoroaster, Lao-Tsze and Mahavira tried to account for them. Not only does he repudiate the Virgin Birth, but he states that opinions on the subject are of little importance, in no way affecting vital Christianity. In this connection he makes the stock remark of the rationalists about the two great teachers of Christianity, St. John and St. Paul, never even distantly alluding to the Virgin Birth. I have often been asked if Dr. Fosdick believes in the divinity, or better, the deity, of our Lord. I hope that he does, and even if in our New Testament we did not have the accounts of Matthew and Luke, the deity of Jesus Christ would everywhere confront us. We must grant, too, that God becoming flesh is a mystery which the Virgin Birth only partially explains. Nevertheless, that is the explanation given in the Gospels, and the only explanation given. Moreover, if we are to take that part of the Gospels as mere pious musing and guessing, will it not weaken our regard for the other parts? If for example the stories of the nativity of Jesus are mere human effort to account for a personality who defied human classification, then who can find fault with the man who says that the ac-

353

counts of the Crucifixion of Jesus are merely imaginations on the part of His followers who wished to have Him die a glorious and sacrificial death? Or that the accounts of the Resurrection are merely the tributes of devotion and admiration, not the records of fact, but stories arising out of the conviction that Christ was too great and holy a man to be held of death, and thus in keeping with other tales of the reappearance and reincarnation of great men? And so with the Ascension and the Second Epiphany. The moment we take this view of the account of the Virgin Birth do we not prepare the way for the repudiation of any other part of the Gospel story by any man who wills to do so?

No intelligent Christian is disturbed by the reference that neither John nor Paul "even distantly allude" to the Virgin Birth of Jesus. It is partly amusing and partly irritating, the way the rationalists make use of Paul and John. When they are talking on the Virgin Birth of Jesus they cite Paul and John as the great authorities of the Church, and yet men who are silent on this subject. But when they are on a subject such as the Atonement, or the fate of the unbelievers in the next, there John and Paul appear in an altogether different light. Now no one knows whether John wrote the Gospel that bears his name; probably not; and as for Paul, he took the simple teachings of a Galilean peasant and grafted upon them a mass of doctrines about sin and atonement and justification by faith which are entirely foreign to true Christianity. For this reason it is amusing to hear them cite John and Paul as on either side when it comes to the Virgin Birth. The fact is that both St. John and St. Paul above all other writers of the New Testament teach the Incarnation of God in Jesus and the supernatural manner of the entrance of the Son of God into this world. The fact that Paul, for example, while he says that Christ was born of woman, does not say that He was born of a virgin, in no way invalidates the authority of Matthew or Luke, or implies that he had never heard of the birth of "that holy thing" in the womb of the Virgin Mary.

J. A. MacCulloch, in the article on Virgin Birth in Hastings' *Encyclopedia of Religion and Ethics*, points out that in the case of Zoroaster and Buddha, to which Dr. Fosdick adverts, actual physical generation through father and mother is implied in the birth stories of Buddha, and in the birth stories of Zoroaster we have his "actual physical generation." Supernatural elements are added, but as Dr. MacCulloch clearly points out, there is no ground whatever for saying that the stories of the births of Zoroaster and Buddha are comparable to the New Testament account of the Virgin Birth of Jesus. But this is a field into which it is not necessary for me to go, for even if there did exist stories of births of great religious leaders through a virgin and without ordinary process of generation, this would in no way repudiate or invalidate the sublime account in the Gospels of St. Matthew and St. Luke, which tell of the conception of Jesus by the power of the Holy Ghost in the womb of the Virgin Mary. The Virgin Birth was universally accepted in the early Church, and it can hardly be denied that to reject the Virgin Birth is to break with historic Christianity. The first denials of the Virgin Birth came mainly from deistical writers in the eighteenth century. This rejection on the part of the deists is now revived by their lineal descendants, the rationalists. It is important to note that while Matthew and Luke are the only Gospels which give the account of the Virgin Birth, these two Gospels are also the only Gospels which profess to record the events of the birth of Jesus. If in John and Mark we had a narrative of the events of the birth of Jesus, and among those events we should find no mention of the Virgin Birth, then the omission would indeed perplex and trouble us. But John and Mark do not profess to record the events of the birth of Jesus, and therefore their omission of the Virgin Birth is insignificant. Certainly no one would be justified in drawing the inference which Dr. Fosdick seems to draw, namely, that because John and Mark are silent on the subject they did not accept the fact of the Virgin Birth.

As for St. Paul, it is well to remember that he makes hardly any reference to the earthly life of Jesus beyond the facts of the Crucifixion and the Resurrection. In his work on the Virgin Birth of Christ, Dr. J. Orr points out the indisputable fact that St. Paul regarded the entry of Christ into the world as no ordinary event, and that in speaking of it Paul always employs "some significant peculiarity of expression," such as, "God sending His Son" (Romans 1:3; 5:12); "becoming in the likeness of men" (Philippians 2:7); and the unusual Greek form in Galatians 4:4, "born of a woman." The simple and yet majestic accounts of Matthew and Luke are integral parts of the narratives and cannot be regarded as interpolations; neither can they be compared, as one would infer Dr. Fosdick compares them, with the pagan myths of miraculous generation. The reader knows that he is moving in a different world.

One would gather from Dr. Fosdick's sermon that belief in the Virgin Birth is of no matter, even to an evangelical Christian, and that it is quite possible to believe in the divinity of Christ without believing in the Virgin Birth. If we put the matter this way, and imagine the New Testament to stand as it is, minus the narrative of the Virgin Birth, that is, that none of us had ever heard of the Virgin Birth, then, of a truth, we could still believe in the divinity of Christ. But when one says, "May I not dismiss the Virgin Birth and still believe in the divinity of Jesus?" the only sensible and logical answer is, "No." And for this reason: The man who rejects the tremendous miracle given in the Gospels as explanation for the entry into this world

355

of Jesus Christ shows thereby that although he may claim to believe in the divinity of Christ, his idea of that divinity must differ from that of those who accept the Virgin Birth. By their fruits ye shall know them, and the real test is the practical test. Applying this test we discover that the great number of those who reject the Virgin Birth also reject the divinity of our Lord. Theoretically, the rationalists might argue that they could still believe in the divinity of Christ although rejecting the Virgin Birth; but as matter of fact and history, the great number of those who repudiate the Virgin Birth also repudiate the divinity of our Lord. If a man really accepts the wonderful fact of the Son of God becoming flesh and entering our humanity he will not stumble at the only New Testament account of the manner of that entry, but will find in it a ground of faith and an instance of the marvellous condescension of the God of all grace. If we had the story of the Son of God without the story of His Virgin Birth, certainly men would outdo the pagans in their wild dreams and guesses as to the manner of His coming. But against all that God has provided by giving us the revelation of the fact that Jesus was "conceived of the Holy Ghost, born of the Virgin Mary."

Dr. Fosdick is not a Presbyterian, but he stands in a Presbyterian pulpit and gets his bread from a Presbyterian congregation. In view of this fact how can his holding the purely naturalistic account of the stories of the birth of Jesus be in harmony with his preaching in the pulpit of a Church whose Creed, never revoked, declares (The Confession of Faith, Chapter VIII, Article XI), "The Son of God—when the fulness of time was come did take upon Him man's nature—being conceived by the power of the Holy Ghost, in the womb of the Virgin Mary, of her substance"? This article of the creed may be impossible for the "modern" mind to hold; it may be myth and rubbish. But myth or fact, truth or rubbish, it is a solemn declaration of the Church from which Dr. Fosdick takes his bread.

II. *The Inspiration of the Bible.* Dr. Fosdick describes two ideas of the inspiration of the Bible, neither of which, however, are held by a great number of intelligent and devout Christians. On the one side there is what he calls the "static (note the word, for it is the word of the rationalists, and should it go out of currency, we know not what they would do) and mechanical theory of inspiration." According to this theory, all the parts of the Bible from the Dukes of Edom to the thirteenth Chapter of First Corinthians were inerrantly dictated by God to men a good deal "as a man might dictate to a stenographer." We pass by irreverence of this statement, with its offense not so much against orthodoxy as against good taste, and remark that those who hold the New Testament idea of inspiration, that holy men of old "spake as they were moved by the Holy Ghost," have never thought of the Holy Ghost dictating to Moses, Isaiah or St. Paul as Dr. Fosdick, for instance, to use his own illustration, might dictate one of his sermons to a stenographer. Nor have the multitudes of Christians ever felt that for Paul to remind Timothy to fetch the cloak which he left at Troas, in the house of Carpus, required the inspiration of the Holy Ghost, or any kind of inspiration save that of the gloom and damp of the Mamertine dungeon. But there are places in the writings of St. Paul where he makes the most careful and solemn claim to divine inspiration, and that what he declares, that is, his magnificent interpretation of the Gospel of Christ, has been revealed to him by the Holy Spirit. Every intelligent Christian knows that it is not correct to say that Christianity depends upon the Scriptures in the historical sense, for Christianity had established itself in the world as a conquering and regenerating power before there was any New Testament. The New Testament was the expression of that Christian life and faith and the record of its establishment. Therefore, every intelligent Christian knows too that while Christianity came before the New Testament, if the New Testament is false, Christianity also must be false. The great question at issue is not any peculiar theory of inspiration, but the credibility and authority of the Bible. Personally, I have never been troubled by the controversies which have raged over the question of inspiration, ranging all the way from harsh, petrified and illogical theories, which would make a genealogical catalogue with its graveyard of names equal authority with St. Paul's statement of the redeeming and reconciling love of God in Christ—all the way from that to Dr. Fosdick's rationalistic theory, namely, that God revealed Himself, or rather misrevealed Himself, in crude and false ways in times past, sanctioning and approving much that was false, but gradually drew away from that misrepresentation and gave a clearer knowledge of Himself in the New Testament, but which representation will undoubtedly be much improved on in the future, since there is no reason to believe that this "progressive" revelation came to a sudden stop with St. John or St. Paul. For me the great question is this: Can we rely upon the Bible as giving us the great facts as to what God requires of man, and that plan of redemption which God has revealed through Jesus Christ? Does it contain the way of Life Eternal? If so, it is inspired of God. Theories of inspiration are of little consequence, for the inspiration of the Holy Spirit is like the wind—thou hearest the sound thereof, but canst not tell whence it cometh or whither it goeth.

But although there is such a thing as accepting the inspiration of the Bible and not being sure as to how it was inspired, that is an altogether different thing from a theory of inspiration which breaks down the whole authority of the book. Whenever we hear men speak as Dr. Fosdick does about the Bible, the question of a mode of inspiration sinks out of sight, and the greater question emerges: Do these men believe that the Bible has any special authority? Do they believe that God spake in times past by the prophets to the fathers in any clearer note than He did to Socrates, Confucius or Buddha? Do they really believe the prophets, to quote the words of Dr. Gore in his recent and notable book, "Belief in God," "were in touch— as other men were not—with reality, with the real God; and that in a long and continuous process, more or less gradual, He was really communicating to them the truth by which men could live, both about the Divine nature and purpose and about human nature?" The Confession of Faith of the Presbyterian Church commences with a declaration about the Scriptures which says: "Although the light of nature and the works of creation and providence do so far manifest the goodness, wisdom and power of God, as to leave men inexcusable; yet they are not sufficient to give that knowledge of God, and of His will, which is necessary unto salvation; therefore it pleased God to reveal Himself and declare His will unto His Church." One puts down a sermon of Dr. Fosdick and all his school with the impression that the light of nature was sufficient for the salvation of men, and that the Bible is but a reflection of that light of nature, coming from man only, and not from God.

I am sure that even the most emancipated modernists will regret Dr. Fosdick's unhappy comparison of the Bible with the Koran, and all believers in the Bible, and who not only talk about it but read it, will indignantly repudiate his assertion that most of the repulsive ideas which are taught in the Koran are taught somewhere in the Bible. I deny that the Bible teaches that "God is an Oriental monarch, fatal submission to his will men's chief duty, the use of force on unbelievers, polygamy and slavery." When we come to appalling statements such as this, the best plan is not to argue but to deny.

PART II.

III. The Second Advent.

I have already intimated that I do not adhere to the premillennial school of the New Testament interpretation. I do believe that the Church has been inexcusably silent and negligent in its teaching as to the future chapters in the drama of Divine redemption, and that this wide neglect has prepared the way for much of the extravagance of the popular premillenarian. Thoughtful conservatives are not a little perplexed over the attitude of some premillenarians, and sometimes feel that their defense of historic Christianity is not altogether a helpful one; and when we hear our premillenarian brethren dwell with more emphasis and zeal upon the mechanism of the temporal kingdom that is to be set up here upon this earth than they do upon the redeeming love of Christ and the conquest of human nature through the mild reign of the Holy Spirit, we are tempted to become impatient with them and to cry out as the princes of the Philistines did, when, about to campaign against Israel, they saw David and his men in their ranks, and said to Achish, "What do these Hebrews here?" But there is one thing about the pre-millenarian concerning which there is no doubt, and that is his loyalty to the Person and the claims of Jesus Christ. However much he may be tempted to write history before it has been made, his absolute loyalty to the Deity of Jesus, His Atonement, and His reign of righteousness and judgment, is never questioned. This is far more than we can say about the rationalists and the modernists. We feel that it is but a poor Christ that they have left us, and only a shadow of the tremendous personality of the New Testament.

If perchance the premillenarian has been a little too sure in his exegesis and in casting the horoscope of the Church and the race, the rationalist has gone to the other extreme and has reduced the great doctrine of the Second Advent of Christ to a mere figure of speech. So Dr. Fosdick regards it, for he says, "They" (that is, the rationalists and modernists) "they, too, say 'Christ is coming!' They say it with all their hearts, but they are not thinking of an external arrival on the clouds. They have assimilated as part of the Divine revelation the exhilarating insight which these recent genera-tions have given us, that development is God's way of working out his will. Man's music has been developed from the rhythmic noise of beaten sticks; man's painting from the crude outlines of the cavemen; man's architecture from the crude huts of primitive men. And these Christians, when they say that Christ is coming mean that slowly it may be, but surely, His will and principles will be worked out by God's grace in human life and institutions, until He shall see of the travail of His soul and be satisfied!" The best possible comment on this idea of the Second Advent of Christ and the final jurisprudence of our species is to set it alongside the mysterious yet mighty utterances of Jesus in the last part of Matthew's Gospel, or the equally mysterious and tremendous utterances of St. Paul and of St. Peter. Whatever Christ or Paul or Peter mean or do not mean, we can be sure of this, that they imply a process of progress and arrival at perfection which is something far different from Dr. Fosdick's mild working out of the tangles of life. The Bible teaches progress and development and a final arrival at a state of universal peace and righteousness, but it also teaches that crisis and cataclysm play their part in bringing the great goal which seers, prophets and poets have saluted afar off and contemplated through their tears. The first advent of Christ was not accounted for by any long-drawn-out natural development, although it did come in the "fulness of time," and it is quite possible that the Second Advent will be just as much of an intervention and interruption as the first advent was. The rationalists do not do justice to this plain portion of the eschatological teaching of the Bible. And even were their absurd dream to come true, even should the world by the slow working out of the powers and principles now lodged in humanity arrive at moral perfection, still the goal would not have been reached, for there would yet remain a fearful contrast between this perfect creature and his environment. So Father Tyrrell, a much more thoughtful modernist than those who today are so vocal, asks: "Shall progress ever wipe away the tears from all eyes? Prolong life as it will, can progress ever conquer death, with its terrors for the dying, it tears for the surviving? Can it ever control the earthquake, the tempest, the lightning, the cruelties of a nature indifferent to the lot of man?" What Father Tyrrell meant by these questions was that not only man, but man's environment, the platform of his civilization and life, must be changed and reconstructed. Have Dr. Fosdick and his fellow-rationalists any prescription for the securing of that great end? They have not, and they know that they have not. Thus, even if it had not been revealed in Scripture, common sense and common experience would demand some such intervention and summing up of human affairs as is involved in the doctrine of the Second Advent.

Then we shall have not only a Messianic race of redeemed men, but a Messianic world, in which there shall be complete and blessed peace not only between man and God, and between man and man, but between man and the beast and between man and the earth. This was the age saluted by rapt Isaiah when he sang, "And the wolf shall dwell with the lamb, and the leopard shall lie down with the kid; and the calf and the young lion and the fatling together; and a little child shall lead them. And the cow and the bear shall feed; their young ones shall lie down together, and the lion shall eat straw like the ox, and the sucking child shall play on the hole of the asp, and the weaned child shall put his hand on the cockatrice's den. They shall not hurt nor destroy in all My holy mountain; for the earth shall be full of the knowledge of the Lord, as the waters cover the sea."

The great error of the Rationalists in their sketch of the future and in their dealing with the New Testament teaching of the coming of Christ, is that they confine themselves to laws and principles, and forget that there is something beyond this. "And these Christians," writes Dr. Fosdick, meaning himself and other Rationalists, "when they say that Christ is coming, mean that slowly it may be, but surely, His will and principles will be worked out by God's grace in human life and institutions, until He shall see of the travail of His soul and be satisfied." Evangelical, New Testament Christians, believe that too. But they believe that the coming of Christ means more than just the establishment of justice in the earth. To them it means also the beatific vision; it means the Presence and the companionship of Him Whom, not having seen, we yet love; on Whom, though now we see Him not, yet believing, we rejoice with joy unspeakable. This and scores of passages like it in the New Testament can have only one meaning, namely, that rich and precious though the present relationship of the believer with Jesus Christ is, there is something yet greater in store. When, according to the old legend, Jesus appeared to Thomas Aquinas and said to him, "Thomas, thou hast written well of Me; what wouldst thou have?" the great schoolman replied, "Thyself, Lord!" that is the consummation of the Christian life and experience. Here we have it in faith and anticipation, but when Christ comes the second time we shall have it in glorious reality. Righteousness is to come and the Church is to be vindicated, and sinners are to be judged, and crooked ways made straight, and the rough places plain; but it ought not to be necessary, yet apparently is, to remind the rationalists that Christ is more than a principle of righteousness and justice, and that the coming of Him upon Whose breast John leaned at the Supper, Who said to the fishermen of Galilee, "Follow Me!" to Peter, "Lovest thou Me?" and to Paul, "Why persecutest thou Me?"—the coming of this Christ must mean nothing less than a personal and blessed and glorious manifestation of Himself to those who have believed on Him, and who, amid the shadows and trials of this world, have followed Him as Lord and Master. To the Rationalists this blessed consummation of the Christian experience seems to mean nothing. They talk about Christ as if He were only a name for a principle, and seem not to know that Jesus to Whom Thomas cried out, "My God and my Lord!" And when Christ comes, how shall they greet Him who in this life, and even as His ministers, have spoken of Him in such a way as to lead men to believe that He was not conceived by the Holy Ghost and born of the Virgin Mary; that He did not take our place and bear our sins on the cursed tree; that He did not rise again from the dead, and that He will not come again in glory? How shall they greet Him, and what shall they say to Him? To talk acceptably to skeptical university boys, or persons inclined to unbelief, and write for rationalistic papers, is one thing; it is another thing to stand before the judgment seat of Christ. Now those great swelling words about "progressive" revelation, "dynamic" Christianity, "the modern mind," etc., etc., sink and shrivel and disappear. No minister should preach or write a sermon which he would not be willing to place in the hands of Jesus should He appear in person. Could the authors of these rationalistic sermons, sermons which tend to destroy men's faith in the Eternal Son of God as their alone Redeemer, meet Christ with confidence, and would they feel like placing in His hands the sermon which has denied Him before men?

IV. *The Atonement.*

Dr. Fosdick does not dwell at length on this central doctrine of Christianity, but in the very sentence in which he caricatures the traditional evangelical belief in the Atonement, he reveals his complete and profound aversion to the New Testament teaching on that great and mysterious subject. He thus describes the theory of the Atonement as held by the Evangelical School: "That the blood of our Lord, shed in a substitutionary death, placates an alienated Deity and makes possible welcome for the returning sinner."

Every Christian knows that there is a difference between the fact of the Atonement and any theory of it. But it is inconceivable that any man should receive the fact of the Atonement, the death of Christ for sin, and not be interested in the explanation of that fact. The rationalists now write of the theology of St. Paul as an intelligent man's honest effort to give some rational explanation of how he is saved, and how it is that the death of Christ makes possible the forgiveness of sin. Why, may we ask, are the rationalists not interested in giving some explanation of the Atonement? If the great primary fact of Christianity, the death of Christ for the remission of sins, is the rock upon which their feet stand, their refuge and their hope, why are they not more interested in the meaning of that fact? Why is it that the only time they talk about the Atonement is when they are assailing the traditional views of historic Christianity? Why is it that the only interest they betray in the Atonement is to deny the explanations of other believers? St. Paul, whom Dr. Fosdick quotes as one of the two great Christian teachers, made the death of Christ, and the substitutionary and vicarious explanation of that death, the one grand theme of his preaching. To the Corinthians he said, "I delivered unto you, first of all, how that Christ died for our sins according to the Scriptures." Is there in the whole world to-day a rationalist or a modernist who can say that to any city or church where he has preached?

At the close of his sermon Dr. Fosdick says, "It is almost unforgivable that men should tithe mint and anise and cummin, and quarrel over them, when the world is perishing for the lack of the weightier matters of the law, justice, mercy and faith." He thus likens the question of the Virgin Birth of our Lord, the Inspiration of the Bible, the Second Advent of Christ, and the atonement to mint, anise and cummin. To me this seems an almost unpardonable flippancy on the part of one who speaks as a teacher of Christianity. Especially astounding it is to hear a man so speak of opinions about the death of the Lord Jesus Christ. Francis Turretin, whom Dale calls the greatest of Calvinistic theologians, evidently thought differently about the

Atonement, for he wrote of it as "the chief part of our salvation, the anchor of Faith, the refuge of Hope, the rule of Charity, the sure foundation of the Christian religion, and the richest treasure of the Christian Church. So long as this doctrine is maintained in its integrity, Christianity itself and the peace and blessedness of all who believe in Jesus Christ, are beyond the reach of danger; but if it is rejected, or in any way impaired the whole structure of the Christian faith must sink into decay and ruin."

Our chief complaint against the rationalist and modernist is not their writings and sayings about the Deity of our Lord, the Bible, the Second Advent, but their rejection of the one great truth of Christianity, that through His death we have remission of our sins and are justified with God.

Dr. Fosdick contends against a conspiracy on the part of those whom he calls "Fundamentalists," and who perhaps so name themselves, to put out of the Church all those who do not agree with them in every particular. I have not heard of such a conspiracy and have never been asked to join it. At the same time, I believe that as long as the Presbyterian Church has not abandoned and repudiated its Confession of Faith, any man in any of its pulpits holding and declaring the views of Dr. Fosdick occupies an anomalous and inconsistent position. Their "New" Theology seems to carry with it a "new" morality also. As for putting them out, that could easily be done, for they are a small minority in the Church; although at present the vocal minority. But I am coming to think less and less of excision and excommunication as a means of preserving the Church from false teaching, not because of any base and ignoble fear on the part of those who might so proceed of being called "heresy hunters," "medieval," etc., but because I am convinced that the far more useful course to pursue is to declare the whole counsel of God so clearly and fearlessly that the whole world may know that there is a difference between what is Christianity and what is not Christianity. However Dr. Fosdick and his companions may worry about processes of excision and ecclesiastical trial, and so being put out of the Church, the sad thing is that in the minds of thousands upon thousands of Christians they are already out of the Church, and no act of an ecclesiastical court could make the fact more real. Our duty is to pray that they may be brought back into the Church and help to build up and adorn where hitherto they have only wounded His mystical Body, which is the Church.

In his celebrated autobiography, John Stuart Mill, in describing the attitude of his father towards Christianity, says that he looked with indignation upon the identification of the worship of the Christian God with Christianity. The son confesses the same aversion, and thinks the day will come when we shall have a Christianity with God left out. For me this sums up better than anything I have ever read the menace of the rationalistic and modernist movement in Protestant Christianity. The movement is slowly secularizing the Church, and if permitted to go unchecked and unchallenged, will ere long produce in our churches a new kind of Christianity, a Christianity of opinions and principles and good purposes, but a Christianity without worship, without God, and without Jesus Christ.

14

NEO-ORTHODOXY AND THE AMERICAN PULPIT
Harold Brack

The neo-orthodox movement in America emerging around 1930 presented a sharp critique of the late nineteenth- and early twentieth-century liberalism. It was particularly distressed with liberalism's uncritical tolerance, its dependence on reason, and its stress on God's immanence. Reinhold Niebuhr and others reasserted the fact of sin, affirmed man's dependence on God and pointed to his mighty acts as set forth in the Bible. Uneasy with liberalism's psychological and sociological approaches, those of the neo-orthodox persuasion protested that the kingdom would not come through sheer human effort or because of some "inherent necessity growing out of the nature of our universe." They declared that the social problem arises out of man's rejection of God's sovereignty and that the resolution of the problem will be by the Grace of God and not simply by the machinations of men.

While neo-orthodoxy warned that the drift from a theological to a psychological and sociological perspective led to an unwarranted optimism, it was not calling for a retreat from preaching on social issues but for a more profound and a more realistic analysis. It demanded that man face his own severe limitations and recognize his utter dependence on God. However, those from a liberal orientation feared that neo-orthodoxy resulted in an over-reaction which, when preached, demoralized men and reduced their sense of responsibility for the social order so that men withdrew from involvement in social issues.

Discussion of these approaches to preaching appeared widely in homiletics textbooks and in lectures on preaching. Estimates of the extent to which the issue affected the bulk of weekly preaching across the nation differ from "significantly" to "minimally." Some suggest that the impact was restricted mainly to centers of theological education and their environs.

The two sermons that follow represent preaching from a liberal stance and preaching from a neo-orthodox position. Both sermons indicate the difficulty of affixing labels. Fosdick's sermon (preached in the mid-thirties) represents a liberal's adjustment in response to neo-orthodoxy. Niebuhr's sermon (preached a decade later) is a product of his critical appraisal of neo-orthodoxy. The sermons represent the two points of view in process rather than doctrinaire or fixed positions. For a fuller context in which to appreciate these sermons read Niebuhr's *An Interpretation of Christian Ethics* published in 1935 and the last four essays in *Adventurous Religion* by Fosdick published in 1926.

Our first sermon "The Church Must Go Beyond Modernism" contains an implicit apologia for liberalism and suggests liberalism's way of meeting the issues raised by neo-orthodoxy.

Fosdick opens with a history of what led up to Christian modernism. He points to the appalling gap between his generation's intellect and its religion. The preacher then grounds his sermon in "the deep and vital experiences of the Christian soul."

He complains that the church had asked men to believe incredible things while clinging to its pre-scientific framework and warns that we must go beyond an intellectual adjustment to modern science to consider whether Christ can morally challenge contemporary culture. He rejects the romantic notion of inevitable progress and calls for a new awareness of a God of moral judgment and speaks

366

of the reality of personal and social sin. While Fosdick accepts the neo-orthodox corrective, he does not appear to carry the matter as deeply. There is no pointing to the exceeding sinfulness of sin. As a matter of fact, he implies that the reaction to the "excrescences of a harsh theology" were justified.

Observing that disgust with "absurdities of the old supernaturalistic theology" led to a turning away from the reality of God to a man-centered culture, he calls for a reaffirmation that God is. However, the signs of God's existence which he cites are "The highest in us . . . goodness, truth, and beauty. . . ."

Finally, Fosdick sounds a strong warning that the church stands in danger of being enslaved by society, of sinking into "undifferentiated identity with this world." Affirming that an adjustment of the Christian faith to the new astronomy, geology, and biology is indispensable, he nevertheless declares that adjustment of the faith must stop short of contemporary nationalism, imperialism, capitalism, and racism.

In his autobiography, Fosdick helps us see this sermon in perspective.

A peril, however, was inherent in our endeavor, which liberalism as a whole was neither wise enough to foresee, nor Christian enough to forestall. We were adjusting Christian thought to a secular culture. . . . We were liberals through and through, but all the more with ominous foreboding we saw the inadequacy of our party and the certainty of revolt against it, unless we could plunge deeper and go farther than mere adjustment to current thinking. We began to drop our concern for fundamentalism and to take for granted the harmonization of scientific and Christian thought. . . . and we began to shout warnings—as one of my sermons in the middle-thirties was entitled—that "The Church Must Go Beyond Modernism.[1]

Now turning to our second sermon, we discover some evidence of Niebuhr's neo-orthodox views in his reference to a "few hardy optimists" and his stress on the forms of

[1] *The Living of These Days* (New York: Harper & Row, 1956), p. 245.

human idolatry as a more significant cause than the idea of "cultural lag." With them go his assertion that "self-righteousness is one of the oldest and most persistent forms of human sin." Niebuhr also denies that ignorance is any justification and goes on to distinguish sin from ignorance. His analysis is summarized in two sentences that succinctly state his critique of liberalism. "Richer resources of faith will be required than those which the liberal culture of the past two centuries has lived by. Its faith grew out of an age of easy achievements and few frustrations; and has little conception of the tragic character of history."

Another important aspect of this sermon is its biblical character. The primary and persistent image is that of "new birth." It draws on both the Old and New Testaments and makes telling use of the words of Jesus and Paul. Niebuhr aptly develops the biblical theme of new birth and skillfully relates it to the contemporary scene. In light of the criticism leveled at neo-orthodox preaching, it is interesting to observe that this sermon does conclude with a declaration of hope.

In the foreword to the volume *Discerning the Signs of the Times* in which this sermon appeared, Niebuhr remarks that these are "sermonic essays" in that they were written after being preached in American colleges and universities. During the latter process they became more theological, and theoretical points were more fully developed than might normally be possible in the traditional sermon.

A few words from Niebuhr describing the category into which this sermon falls will help orient us to it.

The other seeks to interpret certain aspects of the Christian faith in terms of their special relevance to the thought and life of our age. Being a tragic age which has suffered two great world conflicts and which cannot yet be certain that it has the moral resources or the political instruments to avoid further world chaos, the primary theme of this category of sermons is the relation of the historical to the trans-historical elements of the Christian faith." [2]

[2] (New York: Charles Scribner's Sons, 1946), p. ix.

These sermons have significant similarities. They both stress the reality of sin and the reality of God and oppose an easy optimism. Both speak out against nationalism and militarism. Both are historically minded and address themselves to significant issues. The appeal to the Bible as authority is deeper and more pervasive in Niebuhr's sermon than in Fosdick's, but Fosdick also appeals to spiritual experience. Both sermons involve the reader by stimulating him to mentally grapple with the issue as the preacher wrestles with it. This attribute makes them particularly stimulating examples of liberal and neo-orthodox preaching.

Harry Emerson Fosdick*

The Church Must Go Beyond Modernism**

If we are successfully to maintain the thesis that the church must go beyond modernism, we must start by seeing that the church had to go as far as modernism. Fifty years ago, a boy seven years of age was crying himself to sleep at night in terror lest, dying, he should go to hell, and his solicitous mother, out of all patience with the fearful teachings which brought such apparitions to the mind, was trying in vain to comfort him. That boy is preaching to you today and you may be sure that to him the achievements of Christian modernism in the last half century seem not only important but indispensable.

Fifty years ago the intellectual portion of Western civilization had turned one of the most significant mental corners in history and was looking out on a new view of the world. The church, however, was utterly unfitted for the appreciation of that view. Protestant Christianity had been officially formulated in prescientific days. The Augsburg Confession was a notable statement but the men who drew it up, including Luther himself, did not even believe that the earth goes round the sun. The Westminster Confession, for the rigorous acceptance of which the Presbyterian rear-guard still contends, was a memorable document but it was written forty years before Newton published his work on the law of gravitation. Moreover, not only were the mental patterns of Protestant Christianity officially formulated in prescientific days but, as is always true of religion, those patterns were sacred to their believers and the changes forced by the new science seemed impious and sacrilegious.

Youths like myself, therefore, a half century ago faced an appalling lag between our generation's intellect on one side and its religion on the other, with religion asking us to believe incredible things. Behind his playfulness the author of *Through the Looking Glass* had this serious matter in mind when he represented the White Queen as saying to Alice, "I'm just one hundred and one, five months and a day." Said Alice, "I can't believe *that!*" Said the Queen pityingly, "Can't you? Try again: draw a long breath, and shut your eyes." So the church seemed to be speaking to us.

Modernism, therefore, came as a desperately needed way of thinking. It

---

* See chapter 13 for a biographical sketch.
** From *Successful Christian Living* by Harry Emerson Fosdick. Copyright 1937, by Harper & Row, Publishers, Inc. Reprinted by permission of the publishers.

insisted that the deep and vital experiences of the Christian soul with itself, with its fellows, with its God, could be carried over into this new world and understood in the light of the new knowledge. We refused to live bifurcated lives, our intellect in the late nineteenth century and our religion in the early sixteenth. God, we said, is a living God who has never uttered his final word on any subject; why, therefore, should prescientific frameworks of thought be so sacred that forever through them man must seek the Eternal and the Eternal seek man? So we said, and, thanks to modernism, it became true of many an anxious and troubled soul in our time that, as Sam Walter Foss expressed it,

> He saw the boundless scheme dilate,
> In star and blossom, sky and clod;
> And as the universe grew great,
> He dreamed for it a greater God.

The church thus had to go as far as modernism but now the church must go beyond it. For even this brief rehearsal of its history reveals modernism's essential nature; it is primarily an adaptation, an adjustment, an accommodation of Christian faith to contemporary scientific thinking. It started by taking the intellectual culture of a particular period as its criterion and then adjusted Christian teaching to that standard. Herein lies modernism's tendency toward shallowness and transiency; arising out of a temporary intellectual crisis, it took a special type of scientific thinking as standard and became an adaptation to, a harmonization with, the intellectual culture of a particular generation. That, however, is no adequate religion to represent the Eternal and claim the allegiance of the soul. Let it be a modernist who says that to you! Unless the church can go deeper and reach higher than that it will fail indeed.

In the first place, modernism has been excessively preoccupied with intellectualism. Its chosen problem has been somehow to adjust Christian faith to the modern intellect so that a man could be a Christian without throwing his reason away. Modernism's message to the church has been after this fashion: When, long ago, the new music came, far from clinging to old sackbuts and psalteries, you welcomed the full orchestra and such composers as Palestrina, Bach, Beethoven, to the glory of God; when the new art came you did not refuse it but welcomed Cimabue, Giotto, Raphael, and Michelangelo, to the enrichment of your faith; when the new architecture came, far from clinging to primitive catacombs or the old Romanesque, you greeted the Gothic with its expanded spaces and aspiring altitudes; so now, when the new science comes, take that in too, and, however painful the adaptations, adjust your faith to it and assimilate its truths into your Christian thinking.

Surely, that has been a necessary appeal but it centers attention on one problem only—intellectual adjustment to modern science. It approaches the vast field of man's experience and need head first, whereas the deepest experiences of man's soul, whether in religion or out of it, cannot be approached head first. List as you will the soul's deepest experiences and needs —friendship, the love that makes a home, the enjoyment of music, delight in nature, devotion to moral causes, the practise of the presence of God—it is obvious that, whereas, if we are wise, we use our heads on them, nevertheless we do not approach them mainly head first, but heart first, conscience first, imagination first. A man is vastly greater than his logic, and the sweep and ambit of his spiritual experience and need are incalculably wider than his rational processes. So modernism, as such, covers only a segment of the spiritual field and does not nearly compass the range of religion's meaning.

Indeed, the critical need of overpassing modernism is evident in the fact that our personal spiritual problems do not lie there any more. When I was a student in the seminary, the classrooms where the atmosphere grew tense with excitement concerned the higher criticism of the Bible and the harmonization of science and religion. That, however, is no longer the case. The classrooms in the seminary where the atmosphere grows tense today concern Christian ethics and the towering question whether Christ has a moral challenge that can shake this contemporary culture to its foundations and save us from our deadly personal and social sins. So the world has moved far to a place where mere Christian harmonizers, absorbed with the intellectual attempt to adapt faith to science and accommodate Christ to prevalent culture, seem trivial and out of date. Our modern world, as a whole, cries out not so much for souls intellectually adjusted to it as for souls morally maladjusted to it, not most of all for accommodators and adjusters but for intellectual and ethical challengers.

When Paul wrote his first letter to the Corinthians, he said that he had become a Jew to the Jews that he might win the Jews, and he intimated that he had become a Greek to the Greeks that he might win the Greeks. "I am become," he said, "all things to all men, that I may by all means save some." That is a modernistic passage of adjustment and accommodation. But that is not all Paul said. Had it been all, Paul would have sunk from sight in an indistinguishable blend with the Greco-Roman culture of his day and we should never have heard of him When he wrote the second time to the Corinthians he said something else:

Come ye out from among them, and be ye separate,
saith the Lord,
And touch no unclean thing.

Church of Christ, take that to yourself now! Stop this endeavor to harmonize yourself with modern culture and customs as though they were a standard and criterion. Rather, come out from among them. Only an independent standing-ground from which to challenge modern culture can save either it or you.

In the second place, not only has modernism been thus predominantly intellectualistic and therefore partial, but, strange to say, at the same time it has been dangerously sentimental. The reason for this is easy to explain. One of the predominant elements in the intellectual culture of the late nineteenth and early twentieth centuries, to which modernism adjusted itself, was illusory belief in inevitable progress. So many hopeful and promising things were afoot that two whole generations were fairly bewitched into thinking that every day in every way man was growing better and better. Scientific discovery, exploration and invention, the rising tide of economic welfare, the spread of democracy, the increase of humanitarianism, the doctrine of evolution itself, twisted to mean that automatically today has to be better than yesterday and tomorrow better than today—how many elements seduced us in those romantic days into thinking that all was right with the world!

In the intellectual culture to which modernistic Christianity adapted itself, such lush optimism was a powerful factor, and the consequences are everywhere present in the natural predispositions of our thought today. In the little village of Selborne, England, the visitor is shown some trees planted by a former minister near his dwelling, so that he might be spared the view of the village slaughter-house. Those trees are suggestive and symbolic of the sentimental illusions we plant to hide from our eyes the ugly facts of life. Especially we modernistic Christians, dealing, as we were, with thoughts of a kindly God by evolution lifting everything and everybody up, were deeply tempted to live in a fool's paradise behind our lovely trees!

For example, modernistic Christianity largely eliminated from its faith the God of moral judgment. To be sure, in the old theology, the God of moral judgment had been terribly presented so that little children did cry themselves to sleep at night for fear of him and of his hell. Modernism, however, not content with eliminating the excrescences of a harsh theology, became softer yet and created the general impression that there is nothing here to fear at all. One of the most characteristic religious movements of the nineteenth century heralded this summary of faith:

> The Fatherhood of God.
> The Brotherhood of Man.
> The Leadership of Jesus.
> Salvation by Character.

The Progress of Mankind—
onward and upward forever.

Well, if that is the whole creed, this is a lovely world with nothing here to dread at all.

But there *are* things here to dread. Ask the physicians. They will tell us that in a law-abiding world are stern conditions whose fulfilment or non-fulfilment involve bodily destiny. Ask the novelists and dramatists, and at their best they are not lying to us as they reveal the inexorable fatality with which character and conduct work out their implied consequence. Ask the economists. They will tell us there are things to dread which lead to an inevitable economic hell. Ask even the historians and they will talk at times like old preachers about the God of moral judgment, as James Anthony Froude did when he said, "One lesson, and only one, history may be said to repeat with distinctness: that the world is built somehow on moral foundations; that, in the long run, it is well with the good; in the long run, it is ill with the wicked."

Indeed, cannot we use our own eyes to see that there are things here to fear? For this is no longer the late nineteenth and early twentieth centuries. This is the epoch after the first world war shook the earth to its foundations, and the God of judgment has spoken. My soul, what a world, which the gentle modernism of my younger ministry, with its kindly sentiments and limitless optimism, does not fit at all! We must go beyond that. Because I know that I am speaking here to many minds powerfully affected by modernism, I say to you as to myself: Come out of these intellectual cubicles and sentimental retreats which we built by adapting Christian faith to an optimistic era. Underline this: *Sin is real.* Personal and social sin is as terribly real as our forefathers said it was, no matter how we change their way of saying so. And it leads men and nations to damnation as they said it did, no matter how we change their way of picturing it. For these are times, real times, of the kind out of which man's great exploits have commonly been won, in which, if a man is to have a real faith he must gain it from the very teeth of dismay; if he is to have real hope, it must shine, like a Rembrandt portrait, from the dark background of fearful apprehension; if he is to have real character, he must achieve it against the terrific down-drag of an antagonistic world; and if he is to have a real church, it must stand out from the world and challenge it, not be harmonized with it.

In the third place, modernism has even watered down and thinned out the central message and distinctive truth of religion, the reality of God. One does not mean by that, of course, that modernists are atheists. One does mean, however, that the intellectual culture of the late nineteenth and early twentieth centuries, to which modernism adjusted itself, was predominantly man-centered. Man was blowing on his hands and doing such things at such a rate as never had been done or dreamed on earth before. Man was pioneering new truth and building a new social order. You young people who were not here then can hardly imagine with what cheerful and confident trust we confided to man the saving of the world. So the temptation was to relegate God to an advisory capacity, as a kind of chairman of the board of sponsors of our highly successful human enterprise. A poet like Swinburne could even put the prevailing mood into candid words:

> Thou art smitten, thou God, thou art smitten; thy death is upon thee, O Lord. And the love-song of earth as thou diest resounds through the wind of her wings—
> Glory to Man in the highest! for Man is the master of things.

Look out on the world today and try, if you can, to repeat those words of Swinburne and still keep your face straight! At any rate, if ever I needed something deeper to go on than Swinburne's sentimental humanism, with man as the master of things, it is now—a philosophy, namely, a profound philosophy about what is ultimately and eternally real in this universe. We modernists were so disgusted with the absurdities of the old supernaturalistic theology that we were commonly tempted to visit our distaste on theology as a whole and throw it away. But theology means thinking about the central problem of existence—what is ultimately and eternally real in this universe. And in the lurid light of days like these it becomes clearer, as an increasing number of atheists are honestly saying, that if the eternally real is merely material, if the cosmos is a physical fortuity and the earth an accident, if there is no profounder reason for mankind's being here than just that at one stage in the planet's cooling the heat happened to be right, and if we ourselves are "the disease of the agglutinated dust," then to stand on this temporary and accidental earth in the face of this vast cosmos and try lyrically to sing,

> Glory to Man in the highest! for Man is the master of things,

is an absurd piece of sentimental tomfoolery. And because I have been and am a modernist it is proper that I should confess that often the modernistic movement, adjusting itself to a man-centered culture, has encouraged this mood, watered down the thought of the Divine, and, may we be forgiven for this, left souls standing, like the ancient Athenians, before an altar to an Unknown God!

On that point the church must go beyond modernism. We have been all things to all men long enough. We have adapted and adjusted and accommodated and conceded long enough. We have at times gotten so low down that we talked as though the highest compliment that could be paid

375

Almighty God was that a few scientists believed in him. Yet all the time, by right, we had an independent standing-ground and a message of our own in which alone is there hope for humankind. The eternally real is the spiritual. The highest in us comes from the deepest in the universe. Goodness and truth and beauty are not accidents but revelations of creative reality. God is! On that point come out from among them and be ye separate! As the poet imagined Paul saying:

> Whoso has felt the Spirit of the Highest
> cannot confound nor doubt Him nor deny:
> yea with one voice, o world, tho' thou deniest,
> Stand thou on that side, for on this am I.

Finally, modernism has too commonly lost its ethical standing-ground and its power of moral attack. It is a dangerous thing for a great religion to begin adjusting itself to the culture of a special generation. Harmonizing slips easily into compromising. To adjust Christian faith to the new astronomy, the new geology, the new biology, is absolutely indispensable. But suppose that this modernizing process, well started, goes on and Christianity adapts itself to contemporary nationalism, contemporary imperialism, contemporary capitalism, contemporary racialism—harmonizing itself, that is, with the prevailing social *status quo* and the common moral judgments of our time— what then has become of religion, so sunk and submerged in undifferentiated identity with this world?

This lamentable end of a modernizing process, starting with indispensable adaptations and slipping into concession and compromise, is a familiar phenomenon in religious history. For the word "modernism" may not be exclusively identified with the adjustment of Christian faith and practise to the culture of a single era. Modernization is a recurrent habit in every living religion. Early Protestantism, itself, emerging along with a new nationalism and a new capitalism, was in its day modernism, involving itself and us in entanglements and compliances with political and economic ideas in whose presence we still are tempted to be servile. Every era with powerful originative factors in it evokes from religion indispensable adaptations, followed by further concessive acquiescences, which in time must be superseded and outgrown. Early Christianity went out from an old Jewish setting into a new Greek culture and never would have survived if it had not assimilated into its faith the profound insights of Greek philosophy. So in the classic creeds, like that of Nicaea, we have a blending of the old faith with the new philosophy, and in that process John and Paul themselves had already played a part. But, alas, early Christianity in its adjustment of its faith to Greek culture did not stop with adaptation to the insights of

376

philosophy. At last it adapted itself to Constantine, to the licentious court, to war, to the lucrative enjoyment of imperial favors, to the use of bloody persecutions to coerce belief. One after another, it threw away the holiest things that had been entrusted to it by its Lord until, often hardly distinguishable from the culture it lived in, it nearly modernized itself into moral futility. Lift up that history, as it were a mirror, in which to see the peril of our American churches.

It is not in Germany alone that the church stands in danger of being enslaved by society. There the enslavement is outward, deliberate, explicit, organized. Here it is secret, quiet, pervasive, insidious. A powerful culture—social, economic, nationalistic, militaristic—impinging from every side upon the church, cries with persuasive voices, backed by all the sanctions and motives most urgent to the self-interest of man, Adjust yourself, adapt yourself, accommodate yourself!

When Great Britain was as mad about the Boer War as Italy is mad today about the Ethiopian War and all the forces of propaganda had whipped up the frenzy of the people to a fever heat, John Morley one night in Manchester faced an indignant, antagonistic crowd, and pleaded with his countrymen against the war. This in part is what he said: "You may carry fire and sword into the midst of peace and industry: it will be wrong. A war of the strongest government in the world with untold wealth and inexhaustible reserves against this little republic will bring you no glory: it will be wrong. You may make thousands of women widows and thousands of children fatherless: it will be wrong. It may add a new province to your empire: *it will still be wrong.*" John Morley did not call himself a Christian. He called himself an agnostic. But he was far nearer standing where Christ intended his church to stand than the church has often been.

We modernists had better talk to ourselves like this. So had the fundamentalists—but that is not our affair. We have already largely won the battle we started out to win; we have adjusted the Christian faith to the best intelligence of our day and have won the strongest minds and the best abilities of the churches to our side. Fundamentalism is still with us but mostly in the backwaters. The future of the churches, if we will have it so, is in the hands of modernism. Therefore let all modernists lift a new battle cry: We must go beyond modernism! And in that new enterprise the watchword will be not, Accommodate yourself to the prevailing culture! but, Stand out from it and challenge it! For this unescapable fact, which again and again in Christian history has called modernism to its senses, we face: we cannot harmonize Christ himself with modern culture. What Christ does to modern culture is to challenge it.

REINHOLD NIEBUHR

Reinhold Niebuhr was born in Wright City, Missouri, on June 21, 1892. He studied at Elmhurst College and Eden Theological Seminary. He received his B.D. from Yale Divinity School in 1914 and his A.M. in 1915. Ordained in the ministry of the Evangelical Synod of North America, he served as pastor of Bethel Evangelical Church in Detroit from 1915 to 1928. He began teaching at Union Theological Seminary in New York in 1928 as Associate Professor of Philosophy of Religion. In 1930 he became Professor of Applied Christianity and in 1955 Graduate Professor of Ethics and Theology. He delivered the Gifford lectures in 1939 and the Warrick lectures in 1947. He also served as editor of Christianity and Crisis. *He authored several books, including:* Does Civilization Need Religion? *(1927),* Moral Man and Immoral Society *(1932),* Nature and Destiny of Man *(1941),* Christian Realism and Political Problems *(1953),* The Self and the Dramas of History *(1955),* Structures of Nations and Empires *(1963), and* Man's Nature and His Communities *(1965).*

The Age Between the Ages*

"Thus saith Hezekiah, This day is a day of trouble, and of rebuke, and blasphemy: for the children are come to the birth, and there is not strength to bring forth."—II KINGS 19:3.

These pessimistic words were spoken by Hezekiah, King of Judah, when he faced a crisis in Judah's relation with Assyria and was threatened with defeat and enslavement by the great power. The words are as applicable to our own day as to his. We are living in an age between the ages in which children are coming to birth, but there is not strength to bring forth. We can see clearly what ought to be done to bring order and peace into the lives of the nations; but we do not have the strength to do what we ought. A few hardy optimists imagine that the end of the second world war represents the end of our troubles; and that the world is now firmly set upon the path of peace. Yet it does not require a very profound survey of the available historical resources to realize that our day of trouble is not over; that in fact

* Reprinted with the permission of Charles Scribner's Sons from *Discerning the Signs of the Times,* pages 39-56, by Reinhold Niebuhr. Copyright 1946 Charles Scribner's Sons.

this generation of mankind is destined to live in a tragic era between two ages. It is an era when "one age is dead and the other is powerless to be born." The age of absolute national sovereignty is over; but the age of international order under political instruments, powerful enough to regulate the relations of nations and to compose their competing desires, is not yet born. The age of "free enterprise," when the new vitalities of a technical civilization were expected to regulate themselves, is also over. But the age in which justice is to be achieved, and yet freedom maintained, by a wise regulation of the complex economic interdependence of modern man, is powerless to be born.

I

The lack of "strength to bring forth" a newly conceived life, ordained to birth, is a significant weakness of human life not shared by the animals. In animal existence there are always instinctive and vital resources sufficient for every necessary process, including the generative one. Animals bring forth easily, giving birth with little pain, as they die without fear. Human beings are born in pain; and frequently the strength to bring forth must be augmented by all kinds of obstetrical aid. The special difficulties of human birth were matters of observation at a very early date in human history and in the story of the Fall in the book of Genesis the pains of childbirth are interpreted as God's curse upon the sinful Eve: "In sorrow shalt thou bring forth children." There is a profound truth in this myth even though we would not now regard the pains of birth as an explicit punishment of sin. The truth in the myth is that human life distinguishes itself from animal existence by its greater freedom and the consequent possibility of the misuse of freedom. Though the biological processes in man are prompted by instinct, as in animal life, only a few of them are purely instinctive. Generally an area of freedom is left open, where the human will is fused with the instincts of nature. Thus man's sexual life is not limited to the procreative process, but can, by imagination and will, become the source of a wider spiritual and artistic creativity, and also of a destructive perversity.

In the same way the process of birth is not completed by purely instinctive power. It is more painful than animal birth, partly because of physiological reasons, which are, however, related to man's uniqueness in the animal world—the size of the human infant's head, for instance. Being more painful, it can be evaded and avoided, for human freedom has now contrived methods of arresting the natural process of procreation. If it is not avoided, the human will, as well as obstetrical devices, must aid and abet the instinctive forces of nature to create the strength to bring forth. A noted gynecologist once observed that the power to bring forth in the human mother contained a bewildering mixture of spiritual and natural elements. Among the spiritual elements, the fear of death in the mother was marvellously compounded with the desire to bring forth life.

Yet physical birth in human beings is sufficiently close to nature to proceed, on the whole, by nature's laws and forces. It is when men deal with the organisms of their social existence, with their political and economic and cultural institutions, that the pains of birth and the lack of strength to bring forth becomes more fully apparent. All social institutions are partly subject to nature. In the early stages of human existence, at least, they are born, they grow, and die with only slight interventions of the human will. But as these institutions beome more and more the creations of the mind and will, their birth and death are increasingly subject to the defects of the will. Modern social institutions are the artifact of the warrior's prowess, the statesman's skill and the community's imagination. With this development the hiatus between the social task, made urgent by historic development, and the moral power required to do what ought to be done, continually widens.

The fact that world-wide economic and technical interdependence between the nations makes a world-wide system of justice necessary is so obvious that even the most casual observers have become convinced of it. At the beginning of this century, before two world wars had chastened the mood of our culture, it was assumed that the comprehension of an historic task would guarantee its achievement. Since then we have learned that a potential world community may announce itself in history through world conflicts; and that some of the very instruments which were to guarantee the achievement of world-wide community could be used to sharpen conflict and give it global dimensions.

But even now we are not ready to measure the full depth of the problem of man's lack of strength to bring forth the historical new-birth required in a new age. The lack of strength to bring forth is usually interpreted as the consequence of a natural or cultural "lag." The common theory is that the mind is more daring and free in its comprehension of historical tasks than are the emotional and volitional forces which furnish the strength to do. Natural passions and cultural institutions supposedly offer a force of inertia against the more inclusive tasks which the mind envisages.

This idea of a cultural lag is plausible enough, and partly true. But it does not represent the whole truth about the defect of our will. It obscures the positive and spiritual element in our resistance to necessary change. The lower and narrower loyalties which stand against the newer and wider loyalties are armed not merely with the force of natural inertia, but with the guile of spirit and the stubbornness of all forms of idolatry in human history.

II

Consider, for instance, the position of the great powers in the present world arrangements. Three great powers have achieved a dominant position in the world; and the charter of the new world organization gives them an explicit hegemony in world affairs. The new world charter speaks loftily of this arrangement as one in which the nations of the world "confer upon the Security Council [which is the organ of the great nations] primary responsibility for the maintenance of international peace and security." Everyone knows that the smaller nations have not willingly conferred such broad powers upon the great nations. The great nations have assumed their rights and powers. They alone wrote the first draft of the present world charter, which the smaller nations tried vainly to amend in principle— though they succeeded in circumscribing the authority of the great powers in some details.

It is also obvious that the great nations are not absolutely single-minded in their desire to maintain the peace of the world. They undoubtedly desire to do so; but each also desires to preserve or enhance its own power and influence. This is the law in their members which wars against the law that is in their minds. The great nations are "of two minds." This is a collective and vivid expression of a general human situation. The "law in our members" is never merely the inertia of "nature" against the more inclusive duties which the mind envisages. It is a spiritual force, compounded of strength and weakness. It is the pride of the powerful, not wishing to share their power. It is also the anxiety of weakness; for even powerful nations are not as secure as they pretend to be. In their anxiety they seek to make themselves independently secure even against their partners in a common world undertaking; and their very effort to do so partly destroys the common security which they pretend to (and in a measure actually do) seek.

All birth in the realm of man's historic institutions is rebirth. The old self must die in order that the new self may be born. The new self is a truer self, precisely because it is more intimately and organically bound to, and involved in, the life of its partners in the human enterprise. But the new self, whether in men or in nations, can not be born if the old self evades the death of repentance, seeking rather to reestablish itself in its old security and old isolation. The tragic events of recent history have proved that old security to be insecure; and the old isolation to be death. There is, therefore, a genuine desire for a new birth and a wider and more mutual security. But it is not powerful enough to destroy the other and older desires. Thus we see the old human drama on a collective and a world scale. If "the strength to bring forth" is lacking in a new period of history, the lack is therefore something else than a natural or a cultural "lag." There is a positive spiritual force in the power which weakens the will to bring forth.

Whatever our hopes for world peace, we must realize that our prospective security against international anarchy is not as good as that of the Pax Romana. This is not because we are worse than the Romans were, but simply because there are three sources of power, rather than one, in the scheme of order. There are too many possibilities of friction between the three, and too many justified mutual apprehensions, to permit the hope that their combined power will give the world an island of order from which to operate against the sea of international anarchy.

Even if the great powers, which have primary responsibility for world order, were more perfectly agreed than they are, we would still face the problem of transmuting the order, which their authority achieves, into genuine justice. The first task of government is to create order by preponderant power. The second task is to create justice. Justice requires that there be some inner and moral checks upon the wielders of power; and that the community also place some social checks upon them. Neither the inner moral checks, nor the outer social and political checks, are sufficient by themselves. Men are never good enough to wield power over their fellowmen, whatever inner checks of conscience may operate in them, without also being subject to outer and social checks.

The great powers in the present world situation have seen to it that these social and political checks are minimal. Neither the smaller powers nor the subject peoples have been given constitutional instruments adequate for the achievement of genuine justice. The great powers pretend that these checks are not necessary because they, the great powers, are "peace-loving" and just. This is somewhat analogous to the pretensions of absolute monarchs of another age who claimed that they were responsible only to God, and not to their fellowmen. Then, as now, it was argued that a wider sharing of responsibility would encourage anarchy. In both cases there was an element of truth in the contention. There is indeed a period in the growth of both national and international communities in which the constitutional instruments, and the organic sources of social harmony, are not adequate for the achievement of harmony, except upon an absolutistic basis. But in both cases the wielders of power tend to obscure the egoistic corruptions of their sense of responsibility. Ages of international constitutional struggles must intervene before the centers of power in the international community are brought under the same adequate checks which now exist in democratic communities. This struggle will be a long and tortuous one, partly because the self-righteousness of the great powers will resist the efforts at greater justice. This self-righteousness is no natural force of inertia. It is a spiritual force. Self-righteousness is one of the oldest and most persistent forms of human sin. In it the human spirit seeks to obscure the partly conscious sense of being involved in universal human sin; just as the lust for power seeks to overcome the partly acknowledged social and historic insecurity.

Our recent experience with a very explicit and demonic form of national egotism and imperialism, in the Nazi state, tends to aggravate these various forms of national self-righteousness. For the nations which now bear responsibility for world peace and justice are obviously more just than were the Nazis. They are tempted to regard that moral superiority as adequate for the achievement of justice. Yet there have been many wielders of power, in both the national and international community, who have been better than the Nazi tyrants and yet have not been just enough to grant real justice to the weak. The destruction of the most tyrannical centers of power in the community, national or international, does not guarantee justice. It merely creates the minimal conditions under which the struggle for justice may take place with some hope of success.

The will-to-power of the great nations, which involves them in vicious circles of mutual fears, is a manifestation of an age-old force in human history. It accentuates the insecurity which it is intended to destroy. It is never completely overcome in man's history; but every new communal advance requires that it be overcome upon a new level of man's common enterprise. Mutual fears lead so inevitably into overt conflict that one would suppose that the nations would recognize this danger more clearly, and would take more explicit steps for a complete international partnership. The fact that they do not can not be attributed merely to ignorance or the cultural lag. There is an element of perversity in this failure to see the obvious; and in the unwillingness to act upon the facts and implications which are seen. The stupidity of sin is in this darkness. "They became vain in their imaginations, and their foolish heart was darkened," is the way St. Paul describes this fact in human life. That description fits the international situation exactly.

The self-righteousness of the great powers, in their pretension that they are safe custodians and protectors of the rights of small nations and dependent peoples, is also a "vain imagination." Just as the will-to-power is intended to overcome the natural insecurity of men and nations, but actually increases what it would overcome; so also the moral pride of peoples seeks to obscure their common involvement in the sins of nations, but actually accentuates what it intends to hide. Both of these forms of vain imagination contribute to the spiritual impotence which prevents the necessary next step in the development of the human community.

There are, of course, special and peculiar forms of these sins, and special and unique reasons for them, in the case of particular nations, which exhibit the general tendency in variable terms. Thus Russia may have a special form of insecurity, derived from the dogma in its religion of an inexorable conflict between capitalist and communist nations. And its special form of pride may be rooted in the idea that it is the only nation which stands on the other side of a revolution, which, according to its faith, proves that it is purged of the common sins of other peoples. The simplicity with which Russia brands any opponents of its policies as fascists reveals this special form of spiritual pride. Britain may possess a special form of insecurity because she is not quite as strong as the two other partners in the hegemony of nations; and she may possess a special form of pride derived from the superior political astuteness achieved through longer experience in world relations. The phenomenal economic power of the American nation is the source of a special temptation to pride; and the political immaturity of the nation tempts it to a peculiar form of insecurity as it moves into the uncharted waters of world politics. Each one of these special sources of either insecurity or compensating pride is a special hazard to the creation of a world community. Yet they all are merely unique manifestations of the general character of the defect of the human will.

The great powers offer vivid examples of the spiritual impotence of our day. But equally valid illustrations could be drawn from the life of the less potent nations. The smaller as well as the larger nations cling desperately to a form of national sovereignty which is incompatible with the requirements of a new age. Each of them, moreover, has its own characteristic weaknesses. The hurt pride of France and her difficulty in acknowledging to herself that her internal decay contributed to the ignominy of her defeat makes her particularly truculent in her relations with other peoples. Resentment and fear determine her relations to a vanquished, but still potentially more powerful, foe; and the dream of reestablishing her military might seems more important to her than becoming the creative center of a continental reconstruction.

China, whose manifest destiny is to become the center of order in Asia, shows little capacity for fulfilling her appointed task. Lacking sufficient resources for her own unity, she may well be divided by the greater powers into their own spheres of influence. Her impotence will tempt the great powers to venture further into Asia than they ought. The peace of the world is not served by the dominance of western powers in the affairs of Asia. Wherever we turn we find not only general, but specific, forms of spiritual and political impotence. The nations are not prepared to create the kind of moral and political order which a technical civilization requires.

III

The failure of this age to achieve adequate instruments of international order is matched by, and related to, the concomitant failure to solve the problem of economic justice within each nation. Modern technics have centralized economic power and aggravated the problem of achieving justice between the various groups of a national community. While a liberal culture sought for an easy solution of the problem of justice, the growing disproportions of economic power transmuted the static injustices of a feudal-agrarian order into the dynamic injustices of technical civilization.

Russia has presumably solved the problem of justice and security in the realm of economic life; but she has paid a high price for the solution in the loss of political liberties. The totalitarian aspects of the Russian régime obscure the genuine achievements of Russian equalitarianism; and give the privileged classes of the western community the occasion to identify falsely political liberty in general with the anachronistic liberty of the economic oligarchy in capitalistic society. If economic power is not brought under more effective social and political restraint, it may well destroy the securities of the common people to the point of undermining the very fabric of western civilization. Of the great powers, Britain is most likely to solve this problem without the loss of democratic liberties; and America is most likely to make abortive efforts to return to a "free enterprise" system, which is incompatible with the requirements of justice in a highly interdependent world.

The rise of modern fascism was partly occasioned by the inability of western civilization to solve the problem of economic justice. Fascism grew in the soil of social chaos and insecurity; and its coerced unity was an effort of modern nations, rent by class conflict, to avoid the disintegration of their national life. The cure proved worse than the disease. The terrible price which nations paid for neglecting to solve their problem of domestic justice might well have been a warning to the privileged classes of the western world. They have chosen rather to identify any effort at a real cure with this false cure; and to lay the charge of fascism against all efforts of the community to bring economic power under control.

There is something more than mere ignorance in this stupidity. It is also a form of the "vain imagination" which distinguishes sin from ignorance. The pride and power of position insinuates itself into the political judgments of the privileged. It insinuates itself into all judgments; but those who have great treasure are obviously more tempted than those who have less: "Where your treasure is, there will your heart be also." The strength to bring forth a more just social order depends partly upon the ability of the poor to transmute their resentments into genuine instruments of justice; and partly upon the ability of the rich to moderate the stupidity of sinful pride and arrogant defiance of the inevitable.

IV

Since the moral and spiritual resources to achieve a just and stable society in global terms are not yet available, we must be prepared to live for decades, and possibly for centuries, in heart-breaking frustrations, somewhat eased by small advances toward the desired goal.

It will not be easy to live in this age between the ages without being tempted to despair. Richer resources of faith will be required than those which the liberal culture of the past two centuries has lived by. Its faith grew out of an age of easy achievements and few frustrations; and has little conception of the tragic character of history.

These resources can not be enlarged upon here, but two facets of an adequate faith for our age between the ages must be mentioned. The one is a form of hope which gives meaning to life not only by what is accomplished in history. We can not live by historic achievement alone, though we can not live meaningfully without historic achievement. The Christian faith has been at a discount in recent centuries because its confidence that "neither life nor death can separate us from the love of God" seemed a desperate kind of hope which was irrelevant to the needs of men who found all their hopes easily fulfilled in history. There are periods of historic achievement in the life of mankind, just as there are periods of fulfillment in the lives of individuals, when the problem of frustration does not arise as a serious issue. But there are also periods when our hopes so far exceed our grasp that we can not count on historic fulfillments to give completion to our life.

There must be a new appreciation of the meaning of the words of St. Paul that "if in this life only we have hope in Christ, we are of all men most miserable." Without the understanding of this depth of human existence it will be difficult to traverse the age between the ages.

The other resource required for our day is a sense of humility which recognizes the lack of strength to bring forth as a common form of human weakness in which all share. We must avoid the peril of attributing our historic frustration to this or that nation—to Russian intransigence, or "British imperialism," or American pride, or any one of the specific forms which the spiritual inadequacies of our day will take. The temptation to do this will be great because there will be many explicit and unique forms of spiritual failure in our day in this class and that nation. It will be necessary to define and isolate these special forms of social and political failure and to deal with their specific causes. But it is equally important to recognize the common root of the failure of all the nations, lest a combination of our pride and our frustration lead to intolerable resentments toward each other.

Human beings in general are more tragic in their stupidities than we have generally believed; and their stupidities are derived from vain imaginations which only great suffering can eradicate. All our new births are brought about in pain; and the pain and sorrow of re-birth are greater than the pain of natural birth. The periods of gestation for the births of history are, moreover, very long; so long that they try our patience and tempt us to believe that history is sterile. This is not the case. Mankind will finally find political instruments and moral resources adequate for a wholesome communal life on a world-wide scale. But generations and centuries may be required to complete the task.

15

The Ecumenical Movement
John W. Carlton

The ecumenical movement, appropriately hailed as the "great new fact of our time," is the expression of an all-embracing goal of a community of Christians united in the confession of a common faith, bound together by ties of Christian charity, nurtured by Word and sacrament, and manifesting to the world a fellowship that transcends human barriers. It is a serious and sustained attempt to restore visible and functional unity to the body of Christ.

Both historical and pragmatic developments have contributed to the ecumenical advance in our century. The fragmentation of Christendom frustrated missionary advance, a practical exigency which prompted Bishop Charles Henry Brent (1862–1929), the first missionary bishop of the Philippine Islands, to challenge denominational divisions imposed from the West, so obviously irrelevant to converts who had come from the great non-Christian religions. The realities of a world sundered by the conflicting claims of secular humanism, existentialism, and communism dramatize the futility of old sectarian alignments in coping with contemporary issues of life and thought. Moreover, within the past fifty years we have experienced a rediscovery of some essential dimensions of the gospel, giving us a fresh appreciation for the theological reality of the church and correcting our pragmatic concern with institutional prestige and self-preservation.

At the turn of this century relatively little concern for Christian unity appeared except in the trenchant writings of such stalwarts as Josiah Strong, Phillip Schaff, and William Reed Huntington, but the earlier years were not without ecumenical pathfinders. Thomas Campbell (1763–1854) published in 1809 his *Declaration and Address*, an apologia for Christian unity and the fundamental document of the Disciples movement. It appealed for the restoration of the church to its "primitive unity, purity, and prosperity," and for a union of all Christians based upon "the pure spring of Bible truth" without added tests of creed or ritual. Thomas Campbell's son, Alexander (1786–1866) took up this refrain in his *Christianity Restored* (1835). Professor Samuel Simon Schmucker (1799–1873), a distinguished Lutheran, issued in 1838 his *Fraternal Appeal to the American Churches: With a Plan for Catholic Union, on Apostolic Principles*. He called for the formation of the "Apostolic Protestant Church," whose doctrinal *sine qua non* and the uniting basis of the constituent denominations was to be a united confession based upon the "fundamental" doctrines of Protestantism expressed in and common to all Protestant creeds. A significant proposal for church unity was made in 1870 by William Reed Huntington (1838–1918) in *The Church Idea: An Essay Toward Unity*, which outlined a platform of four essentials of Anglicanism on which churches could unite: (1) the Holy Scriptures as the rule and ultimate standard of faith; (2) the primitive creeds as a sufficient statement of faith; (3) the two sacraments ordained by Christ; and (4) the historic episcopate as the keystone of governmental unity. These "essentials" were approved with slight modifications by the American Episcopal House of Bishops and the Anglican Lambeth Conference and became the "Chicago-Lambeth Quadrilateral."

Emerging structures and world gatherings of Christian bodies furthered the goal of Christian unity. The Federal Council of Churches of Christ in America was founded in 1908, with a membership comprised of about thirty

American denominations. The World Missionary Conference at Edinburgh in 1910 convinced leaders such as Bishop Charles Henry Brent that the spirit of God was preparing a new era in the history of Christianity. The forces for unity brought about the World Conference on Faith and Order at Lausanne in 1927, when over four hundred delegates representing more than one hundred church bodies convened, explored their ecclesiastical divisions, and issued a unanimous statement on "The Church's Message to the World." A Continuation Committee carried the deliberations further and summoned the next Conference for Edinburgh in 1937. The Conference on Church, Community, and State at Oxford in 1937 served to bring churches together in common ethical action notwithstanding their doctrinal cleavages. For more than twenty-five years the three major movements calling for cooperation in the missionary task of the church, life and work, and faith and order pursued their independent ways, but such a separation could not continue given those within each movement who envisioned a broader goal. In Amsterdam on August 22, 1948, representatives from 146 churches and 44 countries convened and completed the organization of the World Council of Churches. It adopted as its basis the doctrinal formula: "a fellowship of churches which accepts our Lord Jesus Christ as God and Savior," and it made clear that the Council would have no constitutional authority over member churches, thus disavowing any role as a "super-church."

A significant area of ecumenical achievement has been that of organic church union. The United States has provided conspicuous examples of intraconfessional unions, notably among Lutherans and Methodists. Other lands have witnessed transconfessional unions across denominational lines. The United Church of Canada came into being in 1925. By far the most significant movement for church union was the formation of the Church of South India in 1947, bringing to final reality union negotiations among the Presbyterians, Congregationalists, Episcopalians, and Methodists.

On the American scene an audacious proposal for church union was made in a sermon preached in Grace

Cathedral, San Francisco, by Dr. Eugene Carson Blake, then Stated Clerk of the General Assembly of the United Presbyterian Church in the U.S.A. on December 4, 1960. This sermon accompanies this brief analysis. He proposed that the Protestant Episcopal Church join with his own denomination in inviting the Methodist Church and the United Church of Christ to form a plan of church union "both catholic and reformed." All four denominations mentioned in Dr. Blake's proposal have since had representatives to engage in joint discussions through a body called "The Consultation on Church Union."

The rigid posture of the Roman Catholic Church toward the great ecumenical gatherings at Lausanne, Edinburgh, and Oxford permitted only a modicum of personal and unofficial cooperation, but today there is exciting ecumenical conversation among Roman Catholic, Orthodox, and Protestant bodies. The monumental pontificate of John XXIII led many Protestants to abandon old stereotypes of Catholicism as a closed, complacent, sectarian body. Catholicism today is producing a prodigious amount of biblical work, new theological vigor, and perceptive literature on the ecumenical movement. Augustin Cardinal Bea, a major draftsman in the unfolding designs of Catholic ecumenicity, has hailed the authentic Christian openness that marks the present dialogue and has called for continuing conversations between Catholics and Protestants on matters not yet proclaimed as binding upon all: problems regarding the membership of non-Catholic Christians in the church, problems of the union of all Christians with Christ, questions relating to the constitution of the church, practical matters pertaining to the relief of the suffering and the oppressed, and concerns of public worship, particularly its language and rites.

Now far past the invigorating days when it was "the great new fact of our time," the ecumenical movement is at a more critical stage of its career. The intervening years have brought a more realistic view of residual problems: the need to broaden the base of ecumenical participation, denominational preoccupations that perpetuate ecclesiastical divisions, the fear of losing cherished gains and values in any synthesis of traditions, and large denominational

391

groups such as Southern Baptists, the Lutheran Church (Missouri Synod), "evangelicals," and Pentecostal bodies that continue to remain aloof. Carl F. H. Henry, prominent evangelical conservative, clearly articulates some of the nonecumenical reservations in the accompanying sermon.

In a factually divided Christendom we are committed to yearn, work, and pray for the fullness and fulfillment of the Body of Christ. The Christian community has lived through a long night of isolation. Although we seem to move "with painful gait and slow," perhaps, under God, we are on the way toward the realization of an undivided community of the faithful and hence to a new day in universal church history.

EUGENE CARSON BLAKE

Dr. Eugene Carson Blake, since 1966 the General Secretary of the World Council of Churches, was born in St. Louis, Missouri, on November 7, 1906. He received his formal education at Princeton University, New College, Edinburgh, and the Princeton Theological Seminary. He has served as a professor at Forman Christian College, Lahore, India. From 1932–1935 he was assistant pastor of the St. Nicholas Church in New York City. Subsequent pastorates included the First Presbyterian Church, Albany (1935–1940) and the Pasadena Presbyterian Church (1940–1951). In 1951, he was elected Stated Clerk of the General Assembly of the Presbyterian Church, USA (since 1958 the United Presbyterian Church, U.S.A.), a post relinquished in 1966 when he was chosen General Secretary of the World Council of Churches.

Dr. Blake has been prominently identified with the National Council of the Churches of Christ in the United States, serving as president of this body from 1954–1957, as a member of the General Board, and as chairman of its Committee on Religion and Race. Prior to his election as General Secretary, he was a member of the Central Committee and of the Executive Committee of the World Council of Churches. He has functioned as a trustee of Princeton Theological Seminary, Occidental College, and San Francisco Theological Seminary. Dr. Blake is author of He is Lord of All, The Church in the Next Decade, *and* Challenge to the Church.

A Proposal Toward the Reunion of Christ's Church*

Text: *"Now the God of patience and consolation grant you to be like-minded one toward another according to Christ Jesus! That ye may with one mind and with one mouth glorify God, even the Father of our Lord Jesus Christ. Wherefore receive ye one another as Christ also received us to the glory of God."*—ROMANS: 15:5-7.

This is a significant occasion. When I received the gracious invitation from your Dean and Bishop to preach in this pulpit, on this particular morning,

* *The Challenge to Reunion*, ed. Robert McAfee Brown and David H. Scott (New York: McGraw-Hill, 1963). Reprinted by permission of Dr. Blake.

it became clear to me at once that the occasion demanded not only as good a sermon as God might enable me to prepare and preach, but also a sermon that would deal with the unity of the Church of Jesus Christ realistically —neither glossing over divisions with politeness nor covering them with optimistic generalities.

Led, I pray, by the Holy Spirit, I propose to the Protestant Episcopal Church that it together with The United Presbyterian Church in the United States of America invite The Methodist Church and the United Church of Christ to form with us a plan of church union both catholic and reformed on the basis of the principles I shall later in this sermon suggest. Any other Churches which find that they can accept both the principles and plan would also be warmly invited to unite with us.

I hasten to make it clear that at this stage this is not an official proposal. My position as Stated Clerk of my Church's General Assembly gives me no authority to make such a proposal officially on behalf of my Church. I speak this morning as one of the ministers of my Church privileged and required to preach under the Word of God. I speak as a minister especially privileged —and therefore under a special requirement—especially privileged to have represented my communion for the past nine years in many formal and informal relationships with other communions both inside and outside the ecumenical movement. I speak as one minister of Jesus Christ who believes that God requires us to break through the barriers of nearly 500 years of history to attempt under God to transcend the separate traditions of our Churches, and to find a way together to unite them so that manifesting the unity given us by our Lord Jesus Christ, His Church may be renewed for its mission to our nation and to the world "that the world may believe."

Before setting forth the basic principles of the union which I propose, it is, I think, important to make clear the compelling considerations that have moved me to believe that union ought now to be sought by us and to clear away some possible misunderstanding of reasons and motives for seeking it.

First of all I am moved by the conviction that Jesus Christ, whom all of us confess as our divine Lord and Saviour, wills that His Church be one. This does not mean that His Church must be uniform, authoritarian, or a single mammoth organization. But it does mean that our separate organizations, however much we sincerely try to cooperate in councils, present a tragically divided Church to a tragically divided world. Our divided state makes almost unbelieveable our common Christian claim that Jesus Christ is Lord and that He is the Prince of Peace. The goal of any unity or union in which we ought to be interested was clearly stated by the Central Committee of the World Council of Churches last summer. The unity sought is primarily a local unity, "one which brings all in each place who confess

Jesus Christ as Lord into a fully committed fellowship with one another." The World Council statement emphasized that the unity sought "is not one of uniformity nor a monolithic power structure." The point of church reunion is not to be found chiefly in national or international organization; it is found most fundamentally in local communion and common witness in all the places where men live.

In October, I was at a political dinner at which I had been invited to give the invocation. A gentleman introduced himself to me as we were waiting to go in to the tables and asked me what Church I represented. When I told him, he said, "My wife is a Presbyterian. I am an Episcopalian. We go happily to each other's church. Why don't you Church officials do something about bringing our Churches together?" Many such ordinary Christians wonder why we continue to be divided.

In the *Christian Century* last January, Bishop Pike wrote, ". . . of this I am sure: The Holy Ghost is on our side whenever we break through the barriers between Christian bodies. He will increasingly provide guidance to show the ways in which we can defeat the complacent obstinacy of our national Church bodies in this regard."

And I am sure that Bishop Pike agrees with me that there are many complacencies in local churches among members and ministers that must be disturbed by the Holy Ghost if Christ's will for His Church is to be accomplished in our time and place. For although many American church members are ready to criticize their church leaders for inaction, I fear that just as many are complacently happy in the divided state of the Church.

Another clear reason for moving toward the union of American Churches at this time came home to me with compelling force during the presidential campaign this fall. The religious issue was, you will remember, quite generally discussed even though all the high level politicians attempted to avoid it as much as possible. Now that the election has been decided and nobody really knows how much the religious question figured in the result, I recall the issue to remind you that one result is clear. Every Christian Church, Protestant, Orthodox, Anglican, and Roman Catholic has been weakened by it. Never before have so many Americans agreed that the Christian Churches, divided as they are, cannot be trusted to bring to the American people an objective and authentic word of God on a political issue. Americans more than ever see the Churches of Jesus Christ as competing social groups pulling and hauling, propagandizing and pressuring for their own organizational advantages.

And this is at a time when the United States of America finds herself at a pinnacle of world power and leadership—needing for herself and the whole free world that kind of spiritual vision and inspiration that only the Church of Jesus Christ, renewed and reunited can give. Our culture, our civilization, our world leadership are under the materialistic threat of Marxist communism. But our culture becomes increasingly secular, our civilization becomes increasingly decadent, and our world leadership becomes increasingly confused precisely because their Christian foundations are undermined and eroded. And our divided Churches, all more and more sectarian in fact, are all therefore less and less Christian in influence.

Finally I am moved to propose this step of church union this morning because my proposal grows out of the convictions expressed in 1959 by thirty-four leaders of Presbyterian and Reformed Churches, theologians and administrators, from all over the world in an address to their fellow Christians, made on the occasion of the 400th anniversary of the Calvinist Reformation. We said:

"The occasion we celebrate (i.e. the 400th anniversary of the beginnings of Presbyterianism) makes invitations more appropriate than proclamations. We ourselves are ready to accept all invitations from sister churches to that comparison of opinion and experience in which Christians submit themselves afresh to the Lord of the Church. And we issue our own invitations to all who would, with us, *put their traditions and systems under the judgment of Christ*, seeking his correction, and ready to relinquish what he does not approve.

"All that we claim for the Presbyterian and Reformed Churches we would lay on the altar. We offer it all to our fellow Christians for whatever use it may be to the whole Church. With the whole Church we hold ourselves alert for the surprises with which the Lord of history can alter the tempo of our renewal, and for the *new forms* with which an eternally recreating God can startle us while he secures his Church."

In this spirit and out of this conviction, I now propose the principles upon which a church union of the scope I have suggested may be even now possible of achievement under God.

Let me begin by re-emphasizing the requirement that a reunited Church must be both reformed and catholic. If at this time we are to begin to bridge over the chasm of the Reformation, those of us who are of the Reformation tradition must recapture an appreciation of all that has been preserved by the catholic parts of the Church, and equally those of the catholic tradition must be willing to accept and take to themselves as of God all that nearly five hundred years of Reformation has contributed to the renewal of Christ's Church.

Let me pause here to be quite sure that all you understand exactly the sense in which I am using the word *catholic*. In common parlance in America we often talk about "the Catholic Church" and mean "the Roman Catholic

Church." That is not the meaning of *catholic* that I here use. At the other extreme all our Churches repeat the Apostles' Creed in which we say, "I believe in the Holy Catholic Church." All of us claim to be catholic in the strict sense of confessing that Jesus Christ has established one universal Church in all ages and in all places and that we are at least part of it. Here, however, I have used the word *catholic* in still a third sense when I speak of the "catholic parts of the Church." I refer to those practices and to those understandings of faith and order, of church and sacraments which are catholic in contrast to the protestant or evangelical practices and understandings. I refer specifically, for example, to the Anglo-Catholic or high Church practices and understandings of your own Church. When I say then that the proposal I make is to establish a Church both catholic and reformed, I mean one which unites catholic and reformed understandings and practices in an even broader and deeper way than that already present in your communion.

Such a union as I now propose must have within it the kind of broad and deep agreement which gives promise of much wider union than seems possible at the present moment, looking ultimately to the reunion of the whole of Christ's Church.

First let me list the principles of reunion that are important to all who are of catholic tradition.

1. The reunited Church must have visible and historical continuity with the Church of all ages before and after the Reformation. This will include a ministry which by its orders and ordination is recognized as widely as possible by all other Christian bodies. To this end, I propose that, without adopting any particular theory of historic succession, the reunited Church shall provide at its inception for the consecration of all its bishops by bishops and presbyters both in the apostolic succession and out of it from all over the world from all Christian churches which would authorize or permit them to take part.

I propose further that the whole ministry of the uniting Churches would then be unified at solemn services at which the bishops and representative ministers from each Church would, in humble dependence on God, act and pray that the Holy Spirit would supply to all and through all what each has to contribute and whatever each may need of the fullness of Christ's grace, commission and authority for the exercise of a new larger ministry in this wider visible manifestation of Christ's Holy and Catholic Church. You will note that this proposal implies no questioning of the reality of any previous consecration or ordination, nor any questioning of their having been blessed and used by God. It does imply that a renewal of our obedience to Jesus Christ in this visible uniting of His Church can be the occasion of fresh indwelling of the Holy Spirit and a new *charisma* for us all.

I mention first this principle of visible and historical continuity not because it is necessarily the most important to the catholic Christian but because it is the only basis on which a broad reunion can take place, and because it is and will continue to be the most difficult catholic conviction for evangelicals to understand and to accept. My proposal is simply to cut the Gordian knot of hundreds of years of controversy by establishing in the united Church an historic ministry recognized by all without doubt or scruple. The necessary safeguards and controls of such a ministry will become clear when I am listing the principles of reunion that catholic-minded Christians must grant to evangelicals if there is to be reunion between them.

2. The reunited Church must clearly confess the historic trinitarian faith received from the Apostles and set forth in the Apostles' and Nicene Creeds. Here there is no real issue between the Presbyterian and Episcopal Churches. The difference that must be bridged is the issue between those in all our Churches who stand for a corporate confession of historic faith and those who fear that any required confession is too restrictive. A quarter of a century ago this would have been a sharper issue and more difficult to bridge. The tendency of the Presbyterian Church to be over-legalistic and of the Episcopal Church to be over-traditional have been modified by renewed theological and biblical understanding in our time. Equally the tendency in some of the so-called free Churches to suppose that no belief, that no confession of the faith, was necessary has given way to a general recognition of the necessity of corporate and individual confession of Christian faith as against the secular, humanistic, and atheistic ideologies of our times.

3. The reunited Church must administer the two sacraments, instituted by Christ, the Lord's Supper (or Holy Communion, or Eucharist) and Baptism. These must be understood truly as means of grace by which God's grace and presence are made available to His people. It will not be necessary, I trust, for a precise doctrinal agreement to be reached about the mode of operation of the sacraments so long as the proper catholic concern for their reality is protected so that, with the Word, the Sacrament is recognized as a true means of grace and not merely a symbolic memorial.

Much more could be said. Doubtless there are those of catholic tradition who would like even at this stage to add precise points to protect their consciences and convictions. The above, however, are the basic points and seem to me to be enough to be listed as basic principles if we are willing to add one more word. It must be agreed that every attempt will be made by those drawing up an actual plan of union to include within it those essentials of catholic practice and faith that will enable those of that persuasion to worship and witness joyfully and in good conscience within the fellowship of the united Church.

And now let me list the principles of reunion that are important to all who are of the reformation tradition:

1. The reunited Church must accept the principle of continuing reformation under the Word of God by the guidance of the Holy Spirit. A few years ago I would have felt that here was an issue on which no possible agreement could be reached. The reformation Churches have traditionally found their authority for faith and life in the Scriptures alone. So long as the wording *sola scriptura* is a required, no bridge can be made between catholic and evangelical. But it is now clear in ecumenical conversations that Protestants generally have come to recognize the right place of tradition, just as catholics have generally become aware of the rightness of judging all tradition by the Scriptures as interpreted to the Church by the Holy Spirit.

The point that the Reformation tradition does require from a reunited Church is that God speaking through the Scriptures, must be able to reform the Church from age to age. While the Bible is not a law book or a collection of proof texts, it is God's instrument to speak His Saving Word to Christians and to the Church. If the catholic must insist on taking the sacraments more seriously than some Protestants have sometimes done, so Protestants in the reunited Church must insist on catholics fully accepting the Reformation principle that God has revealed and can reveal Himself and His will more and more fully through the Holy Scriptures. The reunited Church must keep Word and Sacrament equally and intimately united in understanding and appreciation.

2. The reunited Church must be truly democratic in its government, recognizing that the whole people of God are Christ's Church, that all Christians are Christ's ministers even though some in the Church are separated and ordained to the ministry of word and sacrament. You will have noticed that in the first catholic principle which I mentioned. I proposed that the traditional three-fold ministry in the apostolic succession be established in the reunited Church. If evangelical Protestants are to enter such a Church with joy and in conscience there are several subsidiary points that must be made clear in the government and ethos of the reunited Church.

Episcopal churches should recognize that it will be with great reluctance that Presbyterians and Congregationalists will accept bishops in the structure of the Church. I should say, however, that there are many aspects of Episcopacy that American Presbyterians and other non-Episcopal Churches more and more generally recognize as valuable and needed. We Presbyterians for example need pastors of pastors quite desperately, and we know it. But we don't need an aristocratic or authoritarian hierarchy, and we don't believe a reunited Church does either. Furthermore Congregationalists and Presbyterians need to recognize how much of democracy is now practiced in American Episcopal churches. In this diocese I remind you that presbyteries have been already established.

On the positive side we Presbyterians would offer to the reunited Church the office of the ordained ruling elder, elected by the people in their congregations to share fully and equally in the government of the church. It will be important for all entering this union to attempt creatively to develop a new form of government that avoids the monarchical, clerical, and authoritarian tendencies that have been historically the dangers of Episcopal Church government. Equally this new form of government must avoid the bureaucratic dangers that appear to be the chief threat of non-Episcopal Churches. It is the essence of Protestant concern, however, that decisions should generally be made by ordered groups of men under the guidance of the Holy Spirit rather than by a man who has personal authority to impose on others his decision or judgment.

While Protestants more and more recognize that a *catholic* understanding of the sacraments does not necessarily imply a clerical control of the Church nor the priestly abuses that introduced fear and magic into the medieval Church and chiefly caused the Reformation, nevertheless they hold the conviction as strongly as ever that clericalism and priestly control of the Church must be guarded against by a government of the Church in which lay people and ministers share equally.

It will be further important to continue to protect in the united Church the responsible freedom of congregations including the election of their pastors and the responsible freedom of ministers to answer the call of God received through the free action of the people. I may say that this ought to present no great problem since all our Churches are largely *congregational* in this respect. At the same time I would hope that all of those entering into such a union as I here propose would be concerned also to find a way in the context of such freedom to preserve the Methodist ability to find some place of employment of his gifts for every minister who is in good and regular standing. If the reunited Church is to have a dedicated and competent ministry, we must find a better way than any of us has yet found to recruit, educate, and employ a ministry avoiding on the one hand professionalism and on the other that kind of equalitarianism which produces disorder and anarchy in the Church.

3. The reunited Church must seek in a new way to recapture the brotherhood and sense of fellowship of all its members and ministers. Let me illustrate what I mean by a series of suggestions of what might appear on the surface to be minor matters but which if creatively resolved in the reunited

400

Church would not only remove many protestant misgivings but would, I believe, strengthen the witness of the Church to the world. Since it appears to be necessary to have certain inequalities in status in the Church as between members and officers, and as among deacons, presbyters, and bishops, let us make certain that the more status a member or minister has the more simple be his dress and attitude. Let us seek to make it evident in every possible way that in the Church the greatest is the servant of all. "My brother" is a better form of Christian address than "your grace." A simple cassock is generally a better Christian garb for the highest member of the clergy than cope and miter. And must there be grades of reverends, very, right, most, etc.? Do there even need to be any reverends at all? It is actually provided explicitly in the Union Plan of Ceylon that a Bishop shall not be addressed as "My Lord." It would be my hope that those planning for a reunited Church would take the occasion to find many ways to exhibit to each other and to the world that we take seriously our Lord's word, "You know that those who are supposed to rule over the Gentiles lord it over them and their great men exercise authority over them. But it shall not be so among you; but whoever would be great among you must be your servant."

Clearly connected with this will be such matters as finding a way to avoid too great inequities in ministers' salaries, in the richness or grandeur of ecclesiastical establishments, lest the poor be alienated or the world conclude that luxury has sapped the soul of the Church. I speak in the full recognition of the spiritual value of this great Church and the rightness of completing it in beauty. Yet I speak for simplicity and brotherhood as every being the requirement of Christ's Church.

4. Finally the reunited Church must find the way to include within its catholicity (and because of it) a wide diversity of theological formulation of the faith and a variety of worship and liturgy including worship that is non-liturgical.

The great confessions of the Reformation must have their place in the confession, teaching, and history of the reunited Church just as do the ecumenical agreements of the undivided Church. I would hope that such a Reformation confession as the Heidelburg Catechism, partly because of its Lutheran elements, might be lifted up in some acceptable formula as having a proper place in the confession of the whole Church. And further, the reunited Church should, as led by the Holy Spirit under the Word, from time to time seek to confess its united faith to the world in new formulations appropriate to its place and time. Our two Churches, however, need to appreciate better than they have the fact that direct and joyful experience of Jesus Christ as John Wesley knew it can be restricted too much by over-reliance on creedal formulas. Our two Churches need to appreciate better than they have the liberating and creative inspiration of the Holy Spirit in the theological freedom of the congregational churches at their best.

Thus the united Church must avoid that kind of legalistic formulation of doctrine which on the ground of expressing unity of faith in fact produces a sterile uniformity which breeds alternately neglect and schism.

In worship there is great value in a commonly used, loved, and recognized liturgy. But such liturgy ought not to be imposed by authority or to be made binding upon the Holy Spirit or the congregations. More and more it would be our hope that in such a Church, as is here proposed, there would be developed common ways of worship both historic and freshly inspired. But history proves too well that imposed liturgy like imposed formulation of doctrine often destroys the very unity it is designed to strengthen.

Again there are many more things that those of the evangelical tradition in all our Churches would doubtless like at this stage to add as precise points to protect their consciences and convictions. The above, however, seem to be the essential and basic points which such a union as I propose would require if here again we are willing to add one more word. We must agree that every attempt will be made by those drawing up the plan of union to include within it those essentials of reformation faith and practice that will enable those of that persuasion to worship and witness joyfully and with good conscience within the fellowship of the reunited Church.

Here I would insert the assumption that all would understand that the reunited Church must remain in the ecumenical movement and its councils. It must be no less—it must be even more concerned beyond itself, recognizing that its reunion was but a stage and a step toward that unity which Christ requires His Church to manifest. This means also that the reunited Church must provide that such relationships of fellowship, cooperation, and intercommunion as the several Churches now have will be continued; this despite the difficulty and tension that such ambiguous relationships will continue to cause.

In conclusion I would remind you that precise ways of formulating such a reunion as I have sketched have been worked out in several ways particularly in the sub-continent of India in the several plans of union there. One may ask why they have preceded us in this, and alternately why we should look to their example for light and inspiration toward union here.

The answer to these questions is a simple one. Christians in India recognize themselves to be a small and beleaguered minority in a pagan and secular world. They have realized full well that they could not afford the luxury of their divisions. I submit that even though our numbers and wealth and prestige may be greater than theirs, we too need to recognize that we cannot afford longer the luxury of our historic divisions. It is because of this conviction that I have felt impelled to preach this sermon.

There are two results that I pray may, under God, come from it. If there is support for what I have said in my own Church, any or all of our presbyteries may, if they will, overture the General Assembly which meets next May asking that Assembly to make an official proposal. I further hope that the Protestant Episcopal Church, by its own processes will also take an early action in this direction so that in your General Convention next fall the invitation to the Methodist Church and the United Church of Christ may be jointly issued to proceed to draw up a plan of union to which any other Churches of Jesus Christ accepting the bases suggested and the plan developed will be warmly invited to join.

Now I have not forgotten that this is a sermon and that it is an unconscionably long time since I announced my text. To you who have patiently listened to my longer than usual exposition, I ask one thing more: that you pray for the reunion of Christ's Church and that as you think about it and examine your own heart and mind, you do it in the spirit of the Apostle Paul when he addressed the saints and bishops and deacons of the church at Philippi.

Paul wrote, "Complete my joy by being of the same mind, having the same love, being in full accord and of one mind." The Apostle continued: "Do nothing from selfishness or conceit, but in humility count others better than yourselves. Let each of you look not only to his own interests but also to the interests of others. Have this mind among yourselves which you have in Christ Jesus, who though he was in the form of God, did not count equality with God a thing to be grasped, but emptied himself, taking the form of a servant, being born in the likeness of men. And being found in human form, he humbled himself and became obedient unto death, even death on a cross. Therefore God has highly exalted him and bestowed on him the name that is above every name, that at the name of Jesus every knee should bow . . . and every tongue confess that Jesus Christ is Lord to the glory of God the Father."

If you, dear friends, and all others who consider and discuss this proposal do so in this spirit and from this motive, I have no fear but that the eternally recreative God will find His way to renew and reunite His Church.

Carl F. H. Henry

Dr. Carl F. H. Henry was born in New York City on January 22, 1913. He holds degrees from Wheaton College (B.A., M.A.), Northern Baptist Theological Seminary (B.D., Th.D.), and Boston University (Ph.D.). He has done additional graduate study at Loyola University, Indiana University, and the University of Edinburgh. From 1942 to 1947, he was associated with the Northern Baptist Theological Seminary as Assistant Professor and Professor of Theology. In 1947, he became Acting Dean of the Fuller Theological Seminary. In 1956, he was elected Editor of Christianity Today. He was Chairman of the World Congress on Evangelism which convened in Berlin in 1966.

Dr. Henry is a prolific writer. He is the author of A Doorway to Heaven (1941), Successful Church Publicity (1942), Remaking the Modern Mind (1948), The Uneasy Conscience of Modern Fundamentalism (1948), Giving a Reason for Our Hope (1949), The Protestant Dilemma (1949), Notes on the Doctrine of God (1949), Fifty Years of Protestant Theology (1950), The Drift of Western Thought (1951), Glimpses of a Sacred Land (1953), Christian Personal Ethics (1957), Frontiers in Modern Theology (1966), and Evangelicals at the Brink of Crisis (1967). He has also edited significant volumes: Contemporary Theological Thought (1957), Revelation and the Bible (1959), and Baker's Dictionary of Theology (1964).

Christ and His Embattled Legions*

He is the head of the body, the church; . . . that in all things he might have the preeminence.—Col. 1:18.

There is no doubt that the world had never before seen anything comparable to the Christian fellowship—that saintly community of the twice-born in which Jew and Gentile, Greek and barbarian, Scythian and free, master and slave, rich and poor, were all brethren. On the basis of the new birth Christianity shaped a new spiritual community, a new family of men and women—supernational and superracial. Except for the intimacies of marriage,

* *Sermons to Men of Other Faiths and Traditions*, ed. Gerald H. Anderson (Nashville: Abingdon Press, 1966), pp. 141-53.

it was the most intimate fellowship in human history; followers of "the Way" had stronger ties to each other than the natural ties of home and family. Never within the long sweep of human history has the society of mankind witnessed the rise of a community more remarkable for its spiritual kinship than the "fellowship of regenerate sinners" devoted in obedient faith to the crucified and risen Redeemer.

It is small wonder then that today we should wistfully recall this remarkable spiritual phenomenon and hope to recover it. We know all too well that Christendom is now broken into innumerable fragments. And this loss of Christian unity is made doubly conspicuous by the painful fractures in the body of humanity that rise from the communist clash, from racial strife, and from international rivalries. How imperative is the need for some visible manifestation of the unity of the church, lest Christendom itself become inundated by the secular forces that threaten all of twentieth-century life. So what shall I say to the ecumenists, to those who think nothing is more important among Christians than their identification in one world organization?

I

The church would surely die if its life were suspended upon anything peculiar to the twentieth century. If we base the life and health of the church only on some specifically modern development, on any manifestation not first found in the apostolic era, the gates of hell will surely prevail against it. The church of Christ is a supernatural creation. Its life is rooted neither in the present nor even in the past; rather, its life flows from the eternal order. The church is a supernatural creation whose existence is neither spontaneously generated nor self-perpetuated.

We must declare all our modern ecclesiastical organizations and ecumenical developments to be quite perishable commodities; they are not to be confused with the church in its enduring character. Whether, in confessing this temporality, we think of the National Association of Evangelicals, or National Council of Churches, or American Council of Christian Churches, or World Evangelical Fellowship, or International Council of Christian Churches, or International Association for Reformed Faith and Action, or World Council of Churches, the judgment must be the same; all are but creatures of the twentieth century, projected and created either by modern ecclesiasts or by modern denominations.

If the modern church confuses its own initiative with the Lord's bidding, its own activity with the deed of the Lord, it is beguiled by that ancient serpent that says "Ye shall not surely die!" Any church whose life is suspended upon human thought and promotion, upon human effort and engineering, must surely perish.

In no generation does Christ's cause depend ultimately upon the church. Of course, such "pontificating" stirs a sense of shock in today's ecclesiastical circles. Surely, it will be said, if Christ is the New Testament bridegroom, we dare not speak of a divorceable bride—as if he purposes to carry out his mission in the world exclusive of the church! But we must reply, and just as surely, that *not because of any virtue inherent in the bride,* not because of stature in society or worldly adornments, but solely because of the bridegroom—and when and as he is truly the bridegroom—does the church exist as his indispensable instrument. Certainly no bride who is unsure of her bridegroom's identity, or wonders whether she has been widowed by his death or really is kept alive by his spirit, or is deluded by the notion that this spirit is myth, can truly qualify as the bride. First-century Christians were convinced that the authentic church had its life source exclusively in the risen Redeemer. If we mean by the church not merely an institutional organization but rather a spiritual organism, then the church depends for its existence and preservation upon Jesus Christ, incarnate, crucified, risen, ascended, and glorified.

Anyone who remembers that church history is divided into pre-Reformation and post-Reformation periods, and who recalls that biblical history is divided into the old and new dispensations, will grasp the force of what Karl Barth has said: "Certainly God is not tied to the historical Church, but is free and able of these stones to raise up children of Abraham." Certainly. "He that findeth his life shall lose it: and he that loseth his life for my sake shall find it" is a law of faith with incisive relevance for the realm of ecclesiastical reality and perhaps particularly for the ecumenical manifestations of our own day.

When the first Christians contemplated the church, they always had in view an entity created and preserved by Jesus of Nazareth, their Savior and Lord. And if the Christian community today is to speak decisively to men of other faiths and traditions, it will succeed in the apostolic sense only by this same awareness that Jesus Christ alone is the source of the church's life.

II

The unity of Christians is not man-made but is God-given. And only through a larger appropriation of divine resources, and not by the ingenious projection of human resources, can this unity be attained more fully.

The broken witness of Christendom and the fragmentation of Christian forces are woefully tragic. At the very moment in modern times when secular life is disrupted and disfigured by crisis and chaos, the one movement in history whose cohesive and adhesive powers are reputedly divine seems on mainstreet everywhere to be no less divided and disrupted than are worldly agencies. These divisions are sometimes more noticeable among theologically sensitive groups which insist that doctrinal agreement is fundamental to Christian unity than among the theologically tolerant and merger-prone denominations. And yet even the ecumenical development, after a half century of consolidation, has not overcome the basic divisions of Christendom, but alongside the pope of Rome has now established a Geneva-based Central Committee, composed of one hundred men, that is experiencing its own internal problems.

The one high service of the ecumenical movement has been to prick the Christian conscience concerning disunity. Men are called to hear afresh our Lord's high priestly prayer "that they may be one"—even if in the same breath they are then called to identify themselves and their churches with a specific organizational structure as the "approved" means of overcoming this disunity and achieving unity.

Christian unity is indeed a central concern of the New Testament, but it is "union with Christ" that is there first and foremost in view. The Christian religion's primary objective is to restore individuals to personal fellowship with God. In the reality of this mighty reconciliation the first Christians discovered each other. No reader of the New Testament can miss the fact that the driving concern of apostolic Christianity was not church union but union with Christ. This emphasis held priority over any and every other interest in unity; it pervades Christ's priestly prayer in John's Gospel as well as the relevant passages in Paul's epistles. The unity of believers flows from their common life in Christ. In the Protestant Reformation, Martin Luther spoke of being "glued to Christ." Any movement for Christian unity that does not first assure itself of this divine adhesive for its members is foredoomed to future dismemberment. Union with Christ is prerequisite to the believer's union with fellow believers. Church unity in Scripture appears not primarily or essentially in terms of the integration or merger of structurally organized churches, but in the need for each individual's personal union with the living, risen, and omnipresent Savior. Therefore, unless a demand for ecumenical unity or for ecclesiastical union makes clear the biblical importance of the participants' prior union with Christ, identification with such an institutional superstructure can hardly be taken to imply its adherents' union with Christ or to manifest a union of believers.

The Baptist theologian A. H. Strong, who assigned the theme of the believer's union with Christ special emphasis, spoke early in this century of the "great need of rescuing the doctrine from neglect." The recent emphasis on church union has not restored the theme to apostolic priority; the Congregational-Evangelical and Reformed merger confession in 1959, for example, made no mention of this doctrine. If the Christian community is to speak decisively to men of other faiths and traditions, it can hope to succeed in the apostolic sense only by observing this priority of union with Christ.

III

Not only does the church's life flow from the risen Christ, not only does the unity of believers flow from their union with him, but God has already struck the decisive blow in his offensive against Satan, sin, and unbelief. In this battle the crucial development is not church union but an episode that long antedates the twentieth century and modern man. The atonement and resurrecton of Jesus Christ in A.D. 30 is the hinge of history —of both sacred and universal history. Our Lord's "It is finished" assured the defeat and doom of Satan on the one hand and the spiritual victory and vindication of all who trust Christ on the other.

There is danger for the church if it exalts a modern ecclesiastical offensive as the decisive factor in its relationship to the world. Any impression that unbelief can be overcome more effectively by ecumenical integration than by faithful proclamation of Jesus Christ's triumph is false. Some will protest this disjunction as arbitrary antithesizing; they will challenge the right to divorce what the ecumenists have joined together, namely, that Jesus of Nazareth is the only divine Savior and Lord, and that Christian fragmentation is the major obstacle to the world's recognition of him. But, we would ask, is the first thesis really a *test* of ecumenical eligibility, and is the second thesis really *true*?

The theological basis of the World Council may indeed be invoked to demonstrate that twentieth-century ecumenism presupposes first-century theology and evangelism. But this is the crucial point: first-century theology and evangelism must not be simply presupposed, but must be perpetuated. They cannot be subordinated to any other ecclesiastical concern or priority. Across the years ecumenical leadership and affiliation have reflected humanist, liberal, neo-orthodox, and neoliberal as well as evangelical points of view. It is not difficult to list prominent ecumenical theologians who deny such basic Christian doctrines as the virgin birth of Jesus, his messianic self-consciousness, his substitutionary and propitiatory atonement, his bodily resurrection, or his personal and visible return. In Faith and Order conferences the loss of the Bible as an authoritative canon of sacred writings is obvious. Present-day ecumenism distills its theological consensus from the diverse promulgations of contemporary Christendom; the great ecumenical creeds of the past, on the other hand, arose through a determination to champion the scripturally revealed doctrines over against heretical deviations. In this latter case, it was the church's fidelity to the truth of the Holy Scriptures that marked it off from the world; in the former, it is no longer biblical theology but the church's participation in a gigantic ecclesiastical movement that marks it off from the world.

It is no accident of twentieth-century Christianity, therefore, that the ecumenical movement as an ecclesiastical phenomenon has been paralleled by serious theological turbulence. For the third time in our century, Continental Protestantism has tumbled into a morass of doctrinal uncertainty. Sad to say, this theological confusion has been sheltered and even promoted by an ecumenical Christianity which prizes tolerance above truth and union above unction.

Consequently we find a new species of churchman, the ecumenist, who prefers to proclaim the unfulfilled opportunities of ecumenical cooperation above the wonderful works of God. Although sure that the divisions of Christendom constitute the main obstacle to the church's witness to the world, he is nonetheless unsure of the central features of Christ's victory over the world, the flesh, and the devil.

Ecumenical Christianity is, in fact, unclear as to its enemy. Sometimes the foe is identified with competitive ecclesiastical movements or with critics of ecumenical structures. Sometimes the world church's enemy is identified with social evils. Further, the prevalent tendency to discount the reality of Satan leads to a misjudgment of the depth of iniquity, and discourages any admission by ecclesiastical gigantism that institutional concentration of power encourages religious corruption. The New Testament offers a somber and sober lesson in church history. It was through the concerted action of religious and political leaders who misjudged the enmity of Satan that the devil achieved his major triumph. To safeguard the vested interests of the entrenched ecclesiastical hierarchy, they soon faced decisions that led to their rejection and destruction of Jesus Christ himself. A theology unsure of its enemy soon tends to misgauge its friends as well as its foes. The early Christians knew that God's decisive blow against the world's sin and unbelief had been struck by the saving events of the life and work of Christ. They accordingly never allowed the world to rationalize its unbelief on the ground that Christians were few in number and sometimes divided at that. To the Corinthians the apostle Paul wrote that there were "not many" wise, mighty, noble (he might have added, for that matter, *not many believers*), and while he rebuked their divisions, he nonetheless proclaimed "Christ and him crucified" as the openly manifested salvation of God. If

409

the Christian community is to speak decisively to men of other faiths and traditions, it can hope to succeed in the apostolic sense only by keeping the great redemptive deeds of God—and not the church—at the center.

IV

The circle of Christian fellowship has always been broken. Moreover, it always will be broken until the church is reunited with her returning Savior to judge the world and to bless the church. There is no basis in this, however, for accepting the present divisions as ideal. But the Christian community is called both to repentance and to profound humility by the ambiguities of Christian history.

The ranks have always been broken. Among the Twelve was Judas, a disciple of discord, a lackey for the religious hierarchy, and a suicide in the very inner circle of Jesus' chosen companions. What an interfaith tragedy—Judas the suicide, Jesus the crucified, Saul of the Sanhedrin breathing slaughter against the saints and the Christian believers who in turn lowered Paul the convert through a window in Damascus to spare him religious reprisal. The frontiers were fluid, the ranks were broken. Barnabas and Mark broke with Paul; Demetrius left him, and the great apostle spent days, weeks, months, and years in the Mamertine prison. The ranks were broken.

Yet apostolic Christianity had sufficient reserves of power to challenge the world of its day. How did this woeful minority of believers—uninvited by the prideful Gentiles, resisted by the unbelieving Jews—overturn the speculative traditions of their time, burst the seams of the inherited religious tradition, and become a symbol of holiness and hope to a generation gripped by the power of sin and the fear of death? Surely they were outnumbered and, by modern criteria, unorganized and disorganized as well. To the very few wise and wealthy and mighty in their midst they must have seemed ignorant and poor and impotent indeed. What was their secret, whose grand result—as historian W. E. H. Lecky described it in the *History of European Morals*—was that "the greatest religious change in the history of mankind" took place "under the eyes of a brilliant galaxy of philosophers and historians" who disregarded "as simply contemptible an agency which all men must now admit to have been . . . the most powerful moral lever that has ever been applied to the affairs of men"? We need to discover that secret, for the ranks are still broken, and the time for redemption is fast slipping away. The ranks, in fact, are badly broken. Who dares not to be concerned, uneasy, heavyhearted? Who should not hope for, pray for, work for better days for the church of Christ? Who can any longer be unmoved by our Lord's high priestly prayer for unity among his disciples?

Not only have we not achieved that for which the Lord of the church prayed, but we have also lost much that the first disciples of our Lord assuredly possessed. While the early Christians were not one in outward institutional organization, they were notable for their unity in faith and doctrine, united in their submission to the vitalizing lordship of Jesus Christ, and one in mission. The ascended Christ bequeathed them apostles, prophets, evangelists, pastors, and teachers for their full maturity including "the unity of the faith." So faithfully and persuasively did they preach to Jew and Greek alike the saving grace of God in Christ that the God of Abraham, Isaac, and Jacob was glorified as the God and Father of Jesus Christ, and the world wisdom of Greece and Rome yielded before the divine revelation of the Judeo-Christian Scriptures.

Today the ranks are broken at a time when industrial technology has shaped materialistic idols for our generation; when the achievements of science fill men's vision with secular hopes; when the communist terror has unleashed a tide of atheistic naturalism upon mankind; when pagan religions once withstood by evangelical missionaries are launching counter-missionary crusades from Orient to Occident. Our ranks are broken at a time when evolutionary philosophies debunk human dignity and destiny and speak in terms of natural processes alone; when the oncoming generation is promised scientific immunity from the physical consequences of the sins of sex; when international hostilities are so taut, and nuclear missiles so powerful, that the time between the Moscow-Washington hot line and global holocaust must be measured in mere minutes and seconds.

That is not all. The ranks are broken at a time when the best educated generation in human history is ignorant of the Word of God; when physicists and mathematicians and chemists who know the inner secrets of nature are strangers to God's self-revelation; when historians and philosophers who survey the spirits of this age discount the Holy Spirit that once lifted the Western world from the mire of moral corruption; when a teen-age generation that speaks uninhibitedly of the life of sex seems wholly unaware that God's kingdom is barred to all but the twice-born.

The ranks are broken at a time when so much could count to the glory of God. The redemption that is in Christ Jesus could bring incomparable healing to sin-burdened multitudes. The commandments of God could remind nations of those changeless criteria by which they will be divinely judged, and give men everywhere a moral standard by which to judge themselves. Man's reconciliation to God could hold great significance for his search for peace among the nations, and his search for significance in his work. And man's reconciliation to God could hold the greatest significance in his search for meaning in life.

411

May the Head of the church soon visit us with healing for the body. To be authentic, let the church draw its true life from the incarnate and risen Christ. To be truly united, let those who bear Christ's name first examine their union with Jesus Christ in whose death and resurrection God has already vanquished sin and unbelief in our world.

Until Jesus Christ returns in judgment and blessing, our Christian duty is to evangelize a lost generation. Everywhere let men of one faith and doctrine unite in spiritual love and passion to fulfill the Savior's great commission and last command. In our scientific age we can still bring to visibility a prospect of peace and power and progress beyond man's present attainment, and in which men of every race and land can share.

Nobody can guarantee spiritual awakening; the world does not deserve it, and even men of faith cannot command it. But the God of grace has published the conditions, and these still remain in force. God still offers what we do not merit—the forgiveness of our sins and new life and joy. Christ remains the bright hope of our generation; we who bear his name are called to make this hope the touchpoint of our witness to the world.

16

THE THRUST OF THE RADICAL RIGHT
Dale G. Leathers

The current reactionary pulpit is preoccupied with an
issue which gives reactionary rhetoric its unique, if not
bizarre, quality. To reactionaries the most important issue
of the day is whether man is innately bad, vindictive, and
untrustworthy, or intrinsically good, compassionate, and
trustworthy. Reactionaries believe that man's capacity to
sin and for sin is inborn and compulsive. While the reactionary pulpit is convinced that men are very vindictive
and highly untrustworthy, the liberal pulpit makes some
strikingly different assumptions about human nature. The
liberals assume that the Christian must work to convert
his nobler impulses into humanitarian channels, rather
than acting defensively in an attempt to curb his destructive and evil tendencies. J. Irwin Miller, past president,
National Council of Churches of Christ in the USA,
stresses man's mandate to do good when he says that
"Jesus in his own life offered us the example of this
prophetic concept of religion. When he came upon suffering, he stopped to relieve it. When he came upon
injustice, he moved to correct it. When he encountered
wickedness, he spoke out to condemn it." Miller's accompanying address seeks to build a strong biblical
basis for social action. The Rev. W. S. McBirnie, pastor

413

of the United Community Church of Glendale, California, on the other hand, articulates the reactionaries' dissenting position when he asserts that man is not responsible for adjusting social inequities; man must not divert his energies from the sizable task of saving himself.

The assumption that man must necessarily detach himself from social problems and collective solutions for those problems is not what makes the reactionaries' position unusual. Many conservatives of the William Buckley-Russel Kirk mold start with a basic assumption which is very similar. The reactionaries, in contrast to the conservatives, circumscribe this assumption with a series of beliefs about the nature of reality which is anathema to the Buckley conservative. To fully understand how the reactionaries' distinctive ideological position grows beyond this premise one must 1) isolate the basic value propositions which color the reactionary rhetoric; 2) explain the current strategy being employed to make previously unsalable values salable; 3) identify the epistemological problem which that strategy creates.

The reactionary pulpit is a fundamentalist pulpit. Above all others, the value which dominates fundamentalist rhetoric is the value of mistrust. The fundamentalist value of mistrust assumes two forms—the fundamentalist God distrusts man and the fundamentalist distrusts his fellow man. Fundamentalists subscribe to a set of values which minimize, indeed deny, the possibility that man may be the master of his destiny on earth. Dominant among fundamentalist values are commitments to a suspicious God who rightfully distrusts untrustworthy man and punishes man in a literal hell for his lack of trustworthiness. These value commitments emphasize the unknowable nature of an omnipotent God; at the same time they emphasize the unknowing nature of impotent man. Men are born evil and untrustworthy. All groups are conspiratorial because they inevitably are formed by evil men; all men are innately bad men.

Since these values stress the untrustworthy, even loathsome, nature of mankind, the reactionary pulpit concludes that all energies should be directed toward glorifying God, not man. In fact reactionaries argue that man should not be helped through governmental action because he is not worthy of such help. Irving E. Howard enunciates the reactionary position by writing in *The Christian Alternative to Socialism* that "present day Americans are committing idolatry by seeking security and equality through government action. They have put the State in the place of God and, consequently, have set in motion a process which will eventually destroy the fabric of society." The touchstone of reactionary theology is an inversion, if not an outright contradiction of the justifying premise of the Social Gospel: man must not be a keeper of his own brother, because each man best promotes the general interest by promoting his own. Reactionary theology asserts that 1) materialistic and social inequities are sanctioned by God; 2) attempts to equalize opportunity and assure minimum standards of living constitute "thievery" in contravention of "God's law"; and 3) complete governmental disregard for individual needs is true humanitarianism, to cater to the needs of the underprivileged is to glorify man at the expense of God. Elaborated in such a fashion these fundamentalist values provide a rationalization for praising the rich and damning the poor and any efforts to help the poor.

For almost three decades before 1960, fundamentalist values and the political positions for which these values provided sanction were quite unsalable. Fundamentalist values continued to lose popularity from 1930 to 1960, if the success of the values of liberalism is any indication. Specifically since the advent of the New Deal, the fundamentalist has been forced to concede that 1) the Social Gospel is no longer a fanciful theory but an institutional reality in the United States; 2) the welfare state has not collapsed of its own inertia; 3) the vast majority of Americans participating in religious and political life continue to approve both liberal religion and liberal government. The combined weight of these factors supports the conclusion that from 1933 to 1960, the reactionaries championed political positions that simply were not salable.

By 1960, then, the reactionary cause was approaching desperation. For thirty years reactionaries had protested in vain against a liberalism that seemed to be gaining strength at an accelerated rate. How could the reactionary persuader give the fundamentalist hope that his values might be seen as important, once again? The answer came with the development of the anti-Communist issue. The reactionaries have discovered a respectable way to cultivate their values and make them acceptable, to legitimize these values. A remarkable shift in the fortunes of fundamentalism becomes apparent since 1960, as the reactionaries begin to accentuate the threat of Communist subversion inside the United States.

Hargis' accompanying speech attacking the National Council of Churches illustrates how the reactionary pulpit builds its case against the Communist around the value of mistrust. Reactionaries are convinced that the citizens of the United States cannot gain knowledge empirically because the Communists control every major type of institutionalized communication in the United States today. They assert that honest communication would merely subvert the purposes and undermine the actions of the Communist conspirators. In short, for the Communists to prosper they must deceive. Reactionary ministers charge that the Communists are perpetrating an evil plan upon the American people. The Communists have gained virtual control of three sources of institutionalized communication in America—the press, the politician, and the clergyman. The Communist's potential to deceive, therefore, is beyond comprehension.

While the Hargis speech concentrates on the alleged infiltration of liberal churches by Communists, Hargis is more concerned about the sinful alliance between the liberal administrations of Roosevelt, Truman, Kennedy, and Johnson. The copy of the McIntire radio broadcast that follows suggests the reactionaries' growing concern with secular affairs; the UN and UNESCO have long been favorite targets of the reactionary pulpit. The point to keep in mind when reading the Hargis speech and McIntire's radio broadcast is that these preachers have made fundamentalist values respectable by couching their appeals in the vernacular of a Communist threat to basic governmental institutions.

In making his fundamentalist values salable to a larger audience the reactionary preacher creates a burden of exceedingly large proportions. While he is legitimizing his values for one audience, the reactionary is forced to reject the quest for empirical verification. The reactionaries' major problem becomes epistemological in the sense that he is forced to use nonempirical means to acquire knowledge. In rejecting appearances as a major source of knowledge the reactionary alienates the numerous advocates of a powerful philosophical force of this age—empiricism.

The reactionaries' rejection of empirical investigation as the primary means of knowing entails a major assumption. To believe is to know. This assumption is a direct reflection of their two most basic value orientations; the conviction that God's master plan for the day-to-day events in our lives is known only by belief and that, since man is evil and deceitful by nature, one must always be suspicious of appearances. One must not be guided by one's experience because such experience is usually deceiving in a deceitful world.

This epistemological bias circumscribes reactionary rhetoric. The bias is pervasive because of its impact on reactionary values. This bias dictates that reactionary values be nonexperiential. Stressing the value of mistrust does not constitute bias in itself. The insulation of reactionary values from the test of experience is what makes for bias. Values are prejudicial when they are prejudged.

Such bias is, of course, not confined to reactionary rhetoric. Bias is of overriding importance in reactionary rhetoric, because one belief is based on another belief rather than on facts. Since the reactionary views all forms of contemporary communication as untrustworthy, he must deny any factual basis for his beliefs. For this reason the reactionary is unwilling to embrace even the theologically respectable position that one should explain as much as possible by fact before relying on belief. With his antiempirical stance and his call to raze America's institutional framework, the reactionary minister accentuates the cleavage between himself and the conservative.

In conclusion, the real burden of the reactionaries'

fundamentalist values is that it forces the reactionary preacher to face an epistemological dilemma. The reactionary is faced with two alternatives which are both highly undesirable: 1) he can maintain, as he does, that appearances are so uniformly deceiving that anti-Communists cannot gather the necessary facts on which to base wise decisions; or 2) he can maintain that appearances are so uniformly reliable to attract the larger "uncommitted" audience, but if he does do so he must disown the very value orientations from which his persuasion springs. In opting for the first alternative in an age that attaches particular importance to facts the reactionary persuader is forced to bear an extraordinarily heavy burden.

J. Irwin Miller

J. Irwin Miller, an industrialist and churchman from Columbus, Indiana, was the first layman elected president of
the National Council of Churches. A leading layman of the
Disciples of Christ, Mr. Miller has served as board chairman
of the Cummins Engine Company and the Irwin Bank and
Trust Company, both of Columbus, and the Union Starch
and Refining Company of Granite City, Illinois. Mr. Miller
has served the Council since its formation in 1950, when
he represented his denomination as an alternate delegate at
the Council's Constituting Convention.

The Theological Basis for Social Action*

Men often reveal themselves in curious ways, and the wording of the subject
which I have been assigned gives an insight into the minds of American
Protestants of our day. "Social action" was the great phrase of the twenties
and thirties. Prosperity had disappeared "around the corner." The need for
reform was so visible that "social action" required no justification, and
liberal American Protestants wrote it across their banner. But today is another day. We live, prosperous and well-fed, in a world that may at any
minute be ended for us. There seems to be less point in correcting the evils
of our own society. We are more concerned with hanging on to what we
have. We wonder what is to become of us, and we are startled by our new
knowledge of the great creation which we inhabit into a new wonder about
the nature of God and his purposes. "Theology" is the word of these
years. . . .

I wish that there were some phrase better than "social action" around
which to build our discussion. Because of its past, it now makes its appeal
to our emotions, rather than to our intelligence. "Social action" is something
people are either "for" or "against," and, as a term, it is no more exactly
descriptive than "Slave Labor Act" or "Right-to-Work Law." Since, however,
it would not be proper to discuss any term without trying to come to some
reasonable definition of it, I think we should at the beginning make an
effort to determine in what sense we shall deal with our term "social action"
in this paper.

* (New York: National Council of Churches, 1958). An address, printed in pamphlet
form, delivered October 19, 1958, at the Convention of Christian Churches (Disciples of
Christ), St. Louis, Missouri.

I will assume that the first word, "social," refers to the society of which each of us as individuals is a part, and I will further assume that we will be discussing primarily the relations of the individual with that society, which means his relations with other individuals and with other groups of men. Finally, since each of us individually is also a member of many groups, and, as such, has relations and dealings both with individuals and groups, I assume we will also consider the relations of groups of men both with individuals and with other groups of other men.

Now we come to the second word, "action." What kind of action have we in mind? I think it is true that, if by "social action" we referred only to the normal actions and interactions that take place daily in our society between individuals and groups of men, then this term would not possess for us its present high emotional content. It is no surprise therefore to any of us to learn that the word "action" in this term "social action" has taken on a fairly specific meaning for us today and is generally understood to signify action to change certain of man's individual social relationships, customs, acts, methods, or practices. Even here, though, were these changes recommended only in the interest of efficiency and of technical or administrative improvement, the term would not generate any great head of emotional steam. Instead, we have come to understand our word to mean action to change *immoral or bad* existing social relationships, customs, or acts into different relationships, customs, or acts, which those urging the action assert are *moral and good.* . . .

Why then should . . . [the] church even think of plunging into a situation like "social action," where its entrance will produce only more tension, more hostility, and more division?

We Disciples have long taken pride in considering ourselves people of "The Book," and, before we form a conviction based on our own desires only, we like to see what guidance we may receive from the Bible. Let us follow now this ancient tradition, and let us begin by examining the Old Testament.

This earlier portion of our Bible contains many things. There is a good deal of history, and the history here given shows to us a primitive race, whose great glory it is to have worked out an understanding of God and a moral code far in advance of any the world had known. The old Testament also consists of books of the law, which define religious institutions and practices, and which crystallize the moral code of the Jews in an attempt to preserve the great gains of their past. The Old Testament also consists of ecstatic praise of God, as in the Psalms, and, finally, it consists of the writings of the prophets. At the risk of over-simplification, and only for the purpose of this discussion, I would like to discuss the Old Testament as if it consisted, in Jesus's phrase, of "the law and the prophets," and see what we can learn from this.

The books of the law are characterized by very carefully detailed instructions. For example "if (a man's) offering to the Lord is a burnt offering of birds, then he shall bring his offering of turtledoves or of young pigeons. And the priest shall bring it to the altar and wring off its head, and burn it on the altar; and its blood shall be drained out on the side of the altar; and he shall take away its crop with the feathers, and cast it beside the altar on the east side, in the place for ashes; he shall tear it by its wings, but shall not divide it asunder."

Or, "All winged insects that go upon all fours are an abomination to you. Yet among the winged insects that go on all fours, you may eat those which have legs above their feet, with which to leap on earth. Of them you may eat: the locust according to its kind, the bald locust according to its kind, the cricket according to its kind, and the grasshopper according to its kind."

Or, "When you reap the harvest of your land, you shall not reap your field to its very border. . . . You shall not oppress your neighbor nor rob him. . . . you shall not be partial to the poor or defer to the great. . . . You shall not take vengeance or bear any grudge against the sons of your own people, but you shall love your neighbor as yourself. . . ."

This is the manner in which the books of the law are written, and their contribution to mankind is very great. The books of the law taught the ancient Jews how to be sensible of obligation to God, how to live healthfully, and how to avoid offense to other members of their society.

If we now move from the law to the prophets, our first impression is one of surprise, for the prophets appear to be engaged in the carrying out of an attack of great violence against the whole concept of the law. Consider the elaborate instructions for the performance of sacrifices which we have just read, and then proceed to the opening chapter of Isaiah: "What to me is the multitude of your sacrifice? says the Lord; I have had enough of burnt offerings of rams and the fat of fed beasts. . . . When you come to appear before me, who requires of you this trampling of my courts? . . . I cannot endure iniquity and solemn assembly." This is, on its surface, a repudiation of the whole solemn content of the law. What had this prophet in mind? I think the key may very well lie in the last sentence I have quoted: "I cannot endure iniquity and solemn assembly," which is to say, "I cannot endure wickedness and worship."

Religious forms and rites and services of worship have been created and used by men since long before the time of history, and no people has been more concerned with them than the Jews, but the Jews from their very early

421

times began to make use of religious form in a new and special way. Unlike the Egyptians and the Greeks, the religious observances of the Jews were not so much designed to propitiate a god whom they feared, as they were to teach and instruct men about the nature of God, about right conduct and habits, about righteous living. The great moral laws are not easy to make clear, and a major purpose of the forms of religion has been to give visible expression to invisible, abstract ideas. Human beings have a deep need for such expressions, and instinctively they practise all sorts of ceremonies every day. We kiss in an attempt to express physically the invisible reality of love and affection; we shake hands in an attempt to express visibly the invisible idea of friendship; and the ancient Jews sacrificed to express visibly the invisible idea of gratitude and debt to God. Thus a physical act is performed to make clear an invisible, spiritual idea and principle.

The substance of religion is the spiritual idea and the moral principle. One of the means to religion is religious form, which assists men to understand the substance, but form and substance become confused and men begin very easily to forget the difficult ideas and the demanding principles and to content themselves with the forms alone. They mistake the form for the substance, and how easy it is to comfort oneself with the notion that one is a good, religious man simply because he goes to church regularly, contributes liberally, and participates enthusiastically in the ceremonies of the church.

It was against this perversion of religion, this mistaking of form for substance, which permitted men to live in wickedness, to violate the Law of God in their lives, and yet become known to themselves and their societies as religious men, that the prophets preached. And their opposition was nothing reasoned, loving, or tolerant. It was an outraged, violent, excessive thing. Isaiah says: "Incense, and Sabbath, and the keeping of feast days are an abomination to God. When you make many prayers, I will not hear. Put away the evil of your doings, relieve the oppressed, judge for the fatherless, plead for the widow. I am full of burnt offerings. Wash you . . . make you clean. What mean you that you grind the faces of the poor, sayeth the Lord God."

Hosea says, "I desire mercy and not sacrifice."

Micah says this about the religious people of his day: "They covet fields, and seize them; and houses, and take them away; they oppress a man and his house. . . . The rulers give judgment for a bribe; the priests teach for hire; its prophets divine for money. . . . With what shall I come before the Lord? . . . Shall I come before Him with burnt offerings, with calves a year old? Will the Lord be pleased with thousands of rams? . . . Shall I give my firstborn for my transgression, the fruit of my body for the sin of my soul? He

422

has showed you, O man, what is good; and what does the Lord require of you but to do justice, and to love kindness, and to walk humbly with your God? . . .

It is quite clear why the prophets teach this: For the man who embraces the form of religion, mistaking it for the substance, finds in his religion the sweet justification for his selfish and greedy way of life. In another society, the Latin poet Lucretius had also seen such conditions and remarked, "How great are the evils to which religion can persuade men."

What do you imagine was the attitude of the great rulers, priests, merchants, and pillars of the church of that time to the prophets' teaching? Do you suppose they considered these prophets harmless old men, who could do little damage urging people to live better lives, or do you imagine that they may have considered them the most dangerous of people, who, for the safety of all and the preservation of society, must be silenced and exterminated? The prophets disturbed their societies. They criticized unrighteous behavior by religious people, and they identified true religion with righteous living.

Let us now leave the Old Testament, and, moving to the New Testament, ask ourselves to what judgment on this subject our Lord came and what the Gospels and the Epistles have to say about it. Let us begin by examining to see how Jesus commenced his own ministry and in what way he identified himself with the religion of his people.

His formal ministry began after his return from the wilderness and his wrestling with the temptations which confronted him there. Luke tells us, "Jesus returned in the power of the Spirit into Galilee, . . . and he came to Nazareth where he had been brought up; and he went to the synagogue, as his custom was, on the sabbath day. And he stood up to read; and there was given to him the book of the prophet Isaiah. He opened the book and found the place where it was written, 'The Spirit of the Lord is upon me, because he has anointed me to preach good news to the poor. He has sent me to proclaim release to the captives and recovering of sight to the blind, to set at liberty those who are oppressed, to proclaim the acceptable year of the Lord.' And he closed the book, and gave it back to the attendant, and sat down; and the eyes of all in the synagogue were fixed on him. And he began to say to them, 'Today this scripture has been fulfilled in your hearing.' "
At the very start of his ministry, therefore, Jesus identified himself with the prophets and with their overwhelming concern for the social evils of their days, and it was as a prophet, and as the successor to the prophets, that the people of his time first received and first understood him. When Jesus asked the question, "Who do men say that I am?" the disciples answered,

"Some say John the Baptist, others Elijah, and others Jeremiah or one of the prophets."

It could, of course, be true that Jesus felt himself in harmony with part of the tradition of the prophets, and at the same time not in agreement with their whole and very radical notions about the place and merit of form and substance in religion. Let us pursue our investigation further.

We are well acquainted with the Pharisees, the priests, and the Levites of this time. These were the people who took the greatest interest in religion. They corresponded to the ministers, to those in full-time Christian service, and to the leading laymen of our own day, and we know that Jesus was as critical of these persons as the prophets before him had been of the similar groups, not at all because of their dedication to religion, but because of their misunderstanding of the purpose and nature of religion. He makes this very clear when he says, "The scribes and the Pharisees sit on Moses' seat; so practise and observe whatever they tell you, but not what they do; for they preach, but do not practise. . . . They do all their deeds to be seen by men; for they make their phylacteries broad and their fringes long. . . . Woe to you, scribes and Pharisees, . . . you shut the kingdom of heaven against men; for you neither go enter yourselves, nor allow those who would enter to go in. . . . You tithe mint and dill and cummin, and have neglected the weightier matters of the law, justice and mercy and faith; these you ought to have done without neglecting the others." The last sentence is one of the keys to our understanding of Jesus on this point. Tithing, fasting, religious form and observance are not, Jesus tells us, to be neglected. On these points, he says, "Practise and observe whatever they tell you . . ." but such matters are not the real substance of the law. The "weightier matters" are always to be defined in terms of human motives and actions. The "weightier matters" of the law are justice, and mercy, and faith— qualities which cannot be expressed, except in right responses, and right actions in difficult and challenging social situations. Jesus in his own life offered us the example of this prophetic concept of religion. When he came upon suffering, he stopped to relieve it. When he came upon injustice, he moved to correct it. When he encountered wickedness, he spoke out to condemn it.

The story of the good Samaritan makes unmistakably clear his thoughts on this subject. While the tale itself is familiar, its occasion is apt to be forgotten, and it is necessary to remember at least two things, if we are to understand the story: first, that Jesus told it in answer to the question, "What should I do to inherit eternal life?"; and, second, that he selected for it a most peculiar cast of characters. Jesus chose a priest and a Levite for the two persons who passed by the wounded man, two types that would instantly appeal to those to whom he was talking as the most theologically correct persons with whom his hearers would be acquainted; and, as the person who befriended and showed himself neighbor to the wounded man, Jesus chose the Samaritan. Now to Jesus's Jewish hearers, the Samaritan was a religious heretic, a member of their own race, but a man who was theologically so wrong that Jews were forbidden to intermarry with his kind, and Jesus's deliberate implication that the heretic—the man of the wrong faith—might possess the qualifications for eternal life over an orthodox person, over men of the true faith, makes very sharply the ancient point of the prophets, that the substance of religion—the weightier matters of the law— are to be found in the possession, the understanding, and the instinctive practice in daily life of justice, mercy, and faith. The law and the prophets, Jesus is saying, consist first of all not in what man professes about his religion, but in how he is moved to act. Remember these famous words: "So whatever you wish that men would do to you, do so to them; for this is the law and the prophets." The law and the prophets are interpreted in terms of men's actions.

For one final example, consider our Lord's description of the Last Judgment. "Then the King will say to those at his right hand, 'Come, O blessed of my Father, inherit the kingdom prepared for you from the foundation of the world; for I was hungry, and you gave me food, I was thirsty and you gave me drink, I was a stranger and you welcomed me, I was naked and you clothed me, I was sick and you visited me, I was in prison and you came to me.' Then the righteous will answer him, 'Lord, when did we see thee hungry and feed thee, or thirsty and give thee drink? And when did we see thee a stranger and welcome thee, or naked and clothe thee? And when did we see thee sick or in prison and visit thee?' And the King will answer them, 'Truly I say to you, as you did it to one of the least of these my brethren, you did it to me.'"

The Last Judgment, the determination of the righteous, the Lord says, is to be made on the basis of their acts in their daily lives, by their "social actions." "By their fruits, ye shall know them." In the passage which we have just read, Jesus identifies the persons placed at his right hand as "the righteous." Such persons Jesus feels exist in each society. His attitude and concern for them is made clear in his answer to the Pharisees: "Those who are well have no need of a physician, but those who are sick. Go and learn what this means, 'I desire mercy and not sacrifice.' For I came not to call the righteous, but sinners."

Nor is this distinction absent from the writings of Paul and the other authors of the New Testament. Paul defines the Last Judgment in terms like those of Jesus, "By your hard and impenitent heart you are storing up wrath for yourself on the day of wrath when God's righteous judgment will be revealed. For he will render to every man according to his works: to those who by patience in well-doing seek for glory and honor and immortality, he will give eternal life; but for those who are factious and do not obey the truth, but obey wickedness, there will be wrath and fury. There will be tribulation and distress for every human being who does evil, the Jew first and also the Greek, but glory and honor and peace for every one who does good, the Jew first and also the Greek, for God shows no partiality. . . . It is not the hearers of the law who are righteous before God, but the doers of the law who will be justified. When Gentiles who have not the law do by nature what the law requires, they are a law to themselves, even though they do not have the law. They show that what the law requires is written on their hearts, while their conscience also bears witness and their conflicting thoughts accuse or perhaps excuse them on that day when, according to my gospel, God judges the secrets of men by Christ Jesus." In Galatians, Paul sums up this matter dramatically when he says: "The whole law is fulfilled in one word, 'You shall love your neighbor as yourself.'"

By now you have had enough quoting from me, and the thought has undoubtedly occurred to you that, when a person begins to pick and choose, he can appear to prove practically anything by the Bible. There are, of course, many other important portions of the Old and New Testaments which give no expression to this particular concern, and we Disciples are nervously aware that at times we have been tempted to build massive doctrine out of isolated verses. It is possible to use the Scriptures like a bag of golf clubs, the player first deciding what shot he wants to play, then searching his bag for the appropriate club. But the Scriptures are no golf set, no loose anthology of unrelated verses. The Scriptures encompass a growing revelation of the nature and purpose of God for the people of this world, and, when portions of it are excerpted for discussions of this sort, it is the responsibility of the person choosing the passages to make certain that he chooses in such a way as to represent fairly the spirit of the whole. It is for this reason that I have quoted at such length and from so many passages of Scripture.

I think it is fair to conclude that throughout the Bible there is an intense concern with the way men act in their daily lives, with the way groups of men act in their daily lives, and with the way whole classes of men act in their daily lives. This concern when it becomes angry, as it often does, has not been directed at the minor peccadillos of the ignorant and unfortunate individuals, groups, and segments of society, but rather at the unrighteous acts and unrighteous ways of life of the powerful, ruling, influential individuals and groups of societies.

I think we have found further that theological correctness and exact ritual observance are presented primarily as aides to righteousness, but that righteousness itself is to be understood as the heart of religion and as indissolubly connected with salvation and the Last Judgment. Finally, we have seen in both the Old and New Testaments that, when men have confused the form of religion with the substance, they have called down on themselves not so much the admonishment, but the wrath, of God's spokesmen, as we have seen them in the Scriptures. In brief, then, our Lord, the prophets before him, and the apostles after him, provide us with very emphatic evidence of their urgent concern with the behavior of men and women in their daily lives. When these are unfortunate or ignorant men and women, unrighteous behavior is not condoned, but it is criticized with compassion—as with the publicans and the woman taken in adultery. When the individuals are powerful, influential, and controlling in society, unrighteous behavior is condemned with passion and with anger—as with the Pharisees, the rich and the rulers.

Now let us consider the implications of this attitude. Was the anger of the prophets and the anger of Jesus directed at persons merely in relation to their economic status? I think not. Jesus said of those who crucified him, "Forgive them, for they know not what they do," but he was angry with the Pharisees and condemned them—because they knew better. By our standards their behavior wasn't too bad. I doubt if the Pharisees, whom Jesus condemned so strongly, had been committing acts which would be punishable today in a court of law; and I am sure that publicans and the woman taken in adultery would have been subject to legal prosecution today. Yet these latter he forgave, and the Pharisees he condemned—because they knew better.

Jesus nearly always seemed to assume that the people to whom he was talking knew what righteous behavior was. When they asked him questions, he, like Socrates before him, usually elected to reply with a series of questions designed to make his questioner answer his own question. Consider the typical treatment of the lawyer in Luke. He asked Jesus, "What shall I do to inherit eternal life?" Wouldn't it have been only simple charity on Jesus's part to give this young man a direct and forthright answer? But great teachers do not do this, and our Lord replied only with a question, "What is written in the law?" The lawyer answered Jesus correctly, showing that he already possessed this knowledge, but he pursued Jesus with another question, "And who is my neighbor?" Again Jesus makes no direct reply, but merely tells the story about the good Samaritan, at the close of which he asks another question, "Which of these three proved neighbor to the man who fell among the robbers?" So at the last the lawyer has answered all parts of his own question, and Jesus has shown him that he knew the answer all the time. This is no isolated case. Consider Jesus's habit of using the paradox—the statement which on its face appears not to be so. For example, "The last shall be first," "He who would save his life must lose it," "Whosoever hath, to him shall be given, but whosoever hath not, from him shall be taken away even that which he hath," and the like. These statements run counter to people's instincts. Unless the persons to whom Jesus was speaking possessed a deeper and truer sense of righteousness than that by which they were habitually acting, which sense, when provoked, would cause them to recognize the truth which lies at the heart of the paradox, Jesus's sayings would merely have seemed incorrect or foolish to those who heard them. Jesus saw this problem which lies deep in every human being. As a child of God, he comes to know inside himself the way of righteousness. As a child of flesh, with freedom of choice, he is constantly pursuing the appearance rather than the reality, choosing the shadow for the substance, compromising with the right way of the Lord. In the words of Paul, "I do not understand my own actions. . . . I can will what is right, but I cannot do it, for I do not do the good I want, but the evil I do not want is what I do."

Doctor Johnson put all this into a sentence, and this sentence states a principal reason for "social action." He said, "Men need more often to be reminded than to be informed." It is not enough that men or groups of men know what they ought to do or how they ought to behave. No one of us ever acts as well as he knows how to act, and all of us tend to slip and to lower our standards, unless we are constantly called to task and reminded. This applies to you and me. It applies to families. It applies to communities. It applies to corporations, to unions, to schools and universities, to ministers, and to pressure groups, and it applies to governments and to nations. They need reminding, but who is there to do this thankless job? There are ministers of the gospel, but we say: "These fellows are removed from the political and business world. They don't understand its problems. They wouldn't know how to make practical suggestions. They would only confuse the whole matter." There is, of course, you, and there is me. But we don't know all the answers to all the difficult situations of the world, and besides, we are lone, unimportant voices, inaudible, without influence. What we would say would make no difference, and it might get us in trouble.

If numbers then are important to make a Christian voice of concern heard and effective in society, there are whole congregations, or whole communities, or, for instance, this convention, which could speak out in our society against unrighteousness and for more responsible acts and conduct in specific situations. But we say, "What right has anyone or any group to speak for a whole church, let alone for a whole brotherhood? No matter what you say, some members will be honestly and sincerely opposed. So you can't pretend you speak for them. And anyway, how can anyone ever speak for a whole group on any subject?" Thus it turns out that there isn't any one or any group who has either the knowledge or the unchallenged right to speak out with a Christian voice in criticism or in reminder of society's shortcomings.

This appears to leave us at an impasse, unless we reflect upon history. The reasons which appear to disqualify individuals and small and large groups from speaking out today have applied with equal justification to the individuals and groups of every age and time; yet some individuals and some groups did speak. Civilization does not naturally improve. Progress is not inexorable, and the race has often, for a time, gone backward. The evils, the shortcomings, and the wickedness of each age have flourished when its people have been complacent, or silent, or fearful; and in the ages when Christian individuals and Christian groups have been concerned, courageous, and vocal, society has been able to rid itself of many ancient evils and to reach new levels of justice, mercy, and brotherhood.

Our present age is in need of that clear and effective voice of Christian warning, concern, and proposal no less than any other. Certainly this voice is also the voice of fallible individuals and of groups of not wholly pure motives. Certainly this voice often urges answers that are based on misinformation, or upon misunderstandings, or even upon answers that are plain wrong, but, if the voice has a predominantly Christian content, and if it draws the eye, and the mind, and the conscience of society to its evils and to its shortcoming, then such voice is the best possession of any society. It is no less a treasure because it comes to us in earthen vessels.

And now a closing word—other Christians in other times have been challenged by conquerors, by tyrants, by persecution, and by evils present among them like slavery, degradation of men as in the eighteenth century prisons, or nineteenth century child labor. Some Christians have with courage spoken, made their voices heard, paid fearful prices in loss of family, friends, position. Others have paid with their lives. For many, the dramatic price has been easier to endure than the smaller cost of the friend who passes on the street with head averted. But each individual and each group which has spoken out from a Christian heart and Christian conscience has made an imperishable addition to the best force for good in any society, and has played a part in God's purpose for his children.

Our own age possesses its share of both subtle and spectacular evils. The children of the God who, according to the Scriptures, "shows no partiality" and "has made of one blood all nations of men for to dwell on the face of the earth" make distinctions which God does not make, denying to those of different races and colors rights and privileges which they reserve for themselves. Church men are to be found in positions of power in corporations whose dealings with customers, public, and employees are less than open, fair, and honest. Church men are to be found in positions of power in labor unions in which corruption, violence, and lawlessness are commonplace. Church men are to be found in governments—local, state, and national—which fail in the discharge of their sworn responsibilities. Church men are to be found in institutions of learning which compromise with their high calling. All these persons in places of power or influence who know the Law of Christ need reminding, and reminding after the fashion and pattern of our Lord and of the prophets before him.

It is clear then that we are called—both to act and to speak, called by the example of the ancient prophets, and by the example and the words of our Master. It is clear that our society needs a courageous and unmistakable Christian voice. By our response to this call and to this need, you and I will be judged. In the lifetime of this world, we will be judged by those generations to whom we hand on our society, according as it is either better or worse than the one we received, and, at the last time, we will be thus judged by the only wise judge, our Savior.

BILLY JAMES HARGIS

Billy James Hargis was born in 1925 to Laura Lucille and Jimmy Ersal Hargis in the small town of Texarkana, Texas. He grew up during the depression years in a God-fearing and hardworking family. While he finished public school in eleven rather than the customary twelve years, his improved performance during his final years of high school did not suffice to gain him admission when he applied to Texas Christian University. He now expresses satisfaction in being denied admission to the school. The liberal philosophy at the university undoubtedly would have corroded the rigid fundamentalism which has become a Hargis trademark.

As a substitute for Texas Christian he attended Ozark Bible College in Bentonville, Arkansas. Here, at this First Christian denominational school, he completed his study for the ministry in a year and a half and was ordained at the age of eighteen, on May 30, 1943. He subsequently was pastor of the First Christian Church at Sallisaw, Oklahoma, leaving there at age twenty to accept the pastorate at the First Christian Church, Granby, Missouri.

A pivotal point in Hargis' career seemed to come in Sapulpa, Oklahoma. He was visiting a local minister and expressed his personal concern that communist influences might be taking control of Christianity in this country. The fellow pastor's indifferent response—So what?—was an affront which shocked young Hargis to the core of his fundamentalist philosophy. He consequently persuaded his church to pay for a "religious" radio broadcast to warn of communism. The response was so favorable that in 1950, at twenty-five years of age, Hargis resigned his small-town pastorate and incorporated as a "religious, nonprofit-making body" called the Christian Echoes Ministry, Inc.—now popularly known as Christian Crusade. The success of Christian Crusade is conceded by all of Hargis' many foes.

In October, 1967, Hargis listed radio outlets in thirty states in addition to Mexico. He has completed an ultramodern building to house Christian Crusade in Tulsa, Oklahoma, and conducts an anti-communist summer school in Manitou Springs, Colorado. Plans are projected to start his own anti-communist seminary in Tulsa.

Although many of his books are ghostwritten by a complete staff that turns out everything from pamphlets attacking Martin Luther King, to record albums featuring Hargis, Hargis himself is nominal author of The Facts About Communism and Our Churches, Communist America: Must It Be, and The Real Extremists: The Far Left. Christian Cru-

431

sade publishes both a weekly and a monthly newspaper, the Weekly Crusader *and* Christian Crusade. *Despite the fact that Christian Crusade recently lost its tax-exempt status as a religious organization, Hargis shows every indication that he is gaining strength in his drive to become the dominant figure in the reactionary pulpit.*

Communism and the National Council of Churches*

Lenin, the high priest of Communism, whose tactics even today guide the International Communist Conspiracy's drive towards world enslavement, once said, "Any religious idea, any idea of a good God is an abominably nasty thing."

Earl Browder, former head of the Communist Party in America said, "We Communists do not distinguish between good and bad religions, because we think they are all bad."

Communist leaders from Karl Marx to the present day have considered the churches a major enemy and believed all worship of God must be stopped. Karl Marx referred to religion as the "opiate of the people." On July 24, 1954, the Soviet Communist Party newspaper *Pravda* called for a "scientific atheistic" propaganda onslaught against religion—"one of the most tenacious and harmful remains of capitalism."

In the effort to destroy religion in the Soviet Union the Communists nationalized all church property; deprived the church of all income except what they could collect from parishioners, forbade printing of religious literature, and took other measures which made existence of churches difficult. Atheism was taught in schools. Priests begged in the streets of Moscow and other cities. Orthodox churches in Soviet Russia dropped from 46,000 before the Communists took over, to 2,000 in 1948. It is reported that many churches operate underground in the Soviet Union today.

When the Communists found out that their attack on the churches was not very effective outside the big cities, they created what was known as "the living church movement." This was an attack from within the church based on the idea of interpreting the teachings of Christ and the Apostles in a way that would serve Communist purposes. For example, Christ chasing the money changers out of the temple would be interpreted as showing that Christ was an anticapitalist. The general idea was to move the church from

---

* *Communist America: Must It Be* (Tulsa, Oklahoma.: Christian Crusade Publications, 1960). This address has been presented in varying forms at Christian Crusade rallies across the country.

the spiritual to the material and make it an instrument of social strife. This attack from within was a supplement to the attack on churches and synagogues from without.

The Communist war on religion in America has been primarily through the infiltration and influence technique and has proceeded along the same lines as the living church movement in Russia. In the early stages of this plan the Communists decided that with only small forces available it would be necessary to concentrate agents in the seminaries and divinity schools. The obvious purpose of this was to make it possible for a small Communist minority to influence the ideology of future clergymen in the paths which serve the Communist cause. As in the Soviet Union, one major objective was to divert the emphasis of clerical thinking from the spiritual to the material and political. Emphasis was to be placed on immediate Communist social demands. These social demands were of such a nature as to weaken our system of government and prepare it for final conquest by Communism. The Communists have a big advantage in religious organizations because their forces are well organized and their non-Communist fellow members are completely unaware of the conspirator's presence.

Ex-Communist Ben Gitlow testified that the American Communist Party's activities on the religious front were discussed at meetings of the executive committee of the Communist International in Moscow in 1927. At these sessions, attention was called to the effective work which Dr. Harry F. Ward did for Communism in China in 1924.

In the early 1930's, the Communists instructed thousands of their members to rejoin their ancestral religious groups and to operate in cells designed to take control of churches for Communist purposes. They were instructed to utilize the age-old tradition of the sanctity of the churches as a cover for their dastardly deeds. In 1935, the seventh congress of the Communist International instructed members of Young Communist Leagues throughout the world to join all types of youth organizations including those conducted by religious bodies, and to "fight for influence" in these organizations. They were to carry out these ends by struggling for "a broad united front. . . ." Communist effectiveness is counted not by numbers but by influence and a few secret, well disguised Communists in key spots can influence many people and create havoc by controlling sensitive spots. Realizing this, Earl Browder, former head of the American Communist Party, told the comrades in 1931, "The churches are effective propaganda agencies for they reached a membership of 50 million persons in 1930." This appeared in an article in the Communist magazine entitled "The United Front, the Key to Our New Tactical Orientation."

Have the Communist plans for infiltrating and influencing churches succeeded? Earl Browder thinks so. In his book "*What Is Communism*," Browder wrote, ". . . the Communist Party, more than any other labor group, has been able to achieve successful united fronts with church groups on the most important issues of the day. This is not due to any compromise with religion as such on our part. In fact, by going among the religious masses, we are, for the first time, able to bring our anti-religious ideas to them." Who manipulated these united fronts? While he was still head of the Communist Party, Earl Browder spoke before the students of Union Theological Seminary and said, "You may be interested in knowing that we have preachers, preachers active in churches, who are members of the Communist Party." Herbert Philbrick, ex-FBI undercover agent in the Communist Party, also thinks the Communist plan has been successful. In an article in the *Christian Herald*, Philbrick wrote, "For nine long years I was a volunteer counterspy for the FBI, observing and participating in Communist strategy from the grass roots to high levels. I know that the Communist threat to your church is greater now than at any time in 20 years. I know how the Reds have planted secret Communists in pulpits, how they have infiltrated seminaries, how they use good and unsuspecting Protestants, Catholics, and Jews they have duped. . . ."

During May of 1953, Dr. Charles Lowry of All Saints Episcopal Church in Chevy Chase, Maryland, warned that Communists have operated in the nation's theological schools for 30 years. There is much evidence to show that the Communists have been highly successful in influencing clergymen through the seminaries. . . .

In discussing the Communist influence within the National Council of Churches, we are not discussing the millions of good American church people whose denominations belong to the National Council. We are discussing the leadership of this vast organization, the policies adopted by it, and the Communist effort to pervert it into a vast tool for the destruction of America.

The National Council of Churches came into existence officially in Cleveland, Ohio on November 29, 1950 when the old Federal Council of Churches reorganized and merged with several other interdenominational agencies. There were 358 clergymen who were voting delegates to the constituting convention of the National Council of Churches. In an article in our November 1957 *Christian Crusade* magazine, Dr. J. B. Matthews, the veteran anti-communist expert, reported that 123 out of these 358 had a record of affiliation with Communist projects and enterprises.

In order to get away from the taint of Red fellow travellers and the pro-communist activities of leaders in the old Federal Council of Churches, National Council leaders have tried to claim that there is no relationship between the Federal Council and the National Council of Churches. This is not true. . . .

The Federal Council's activities, policies and objectives were continued and expanded by the National Council of Churches.

Communist-front activities have been a popular pastime among leaders of the Federal and National Council of Churches for years. Some of the Federal and National Council presidents have been vigorous and dedicated Communist-fronters. For example, look at the record of the current president of the National Council of Churches. But first, let's ponder the real meaning of a Communist front.

Communist-front organizations are just as essential a part of the Communist conspiracy as the Communist Press, their training schools, and espionage cells. All are directed by a central high command and are coordinated to achieve the overthrow of our government by force and violence. It is a deliberate tactic of the Communists to conceal the complete integration of the Communist-front apparatus with the whole Communist conspiracy. Deceitfulness is the essence of the front organization. Communists strive to get the names of "reputable" people on the letterhead of their front groups to further the deception of Americans.

Testifying before the House Committee on Appropriations on December 9, 1953, FBI Director, J. Edgar Hoover, said that "one of the principal mediums for the attainment of the goal of the Communist Party is through Communist-front organizations." There is no question as to the importance of Communist fronts to the subversive purposes of this satanic conspiracy. Anyone who supports a Communist-front organization is supporting the Communist conspiracy and helping to enslave the American people. Some innocent joiners of fronts have seen their mistake, admitted it and spoken out against these fronts and the Communist Conspiracy which initiated them. However, we have not seen anything so frank coming from the front joiners in the National Council.

Now, let us look at just a portion of the Communist-front record of present president of the National Council of Churches, Dr. Edwin T. Dahlberg of St. Louis, Missouri. The official publication of the National Americanism Commission of the American Legion, issued from the American Legion offices in Indianapolis, January 15, 1958, called *The American Legion Firing Line*, revealed the Communist-front record of Dr. Dahlberg.

"During its Triennial General Assembly held at St. Louis, Missouri, in December 1957, Rev. Dr. Edwin Theodore Dahlberg was elected President of the interdenominational National Council of Churches of Christ in the U.S.A. for a three-year term. The National Council represents 34 constituent Protestant and Eastern Orthodox denominations which have a collective membership totalling over 37,000,000. As a co-operating organization of the World Council of Churches, the National Council's General Secretariat is located at 297 Fourth Avenue in New York City.

"Born in Fergus Falls, Minnesota, on December 27, 1892, Dahlberg was ordained in the Baptist ministry in 1918. He is currently the pastor of Delmar Baptist Church in St. Louis. Dahlberg was President of the Northern Baptist Convention from 1946 through 1948, and served for six years as a member of the Central Committee of the World Council of Churches. He was previously active in the National Council and has been reported to be a 'prominent Christian pacifist.' Speaking before the General Assembly's December 6th session on the subject of war prevention, Dahlberg declared that it was 'utter folly and futility' to spend 40 billion on a system of defense that 'never in the world can defend us.'

"In 1942, Dahlberg was listed as having favored Presidential clemency for the release of Communist Party leader Earl Browder, who was then serving a four-year term at Atlanta Federal Penitentiary for 'perjury committed in connection with his false passports.' Dahlberg's name had appeared on stationery of the Communist Citizens Committee to free Earl Browder. The following year, he signed an Open Letter to President Roosevelt urging that Harry Bridges' deportation order be 'set aside.' This petition was circularized by the subversive Citizen's Victory Committee for Harry Bridges.

"According to a Press Release dated October 31, 1947, Dahlberg was an 'original sponsor' of a statement endorsing publication and distribution of a report of seven clergymen who visited Yugoslavia during the summer of that same year. The report, *Religion in Yugoslavia*, stated there was 'fundamental freedom—freedom of worship—existing in (Communist) Yugoslavia.' Among the seven authors of this report were William Howard Melish, Guy Emery Shipler and Claude Williams. In 1949, Dahlberg was a member of a committee of five who organized a Conference for Peaceful Alternatives to the Atlantic Pact, which was held in Washington, D. C. This Conference 'resulted in the formation of a (Communist) front organization known as the Committee for Peaceful Alternatives to the Atlantic Pact.'

"In 1952, Dahlberg signed an Open Letter urging repeal of the McCarran Internal Security Act, which was distributed by the subversive National Committee to repeal the McCarran Act. His name was also listed on the Committee's 1957 letterhead as an 'initiator' of the organization. On page 2 of the August 1957 edition of *That Justice Shall Be Done*, an organ of the Communist National Committee to Secure Justice for Morton Sobell, Dahlberg was listed among others as having written a letter to President Eisenhower urging clemency for the convicted Soviet spy. Last July, he signed a telegram to the President urging the banning of all hydrogen-bomb tests by the United States Government. A 1957 letterhead of the Fellowship of Reconciliation, a national pacifist organization, listed Dahlberg as a member of its Advisory Council. This group has been recently agitating for the release of imprisoned Communist Party leaders convicted under the Smith Act."

In a magazine article during 1953, J. B. Matthews pointed out that the Communist Party of the United States had placed more and more reliance on the ranks of the Protestant clergy to provide the fellow travelers for front groups. He wrote that, "The largest single group supporting the Communist apparatus in the United States today is composed of Protestant clergymen. . . . Clergymen outnumber professors two to one in supporting the Communist-front apparatus of the Kremlin conspiracy. . . ."

Our present immigration law, the McCarran-Walter Immigration and Nationality Act, is the result of four years of the most intensive and objective study by a joint Senate and House Committee of Congress. This law was endorsed by the CIA, the Department of Justice, the Immigration and Naturalization Service and the Visa and Passport divisions of the State Department. It is considered to be the best immigration law in our nation's history, by informed, patriotic individuals and organizations. This immigration law is America's first line of defense, and naturally that makes it an A-1 priority target of the atheistic Communist Conspiracy.

From the time of its passage, over President Truman's veto, the McCarran-Walter Immigration Act has been attacked most viciously by the Communist Press and left-wing pro-communist sources. During the sixteenth National Convention of the Communist Party in New York on February 12, 1957, the conspirators adopted a resolution on this important matter. The secret text of this unanimously adopted resolution was obtained by Representative Francis Walter. Among other things, it said, "The 16th National Convention therefore instructs the incoming national committee to take all necessary steps to place this work on a high priority basis, including: 'A two-day working conference on a national basis . . . to prepare a plan of work . . . against . . . the McCarran-Walter Law.'" The Communist conspirators have created over 180 front organizations to work for the destruction of our immigration law, America's first line of defense.

Prominent church leaders and organizations in the United States were working to get the immigration flood gates into America opened before the McCarran-Walter Act was passed. In a meeting during March, 1942, the Federal Council of Churches (predecessor of the National Council of Churches) called for world-wide freedom of immigration. Since the passage of the McCarran-Walter Immigration Act in 1950, the National Council of Churches and some of the modernist church leaders in the United States have called for crippling amendments time and time again. They have propagandized Congress for passage of amendments which would open wide the gates of our first line of defense.

It is obvious that Congressional Committees investigating Communism would be a prime target of Communist Conspiracy smear attacks and they have been from the early days of such investigations. On January 5, 1959, Radio Moscow said, ". . . The officials of the notorious U. S. Congressional Un-American Activities Committee lost what reason they had left and have become an object of ridicule of the entire world . . . the committee members hate everything progressive and nurture a practically bestial hatred of the Soviet Union. . . ." This quote is typical of the attacks on the House Un-American Activities and other congressional committees investigating Communism by Moscow's fifth column in America, through the years of Communism's war against our land.

Apostate church leaders in the United States of America have not failed the Communist conspiracy in this important fight against our nation. They have attacked committees exposing America's deadly enemies with a blindness that is astounding. They have attacked consistently for years and years. Typical of these blind unfounded attacks against our patriotic anti-Communist Congressional Committees was the viciously unfair attack contained in the famous ". . . Letter to Presbyterians," which was unanimously adopted by the General Council of the General Assembly of the Presbyterian Church in the United States of America on October 21, 1953. Without the slightest thread of evidence these brain-washed Presbyterian leaders proclaimed that ". . . subtle but potent assault upon basic human rights is now in progress. Some Congressional inquiries have revealed a distinct tendency to become inquisitions. These inquisitions . . . begin to constitute a threat to freedom of thought in this country. Treason and dissent are being confused," etc. This letter went out to Presbyterian churches around America with this and other smear attacks against our land. . . .

The Soviet Embassy in Buenos Aires, Argentina, featured [Joseph] Hromadka in their Soviet publication, July 1958, as one of the great fighters for peace and a winner of the Lenin peace prize. In their commendation of him, the Reds said, "He accomplishes a great work in the World Council of Churches."

These leaders of the ecumenical movement and National Council of Churches in the United States are regularly collaborating with Hromadka. February 8 to 12, 1960, in Buenos Aires, Argentina, Hromadka sat together with members of the executive committee. The National Council leaders included Dr. Eugene Carson Blake, stated clerk of the General Assembly of the United Presbyterian Church in the U.S.A., and Dr. Franklin Clark Fry, president of the United Lutheran Church.

During 1956, a delegation of eight men from the Soviet Union, posing as clergymen, visited the United States under the sponsorship of the National Council of Churches. This visit was in return for a visit to Moscow by eight National Council leaders earlier in the year. During this visit to Moscow, America's so-called Protestant leaders were entertained by a high official in the Soviet Secret Police, Major General Georgi Karpov who runs the churches in the Soviet Union for the Kremlin.

When the delegation of eight so-called clergymen from the Soviet Union returned the visit to the United States in June, 1956, they were headed by Metropolitan Nicolai, a vicious Communist enemy of our nation and freedom everywhere. Informed Americans tried to warn our people and our leaders about these men and the real purpose of their visit. These warnings were ridiculed, even though they were backed up with documented facts that could not be contested. National Council leaders presented Nicolai and his fellow communist agents to duped church members around America as great Christian leaders. Nicolai's vicious germ warfare lie and other blatant lies against America were conveniently ignored.

A strong protest against this visit by Communist agents wearing the robes of the clergy was made by the Russian Orthodox Church in exile at their diocesan convention. They passed a resolution protesting the Soviet visitors posing as the loyal representatives of the Russian Orthodox Church and the Russian people. They said that this so-called clergymen group was "a small group of people actively collaborating with the Godless Communist government in Russia." Of course, the National Council leaders ignored this warning. These strange preachers have little use for refugee clergymen who actively oppose international Communism.

On May 5, 1959, Peter S. Deriabian, former officer in the Soviet Secret Police, testified before the House Un-American Activities Committee and exposed Metropolitan Nicolai as an agent of the Soviet Secret Police. An article by him which also contained this exposure appeared in *Life* magazine. This further exposure of the already exposed Nicolai did not faze National Council of Churches leaders. They are still going ahead with their plans for establishing co-operation with the Soviet Secret Police run churches in the Soviet Union. They have remained quiet about the exposure of Metropolitan Nicolai and still consider him a Christian leader. If there was ever a day when the Biblical warning to "beware of false prophets, which come to you in sheep's clothing," was needed in our nation, it is today.

On Friday, February 19, 1960, Congressman Francis Walter of the House Un-American Activities Committee said in Washington, "Secretary of Defense, Thomas E. Gates, Jr., would have done well to have investigated the facts respecting the bureaucracy which runs the National Council of Churches before he issued his groveling apology to them over the contents of the Air Force Manual. The leadership of the National Council of Churches which fraudulently claims to speak for 38 million American Protestants, has in the aggregate a record of hundreds of affiliations with Communist fronts and causes. The Fifth World Order Study Conference held in Cleveland, Ohio, in 1958 under the auspices of the National Council of Churches of Christ in the U.S.A., went on record in favor of diplomatic recognition of Red China by the United States and the seating of that government in the United Nations. Not one word was uttered there against the inhumanities of the atheistic Communist regime nor any mention made concerning its aggressive acts in which scores of hundreds of American boys were murdered."

The first evidence we have of support for Red China by a well-known National Council clergyman was the call for recognition of Red China and its admission to the U.N. by the Presbyterian leader, Dr. John A. Mackay, during December of 1949—less than three months after the Communist conspiracy took over that unfortunate nation. This was followed by occasional plugs in behalf of Red China by others within the National Council of Churches. The drive on behalf of this extremely important Communist objective seemed to pick up speed during 1958. On June 30, 1958 the Congregational Christian Churches requested the State Department to re-appraise American relations with "the people of mainland China," meaning the tyrannical dictators who rule the people. Frederick Nolde, director of international affaris of the National Council told 1,500 church women in Toronto, Canada during October 1958 that there could be no progress towards agreements on the world's most pressing problems without participation by the "People's Republic of China," meaning the cruel Communist dictatorship on China's mainland.

The big blow at the suffering Chinese people by the National Council's leadership came at their Fifth World Order Study Conference in Cleveland on November 22, 1958. The 600 delegates to this meeting passed a resolution urging the United States government to recognize the Red dictatorship on China's mainland and agree to their admittance to the United Nations. In other words they blatantly called for a sell-out of the Chinese people. They used the Communist conspiracy's whitewash term in referring to Red China by calling it "the People's Republic of China." They said that by excluding this murderous regime which they called "the effective government on the mainland of China," we would help to "preserve a false image of the United States ... in the minds of the Chinese people."

In adopting this stupid and suicidal surrender resolution, National Council leaders were not only striking at our sinking nation, but as I suggested earlier, they were kicking the poor oppressed Chinese people right in the face. The very wording of their surrender resolution promoted the satanic lie that the Communist dictatorship was approved by the people, and was therefore their legitimate representative. Imagine churchmen saying that by not recognizing this pack of crazed murderers who are trying to abolish Chinese family life we give the Chinese people a "false image" of the United States. . . .

Christian Americans, think of the additional souls that could be brought to the saving grace of our Lord Jesus Christ if the money, time and effort put into promotion of pro-communist goals by the National Council of Churches were put into bringing the true gospel to the unsaved. Think of the good which could be accomplished for our nation in its time of such great peril, if National Council leaders diverted their efforts from support of Communist and Socialist objectives into support of the anti-Communist cause.

America is greatly in need of your prayers. Please pray for an awakening among the innocent people in many of our large denominations who have no conception of the damage being done to America and Christianity by their left-wing leaders.

CARL McINTIRE

Carl McIntire represents a reactionary pulpit of an earlier era. Unlike Billy James Hargis, McIntire was originally more concerned with the alleged alliance between liberal religion and liberal government, than the alliance between liberal government and communism. Since 1960, nonetheless, McIntire has also focused his attention on the secular problem of the sinful liberal.

McIntire was born in Ypsilanti, Michigan, on May 17, 1906, and grew up in Durant, Oklahoma. Interestingly, this region is the heartland of fundamentalism. It is, indeed, from nearby Tulsa, Oklahoma, that men like Oral Roberts and Billy James Hargis warn that we should seek heaven and shun hell. McIntire took his undergraduate work at Park College, Parkville, Missouri. At twenty-three years of age he received his A.B. degree and moved to Princeton Theological Seminary. Once there, he developed a deep admiration for the fundamentalist scholar, Dr. J. Gresham Machen. This association proved to be most pivotal in the bitterly controversial ministry of Carl McIntire.

The religious values to which Dr. Machen subscribed were not generally accepted in the late 1920's and early 1930's. In fact, with the dissatisfaction with Herbert Hoover's brand of self-reliance so fresh in the minds of depression victims, Machen's beliefs were particularly unsuited to the time. Dr. Machen was devoted to a form of biblical individualism which brooked no interference by the state to help those who cannot help themselves. He felt the Social Gospel emphasis at Princeton Theological Seminary was beginning to compromise his principles. When Machen left Princeton to set up his own Westminster Seminary in Chestnut Hill, Pennsylvania, in 1931, McIntire followed. Both men bitterly attacked the apparent endorsement of the welfare measures of Franklin Roosevelt's New Deal by the United Presbyterian Church of America. In 1936, McIntire and Machen were brought to trial before the General Assembly of the Presbyterian Church for, among other things, "breaking certain of the Ten Commandments," "causing dissension and strife," and "engendering suspicion and ill will among Presbyterians." Both men were expelled.

Stripped of a national religious body of his own, Carl McIntire founded the American Council of Christian Churches in 1941, and started work in 1947 to form the International Council of Christian Churches. Both organizations are dedicated to the destruction of any type of religious collectivism and their chief target has been the National Council of Churches.

McIntire had preached on a single radio station for two decades, but had failed to reach more than a very small audience. However, in the early 1960's his monthly newspaper, the Christian Beacon, *set up a subsidiary called the Twentieth Century Reformation Hour to broadcast his dissident views. Suddenly, he began adding stations to his radio network. By 1963, he had 576 stations for his use; by 1965, there were 750; and in 1967, he claimed over one thousand. The Twentieth Century Reformation Hour is thirty minutes long and features an assistant pastor, Charles Richter (Amen Charlie) who confines his remarks to "A-men" and "That's right."*

Unlike Hargis, McIntire is pastor of his own independent Presbyterian church in Collingswood, New Jersey. Like Hargis, McIntire conducts his own anti-communist summer school at Cape May, New Jersey. McIntire has purchased and remodeled an old hotel now known as the Christian Admiral. At present, McIntire is probably the most influential figure in the reactionary pulpit because he possesses the largest radio ministry of any reactionary.

Twentieth Century Reformation Hour*

ANNOUNCER: This is the Twentieth Century Reformation Hour by tape recording from Collingswood, New Jersey under the direction of Carl McIntire. Carl McIntire is editor of the *Christian Beacon*, a weekly religious newspaper and pastor of the Bible Presbyterian Church of Collingswood, New Jersey. Now, here is Dr. McIntire with his cheery greeting.

Good morning! Good morning, everybody. Yes, this is Carl McIntire and Dr. Charles E. Richter and we're right in the middle of our discussion of *Look* magazine, this January 26th issue that has four major articles, dealing with what they call "Conspiracy U.S.A." and they've bundled together in one big package almost everybody who's been active over on what we call the Conservative side and they would tell the whole nation that there is a conspiracy on to destroy the United States of America. It's utterly fantastic! I have been dealing at great length with the first article by Senator Church from Idaho. Today, we're going to start on the second article, "Arthur Larson!" and then we have the third article before us, "A Plot that Flopped" and then the fourth article dealing with "Mental Health," and I'm going to

* Golden Valley, Minnesota, Radio Station KQRS, January 29, 1965.

deal with these future articles just as I've been discussing the Senator Church article.

Nothing that's happened in recent years is quite as important as all this, because here is an open campaign that's being launched now all over the United States to discredit those of us who are standing up for the Bible, for the Ten Commandments, for the Word of God, to get the Bible back in school, those of us who are the anti-communists. And they're going to ask the American people as Senator Church does to repudiate every one of us. I don't think they can do it. We're giving you the facts, we're asking now for one thousand radio stations. We've launched a campaign to raise a million dollars. We're all challenged; we're all inspired; we're all on the firing line and I want to get everybody who listens to this broadcast to get in this great struggle with us and let's preserve a free America! And let's defend the faith that our fathers had. And now a word of prayer.

Our Father, we thank Thee that Thou art our God. Thou art faithful from generation to generation. Thy Word is true from the Beginning and everyone of Thy righteous judgments endureth forever. And Thou hast told us that the fear of the Lord is the beginning of wisdom and to depart from evil—that is understanding. And wilt Thou give us an understanding of evil, that we may not follow it. And we thank Thee for the great text that Thou hast set before us, "Thou shalt not follow a multitude to do evil." Oh God, keep us in the straight and narrow path that leadeth unto Life and may we listen to the words of our Saviour as He said to each one of us, "Take up thy cross and follow me." Now be with our many listeners and we ask that Thou wilt hear our prayers. We ask that Thou wilt strengthen us for the battle. We ask that Thou wilt undergird these radio stations with committees and with local support. And now we ask that Thou wilt give us one-million dollars. Father, we're asking for it. And we're out here struggling. We're lifting up a standard. We desire Thy help now that men may know that there is a God in Israel. These things we ask for the sake of Jesus Christ our Lord. Amen. (*Amen!*)

Charlie, you're a little late this morning. (*Yes, I'll tell you, we had a lot of snow and it was quite a time to clean it off the car. Those things will happen you know.*)

Well, I've been giving you people some of these wonderful texts in which we have references from the lips of Jesus, concerning following him. And I told you we'd spend a few days in this tenth chapter of Matthew where Jesus said, "He that taketh not up His cross and followeth after Me is not worthy of Me." We want to be worthy of Him, beloved. We want to help carry the standard. And then in verse 39, "He that findeth his life shall lose it, and he that loseth his life for My sake, shall find it." Now while you people are sitting out there saying, Well, now I appreciate what Dr. McIntire is doing and I think it's fine and I just thank God that he's doing what he is, but that's not for me. Yes, ladies and gentlemen, it is for you. Then some of you sit out there and you say, Well, I know Mrs. Jones, she's all right, she's active in the church, and she's active in these things down in the Club. But I can't get too active in these things, because it might hurt my husband's business. It might cause me to—well, I might have a little trouble. Beloved, Jesus Christ said that "He that findeth his life shall lose it," and when great issues of truth and righteousness and freedom and morality are at stake, we need to have the spirit of Patrick Henry who said, "Give me liberty, or give me death." (Amen!) And Jesus Christ said, "He that loseth his life"—he that giveth up his life for my sake shall find it. And a lot of you people ought to give up an awful lot of things that you're doing right now. And use your time in the great struggle to maintain and proclaim the gospel of Jesus Christ. You just need to lose your life. Amen Charlie and I are losing ours. We're just giving everything we have and furthermore, one of the nice things about our giving is that we're having such joy about it. (Amen.) Oh, the days are dark. The Bible says they will be fierce. But we're in this thing with the joy that only Christ gives because we're struggling for the liberty that only our grandchildren shall enjoy. And we're preaching the gospel that saves lost sinners and brings them home to Jesus Christ and gives them everlasting life. (Yes!) My friend, I appeal to you to lose your life in this struggle. I appeal to you to make the sacrifice necessary in your time, and in your money and in your stewardship. Make these sacrifices now. And Jesus Christ says you'll find your life. You'll find it. God bless you folks, don't you love the Bible? Yes, don't you love the Word of God? You know that blessed text comes to my mind, "Thy Word is sweet unto my taste, it's sweeter than honey in the honeycomb."

[Here follows approximately a seven minute appeal for letters and funds to be sent to the program.]

I just can't tell you the shock that's hit us and hit the people of our church here and everybody to see *Look* magazine come out and say that I'm a part of a conspiracy that's going to destroy the U.S.A. Utterly fantastic!

And I've been dealing now with the first of these articles and let's turn to the second one for a few days, "A Republican Looks at Extremism—A Visit with Arthur Larson." Do you see this Charlie? (Yes.) It's written by *Look's* senior editor and we have here four pages and there's only an equal of about one page of script—the rest are the most glamorous pictures. . . . But this title, "A Republican Looks at Extremism" obviously is pointed. It

445

has undoubtedly the reflection that there was a republican candidate for the presidency by the name of Barry Goldwater who made the statement concerning extremism when he accepted the nomination in San Francisco that literally sent shivers and thrills across this nation. "Extremism in the behalf of liberty is not a vice." That's what Senator Goldwater said.

Now we've got an article—"A Republican Looks at Extremism." And of course, this is the general overall attack now to make this extremism a bad word, a dirty word so that every time it's used somewhere, people will say, "Oh, yes that crowd!" And it's a part of a general, psychological situation that's seeking to be built up here in this country against those over on the conservative side who've been very active.

Now, I think I must say, so far as the report concerning Mr. Larson is concerned, that it is somewhat milder than the one on the senator. The article here by Mr. Larson doesn't go quite as strong as the senator went with these things and yet obviously they are together. And the article begins by saying Arthur Larson is a tall, blond, dignified scholar. So we now are introduced into the presence of a scholar and then a little later we have a statement here concerning the "Niagara of Noxious Literature" that is supposed to be put out by the right wing—every thing from nasty little throwaways to books containing a facade of scholarship. So the right wing has a facade of scholarship, but the group that's seeking now to expose extremism is being led by a dignified scholar. Now that contrast is immediately here in the first two columns where the article begins.

Well, we're told concerning Mr. Larson, "You know," he confides, "I really don't know any people who think the way extremists do." Well, I'm not sure he's all that naïve, but perhaps he doesn't, and maybe if he did know more people who think the way extremists do, I think if he had the opportunity to know Amen Charlie, he'd think he was a pretty nice fellow. I think if he had the opportunity to meet a great many of the people whom I've met, who are members of the John Birch Society, he would discover they're very fine Americans and citizens standing for the best things a community could stand for. I think if he had a little personal contact with some of these people and could talk with them that maybe his attitude would change. In fact, I would like to meet him myself. Maybe if I had a chance to meet him and sit down and talk to him, we could persuade him that there is a relationship between what he calls extremism and our devotion to the moral teachings of the Word of God.

Then we come on down a little further and we notice here that he says they were in a dilemma for sometime as to how to deal with what they call the "right wing." Would they fight back? Or would they ignore them? And he's come to the conclusion that you can't ignore them any more and he wished they would have started long before they did. So, ladies and gentlemen, we're confronted now with an organized effort—and *Look* magazine certainly represents this effort—to fight back at what they call the "right wing." And when they come to fight back as they say, we're going to stand right up to them and not only are we going to stand right up to them, but we're going to do what I am doing now. I am taking these four articles just as they're written. I am photographically reproducing it and I have already written a point-by-point analysis of each one of them and I'll send this to you free and post-paid. And they want to start fighting back, we'll just give you everything that they say. And then we'll turn around and point out for you the clean, clear refutation with evidence and documentation that the so-called right wing is not a conspiracy which is seeking to destroy America; that those of us over here on the conservative side are lifting our voices just as I'm lifting my voice at the present time in order that we may persuade you people that this nation faces the greatest peril, the greatest threat, the greatest danger its ever had in all the history of its existence. (*That's right.*) We face a diabolical conspiracy headed out of the communist world which is determined to bring down the destruction of this great republic. (*That's right!*) And don't you sit back and smirk and smile and belittle this conspiracy. The communists are moving on out and they intend to rule the world!

And now, we're told here that Mr. Larson and his group intend to send speakers out across the country to inform the people on the way in which the right-wing operates. Now, I hope they do send these speakers because if they send them out, they're going to have some speakers trailing them, as truth squads. And if they send them out in various groups or send them around the country, I want you people to let us know in here who they are, where they are. We'll report it for you.

Listen, ladies and gentlemen, we're getting into some of the greatest days of broadcasting we've ever had. Now what interests me about what they say about sending out these speakers to expose the right wing—there's no suggestion that they have a dialogue with the right wing. Isn't that interesting?

Oh yes, we're having dialogues with the communists, and we're having dialogues among the left wingers all the time if you want to talk about dialogues. As a matter of fact, we're talking about a reproachment [sic], we're talking about doing business with the "reds"—oh, we're just being so nice to the "reds" but there's no talk about a reproach [sic] with the so-called right wing. There's only a campaign of repudiation. That's what we have here from the words of the senator, and ladies and gentlemen, if there's anything that America ought to unite to repudiate, we ought to unite to repudiate the American conspiracy. (*Amen!*) There should be a union among all Americans to expose the Communists and to keep the pledges and the promises that we made to our brethren and to our friends in the "iron-curtain" countries. We said we would work for their liberation! What ever happened to those promises?

Well, now let's go back and I want to take up some of these specific things that Mr. Larson deals with here. And among them of course is his estimate of the recent political campaign. And he says that these 26 million republicans who voted for Goldwater were just loyal republicans—not extremists! In other words, the vast majority of those who backed Goldwater were not extremists. So what they're trying to do is separate the men who've been out in front, the men who have been carrying the burden of some of these great issues—like myself and others—trying to separate them from what they would characterize as responsible conservatives. This is their tactics. Ladies and gentlemen, we can't let them do it! Carl McIntire sits here and I'm a part of a great religious movement in this country. I'm the president of a council of churches that has 39 Protestant denominations in it. And one of the things that struck me as I read these articles where my name is mentioned—and I think it's true of others too, not all of them, but certainly true of a number of them—there's no identification given concerning us—our location—where we operate—where we come from—in my case, you see, they just say, Reverend Carl McIntire. You see it, Charlie? They don't say Collingswood, New Jersey. I think they wouldn't dare say Collingswood, New Jersey for fear . . . somebody might write Dr. Carl McIntire and see what he would have to say about these articles. If anybody would write me, I would give them what I'm giving to you right now on this broadcast—a complete rebuttal, a complete answer to everything that is said here. Isn't it interesting that when they refer to our broadcast they just say radio—with six hundred and seventeen stations—they don't even use the name, Twentieth Century Reformation. No, they simply are seeking to create in the public mind the idea that Carl McIntire is a part of a conspiracy. They no longer identify him in any way, shape or form and you people who are listening to this broadcast, you know who we are. We're pastor of a great church; we've been here 31 years. We are standing up for what we believe to be right and honorable and honest in this blessed land of ours. (Amen!) We've got a perfect right to do it! And when you see this strategy, this tactic, for instance, they have here the American future—no indication as to any part of the country where its headquarters might be located or anything of that kind. It's perfectly clear, the strategy and the tactic that's being used. You know, if we had a Federal Press Commission, which we don't have and which we don't want, and the Federal Press Commission had a so-called "fairness" doctrine—which we don't like and don't approve of—*Look* magazine could be required by the Federal Press Commission to carry equal space so we would have opportunity to answer *Look* magazine. (*That's right.*) Do you think *Look* magazine would give Carl McIntire a page or a half a page or any section in order to give a refutation to the things that are said here about us being a part of a conspiracy? Do you think they would do a thing like that?

Of course, they ought to do it—they ought to be willing to do it. But I'm taking *Look* and reproducing these articles and then I'm giving you this point-by-point refutation of each one of them.

Now in regard to the majority of the people who voted for Goldwater just being loyal republicans and not extremists. We're told in the same paragraph that Larson is casting a cold eye on the far-right groups that Goldwater refused to disavow. So there's no question but what these articles do have a political implication. No question but what they're trying to deal with the issues that were raised during the last political campaign. But their problem is they have involved men like Carl McIntire who is not dealing specifically and directly with the political issues—I'm dealing with the religious and spiritual problems (*Amen.*) that underlie this great attack of the Communists upon us, (*That's right!*) and our indifference and our no-win policy and the things which relate directly to this great struggle in which we're engaged.

Well, we come on down here to C. B. and Kent Courtney. Now they don't tell you they're from New Orleans. And then they refer to Dan Smoot and they don't tell you that Dan Smoot is from Dallas, Texas, but they do say here that the Courtneys have put out bumper stickers claiming 26 million Americans can't be wrong. And Smoot is reported to have presented some figures that the conservative cause is fifty-two times as powerful as in 1956. What's actually behind all this, I think, is that these leaders are afraid that the 26 million who voted for Goldwater may be able to persuade another 15 million in four years and then the conservatives would have the majority in any election and I think that's possibly what's behind all this.

But now when we get on a little further, we have the report here that the radio broadcasts are being monitored. And we thought the National Council of Civic Responsibility which Mr. Larson heads were monitoring these programs itself, but it turns out now that it's done through group research . . . they're monitoring these broadcasts and we're thankful they are and I hope that if they'll just listen to them it may be the gospel that we preach may get through—just a little bit to some of these gentlemen. (*Amen!*)

Maybe this gospel may get through! And wouldn't it be marvelous if in the providence of God that some of these men might get converted and find out what it means to be "born again" and actually come over and join our camp (*Amen.*) in this great battle to preserve our heritage and freedom.

[Here follows an appeal of about one minute in length for the campaign to raise $1 million.]

When the Senator from Idaho makes his other speeches as he's promised us, I'll reproduce them in full. We'll give you the answer to them and this is the kind of debating and this is the kind of an appeal to the conscience of the people of this country which I believe will bring real conviction.

And thank you for listening!

17

POPULAR VS. EXPERIMENTAL RELIGION
Leroy Davis

During the years immediately following the Second World War, the religious institutions of America largely attempted to reestablish the patterns they had maintained prior to that conflict. Primary emphasis was placed upon the kind of activities which resulted in increased membership and budgets. Comfort and lack of discord were pursued. These trends could be designated as an ecclesiastical return to normalcy. However, the war had fostered an increased awareness in some quarters of the church of philosophical existentialism and other questioning movements. During the 1950's a new legal approach to Negro rights developed and became a part of an increased social awareness in some parts of the church. In addition, some European developments in theology were more fully appreciated, which contributed to a more fluid approach to theology and ethics. These developments contributed to a new and differing approach to church life. During the 1960's these two approaches tended to become polarized, achieving notable differences in regard to politics and ethics. The two approaches have been designated as popular and experimental.

A corresponding type of preaching has developed for each approach to church life. Two sermons have been chosen to illustrate the polar position of each approach, "God Revealed in Christ" by D. Reginald Thomas and "The Context of Decision" by Lloyd J. Averill.

Typical of popular sermons, "God Revealed in Christ" is ostensibly based upon a verse taken from the Bible. The assumption inherent in this approach is that the biblical materials contain self-evident truths which can be presented in isolation from one another. In this particular case the text is from the Prologue of St. John as quoted in the King James version. Because the truths are considered to be self-evident, there is little exegesis of the passage. Thus, the concepts inherent to the scriptural argument, eg., word, flesh, glory, grace, truth, are treated as if their meaning is what one would assume them to mean in ordinary conversation.

The experimental approach of Mr. Averill is based upon the assumption that religious insights can be developed from an analysis of human situations. Therefore, the text used by this preacher is from Jean-Paul Sartre. This sermon is based upon a subjective approach to understanding, which leads to its fluid or contextual character. The insights which undergird the sermon are not treated as divine truth but as human situational understandings.

There may be little difference, in the final analysis, between these two approaches to preaching since the former does not really utilize biblical materials any more than does the latter. Both sermons represent the preacher's opinions about the topics under consideration. In the latter case, it was not felt appropriate to base decision-making upon the many pertinent biblical passages. In the former case it was not felt necessary to adhere to the concepts inherent in the text. Either way the preacher has engaged in a radical subjectivism. Mr. Thomas chose to base his presentation upon a self-evident reading of scripture. Mr. Averill chose to base his upon an analysis of the life situations he has encountered or read about. Both approaches deny the existence of an external, unique, and well defined standard.

The radical subjectivism of both preachers renders other distinctions hyperbolic. For example, in "God Revealed in Christ" the preacher argues from the position of having a specific and unalterable truth in his possession, but the truth propounded is not derived from the text which is supposedly so absolute and self-validating that a life-saving presentation can be based upon it. The other preacher argues as if there were no absolutes which are pertinent to his problem. The fact that the former sermon utilizes a biblical text and the latter does not as the base of the sermon is meaningless as a distinction since both are subjective presentations. The former is no more objective than the latter. The real difference between the two approaches is that the former has a solution for a problem asked only by the preacher, and the latter no answer for a question asked by mankind. On a superficial level, this hyperbolic distinction results in the observation that popular preaching tends to result in facile answers and experimental preaching in the endless description of problems.

When specific revelation of self-evident truths is used as a base, a sermon tends to deal with the preacher's insights relative to that special revelation. The sermon, then, tends to be removed from human life. Without exegesis, biblical insights become self-evident truths which are merely pegs upon which the preacher can hang his own opinions about "religion." Biblical insights, according to this approach, tend to be elevated into a position of artificial truth and are then not subject to critical scrutiny. On the other hand, when an analysis of contemporary human events is used as a base, the sermon tends to contain a great deal of situational material and is not "religious."

Many people conclude, primarily from listening to preachers, that biblical insights are outdated or that they do not exist. These conclusions are appropriate to and consistent with preaching which is radically subjective because a subjective approach penetrates only into itself, the subjective perceiving individual. If preaching does not really deal with biblical materials, preferring to use them only as self-evident truths or as human insights, the allegation that the biblical materials are irrelevant or nonexistent is preposterous if the argument is based upon what is contained in sermons. While the experimental

453

approach represents an attempt to relate biblical understanding to men, it really represents only a shift in emphasis away from biblical literalism. It has remained as subjective as the popular approach. It would be interesting to examine the development of the various "God-is-dead" ideas in relation to the radical subjectivism of preaching. It is certainly possible to understand how relatively theologically uneducated persons could intelligently conclude that God is dead. Radical subjectivism in any form constitutes a denial of the external reality of God. That is why experimentalism, like popularism, will fail to achieve its purpose of bringing men in relation with God. The final break with external reality is the emergence of hallucination. Radical subjectivism in the pulpit still has the trappings of externality. Should middle-class morality ever be sufficiently shaken, the future of subjective preaching could contain some kind of psychedelic speaking in tongues. It is the natural extension of the present trend.

The issue with which preaching must wrestle is ontological. However God has been viewed in the past, he has been seen as an external reality. If there is going to be a whole-hearted commitment to subjectivism in preaching, reality is going to have to be redefined. The question to be faced is whether hallucination, the extreme form of subjectivity, constitutes reality. These are weighty matters, but ones which will be faced one way or another during the 1970's.

The structure of these sermons is consistent with the approach of each. Thomas' sermon is a typical three-part variety. Averill's is structureless. In fairness to the two preachers who have been kind enough to allow the use of their sermons, it must be stated that these sermons have been chosen because they represent the extremities of the polarity under consideration and may or may not be representative of those customarily preached by these men.

D. REGINALD THOMAS

D. Reginald Thomas, D.D., Senior Minister of the Brick Presbyterian Church in New York City, 1965-70, was born of Welsh parents in London, England, in 1914. He graduated from the University College of Wales and from the Theological College of Aberyswyth in Wales. He was ordained as a minister of the Presbyterian Church of Wales in 1944. Following his ordination, Dr. Thomas served two congregations in Wales. In 1955, he accepted a call to the First Presbyterian Church in Germantown, Pennsylvania.

Dr. Thomas received the honorary Doctor of Divinity degree from Temple University. Because of his many contributions in the field of ecumenical relations, Dr. Thomas was chosen to represent the Presbyterian Church of Wales at the World Council of Churches meeting at Evanston, Illinois in 1954. He prepared a film entitled, "Land Where our Fathers Died," which received a top award from the Freedoms Foundation. Dr. Thomas has conducted radio services for the British Broadcasting System and for the National Broadcasting Company. He was the National Church Preacher for 1969 and is the author of the books, Love So Amazing and To Know God's Way.

God Revealed in Christ*

And the Word was made flesh, and dwelt among us, (and we beheld his glory, the glory as of the only begotten of the Father) full of grace and truth—JN. 1:14.

Once again, we have come to Christmas, when we remember the amazing fact upon which the whole of the good news of the Gospel depends and without which it ceases to be a Gospel at all. We have come to the time when with gratitude we remember the fact of God's great condescension to us in the person of Jesus Christ. "The word was made flesh and dwelt among us," said John in the opening chapter of his Gospel. "In the beginning was the Word, and the Word was with God, and the Word was God. The same was in the beginning with God" (Jn. 1:1-2). In the incarnation, this word was made flesh and tabernacles among men.

We remember God's condescension to us in a Word made flesh; that is, the Word. The mind, the divine thought became flesh so that in that

* Reprinted by permission of the author.

455

communicable form we might see it, appreciate it, love it, and give ourselves to it. But since the Word became flesh, we no longer talk about "it." Rather Him. We see Him; appreciate Him; love Him, and give ourselves to Him in whom this Word was clothed with flesh. We are restating our faith in this truth—that behind all the discovery of religious truth which man has accomplished is the willingness of God to make the truth known to man. We restate this truth—that if it is our duty to seek God, as it most certainly is, there is only sense in our seeking, because God first of all sought us.

If you take a faith in a revealed God out of religion, then you are taking away something that is absolutely vital to it and upon which it actually depends. Revelation is God revealing Himself in Christ. As we come to Christmas again, we are reasserting this truth—that if you take revelation out of religion, then you are left only with a form of religion but a dead form. If you will allow me to use a phrase that is usually applied in an entirely different context, let me put it this way; take revelation out of religion and what is left is "beautiful but dumb."

We come to these familiar words, "The word became flesh and dwelt among men" and out of this phrase, let us note three very simple and obvious reflections. The first, the necessity of revelation in religion; the second, the evidence of revelation in religion and the third, the compulsion of revelation in religion.

Let us go then to the first of these thoughts; the necessity of revelation in religion. Revelation is a necessity only in religious truth. Mark that, only in religious truth for revelation is not a necessity for all kinds of truth. For example, revelation is not necessary for mathematical truth or scientific truth, but in religious truth which is the truth about the character of God and the way in which He deals with men, revelation is absolutely essential. For in religious truth, any attainment on the part of man in his appreciation of it depends first of all upon the revealing activity of God. It depends first of all upon the willingness of God to disclose Himself and His purposes.

Now, I know that there is a very real sense in which it is true to say that God made the reality of the truth which the scientist has discovered. It is also true to say that God created the mind which made the discovery, and which having made the discovery, understood it. In a sense, I suppose, one may say that the particular discovery on the part of the scientist is the design of God, but at the same time that kind of discovery, as in the case of scientific truth, is quite different from man's attainment and achievement in religious truth.

A scientist, for example, has no sense of a person thrusting himself into his life. You see, the truth which the scientist discovers was there all the time. It was hidden, dormant, and then it is laid bare and appreciated by the activity of an inquiring mind, but if the scientist had not sought it, if he had not experimented, the truth would never have been found, and that truth would never have come in search of the scientist. But the genius of all religious discovery is in this, that it has in it not so much the sense of you finding something, but of something or rather from the Christian point of view of someone finding you. In religious truth, the activity is not on your side; it is on the other side; God's side. There has been a deliberate entrance into your life and into your experience and that is why in the one case—that of the scientist—we speak of discovery. This man found something, but in the case of religious truth we speak of revelation. This is something in which God has taken the initiative and which God has disclosed. God is not actively at work revealing Himself in science. He is at work there, but not in the same sense that He was actively at work revealing Himself in Jesus Christ. "The Word became flesh and dwelt among men." That was not a movement initiated by man toward God. Rather it is a movement initiated by God for the sake of man, and this faith in revelation, in revealed truth is absolutely necessary to any kind of religious truth and religious experience. Thus first of all, we see the necessity of revelation in religion.

Second, we see the evidence of revelation in religion. For example, there are some things in life which God seems to have left for us to find out for ourselves. There are other things in which He quite obviously has not left us to find out for ourselves. Now scientific truth belongs to the former. These are things upon which a man can experiment and inquire and discover for himself, but on the other hand religious truth, which is the knowledge of God and His way with man, belongs to the latter class. These are things that we are not left to find out for ourselves.

Well, take for example the realm of nature of which man knows so much, and yet which nowadays we see quite obviously that it is a vast undiscovered continent. Now nature does not help man except insofar as he is willing to try, to test, to probe, and to inquire. Nature does not help man except insofar as he is willing to try and persuade mother nature to serve his purposes. It is then that man discovers things for himself, but this is certainly not true of religion. In religious truth, there is always the sense of a personal purpose intruding itself into one's life. In revelation, God gives Himself to us, and this is a supreme discovery, but we do not make it ourselves.

Now the truth of what I am saying is amply illustrated in the textbook of our faith—the Bible. For example, throughout the Old Testament the assumption is always made that the faith of Israel with all its consequences, its joys, and its privileges was not so much achieved by Israel as given by God. That was the faith of the Israelites from first to last. The ancient Hebrew never thought of man as having lifted himself up by his shoelaces to God.

457

For him, the truth was that it was always God who spoke first, and it was man's task to listen and to respond. Therefore, they always used these words, "Thus saith the Lord" or "The Lord hath spoken it." God was always thought of as having broken into the life of His appointed people for His chosen servant.

Even while this truth of the evidence of religion is illustrated aptly in the Old Testament, how much more in the New Testament in which we have the doctrine of the incarnation, the Word becoming flesh and dwelling with man. The New Testament teaches that God deliberately and intentionally unveiled Himself to man in the person, in the coming and in the work of Jesus Christ. The New Testament does not for one moment regard Jesus as simply the product of the human race or as something that grew up out of a culture and refinements of humanity. The New Testament regards our Lord as One who came to man from above. One sent from God to man, One in whom God was taking the initiative, revealing Himself to man in the form of man but in One who was God as well as man.

Consider Jesus Christ in His ministry. He never spoke a word which needed to be modified or corrected or withdrawn. He never once sought advice. He never confessed a sin. He never asked for or permitted a prayer to be spoken on His behalf. He was of human ancestry and that can be traced. He was of human appearance, of human constitution, and limited as we are by reason of the flesh, time and space. He could suffer through the flesh and yet, He annunciated the highest standard of morality. He assumed superiority over every prior revelation. He invinced a sublime self-consciousness of His own person and work. He lived a blameless, stainless, sinless life. In Him, that word which I referred to as "beautiful but dumb," became beautiful and vocal. It is God saying to man in man's language and in man's situation, "This is what My love is like. This is what My compassion is like. This is the measure of My judgment. This is how I will reconcile you to Myself."

So then we have the necessity of revelation, and we have the evidence of revelation and that necessity and evidence leads us to the third and final thought; the compulsion of revelation. If it is true, as Christianity asserts, that God comes to you, then there are certain compelling thoughts that follow. The first is this—if it is God who is speaking, then you must listen. A simple thought, but let me repeat it. "If it is God who is speaking in Jesus Christ, you must listen."

There is a sense I know in which we seek God, but there is a danger in our seeking unless we have first of all recognized this tremendous truth—that God first of all came to us in this person who lived on earth nearly two thousand years ago. For some people, whom I know, the thought of God is extremely illusive and because that is true, there is a tendency on our part to conceive of God in our own image. We want a God who will assist us, who agrees with us, and who will second the motion that we make, not a God who disagrees, who disciplines, or whom we have to serve. We want a God who will respect our wishes and obey our commands, not a God who commands us.

It is right that we should seek God. The Scriptures tell us to seek Him and to seek Him diligently, but such seeking of itself is dangerous. The danger is that we are apt to discover the God that we want to find. As we set out upon our search, that danger can only be avoided by believing that the God we are seeking first of all revealed Himself, His nature, His intent in Jesus Christ.

Now the other compelling thought that follows upon revelation is a thought that will save us from doing what so many earnest and devout people do. As a minister, I have met those who sort of hover between a lazy optimism on the one hand and a lazy pessimism on the other. If things are going well, they lose their sense of urgency. If things are not going well, they lose their sense of the worthwhileness of the cause of Christ. It is difficult even for the best disciple to keep himself poised somewhere between that kind of pessimism and optimism. The safety of the disciple is that he continually comes back to this point that inasmuch as the Word became flesh, inasmuch as God has revealed Himself, then the cause for which God did all of this must eventually prosper and triumph. God is living and in Jesus Christ, in His life, in His death, in His resurrection, He has demonstrated that what He intends must come to pass, for in Christ, God has entered the realm of history. He did it in a person who was born in a place that you can mark on the map at a time that you can check on a calendar. God in Christ has touched this world in the context of history and history is His. God has touched human life, and He is the Lord of life.

It is this faith in the initiative and activity of God which keeps a disciple free from this pessimism in which he doubts the value of Christ's cause and safe from that optimism in which he thinks that since things are going so well, little or nothing is required of him. Here then is the great news for a world such as this—a world which causes so much concern and anxiety. Here is the great news of any personal life that may be distraught or distressed or weighed down with a sense of failure and inadequacy or in sorrow. God came to this world in Jesus and by His Holy Spirit, He still comes. God is with us and blessed be His name.

LLOYD J. AVERILL

Dr. Lloyd J. Averill, Dean at Elkins Davis College, has been Distinguished Visiting Professor at Ottawa and Baker Universities and at Park College. Over the past decade he has been a lecturer and preacher in more than sixty colleges and universities. He served as Associate Director of Field Work and Instructor in Practical Theology at Colgate Rochester Divinity School from 1951 to 1954 and as Vice President and Professor of Religion at Kalamazoo College from 1954 to 1967. He is past President of the Council of Protestant Colleges and Universities.

Dr. Averill received his undergraduate degree from the University of Wisconsin, his Master of Arts degree from the University of Rochester, and the degrees of Bachelor of Divinity and Master of Theology from Colgate Rochester Divinity School. He has pursued additional graduate study at the University of Cambridge. Dr. Averill is the recipient of honorary doctoral degrees from several colleges and universities; among them Lewis and Clark, William Jewell, Carroll, Augustana, and Tusculum. He is the author of A Strategy for the Protestant College, American Theology in the Liberal Tradition, *and* Between Faith and Unfaith. *He is a frequent contributor to* Christian Century, The Pulpit, Liberal Education, The Christian Scholar, Current Issues in Higher Education, *and other periodicals. His sermon "What you Worship as Unknown," appears in* Rockefeller Chapel Sermons, *edited by Donovan Smucker.*

The Context of Decision*

Jean-Paul Sartre, in his latest drama, *The Condemned of Altona*, gives to one of the characters in the drama an utterance which is poignantly personal for many of us. Werner von Gerlach is offered control of a vast industrial empire, and his reply to that choice expresses the near-terror which is felt by many a man and woman even in the presence of lesser decisions:

To decide. To decide. To be responsible for everything. Alone. . . . There are so many cogs in the machine. Suppose one of them were to jam. . . .

* Reprinted by permission of the author.

What is there about decision that frightens us? There is, for one thing, the fear that if we refuse the challenge when someone says, "Choose!" it will be an admission of weakness. Decisiveness is, after all, one of the great American virtues. Its virtuousness is seen in the fact that it is one of the chief traits of that epic hero of American folklore, the successful business-man. The popular image of the American executive-type is a man who is able to make impeccable, near-infallible decisions within moments after a problem is handed to him. It is something like that image that intimidates us in the presence of our own decisions and threatens to charge us with weakness if we hesitate.

One of von Gerlach's words suggests a second element which deepens our fright in the presence of decisions. It is the word. "Alone." We are dis-turbed by the loneliness to which we seem to be condemned in our choices, and yet we fear there is no alternative. There was a time, not so very long ago, when most college students seemed able to entertain quite calmly the idea of consulting a psychiatrist when serious difficulty arose, but there is some evidence to suggest that a change of attitude has taken place. Such con-sultation is now looked upon by many with suspicion. Indeed, some of us scarcely dare to consult anyone when we are faced with a difficult decision, lest it be an open admission of weakness. More than one conversation in my office has been opened by the visitor with words of embarrassed apology, "I know I ought to be able to handle this myself." Independence, after all, is another of our great American virtues. Our folklore places a premium on self-reliance. Maturity is defined in terms of self-sufficiency. Then actively to seek the help of another person when we are faced with a decision is virtually to confess our immaturity.

It is another French man of letters, Andre Gide, who expresses a third frightening element in decision. "All our life long," Gide writes, "we have been tormented by the uncertainty of our paths. How can I put it? All choice, when one comes to think of it, is terrifying: liberty when there is no duty to guide it, terrifying." Man is free, Gide is saying, and his freedom means that he cannot appeal to any precedent for help in the decisions he faces. Many of us believe that too. No problem which another man has faced can provide guidance for me, because no one else has ever faced quite my problem before. Rugged individualism is still another of the great American virtues, and only the weak are unwilling to create their own precedents.

And there is one other element in decision which frightens us. It is the element of uncertainty which reaches ominously from the moment of de-cision into the opaqueness of the future. Said Werner von Gerlach in Sartre's drama, "There are so many cogs in the machine. Suppose one of them were to jam. . . ." That question can be translated readily into the questions we ask about the critical decisions which face us. Many of you find that your aptitudes and interests could lead you into any of two or three professional fields. How can you be sure that one is really better than another? Certainly there is a high incidence of professional failure every year. Do you dare to choose one over the others without being certain of success in advance? Would it not be better to withhold decision until the evidence is clear? Some of you have found yourselves, during these college years, attracted to more than one young man or young woman. How can you be sure that one of them will really make a better husband or wife than another? Certainly there is a high incidence of marital failure every year. Do you dare to choose one over the others without being certain of success in advance? Would it not be better to withhold decision until the evidence is clear? After all, caution is another of the great American virtues. It has not always been so, but it has been increasingly so in the last decade and a half. We are living in a dangerous world and the smart move is the safe one.

Now, let me admit what some of you may be thinking, that I have overstated the situation. Of course I have. It has not been my purpose to draw the picture of any single individual as he stands in the moment of decision. It is unlikely that any of you will find all of these factors at work in you in the presence of any single choice. Rather what I have attempted to draw is a kind of composite portrait of many of us. Probably other factors, as relevant at least as any I have noted, have escaped my attention. But this I have observed with some regularity, that in these college years significant decisions produce the real crisis; and crisis deepens into trouble when men and women do not know what to do with their decisions. I am convinced that the four elements which I have noted are among the chief reasons why crisis deepens into trouble, and I want now to try to suggest some ways of approaching our decisions, not for the purpose of avoiding crisis but of meeting it constructively and confidently.

II

So then let us return to the first of those four elements which often prevent us from dealing with our decisions creatively. It is the fear that if we refuse the challenge when some one says, "Choose!" it will be an admission of weakness. On the contrary, I should like to give you a good conscience about refusing to make certain kinds of decisions. You are under no obligation to make tomorrow's decisions today. Whenever you are pressed for decisions of the "what-are-you-going-to-be-when-you-grow-up" variety, it is a sign both of strength and intelligence to reply, "That is not a proper choice for me now."

Jesus spoke once with unembellished directness on precisely this point. His words to the prematurely anxious of his own time ought to quiet our own premature anxiety. Said he, "Take no thought for the morrow: for the morrow shall take thought for the things of itself. Sufficient unto the day is the evil thereof." Or as the Revised Standard Version has it, "Do not be anxious about tomorrow, for tomorrow will be anxious for itself. Let the day's own trouble be sufficient for the day."

We live in a society which is so oriented toward the future that we are all but incapable of appreciating the significance of the moment. One of the most acute observers of the American college has written of the contemporary student, "He seems to spend his life searching for the answer to the question, 'When does life begin?'" In Will Oursler's novel, *New York, New York,* one character speaks for many a college student: " 'Someday I may do something terribly important,' Jackie told him solemnly. 'That's what I'm working on now. Thinking I've got to think it all out, so I won't make a mistake.' " Are there, then, no terribly important things to be done now? Many of us, I think, are convinced the answer to that is no and the result is that we move through our four years of college in almost total ignorance of the depth and range of life—real life—which is opened all about us.

Perhaps this is not so surprising. When you find yourself needing to make conversation with a small child, what is the very first question you are likely to ask him? "What are you going to be when you grow up?" That has become the test question of our culture. We have been systematically schooled to believe that life is something that begins some time in the future. We do not ask a young man, "What kind of person are you now?" but "What are you going to be?" Too seldom have young people in our society been encouraged to take responsibility for life now, within the full reach of their capacity. Even in college there is too much perpetuation of the conditions of childhood. And the result is that, when we are grown, many of us are not "grown up." College students who ask, "When does life begin?" very soon become professional men and housewives asking, "When does life begin?"

There is a character in one of Jean-Paul Sartre's novels who fits our problem, a professor who is not really a man because he has never chosen to be a man and is therefore nothing. When he comes to the full realization of his nothingness, he says, "I have led a toothless life. I have never bitten into anything. I was waiting. I was saving myself for later on, and I have just noticed that my teeth are gone."

463

III

You are under no obligation to make tomorrow's decisions today. "Take no thought for the morrow," says Jesus, "For the morrow shall take thought for the things of itself. Sufficient unto the day is the evil thereof." But these words of Jesus do not stand by themselves in the Gospel of Matthew. They are preceded by some other words without which their statement is incomplete. These words: "Seek first the kingdom of God and his righteousness, and all these things shall be yours as well."

If we are not required to make tomorrow's decisions today, we are required to make today's decisions today, and that is responsibility enough to occupy any of us. What Jesus has enunciated here is, I am persuaded, the first principle of religious life. But it is more than that. It is the first principle of all life. It is the character of our decisions today that sets limits to the possibility of our decisions tomorrow. The Apostle Paul put the matter no less pointedly when he wrote, "Whatsoever a man soweth, that shall he also reap."

Then I have not really given you a way through the frightening problems of decision at all. If I have given you a good conscience about refusing to make certain kinds of choices, I have left you with other choices no less demanding. The question, what shall I do now, may be no less difficult for many of you than the question, what shall I do four years from now. And in the presence of this immediate question, you may feel as Werner von Gerlach felt: alone.

But the truth is that we are not alone, you and I. My own thinking is very much in debt to the existentialists, and I honor them for the courage with which they have made us face some of the facts of our human experience which we might prefer to forget. Some of you have heard me say before that one of the best definitions of existentialism I know is that "no one can take your bath for you." The existentialist philosophers and dramatists have made us see that each of us is an accountable individual, and we cannot assign responsibility for our actions to anyone else. As no one can do my dying for me, so no one can do my living for me. And no one finally can make my decisions for me. Most of us, I think have come to accept that. The person who comes into my office and prefaces his remarks by saying, "I know you can't tell me what I must do," acknowledges just what the existentialists have been telling us.

But I think the time has come for us to see that in another respect the existentialists have sold us a bill of goods, and the product is shoddy. They have become so preoccupied with the lonely individual that that is all they see, and as a consequence, they have falsified the human situation. The Jewish philosopher and theologian, Martin Buber, was once an orthodox existentialist; but Buber was too sensitive an observer of human life to be satisfied with this view of lonely man. While it is true, it is only part of the truth. The other part of the truth is supplied in Buber's trenchant phrase, "Real life is meeting."

How do you men know what it is really to be a man? How do you women know what it is really to be a woman? Is that something you are given simply by internal reflection, by gazing inward upon your own ego until you compel it to give up its secret? Of course not. There are two experiences that tell me what it is to be a man. One is meeting another man, coming into contact with one of my own sex who gets hold of my life in such a way that I want to become like him. When that happens, I begin to understand what it is to be a man because I have a model to follow. The other experience is meeting a woman, coming into contact with one of the opposite sex who gets hold of my life in such a way that I understand how my life as a man is incapable of completing itself, that it must be complemented by hers.

Reliable self-knowledge is one of the conditions of intelligent and effective choice. My decisions go awry most often because my self-estimate is distorted. But real understanding of myself never comes in isolation. It is the product of our human interaction. It comes in meeting another. I cannot estimate myself aright until I am prepared to take seriously the estimate others make of me. Of course I cannot allow myself to capitulate simply to what others think of me. That would obliterate my own individuality. But I must nevertheless allow their estimates to correct my own—to prod me into larger expectation when I would have been satisfied with the lesser, to make my expectation more modest when my ambition outruns my real capacity.

The self-made man is a myth. There is a proverb which says, "Pygmies standing on the shoulders of giants can see farther than the giants." The one who claims to be a self-made man is only a pygmy who doesn't know that he is not standing on his own feet. "We are members one of another." That phrase comes out of the New Testament, and it describes the real truth of our human condition. It does not deny our individuality. "There are many members," says Paul, "and not all members have the same function." But we comprise one body, bound together by influences so fragile they are sometimes scarcely seen, yet so indelible that they can never be erased from our lives. If, in the moment of decision, I shut myself up in lonely isolation, I cut the only links which make wise decision possible.

IV

Then is it really true that we cannot appeal to any precedent for help in the decisions which face us? That was the third fear we noted, and it becomes pertinent just here. Is it really the case, as the Frenchman Gide suggests, that our freedom is rudderless with nothing to guide it? Is it finally so that no problem which another man has faced can provide guidance for me, because no one else has ever faced quite my problem before?

Well, in one sense, of course, it is true. I am I. I am a unique, unrepeatable human event. There has been no person before, and none will come after, quite like me. But if I am thus different from other men, the continuity of my experience with the experiences of other men is at least as real a fact about me. It is precisely because my humanity is not radically different that it is possible for another man to become a model for me.

When Harry Emerson Fosdick was minister of the Riverside Church in New York City, many a Columbia University student, deep in despair, found his way into the minister's study. Often the student would start to say, "Dr. Fosdick, let me tell you I feel." But Dr. Fosdick would stop him and say, "Wait a moment. Let *me* tell you how you feel." And then the minister would describe the life of despair with such accuracy and vividness that the student saw his own experience mirrored in the description. Sometimes it was for him the beginning of the way out, this discovery that he was not the only one to feel as he felt, this discovery that another had been there before him. This was no academic recital for Dr. Fosdick, gleaned from psychiatric texts. As a young man he had spent a time in a mental institution until he found his own sense of balance returning; and years later in the study of the Riverside Church it provided that human connection with the experience of others which helped more than one person through difficult times.

I think we might be surprised at the understanding others are prepared to give us—understanding for the most apparently unique problems—understanding in the most apparently unlikely places, because some one has been there before us. This, indeed, is the significance of the figure of Christ in the Christian faith. His was not a protected, privileged kind of humanity. Catalog the crises which afflict our human kind, and there is scarcely one he did not know. Failure, betrayal by friends, rejection by family, empty acclaim, temptation to selfishness, mental anguish, physical torment, threat of death: our experiences, perhaps, and his as well. In itself that might not be significant. That would not make him admirable, only pitiable. What is significant is this: those experiences did not control him; he controlled them. I am offered a part in that life of victory. It is no empty offer. I will become a Christian when I accept Christ as the precedent for my life. I can become a Christian because he has been there before me.

V

If only we dared to make such a choice. But how do we know that the claims the Christian faith makes for Christ are really true? How can we be sure that God was in Christ, as some Christian seems always to be saying? How can we tell in advance that the way of love which Christ taught is really practicable in our kind of world? How do we even know for certain that God exists? Indeed, some of us become periodically impatient that, if he exists, he should declare himself to us more openly more unequivocally. If only he were to do that, then we should be prepared to believe.

Of course, there is no way to be sure of any of these things in advance. And it is not simply the absence of a clearly visible God which creates uncertainty in our decisions. Religious commitment is by no means the only issue which mocks us with the openness of its outcome: to pledge or not to pledge, to go steady or not to go steady, to apply to this graduate school or that one, to prepare for this vocation or the other, to marry now or to marry later. If only we could see the end of the beginning.

When I started work on this sermon yesterday, I had a very frustrating experience. I should have been able to anticipate it, because it happens every time, but there it was again. I had a set of ideas that seemed reasonably pertinent, reasonably important. I had even jotted some of them down. For a time I sat and looked at my notes, trying to figure out how to tie the thing together, how to give it pungency of illustration, development of idea, relevance of application. I wanted to see it whole before I began to write. The trouble was that the longer I sat and studied those notes, the emptier my head became and the greater my mental paralysis. I got absolutely nowhere until I sat down at my typewriter and wrote a first tentative sentence. It gradually became modified, but one sentence led to another, phrased and rephrased; one idea led to another, cast and recast. Implications emerged that I had never seen before. Some things I had originally intended to include simply did not fit and had to be left out. Some illustrations that had never occurred to me suddenly turned up, drawn out in the process of free association of ideas.

Life is just this kind of process of free association of actions and ideas. Insist on seeing the end from the beginning, insist on seeing it whole before you take hold of one of the parts, and the result is paralysis of the will. But when you have an idea, and ideal, a cause, a course of action which seems worthy, and when you dare to take that first tentative step out upon it, other steps follow. Sometimes you step back temporarily. At times you may step back all the way, to begin again on a slightly different direction. But one step leads to another, experiences appear which you could never have anticipated, opportunities open which you could not have planned, satisfactions emerge which you had never even guessed. All because you dared to take that first step.

There is no other way. In the Gospel of John, Jesus puts it this way: *he that does the work* shall know of the doctrine whether it be true.

VI

How then will you face your choice? You are under no obligations to make tomorrow's decisions today, but we are required to make today's decisions today—not in loneliness but in meeting, not adrift and rudderless but in the presence of those who have been there before us, not with all answers in advance, but with the wonder and expectation of those who dare to take the first step.

18

THE SEPARATION OF CHURCH AND STATE
Charles Stewart

The controversy over the separation of church and state has been a part of America life since the earliest colonial period. Most of the original colonies were settled according to religious belief, and the majority sect tended to become the established church with state enforcement of its beliefs and practices. On the eve of the Revolutionary War, only four colonies had no established churches and Rhode Island alone had complete separation of church and state and no laws unfavorable to Catholics and non-Christians.

The Revolutionary and early constitutional periods saw remarkable changes in church-state relationships in America. The intermingling of religions during the war, accompanied by a wave of religious indifference and skepticism, created a more tolerant atmosphere and lessened the influence of established churches. In December of 1785, the Virginia Assembly passed an act guaranteeing religious freedom and no established church in Virginia. This act served as an impetus for other states to remove religious strictures and for national action at the Constitutional Convention in 1787 and the first session of

Congress in 1789. The first clause of the First Amendment to the Constitution read: "Congress shall make no law respecting an establishment of religion, or prohibiting the free exercise thereof. . . ."

Many of the "founding fathers," Thomas Jefferson in particular, were optimistic that the Constitution had effectively erected "a wall of separation between church and state." It took decades, however, for the last vestiges of religious intolerance to be removed from the statutes and constitutions of the original states. Generations of clergy have debated state limitations on religion, tax exemption of churches, governmental aid to parochial schools, religious observances in public schools, and even the proper degree of separation between church and state.

Since the early nineteenth century, Protestants have viewed with alarm the ever growing Roman Catholic minority in America. Papal claims of complete control over church members and pronouncements against separation of church and state have convinced Protestant spokesmen that the "wall of separation" was in grave danger. Groups like the American or Know Nothing Party have tried to prevent Catholics from gaining any local, state, or national political office. Above all, Protestants have feared either a Catholic or pro-Catholic candidate winning the presidency. The so-called religious issue, usually the assertion that the Catholic Church was controlling one of the presidential candidates, entered into the elections of 1856, 1876, 1884, and 1896.

The twentieth century has witnessed continued furor over the separation of church and state. Old issues have remained unresolved, and new controversies, often with the Roman Catholic Church at the center, have arisen over birth control, federal aid for parochial schools, bus transportation for students in parochial schools, and prayer in public schools. The religious issue haunted Presidents Theodore Roosevelt, Taft, and Wilson, while in 1928 the first practicing Catholic, Alfred E. Smith, won the Democratic nomination for president. The religious issue played a major role in the 1928 campaign and in Smith's defeat. Since World War II, the United States

Supreme Court has played an increasing role in determining violations of the constitutional provisions separating church and state.

The decade of the 1960's could prove to be the peak of controversy over the separation of church and state. Its first year saw the nomination and election of the first Roman Catholic president; its second year has been called the "most important single year in the legal history of American church and state relations" because of the volume of court cases; and succeeding years have witnessed a continuing series of momentous Supreme Court decisions concerning governmental sponsorship of religious activities. The American pulpit has been as active in these controversies as it has in all church-state matters since the colonial period. Nowhere has pulpit involvement been better exemplified than in the 1960 election and the reaction to the Supreme Court decisions concerning religious exercises in the public schools.

THE 1960 ELECTION

Months before John F. Kennedy announced his candidacy for the Democratic Party's presidential nomination, Protestant pulpits began to tell congregations of the Roman Catholic threat to religious liberty and the separation of church and state. Preaching on the "religious issue" seemed to intensify each time Kennedy took a step closer to the presidency, and it continued until election eve.

The thesis of most anti-Catholic sermons was that the Roman Catholic Church, in theory and in practice, was opposed to the American traditions of religious liberty and the separation of church and state. The basic strategy was to present simple, well supported arguments and then to challenge Kennedy and the Catholic hierarchy to disprove or even to deny the charges as made. Wherever possible, clergymen relied on Catholic sources for their supporting materials. They provided a variety of evidence from foreign and American sources and from historic and very recent dates to show, first, that the beliefs and practices of the Catholic Church were prevalent in

471

America as well as in distant foreign countries and, second, that the Church's positions were long-standing and still believed and practiced. Preachers generally paid little heed to candidate Kennedy because they said he would follow, indeed that he had to follow, his Church's dictates.

The majority of clergymen who opposed the religious issue refrained from preaching on it lest their very discussions serve as admissions that religion was a legitimate campaign issue. As the campaign progressed, however, some clergymen (Protestant, Catholic, and Jewish) felt compelled to answer the mounting charges against Kennedy and Catholicism. They feared that a rise of religious intolerance and dissension would result if the anti-Catholic sermons remained unchallenged.

The strategy of pro-Catholic sermons was defensive in nature, an attempt only to answer the charges against the Catholic Church and not to provide new counter-arguments. Clerics admitted the existence of Catholic pronouncements against both religious liberty and the separation of church and state and admitted acts of persecution in some Catholic countries. They argued, however, that there was no "official" Catholic position on the issue of church and state. Anti-Catholic preachers were accused of carefully selecting only those pronouncements and examples that would prove their thesis, while ignoring Catholic support of the wall between church and state, religious liberty, and Catholic countries where no intolerance could be found. Some pro-Catholic clergy pointed out that their opposition, both here and abroad, was guilty of the very practices for which they were condemning the Catholic Church. The sermons in this volume by James William Morgan and Carroll Brooks Ellis serve to illustrate the polarity of the issue and arguments used.

Postelection studies have shown that the religious issue did play a major role in the 1960 election, and that it did deny many votes to Kennedy. John Kennedy managed to win, however, and the religious issue may never again be a strong factor in national politics.

472

PRAYER AND BIBLE READING IN THE PUBLIC SCHOOLS

On June 25, 1962, the Supreme Court declared that a prayer prescribed for the New York public schools was a violation of the First Amendment's guarantees of religious freedom and the separation of church and state. Reaction from the pulpit was immediate and vocal. Generally, Catholic and conservative Protestant clergy condemned the decision while Jewish and liberal Protestant clerics defended and even praised the court's action. The controversy received new life when, on June 17, 1963, the Court decided that required Bible reading and recitation of the Lord's Prayer as specified in statutes of Pennsylvania and Maryland were also unconstitutional.

Preaching against the Court's decisions has tended to be highly emotional with little consideration of what the Court actually said. A common tactic, for example, has been to discredit the Court by suggesting that it is communistic and atheistic, or at least that it is consciously supporting Communists and atheists against loyal, Christian Americans. Clergymen have argued that the decisions on prayer and Bible reading were erroneous because, first, the Court made an excessively narrow interpretation of the Constitution; second, the actions were contrary to American history and traditions; third, the decisions were part of a sinister plot to remove God from all aspects of American life; and, fourth, that the Court was allowing minorities to usurp the powers of the majority. The only solution, they argued, was a constitutional amendment that would allow religious exercises in the public schools.

Clergymen favoring the Court's decisions have attacked anti-Court sermons at their weakest spot—lack of consideration of what the Court actually said and did. They quoted at length from the decisions, cited reasons why the Court could have acted only the way it did, and showed why prescribed prayers and Bible readings were dangerous breaches of the wall between church and state. Pro-Court preachers have frequently evaluated the practices ruled unconstitutional, and tried to show that they were of questionable religious value. For a solution, clergymen proposed increased prayer in both the home and the church. A constitutional amendment, they warned, could lead to state prescribed religion in other areas of American life. This issue and delineating arguments are illustrated in the accompanying sermons by Donald W. Morgan and Marion L. Matics.

The controversy over the Supreme Court's actions has not ended, but it has gradually lessened and the decisions have gained increasing support. Dozens of bills have been introduced into both houses of Congress with the express purpose of overruling the Court. The Senate and the House have held public hearings on proposed constitutional amendments. Thus far no bill for amendment has posed a serious threat to the Court's actions.

JAMES W. MORGAN

*James William Morgan was born in Dallas, Texas, on
April 24, 1914, and has spent nearly all of his life in his
native state. He received a Bachelor of Arts Degree from
Southern Methodist University in 1935, and a Bachelor of
Divinity Degree from Perkins School of Theology at Southern
Methodist in 1937. Morgan served churches in Corpus Chris-
ti, Seguin, Georgetown, and San Antonio before assuming
his present position at the University Methodist Church in
Austin, Texas, in June of 1959. He has served on many im-
portant national and international committees of The United
Methodist Church and has contributed articles to* Christian
Century, The Pulpit, *and* Together. *"Reformation Day and
the Election" was delivered in the University Methodist
Church, Austin, Texas, on October 30, 1960.*

Reformation Day and the Election[*]

Four hundred forty-three years ago tomorrow, a Roman Catholic monk
named Martin Luther nailed his ninety-five theses to the church door at
Wittenberg, initiating a debate that eventually brought into being what is
loosely known as the Protestant Church or the Reformation. He was not the
first or the last to engage in that great struggle. The Roman Catholic Church
was itself greatly changed, but the most obvious result was a distinct polariz-
ing of the Christian movement. The central creed of all Christian churches
remained, and still is, the Apostles' Creed which we have repeated this
morning. But when we join in saying, "I believe in the Holy Catholic
Church," we all stand under the judgment of God that we are a divided
Body of Christ, even though we know our Lord has prayed that we might
be One.

This Sunday on the church calendar comes at a peculiar moment in our
American history when the conflict between Protestant and Catholic has
erupted in many ways. Right after the conventions I wrote an editorial in
which I tried to state that religion is not *the* issue. I promised myself that
this would be all I would say. As the weeks have gone by, I have sadly
realized that I cannot possibly speak on this Reformation Sunday and ignore
this issue. I would be an ostrich, making our faith wholly irrelevant if I

[*] Reprinted by permission of the author.

dared to witness to Reformation Doctrine without reference to what has been happening in recent weeks.

But oh how difficult it is to thread your way through these issues and be fair! How painful to speak in an atmosphere where our emotions are intensified as they always are by a presidential campaign. If my main concern were to please people, I should have chosen another topic, chosen to ignore the day, or had a visiting speaker.

The very matter of speaking on this subject raises some real questions as to the propriety of such a theme in the pulpit. Several years ago a prominent theologian began a new semester with these words:

I have made a point never to speak about current politics in my lectures, and I think I shall not do so in the future. However, it would seem to me unnatural were I to ignore today the political situation in which we begin this new semester. The significance of political happenings for our entire existence has been brought home to us in such a way that we cannot evade the duty of reflecting on the meaning of our theological work in *this* situation.

That was Rudolf Bultmann speaking in 1933 in Germany, roughly one month after Hitler received full power. It is easy to say that politics shall never invade the pulpit, but who would deny that the church in Germany was doomed as irrelevant if the pulpit did not deal with those issues affecting the body, mind, soul, and spirit of all people.

Today, in America, we are faced with a most divisive force in our common life. There is evidence that a small group of little known churches are turning this Reformation Sunday into an anti-Catholic rally. Neighbor is being pitted against neighbor. The fabric of our national solidarity is being threatened. The invitation to the Holy Communion is being threatened when it asks if we are "in love and charity with our neighbors." So, painful or not, offensive or not, I must declare the Gospel this morning as I see it, relevant to the current situation.

It is the principle of the religious issue, and this alone, that I am concerned about this morning. It would be sheer arrogance on my part to tell you to vote for either candidate or either party, or even to suggest in any way that God's will favors one side or the other. But it seems infinitely clear that we as Christians must face the terrible consequences in our common life of the forces that would pit Protestant against Roman Catholic in this election.

I

Let us begin by recognizing that there are not just two sides to this question, but many sides. May I try to describe four positions:

A. First, the position of pure prejudice which is the only position that I will label as bigoted. This is the stand that makes the candidate's Roman Catholicism the supreme issue just because they cannot tolerate Roman Catholics. This is the position that would vote against a Roman Catholic no matter who was running against him. This I do not hesitate to label as bigoted, even though I resent the label being attached to all who dare to discuss the issue. You will discover that I have serious differences with our Roman Catholic brethren, but they are still my Christian brothers. Because we both stand under the judgment of God, I must acknowledge and treat them as my brothers, even as I would desire them to treat me.

Therefore, we must resist with all our power the fanatic prejudice that has been released in this campaign. The judgment of God has fallen upon some of the lies and hatred that have been called forth. That anyone would dare to use the false oath of the Knights of Columbus or the equally bogus Protocols of the Elders of Zion indicates that they are either sick or are willing to use a lie to promote their cause. You see, I can have no religious freedom, nor freedom from lies, unless I am also willing to protect my brother's rights in the same way. Yet, when we Protestants let these lies continue to float around, we stand under the judgment of God. And, I refer to all the silly stories of prejudice we hear about guns in the basements of Roman churches, the immorality of priests and nuns, and all the other foolishness of prejudice. Brethren, in the name of God and truth, let us fight such lies wherever we find them.

B. A second stance or position that is being taken might well be as dangerous—though it appears just the opposite. This is the naïve attitude that runs around under the banner of tolerance. It seems to say: Religion makes no difference, this is a political campaign and religion has nothing to do with it. Now this is mainly thoughtless. Such people believe they are speaking a word for tolerance, but what they are saying is that religion doesn't make any difference. This is the idea of the compartmentalized man, that he can keep his religion in one section of his brain and his politics in another and never the twain shall meet. Such a man is dangerous. It is obvious that I do not believe the denominational affiliation of the candidates is *the* issue in this campaign, but let us not jump to the conclusion that our faith makes no difference. If Mr. Criswell, a Southern Baptist in Dallas, were running for president, I would more than likely vote against him because of his personal religious convictions that no Roman Catholic should be allowed to hold any public office. But I would never find the religious convictions of a Southern Baptist like Blake Smith to be a bar to public office. A Mennonite would hardly make a good Secretary of Defense, and it is not likely that we shall appoint a Christain Scientist as Secretary of Health, Education, and Welfare. So, the supposed tolerance of this position is really saying that religious faith is nothing. Actually, it is our religious faith that causes us to choose as responsibly as we know how, knowing that our choices stand before the judgment bar of God.

C. A third position is taken by a thoughtful few whom I respect and cannot call bigoted, but with whom I heartily disagree. This position, without prejudice, believes that the Vatican itself must make some guarantees and some changes in her stand on church-state relationships and the rights of people whom she considers in error before a Roman Catholic can serve in good conscience as president of the United States. I do not believe this position is realistic in this particular situation, but it cannot accurately be called bigoted.

D. A fourth position I defend: That in this particular situation, with these particular candidates, given the assurances that have been given, we must not let the denominational affiliation of the candidates be *the* deciding factor.

II

Let us consider our differences, for we do not help this matter by denying that differences exist. They are great and serious differences, but the matter at stake is whether or not we have created a constitution and a culture in which the very great differences can live together with mutual respect and understanding.

The Roman Church as a church represents the principle of authority. The Protestant Church at the opposite pole represents the principle of freedom and individual conscience. Who is to say that America is to exist without either of these principles? We Protestants are always in danger of allowing freedom to degenerate into license, whereas our Roman Catholic brethren are always in danger of allowing their principle of authority to deny the freedom of individual responsibility. There is much evidence that we have had a wholesome influence upon each other in this regard.

In preparation, I re-read all the Vatican pronouncements and encyclicals I felt to be pertinent to this problem of the Roman Catholic and the American Constitution. There are not many subjects on which Rome has not had something to say. There are many statements stemming from Rome's conviction that she is the only Christian Church which can be used as fuel for the fire. But this is to ignore the vast amount of excellent work that has been done in America which is the truer expression of the vast majority of Roman Catholic laymen and clergy. I shall use only two such statements. The first is from the famous statement of the Roman Catholic Bishops issued in 1948, twelve years ago:

We feel with deep conviction that for the sake of both good citizenship and religion there should be a reaffirmation of our original American tradition of free cooperation between government and religious bodies—cooperation involving no special privilege to any group and no restriction on the religious liberty of any citizen. We solemnly disclaim any intent or desire to alter this prudent and fair American Policy of government dealing with the delicate problems that have their source in the divided religious allegiance of our citizens. We call upon our Catholic people to seek in their faith an inspiration and a guide in making an informed contribution to good citizenship.

And the other statement from Archbishop John T. McNicholas, speaking also in 1948:

We deny absolutely and without any qualification that the Catholic Bishops in the United States are seeking a union of Church and State by any endeavors whatsoever, either proximate or remote. If tomorrow Catholics constitute a majority of our country, they would not seek a Union of Church and State. They would, then, as now, uphold the Constitution and all its Amendments, recognizing the moral obligation imposed on all Catholics to observe and defend the Constitution and its Amendments.

I cannot deny that there are many statements from the Vatican which seem to contradict such American pronouncements, but the significant thing is that Rome has not silenced these opinions and this speaks volumes.

Of course, there are differences and pressures because of these differences. This is the meaning of both government and democracy. We wouldn't be holding an election if there were no differences. But this is the Protestant principle that both Catholic and Protestant, both Democrat and Republiccan, all stand under the judgment of Almighty God. We are given the freedom to act and to choose, but all our acts and choices stand under the judgment of God.

III

A second matter we must examine. We are always in danger of becoming what we say we abhor. Have you not felt this judgment at times in our quarrel with Russia, that we find ourselves doing and saying those things dangerously close to our accusations of Russia? This so often shows itself in our Protestant quarrels with Rome. The Roman church is predicated on the

479

belief that she is the only true church; therefore, many of her pronouncements are offensive to Protestants. I was pleased to see Pope John remove the
word "heretic" as it applies to Protestants and substitute, "separated brethren." But while we complain, we must also look at some of our pronouncements about Rome. Both of us must recognize that our words and persecutions of each other both stand condemned of God.

One of the peculiarities of this present time is the accusation that Rome
is so monolithic and authoritarian that she always votes as a solid block,
denying the right of individual choice. Our own experiences with our Roman Catholic friends should make us know this is not true. There are Roman
Catholic Republicans and Roman Catholic Democrats. Doubtless some
Roman Catholics are voting for Mr. Kennedy just because he is Roman Catholic; and there are others voting against him from fear that a Roman Catholic
in the White House would blame Roman Catholics for all that goes wrong.
Undoubtedly, the hatemongering has driven some Roman Catholics, as well
as Protestants, to vote for Mr. Kennedy out of sympathy.

But the significant thing to see is that certain groups of Protestants have
become monolithic in demanding that their members vote against the
Roman Catholic just because he is a Roman Catholic. The very church
most vocal for individual conscience has also been the most monolithic
and authoritarian. When one of their distinguished members dared to defy
that stand here in Austin, he was overwhelmingly censured. How odd that
we should accuse the Roman Catholics of telling members how to vote and
use this to tell our members how to vote. Protestants are defeating the very
principle they were responsible for writing into the Constitution.

God is concerned that we bring to our vote the best study and counsel
we can secure, but there is no theological principle that permits any church
or any person to declare that it is clearly God's will that we vote one way
or the other. I enjoyed the wag who told of two priests discussing the
issue. One declared to the other: "I'm not going to vote for Mr. Kennedy.
I don't want the Vatican run from Washington."

IV

Finally, I think it is time for us to ring the bell for American Freedom.
America is the greatest experiment the world has ever known. We have
dared to say that all races, all colors, all creeds can live together here in
freedom. The way this religious issue has been raised in this campaign
threatens all we hold dear. In so much that has been said there is the
declaration that we must never elect a Roman Catholic, that forty million

Americans must be denied certain constitutional rights, that henceforth this is a Protestant country in which Roman Catholics are merely tolerated but denied full privileges as Americans.

Brethren, let us be done with the hysterical fear gripping America. We act as though the Constitution and the American system of government will fall if we really exercise the freedoms we claim in the Constitution. One of the tragedies of all political races is that we begin to think with our emotions. We have two shrewd, brilliant young men running for our highest office—we do not have a political saviour in either of them, nor a political anti-Christ.

The percentage of Roman Catholics in this country has not appreciably changed since unlimited immigration stopped years ago. Yet Protestants are acting as though every one will suddenly become a Roman Catholic if a Roman Catholic president is elected. What sort of fear is this? It is the greatness of America that Protestant or Catholic is free to persuade all America to be Protestant or Catholic. Are we Protestants so fearful of our own witness that we believe this witness to the Word of God will no longer prevail? Actually, the demonstration here has permitted religious freedom to arise in many places such as France and Ireland, predominantly Catholic. Not all Roman Catholic countries are like Spain.

But America is living in a fishbowl and the whole world is watching and wondering if we believe the freedoms we so loudly proclaim.

Oh, the greatness of America. Here two city boys, Mr. Nixon and Mr. Kennedy, are bleeding for the farmers. A Protestant Eisenhower has declared a position on birth control acceptable to the Roman Catholics and Roman Catholics Kennedy and Brown have taken a position acceptable to the Protestants. A great general, Eisenhower, uses his military prestige to resist spending more on the military, and a Texan, Lyndon Johnson, is the only Senate Leader since Reconstruction to get a civil rights bill through. A Roman Catholic Kennedy promises no federal aid to parochial schools, and a Protestant Lodge takes the opposite side. Mr. Criswell says Mr. Kennedy is lying, and I am awaiting his pronouncement on Mr. Lodge. Rich boy Roosevelt did favors for his poor constituents, and poor boy Eisenhower has done favors for his rich constituents. "In such a political system a Protestant office holder has no choice but to look after his Catholic constituents. And vice versa." Even the *Wall Street Journal* which could hardly be put in the Democratic Camp has said: ". . . a Catholic cardinal would find it far easier to present his political views to a Protestant President than to this man from his own church." We're far too complex a people to be settled with a label.

What I have tried to say is really quite simple. Vote for the candidate or party of your choice, based upon your studied belief as to which man or party can best lead the nation and the world in these critical days—but don't let your decision rest *solely* upon the denominational affiliation of either candidate.

Let us pray:

Grant, O Lord, that against the confusion of false choices and the restlessness of our unsure desires we may know that in thy will is our peace; through Jesus Christ our Lord. Amen.

CARROLL BROOKS ELLIS

Carroll Brooks Ellis was born in Booneville, Mississippi, on May 24, 1919. He spent much of his early life in Texas, where he began preaching in 1936 and where he received a Bachelor of Science Degree from North Texas State College in 1941. Ellis has long pursued two professions, preaching and college teaching. He has been a minister at Churches of Christ in Plano and Austin, Texas, Baton Rouge, Louisiana, and different churches in Nashville, Tennessee. Ellis was an instructor in speech at Louisiana State University from 1945 to 1949, and received both the Master of Arts and Doctor of Philosophy Degrees from that institution. He has been on the faculty of David Lipscomb College since 1949, where he is currently a Professor of Speech and Chairman of the Speech Department. Along with his many duties as minister and professor, he has spoken frequently on lectureships at various colleges and on programs of the Speech Association of America. The Sermon "Religion and the Presidency" was delivered on July 10, 1960 in the Waverly-Belmont Church of Christ in Nashville, Tennessee.

Religion and the Presidency*

The man who occupies the office of president of the United States has the number one position in the world. He has power which would make Caesar, Genghis Khan, or Napoleon bite his nails with envy. By the Constitution he is hailed as the Chief of State; that is, he is the ceremonial head of the government. In President Taft's words, he is the "personal embodiment and representative of the dignity and majesty of America." He is the Chief Executive. He not only reigns, but he rules. He is responsible for the ethics, loyalty, and efficiency of the American government.

President Truman had a sign on his desk, "The Buck Stops Here." Others can blame another individual, but the final responsibility rests upon the president. He is the Chief Diplomat; that is, the prime officer in international relations. The president is the Commander-in-Chief of the Armed Forces of the United States. While he cannot declare war, his handling of the armed forces might easily provoke a war. He is the Chief Legislator, responsible for guiding Congress in much of its legislative activity. In addi-

* Reprinted by permission of the author.

tion, he must play the role of the Voice of the People. At the present time, he must serve as the leader of the Coalition of Free Nations. The presidency unites power, drama, and prestige as does no other office in the world.

It is always important to consider carefully the qualifications of any man who is to be handed this much power. Once in office, he cannot be removed without a major political upheaval or revolution. His decisions will affect the destiny of millions. Not only the candidate's experience, ability, general political beliefs, and health should be considered; but his religion, as well. Religion, admittedly, is a delicate matter and often controversial; but it is an inescapable part of the life of every individual. In most instances, the basic philosophy of an individual is more important even than isolated acts or statements. The religious commitment of any individual is an indication of his training and general outlook upon life. The religious beliefs of every man who has sought the office of president have always been held up to public scrutiny, and they should be. If the basic philosophy of an individual is opposed to the responsibilities placed upon him in his office, he is not qualified to serve in this capacity. The religious position of some does disqualify them from certain offices. For example, a Christian Scientist could not serve as Secretary of Health. Neither could a practicing Quaker be qualified as Secretary of War. A Jehovah's Witness would certainly not be qualified to make flags.

NEVER A CATHOLIC PRESIDENT

For a period of one hundred and seventy-one years no Catholic has been elected president of the United States. In 1928, a Catholic, Alfred E. Smith, was defeated, partly at least, because of his religious affiliation. There is a solid reason why the citizens of our free nation have never elected a Catholic to the highest office of the land. This action has not been taken because Catholics are not loyal and patriotic American citizens, but because the nature of their religious affiliation places them in a position where they could be made to serve as tools for the dissolution of American freedom and liberties. It is true that Catholics have been elected to public offices, but they have come mainly from sections where there was a predominant Catholic population. In several large cities they have had a practical monopoly on the position of mayor and other municipal offices. In a nationwide contest, however, they have not been successful. This has been true because the majority of Americans have recognized the Roman Catholic Church is not just a religious organization, but a temporal power-oriented group which seeks whenever possible to use civil authority to further her own ends.

It goes without saying that to take such a position immediately will cause the label of intolerance, narrow-mindedness, and bigotry to be charged by the Catholic Church. These tactics have been used from the days of the burning of John Huss, the murder of Ulrich Zwingli, the personal vilification of Martin Luther and John Calvin, to the present day. All who have opposed the pretensions of the Roman Catholic Church have been labeled as heretics and renegades. A position of infallibility is supposedly above criticism and not subject to reform. It is true the tactics of the Ku Klux Klan and other radical groups have left a blot upon our national character, but the persecution and bigotry of the Catholic Church are not only a matter of history but of the current scene. Indeed, it is hard to learn the lesson of tolerance from the point of a sword.

REASON FOR OPPOSITION

Because of Catholic ownership and pressure our channels of communications often give a distorted picture of Roman Catholicism. Rarely, indeed, have they given full play even to the expression of Catholics who oppose the hierarchy and the Catholic procedure. A notable exception did occur in an article published in *The Atlantic Monthly*, in 1928, by an American priest who, for his own protection, remained anonymous. His explanation for anti-Catholic feeling is particularly astute and correct. "We are a people self-ostracized," said the priest. "We must have our own schools, our own charities, our own graveyards. We are the modern Pharisees who will not sit with Publicans. Bitterly we complain of the prejudice that has risen against us. We may thank our own aloofness for it. The spirit of segregation is diametrically opposed to the spirit of Christ." Indeed, the spirit of segregation, coupled with the arrogance and dogmatism of Roman Catholicism, is responsible for the reaction against it. Indeed, for every action there is a reaction.

It should be kept in mind also that those who complain of bigotry in opposing a Roman Catholic president of the United States are delighted to uphold the laws of Catholic countries like Spain, Argentina, and Paraguay, which exclude all Protestants and Jews from the highest state offices. In most Catholic countries, a person cannot even receive a commission in the Army unless he is a "loyal Son of Rome."

It must not be assumed, however, that to oppose the political philosophy of the Roman Catholic Church and its methodology automatically places one on the lunatic fringe. It is possible to oppose ideology without unfairness or vulgarity. It is well recognized that the rank-and-file members of the Roman Catholic Church have no control over the Roman hierarchy or the action of the papacy. By various circumstances they have placed themselves in a situation of abject subserviency to a system over which they have no control. Many of those who have been born into this religious affiliation have been so blinded by devotional and personal elements as to be unable to see the social and political implications for America. It is the system, not the people, which needs examination. It is my contention that in at least three areas the position of the Roman Catholic Church disqualifies any of its members to occupy the office of president of United States.

UNION OF CHURCH AND STATE

The Roman Catholic position places the ecclesiastical organization above the state. The ideal relationship is one in which the civil government will foster the teaching and claims of Catholicism. It would be possible to quote from Augustine, the doctrinal parent of Catholicism, or the cataloger, Thomas Aquinas, to support the view that the Pope is by divine right lord of thrones and all earthly things. When Pope Pius V proposed to uncrown Queen Elizabeth I in 1570 and release her subjects from civil allegiance to her, he was following a well established doctrinal pattern. In this instance, he was not able to remove a civil power, but in many instances the papacy has been successful. In the past, leading American Catholic clergymen attempted to get Rome to declare the doctrine of separation of church and state was legal for America, but they were promptly rebuked by Pope Leo XIII, and came back into line.

The Roman Catholic Church has accepted the idea of separation of church and state in America, but according to *Living Our Faith*, by Flynn, Loretto, and Simeon, a book widely used in Catholic schools, "It is still a compromise and . . . the lesser of two evils." The present official position of the Roman Catholic Church is stated in a book by Ostheimer and Delaney, *Christian Principles and National Problems*, under the imprimatur of Cardinal Spellman:

The doctrine of the church . . . is that the State might profess and promote, not any religion, but the one true form of worship founded by Christ and continuing today in the Catholic Church alone. Such a public profession . . . will of necessity bring the State into some relation with Catholicism, the only complete expression of God's revealed Truth. An ideal is when the Church and State would be united in their efforts. (p. 98.)

In spite of the failure to achieve union of church and state in America, the papacy has not given up the ideal. Neither has it given up the attempt to control the thoughts of its people. It is ultimately true that those who control the thoughts of citizens can in time control the government. The strong basis from which the Pope operates is his pretention to have the power to determine to a large extent the destiny of a man's soul in eternity. Is thought control still the philosophy of the Catholic Church? In May of this year, 1960, the official newspaper of the Vatican, *Observatore Romano*, published a special article labeled "Authoritatively Binding on all the Church." This article said, "The Church has full power of jurisdiction over all the faithful to guide and direct them on the plane of ideas and action. The church has the duty and the right to intervene even in the political field. A Catholic can never (prescind) (detach himself) from the teachings and directives of the church. In every section of his activity he must inspire his private and public conduct by the laws, orientation, and instruction of the Hierarchy."

The doctrine of the union of the church and state is unscriptural and unAmerican. God should be placed first in life. When there is a conflict between the state and God, "we must obey God rather than men" (Acts 5:29). The difficulty arises because every Catholic is taught to believe the Pope is the personal representative of God. When he speaks as the official head of the church, he speaks as God. One who listens to the Pope as the voice of God is unqualified to speak for the American people.

The system of free public education is a cornerstone of our democracy. Wisely our forefathers, fleeing from religious tyranny, recognized the state should not be committed to religious instruction. This did not mean our forefathers were antireligious, but that they were antisectarian. Supreme Court Justice Black, in a recent decision, wrote "No tax in any amount, large or small, can be levied to support any religious activity or institutions, whatever they may be called or whatever form they may adopt to teach or practice religion." This has been in harmony with the American tradition.

The priests of the Roman Catholic Church, however, insist they have been appointed by God to control education. This is stated by Pope Pius XI in his encyclical, *The Christian Education of Youth*. The Catholic Church believes that the priests should either (1) administer all schools, or (2) direct religious teaching in all schools, or (3) failing in either of these, develop their own private system of schools which their followers are required to attend. Canon Law 1374 of the Roman Catholic Church states "Catholic children may not attend non-Catholic mutual or mixed schools"; that is, those which are open also to non-Catholic. The only exception is under the permission of the bishop.

The Roman Catholic Church certainly has the right to establish its own schools and to insist on Catholics sending their children to them. The fact that this has serious educational disadvantages and often substitutes training and indoctrination for real learning is their concern.

The official position of the Roman Catholic Church is to petition and receive tax money, money from the public treasury, for supporting its denominational schools. Cardinal McIntyre, Roman Catholic prelate of Los Angeles, has urged federal subsidies to his denominational schools on the basis of aid to the pupils. The Knights of Columbus are now urging tax monies for Roman Catholic private schools. In some twenty-six states they have already received some auxiliary aid from the public treasury, which is unconstitutional; but the power which they have and the continual pressure which they exert has worn down the opposition. With more Catholic officials in office than ever before, they have been successful. There can be no doubt that the goal of the Roman Catholic Church is to have the state support of their schools, schools in which history is taught from a Catholic bias, the mass is held each morning in connection with schools, and a rigid system of indoctrination is engaged in. Again I say the Catholic Church has the right under the Constitution to maintain and support its own schools; but it does not have the right to demand those who do not believe its doctrine to support them. Government support of parochial schools is a step in erasing the traditional line between church and state.

AGAINST RELIGIOUS LIBERTY

The Roman Catholic Church has prospered in the freedom of American democracy. Yet Catholics do not believe freedom of worship should be granted to those who differ from them. In the Jesuit Journal, *Civilta Cattolica*, in April of 1948, they published the following statement:

In some countries Catholics will be obliged to ask full religious freedom for all, resigned to being forced to cohabitate where they alone should rightfully be allowed to live; but in doing this the church does not renounce her thesis which remains the most imperative of her laws, but merely adapts herself to the factual conditions which must be taken into account in practical affairs.

The tenor of this teaching is clear. Freedom of worship is of value to them only when they are in danger of losing it for themselves. In countries where Catholic control is assured, they have outlawed all religious activities except their own. We all remember the treatment which was accorded to gospel preachers in Italy several years ago. They were stoned, jailed, and not allowed to place signs on a place of worship. Recently, three Baptist churches have been closed in Spain, and there are numerous present-day examples of persecution and of discrimination against Protestants in all Catholic countries. The question of the Catholic stand on religious liberty is not an academic one, but is one which can be demonstrated by literally thousands of cases in our present-day world. The Roman Catholic Church has not so boldly acted in America because they have not had the power to do so, but they subtly have used many means to destroy the religious liberty of others.

The Catholic Church boasts of its intolerance because it only has the truth and must oppose error in every form. A loyal Catholic is not permitted by his church to attend religious services of any other group. John Kennedy accepted an invitation to represent the Catholic faith at the dedication for the Chapel of the Four Chaplains in Philadelphia, Pennsylvania. This was not in connection with any religious institution but was a nonsectarian affair. When he was asked to do so by Cardinal Dougherty he rescinded his acceptance and did not attend. A Catholic president would not be allowed by his church to attend Waverly-Belmont Church of Christ if he were in town.

I do not deny the right of the Roman Catholic Church to believe what it desires to believe. I will not agree with them and will use all peaceful means of persuasion to lead them to a more perfect knowledge and understanding. Catholicism, however, does not believe in my right to be a member of the Church of Christ. They do not believe in the right of a person who believes Baptist doctrine to be a member of the Baptist Church, or a person to be a member of the Methodist Church. Any monopolistic system contains a threat to freedom. Hard orthodoxy always leads to persecutions and inquisitions. As Dr. Reinhold Neibuhr has pointed out, the bitter hatred of communism by Catholicism is due to the fact that these two are "rival absolutists." Certainly, I am disturbed by Roman Catholic claims even in a country where they are not as yet able to enforce them.

CATHOLICS WANT CATHOLIC PRESIDENT

I am not surprised the Catholic Church is interested in having one of its members as president. It is interesting to note that those who are most insistent and are the most outspoken leaders for a Catholic president are the members of the Roman Catholic Church. I would not say the election of the Roman Catholic president would mean the immediate dissolution of American liberties. In fact, the first Catholic president might make every effort to stay clear of the influence of the Roman Catholic Church. Yet his election would pave the way for the second and the third, and perhaps would mark the beginning of the loss of American freedom.

To take a position against a Catholic president is not to have hatred or malice for any individual. I do believe one who has in the past supported and continues to support the Roman Catholic system has placed himself in a position where it would be impossible for those who believe in separation of church and state, in public education, and in religious liberty to support him. The religious affiliation of a candidate is a matter of public concern when the religious commitment endangers the basic principles of our nation. May God grant us the courage to protest firmly but lovingly against a system which has deprived millions of their religious liberty and could remove ours.

Donald W. Morgan

Born in Arlington, Massachusetts, February 19, 1925, Donald W. Morgan was reared in historical Lexington. He was granted a Bachelor of Science Degree (magna cum laude) from Tufts College in 1950. Three years later he received a Bachelor of Divinity Degree from Union Theological Seminary. The Rev. Mr. Morgan was pastor of the United Church in Northfield, Vermont, and the First Congregational Church in Litchfield, Connecticut, before becoming the Senior Minister at the Congregational Church (United Church of Christ) in Rutland, Vermont, in 1962. He delivered his sermon "The Supreme Court Decisions: Their Meaning For Us" on September 8, 1963, in his Rutland Church.

The Supreme Court Decisions: Their Meaning for Us*

Within the past year two historic decisions of the Supreme Court have reverberated across the land. The rumblings have yet to subside. Both decisions had to do with religious observances in public schools, and both have received, even in religious circles, mixed, sometimes heated reactions. The first of these decisions, that of a year ago, has been identified as "The Regents' Prayer Decisions"; the other, that of this summer, has been called "The Bible Reading Decisions." Both were focused upon the widespread practice of morning devotions in public schools. And both have stirred up a hornet's nest of approval and disapproval, praise and calumny, criticism and countercriticism.

Now, understandably deep concern has been registered among Christian people. Understandably many of us have received the news of these decisions with shock, bewilderment, even resentment. For what, we wonder, does this mean for the cause of religion in our land? What does this mean for the future influence of the Christian faith throughout the world? What does this mean for our republic, for America—founded largely upon fundamental Christian principles concerning man and God? Have the floodgates been opened to irreligion? Is secularism now the official faith of our country? And will the inevitable consequences of these two decisions set the stage for

* Reprinted by permission of the author.

the gradual demise of vital faith and the slow death of vigorous religion?

These decisions have not only precipitated fear and foreboding among many; they have also occasioned humor, sometimes biting and bitter humor. There is, for instance, the story circulating of a teacher returning to her classroom and observing several boys crouched in a corner, doing something on their knees. "Boys!" she exclaims with apprehension in her voice, "what are you doing?" "Rolling dice, teacher" comes their uneasy reply. "Oh, that is all right! For a moment I thought you were praying." Or there is the cartoon which appeared in several newspaper and news magazines this summer. An irate father exploded from his breakfast table, pounding the table with one hand, clutching the morning paper with the other. "What do they think we're going to do?" he shouts. "Pray with the children at home?"

At any rate, not an American alive to the issues of the day and not a Christian alert to the cause of his Lord has failed to ask searching questions about the meaning and impact of these historic decisions. "What does it all mean? What does it portend for our nation? More importantly, what does it portend for the cause of Jesus Christ? And what should be our response as thinking and committed Christians?" It is with the hope of shedding some helpful light upon the answer to those questions, that we deal with the matter before us this morning.

I

First of all, what precisely were these decisions? Certainly at the outset we need clarification there. For no good can come of sweeping, extravagant claims. We need to be on guard against careless generalizations and idle speculation which may have little or nothing to do with the actual situation before us. What, in a few words, did these two historic decisions assert?

Look at the Regents' Prayer decision. It was in 1951 that the New York state board of regents, an agency created by the legislature, directed that this prayer be used in the morning exercises of the schools of the state: "Almighty God, we acknowledge our dependence upon Thee, and we beg Thy blessings upon us, our parents, our teachers and our country." That would seem innocuous and harmless enough, though a Christian might have some misgivings. The prayer is largely self-centered and heavily nationalistic; it runs counter to the counsels and examples of Christ as to the appropriate use and phrasing of prayer. But our misgivings are mild. In any case, the issue was brought before the Supreme Court. Basing its judgment on the First Amendment, the Court declared the prayer unconstitutional. It averred that "in this country it is no part of the business of government to compose official prayers" and thus in this way "to promote a program to further religious beliefs."

Look now at the Bible Reading decision. It was in 1905 that the Baltimore Board of School Commissioners adopted a regulation which required the reading of the Bible and/or the recitation of the Lord's Prayer at the opening of the school day. In Pennsylvania a law with similar provisions was in effect. These twin requirements in two states were questioned and in time brought before the Supreme Court. After long deliberation, the Court ruled unconstitutional any such religious ceremony or devotional practice. "The place of religion in our society," affirmed the Court, "is an exalted one, achieved through a long tradition of reliance on the home, the church, and the inviolable citadel of the individual heart and mind. We have come to recognize through bitter experience that it is not within the power of government to invade that citadel, whether its purpose or effect be to aid or oppose; to advance or retard."

So spoke the Court in two of the most controversial decisions of our time.

II

Now, in the second place, consider why not a few thoughtful people, despite perhaps initial disappointment and regret, have come to accept these decisions. Certainly those of strong religious convictions were given pause. Certainly those of deep religious faith were disturbed. And certainly those, like your minister, whose concern for the cause of Christ has led them to devote their lives in its service—certainly they have acutely felt the impact of these decisions of the Court. Why then have many accepted these judgments?

Perhaps because they understand that in democratic America when the Supreme Court speaks, responsible citizens must listen. Our freedom is upheld by law. Justice is protected by our legal system. Liberty with order is preserved by the processes wherein the Supreme Court necessarily gives final and conclusive judgments. "It is too late in our history," asserted Congressman Robert Taft, Jr., of Ohio—"It is too late in our history to deny that the Constitution, as interpreted by the [Supreme] Court, is the supreme law of the land." Perhaps these people have understood that recklessly to undermine that court is to undermine democracy itself and to cast a vote for anarchy.

Perhaps that is why, or perhaps there is another reason for their acceptance of the decisions. Perhaps these people have recognized, in the light of history faithfully read, that these latter-day affirmations of the separation of church and state in America are simply the inevitable issue of the birth of the republic itself. How early some of the wisest of our founding fathers, such as Jefferson and Madison, declared the necessity of this division! Yet how slowly the full implications of the doctrine have been fulfilled! It was as late as 1818 that there was an end to state-supported religion in Connecticut, and it was as late as 1832 that there was an end to state-supported religion in Massachusetts. Charles Beecher, son of the most noted minister in America at that time, Lyman Beecher, has described the effect upon his father of the shelving of Congregationalism as the official, tax-supported religion of Connecticut. "I remember seeing father, the day after the election, sitting on one of the old-fashioned, rush-bottomed kitchen chairs, his head drooping on his breast, and his arms hanging down. 'Father,' said I, 'what are you thinking of?' He answered solemnly, 'The Church of God.' " What exactly was the cause of Beecher's gloom? It was the election of the antiestablishment Fusion Party. For in May, 1818, the party which campaigned for the disestablishment of Congregationalism had won the election. That event, in the minds of many, meant the doom of the Christian character of the state and of the nation. "It was," Beecher later wrote, "a time of great depression and suffering. . . . It was as dark a day as ever I saw. The odium thrown upon the ministry was inconceivable. The injury done to the cause of Christ, as we then supposed, was irreparable. For several days I suffered what no tongue can tell." Ah, but time revealed that this was by no means the end of religion in America! And if not then, why now?

Other realizations have led thoughtful people to the acceptance of these decisions of the Supreme Court. For instance, isn't it true that to give the state, whatever our motive, the right to enforce one prayer is to give it the right in time to enforce any prayer? Yet some prayers are so blatantly unchristian that they are an affront to God and a curse upon our lips. To approve the Regents' prayer because we find it relatively innocent is to leave us with no recourse in the face of a prayer which Christian men of conscience dare not recite.

Or again, isn't it true that if the state can require the reading, and seeming acceptance, of the Bible, it can in another time and place require the reading with like acquiescence, of non-Christian writings? You say, how unlikely? Think again! Think hard! In certain school districts of Hawaii the Buddhists enjoy a majority. Hence, by the same token, they could require the reading, not of Christian scriptures, but of Buddhist scriptures. And if we condone such readings here and now because they agree with our convictions, what grounds would we have for refusing such readings there and then which are contrary to our convictions? We would have none!

Or again, isn't it true that to enforce religious observances in the classroom upon little children of tender age is to subject some of them to unfair

494

pressures? What of the Jewish child when the Lord's Prayer is said? Or what of the Catholic child when the King James' Version is used? Or what of the Protestant child when the Lord's Prayer ends abruptly, according to Catholic practice, with "and deliver us from evil," while omitting "for thine is the kingdom, and the power, and glory"? To an adult, this may be tolerable; but to a child it is the rejection of things he holds dear.

Again, isn't it true that to allow the state to compose and compel the use of prayers, or to direct and require the devotional reading of religious writings—that this is an unhealthy reliance upon the power of the state to do the work of the church and of the home? History is full of evidence that such unholy alliances of the church and state mean either corrupt religion or dead religion or both. Take present-day examples, take Sweden, take Spain, take Italy. Take any nation where the church is supported by the state.

Again, isn't it true that such daily exercises heaped upon teachers, willing or unwilling, suited or unsuited, can, instead of inculcating reverence and respect, breed lifelong resistance to vital religion? "Religion," said one minister, "is cheapened, not sustained, by the tawdry, perfunctory attention given it in the public school morning devotion. . . . Such exercises condition children to think religion dull as dishwater."

Or finally, isn't it true that to allow the state, however innocent at the moment it seems, to intrude upon the affairs of religion and conscience, that to do this is to fall into the ancient evil of ancient Rome. Those Christians back there, why did they suffer persecution? Because they were Christians? No, but because they refused to bow down to all the gods sanctioned by the state and to acknowledge a general religion. They would not compromise their faith; they would not compromise their Lord. Shall we then, the heirs of so rich a heritage, blindly succumb to the same evil and become party to the same injustice? God forbid! Whatever our excuse, God forbid!

So many a thoughtful person, having hearkened to the voice of the Court and pondered its judgment with depth and perspective, has accepted its verdict!

III

But dare we leave the matter there? Isn't there one question more crying out to be answered? And isn't it this: What do these decisions mean for us? for you and me? for mothers, and fathers, and children? for any one of us who fancies himself at all interested in preserving and advancing Christian values in our society, in our nation, and in our own lives? The artificial supports are being pulled out, so where must the enduring supports be found? The answer is simple, but has its impact been felt?

For it means the home must do its homework. If because of our weakness and lack of self-discipline and want of faith, we must turn over to the state the nurture of character and religious conviction in our children, so be it, but it won't be democracy, and it won't be Christianity. It will be eventual tyranny and it will be a good deal less than Christianity. The alternative is the home doing its job; mothers and fathers fulfilling their God-given responsibility and not running out on it because it is inconvenient or too demanding or interferes with a game of golf. It means prayer in the home. It means worship in the home. It means Bible reading and the sharing of faith in the home. And it means church in the home. Said that noted Boston physician, the late Dr. Richard Cabot, "In my childhood I was guided not so much by the authority of my parents as by the Higher Authority to which I saw them looking up."

And it means that the church must do its churchwork. How often, alas, the church has degenerated into a social center or a cliquey club. But a church existing first and foremost in every realm for worship and learning, for service and mission, by and for everyone, this we too seldom behold on the current scene. In this year 1963, the church must return to its chief business—providing the home base for the christianizing of all men and all society, right here in Rutland but no less to the distant corners of the world! The church must be the church because nothing else, not even the state, now will do its work for it!

What then do these historic court decisions mean? The end of vital religion in America? The decline of Christian influence throughout our land? But why? You remember poor Lyman Beecher and thousands like him back in 1818 bemoaning the certain death of the church? But now, what really came of that disturbing development? Why an extraordinary resurgence of religion beyond all expectation! And Beecher himself later celebrated it and rejoiced in it. Said he: "It cut the churches loose from dependence on state support, . . . threw them wholly on their own resources and God," and "the effect . . . was just the reverse of the expectation." This may mean a new day, a new birth of faith for us all, and everything now depends on whether you and I, professing Christians, are made of the stuff that the times demand!

Marion L. Matics

Marion L. Matics was born in Suffolk, Virginia, on July 17, 1917. He grew up in the North and received a Bachelor of Arts Degree from the University of Chicago and a Master of Arts Degree from Harvard University. The Rev. Mr. Matics went on to receive an S.T.B. Degree from General Theological Seminary in New York and a Doctor of Philosophy Degree from Columbia University. He served a number of Episcopal churches in New Jersey and New York before becoming rector of Brooklyn's Christ Church Bay Ridge in 1961. Articles of his have appeared in various church magazines. He delivered "Obituary for Children's Prayers" at Christ Church Bay Ridge on June 23, 1963.

Obituary for Children's Prayers*

Last week the Supreme Court of the United States of America declared unconstitutional the reading of the Bible and the saying of the Lord's Prayer in the public schools of the nation. Although such modest religious exercises have been a part of public school tradition and of national life since the arrival of the Pilgrim Fathers, the decision in itself will not ruin the nation, but it is another straw in the rising wind of secularism. In fact, the nation as a whole did not seem to notice this historic and infamous decision very much. It did not create nearly as great a stir as the outlawing of the New York State Regents' Prayer about this time last year, partly because this has been such a news-filled week. We have had further evidence of Communist superiority in outer space, with the Soviet man and the Soviet woman whirling around the earth, showing up our space experts to be feeble amateurs, and providing further indication that our program is bogged down in the mire of politics and God knows what kind of incompetence behind the scenes. Last week we read about the nation torn with racial strife, with threats and counterthreats of violence, and the voice of sanity, if it exists, is lost in the tumult of the bigotry and the shouting. We read about the opening of *Cleopatra*, the papal election, and, most of all perhaps, the great Profumo scandal from across the sea. This latter event provided many lascivious details to drool over that may not make for sound government, or wholesome

---

* Reprinted by permission of the author.

family life, or a happy people, but which certainly sell the papers and are good for conversation. The extreme example of its exploitation, perhaps, is this week's *Life* magazine, a periodical frequently given to a high moralizing tone, which features attractive colored pictures of the principal call girl in revealing costumes and positions. I am referring not to last week's issue with the papal funeral on the cover, but to this week's edition which flaunts a cover photo of Shirley MacLaine as a prostitute.

So, the American people have had a lot to think about; and they have not had much time to be worried because children no longer can read the Bible nor say the Lord's Prayer in the public schools. As the *New York Times* put it, the attitude of many was summed up in the words, "I couldn't care less."

The attitude of our various religious groups is also most interesting. Conservative, fundamentalist Protestants, along with the members of the Roman Catholic Church, have generally denounced the Supreme Court decision. The more liberal Protestants have supported it, and, indeed, have attempted to prepare their people for its coming—for example, as in recent statements issued by the General Assembly of the Presbyterian Church and by the National Council of Churches; and Jewish opinion has been even more enthusiastically favorable. At least, the fundamentalists and the Catholics, whatever their strength and weaknesses, are truly interested in religion as such—the great fact that God exists and that there are basic moral teachings which must be observed if life is to have any meaning or validity—whereas, it might be said of the others that sometimes they appear to be more interested in the causes and subsidiary issues of religion, as, for instance, the delicate problem of freedom of conscience, than in the substance of religion itself. That is not to say that freedom of conscience can be bypassed or ignored, but it is to say that there are other issues which are more fundamental. Freedom in the abstract is a meaningless cipher: The question is, freedom from what, and for what?

When the early settlers came to this country, they sought freedom to worship God as they pleased, without being told how to do it by any church from overseas. They were bitterly opposed to the establishment of a state church; but they were not particularly interested in the freedom *not* to worship God, although in due time they came to realize that even this freedom was necessary. However, it was furtherest from their thought that the nation should be neutral concerning our basic theistic belief and the moral principles of the Bible from which the rights of man are essentially derived. It was their opinion that, just because man is a child of God and endowed by his Creator with certain unalienable rights, he deserves to be free from tyranny of any sort.

498

This great point is made even in the pathetically garbled Majority Opinion written by Justice Tom C. Clark. While setting up one straw man after another, and knocking them over—like the issue of the state church which was decided so long ago—he proceeds to write:

The fact that the Founding Fathers believed devotedly that there was a God and that the unalienable rights of man were rooted in Him is clearly evidenced in their writings, from the Mayflower Compact to the Constitution itself. This background is evidenced today in our public life through the continuation in our oaths of office from the Presidency to the alderman of the final supplication, "So help me God."

He refers to the opening prayer in each house of Congress, and to the opening of the Supreme Court by a short ceremony in which the crier invokes the grace of God—"God save the United States and this honorable court." He refers to chaplains in military service, and to the pervasive influence of religion in many aspects of the national life. He quotes other cases. As late as 1952 the Court ruled, "We are a religious people whose institutions presuppose a Supreme Being."

As late as 1962 the Court remarked: "The history of man is inseparable from the history of religion. And . . . since the beginning of that history many people have devoutly believed that 'more things are wrought by prayer than this world dreams of.' "

On the basis of these and other examples, Justice Clark writes:

It can be truly said, therefore, that today, as in the beginning, our national life reflects a religious people who, in the words of Madison, are "earnestly praying, as . . . in duty bound, that the Supreme Law-giver of the universe . . . guide them into every measure which may be worthy of His . . . blessing."

Indeed so. Although America is a pluralistic society—neither Protestant, Catholic nor Jewish—it has been, until now, a theistic society which finds in the Judaeo-Christian tradition its basic philosophy of freedom. It has taken for granted that, whatever a man's particular version of religion, he ought generally to be able to join in the last verse of the hymn "America."

When the children said the Lord's Prayer in school, they were saying an ancient Jewish prayer, written by a Jew, and derived line-by-line from the Old Testament. They were acknowledging, not Jesus, but Almighty God, the Father and Creator of all men. When they read from the Bible, without comment, a brief passage or two, perhaps their devotional life was not being greatly enriched, but at least they were being taught respect for the fundamental religious tradition which has made this nation great. Even so, they were not coerced, and any child could be excused from this innocent religious

499

exercise. Of course, Mrs. Murray of Baltimore, the atheist who brought the issue to the Court, complained that other children had made fun of her son whom she wished to bring up as an atheist like herself. And of course the son should be protected, as any member of a minority should be protected; but does this mean that the majority should, therefore, be deprived of *their* rights? Suppose the child had been a vegetarian, instead of an atheist, wouldn't the other children have made fun of him until restrained by their teachers? And would this mean that the school cafeteria would have to stop serving meat? If you want to be in the minority, then, you should be able to stand being a little different, and you should respect the rights of others as you demand that they respect your rights. In other words, because one child is to be an atheist is no reason why public prayers are to be denied to an entire school.

Nonetheless, the 1st Amendment reads, "Congress shall make no law respecting an establishment of religion . . ." and so prayers and Bible reading are out, although Congress has made no such law, and how the one follows from the other is something which I leave to the murky mind of the lawyers and of the Court. It is only a straw in the wind, but it is a particular blow to the Protestant Church which always has befriended the public school system, while others have been belittling and tearing it down. Now the cry will go up for more parochial schools, and they will work their divisive influence and the cry will increase for the support of those denominational schools from the public treasury—a point on which the Supreme Court has been more than a little soft in the past.

Now there is to be another suit, sponsored by the American Civil Liberties Union, designed to eliminate the phrase "under God" from the pledge of allegiance to the flag. It looks like we made a mistake when this phrase was introduced by Congress in 1954. Perhaps the pledge should read "NOT under God" so that there can be no mistake that America is a superficial, cheerless, cold, secularized, materialistic society interested only in soft living and material comforts.

Meanwhile, the moral fabric continues to deteriorate, and our children and young people are quick to sense the trend. Last week's paper told of eight hundred teen-agers at a beer-drinking brawl on a parking field at Jones Beach; the Darien School Parents in Fairfield County, Connecticut, issued a report saying that teen-age behaviour in that town had reached a "point of alarm"; the P.T.A. in Chappaqua, New York, stated that shop lifting has become a game among their youth; the police arrested twenty-two boys near Smithtown, Long Island, about to engage in a rumble with hunting knives and other weapons; a judge in the Nassau County District Court declared that teen-age gangs, especially around Freeport, were "terrorizing neighborhoods"; on the eve of Memorial Day vandals in the Holy Sepulchre Cemetary, New Rochelle, overturned or destroyed 264 headstones, creating damage estimated at a hundred thousand dollars. By all means, keep our children protected from the Lord's Prayer and from Bible reading in the schools. They might learn to believe in God. They might learn decency and self-respect. Wouldn't it be terrible if they learned the Ten Commandments?

For us there remains neither a word of comfort nor a message of inspiration. Only an obituary for a society changing not always for the best. Only a eulogy for the values which made America great. Only a lamentation and a cry of protest. Only a statement of sad regret.

19

The Pulpit and Race Relations
1954–1966
William M. Pinson, Jr.

Preaching on race did not begin in America in 1954. It began almost at the time of the coming of the first settlers. Theological questions had to be resolved concerning the status of Indians and Negro slaves. For example, did they have souls? Were they human beings? What rights had they?

The first large outburst of preaching on race occurred, however, during the abolition movement. From the early 1800's through the Civil War period both pro- and anti-slavery sermons were preached. By the time the War Between the States was fought abolition preachers were mainly Northern, and slavery advocates were chiefly Southern.

The next noticeable round of preaching on race came with the 1954 ruling of the Supreme Court of the United States against segregation. Preaching was related to the civil rights movement in the 1950's and 1960's. In the beginning, the segregationists were the most outspoken. But as the civil rights movement picked up steam, the segregationist outbursts were buried under a barrage of integrationist preaching.

In the controversy over race, some preachers were

militant and outspoken. Others were mild. Most were silent. Courage was called for in the stand taken by many. Numerous pastors lost their jobs speaking out against segregation. Many segregationists suffered ridicule from the press, the academic community, and in some instances the public at large.

THE ISSUE

The central issue in the controversy was, "Is segregation right or wrong, Christian or unchristian?"

Segregationist preachers declared that integration was a moral, political, biological, and economic evil. Morally, it was sinful because the Bible taught that God commanded segregation. Politically, it was wrong because the government was forcing people to do what they did not want. Further, integration was declared part of a Communist plot to wreck America. Biologically, it was harmful because mixed races were said to be weak races. Segregationists insisted that to keep the white race pure and undefiled was best for everyone—including the Negro. Only by remaining pure could the white race maintain its superiority. Economically, it was foolish to force the Negro to be accepted by business and industry as an equal.

Antisegregation preachers insisted that segregation was a moral, political, psychological, and economic evil. They countered point for point the attack of the segregationists. Morally, segregation was wrong because it violated the way and will of God. A God of love and justice could not possibly approve prejudice, discrimination, and injustice in regard to race. Politically, segregation was deemed intolerable in a nation which promised liberty and justice for all. Psychologically, segregation was considered harmful because it produced a sense of inferiority, frustration, and hate on the part of the Negro. Economically, segregation was declared too expensive to tolerate.

The issues were clear cut. One group supported a practice which had long been tolerated in American life and was now under attack. The other group strongly opposed the practice and cheered the attack of the government on segregation. Both sides felt strongly that their position was correct. Compromise was really no live option. In fact, it was sometimes said or insinuated, parcularly by the segregationists, that to hold the counter position was to be outside the Christian fold.

Initially most of the preaching majored on the central issue of segregation and the decision of the Supreme Court. As the civil rights movement expanded, scores of related issues were dealt with, such as legislation, demonstrations, civil rights organizations, open housing, the right to vote, federal intervention, and the correct way to evoke social change. Often men united in their opposition to segregation were divided in their opinions on these issues.

The stands taken by preachers on race cut across denominational, racial, theological, and geographical lines. Most denominations had within their ranks both outspoken integrationists and militant segregationists. Both Negroes and whites stood in each camp. The North and the South contained spokesmen for each position. Most preachers to the theological left were integrationists. But so were many conservatives.

The bulk of the preaching centered on the relations between white and Negro. Scattered emphases were directed to race and human relations in general. A few sermons majored on the plight of the Indian or Latin American. Some stressed the problem of prejudice in general. But for the most part, the main concern was over Negro-white tensions and segregation.

APPROACH

Most sermons preached on race from 1954 to 1966 were not coldly analytical and dispassionate. To the contrary, dogmatism and emotion prevailed.

The segregationists majored on the threat of intermarriage. They opposed integration because they felt that it would lead to intermarriage. Intermarriage was wrong, said the segregationists, because it was forbidden by the Bible and because the Negro was inherently inferior. To mix white and Negro blood could lead only to the weakening of the white race. Segregationists insisted that no great civilization had survived racial mongrelization. They often saw integration as a Communist plot to ruin America.

Segregationists appealed to other fears. The Negro was diseased. He was immoral. He was mentally inferior. Thus, contact with him could only work to the detriment of the white man. Segregationists appealed to religious conviction, reason, and pride of race. They used the Bible, usually in a proof-text fashion, to prove that God was the original segregationist. They insisted that to be for integration was to be against God and the Bible.

The integrationist preachers scoffed at the idea that the Bible taught segregation. Verse by verse they refuted the exegesis of the segregationists. Although they did trot out verses to bolster their position, in the main they rested their case more on the general emphasis of the Bible than on specific texts. They stressed, for example, the fatherhood of God and brotherhood of man, the demands of God for love and justice, and the ministry of Jesus to every man regardless of race or national origin.

Some integrationist sermons played on men's fears. For example, they warned that segregation gave the Communists a propaganda tool to use against America. Most, however, appealed to love, a sense of fair play, law and order, justice, and concern for the underdog.

In each camp sermons were both direct and indirect. Often preachers took advantage of specific events—court decisions, legislation, or racial crises—to present their views. Both camps refused to limit their statements to what the churches should do. They prescribed policies for schools, governments, and businesses. Neither were they content to rest their case on purely biblical material. They utilized law, history, anthropology, psychology, economics, political science, genetics, and sociology in their appeals.

The following two sermons illustrate some of the factors presented in this brief essay. Both preachers have similar backgrounds, are pastors of Southern Baptist churches, are conservative in their theology, and are actively involved in the racial crisis. Yet they hold deeply differing points of view. Some desegregationists may feel that Dr. Dale Cowling's sermon does not make a strong enough case for integration. When one remembers the geographical and historical setting, the purpose for which it was delivered, and subsequent events, it seems a strong statement indeed. At the time this essay was written, each man was still pastoring the church to which his sermon was preached and each was continuing to speak his convictions on race.

DALE COWLING

Dr. Dale Cowling is pastor of the Second Baptist Church, Little Rock, Arkansas. His downtown church is affiliated with the Southern Baptist Convention. Dr. Cowling was born in Arkansas; he is a graduate of Ouachita Baptist College, Arkadelphia, Arkansas. He holds two earned graduate degrees, the M.R.E. and the D.R.E., from Southwestern Baptist Theological Seminary, Fort Worth, Texas. Prior to becoming pastor of the church where he now serves, he was director of Baptist student work for Arkansas Baptists. The sermon, "A Pastor Looks at Integration in Little Rock," was preached on the Sunday in 1957 before the governor of Arkansas called out the National Guard and closed the schools in Little Rock.

A Pastor Looks at Integration*

Every thoughtful Christian citizen is concerned about the tremendous problem we are facing with regard to the racial integration of our public schools. Almost everyone has some opinions on the matter.

Surely, none of us want our community to be torn with strife with the attendant hurtful consequences and unfavorable publicity.

In the light of the situation before us and under what I believe to be divine leadership, it is my purpose this morning to simply talk with you as my beloved church family. I can do this because I know your heart. Regardless of what your view toward integration may be, your deepest concern is to take the course that is becoming to a follower of Christ. Even if you have an extreme position either for or against integration, I am confident that you want to feel that your stand is pleasing to our Savior and God.

I. *First, we need to clearly consider, what is the real problem in integration?*

If we can agree upon the major problem, then we will be in a much better position to reach the solution. It is both interesting and amazing to find the many different bases of argument from different individuals.

1. Because there are so many diverse points of view, it seems necessary to take a negative look at the real problem. We must eliminate some things that distort our judgment of what the real problem is.

(a) There are those who base their extreme opposition to integration upon

* Reprinted by permission of the author.

their interpretation of the Scriptures. These individuals are sincere beyond question. They are simply greatly mistaken in their efforts to prove that God has marked the Negro race and relegated it to the role of servant. Those who take this point of view try to establish as a fact that the Negro race descended from Ham, and that the curse put upon Ham is upon the whole Negro race; thus, indicating that they are to forever live in the role of servants. A serious study of this section of Scripture and history soon points out the fact that this is only the conjecture of man. We might as well reason that the Negro is descendant of any other Old Testament character.

There are others who would make much of the fact that God constantly urged the Hebrew people to stay within their own race. We must not forget, however, that God's purpose was to produce a race loyal to Jehovah God so as to bring forth the Messiah. To mix heathen races threatened to contaminate Jehovah worship. Since the coming of the Savior, the clear insistence of the Word of God is that "in Christ there is neither bond nor free, Greek or Hebrew."

(b) There are those who feel sincerely that the Negro race possesses an inferior intelligence. These individuals argue that the basic IQ of the Negro is inferior to that of the white. This view is contrary to our best scientific evidence. It has been definitely established that a Negro and a white child, given an equal environment and opportunity, will show an equal grasp of things. It is true that because of poor background and environment, the Negro child's mentality is developed less at a given age than that of a white child with superior opportunity and background. It is also true, however, that a white child with a poor environment and background will fail to develop as rapidly as another white child with better opportunity. We argue against scientific truth when we say that the Negro is inferior in intelligence.

(c) There are those who honestly feel that the Negro race is inferior from a physical point of view. They point out the high rate of certain diseases within the Negro race. They argue that the Negro is more susceptible to social diseases in particular. Again, scientific facts will not substantiate this view. If the rate of social diseases among Negro people is higher than among whites, it is again because of environment and background. In fact, we would find groups of white people whose environment is very poor who would also show a high rate of social diseases.

Another statement taken for granted by many sincere people is that all Negroes smell badly. Many scientific experiments have been conducted taking perspiration from the glands of Negroes and whites only to find that there is no difference. The matter of body odor is again one of environment and economic condition which discourages either the opportunity or the tendency to liberally apply soap and water. Any person, colored or white, who goes without bathing will be sure to perfume the atmosphere.

These are the three most often heard statements designed to prove that the basic problem in integration consists of the inferiority of the Negro race and the teachings of the Word of God. There are many other arguments which are in reality nothing more than our prejudices. These are enough, however, to bring us face to face with the major problem.

2. It becomes apparent that, the real problem is a social one. It has to do with the changing of long-established traditions. It throws us into social relationships that are unfamiliar to us. It cuts across the established pattern and is, therefore, upsetting to us. We are afraid of the outcome if the races associate together in school. We wonder what it will produce. Our greatest fear is that it will result directly in mixed marriages. Our fears of these new social relationships are so great until they keep us from looking calmly at other communities where they have already been met. Surely, the same culture, training, and background that operates presently in the choice of our friends will continue to operate. We do not choose to cultivate certain people as friends or marriage partners even within the white race. We teach our children to choose companions. Surely those teachings will continue to operate and produce good results even in an integrated society. Be that as it may, we are at least agreed that our great problem is a social one. It involves a change in society.

3. Our school board has been wise to recognize the social nature of our problem. In my judgment, the board has chosen a wise course of action in dealing with the social aspects of the problem. They have taken three years to prepare for the beginning of integration. During this time, they have sought to educate and prepare our society to make the best of a serious social problem thrust upon us.

The school board has been wise again in coming to a decision of gradual integration. This plan of gradual integration had to be one that would be accepted by both Negro and white groups to avoid unnecessary problems from either side. By beginning the integration in the senior year, the school board has avoided the more serious emotional problems in the minds of adults in the integration of little children. The plan provides for a small beginning and will provide a helpful proving ground for further action.

The school board has also been very thoughtful and wise in providing personal instructions for the pupils to be integrated, by the Superintendent of Schools, as well as by some of the most thoughtful Negro leaders.

All in all, it seems to me that good groundwork has been laid to do as much as possible toward overcoming the great social problems of integration.

4. It also seems that our citizens have in a majority expressed approval

of this procedure and confidence in the school board's leadership. You may remember that in our last school board election, the candidates who were avowed foes of integration were defeated by those whose stated purpose was to follow the gradual processes already established by the school board. This indicates that although our citizens probably would not have chosen integration on their own, they were committed to this plan which seems to offer the best solution.

II. *Second, we should consider, "What brought on the crisis of this problem?"*

We must remember that the decision to integrate our schools was not a local one. It was not the choice of our school board. It does not simply involve our community nor even the communities within our state. It is a national affair. We must remember that the situation came about by the interpretation of the Constitution of the United States of America by the highest court of our land. Whether we agree with the interpretation or not, we still face the fact that our properly constituted authority has so judged.

One seriously wonders if the high court could have interpreted otherwise. We must remember that the very heart of America is freedom. Her strength has been her rebellion against caste systems and her insistence upon the worth of every individual. The design of our Constitution was to provide this freedom for all.

At any rate, whether we sympathize with or rebel against the decision of the Supreme Court, the die is cast. I personally cannot foresee a change in the decision.

Our decision, then, becomes, "What attitude must a Christian take toward civil authority?" Can we as Christians be outlaws to our civil authority? Romans 13:1-7 gives us a very pointed answer to this question: "Let every soul be subject unto the higher powers (civil authority) . . . the powers that be are ordained of God. Whosoever therefore resisteth the power, resisteth the ordinance of God. . . . Wherefore ye must needs be subject, not only for wrath, but also for conscience sake."

This is the same thought Illustrated by Jesus when he, though he was the Son of God and certainly not subject to civil rulers by necessity, made it clear that he paid his taxes and stated that we are to "pay tribute to whom tribute is due." We as Christians surely cannot justify ourselves in taking the law unto our own hands. If we must disagree with the law, then we ought to do it through legal means—not by becoming outlaws and resorting to acts of violence.

III. *Third, we should earnestly seek to know, "What principles does the New Testament set forth that apply to this situation?"*

We have already established the fact that Christians ought to be obedient to civil authority and to abide by the laws of the land. Whatever reactions a Christian makes to a given situation ought to come within the framework of our existing law.

Now, we turn to try to find the principles set forth in the New Testament which will help us form our Christian position with regard to this serious matter.

1. Let us consider Jesus' example.

We must remember that our Savior brought great criticism upon himself in that he openly cut across established social patterns.

(1) We have the example of him talking with a Samaritan woman at the well of Jacob. A Samaritan was a Jew with mixed blood and looked upon by other Jews as a dog. A good Jew had nothing to do with a Samaritan; yet, Jesus felt compassion for this woman, led her to the Christian faith, and spent some days in her Samaritan village preaching to her town's people. The Scriptures bear evidence that many of them were converted.

(2) On another occasion, Jesus cut across racial boundaries by healing the servant of a Roman centurion. The centurion was without question a Gentile. Yet, Jesus said, "I have not found so great a faith even in Israel."

(3) One of the beautiful stories of the New Testament is that one of the Good Samaritan told by Jesus. When a dying Jew was passed by a priest and Levite of his own race he was rescued by a Samaritan and saved from death. This story in Jesus' day was loaded with TNT. Yet, he used it to illustrate the fact that we all are neighbors regardless of race.

2. We also have some meaningful examples from the experiences of the early Christians.

(1) One of the most significant of these is that of the conversion of Cornelius, a Greek, by the preaching of Peter, a strict Jew. The Bible makes it clear that God led Peter to go to Cornelius and deliver his word. Peter himself testified that he learned that, "God is no respector of persons, for he sent the holy Spirit upon the Greeks in Cornelius's house just as he had sent him upon the Jews on the Day of Pentecost."

(2) Another meaningful example is that of the Holy Spirit sending Phillip, the evangelist, away from a successful revival to the desert of Gaza where he had arranged for him to ride in the chariot with an Ethiopian eunuch and lead the eunuch to faith in Christ.

(3) One of the most beautiful and pungent pleas on behalf of one for another is found in the letter of Philemon where Paul is writing to Philemon on behalf of Onesimus, his runaway slave. Onesimus had run away from Philemon after stealing some of his property. In that day, a runaway slave could be crucified or put to death in some other way. Somehow, in God's providence, Onesimus had gone to Rome and had either been arrested and

put in prison or in some way came to the prison where Paul was a prisoner. Paul had led Onesimus to faith in Christ. Now, he is sending the runaway slave, who had become a Christian, back to his master who has the right to put him to death. Paul pleads with Philemon to receive Onesimus not as a slave but as a brother in Christ.

(4) Another principle not to be overlooked is the one declared by the apostle Paul in his message on Mars Hill in Athens. Paul declared, as recorded in Acts 17:26, "And God hath made of one blood all nations of men for to dwell on all the face of the earth. . . ." This is a clear statement of the unity of the human race.

3. We not only have these direct teachings concerning our relationship to other races, but we also must not forget Jesus' beautiful teachings in the Sermon on the Mount. The believer who practices the true Christian spirit will:

(1) Turn the other cheek. He will not strike back.

(2) Give the cloak also. He will not be contentious and ugly in spirit.

(3) He will return good for evil and will even be able to love his enemies.

(4) Jesus concluded, "Blessed are the peacemakers."

It is quite evident, then, that the Savior loves the spirit of peacefulness and humility and compassion. This attitude is certainly one for which we should pray in our Christian lives.

Conclusion

In the light of the social nature of our problem, the ruling of the highest court of our land, the insistence of God's Word that we pay respect and obedience to civil authority, the broad principles of love, brotherhood, and Christian patience laid down in the New Testament, I would implore you to:

1. Determine that you as an individual will have nothing to do with any threat of violence or gathering of a mob, incident to the opening of school.

2. Determine that you as a student will not be a party to embarrassing or intimidating a colored student.

3. Determine as a Christian to earnestly pray for the best solution to the problems incident to our local and national situation.

4. Determine to maintain an attitude of calmness and confidence in the peaceful solution of the problem.

CAREY DANIEL

Dr. Carey Daniel has been pastor of the First Baptist Church of West Dallas, Dallas, Texas, since 1948. The church is affiliated with the Southern Baptist Convention. His parents were Southern Baptist missionaries to China and he spent seven years there. For three years he was enrolled in Baylor University, Waco, Texas. Later he attended Southwestern Baptist Theological Seminary, Fort Worth, Texas. He has served as president of the White Citizens' Church Council and the Citizens' Council of America for Segregation. "God the Original Segregationist" was delivered on Sunday morning, May 23, 1954, just after the famous ruling by the Supreme Court of the United States against segregation.

God the Original Segregationist *

OLD TESTAMENT TEXT—GENESIS 10:32; 11:1-9

"These are the families of the sons of Noah, after their generations, in their nations: and by these were the NATIONS DIVIDED in the earth after the flood. (The Bible word for race is always 'nation').

"And the whole earth was of one language, and one speech. . . . And they said, Go to, let us build us a city and a tower, whose top may reach unto heaven; and let us make us a name, LEST WE BE SCATTERED ABROAD UPON THE FACE OF THE WHOLE EARTH. And the Lord came down to see the city and the tower, which the children of man builded. And the Lord said, Behold, THE PEOPLE IS ONE, and they have all one language; and this they begin to do: and now nothing will be restrained from them, which they have imagined to do. Go to, let us go down, and there confound their language, that they may not understand one another's speech. So the LORD SCATTERED them abroad from thence upon the face of all the earth: and they left off to build the city. Therefore is the name of it called Babel; because the Lord did there confound the language of all the earth: and from thence did the LORD SCATTER them abroad upon the face of all the earth."

NEW TESTAMENT TEXT—Acts 17:26, 27

"And (God) hath made of one blood all nations of men for to dwell on all the face of the earth, and hath determined the times before appointed, AND THE BOUNDS OF THEIR HABITATION: that they should seek the Lord, if haply they might feel after him and find him, though he be not far from every one of us."

* The author granted permission to use this sermon with the understanding that the following statement be made: This sermon may be purchased in booklet form from the author, 2302 Lawndale Drive, Dallas 11, Texas, for $.35 postpaid.

Our Lord God Himself was the Original Segregationist. When first He separated the black race from the white and lighter skinned races He did not simply put them in different parts of town. He did not even put them in different towns or states. Nay, He did not even put them in adjoining countries.

He put the black race on a huge continent to themselves, segregated from the other races by oceans of water to the west, south and east, and by the vast stretches of the almost impassable Sahara Desert to the North.

After the flood of Noah's day God made a sharp division in the lands He allotted to Shem, Ham and Japheth, the sons of Noah, who headed the three great branches of the human family. Our text plainly declares that by these three "were the nations *divided* in the earth after the flood."

The descendants of Shem were to become the Semitic race, the chief representatives of which are the Jews. In fact the Jews and Jew-related Arabs are almost the only people who can accurately trace their lineage and positively prove they are Semitic, though others claim to be and still others are called Semitic only because of their language and not their racial origin.

The descendants of Ham were to become the Negro race. The very name Ham comes from an Egyptian word "kem" meaning "Black" (see *Young's Analytical Concordance*, James Hasting's *Dictionary of the Bible* or any other reliable Bible dictionary). And in Bible times, unlike modern times, names had meanings.

The descendants of Japheth were to become the other Gentile races. His was to be the "enlarged" family (Genesis 9:27) whose members were to comprise the great majority of the world's population.

To Shem and his offspring was granted not only what is known as "the land of Israel" but also a vast territory south and east of there, extending all the way to the river Euphrates (Deut. 1:7, 8 and Josh. 1:2,4). This was much larger than the land they actually occupied.

To Ham and his posterity was granted the enormous continent of Africa, the second largest body of land in the whole world, surpassed in size only by the double Eurasian continent. That is why Egypt in particular and Africa in general are called "the land of Ham" (Psalms 105:23-38 and 106:21, 22). The ancient Egyptians were the children of Mizraim, a son of Ham. In fact Ham is the only son of Noah for whom a country was ever named.

The Canaanites (the only children of Ham who were specifically cursed to be a servile race) were temporarily allowed to occupy a narrow strip of the Promised Land along the Mediterranean coast, extending as far north as to include Sidon, the twin city of Tyre, and as far east in one place as to include Sodom and Gomorrah (Gen. 10:19). Anyone familiar

514

with the Biblical history of those cities during that period can readily understand why we here in the South are determined to maintain segregation.

But even those servant people were to live in a different part of the country from the children of Shem, with at least a geographic line between them. When later they dared to violate God's sacred law of segregation by moving into and claiming the land farther east, so that the Hebrew territory became known as "the land of Canaan," the Lord justly commanded His chosen people to wage war upon them and "utterly destroy them" (Deut. 7:1,2).

To Japheth and his posterity were given "the isles of the Gentiles" (Gen. 10:5). The word "isles" here means "coasts" or "settlements," and the phrase "the isles of the Gentiles" is further defined in Isaiah 41:1-5 and 49:1-6 as including all territories "to the ends of the earth." In other words Japheth's children were to have all the rest of the world. That was only fair, since they were to be so much more numerous.

These Scriptures show that we white Gentiles are living in that part of the earth which God assigned to us. They also belie the vile slander that our forefathers "stole" this country from the Indians—those wandering tribes who had no organized nation, and whom our ancestors were compelled to fight in defense of their wives and children.

We have no reason to suppose that God did not make known to Noah and his children His divine plan for racial segregation immediately after the flood. But they were all slow to obey. Three generations passed and they were still all living together.

KING NIMROD THE ORIGINAL INTEGRATIONIST

Ham had a grandson named Nimrod, which means Rebel or "Let us Rebel." He was "a mighty one in the earth," a powerful leader and an influential monarch—so much so that he became the commander of the builders of the Tower of Babel. He was most likely the one who first conceived the idea because "the beginning of his kingdom was Babel" (Gen. 10:10). He was so obviously the mouthpiece of the Devil that I might have done better if I had entitled this section "Satan the Original Integrationist."

Nimrod was a twofold rebel, a double-dyed anarchist. He rebelled against both God's plan of salvation and God's plan of racial segregation. This is shown by the two reasons given for the building of "the tower whose top may reach unto heaven":

First, to "make us a name." Nimrod ignored the "Name Above Every Name," the Lord Jesus Christ. The whole Bible was written primarily to teach us that salvation is entirely the work of God and not of man and that

515

it comes down from above and not up from beneath. "Where is boasting then? It is excluded. By what law? of works? Nay, but by the law of faith. Therefore we conclude that a man is justified by faith without the deeds of the law" (Rom. 3:27, 28).

Secondly, "lest we be scattered abroad upon the face of the whole earth." That was just exactly what the Lord had told them to do many years before then—to scatter and separate from one another racially. When they persistently refused to do so God *himself* scattered them.

(The chapter divisions of Scripture were placed there by men, not by God; and one of the most unfortunate in the whole Bible is the one between the tenth and eleventh chapters of Genesis. The last verse of the tenth chapter is an integral part of the story of the Babel-builders. Without it we might suppose that the "scattering" was merely a dispersion of individuals or families; but with it we can see plainly that it was also a separation of nations, or races.)

Not only did God want these three races to be segregated, but He also wanted to remove from them all temptation to reunite later on. So He "confounded their speech"—that is, He gave them different languages. In this connection it is interesting to note that most linguistic scholars now agree that all modern languages can be traced back to the three "parent tongues," the Semitic, the Aryan and the Turanian.

ABRAHAM THE SEGREGATIONIST

Abraham was called of God to leave his father's people and to begin the formation of what was soon to become the most strictly separated and rigidly segregated race ever to inhabit the earth—the Jewish race. The Lord intended that His chosen people should always be a good example to the surrounding heathen nations and Gentile races in all kinds of purity, especially racial purity (Num. 25).

When Abraham instructed his servant to go and find a bride for his son Isaac he commanded under divine inspiration that she was not to be a Negress. "I will make thee to swear by the Lord," he demanded, "that thou shalt not take a wife unto my son of the daughters of the Canaanites." (Gen. 24:3).

MOSES THE SEGREGATIONIST

God thundered through the lips of Moses such stern warnings against the intermarriage of Jews and Gentiles that the Jews to this day have maintained an amazing racial purity. Moses' own marriages to the two Gentile women took place before those warnings were given. He was a very old man then, approaching 100 years of age, and it is doubtful that those Gentile wives were even living at that time.

That noble prophet was inspired of the Lord to devote a whole chapter of his book of Deuteronomy to forbid the comingling of his people with Negroes. It begins like this:

"When the Lord thy God shall bring thee into the land whither thou goest to possess it, and hath cast out many nations before thee, the Hittites, and the Girgashites, and the Amorites, and the Canaanites, and the Perizzites, and the Hivites, and the Jebusites (nearly all of these were descendants of Ham—see Gen. 10), seven nations greater and mightier than thou; and when the Lord thy God shall deliver them before thee, thou shalt smite them, and utterly destroy them; thou shall make no covenant with them, nor show mercy unto them: *neither shalt thou make marriages with them*; thy daughter thou shalt not give unto his son, nor his daughter shalt thou take unto thy son" (Deut. 7:1-3).

NEHEMIAH THE SEGREGATIONIST

In pronouncing a divine curse on interracial marriage Nehemiah even went so far as to knock his people down and snatch them baldheaded to enforce segregation. "And I contended with them and cursed them," he declared, "and smote certain of them, and plucked off their hair, and made them swear by God, saying, Ye shall not give your daughters unto their sons, nor take their daughters unto your sons, or for yourselves" (Neh. 13:25).

HABAKKUK THE SEGREGATIONIST

In the last chapter of one of the last short books of the Old Testament we find the inspired prophet Habakkuk referring to the Babel segregation which we have already described from the first book of the Old Testament. "He (God) stood, and measured the earth; he beheld, and *drove asunder the nations*," proclaimed that prophet. "*His ways are everlasting* (showing that He intends for this segregated condition to continue at least as long as this present world shall last). I saw the tents of Cushan (Cush was the father of Nimrod) in affliction. . . ." (Hab. 3:6, 7).

When the Bible speaks of Marriage it says, "What God hath joined together, let not man put asunder." But when the Bible speaks of Racial Segregation, with its natural prevention of intermarriage, it says that *what God hath put asunder, let not man join together*. In "driving asunder" that first unholy bunch of One-Worlders, the Lord has given us a good idea of what He thinks about the present-day bunch, and of what He is planning eventually to do with them.

Thus we might almost say that the Old Testament begins and ends with the doctrine of Racial Segregation.

JESUS THE SEGREGATIONIST

"But can it be proven," we are sometimes asked, "that Jesus Himself was a segregationist?"

The burden of proof, my dear friend, rests with you to prove that He was *not* a segregationist. The very question implies unbelief in the Lordship of Christ or at last a woeful ignorance of the Old Testament. Jesus was the very same identical God who spoke through the lips of Moses, Abraham, Nehemiah and Habakkuk; and He never once repudiated a single statement He ever made. If so, our God is divided against Himself and His kingdom cannot stand.

To the contrary, Jesus said: "Think not that I am come to destroy the law, or the prophets: I am not come to destroy, but to fulfill. For verily I say unto you, Till heaven and earth pass, one jot or one tittle shall in no wise pass from the law, till all be fulfilled" (Matt. 5:17, 18). We need not look beyond that statement for proof that the incarnation of God in Christ did not change His views on racial segregation.

"But did not Jesus request the Father in His prayer of intercession that His believers would all be 'one'? (Jn. 17:11) Would it not be wrong and sinful for us to do anything that would in any way hinder or prevent that perfect unity for which He prayed?"

Indeed it would. But remember, the "oneness" for which He prayed was purely spiritual and not physical. When I was living in China as the son of a missionary I was one in spirit with every born-again Christian in my native homeland, even though we were separated physically by the widest ocean in the world.

Neither Jesus nor Paul apologized for racial discrimination when they taught that even the universal Gospel of salvation was to be preached to the Jew first. "Go not into the way of the Gentiles," Christ first told His disciples, "but go rather to the lost sheep of the house of Israel" (Matt. 10:5, 6).

PAUL THE SEGREGATIONIST

"But does not the Apostle Paul say that Christ has 'broken down the middle wall of partition between us' "? (Eph. 2:14)

Yes, but the next verse (usually omitted by the race-mixers) explains just what kind of "wall" He has broken down:—"Having abolished in His flesh the *enmity*"—the wall of hatred, not only between sinners and their God, but also the wall of hatred and race prejudice between Jews and Gentiles which had prevented effective missionary work.

Certainly Paul could not have meant that Jesus broke down the walls of racial segregation which God Himself had erected. If Paul had meant that he would never have told the Athenians:

"And (God) hath made of one blood (the word "blood" is omitted from the A.S.V. and the best manuscripts) all nations of men for to dwell on all the face of the earth, and hath determined the times before appointed, *and the bounds of their habitation:*

"That they should seek the Lord, if haply they might feel after Him and find Him, though He be not far from every one of us" (Acts 17:26, 27).

Here again is another passage the integrationists love to mutilate. Their favorite sport is quoting the first half of the 26th verse and leaving out the last half.

The Lord worked from "one" to "all nations of men." Those who oppose segregation want to reverse the divine process and work from "all nations of men" back to "one" race. The ultimate goal of the race-mixers, of course, is the intermarriage of whites and blacks. But if God wanted only one race to inhabit His earth all He had to do was to retain the "status quo" and leave things as they were at the beginning. Integration therefore is not progress but retrogression, not godliness but "devilution."

This passage of Paul's concludes by revealing God's high purpose in segregation. *"that they should seek the Lord, if haply they might feel after him and find him."* According to the race-mixers the best way to win souls to Christ, to spread the Gospel and to advance the kingdom of our Savior would be to mix the whites and blacks in our schools and churches so that they could study and worship together. But according to the Word of God it is segregation, not integration, which accomplishes this purpose in the best way.

If there is no connection between segregation and soul-winning then I must be frank to say that I would have no interest in segregation. When I was ordained to the ministry I made a solemn vow to God that in my preaching I would be "determined to know nothing save Christ and Him Crucified." But this Scripture and others link those two subjects inextricably.

SEGREGATION AS AN AID TO SOUL-WINNING

Often a Christian is thrown together socially with some member of another race, belonging to a different cultural world, so that they fall in love and marry. But seldom do they stay together long. And even when they do there is usually so much friction and quarreling between them that the children of such marriages are likely to conclude, "If this is a Christian home I would rather be an infidel"—and who can blame them?

And just as racial amalgamation is a foe of the gospel of Jesus, so racial segregation is a close friend and handmaiden to it. Why is it that whenever we hear of a missionary going to Africa it is nearly always a White man and practically never a Negro? If the colored folks are our equals, as the race-mixers would have us believe, then they should be willing and able to assume equal responsibilities with us, especially in a matter like that.

Just think how much more readily the Africans would listen to a member of their own race than to a foreigner. Jesus must have had that thought in mind when He chose as one of His disciples to whom He was to give the Great Commission a Negro—Simon the Canaanite (Matt. 10:4).

Booker T. Washington is reported to have taught his pupils repeatedly that "Our people were brought to this country in the Providence of God that they might learn the White man's religion and take it back to Africa!"

RACE-MIXING AND IMMORALITY

The Lord Jesus Christ and the Apostle Paul spent most of their earthly lives in the world's most sternly segregated nation, the land of Israel. Both were loud in their condemnation of every kind, shape and form of sin they found around them. We may be sure that if segregation is sinful and immoral, as we are so often told these days, they would both have opposed it instead of defending it.

Even if they had been completely silent on the subject—which they definitely were not—their very silence would have betokened approval, not disapproval. But instead, they were both constantly endorsing the entire Old Testament, a book so strongly pro-segregation that it taught God's praise of the death penalty for both a Jew and a Gentile who would dare to live together as man and wife (Numbers 25).

The Lord was a little more lenient with those Jews who had just returned from Persian captivity and married foreigners, demanding only divorce instead of death. But He also required that those Hebrews be separated from their own mixed-breed children. The confession of their sin is found in Ezra 10:2 and 3.

"We have transgressed against our God, and have taken strange (foreign) wives of the people of the (Persian) land; yet now there is hope in Israel concerning this thing. Now therefore let us make a covenant with our God to put away (divorce) all the wives, and such as are born of them, according to the counsel of my lord, and of those that tremble at the commandment of our God; and let it be done according to the law. . . .

"And Ezra and the priest stood up, and said unto them, Ye have transgressed, and have taken strange wives, to increase the trespass of Israel. Now therefore make confession to the Lord God of your fathers, and do His pleasure: and separate yourselves from the people of the land, and from the strange wives. Then all the congregation answered and said with a loud voice, As thou hast said, so must we do" (Ezra 10: 10-12).

Some will raise the usual objection that these were Old Testament instructions and do not apply to us who are "living under the New Testament." But it is the New Testament, remember, which tells us that "All Scripture is given by inspiration of God, and is profitable for (our) doctrine, for reproof, for correction, for instruction in righteousness" (2 Tim. 3:16)

THOSE "MIXED MULTITUDES"

Thus did Ezra and Nehemiah in their day "separate from Israel the mixed multitude" (Neh. 13:3). The first "mixed multitude"—the one that so foolishly followed Moses out of Egypt—was destroyed by the hand of God.

When the Lord told Moses to lead the children of Israel away from the Egyptians (Ex. 7:5) He meant that they were to be separated from *all* the Egyptians, including those who were partially Egyptian and partially Hebrew. But Moses thoughtlessly allowed those mixed-breeds to follow him, because "a mixed multitude went up also with them" (Ex. 12:37).

He soon learned from bitter experience that he should have left them in Africa. They proved to be a constant source of weakness, division and trouble. They were the ringleaders of the rebels who complained about the heavenly manna, that wonderful "angels' food," and who cried so "lustfully" for a return to the fleshpots of Egypt (Num. 11:4-6).

As a result, "the Lord smote the people with a very great plague, and . . . there they buried the people that lusted"—which included the mixed multitude (Num. 11:33, 34). The Bible, unlike United Nations propaganda, never paints a pretty picture of race-mixing.

But it does paint a gorgeous picture of the blessings of segregation. After all, racial separation is only one of several forms of segregation enjoined in God's Word. There is also the Spiritual Segregation of believers and unbelievers (2 Cor. 6:14-18), the Socio-Economic Segregation of the servant class and the master class (Eph. 6:5—another distinction the Communists and their dupes are trying to erase), the Family Segregation of parents and children when the latter marry (Gen. 2:24, Matt. 19:5), and even the

Marital Segregation of husbands and wives during the daytime. The wife's place is in the home (Tit. 2:4, 5) and the husband's place is in the business or agricultural world (Gen. 3:16-19).

Why should Racial Segregation be the only kind to cause such horror and such frequent misquotations of Galatians 3:28:—"There is neither Jew nor Greek, there is neither bond nor free, there is neither male nor female; for ye are all one in Christ Jesus." Even in those race-mixing churches where that verse is parroted the loudest they segregate the sexes by having separate class rooms and rest rooms for their men and women!

The flood of Noah's time was caused by the intermarriage of two races that God had separated—the descendants of the rightous Seth (the "sons of God") and those of the wicked Cain (the "daughters of men"). See Genesis 6:1-7.

20

The Challenge of the Secular
Leroy Davis

During the past two or three decades the institutional church has been repeatedly challenged by events and developments in the secular world. Crises have arisen requiring the institution to respond. Although it might appear that a spectrum of possible responses would be available to church leaders, the responses to the challenge of the secular have tended to be limited to two polar positions. With some exceptions, church leaders have tended to stress additional disengagement from the secular or have advocated a radical engagement with the secular.

In the context of preaching these polar positions are not presented as engagement versus disengagement or involvement versus noninvolvement. They are presented as a debate over the procedure of engagement. For many reasons—among them is considerable pressure from national church officials—there is very little preaching which advocates disengagement. Those preachers, who might tend toward the view that the church ought not to be engaged with the secular, appear to speak in terms of optional individual involvement with the secular. Those preachers who tend to advocate engagement do so in terms of institutional participation. Both polar positions tend to advocate engagement and debate only the means.

Undergirding these differences of procedure is, however,

a fundamental disagreement about the nature of the church. There is a basic polarity of views reflected in preaching which deals with secular issues. The fundamental attitude conveyed by preaching which emphasizes institutional involvement in the secular is here called instrumental. The basic attitude of the preaching which emphasizes individual participation in the secular we have called expressive. The latter attitude tends to emphasize the eternal aspects of the faith, personal growth to greater belief, a pastoral attitude toward home and family, and similar things. It is concerned to preserve and maintain the structures of which it is a part. The former attitude, on the contrary, tends to emphasize current human needs, community action, a general concern for all persons, and the like. It is concerned to change the structures of which it is a part. Advocates of both positions rightly consider that they represent valid traditions in Judeo-Christian history.

It is important to state that engagement with the secular during the period under consideration has meant not a general kind of involvement with ordinary secular phenomena, but a participation in specific problem areas. The institutional church has been in the position of responding to problems. Since the church follows rather than leads, it must constantly make decisions about how it will respond to the life about it. When situations such as the war in Vietnam, or riots in cities, or decreased employment due to automation, or pollution arise, the church decides whether it will become involved or not with the specific problem.

Derivative from the fact that the institutional church tends to respond to change and problems, rather than initiate them, has come a hardening of popular views regarding the relationship of the religious and the secular which are reflected in preaching. Most persons tend, it is probably fair to say, to view civil disturbance, for example, as a secular rather than a religious phenomenon. The categories by which persons understand phenomena are largely dependent upon what they see happening, rather than upon reflective thought. Thus, when a secular agency like the police deals with civil disturbance, it seems to most persons that civil disturbances are secular phenomena. Only when the institutional church is involved in such a way as to be clearly seen in events are problems seen as having a religious dimension. Civil disturbance becomes a religious concern through institutional activity in the problem area. If, however, the institution chooses to restrict its activity to worship and ecumenism and building bigger churches, then these things become identified as the province of religion. Within certain legal limits, the institutional church defines the secular and the religious by what it chooses to become institutionally engaged with.

It is worth noting the change which has taken place in the attitude of persons toward the secular. Until fairly recently the secular was defined basically as a negation of the sacred or the religious. It was seen as a lower or inferior level of existence. Even after this viewpoint lost its force persons did tend to pay it the lip service owed the dead. This is not true any longer. For most laity, and probably most clergy, the secular has become the higher or superior level. There is little doubt that even though persons attend and support religious institutions, their real concerns are with occupational advancement, income, property rights, pleasure, secure retirement, and the like. For most persons the secular world is the only world which exists. For them any activity undertaken by a religious institution constitutes an intrusion by a really phony outfit into the vital areas of life. The secular, instead of being used and interpreted through the religious, has come to represent an end in itself. The operational definitions of sacred and secular have been taken from the established institutional church. When those definitions are accepted, then persons who attempt to be truly religious by bringing all of life under a religious outlook are labeled secularists because they are involved in concerns outside the institution. Such is the dilemma of semantics.

This dilemma is heightened because the operational definitions of the institution are being challenged by new approaches. Even the meaning of "church" is unclear. This has partially come about because many instrumentalists have found it either difficult or impossible to build what they consider to be a true church community through the institutional church. They have turned to the formation of various organizations intended to further specific purposes. They have created an organizational church which exists alongside the institutional church. To many the SCLC is a church in the most profound sense. To others, however, only the Circuit Riders constitute the true church. Both of these "churches" derive their vitality from sources outside the institution and have independent lives. They can, obviously, be useful in increasing the kingdom of God or they can kill it. In any event, the instrumental approach has given living expression to a new definition of church.

In order to bring a measure of clarity into this dilemma where religious and secular have come to mean their essential opposites, and where even the term church cannot be operationally agreed upon, we have chosen to utilize two new behavioral terms to describe the polarity under consideration, rather than seek to redefine older terms. In summary, the expressive view emphasizes traditional theological language, edifice-centered religious activity, and change in the souls of individuals. The instrumental view is characterized by its restated theological language in terms of contemporary disciplines, its activity outside the parochial walls, and its desire to change the structures of society.

We chose two sermons to illustrate the expressive-instrumental polar response to the secular. The first, representing the instrumental outlook is by David O. Woodyard. The second, representing the expressive pole is by Herschel H. Hobbs. It is probably not incidental that the Rev. Dr. Hobbs, who is pastor of the First Baptist Church of Oklahoma City, has served parishes for many years, while Mr. Woodyard, who is Dean of the Chapel at Denison University, is considerably younger and is a university chaplain. Their approaches to the secular, regardless of causative factors are strikingly different. While it would have been possible to select other preachers whose sermonic material is more extreme, we have chosen the work of these responsible gentlemen.

me and every person whom I meet until my stereotypes and prejudices fade away.

Now this Christ makes a demand of me as He does of every man who would call himself a Christian. And very simply it is that I see each Negro as a person. He is not essentially ignorant, essentially black, essentially limited in potentiality, but essentially a human being—one who has needs of love and forgiveness as I do, one who cares for his children as I care for mine, one who works, and struggles, and dreams as I do.

And this is all the Negro is ultimately asking of us. He doesn't want to marry your sister, her skin is too colorless; he probably doesn't want to belong to your country club, its activities would not appeal to him; he doesn't want many of the "things" you and I feel are so essential, to him they would be a burden. All he wants is personhood, the kind of personhood which can only come when he is treated as a person. A friend of mine, a white pastor in the South, went to call on Martin Luther King the second day of his imprisonment in Birmingham. He was met by "Bull" Connors, [sic] the Director of Safety, who prides himself on controlling the situation there. The pastor said, "I want to see Dr. Martin Luther King." Connors replied, "We have no Dr. Martin Luther King here." Then he said, "I want to see Mr. Martin Luther King." Connors replied, "We have no Mr. Martin Luther King here." A third time he asked, "I want to see Martin Luther King." And again Connors replied, "We have no Martin Luther King here. All we got is a goddam nigger." If you can escape this incident because it is from the South, listen to this voice from the North. I am sorry to say these are the words of a prominent Denison alum. Boastfully he said, "I am the best friend the nigger's got. At Christmas I give the nigger at the country club a bottle of whiskey. When the son of the nigger who cleans our house needed a job, I got him one. I even have some niggers doing menial tasks in my business. I'm the best friend the nigger has—but he has his place and it's serving his betters." Well, the Negro is tired of being a nigger taking the scraps from under the white man's table. He wants to be a person.

Now many of us who are sympathetic with the Negro cause are unsympathetic with the ways in which he is struggling to secure his rights. This is an issue upon which men of honor disagree. But I beg each of you, as I struggle myself, to reach behind our disagreements on the method and understand that the Negro is tired of waiting for us to bestow upon him his rights as a person.

Listen to Martin Luther King. "For years now I have heard the word 'wait!' . . . This 'wait' has almost always meant 'never.' . . . We have waited for three hundred and forty years. . . . I guess it is easy for those who have never felt the stinging darts of segregation to say 'wait.' But when you have seen vicious mobs lynch your mothers and fathers at will and drown your sisters and brothers at whim; when you have seen hate-filled policemen curse, kick, brutalize, and even kill your black brother with impunity; when you see the vast majority of your twenty million Negro brothers smothering in an air-tight cage of poverty in the midst of an affluent society; when you suddenly find your tongue twisted and your speech stammering as you seek to explain to your six-year-old daughter why she can't go to the public amusement park that has just been advertised on television, and see the tears welling up in her little eyes when she is told that Funtown is closed to colored children, and see the depressing clouds of inferiority begin to form in her little mental sky; . . . when you are harried day and haunted night by the fact that you are a Negro, . . . then you will understand why we find it difficult to wait." There are many things the Negro is doing which I feel to be unwise or imprudent. But when I think of how he has been abused as promises for a better tomorrow have rung their hollow hope, I only wonder that murder is not his daily intent. I'm afraid it would be mine.

But some by now are asking, "What can I do?" No one can answer that question for you. Each of us must find that form in which he can give witness to his convictions. Yet there is one response upon which all Christians can agree and which can be the format of every word and deed. And it is the recognition of who the Negro really is—whether he is rich or poor, clean or dirty, respectable or disreputable. He is the neighbor for whom I am responsible to God; in him I am to recognize Christ and the demands he has upon me. Jesus spoke of a day when there would be a separation between the faithful and the unfaithful to him. To those who were to inherit his kingdom he said, ". . . I was hungry, and you gave me food, I was thirsty and you gave me drink, I was a stranger and you welcomed me, I was naked and you clothed me, I was sick and you visited me, I was in prison and you came to me." And when they asked when they had done this for him, he replied, "Truly, I say to you, as you did it unto one of the least of these my brethren, you did it to me."

Some of you are familiar with the Glass family which J. D. Salinger has fictionalized in a continuing epic. Each of the seven children in this household is brilliant and their talents are displayed on a quiz program called "It's a Wise Child." Seymour, the eldest, has told the others that they ought always to shine their shoes for "the Fat Lady" somewhere in the audience, an unknown woman who is lonely, unattractive, and suffering. They are to care about her as if they knew her, for she knows them. Some years later Franny has an emotional breakdown and her brother Zooey struggles to bring her out of it. Finally he says to her, ". . . I'll tell you a terrible secret [Franny]—are you listening to me? There isn't anyone out there who isn't Seymour's Fat Lady. . . . Don't you know that? . . . And don't you know—listen to me, now—don't you know who that Fat Lady really is? . . . It's Christ Himself. Christ Himself, buddy."

Don't you know who the Negro is, the neighbor with darkened skin and troubled spirit? Don't you know who he really is? "It's Christ Himself. Christ Himself, buddy." Unless you come to him aware of your sin and his need, you will never know the One called Christ. "I was hungry and you gave me food, . . . thirsty and you gave me drink, . . . a stranger and you welcomed me, . . . naked and you clothed me, . . . sick and you visited me, . . . in prison and you came to me." "It's Christ Himself, buddy." And his face is black.

Herschel H. Hobbs

Herschel H. Hobbs was born at Talladega Springs, Alabama, in 1907. He later moved to Birmingham and graduated from Howard College. In 1941 Howard College presented him with the honorary doctor of divinity degree. Dr. Hobbs served as pastor of Calvary Baptist Church in Birmingham. Later he was pastor of Clayton Street Church, Montgomery, Emmanuel Church in Alexandria, Louisiana, and Dauphin Way Church in Mobile. In 1949 he was called to the First Baptist Church of Oklahoma City, where he is serving at the present time. In 1961 he was elected president of the Southern Baptist Convention. He has preached on The Baptist Hour since 1958 and is now permanent preacher for this international radio broadcast. He has been a member of the Foreign Mission Board, the convention's executive committee, the new program planning committee, and the theological education committee of the Southern Baptist Convention. Despite the fact that Dr. Hobbs is a much sought after preacher, a diligent Bible student, and the author of more than a dozen books, he is best known and admired for his warmth and concern for persons.

More Than Religion*

"What good thing shall I do, that I may have eternal life?"—MATT. 16:19.

A pagan woman, holding a sick child, wept as she murmured her prayers before an idol. A missionary asked her, "Little mother, to whom are you praying?" She replied, "I do not know. But surely there is somebody out there who will hear and heal my sick baby."

What a contrast between this pathetic story and the one of Him who said, "Suffer little children to come unto me . . ." At a time of international crisis, social unrest and personal need, it is important to remember God's laws, the foundation stones of moral and spiritual relationships.

As we study the first Commandment of God's laws, "Thou shalt have no other gods before me," let us note first the requirement; second, the reason; and third, the revelation.

* Reprinted by permission of the Radio and Television Commission of the Southern Baptist Convention. This sermon was originally broadcast on *The Baptist Hour*, 1961.

THE REQUIREMENT

"Thou shalt have no other gods before me." What is involved in this commandment? Note that it says nothing about atheism. To the contrary it assumes the religious nature of man. It recognizes that each of us will have an object of worship. Charles Darwin is reported as saying that if and when the so-called "missing link" of the theory of evolution is found, it will have no capacity for worship. No such link has been found.

The first commandment not only recognizes the existence of God, but it also takes into account the fact of false gods. But it further identifies Jehovah, the God of the Hebrews, as the one true God. "I am Jehovah thy God . . . thou shalt have no other gods before me." Thus it sets monotheism, the worship of one God, over against polytheism, the worship of many gods. Nor does it say that it is permissible to worship any one of the pagan gods. Literally, "I am Jehovah thy Elohim . . . thou shalt have no other elohim before me" or besides me.

Like Paul in Athens, Moses lived among nations that were "very religious." They had gods of all kinds and for every purpose. To the Israelites Jehovah said, "You are to have none of these gods in place of me." It was another way of saying that it is not sufficient simply to be religious. Your religion must be centered in the worship and will of the one true God.

A man came to a pastor with a problem. In the midst of the interview the pastor asked if he were a Christian. To which he replied, "Well, I am a religious man, if that is what you mean." But is that what he meant?

I have traveled about the world a bit. And I have seen many forms of religion. I have observed the kind of men and women they produce. I have looked into their blank faces as they went through meaningless forms of worship. I have seen men clap their hands or ring bells before pagan altars in order to get a god's attention. Can such a religion satisfy the deepest longings of the soul?

No, religion is not enough! The heart of man demands more than religion. It calls for an experience with the living God. That is why Jehovah says, "Thou shalt have no other gods before me."

THE REASON

Why does God begin with this commandment? Because it is the only basis of a truly soul-satisfying religious experience. If you will examine the Ten Commandments you will find that the first four deal with your relation to God, while the other six are concerned with your relation to other men. It is God's way of saying that true religion begins with God, not with men.

There is a type of modern religion called Humanism. It places religion on the basis of man and his relation to other men. It is designed to change a man's environment, but is powerless to change the man. It fills his stomach, but leaves him with an empty soul. Thus it leaves much to be desired. Now, do not misunderstand me. True religion does have a social aspect. But it does not begin there. It begins with a right relation with God, and from that relationship expresses itself in a right relationship toward men. Anything short of that leaves a void in your heart.

Take as an example the rich young ruler (Matt. 19:16ff.). He came to Jesus with a question. "Good Master, what good thing shall I do, that I may have eternal life?" There is no reason to doubt his sincerity. Certainly Jesus did not do so. It is quite evident that he was searching for a deeper, soul-satisfying religious experience.

Note Jesus' response. ". . . if thou wilt enter into life, do the commandments." When the young man asked, "Which?" Jesus quoted, "Thou shalt do no murder, Thou shalt not commit adultery, Thou shalt not steal, Thou shalt not bear false witness, Honour thy father and thy mother: and, Thou shalt love thy neighbour as thyself."

Note further the commandments quoted by Jesus. He omitted the first four having to do with the young man's relation to God, quoting only those regarding his relationship to men.

Now note the youth's reply. "All these things have I kept from my youth up: what lack I yet?" All his life he had treated his fellow man right. His religion was a type of Humanism. It had centered in his relations to men, with no regard to his relation to God. And it had brought him no satisfaction!

That is exactly what Jesus wanted him to see. That is why He did not begin by quoting, "Thou shalt have no other gods before me." When Jesus said, "If thou wilt be perfect [complete or reach the true goal of your life], go and sell that thou hast, and give to the poor . . . and come and follow me," that was His way of quoting the first commandment. The youth was making his possessions his god, and he was to have no other gods before Jehovah.

Do I need to apply this truth further? You can work your fingers to the bone keeping those commandments which relate you to men. You may do much good for others, but it will leave an aching void in your own soul. You are, perhaps, even now crying, "What lack I yet?" The answer is that you must begin with God. First, rightly relate yourself to Him, and your service to men will become a soul-satisfying joy, and not merely a chore in social service. That is why God says, "Thou shalt have no other gods before me."

THE REVELATION

How may you come to know Him and enthrone Him in your heart? The answer is found in Jesus Christ. In the eighth century B.C., Isaiah wrote, "Therefore the Lord (Jehovah) himself shall give you a sign; Behold a virgin shall conceive, and bear a son, and shall call his name Immanuel" (7:14), which means "God with us." Matthew records its fulfilment in the birth of Jesus. ". . . Thou shalt call his name JESUS, for he shall save his people from their sins" (1:21). Now "Jesus" means Jehovah is salvation. He is God with us in saving power.

It is well at this point to recall the meaning of the word Jehovah. The names most often used in the Old Testament for God are *Elohim* and *Jehovah*. The former is used 2,550 times, the latter appears 6,823 times. *Elohim* expresses the power and majesty of God. *Jehovah* is the name which designates Him as Redeemer. So the greater emphasis is upon God as Redeemer or Saviour. The full revelation of God as such is seen in Jesus, *Jehovah* is salvation.

Of Himself, Jesus said, "He that hath seen me hath seen the Father . . ." (John 4:9). "I am the way, the truth, and the life: no man cometh unto the Father, but by me" (14:6). So you can have a right relationship to God only as you do so through Jesus Christ.

The city of Corinth had many gods. It is significant, therefore, that to the Corinthian Christians Paul wrote, "For though there be that are called gods [so-called gods], whether in heaven or in earth . . . but to us there is but one God, the Father . . . and one Lord Jesus Christ, by whom are all things, and we by Him" (I Cor. 8:5-6).

So we return to this first commandment. "Thou shalt have no other gods before me." God is saying that you should remove from your life anything and everything which comes between you and the true and living God. Any form of religion which does less cannot suffice for man, or for you as an individual man, woman, or child. This can be done only as you enthrone in your life God's revelation of Himself through His Son, Jesus Christ.

It is high time that the world took the road back from the brink of disaster. The free world is responding to President John F. Kennedy's call to strengthen our ability to resist the forces of tyranny. And that is as it should be. But that can serve only as a deterrent to evil. Evil can be destroyed only as it is dethroned from our hearts. We must begin somewhere. Why not begin in you and me? Why not begin with God in Christ? Some of us have already trusted in Him as our Saviour. Let us rededicate our entire beings to Him. Others of you have never given yourselves to Him. I beg that you will do so now as you receive Him through faith into your hearts.

INDEX